COLLECTIBLE TOYS AND GAMES

of the Twenties and Thirties
from Sears, Roebuck and Co. Catalogs

Edited by
JAMES SPERO

DOVER PUBLICATIONS, INC., NEW YORK

Copyright © 1988 by Dover Publications, Inc.
All rights reserved under Pan American and International Copyright Conventions.

Published in Canada by General Publishing Company, Ltd., 30 Lesmill Road, Don Mills, Toronto, Ontario.
Published in the United Kingdom by Constable and Company, Ltd.

Collectible Toys and Games of the Twenties and Thirties from Sears, Roebuck and Co. Catalogs is a new work, first published by Dover Publications, Inc., in 1988.

Manufactured in the United States of America
Dover Publications, Inc., 31 East 2nd Street, Mineola, N.Y. 11501

Library of Congress Cataloging-in-Publication Data

Collectible toys and games of the twenties and thirties from Sears,
    Roebuck and Co. catalogs / edited by James Spero.
        p.   cm.
    ISBN 0-486-25827-0 (pbk.)
    1. Sears, Roebuck and Company—Catalogs. 2. Toys—Catalogs.
3. Games—Catalogs.   I. Spero, James.
NK9509.C64   1988
688.7′0973′075—dc 19   88-28207
                                                                        CIP

PUBLISHER'S NOTE

THIS VOLUME CONTAINS a selection of the toy pages from the Fall/Winter catalogs of Sears, Roebuck and Co., 1921–39. (These catalogs were, of course, intended for the Christmas season. The Spring/Summer catalogs contained a drastically reduced toy section.) Since there was considerable duplication of material from year to year, the selection has been made to present as great a variety as possible. (Dolls and related materials have already been treated in *Collectible Dolls and Accessories of the Twenties and Thirties from Sears, Roebuck and Co. Catalogs*; Dover ISBN 0-486-25107-1.)

Here is a full representation of the toys that delighted the children of the period (as similar toys, different only in their packaging and electronic gadgetry, find favor today), from the wind-ups, board games and construction toys to costumes, electric trains, toy instruments and bicycles and wagons. Fullest representation is given for 1921; thereafter, only pages featuring significant additions or changes are included (such as the considerable redesign of toys in the mid-1930s to reflect the trend toward streamlining).

The pages are presented in sequence, save when a slight rearrangement was necessary to preserve a heading running across a double-page spread. In many cases, where only one page of a double-page spread is shown, the part of the head appearing on the page is reproduced unaltered.

CONTENTS

Parlor Games

Combination Game Board
57 Games $5.39

Well made, standard combination game board. It will furnish amusement for the entire family, young and old. Makes a most acceptable present which will be used at all times. Equipped with reversible net pockets. Complete with full set of equipment to play fifty-seven games, such as crokinole, carroms, checkers, parlor pool, tenpins, etc. Full instructions for playing all of them. The panel is made of three-ply maple veneer, natural wood finish. Crokinole and checker sections are artistically stenciled on the polished surface of the wood, producing a pleasing effect. Size, 28½ inches square.

Equipment.

(1) Two 26-inch Cues.
(2) One set 3-inch Tenpins.
(3) One set 29 Crokinole and Carrom Rings.
(4) One Tenpin Backstop.
(5) Six Wood Flies, 3 green, 3 yellow.
(6) One Dice Cup, 2 Dice.
(7) Three Wood Tops.

Shipping weight, outfit complete, 11½ pounds. On account of size, this board is unmailable.
79F489¼—Price, complete........ **$5.39**

Complete set of twenty-nine Crokinole and Carrom Rings, made of hardwood, in pasteboard box. Shipping weight, 8 ounces.
49F480—Price........ **33c**

Parcheesi.

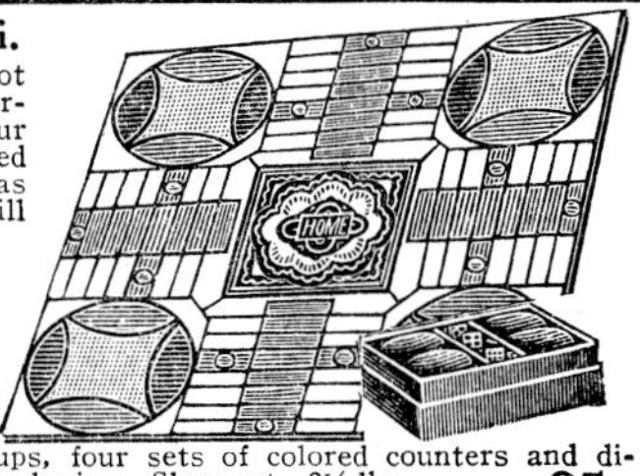

Who has not heard of parcheesi? Your father played it when he was a boy, and still it retains its fascination for all. Consists of 18¼x18¼ inch folding board, dice, four cups, four sets of colored counters and directions for playing. Shpg. wt., 2⅛ lbs.
49F100—Price........ **95c**

Small Pocket Size Parcheesi.
Cloth covered folding board, 8¼ inches square, 4⅛ inches wide folded. Printed in colors. Sixteen colored composition men and a totum spinner which takes the place of dice. Packed in folding cover. Shipping weight, 5 ounces.
49F103—Price........ **47c**

Cortella.

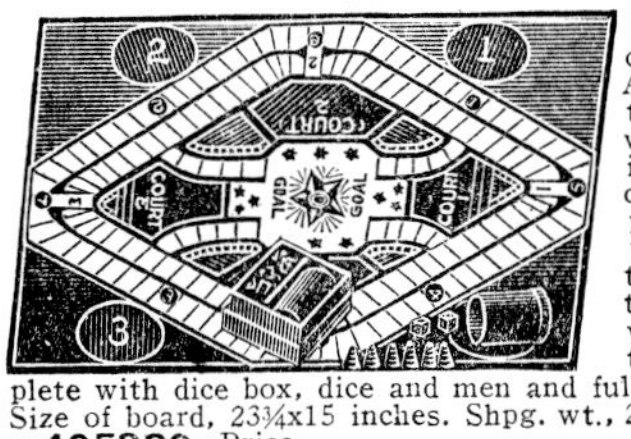

A dandy, exciting game. A race for two to four people with capturing of pieces, confining of prisoners in the king's castle, requires thought as well as luck to win. Complete with dice box, dice and men and full instructions. Size of board, 23¾x15 inches. Shpg. wt., 2 lbs.
49F289—Price........ **79c**

8-Game Combination Board.

Has full equipment for playing eight games. Crokinole, checkers and many others. Made of good grade wood, mission finish edge, polished center, smoothly finished. Diameter, 30½ inches. Shipping weight, 11¼ lbs.
Unmailable.
79F490¼ Price........ **$3.45**

Exciting Auto Race.

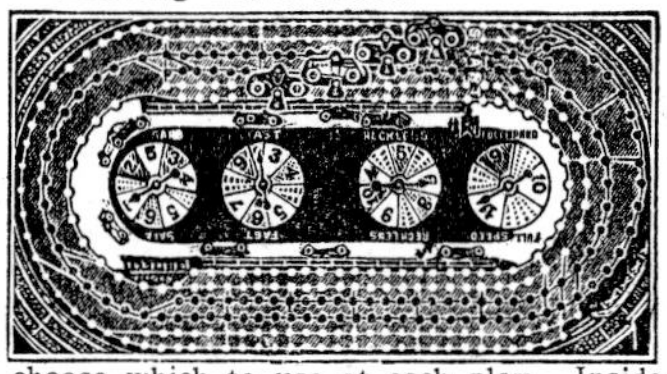

A game with many thrills, you can use the fast, reckless, or full speed spinners which advance your man much faster, but with greater danger. Four speeds. You choose which to use at each play. Inside track is shorter than outside. A good player on the outside can work his man in and get the inside track.
Board measures 12½x24 inches, made of extra heavy cardboard, beautifully lithographed in colors. From two to eight can play. Shipping weight, 1½ lbs.
49F154—Price........ **79c**

Ouija Mystery Board

Interesting and mystifying. Great mirth making game for parties. Apparently answers questions concerning past, present and future. Full directions accompany each board. Nicely finished. Small felt tipped table on which you place your hands, slides about on larger board, pointing out letters as words are spelled.

Genuine Fuld Ouija Board, 89c.
Manufactured by the originator of the famous ouija board. Many people prefer this genuine Fuld board, even at the little higher price. Size, 18x12½ inches. Shipping weight, 3 lbs.
79F129¼—Price........ **89c**

Larger Size Imitation Ouija Board, 98c.
Size, 22x15 inches. Shipping weight, 3½ pounds.
79F163¼—Price........ **98c**

Small Size Imitation Ouija Board, 47c.
Size, 15x12½ inches. Shipping weight, 3 pounds.
49F110—Price........ **47c**

Ring My Nose.

Colored clown target with long nose. Four rings to throw. Box, 9x14 inches. Shipping wt., 8 oz.
49F136 Price........ **39c**

NINE PIN SET, 57c

Wonderful value. A dandy set of painted Nine Pins. Each pin 7 inches high. Two balls, 1⅝ inches diameter. Several different color pins in each set. Shipping weight, 2¾ pounds.
49F185—Price........ **57c**

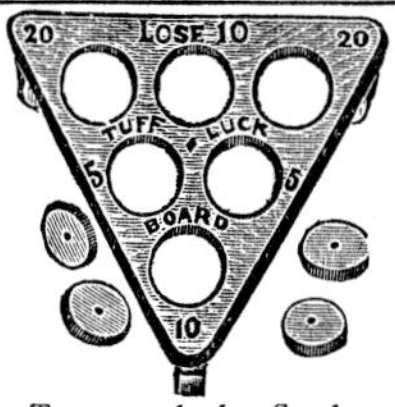

Try your luck. See how good your eye is; 13-inch triangle shaped board, made of three-ply veneer. Six holes, about 2½ inches in diameter, each numbered. Four assorted colored discs, about 1¼ inches in diameter, are furnished for tossing. Shipping wt., 1 pound.
49F107—Price........ **39c**

Fortune Teller.

Colored cardboard figure, 6½x8¼ inches, points out fortune on wheel. Full directions. Great for parties, packed in neat box. Shipping weight, 5 oz.
49F130—Price........ **33c**

Checkers and Backgammon.

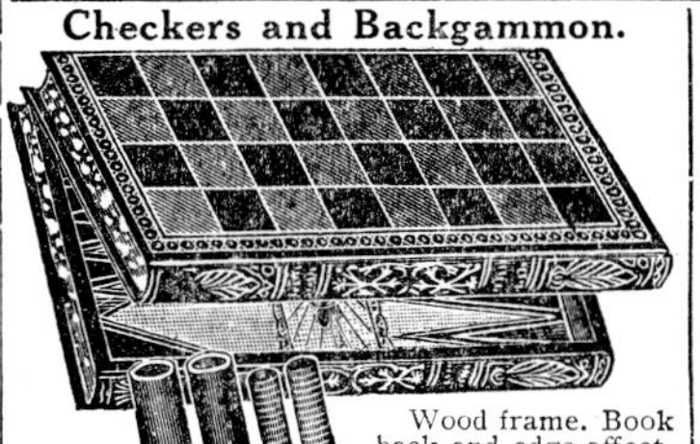

Wood frame. Book back and edge effect. Fancy heavy paper covered. Printed in red, black and gilt. Gloss finish. Backgammon board inside. Complete with checkers, dice cup and dice. Size, 16x14¼ inches. Has 1½-inch squares. Shipping weight, 1¾ pounds.
49F116—Price........ **$1.39**

Our 79-Cent Board.
Lighter weight wood frame. Gloss finish. Complete with checkers, no dice cup or dice. Size, 18x17⅝ inches. Has 1¹¹⁄₁₆-inch squares. Shipping weight, 2 lbs.
49F119—Price........ **79c**

Our 45-Cent Board.
Size, 15x15 inches. Has 1½-inch squares. Shipping weight, 1⅝ pounds.
49F125—Price........ **45c**

Our 25-Cent Board.
Size, 12x12 inches. Hardly as well finished. Shipping weight, 1½ lbs.
49F122—Price........ **25c**

Lotto Game.

Cardboard box, resembles trunk. Size, 6¾x4x1¾ inches. Complete with twelve cards, wood counters. Full instructions. Shipping weight, 1⅛ pounds.
49F145—Price........ **21c**

5-Game Combination Board.

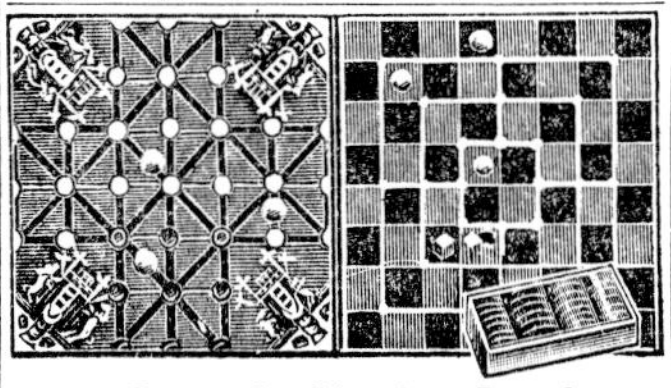

Attack, Checkers, Nine Men Morris, Solitaire and Running the Blockade. Full instructions and men. Board, 26¾x13½ in. Shipping weight, 1½ pounds.
49F121—Price, complete........ **89c**

Chessmen. Staunton Pattern.

We have four grades Staunton chessmen.

49F198—Loaded bottoms with felt pads. Height of King, 2⅝ inches. Shipping weight, 1½ pounds.
Price, per set........ **$2.98**

49F199—Same as above, only bottoms not loaded and no felt pads. Height of King, 2¼ inches. Shipping wt., 11 oz.
Price, per set........ **$1.39**

49F200—Height of King, 2⁹⁄₁₆ inches. White and red enameled. Shipping wt., 11 ounces. Price........ **98c**

49F194—Nicely turned and varnished. Height of King, 2⅝ inches. Shipping wt., 10 ounces. Price, per set........ **67c**

Chess Board.

Size, open, 14x14 inches. Folds in center. Made of ³⁄₁₆-inch composition board with cloth hinge. Red and black 1½-inch squares. Excellent quality. Shipping wt., 14 oz.
49F131 Price........ **39c**

Keeping Up With the Joneses.
Based on the famous cartoons.

A rip roaring funny game. Two, three or four can play. Sixteen men, two dice cups and dice, also full instructions. Board, 18 inches square, lithographed in colors, featuring the famous cartoon characters. Absolutely new. Shpg. wt., 1½ lbs.
49F169—Price........ **89c**

GAMES FOR ALL

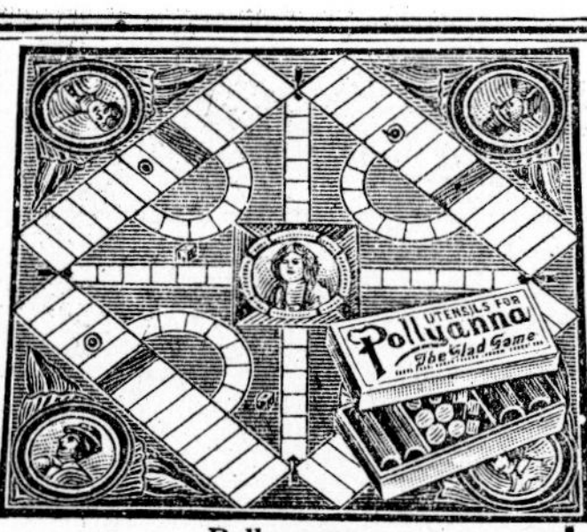

Pollyanna.
• Similar to Parcheesi, but different enough to make a delightful change. Has had a tremendous sale since being introduced. Board measures 18⅝x18¾ inches. Complete with four cups, dice and men. Up to four can play. Shipping weight, 1½ pounds.
49F120—Price........ **$1.67**

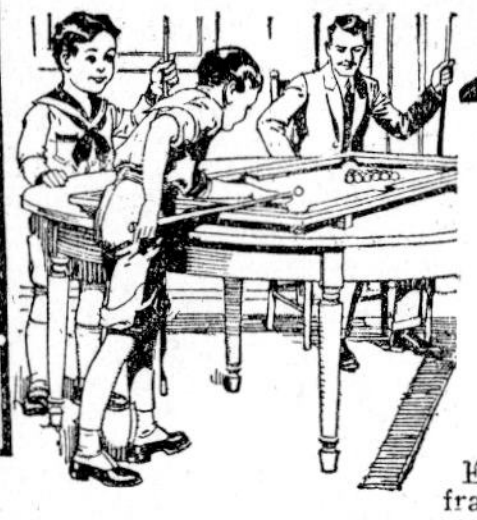

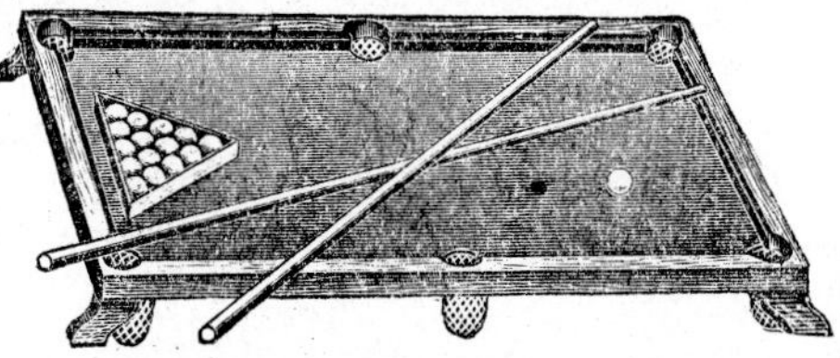

BOYS' SMALL SIZE POOL TABLE.
Everyone enjoys playing pool. Dark mahogany finish wood frame tables, bed covered with green billiard cloth. Rubber cushions. Six net pockets. Two sizes. Fully equipped with cues and fifteen numbered composition balls, different colors and wood triangle frame.

Popular size. Inside measurement, 40x20 inches. Two 32-inch cues; balls, 1¼ in. in diameter. Shipping wt., 15 lbs.
79F486¼—Price........ **$6.87**

Inside measurement, 15x30 inches. Two 27-inch cues; balls, 15/16 inch in diameter. Shipping weight, 7¼ pounds.
79F485¼—Price........ **$4.98**

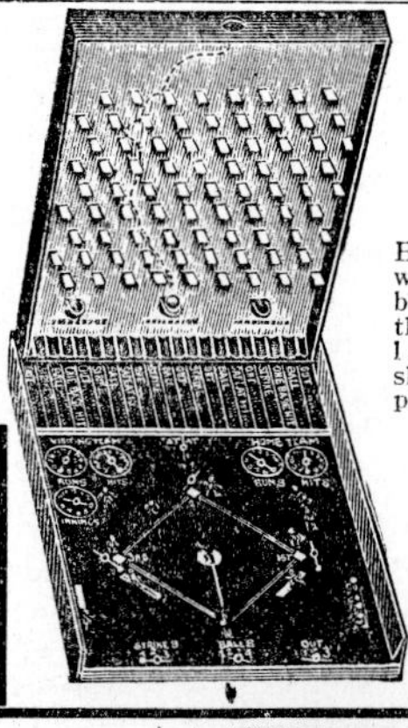

Baseball Game.
Baseball diamond with eight dials to show progress of game. Nearly all plays of real game possible. Has metal field with pegs. Steel ball rolls down these pegs and lands in groove showing result of play, such as ball, fly, strike, foul, out, home run; also new positions of base runners. Full directions. Size of box, about 6x9 in. Shipping weight, 1½ lbs.
49F132 Price.. **89c**

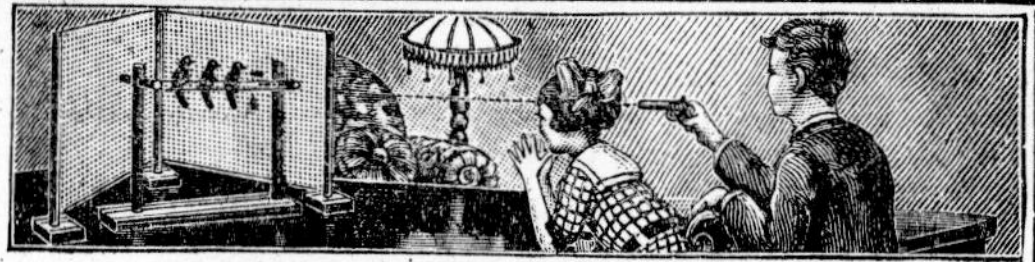

Shoot the Birds Off the Wire.
Miniature telephone poles with rubber bands for wires, and three 3¼-inch colored birds. Corks are furnished for shooting. The metal air pistol will shoot accurately. A screen stops the corks. Really improves markmanship. Everyone wants to play. Box measures 18¼x8 inches. Shipping weight, 2¼ pounds.
49F141—Price........ **98c**

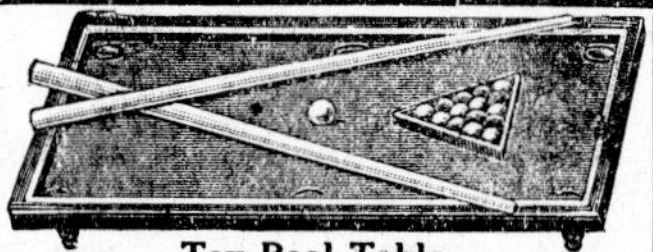

Toy Pool Table.
Complete with two 20-inch cues, a triangle, fifteen 1⅛-inch numbered composition balls and a cue ball. Six metal depression pockets. Felt covered table measures 10¾x19¾ in. inside. Shipping weight, 3¼ pounds.
49F208—Price, complete.. **$1.87**

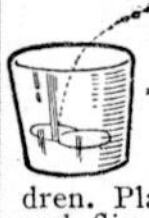

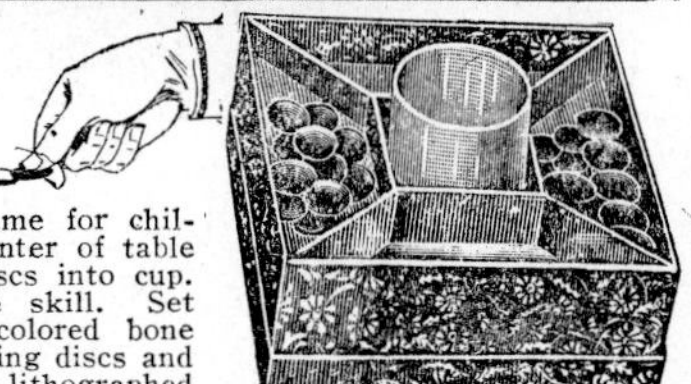

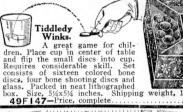

Tiddledy Winks.
A great game for children. Place cup in center of table and flip the small discs into cup. Requires considerable skill. Set consists of sixteen colored bone discs, four bone shooting discs and glass. Packed in neat lithographed box. Size, 5¼x5¼ inches. Shipping weight, 12 ounces.
49F147—Price, complete........ **25c**

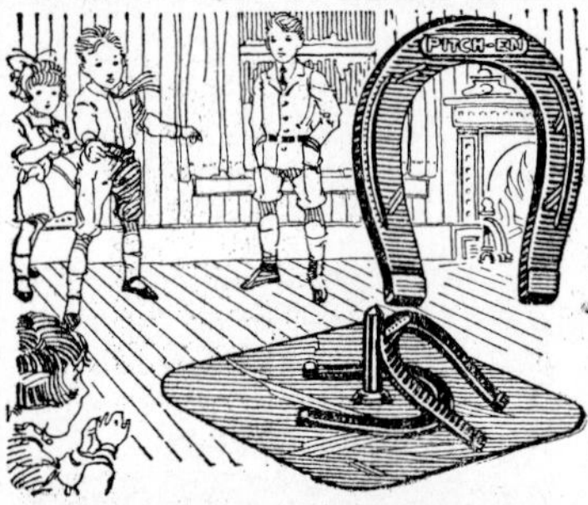

Pitchem

Indoor Horseshoes.
Full Size Rubber Horseshoes. Will Not Injure Furniture or Floors.

A practical game of Indoor Horseshoes, consisting of four full size horseshoes, made of rubber, and two pegs firmly fastened in nicely enameled broad metal plates to set on floor. You can get ringers and "leaners" just like outdoors. The rubber shoes will not injure the finest furniture, should they strike it. Have a jolly good time this Winter, playing this old familiar game indoors. Outfit packed in neat box. Size, 12¼x12¼ inches. Average shipping weight, 3⅛ pounds.
49F128—Price, per set...... **$1.39**

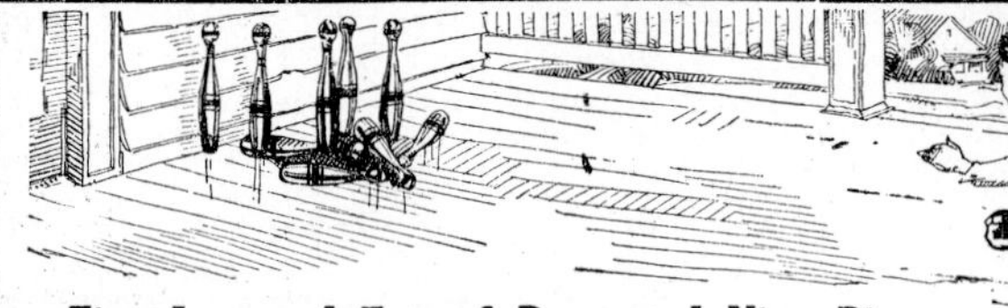

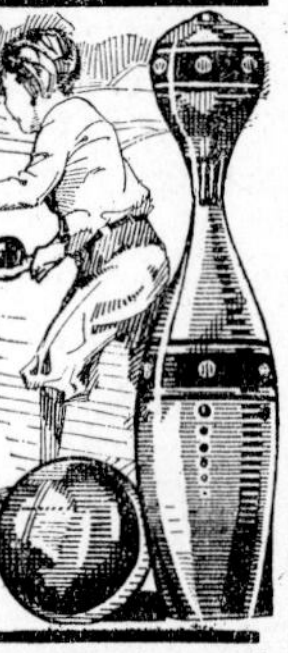

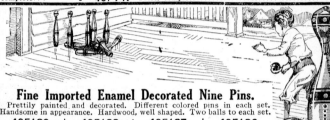

Fine Imported Enamel Decorated Nine Pins.
Prettily painted and decorated. Different colored pins in each set. Handsome in appearance. Hardwood, well shaped. Two balls to each set.

49F189	**49F188**	**49F187**	**49F186**
Height, pin, 7 in. Balls, 1⅝ in. Shipping wt., 2¾ lbs. Price.... **98c**	Height, pin, 5¾ in. Balls, 1⅝ in. Shipping wt., 2½ lbs. Price.... **69c**	Height, pin, 5 in. Balls, 1⅛ in. Shipping wt., 2¼ lbs. Price.... **47c**	Height, pin, 4 in. Balls, 1⅛ in. Shipping wt., 1¾ lbs. Price.. **33c**

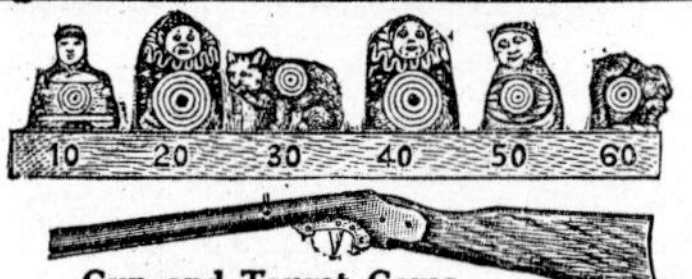

Gun and Target Game.
Consists of a 9½-inch good spring gun with blued steel barrel and wood stock and a 13¾-inch novelty wooden target set. The gun shoots little wooden bullets with just enough force to knock the targets over. Targets are numbered for scoring. A game with lots of competition. Shipping weight, 12 oz.
49F106—Price........ **98c**

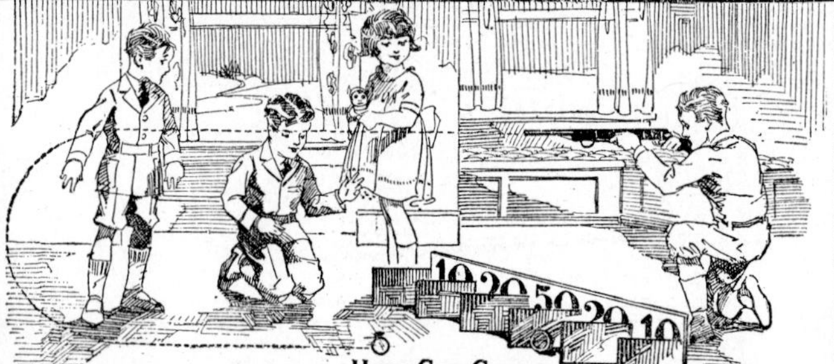

Hoop Gun Game.
It really shoots. It cannot possibly hurt anyone. The gun shoots small wooden hoops, giving them a swift reverse motion which causes them to roll back when hoop strikes the floor. With the gun comes a target. The game is to have the hoop roll back into the stall that counts most. Gun has wooden barrel and stock and measures over all 27 in. Target, 3½ in. high and 30 in. long. Shpg. wt., abt. 2½ lbs.
49F5606—Price, complete, special at........ **$1.00**

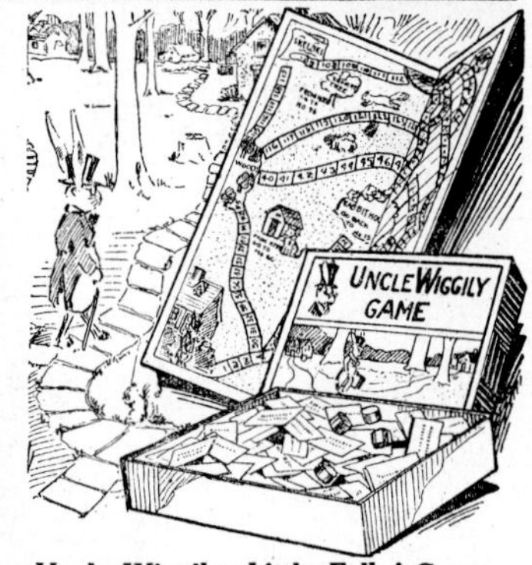

Uncle Wiggily—Little Folks' Game.
From two to four can play and each has a wooden "Uncle Wiggily" to move. Uncle Wiggily wants to get to Doctor O'Possum's office. 140 cards tell with funny verses and directions how many hops forward or backward Uncle Wiggily can take. There are many traps and pitfalls to beware of. The first Uncle Wiggily to reach Dr. O'Possum's wins. Folding cardboard game board, size 16 inches square. Directions for playing. Shipping wt., 1½ pounds.
49F104—Price........ **59c**

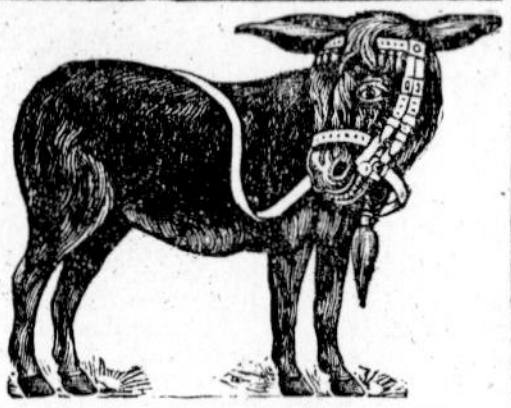

Donkey Party.
Starched cloth sheet, 18¼x30 in. With picture of donkey without tail, 24 loose tails to be attached. Blindfold everybody, give each a donkey tail and have him pin it on the donkey. The one who pins a tail nearest where it belongs wins. A dandy game for parties. Shipping weight, 5 ounces.
49F135—Price........ **19c**

Baseball Game.

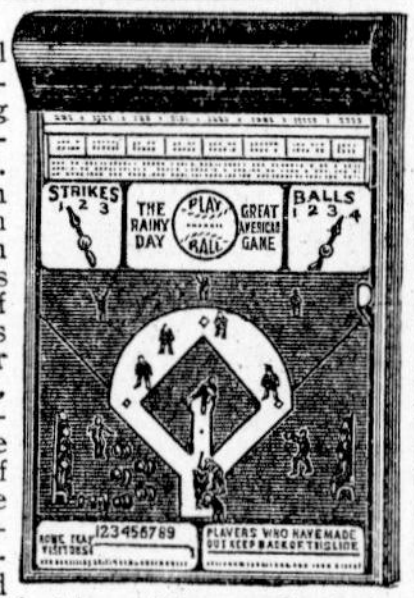

A wood and steel box with partly concealed revolving drum showing movement of players. Nine men on each side. Place player in batter's box, push lever, which revolves drum. The result of the play shows whether ball or strike, fair or foul, hit or any one of almost 300 possible combinations of plays that can be made on a real diamond. The players move around the bases in regular fashion. The crack of the bat against the ball is all that is missing to give all the thrills of a real game. The rules of regular baseball apply. For baseball fans this game is a boon. Women also take great interest and soon become ardent players. Box measures about 14⅛x8⅞ inches. Compartment under playing field for storing men. Shipping weight, 2 pounds.
49F133—Price........ **$1.39**

"Cootie" Game, 21c.

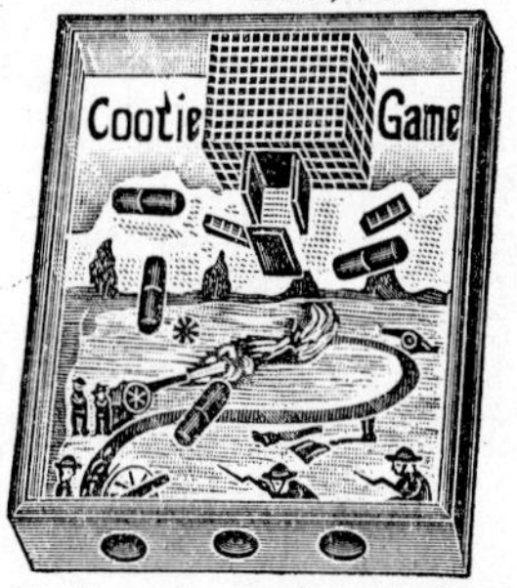

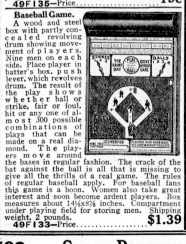

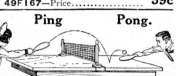

Don't neglect to buy it. Most popular and fastest selling game. Over five million games sold last year. Fun and laughter by the hour. Anyone can play. Enjoyed by all ages. Metal frame box, 4x5 inches, with glass top, containing four colored capsules with weight in end, rolling, tumbling, turning everywhere but where you want them. Person getting all four in wire cage in shortest time wins, and it is a real job to keep them all in. Also try timing each person until all cooties are in cage and note the fun. A dandy game. Shipping weight, 10 oz.
49F134 Price........ **21c**

Geographical Lotto.

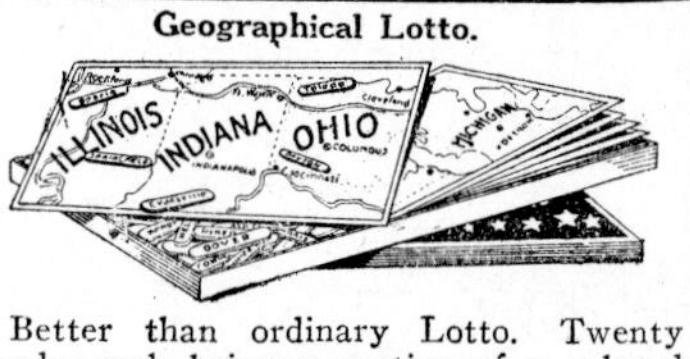

Better than ordinary Lotto. Twenty cards, each being a section of a colored map of the U. S., and showing names and locations of twelve cities. Also 227 smaller counter cards, each with name of city. The player whose cities are first covered wins. Full instructions. Size of box, 6x11½ inches. Well made of good materials. Shipping weight, 1 pound.
49F167—Price........ **59c**

Ping Pong.

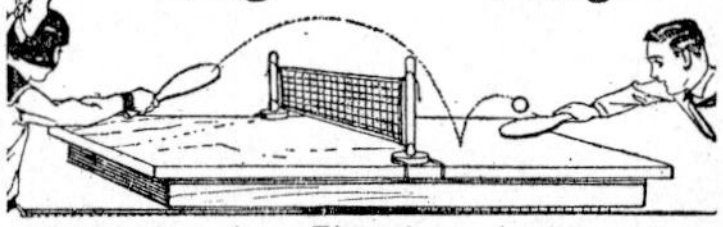

Regulation size. Fine three-ply veneer racquets with shaped handles, 11⅝x5⅜ inches. Taped edge net, 5½x41 inches, and posts and standards with clips for attaching to table, also three balls and set of instructions and rules for playing. Ping Pong is indoor tennis and is intensely interesting for all ages. Each set in box, size 7x15 inches. Shipping weight, 1¾ pounds.
49F171—Price........ **$1.67**

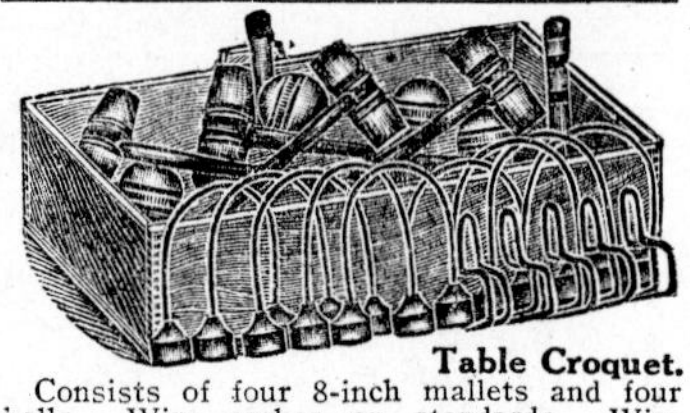

Table Croquet.
Consists of four 8-inch mallets and four balls. Wire arches on standards. Wire clamps to hold up tape to prevent balls from rolling off table. Packed in cardboard box, size 7¼x11¼ in. Shpg. wt., 1¾ lbs.
49F111—Price, complete........ **87c**

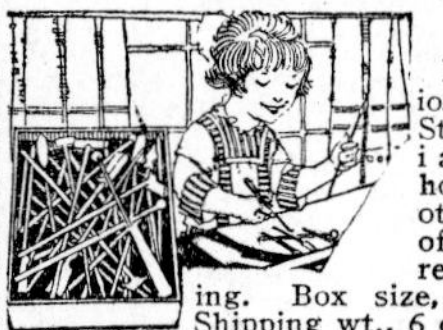

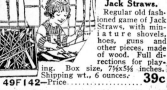

Jack Straws.
Regular old fashioned game of Jack Straws, with miniature shovels, hoes, guns and other pieces, made of wood. Full directions for playing. Box size, 7⅝x5⅝ inches. Shipping wt., 6 ounces.
49F142—Price........ **39c**

Indoor Games

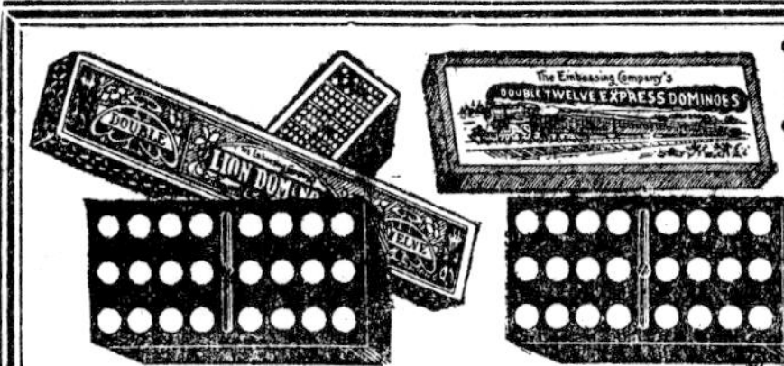

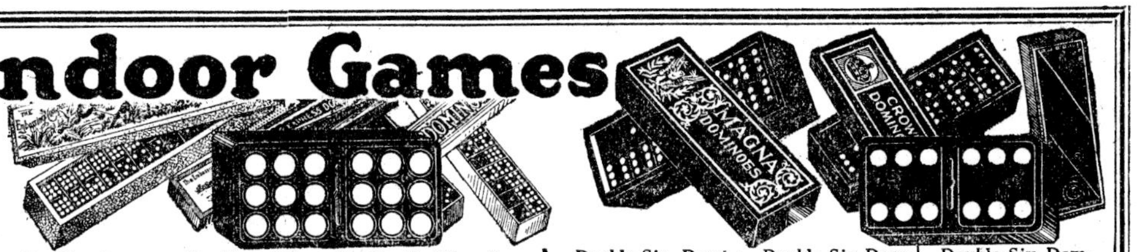

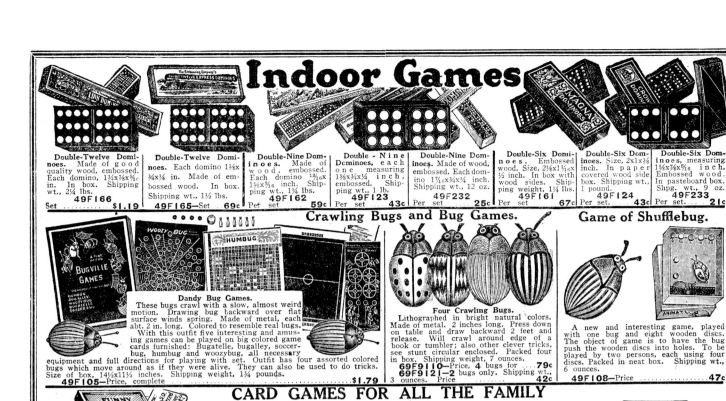

Double-Twelve Dominoes. Made of good quality wood, embossed. Each domino, 1¾x⅞x5⁄16 in. In box. Shipping wt., 2¼ lbs.
49F166
Set $1.19

Double-Twelve Dominoes. Each domino 1⅝x¾x¼ in. Made of embossed wood. In box. Shipping wt., 1½ lbs.
49F165—Set 69c

Double-Nine Dominoes. Made of wood, embossed. Each domino 1 3⁄16x1⅝x5⁄16 inch. Shipping wt., 1¼ lbs.
49F162
Per set 59c

Double-Nine Dominoes, each one measuring 1⅝x¾x¼ inch, embossed. Shipping wt., 1 lb.
49F123
Per set 43c

Double-Nine Dominoes. Made of wood, embossed. Each domino 1 7⁄16x¾x¼ inch. Shipping wt., 12 oz.
49F232
Per set 25c

Double-Six Dominoes. Embossed wood. Size, 2⅛x1 1⁄16x½ inch. In box with wood sides. Shipping weight, 1¼ lbs.
49F161
Per set 67c

Double-Six Dominoes. Size, 2x1x⅜ inch. In paper covered wood side box. Shipping wt., 1 pound.
49F124
Per set. 43c

Double-Six Dominoes, measuring 1⅝x⅞x5⁄16 inch. Embossed wood. In pasteboard box. Shpg. wt., 9 oz.
49F233
Per set. 21c

Crawling Bugs and Bug Games.

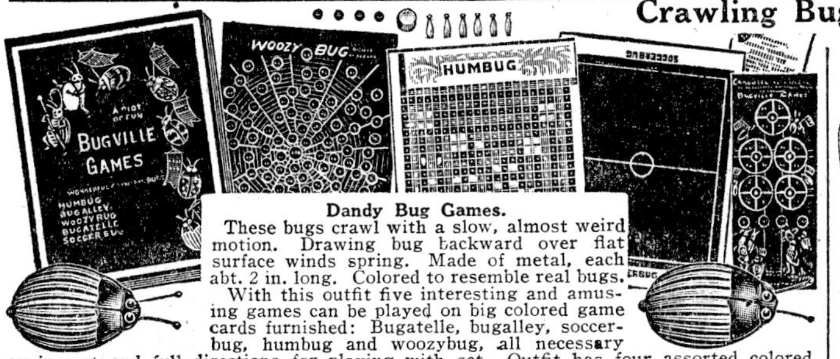

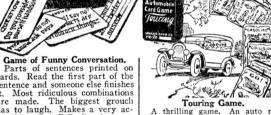

Dandy Bug Games.
These bugs crawl with a slow, almost weird motion. Drawing bug backward over flat surface winds spring. Made of metal, each abt. 2 in. long. Colored to resemble real bugs. With this outfit five interesting and amusing games can be played on big colored game cards furnished: Bugatelle, bugalley, soccer-bug, humbug and woozybug, all necessary equipment and full directions for playing with set. Outfit has four assorted colored bugs which move around as if they were alive. They can also be used to do tricks. Size of box, 14½x11½ inches. Shipping weight, 1¾ pounds.
49F105—Price, complete $1.79

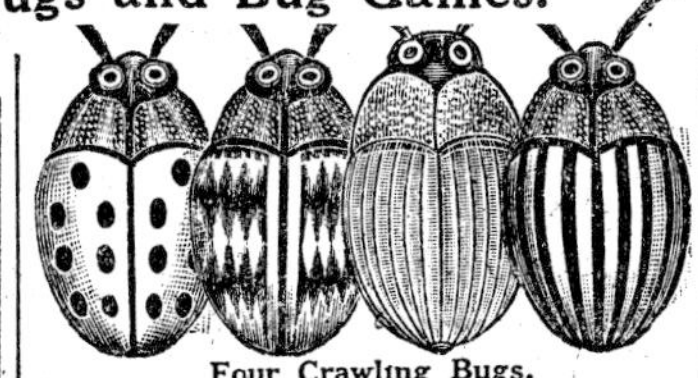

Four Crawling Bugs.
Lithographed in bright natural colors. Made of metal. 2 inches long. Press down on table and draw backward 2 feet and release. Will crawl around edge of a book or tumbler; also other clever tricks, see stunt circular enclosed. Packed four in box. Shipping weight, 7 ounces.
69F9110—Price, 4 bugs for 79c
69F9121—2 bugs only. Shipping wt., 3 ounces. Price 42c

Game of Shufflebug.

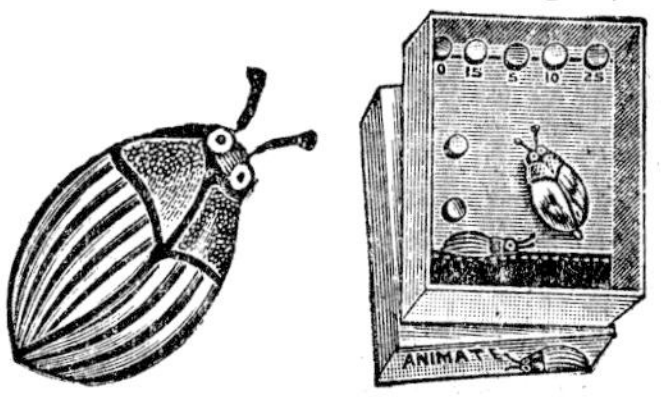

A new and interesting game, played with one bug and eight wooden discs. The object of game is to have the bug push the wooden discs into holes. To be played by two persons, each using four discs. Packed in neat box. Shipping wt., 6 ounces.
49F108—Price 47c

CARD GAMES FOR ALL THE FAMILY

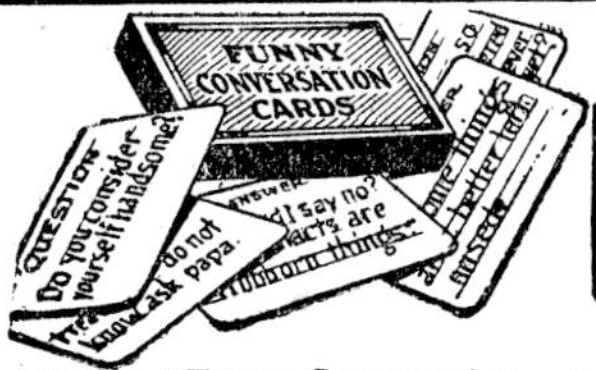

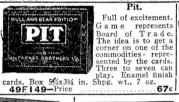

Game of Funny Conversation.
Parts of sentences printed on cards. Read the first part of the sentence and someone else finishes it. Most ridiculous combinations are made. The biggest grouch has to laugh. Makes a very acceptable gift. Full directions are included with each package. Size of box, 7½x5½ in. Shpg. wt., 8 oz.
49F255—Price 39c

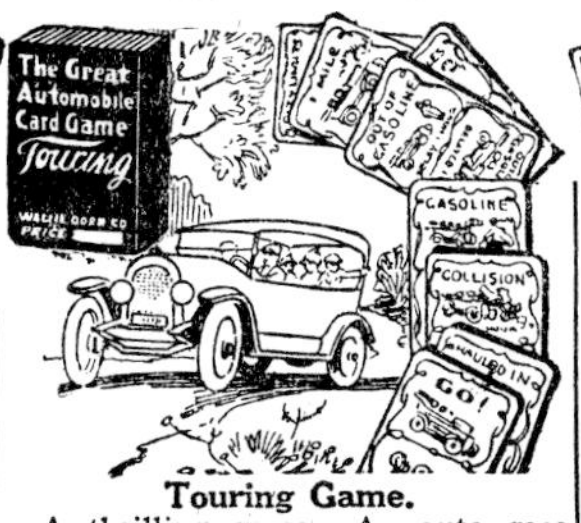

Touring Game.
A thrilling game. An auto race for 50 miles. Any number of persons up to six can play. Up to date and exciting. Shipping weight, 8 oz.
49F150—Price 59c

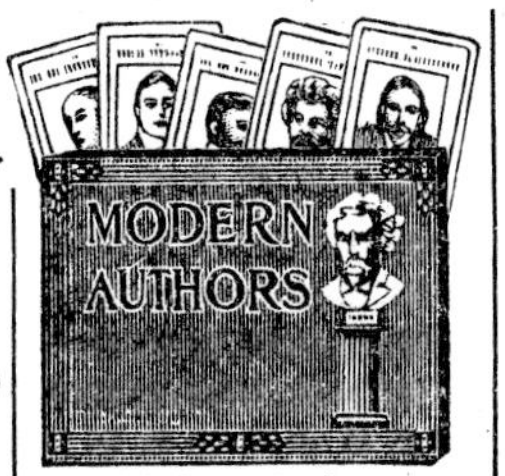

Modern Authors.
Enamel finish cards, in box with directions for playing. Two or more can play. Size of box, 7½x5½ in. Shpg. wt., 7 oz.
49F156—Price 39c

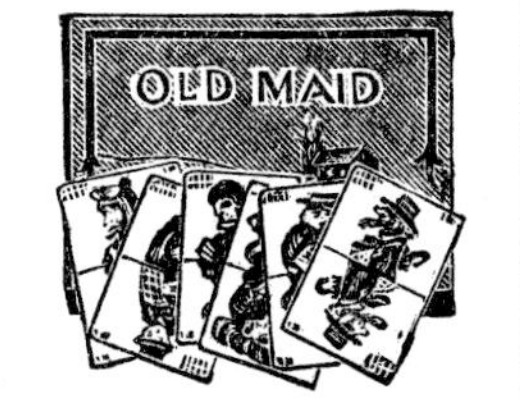

Old Maid Game.
Enamel finish cards, in colors, in neat box. Small children can play it. Size of box, 7½x5½ inches. Shipping weight, 6 ounces.
49F157—Price 39c

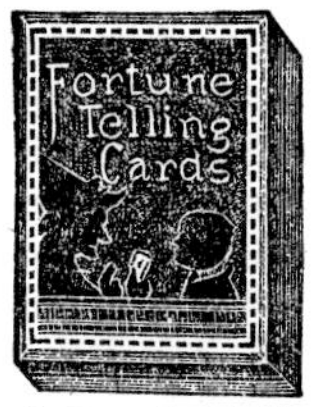

Children's Fortune Telling Card Game.
A funny fortune telling game for children. Queer pictures. Cards packed in neat box 7½x5½ inches. Shipping weight, 6 ounces.
49F144—Price 43c

Bunco, the Exciting Game.

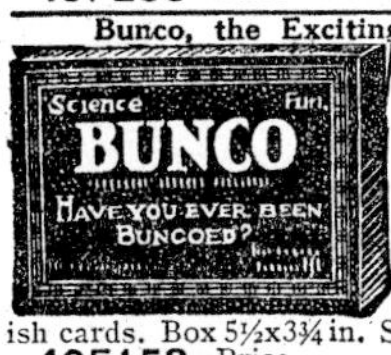

Popular game for progressive parties or individual tables. From two to seven can play. 115 enamel finish cards. Box 5½x3¾ in. Shpg.wt.,10 oz.
49F152—Price 49c

Pit.

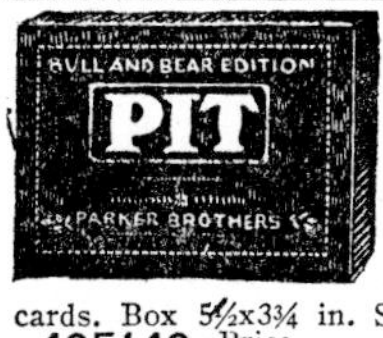

Full of excitement. Game represents Board of Trade. The idea is to get a corner on one of the commodities represented by the cards. Three to seven can play. Enamel finish cards. Box 5½x3¾ in. Shpg. wt., 7 oz.
49F149—Price 67c

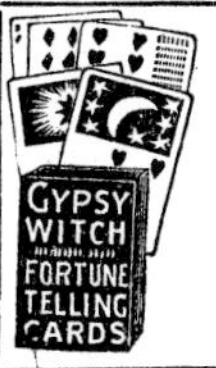

Tell Your Friends' Fortunes.
Gypsy Witch Fortune Telling Cards. For grown people. The meaning and symbols of cards explained. **You can tell fortunes with these cards.** Good quality cards, printed in colors. Complete directions with each set. Shpg. wt., 4 oz.
49F153—Price 59c

Flinch.
They are always ready to play flinch. Get out the flinch deck and watch the folks all smile and draw up their chairs to the table. Consists of 150 cards, with full directions for playing. Nicely packed in neat box. Shipping weight, 11 ounces.

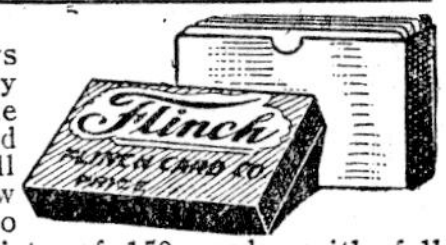

49F151—Price 67c

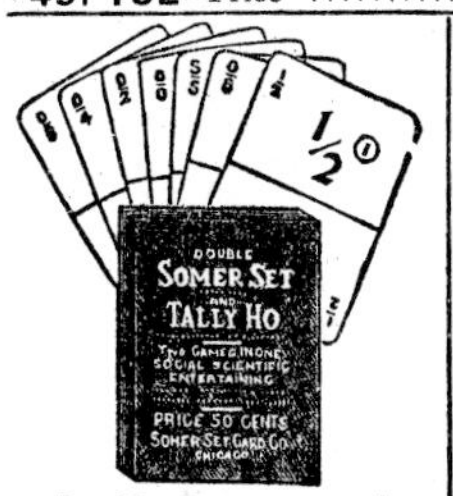

Double Somerset and Tally Ho.
Combines two games in one. Simple for young folks, and interesting for grown-ups. Shpg. wt., 4 oz.
49F196—Price 67c

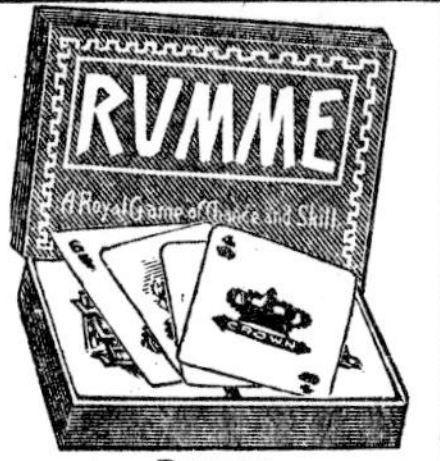

Rumme.
Ten other games besides rumme can be played. Enamel finish cards in cardboard box, 5¼x3¾ in. Full directions with each. Shipping weight, 7 ounces.
49F159—Price 67c

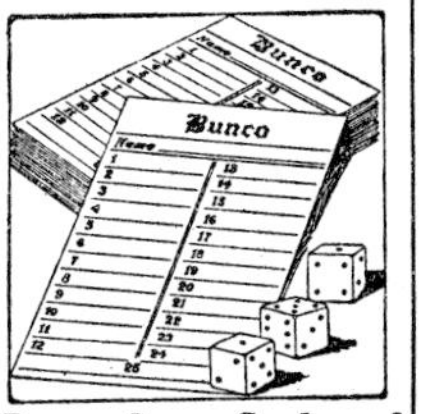

Bunco Score Cards and Dice.
100 Bunco score cards, size 3x3¾ inches, and three ½-inch Bunco dice. Shipping wt., 6 oz.
49F206—Price.... 25c

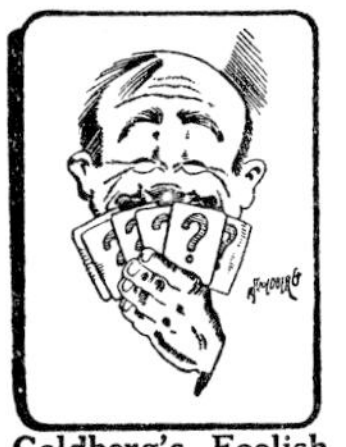

Goldberg's Foolish Questions.
Easily learned. Ask the foolish questions and you will surely enjoy the answers. Box 5¼x3¾ inches. Shipping wt., 4 oz.
49F237—Price 25c

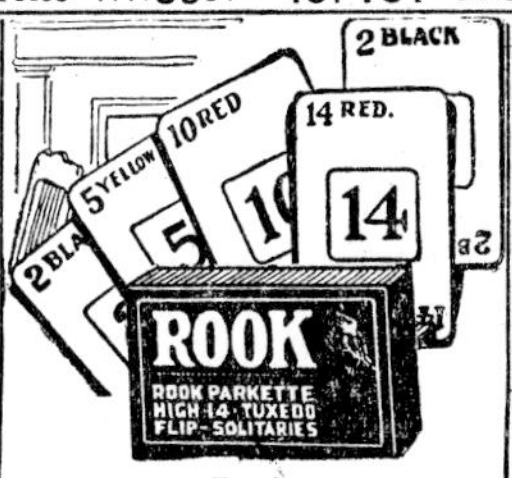

Rook.
Ten rattling good games for adults and children can be played with rook cards. Enamel finish with fancy backs. Box, 5¼x3¾ inches. Shipping wt., 8 oz.
49F148—Price 67c

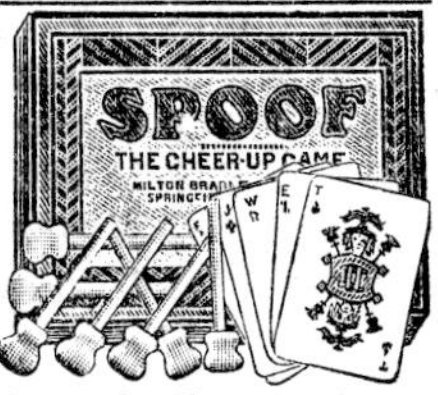

Spoof, the Cheer-Up Game.
Will develop quick thinking. Fifty-two enameled cards and seven wooden batons. Up to seven can play. Box, 7½x5½ in. Shipping wt., 10 oz.
49F158—Price ... 67c

PLAYING CARDS, DICE AND POKER CHIPS

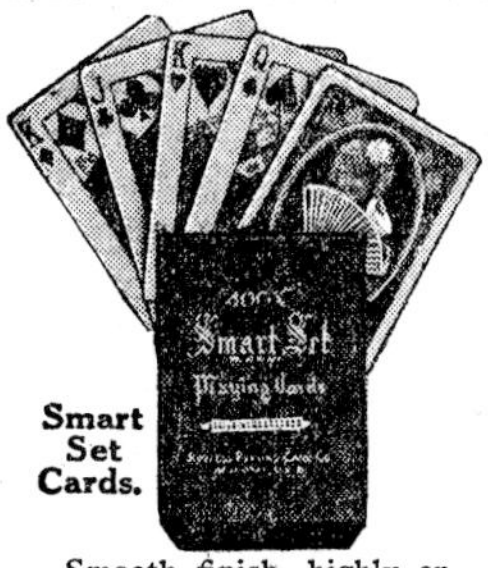

Smart Set Cards.
Smooth finish, highly enameled. Gold burnished edges. Picture backs in assorted designs. Regulation size. Each set in telescope box. Shpg. wt., 5 oz.
49F285—Price 50c

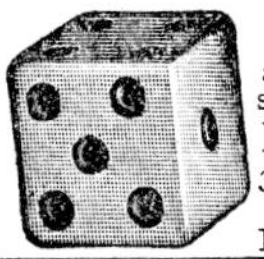

Celluloid Dice.
Transparent, smooth and light; 9⁄16 inch square. Red with white spots. Five dice to set. Shipping wt., 3 ounces.
49F234
Per set 79c

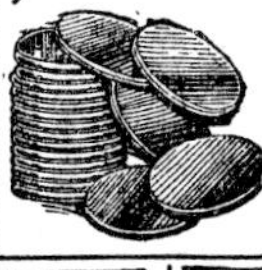

U. S. Playing Card Co.'s Poker Chips.
One hundred 1½-inch composition poker chips. So called unbreakable. Fifty white, twenty-five blue and twenty-five red. Shipping wt., 2⅜ pounds.
49F261—Price $1.39

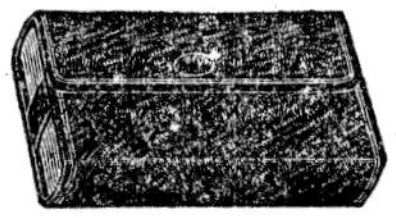

For a Gift. Cards in Leather Case.
Genuine leather covered case and deck of whist size gold edge playing cards. Shipping weight, 6 ounces.
49F170
Price, complete.. 98c

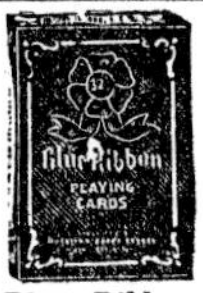

Blue Ribbon.
High grade linen finish cards. Shipping wt., 4 oz.
49F282
Price 45c

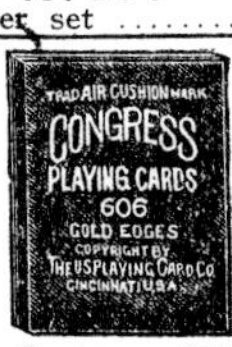

Congress 606.
Burnished gold edges. Assorted art backs. Linen finish. Shipping wt., 4 oz.
49F252
Price....... 67c

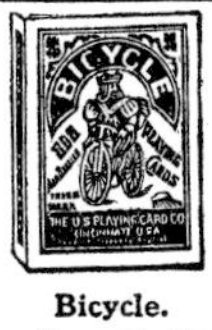

Bicycle.
One of the best known cards. Linen finish. Shipping wt., 4 oz.
49F250
Price 47c

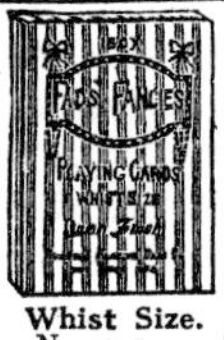

Whist Size.
Narrow. Linen finish. Gilt edges. Telescope case. Shpg. wt., 4 oz.
49F251
Price 59c

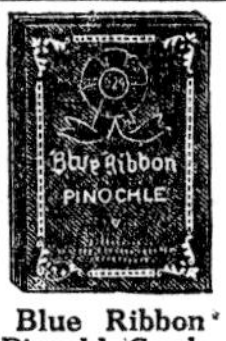

Blue Ribbon Pinochle Cards.
Linen finish cards. Shipping weight, 4 ounces.
49F284
Price 45c

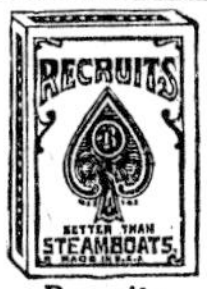

Recruits.
Medium grade enamel finish. Shipping weight, 4 oz.
49F160
Price 29c

Dice Cup With Dice.

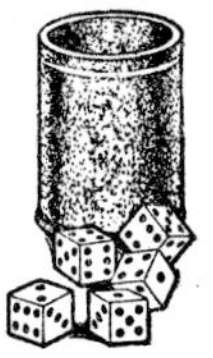

Leather dice cup and five 7⁄16-inch smooth ivory color dice. Shipping wt., 4 ounces.
49F218
Price 79c

SEARS, ROEBUCK AND CO. 2599

Paints and Educational Toys

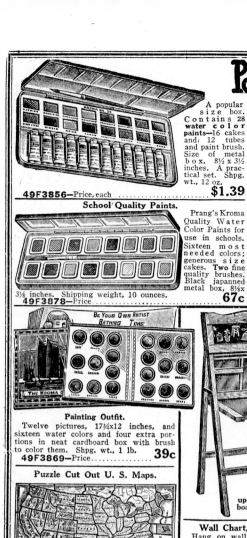

A popular size box. Contains 28 water color paints—16 cakes and 12 tubes and paint brush. Size of metal box, 8½ x 3½ inches. A practical set. Shpg. wt., 12 oz.
49F3856—Price, each **$1.39**

School Quality Paints.

Prang's Kroma Quality Water Color Paints for use in schools. Sixteen most needed colors; generous size cakes. Two fine quality brushes. Black japanned metal box, 8½x3⅛ inches. Shipping weight, 10 ounces.
49F3878—Price **67c**

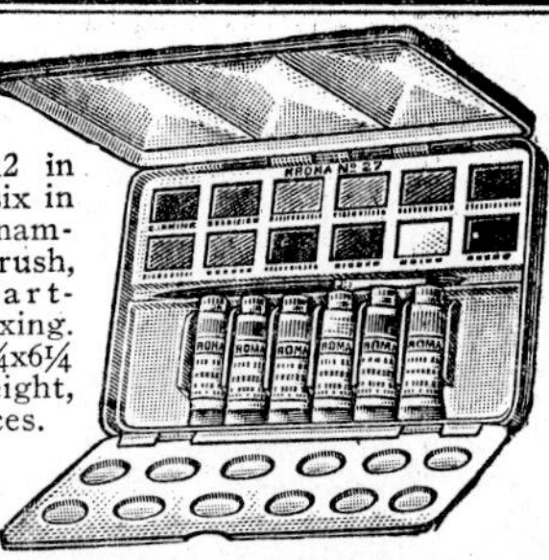

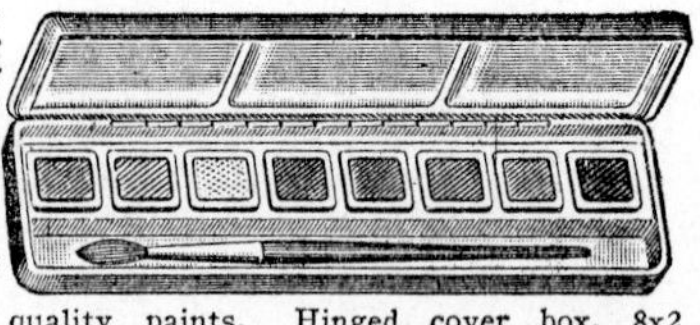

Eighteen water color paints, 12 in cake form and six in tubes, white enameled pallette, brush, separate compartments for mixing. Metal box, 3¾x6¼ in. Shipping weight, packed, 12 ounces.
49F3855 Price, each..... **98c**

Consists of **THIRTY-TWO EXCELLENT QUALITY WATER COLOR PAINTS** for school use—sixteen cakes and sixteen tubes. Also two brushes and compartments for mixing. A practical set of colors. Japanned metal, hinged cover box, 9x4½ inches. The best set to buy if quality is desired. Shipping weight, 1¼ pounds.
49F3858—Price **$2.39**

Eight water color paints in metal box with paint brush. Fine for school work. Standard quality paints. Hinged cover box, 8x2 inches. Shipping weight, 8 ounces.
49F3877—Price **39c**

Painting Outfit.

Twelve pictures, 17¾x12 inches, and sixteen water colors and four extra portions in neat cardboard box with brush to color them. Shpg. wt., 1 lb.
49F3869—Price **39c**

Puzzle Cut Out U. S. Maps.

Cut out maps of the U. S. Nicely colored. States cut out on state lines where possible. Principal cities, rivers, mountains and lakes shown. Size, 19¾x12¼ inches.

Our Best Map.	Our Medium Priced.
Made of three-ply veneer wood. Shpg. weight, 1⅝ lbs.	Made on heavy cardboard. Shipping weight, 1⅛ lbs.
49F3871 Price........ **98c**	**49F3870** Price **45c**

Combination Chart—Blackboard—Desk.

Strong hardwood. Mission finished frame. The writing desk top is finished in cherry color and on reverse side is a fine blackboard 17x18 inches. When the board is down it forms writing desk. Has large revolving chart showing alphabet, numbers, animals and other designs for the child to copy on the board. Offers an unusual opportunity for teaching young children alphabet and numbers. Height, opened for use, about 44½ inches; writing desk surface, about 24½ inches above floor. Good quality eraser and box of crayon sent with each board. Shipping weight, 15 pounds. **Unmailable.**
79F3812¼—Price.................. **$4.79**

Desk folds up, bringing blackboard into place.

Wall Chart, Desk and Blackboard.

Hang on wall at convenient height. Has long revolving scroll of charts. Same as furnished in 79F3812¼ described above; 16½x17¼-inch blackboard surface, complete with assorted color crayons and eraser. Height, 26½ inches; width, 22 inches. Shipping weight, 12½ pounds.
79F3873¼—Price.................. **$3.98**

Universal Spelling Board.

Fifty-six ⅞-inch lettered blocks of hardwood to be moved in slots to form words and sentences. Size, 13½x9 in. Shipping weight, 2¼ pounds.
49F3838—Price **$1.47**

Animal Stencils.

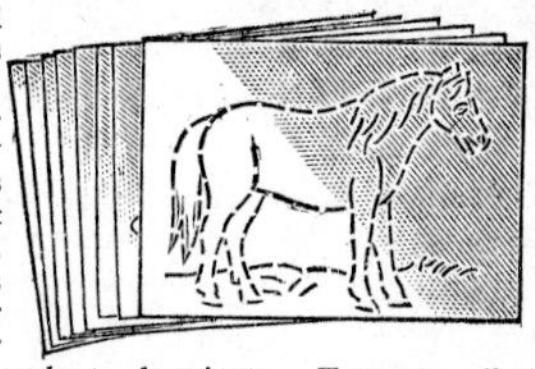

Cardboard with stencils of animals. To make pictures follow the cut lines with the point of a pencil. Soon teaches a child proper proportions for making independent drawings. Ten stencils, size 4½x6½ inches. Come packed in neat box. Shipping weight, 2 ounces.
49F3826—Price **29c**

As Blackboard. As Desk.

A Big Value Paint Box.

23 separate colors (21 cakes and 2 tubes) in partition metal box with good grade brush. Size of box, 7x3½ in. Our best value in paints. Shpg. wt., 8 oz.
49F3852—Price **39c**

Complete Painting Outfit.

Box contains twenty-four cakes of water color paint, two mixing pans and a brush, a painting book, with pretty childhood pictures in outline to paint. Size box, 13⅝x7⅞ inches. Shipping wt., 1 lb.
49F3864—Price, complete..... **39c**

Embroidery Set.

Six-inch hoop, thimble, needle, five skeins colored embroidery cotton, four doilies and sheets with designs. Box, 10x6½ in. Shpg. wt., 1 lb.
49F3816 Price **59c**

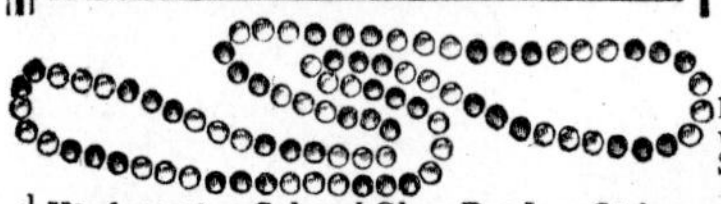

Story Sewing Cards.

Twelve Picture Sewing Cards, plainly perforated for sewing. Five skeins assorted colored threads and needle. Size, 7½x 5⅝ in. Shipping weight, 10 oz.
49F3814 Price, per set **25c**

Kindergarten Colored Glass Beads on String.

An extra fine string of colored glass beads, each about ¼ inch in diameter. About 160 assorted colored beads to string. Teaches child colors, how to count and furnishes amusement. Shipping weight, 8 ounces.
49F3803—Price **25c**

Glass Beads for Stringing.

Four bags of imported colored glass beads. About 225 assorted color glass beads; each bag different size beads. Size of each bag, about 2x3 in. Shpg. wt., 8 ounces.
49F3815—Price...... **25c**

See If Your Child Is Artistic.

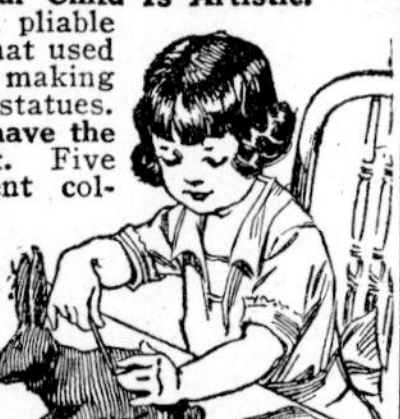

Plasticine is a pliable clay similar to that used by sculptors in making models of big statues. **Your child may have the sculptor's talent.** Five packages different colored Plasticine, modeling stick and a book of beginner's lessons. Size box, 9x7½ in. Shipping wt., 1⅛ lbs.
49F3834—Price **45c**

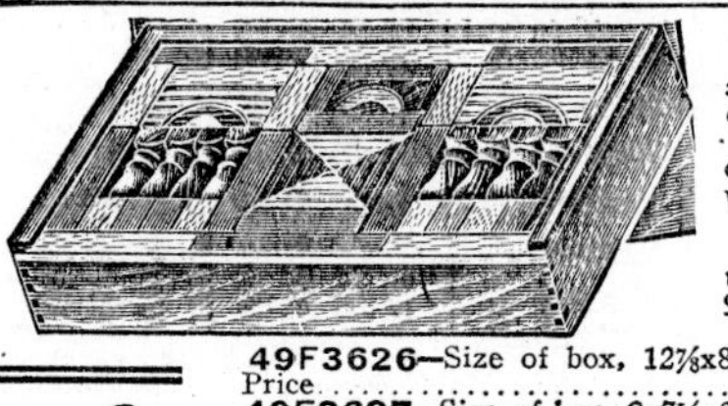

WOOD BEADS FOR STRINGING

33c Special. Consists of about 100 assorted colored round wooden beads and two colored cords. Packed in wooden box with slide cover. Shipping weight, 8 ounces.
49F3831 Per set **33c**

A Popular Box. Set of assorted colored wooden beads with two strong stringing cords. About 175 wooden beads, assorted shapes. Wooden box. Shipping wt., 1 lb.
49F3813 Price, per set **67c**

Our Largest Bead Assortment. Six strings, 350 beads, assorted colors and shapes. Some square, round, oval and cylindrical. Wooden box. Shipping weight, 1¼ pounds.
49F3810 Price **98c**

Imported Architectural Blocks.

Fine, clear hardwood. Turned columns and odd shaped blocks. Two layers in each box. Packed in wood boxes.
79F3631¼—Our largest set. Size of box, 19½x12½x3¼ inches. Shipping weight, 16 pounds. Price **$4.89**
79F3625¼—Medium size. Box measures 15x10¼x3¾ inches. Shipping weight, 9½ pounds. Price **$2.98**
49F3626—Size of box, 12⅞x8¼x2¼ in. Shipping wt., 5 lbs. Price **1.39**
49F3627—Size of box, 9x7¼x2¼ inches. Shipping weight, 3 pounds. Price .... **.69**

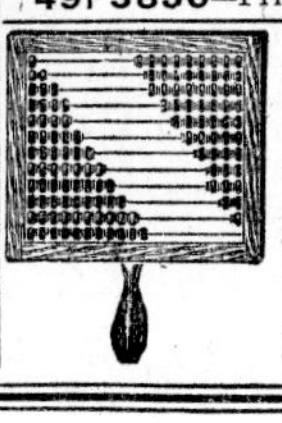

Rubber Stamp Circus.

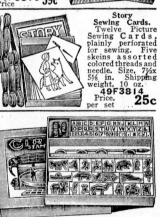

You can have a circus on paper. Rubber stamps with ink pad, ruler, water color paints and a brush for coloring the pictures. The stamps are all on wooden holders. Size box, 8½x8½ in. Shipping weight, 1⅜ pounds.
49F3850—Price, per set....... **89c**

Numeral Frame.

One hundred assorted colored beads on wires. Varnished wooden frame and handle. Size, 10⅝x9½ in. Shpg. wt., 1 lb.
49F3832 Price **50c**

Toys For The Baby

Get Baby a Bow Wow.

BOW WOW

MEOW

BOW WOW

Tom Tinker. He is made of nice smooth wooden balls strung on strong cords which extend to a handle ball above his head. His many colors are made from harmless dyes that do not come off. About 7 inches high. Packed in pretty box. Shipping wt., 10 oz.
49F7223—Price.... **57c**

Belle Tinker. Tom's twin sister, never out of sorts, always gracious. Her colorings are all her own and will not come off. She is made of bell shaped wooden pieces strung on heavy cords. Bright colors. About 6¼ inches high. Packed in pretty box. Shipping weight, 12 oz.
49F7224 Price.............. **55c**

He Barks. Yes, his bark is much worse than his bite. In fact he never bites at all, for he is only a little cloth covered toy dog. Well shaped and marked to resemble a Boston Bull. Big glass eyes and pert little ears. When baby presses his head down he opens his mouth and barks. Height, about 6¾ inches. Shipping weight, 1 pound.
49F4087—Price **33c**

Meow! Meow! Kitty. Dear Little Kitty! See how she opens her little pink mouth and cries when baby presses her head. Tiny hands soon learn how to make kitty meow. Naturally striped, cloth covered body. Big glass eyes. Collar with bell. About 6¼ in. high. Shipping weight, 7 ounces.
49F4089—Price **33c**

Beware the Dog!! He has a baby size bark to fit his small body. Babies love to hold him. Light enough to carry around. Enough like a real doggie to catch the fancy. A little mouth that opens when baby presses on his head to make him bark. A collar and a bell. Two sizes.
49F4088 — Large size, 8x7 inches. Shipping weight, 12 ounces. **39c**
49F4013—Small size, 6x5¼ inches. Shipping weight, 8 ounces. **25c**

Floating Toys for Baby's Bath.

White Rubber Animals. Just the Thing for the Baby. Assorted white rubber animals with whistles.
49F4406 — Small size, about 4¾x2¼ inches. Shipping weight, 5 ounces. Price, each **17c**
49F4428—Large size, about 5x3½ inches. Shipping weight, 7 ounces. Price **27c**

When Bathing Baby. A few of these floating toys placed in the tub will keep him amused. Proportioned true to life in realistic colors. A large assortment, some of them shown above. About 2 in. long.
69F7858 — Twelve Floating Animals. Shpg. wt., 6 oz. Price **97c**
69F7850—Six Floating Animals. Shipping weight, 4 oz. Price **49c**

The wash rag usually brings tears to baby's eyes. But it need not. These little dollies are water babies. They float, and they will keep baby happy even at bath time.
49F7229—Betsy Bobs. Rubber sponge body; cork head. Height, 5¼ in. Shpg. wt., 3 oz. **39c**
49F7227—Bobby Bobs. All cork. Reinforced. Hand painted. Height, 7¾ in. Shpg. wt., 6 oz. Price **39c**
49F7228—Pretty little doll with sponge rubber dress. Height, 4¼ inches. Shpg. wt., 3 oz. Price **39c**

No Tears at Bath Time.

Red Rubber Dog. Red rubber dog with whistle. Size over all, 5x4¼ inches. Shipping weight, 5 ounces.
49F4436—Price. **45c**

Red Rubber Cat. Heavy red rubber. Complete with whistle. Size over all, 4¾x2 inches. Shipping weight, 5 ounces.
49F4433—Price. **25c**

Angora Kitten. Natural colors, real fur. Glass eyes, pink mouth. Kitten voice. Soft and cuddly; very lifelike. In position shown, about 5½ inches high by 5 inches long. Shipping weight, 8 ounces. **49F4098**—Price **97c**

Babies Rattles

Roly-Polys

Imported roly-polys, made of composition and papier mache. Handsomely colored. Round bottom weighted. When tipped over always sits up again. Babies want them. Clowns and other assorted funny figures. Movable heads.

	Height, Inches	Shpg. Wt., Lbs.	Price
49F7015	16½	4	$1.98
49F7006	12	3	1.47
49F7009	9¾	1½	.98
49F7005	9	1½	.79
49F7004	7½	1	.49
49F7010	4¼	¾	.25

Wonder What This Is ? Unhook the lid, quick as a wink up it comes, and a queer little man, with reddish whiskers, or a funny clown or some other strange figure sticks his head out at you with a little squeak. Surprise boxes were loads of fun even when we were kids. They are as popular now as then. Size of box, 4x4x7 inches high. Shipping weight, 10 ounces.
49F5712—Price..... **29c**

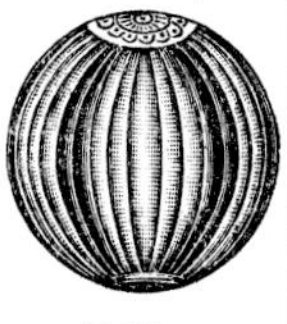

Rubber Whistle Ball. Fluted rubber ball. Decorated in several colors. Well made and finished. Whistle in end. Diameter, 2¼ inches. Shipping weight, 4 oz.
69F7723 Price..... **8c**

Rattle. Daintily colored celluloid in assorted designs. Length, abt. 6 in. Shpg. wt., 5 oz.
69F9162 Price .. **49c**

Rattle. Nicely decorated, strong and substantial celluloid. Length, about 5¾ in. Shpg. wt., 5 ounces.
69F9165 Price .. **33c**

Pyralin Egg Shape Rattle. Brightly colored, twisted handle. Length, 5 inches. Egg is 2¾ in. long. Shipping wt., 2 ounces.
69F9168 Price ... **10c**

Rattle. Celluloid, two color rattle. Length, abt. 5¼ in. Shpg. wt., 2 oz.
69F9163 Price ... **19c**

A B C Rattle With Teething Ring. Gray rubber with alphabet. Good for teething. Length, abt. 4 inches. Shipping wt., 4 oz.
49F4401 Price ... **10c**

Baby Face Rubber Rattle. About 4¾ in. long. Good grade white rubber. Assorted designs. Round ring on end for teething ring. Small bell inside of head. Shpg. wt., 2 oz.
49F4408 Price **19c**

The Daintiest of Toys for Dainty Babies.

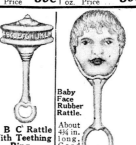

Sitting Bunny. Av. shpg. wt., 6 oz.

Kitty Cat. Washable terry cloth. Stuffed with kapoc. Legs, tail, eyes, etc., painted with waterproof colors. Ribbon bow. Height, 7¾ in. Shpg. wt., 6 oz.
49F4000 **79c**

These darling stuffed kitties and bunnies are made of the daintiest of washable cotton crepe, with features carefully embroidered in pretty colors. Stuffed with light weight, fluffy kapoc. Not out of place in any baby's crib. Very fine quality.
49F4015—Slumber Pillow Kitty. Removable cloth slip, easily washed. Size, about 10x10 in. Shipping wt., 1 lb. Price **98c**
49F4009— Kitty. Height, about 7¼ inches. Shipping wt., 8 oz. Price **98c**
49F4004 Bunny. Height, abt.10½ in. Shpg. wt., 10 oz. Price **98c**

Good quality terry cloth (Turkish toweling), stuffed with light, fluffy kapoc. Can be washed. Measures abt. 9¾ inches. Ribbon bow.
49F4002 **67c**

Humpty Dumpty. Made of soft heavy white washable material. Buy this for baby. Eyes and other features painted in waterproof colors. Legs with bells at feet. When baby squeezes Humpty he squeaks. Height, when seated about 7½ in., or 11½ in. long, including legs. Shipping weight, 10 ounces.
49F7210—Price. **69c**

Baby Bunting. A cunning little toy, wearing a soft white baby bunting with hood and pink lined bunny ears. Two little bells down front. A delightful light weight plaything for baby. Height, over all, 8 inches. Shipping wt., 7 ounces.
49F7241—Price. **79c**

Carriage Ball. Hang this pretty, brightly decorated 2¼-inch celluloid ball from hood of baby's carriage. String with ribbon. Average shipping wt., 3 oz.
69F9164 Price **33c**

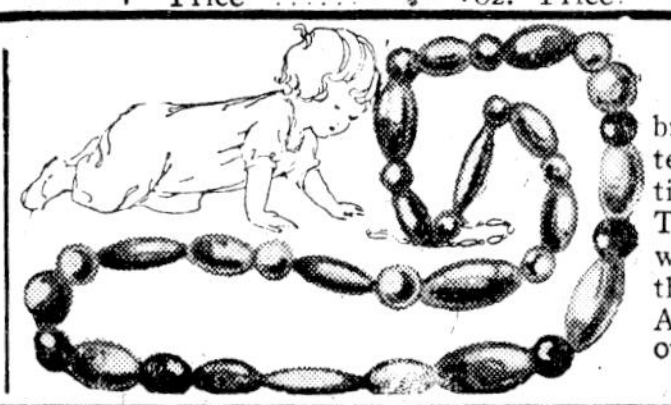

Creeping Beads. Thirty-six large size, brightly colored beads, fastened on heavy string and tied. They catch baby's eye. Throw string on floor and watch baby creep to get them. Endless fun for baby. Average shipping weight, 4 ounces.
49F3825—Price.. **59c**

MUSICAL TOYS

Schoenhut's Quality Toy Pianos.

These pianos are all carefully tuned so that simple melodies can be played. Wood frames shaped like ordinary upright piano stained to represent rosewood and nicely varnished. Decorated front, wood keys painted white with black markings to represent the black keys of a real piano. Each piano packed in strong shipping carton. Furnished in eight sizes as described below.

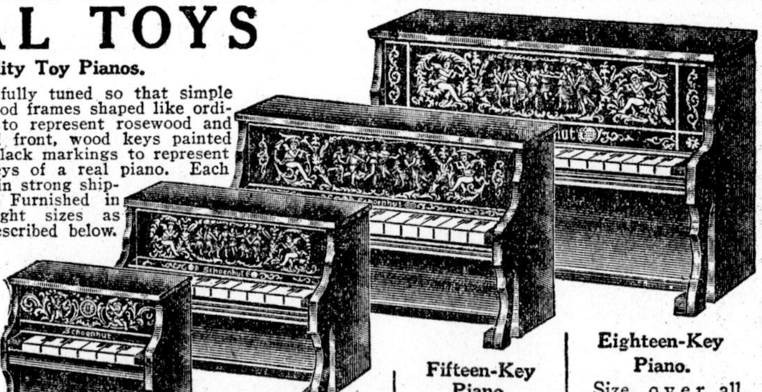

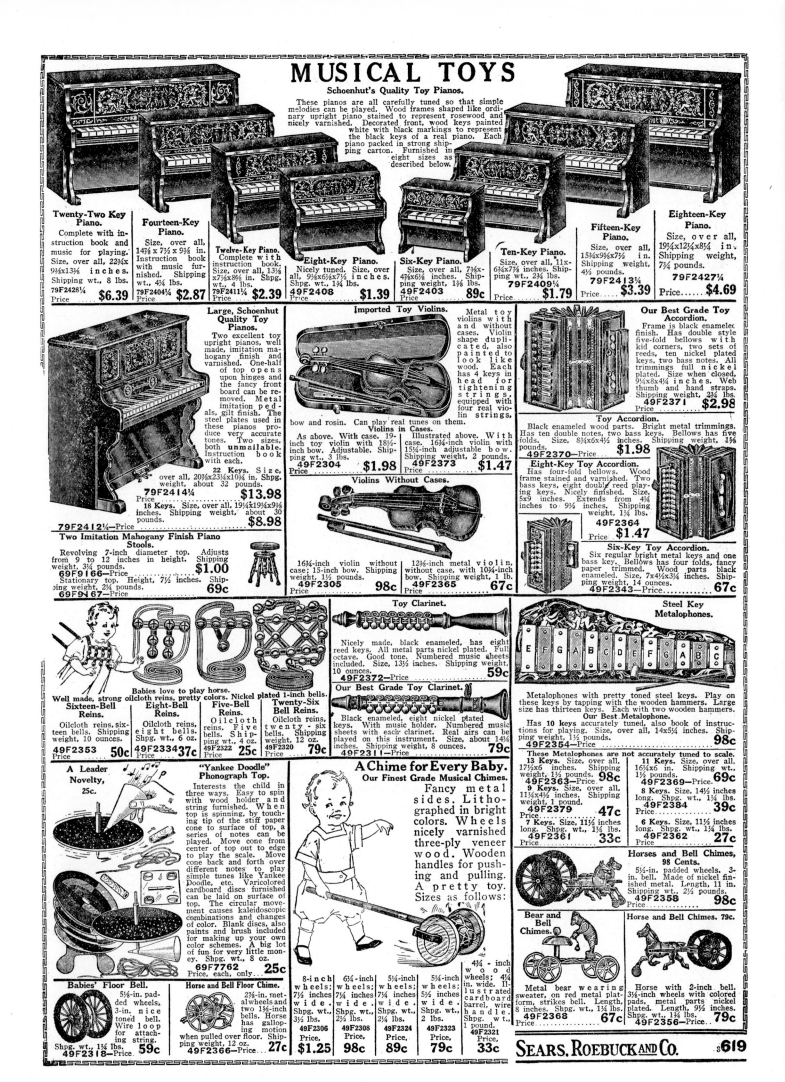

Twenty-Two Key Piano. Complete with instruction book and music for playing. Size, over all, 22¾x9⅜x13⅛ inches. Shipping wt., 8 lbs. 79F2428¼ Price **$6.39**

Fourteen-Key Piano. Size, over all, 14⅞ x 7½ x 9⅜ in. Instruction book with music furnished. Shipping wt., 4¼ lbs. 79F2404¼ Price **$2.87**

Twelve-Key Piano. Complete with instruction book. Size, over all, 13⅛x7⅛x8⅝ in. Shpg. wt., 4 lbs. 79F2411¼ Price **$2.39**

Eight-Key Piano. Nicely tuned. Size, over all, 9⅛x6⅛x7½ inches. Shpg. wt., 1¾ lbs. 49F2408 Price **$1.39**

Six-Key Piano. Size, over all, 7⅜x4⅞x6⅛ inches. Shipping weight, 1⅛ lbs. 49F2403 **89c**

Ten-Key Piano. Size, over all, 11x6¾x7⅞ inches. Shipping wt., 2¾ lbs. 79F2409¼ Price **$1.79**

Fifteen-Key Piano. Size, over all, 15¾x9⅝x7½ in. Shipping weight, 4½ pounds. 79F2413¼ Price..... **$3.39**

Eighteen-Key Piano. Size, over all, 19¼x12¼x8¾ in. Shipping weight, 7¾ pounds. 79F2427¼ Price...... **$4.69**

Large, Schoenhut Quality Toy Pianos.

Two excellent toy upright pianos, well made, imitation mahogany finish and varnished. One-half of top opens upon hinges and the fancy front board can be removed. Metal imitation pedals, gilt finish. The steel plates used in these pianos produce very accurate tones. Two sizes, both **unmailable.** Instruction book with each.

22 Keys. Size, over all, 20⅞x23¼x10¾ in. Shpg. weight, about 32 pounds. 79F2414¼ Price **$13.98**

18 Keys. Size, over all, 19¼x19¼x9⅜ inches. Shipping weight, about 30 pounds. 79F2412¼—Price **$8.98**

Two Imitation Mahogany Finish Piano Stools.

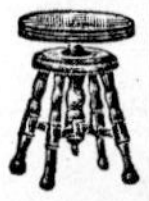

Revolving 7-inch diameter top. Adjusts from 9 to 12 inches in height. Shipping weight, 3¾ pounds. 69F9166—Price **$1.00**

Stationary top. Height, 7½ inches. Shipping weight, 2¼ pounds. 69F9167—Price **69c**

Imported Toy Violins.

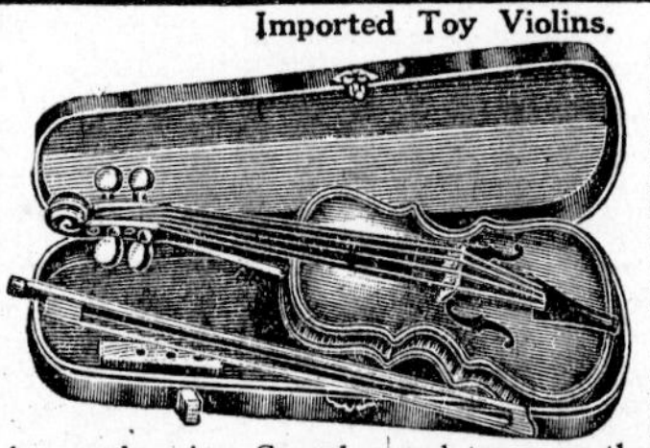

Metal toy violins with and without cases. Violin shape duplicated, also painted to look like wood. Each has 4 keys in head for tightening strings, equipped with four real violin strings, bow and rosin. Can play real tunes on them.

Violins in Cases.

As above. With case. 19-inch toy violin with 18½-inch bow. Adjustable. Shipping wt., 3 lbs. 49F2304 Price **$1.98**

Illustrated above. With case. 16¾-inch violin with 15¼-inch adjustable bow. Shipping weight, 2 pounds. 49F2373 Price **$1.47**

Violins Without Cases.

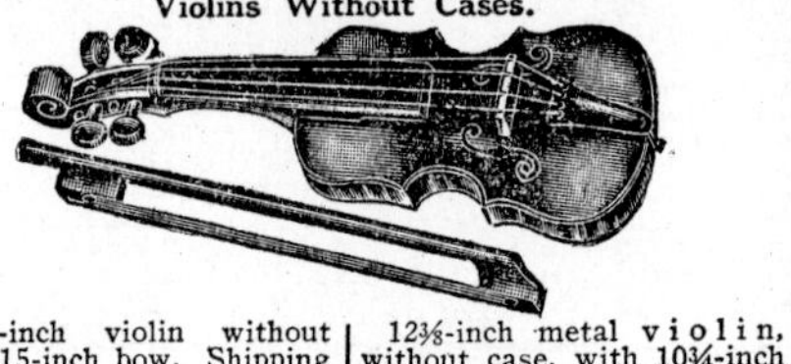

16¾-inch violin without case; 15-inch bow. Shipping weight, 1½ pounds. 49F2305 Price **98c**

12⅜-inch metal violin, without case, with 10¾-inch bow. Shipping weight, 1 lb. 49F2365 Price **67c**

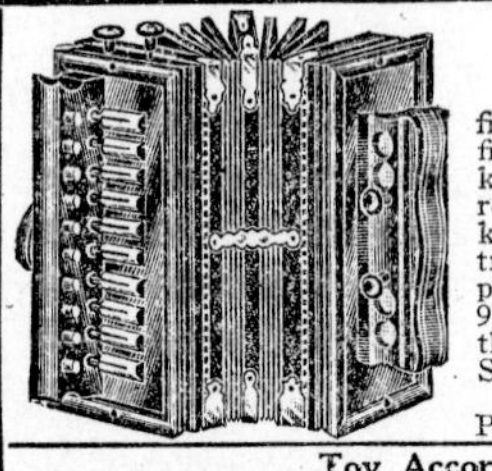

Our Best Grade Toy Accordion.

Frame is black enameled finish. Has double style five-fold bellows with kid corners, two sets of reeds, ten nickel plated keys, two bass notes. All trimmings full nickel plated. Size when closed, 9¼x8x4¼ inches. Web thumb and hand straps. Shipping weight, 2¾ lbs. 49F2371 Price **$2.98**

Toy Accordion.

Black enameled wood parts. Bright metal trimmings. Has ten double notes, two bass keys. Bellows has five folds. Size, 8¾x6x4½ inches. Shipping weight, 1⅝ pounds. 49F2370—Price **$1.98**

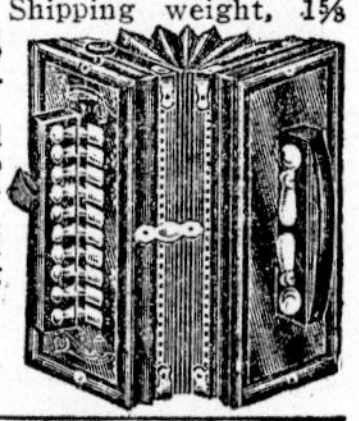

Eight-Key Toy Accordion.

Has four-fold bellows. Wood frame stained and varnished. Two bass keys, eight double reed playing keys. Nicely finished. Size, 5x9 inches. Extends from 4¼ inches to 9½ inches. Shipping weight, 1¼ lbs. 49F2364 Price **$1.47**

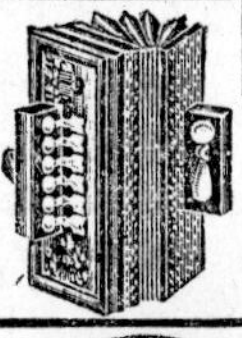

Six-Key Toy Accordion.

Six regular bright metal keys and one bass key. Bellows has four folds, fancy paper trimmed. Wood parts black enameled. Size, 7x4½x3¼ inches. Shipping weight, 14 ounces. 49F2343—Price **67c**

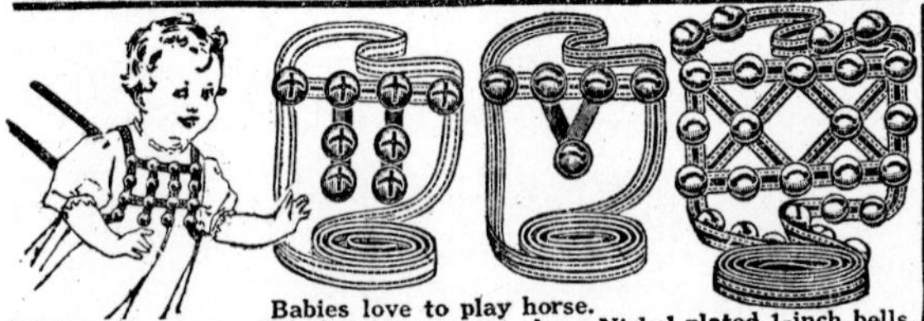

Babies love to play horse. Well made, strong oilcloth reins, pretty colors. Nickel plated 1-inch bells.

Sixteen-Bell Reins. Oilcloth reins, sixteen bells. Shipping weight, 10 ounces. 49F2353 Price **50c**

Eight-Bell Reins. Oilcloth reins, eight bells. Shpg. wt., 6 oz. 49F2334 Price **37c**

Five-Bell Reins. Oilcloth reins. Five bells. Shipping wt., 4 oz. 49F2322 Price **25c**

Twenty-Six Bell Reins. Oilcloth reins, twenty-six bells. Shipping weight, 12 oz. 49F2320 Price **79c**

Toy Clarinet.

Nicely made, black enameled, has eight reed keys. All metal parts nickel plated. Full octave. Good tone. Numbered music sheets included. Size, 13½ inches. Shipping weight, 10 ounces. 49F2372—Price **59c**

Our Best Grade Toy Clarinet.

Black enameled, eight nickel plated keys. With music holder. Numbered music sheets with each clarinet. Real airs can be played on this instrument. Size, about 14¼ inches. Shipping weight, 8 ounces. 49F2311—Price **79c**

Steel Key Metalophones.

Metalophones with pretty toned steel keys. Play on these keys by tapping with the wooden hammers. Large size has thirteen keys. Each with two wooden hammers.

Our Best Metalophone.

Has **10 keys** accurately tuned, also book of instructions for playing. Size, over all, 14x5¼ inches. Shipping weight, 1½ pounds. 49F2354—Price **98c**

These Metalophones are not accurately tuned to scale.

13 Keys. Size, over all, 17½x6 inches. Shipping weight, 1½ pounds. 49F2363—Price **98c**

11 Keys. Size, over all, 16¼x6 in. Shipping wt., 1½ pounds. 49F2369—Price **69c**

9 Keys. Size, over all, 11¼x4½ inches. Shipping weight, 1 pound. 49F2379 Price **47c**

8 Keys. Size, 14½ inches long. Shpg. wt., 1¼ lbs. 49F2384 Price **39c**

7 Keys. Size, 11½ inches long. Shpg. wt., 1¼ lbs. 49F2361 Price **33c**

6 Keys. Size, 11½ inches long. Shpg. wt., 1¼ lbs. 49F2362 Price **27c**

A Leader Novelty, 25c.

"Yankee Doodle" Phonograph Top.

Interests the child in three ways. Easy to spin with wood holder and string furnished. When top is spinning, by touching tip of the stiff paper cone to surface of top, a series of notes can be played. Move cone from center of top out to edge to play the scale. Move cone back and forth over different notes to play simple tunes like Yankee Doodle, etc. Varicolored cardboard discs furnished can be laid on surface of top. The circular movement causes kaleidoscopic combinations and changes of color. Blank discs, also paints and brush included for making up your own color schemes. A big lot of fun for very little money. Shpg. wt., 8 oz. 69F7762 Price, each, only **25c**

A Chime for Every Baby.

Our Finest Grade Musical Chimes.

Fancy metal sides. Lithographed in bright colors. Wheels nicely varnished three-ply veneer wood. Wooden handles for pushing and pulling. A pretty toy. Sizes as follows:

8-inch wheels; 7½ inches wide. Shpg. wt., 3½ lbs.	6¼-inch wheels; 7¼ inches wide. Shpg. wt., 2½ lbs.	5¼-inch wheels; 7¼ inches wide. Shpg. wt., 2¼ lbs.	5¼-inch wheels; 5½ inches wide. Shpg. wt., 2 lbs.	4¾-inch wood wheels; 4¼ in. wide. Illustrated cardboard barrel, wire handle. Shpg. wt., 1 pound.
49F2306 Price, **$1.25**	49F2308 Price, **98c**	49F2324 Price, **89c**	49F2323 Price, **79c**	49F2321 Price, **33c**

Horses and Bell Chimes, 98 Cents.

5½-in. padded wheels. 3-in. bell. Made of nickel finished metal. Length, 11 in. Shipping wt., 2½ pounds. 49F2358 Price **98c**

Bear and Bell Chimes.

Metal bear wearing sweater, on red metal platform, strikes bell. Length, 8 inches. Shpg. wt., 1¼ lbs. 49F2368 Price **67c**

Horse and Bell Chimes. 79c.

Horse with 2-inch bell. 3⅛-inch wheels with colored pads, metal parts nickel plated. Length, 9½ inches. Shpg. wt., 1¼ lbs. 49F2356—Price **79c**

Babies' Floor Bell.

5⅛-in. padded wheels, 3-in. nice toned bell. Wire loop for attaching string. Shpg. wt., 1¼ lbs. 49F2318—Price **59c**

Horse and Bell Floor Chime.

2⅞-in. metal wheels and two 1⅝-inch bells. Horse has galloping motion when pulled over floor. Shipping weight, 12 oz. 49F2366—Price **27c**

UNIVERSAL MECHANICAL TOYS

Scissors Grinder.
See the Sparks Fly.
Wind the spring and the man pedals vigorously, causing showers of sparks. Man and machine made of metal. Height of man, 5½ in. Total length of toy, 6½ inches. Shipping weight, 12 ounces.
49F5791—Price............. **59c**

Flying Airplanes.

Turn crank and these airships fly around in circles with propellers whirling. This is a large toy when set up and very showy, as it is very handsomely finished. Has a man in each airplane. Speed of airplanes depends upon how fast the crank is turned. Made of wood and metal. Nothing to get out of order. A dandy action toy. Shipping weight, 1¾ pounds.
49F5762—Price............. **98c**

Naughty Boy.
While father is trying to drive in a dignified manner his young son continually pulls at the steering lever, causing the car to run most every way. Decorated in fancy colors. Size, 4¾x4½x3 inches. Shipping weight, 9 oz.
49F5721 Price....... **39c**

Crazy Clown.
Very amusing clown driving a little car which runs around floor in a very comical zigzag manner. Excellent spring motor. A toy wonder. Size, 5½x4¼ in. Shpg. wt., 10 oz.
49F5783 Price **39c**

Butting Goat and Clown.
Goat butts clown in wagon around floor in a very amusing manner. Nicely decorated in lifelike colors. Strong spring motor provides lots of action. Size, 7¼x6 inches. Shpg. wt., 14 ounces.
49F5781 Price **98c**

Mechanical Street Roller.
A splendid toy. See page 627 for full description. Shpg. wt., 1½ lbs.
49F5763 Price, **$1.39**

Joke Mouse.
Runs along the floor. See the girls run. For full description see page 629. Shpg. wt., 3 ounces.
49F6305—Price............. **19c**

See the Puff of Smoke at Each Shot.

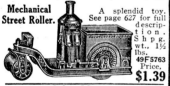

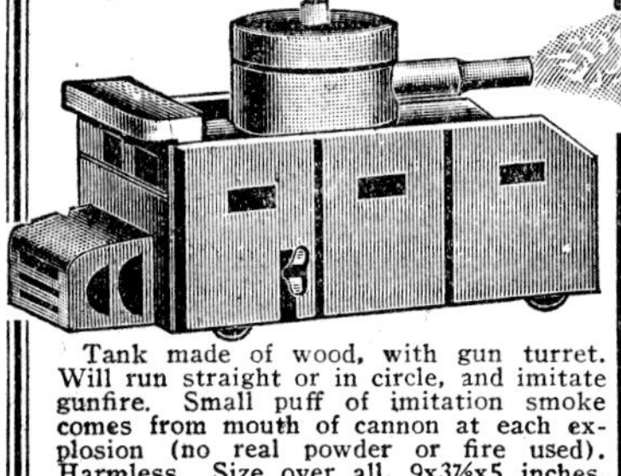

Tank made of wood, with gun turret. Will run straight or in circle, and imitate gunfire. Small puff of imitation smoke comes from mouth of cannon at each explosion (no real powder or fire used). Harmless. Size over all, 9x3⅞x5 inches. Shipping weight, 2 lbs. 3 oz.
49F5749—Price............. **$1.39**

Handsomely Colored Racer.
Cranking Model, Spare Wheel.
Mechanical racing roadster, made of sheet steel, nicely enameled and finished in bright yellow, with black stripes and red wheels. Cranking car winds the spring, then watch auto go. Adjustable and can be made to run in circle or in straight line. Complete with metal driver. Size, over all, 9½x3¾x3½ in. Shipping wt., 1 lb.
49F5011—Price............. **98c**

Ambulance.
Metal, finished in colors. Crank winds up. Strong spring motor. Size, 8¼x5¾ in. Shpg. wt., 2¾ lbs.
49F5003—Price, each......... **98c**

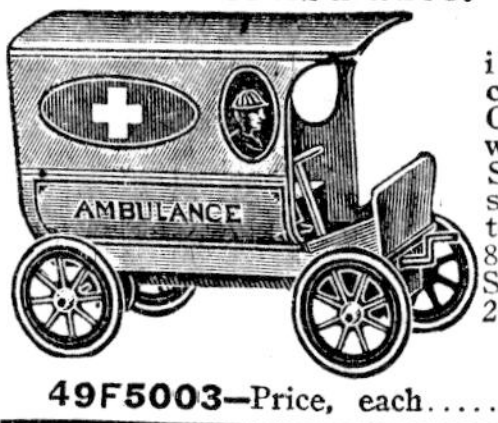

U. S. Mail.
Painted delivery auto. Sheet steel with a good spring wound by crank. Metal driver. Size, 7½x 4¼x5¾ in. Shpg. wt., 2¾ lbs.
49F5007—Price............. **98c**

The Wise Beetle.
Immense metal beetle decorated in lifelike colors. Wind up the strong spring motor, put beetle on smooth table and he will crawl away in a hurry, and when he comes to the edge of the table he turns and follows around the edge, seemingly looking for a way down. He will not fall off. Size, 7¼ inches long and 4¼ inches wide over all. Shpg. wt., 15 oz.
49F5728—Price............. **45c**

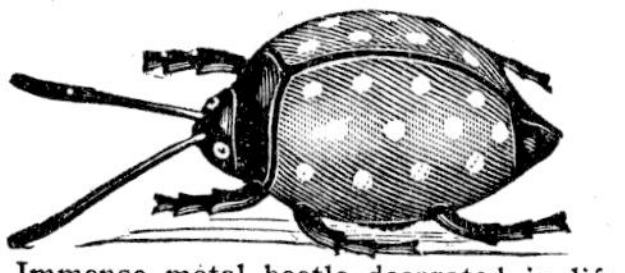

Cat and Mouse.
Kitty is on wheels. Wind up the clockwork motor and see her push the mouse trap over the floor while the little mouse races around, seemingly trying to find a way out. Very realistic. Total length, about 11 inches. Metal painted in natural colors. Shpg. wt., 12 oz.
49F5727—Price............. **59c**

Moving Turtle.

Watch this turtle make its way over the floor. Realistic in action and coloring. Draw backwards on table or floor and release. Nothing to wind. Hairspring mechanism concealed. About 2 inches long. Shpg. wt., 2 oz.
49F5774—Price............. **39c**

Mechanical Goose With Movable Wings.
When wound goose darts across the floor on wheels flapping its wings in a very natural manner and at the same time quacking. Made of metal and painted in natural looking colors. Good spring motor and well made throughout. A toy that every child will enjoy. Shipping weight, 1 pound.
49F5797—Price............. **39c**

Metal Duck.
Friction motor. Waddles from side to side. Made of prettily lithographed metal. Size, 4x2x3 in. Shpg. wt., 8 oz.
49F5725 Price **39c**

Peacock With Voice.
Nicely enameled in colors. Very lifelike. Walks around floor, squawking as it walks. Size, 9¾x6¾ inches. Shipping weight, 14 ounces.
49F5771 Price, special at **89c**

Two Walking Toys

The Chinaman Pulls His Cart.
Nicely decorated in snappy colors to imitate Chinaman and cart. When wound up and released he walks along in a manner most lifelike, drawing his cart after him. The cart is large enough for very small toys and he will pull them, too. Very interesting mechanical toy. Made entirely of metal. Size, 4⅝ x 5⅜ inches. Shipping weight, 14 ounces.
49F5717—Price............. **39c**

The Negro Porter Pushes His Cart.
Wind it up and the porter walks across floor, pushing the cart ahead of him. The legs move just as though he were actually walking.
Made of metal, nicely lithographed in attractive colors. Size, over all, 6¼x5¾x2½ in. Shipping weight, 10 ounces.
49F5759—Price............. **39c**

Walbert Reversing Street Car

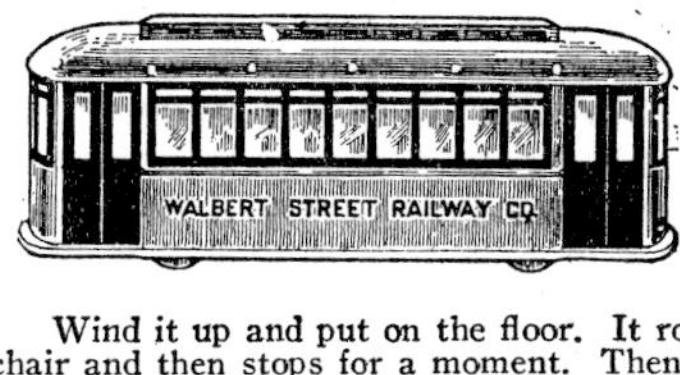

Wind it up and put on the floor. It rolls along until it bumps into a wall or chair and then stops for a moment. Then you hear the bell ring twice just like when the conductor of a real car rings the bell for the motorman to start back, and the car starts back, stopping again when it strikes a solid object. This is kept up until the strong spring runs down. Size, 14x4x4 inches. Painted in bright colors, packed well to insure safe delivery. Shipping weight, 5 pounds.
49F5737—Price............. **$3.98**

Mechanical Trolley Car.

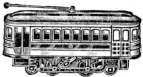

Pretty colors. Made of metal and shaped like a real car with round ends, adjustable trolley. When wound runs along floor. Substantially made with excellent clockwork motor. Will run on floor or carpet. Size, 10½x5½ inches. Shipping weight, 1¾ pounds.
49F5113—Price.................. **89c**

Duck Waddles.
Handsomely colored metal. Spring motor, runs over floor or carpet, wabbling from side to side. Size, 6½x4¼ in. Shipping wt., 6 oz.
49F5757 Price, each **39c**

Rooster and Duck.

Very naturally colored. Comical struggle for possession of frog. Runs around floor in a very funny manner. One of our best toys. Size, 11 inches long. Shipping weight, 12 ounces.
49F5778—Price.................. **59c**

Knife Sharpener.

Standing at his work bench this little man will busy himself at sharpening a knife he holds in his hands. If you wind up the strong spring motor the grindstone turns and real sparks fly from the knife. Height, of man, 4 inches. Length of toy over all, 4½ inches. Shipping weight, 12 ounces.
49F5792—Price.................. **39c**

Man on Motorcycle.
Very realistic. Naturally colored. When wound, man propels motorcycle around room in a very natural manner. Size, 7¾x5¾ inches. Shipping weight, 12 ounces.
49F5732 Price, **59c**

Pony and Cart.
Wind this toy up and watch it run along the floor. Cart large enough for small toys. Made entirely of metal, nicely painted in attractive colors. Length, about 7½ inches. Shipping wt., 10 oz.
49F5767—Price............. **33c**

Clown and Pig.

Clown tries to lead pig by ears. If you ever tried leading a pig you will know how funny this toy is. Made of metal painted natural colors. Size, 7½x6 inches. Shipping weight, 10 oz.
49F5776—Price............. **43c**

Panama Pile Driver.
Put marbles in chute at top and hammer goes up and down until all the marbles have been brought down. Comes complete with twelve marbles. Size, set up, 17x12½ in. Shipping wt., 2½ lbs.
49F5822 Price, **$1.39**

FRICTION TOYS

These new friction toys are an American invention and very popular. No springs to break. Merely put the toy on the floor, push forward two or three times, putting pressure directly above friction motor, and see it go ahead.

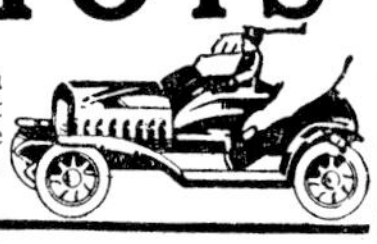

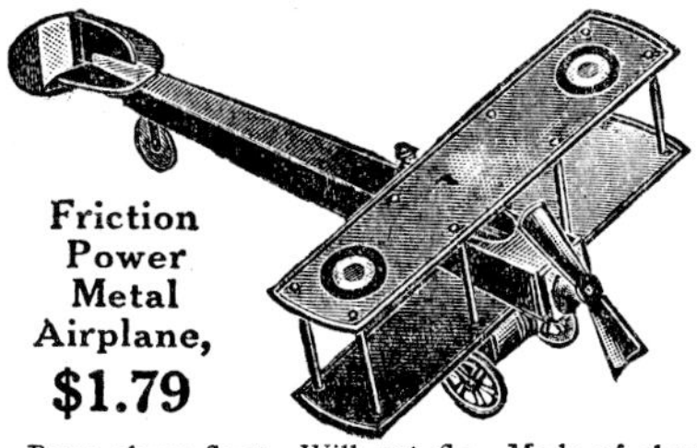

Friction Power Metal Airplane, $1.79

Runs along floor. Will not fly. Made of sheet steel nicely painted and decorated. Equipped with friction motor. Can also be used as a pull toy. Size over all, length, about 16¾ inches; width, 10¾ inches; height, 5¾ inches. Propeller at the front of machine revolves when toy is in motion. Shipping weight, 4¼ pounds.
79F5700¼—Price.................. **$1.79**

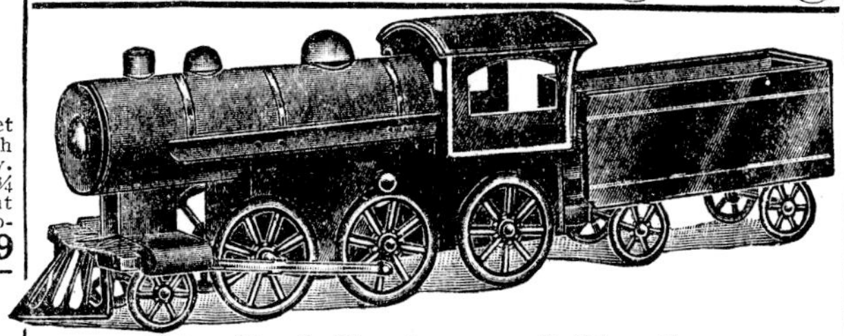

Big Red Engine and Tender

Made of sheet steel, brightly enameled, with gilt decorations. Equipped with friction motor. Engine is of the large camel back type, with eight wheels, while tender has four wheels. This is a very fine present for the little boy and one that he will appreciate. Length over all, about 24 inches. Shipping weight, 6¼ pounds.
79F5708¼—Price, complete.................................... **$1.79**

Similar to above, only engine has four wheels instead of eight and size is smaller. Length, over all, 17 inches. Shipping weight, 3 pounds.
79F5719¼—Price.. **$1.39**

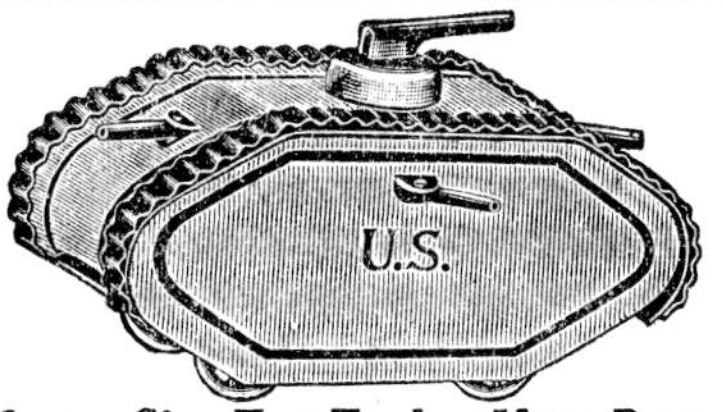

Large Size Toy Tank. Very Prettily Finished.

Made of sheet steel, nicely decorated and trimmed in colors. Has five dummy cannon and imitation caterpillar treads. Guns can be pointed in different directions. Equipped with friction motor and will run easily over floor under its own power. No key to wind. Size over all, 12¼x4¾x6½ in. Shpg. wt., 3½ lbs.
79F5705¼—Price.............. **$1.39**

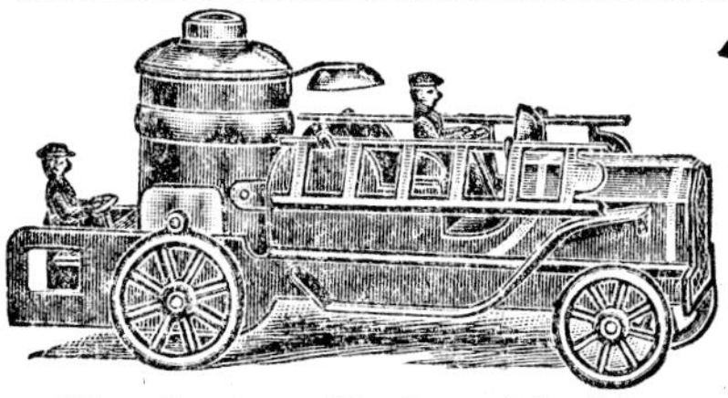

Fire Engine—Hook and Ladder.

These toys made of metal and painted in pretty colors. Each has two men. Friction motor.

Engine illustrated above. Size, 14½x4¾x7 in. Has two 7-in. ladders. Shpg. wt., 4¾ lbs.
79F5711¼—Price.................... **$1.79**

Hook and Ladder Truck. (Not illustrated.) Two 14-inch detachable metal ladders and one attached extension ladder. Turn crank and extends to about 25 inches in height. Size over all, 19½x4¼x7⅝ inches. Shipping weight, 4½ pounds.
79F5715¼—Price.................... **$1.79**

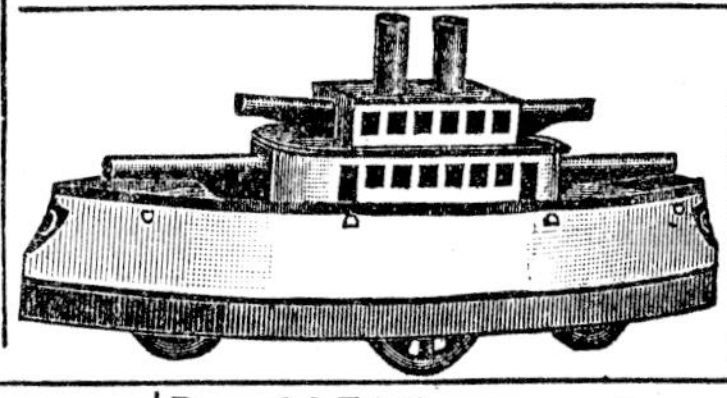

Friction Battleship.

battleship. Attractively decorated. Made of sheet metal. Has dummy guns. Equipped with a friction motor. Size over all, 15x7¼x3½ inches. Shipping weight, 2¾ pounds.
79F5739¼
Price.............. **$1.39**

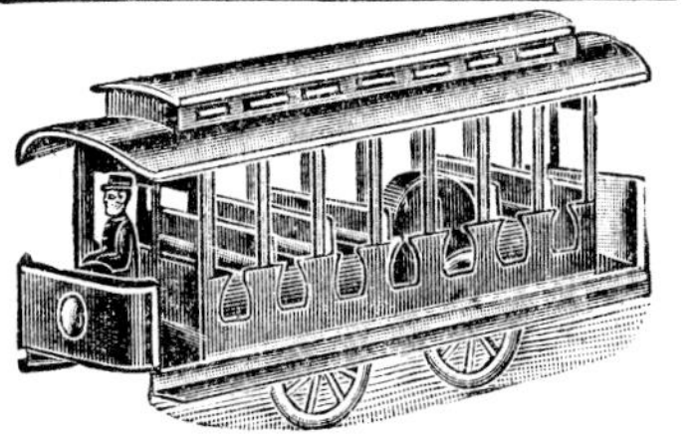

Street Car With Seats for Paper Dolls.

Has friction motor. Press down on top of car, push along floor and release, and car moves along on its own power. Made of sheet metal, nicely painted and decorated. Seats that child can use for little toys and paper dolls. Complete with motorman. Size over all: Length, about 13¾ inches; height, 6½ inches; width, 4⅝ inches. Shpg. wt., 3¼ lbs.
79F5775¼—Price.............. **$1.69**

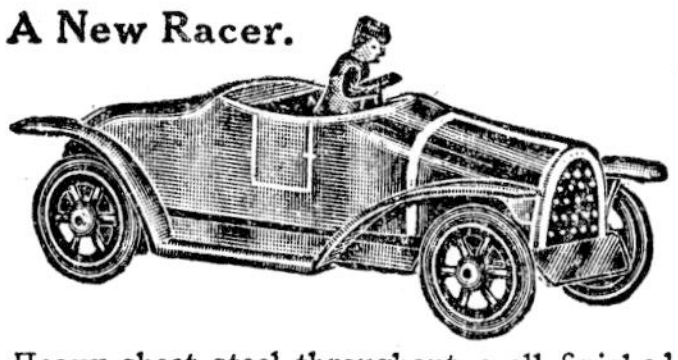

A New Racer.

Equipped with a new friction motor and gear encased underneath car. Produces high speed and will run a considerable distance either in circle or a straight line. Heavy sheet steel throughout, well finished edges and entire car very nicely painted and trimmed. Size over all, 10¾x4¾x3¼ inches. Shipping weight, 2 pounds.
49F5806—Price.............................. **98c**

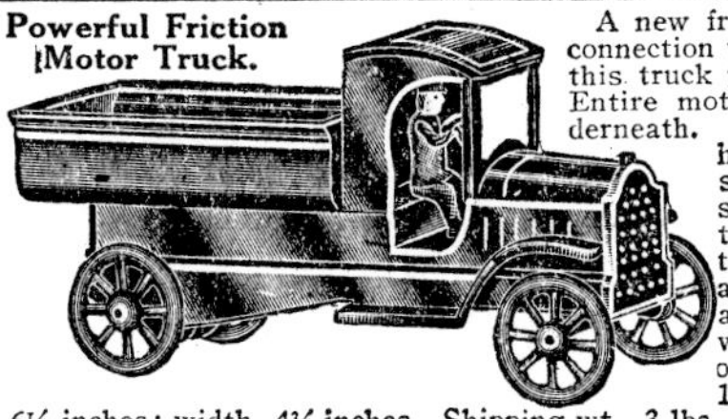

Powerful Friction Motor Truck.

A new friction motor in connection with gear gives this truck powerful speed. Entire motor encased underneath. Well made of heavy sheet steel and all sharp edges turned in. Prettily painted in attractive colors and trimmed with gilt. Size over all: Length, 13 in.; height, 6¼ inches; width, 4¾ inches. Shipping wt., 3 lbs.
79F5825¼—Price.............................. **$1.19**

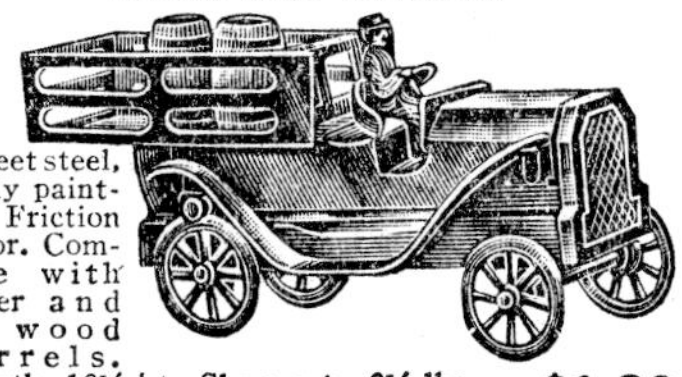

Truck and Barrels.

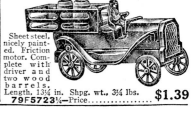

Sheet steel, nicely painted. Friction motor. Complete with driver and two wood barrels. Length, 13¼ in. Shpg. wt., 3¼ lbs.
79F5723¼—Price.............. **$1.39**

This Friction Floor Train, 3½ Feet Long, for $1.98.

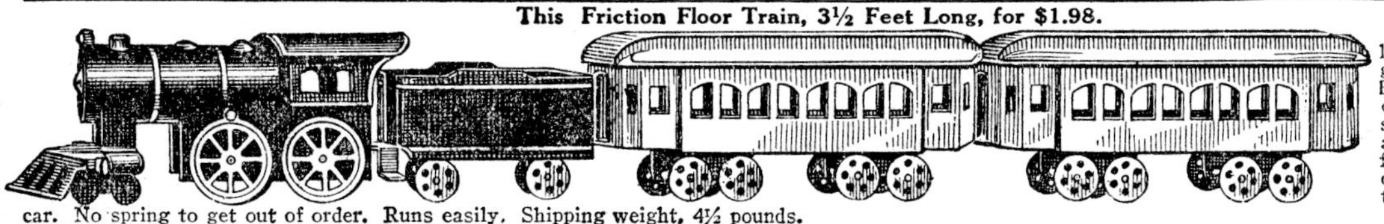

Large friction train, about 42 inches long over all, consisting of 18-inch engine and two cars, each 12 inches long. Has good friction motor, or can be pulled over floor with string. Made of sheet steel, nicely painted in attractive colors and with gilt decorations. Engine has four large movable wheels and four small dummy wheels, four small wheels on tender and eight wheels on each Pullman car. No spring to get out of order. Runs easily. Shipping weight, 4½ pounds.
79F5276¼—Price, complete.............................. **$1.98**

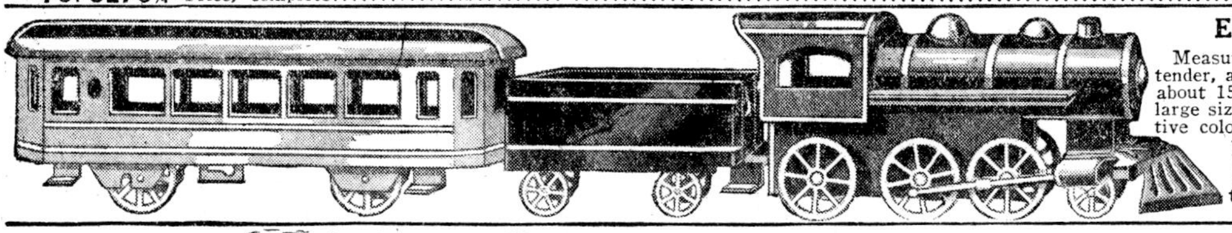

Extra Big Train to Pull, $2.39.

Measures over all, about 40 inches. Large engine and tender, about 23½ inches long, 6½ inches high, and a car about 15¾ inches long and about 5¾ inches high, with large size wheels. Made of sheet steel painted in attractive colors and trimmed in gilt. Engine has six large wheels. Tender large enough to haul small blocks. **This is not a friction train** and does not run on track, but is intended for pulling over the floor with string. Shpg. wt., 6¾ lbs.
79F5277¼—Price, complete....... **$2.39**

Iron Trains to Pull Over Floor.

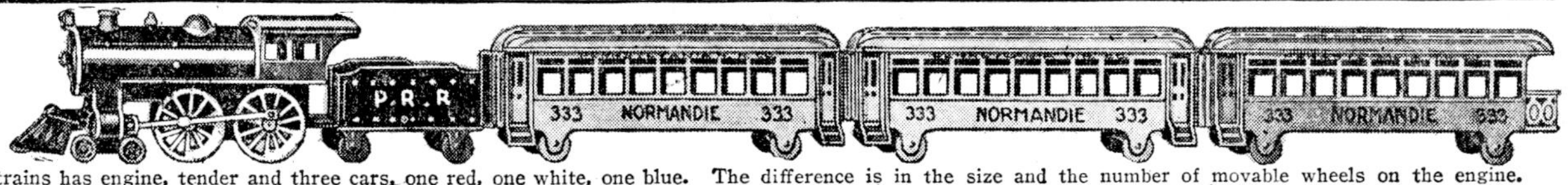

Each of these trains has engine, tender and three cars, one red, one white, one blue. The difference is in the size and the number of movable wheels on the engine.

37-Inch Length Train. Four movable wheels on engine. Shipping weight, 7¼ pounds.
79F5281¼
Price.................... **$1.98**

32-Inch Length Train. Four movable wheels on engine. Shipping weight, 6¼ pounds.
49F5285
Price.................... **$1.79**

27-Inch Length Train. Two movable wheels on engine. Shipping weight, 4⅞ pounds.
49F5286
Price.................... **$1.39**

25-Inch Length Train. Two movable wheels on engine. Shipping weight, 3⅜ pounds.
49F5280
Price.................... **98c**

21-Inch Length Train. Two movable wheels on engine. Shipping weight, 3 pounds.
49F5284
Price.................... **67c**

CAST IRON TOYS

Cast Iron Nicely Painted Auto to Pull Along Floor. 25c

A Dandy Hook and Ladder With Two Ladders.

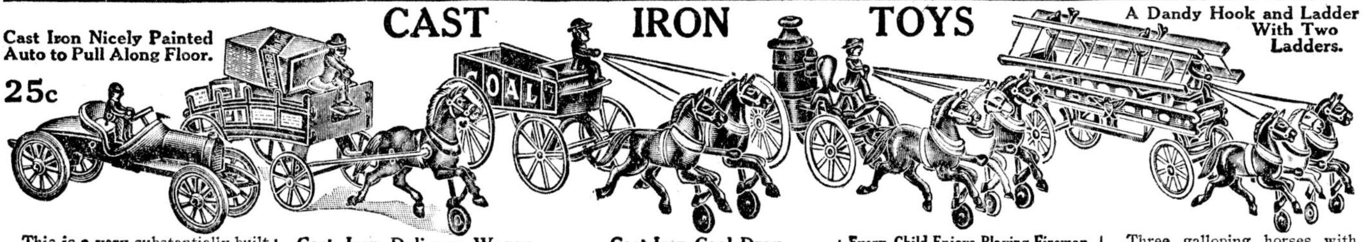

This is a very substantially built car. Has no motor, but is to be pulled with string. Attractively finished in colors. Iron man included. 7½ inches long. Shipping weight, 1¼ pounds.
49F5001—Price........ **25c**

Cast Iron Delivery Wagon. Nicely painted and trimmed cast iron and sheet metal. The length over all is about 11¼ inches. Seat is 3¾ inches high. Complete with dummy packages of food and cast iron driver. Shpg. wt., 1⅞ lbs.
69F7600
Price **59c**

Cast Iron Coal Dray. These horses can be detached from wagon and measure about 5½x4⅛ inches over all. Painted black with gilt trimming. Wagon is nicely painted. The body of wagon measures about 5x2 in. Total length, 12 in. Cast iron driver. Shpg. wt., 2½ lbs.
69F7601—Price........ **89c**

Every Child Enjoys Playing Fireman. Red cast iron fire engine with yellow wheels. Three galloping horses, two painted black, one white, each measuring about 5½x4⅛ inches over all. The length over all is about 12½ inches. Complete with cast iron driver. Shpg. wt., 3½ lbs.
69F7603—Price...... **98c**

Three galloping horses with hook and ladder. Horses measure about 5½x4⅛ inches over all. Two 10-inch ladders. Ladders wood, balance cast iron. Wagon part finished in four colors. Length, over all, about 16 in. Two men riders. Shipping weight, 4 pounds.
69F7602—Price...... **98c**

Floor Toys

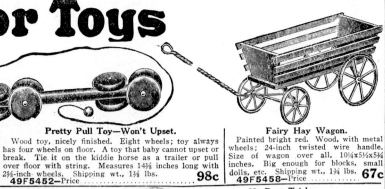

Figures Whirl.
To pull over floor or sidewalk. Finished in bright waterproof colors. Figures whirl around. Made of hardwood and steel. Size, over all, 8¼x7½ inches; 2⅝-inch wheels. Shipping wt., 1½ pounds.
49F5450—Price............ **98c**

Tumble Balls.
Finished in bright waterproof colors. Balls slides up and down. Made of hardwood on steel frame; 2⅝-inch wheels. Size, 9¼x8⅝ inches. Shipping weight, 2 pounds.
49F5451—Price........ **98c**

Pretty Pull Toy—Won't Upset.
Wood toy, nicely finished. Eight wheels; toy always has four wheels on floor. A toy that baby cannot upset or break. Tie it on the kiddie horse as a trailer or pull over floor with string. Measures 14⅜ inches long with 2⅝-inch wheels. Shipping wt., 1⅜ lbs.
49F5452—Price........... **98c**

Fairy Hay Wagon.
Painted bright red. Wood, with metal wheels; 24-inch twisted wire handle. Size of wagon over all, 10¼x5½x5¾ inches. Big enough for blocks, small dolls, etc. Shipping wt., 1¾ lbs.
49F5458—Price......... **67c**

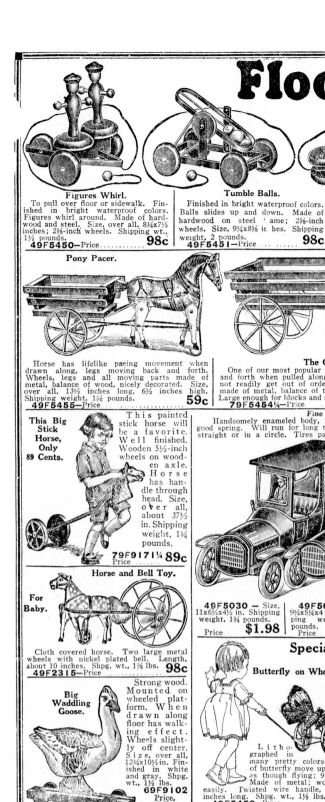

Pony Pacer.
Horse has lifelike pacing movement when drawn along, legs moving back and forth. Wheels, legs and all moving parts made of metal, balance of wood, nicely decorated. Size, over all, 13½ inches long, 6½ inches high. Shipping weight, 1½ pounds.
49F5455—Price.............. **59c**

The Gray Beauty Pacers.
One of our most popular toys. Horses are lifelike, legs moving back and forth when pulled along. This toy is well made and durable; will not readily get out of order. Wheels, legs and all moving parts are made of metal, balance of toy is wood. Size, over all, 18½x6½ inches. Large enough for blocks and small toys. Shpg. wt., packed, 2¼ lbs.
79F5454¼—Price.............. **98c**

He Does Tricks. 
Elephant mounted on platform can be pulled around. Movable legs. Elephant can be made to stand on head, sit down, lie on back or stand on front or hind legs only, or stand on platform or behind platform. Wheels and legs made of metal, balance of wood. Size, over all, natural position on platform, 10x9 inches. Shipping weight, 1¼ pounds.
49F5463—Price... **59c**
Elephant without platform. Has jointed movable metal legs. Size, over all, natural position, 8½x7⅝ inches. Shipping weight, 10 ounces.
49F5462—Price............ **25c**

This Big Stick Horse, Only 89 Cents.
This painted stick horse will be a favorite. Well finished. Wooden 5½-inch wheels on wooden axle. Horse has handle through head. Size, over all, about 37½ in. Shipping weight, 1¾ pounds.
79F9171¼—Price.............. **89c**

Horse and Bell Toy.
For Baby.
Cloth covered horse. Two large metal wheels with nickel plated bell. Length, about 10 inches. Shpg. wt., 1⅛ lbs.
49F2315—Price.............. **98c**

Big Waddling Goose.
Strong wood. Mounted on wheeled platform. When drawn along floor has walking effect. Wheels slightly off center. Size, over all, 12¼x10½ in. Finished in white and gray. Shpg. wt., 1½ lbs.
69F9102—Price.............. **25c**

Big Moo Cow.
Papier mache form covered with Canton flannel. Brown and white color. Glass eyes, and very natural shape and appearance. When tipped forward the cow emits a lifelike "moo." Size, 12x8¾ in. Shipping weight, 1½ pounds.
49F4014—Price.............. **98c**

Auto Racer.
Heavy sheet steel, nicely painted. Spring mechanism. Long hood like real racer. Length, over all, 9⅛ in. Complete with metal driver. Shpg. wt., 2½ pounds.
49F5713—Price, each........ **98c**

Fine Imported Toy Limousines.
Handsomely enameled body, hood, top and fenders, metal chauffeur, movable doors, good spring. Will run for long time. Adjustable front wheels by which car can be run straight or in a circle. Tires painted to look like rubber. Come in four sizes. Three larger sizes have hinged doors that open.

49F5030 — Size, 11x6½x4½ in. Shipping weight, 1¾ pounds. Price.... **$1.98**	**49F5031**—Size, 9½x5¼x4 in. Shipping weight, 1½ pounds. Price.... **$1.48**	**49F5032**—Size, 8¼x4¾x3¾ in. Shpg. weight, 1 pound. Price.... **98c**	**49F5033** — Size, 7x4x3⅜ in. Stationary doors. Shipping wt., 12 ounces. Price.... **67c**

Special Floor Toys for the Baby.

Butterfly on Wheels.
Lithographed in many pretty colors. Wings of butterfly move up and down as though flying; 9 in. wide. Made of metal; won't break easily. Twisted wire handle, about 20 inches long. Shpg. wt., 1½ lbs.
49F5459—Price.............. **59c**

Black Cloth Covered Platform Horses.
Large natural shaped black cloth covered horses on strong wood frames. Exceptionally well made.
Mounted on varnished platform. To be drawn on floor or sidewalk. Horses have saddle, bridle and trappings in artificial leather and cloth saddle blanket. Come in three sizes as shown.
79F7500¼—Size, 17¾x18 in. Shpg. wt., 3¼ lbs. Price.... **$1.98**
69F7501—Size, 10¾x11½ in. Shpg. wt., 1⅜ lbs. Price.... **1.00**
69F7502—Size, 8½x7½ in. Shpg. wt., 14 ounces. Price.... **.67**

Galloping Pony in Wheel.
Wheel measures about 12¼ inches in diameter; painted wood rim. Wire spokes. Horse, 7½x6½ in., made of wood and metal, nicely colored. Twisted wire handle, about 21 in. long. Shpg. wt., 1½ lbs.
49F5456—Price.............. **59c**

Dappled Cloth Covered Platform Horses.
Artificial leather bridle and saddle, with cloth saddle blanket and trappings on bridle. Horse is white with brown spots, cloth covered. Nicely formed. Glass eyes. Each horse on wood platform with four wheels.
79F7540¼—Size, 12½x12½ in. Shpg. wt., 2¾ lbs. Price.... **$2.39**
79F7541¼—Size, 11½x11¼ in. Shpg. wt., 1¾ lbs. Price.... **1.98**
69F7542—Size, 9⅞x9¾ in. Shpg. wt., 1⅜ lbs. Price.... **1.47**
69F7543—Size, 9x9 in. Shipping weight, 1¼ lbs. Price.... **98c**

Donkey and Dump Cart for 39 Cents.

Wooden donkey on wheeled platform attached to dump cart. Metal wheels. Length, over all, 15 inches; height of donkey, 6¾ in. Shpg. wt., 1¼ lbs.
69F7609—Price........ **39c**

A Large Mechanical Limousine.
Big Value.

Made of light weight metal, attractively colored. Size, 10½x4x4¾ in. Strong spring. Doors open. Will run in circle or straight. Shipping weight, 1¾ pounds.
49F5005—Price.............. **89c**

Big Value—Mechanical Auto for 21 Cents.
Made of light weight metal, nicely lithographed in several colors. Good grade spring. Will run in circle or straight. Size, 5¾x3¼x2¾ in. Shpg.wt., 10 oz. **21c**
49F5000—Price..............

Real Cranking Auto Truck.

Made of sheet steel. Finished in colors. Has crank in front which winds big spring. Metal driver. Size, over all, 9x4x3½ in. Shipping weight, 1¾ pounds.
49F5012—Price.............. **79c**

Made of Wood.
Pull on Floor or Run on Pulley.
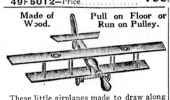
These little airplanes made to draw along the floor or run on a string through the air. Modeled after real airplanes. Nicely finished and trimmed with red, white and blue decorations. Propeller turns.
69F7637—Size, 20x14½x4¼ in. Shpg. wt., 3½ lbs. Price....... **89c**
69F7638—Size, 16⅞x13¼x3½ in. Shpg. wt., 3 lbs. Price....... **67c**
69F7639—Size, 14½x11½x3⅜ in. Shpg. wt., 2¼ lbs. Price....... **47c**

Stock Farm

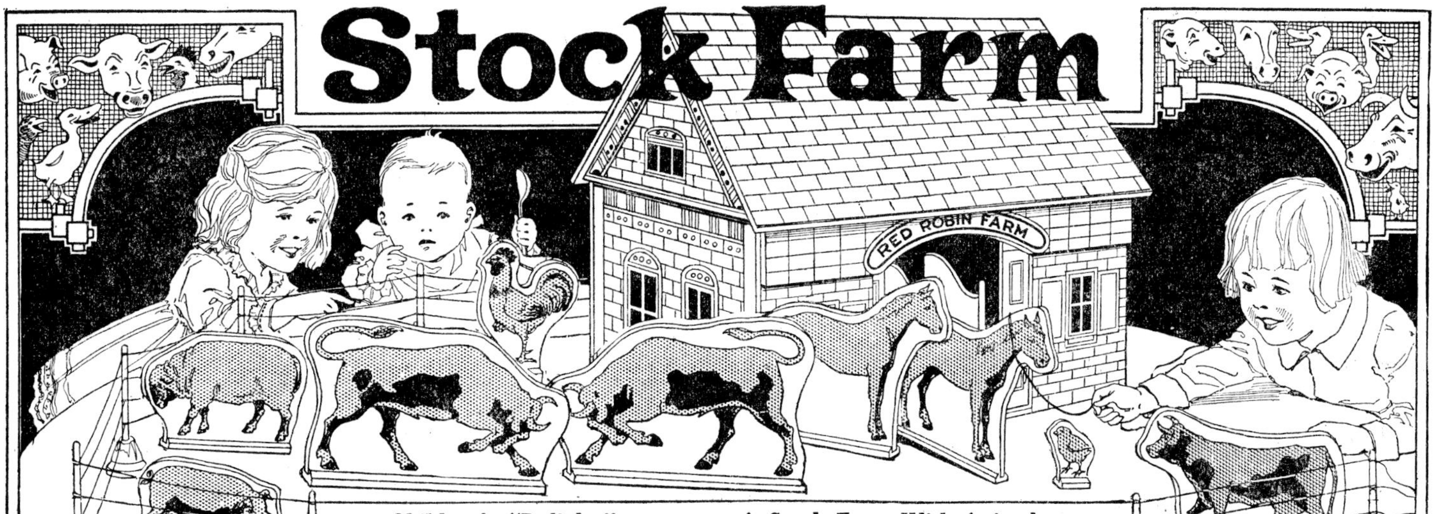

Children's "Delight." **A Stock Farm With Animals.**

What sport for all the youngsters with this stock farm. They play for hours, opening and closing the sliding doors, putting the animals into the stalls and feeding them imaginary hay and grain in the feed box. A box of tooth picks makes an ideal rail fence, or with some old spools cut in half and twigs or pencils inserted for fence posts, and with a spool of mother's thread, a fine fence can be built. The barn measures 13¼ inches long, 11⅜ inches high and 9⅛ inches wide over all. In it are packed an assortment of nine wooden farm animals, each on small platform. The barn is made of good grade wood, nicely decorated. Sliding doors. Stall partitions and feed boxes inside. Roof is detachable. Fence materials shown in illustration not included. Shipping weight, 7 pounds.

79F8120¼—Priced special at **$1.33**

Transfer Pictures, 240 for 19c.

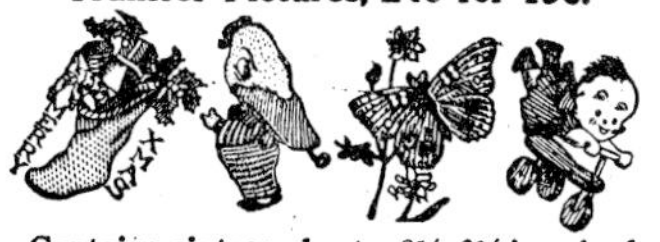

Contains sixteen sheets, 8⅝x3¾ in. of colored transfer pictures, fifteen on each sheet. Subjects are assorted. Wet picture, press face down and it transfers to album or almost any surface. Shpg. wt., 2 oz.

69F9112—Price, per set........ **19c**

You Can Really Talk Over These Phones.

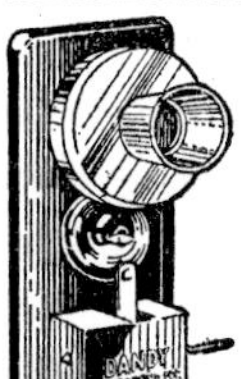

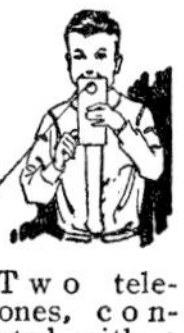

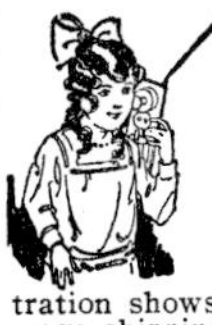

Two telephones, connected with a long cord. Metal, with transmitter, which also acts as a receiver. Built on scientific principles and while there is nothing electric about them, if the cord is stretched tightly between the phones, and touches nothing intervening, the sound waves travel along the cord and **low spoken words can be heard distinctly at the other end.** Illustration shows one of the two phones. Average shipping weight, 12 ounces.

69F9155—Price **39c**

Kemical Magik.

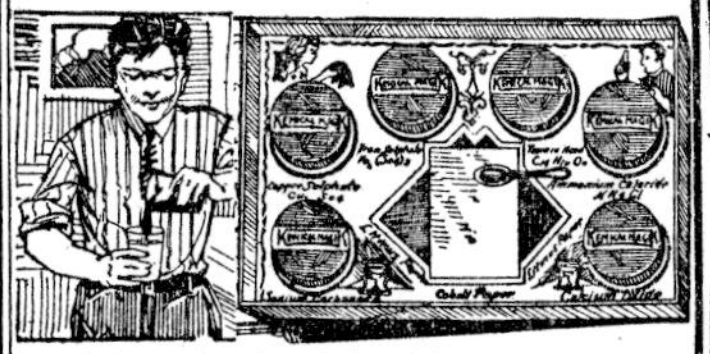

Looks Like Magic.

Simple harmless experiments made easy with this set and explained so a child will understand and remember. Turn water to milk; or give a bright copper finish to the butcher knife; or write a letter with water; other tricks as startling. A child can perform these tricks. Shpg. wt., 12 oz.

49F6008—Price **42c**

For the Artistic Child.

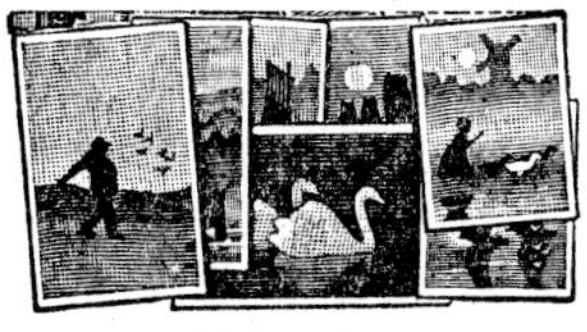

Children Make These Pictures.

Pretty enough to frame. Each outfit contains all necessary materials, enough to make a great number of pictures. Full instructions furnished with each set. Comes in two sizes.

Medium Size, about 30 prepared backgrounds and about 1 dozen card mounts. Shpg. wt., 12 oz.

49F3805 Price..... ... **69c**

Large Size, big assortment of 48 prepared backgrounds, about 24 mounts, and a number of cut stencils. Shpg. wt., 2½ pounds.

49F3806 Price **$1.39**

The Home Five-Coin Bank.

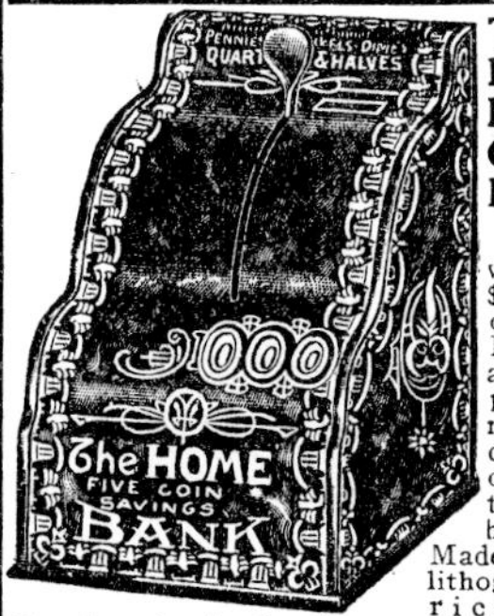

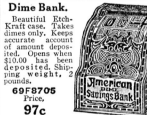

Opens when $10.00 is deposited. Registers and adds pennies, nickels, dimes, quarters and halves. Made of steel, lithographed in rich colors. Popular size bank. Size, over all, 7x6⅞x4¾ inches. Shpg. wt., 3 lbs.

69F8701—Price **$2.98**

Three-Coin Bank.

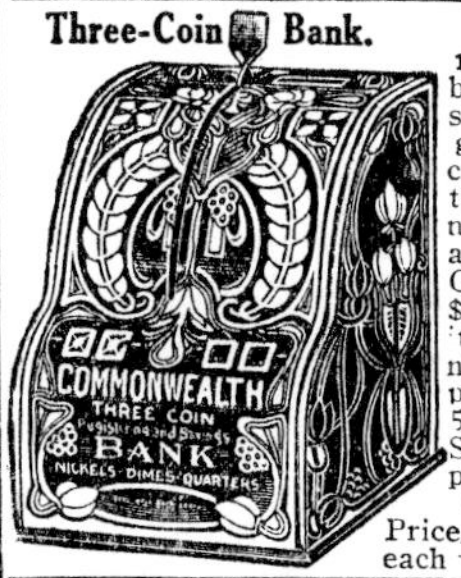

Three-coin registering bank made of steel, lithographed in rich colors. Registers and adds nickels, dimes and quarters. Opens when $10 is deposited. Makes a nice looking present. Size, 5x5⅜x4 inches. Shpg. wt., 2¼ pounds.

69F8700 Price, each **$1.79**

Home Savings Bank.

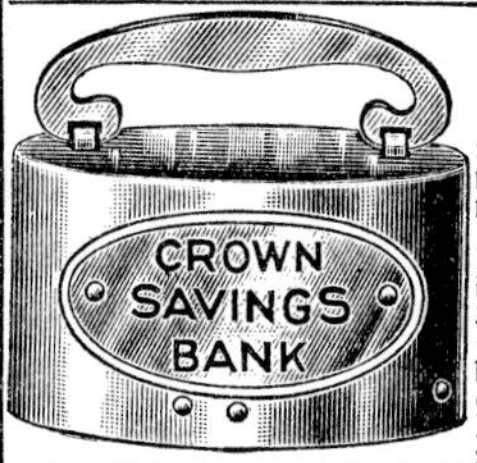

Beautifully nickel plated and polished oval steel bank. Height, 2¼ in. Length, 3⅞ inches. Opening in bottom for coins. Money cannot be taken out until bank is unlocked. Key furnished. Black enameled plate on front. Each in box. Shipping weight, 10 oz.

69F8708—Price **97c**

Cute Puppy Bank.

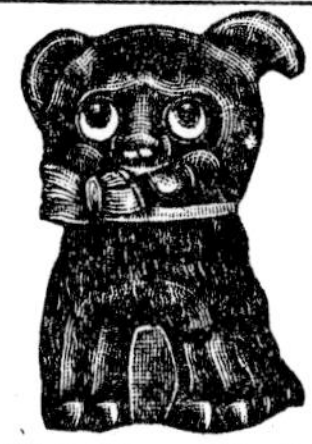

Cute puppy. Popular with kiddies. Made of iron, nicely painted and finished. Size over all, about 4x2½ inches. Shipping weight, 1½ lbs.

69F8715 Price, each **25c**

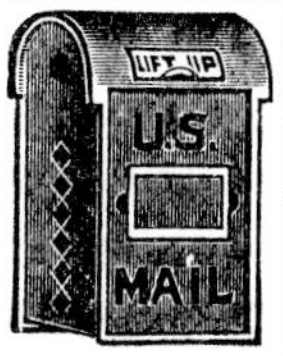

Deposit coins just like letters. Made of iron. Painted green with gilt lettering. Size, 4⅜x2¾x1⅝ inches. Shipping weight, 1¼ pounds.

69F8713 Price **19c**

Provident Four-Coin Bank.

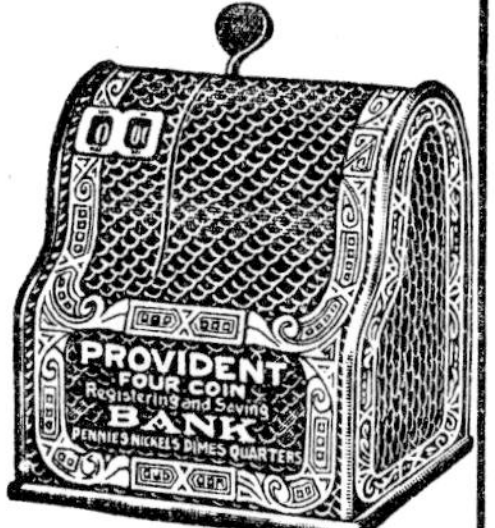

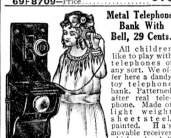

A four-coin registering bank. Opens automatically when a total of $10.00 is deposited. Registers and adds pennies, nickels, dimes and quarters. Made of sheet steel, lithographed in rich colors. Size over all, 5x4¼x4¾ in. Shpg. wt., 2⅛ lbs.

69F8702—Price, each........ **$2.25**

Dime Bank.

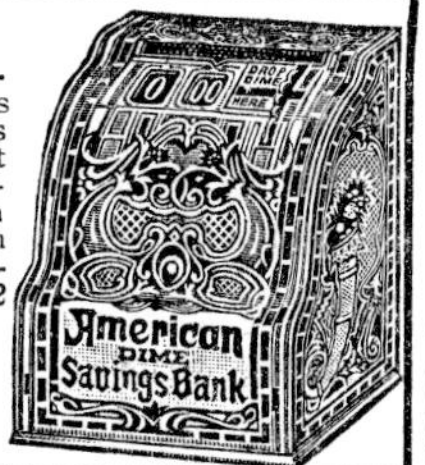

Beautiful Etch-Kraft case. Takes dimes only. Keeps accurate account of amount deposited. Opens when $10.00 has been deposited. Shipping weight, 2 pounds.

69F8705 Price, **97c**

Penny Bank.

Exactly same as dime bank, except takes pennies only. Opens when $1.00 has been deposited. Shipping weight, 2 lbs.

69F8709—Price **97c**

Metal Telephone Bank With Bell, 29 Cents.

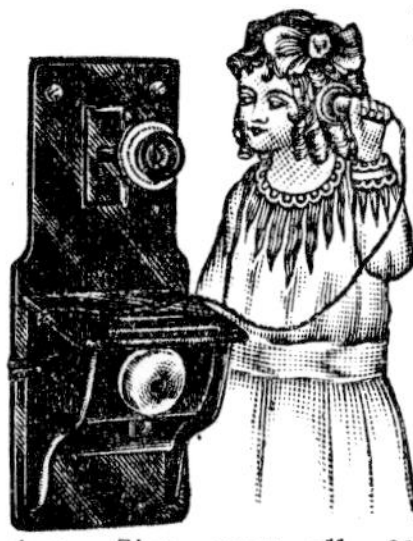

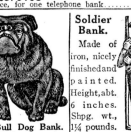

All children like to play with telephones of any sort. We offer here a dandy toy telephone bank. Patterned after real telephone. Made of light weight sheet steel, painted. Has movable receiver which makes bell ring. Size, over all, 9⅝x4¼x2⅞ inches. Shipping weight, 14 ounces.

69F9158 Price, for one telephone bank........ **29c**

Bull Dog Bank.

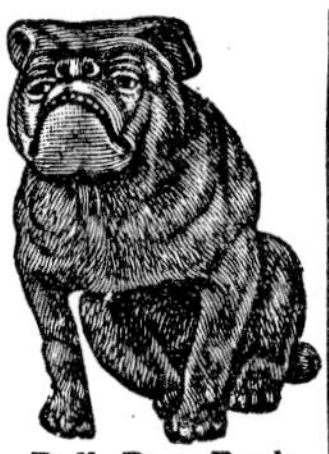

Made of iron, nicely painted. Size, 4½x3⅞ inches. Shpg. wt., 1⅝ lbs.

69F8719 Price **23c**

Soldier Bank.

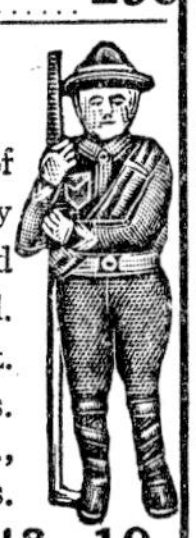

Made of iron, nicely finished and painted. Height, abt. 6 inches. Shpg. wt., 1¼ pounds.

69F8718 Price........ **19c**

4 Bugs, 79 Cents. Assorted Kinds.

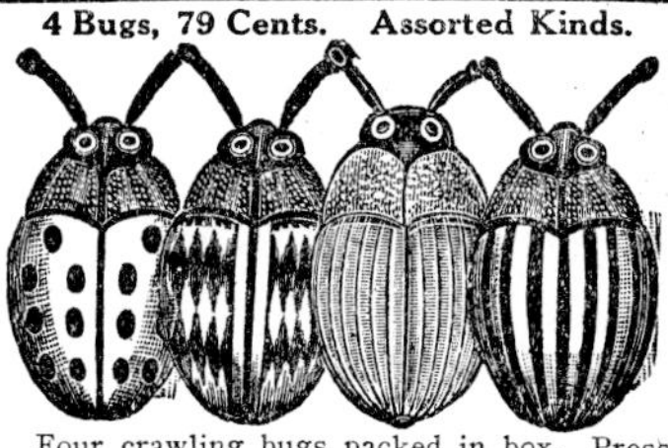

Four crawling bugs packed in box. Press on floor, draw back two feet and release. You can race them and do many other stunts with them. Bugs made of metal, lithographed in colors. About 2 inches long over all. In neat gift box. Shipping wt., 7 oz.

69F9110—Price, 4 bugs for..... **79c**

69F9121—Price, 2 bugs for **42c**

Bugs and Cutup Toys.

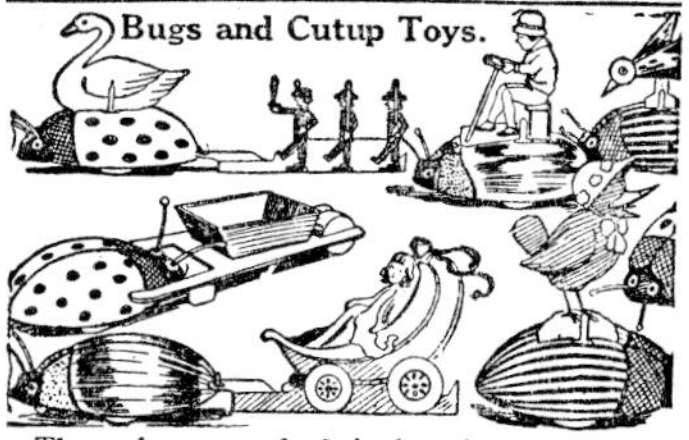

Three bugs, each 2 inches long, made of metal, decorated in natural colors to look like real bugs. Place one on table and draw backward about 2 feet. Release bug and it crawls away slowly. Also a number of little vehicles for bugs to push or pull, and other **fanciful colored cutouts** to ride on top. Shipping weight, 1 pound.

69F9115—Price, complete **$1.79**

Our 89c Assortment.

Similar to large set but two bugs and smaller number of cut up toys. Shipping weight, 1 pound.

69F9118—Price.................. **89c**

Three Bubbler Outfits for 25 Cents.

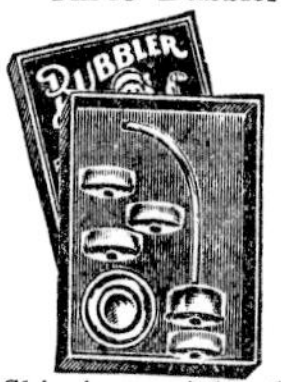

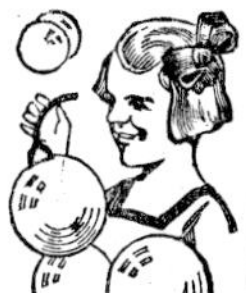

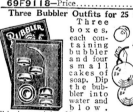

Three boxes, each containing bubbler and four small cakes of soap. Dip the bubbler into water and blow. Shipping weight, 11 ounces.

69F9152—Price, 3 boxes for..... **25c**

Roll It Away and It Comes Back.

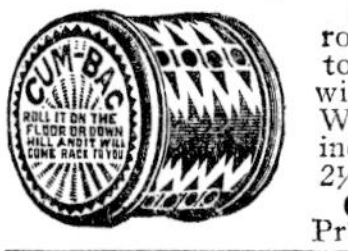

Cylinder shape with round metal ends. Roll toy along the floor and it will" Kum Back" to you. Will even roll up slight incline. Size, about 2½x2½ in. Shpg. wt., 6 oz.

69F9123 Price **8c**

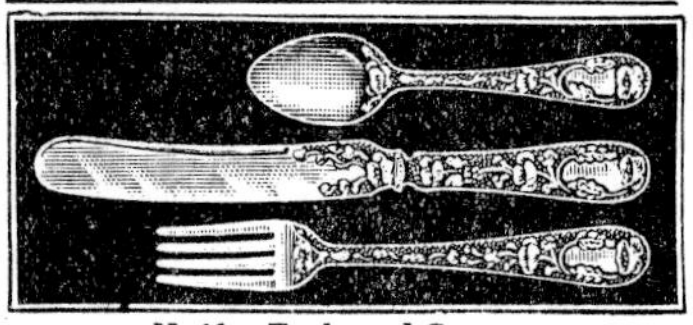

Knife, Fork and Spoon.

Bright metal finish. Suitable for baby. Assorted designs. Packed in box. Shipping weight, 6 ounces.

49F1950—Price, per set........ **17c**

MISCELLANEOUS TOYS

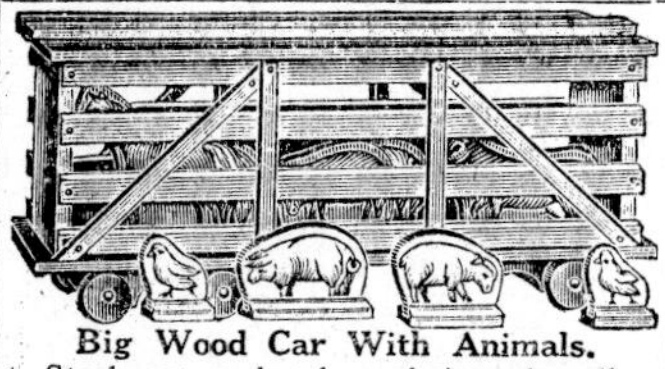

Big Wood Car With Animals.
Stock car made of wood, in red, yellow and black, substantially put together. Each car has various domestic animals and fowls in it. Top of car is removable. Can be used as pull toy as well. Measures 16⅝x6¾x8 inches and has 9 animals, including fowls. Shpg. wt., 3¼ lbs.
79F8123¼—Price **$1.00**

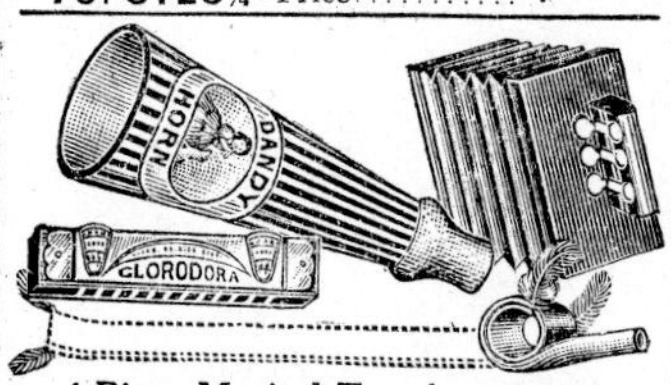

4-Piece Musical Toy Assortment.
Seven-Inch Heavy Cardboard Carnival Horn with wooden mouthpiece; Three-Key Toy Accordion, 2⅛x3⅝ inches; Ten-Note Mouth Organ, about 4 inches long and Whistling Blowout Toy with tickler. Shipping weight, 14 ounces.
49F2310—Price, all 4 for..... **29c**

MUTT AND JEFF BALLOON ASSORTMENT

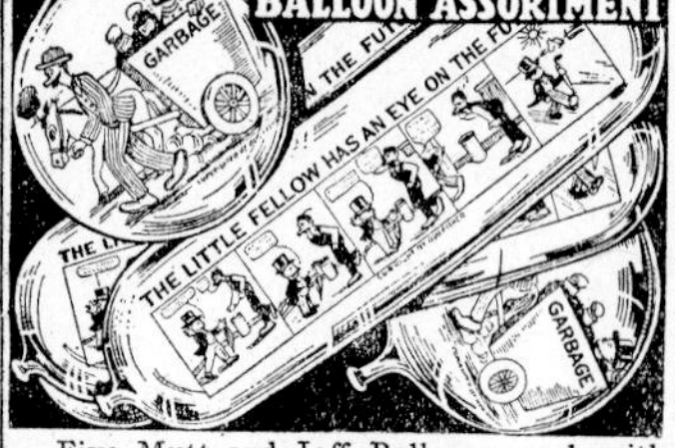

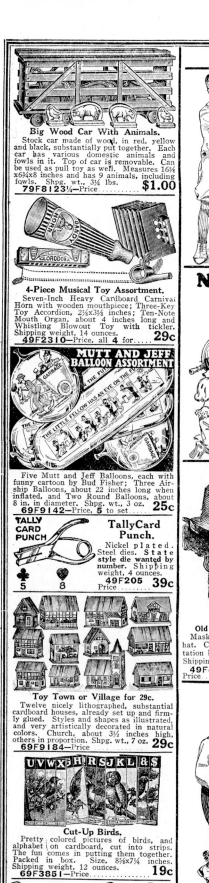

Five Mutt and Jeff Balloons, each with funny cartoon by Bud Fisher; Three Airship Balloons, about 22 inches long when inflated, and Two Round Balloons, about 8 in. in diameter. Shpg. wt., 3 oz.
69F9142—Price, 5 to set..... **25c**

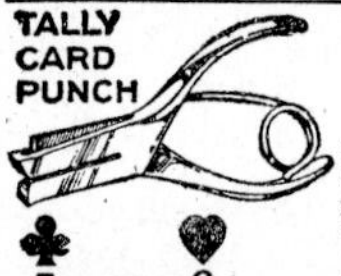

TallyCard Punch.
Nickel plated. Steel dies. State style die wanted by number. Shipping weight, 4 ounces.
49F205 Price **39c**

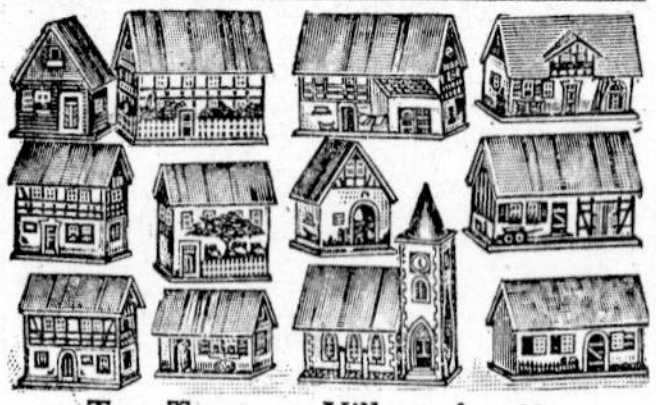

Toy Town or Village for 29c.
Twelve nicely lithographed, substantial cardboard houses, already set up and firmly glued. Styles and shapes as illustrated, and very artistically decorated in natural colors. Church, about 3½ inches high, others in proportion. Shpg. wt., 7 oz.
69F9184—Price **29c**

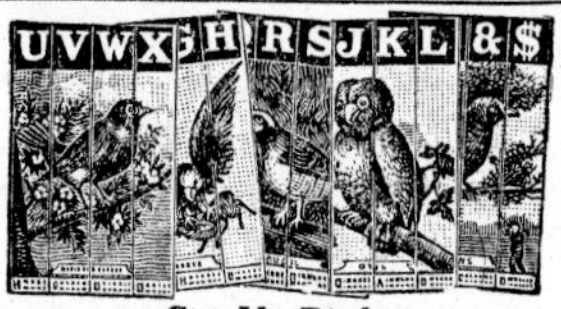

Cut-Up Birds.
Pretty colored pictures of birds, and alphabet on cardboard, cut into strips. The fun comes in putting them together. Packed in box. Size, 8⅝x7¼ inches. Shipping weight, 12 ounces.
69F3851—Price................ **19c**

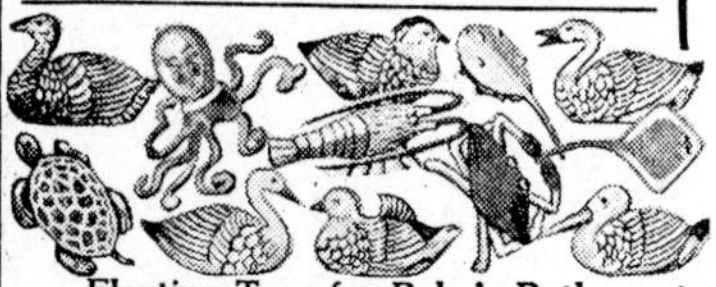

Floating Toys for Baby's Bath.
Twelve Assorted Floating Toys. Models of ocean fish and water birds. Unusually well reproduced in natural colors. Larger children will be interested in these small models of fish and fowls. Put them in baby's bath to amuse him. About 2½ inches long. Shipping wt., 4 oz.
69F7851—Price, 12 for..... **98c**

BALLOONS

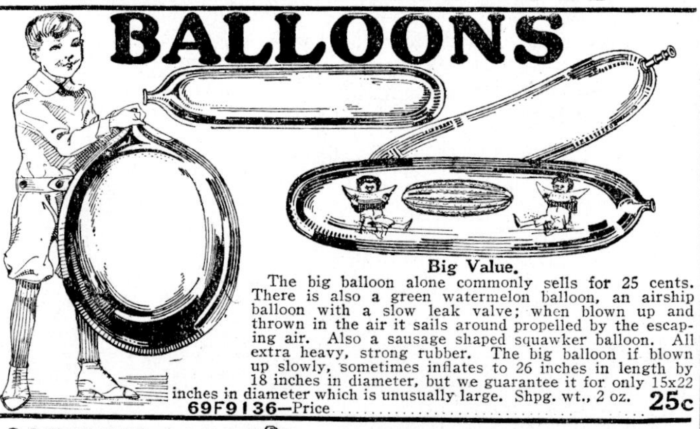

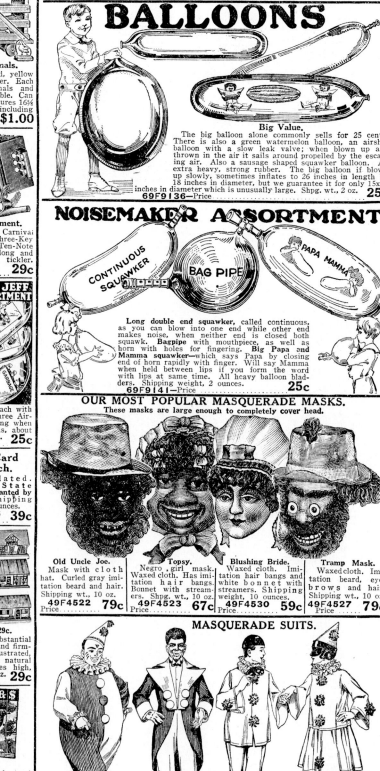

Big Value.
The big balloon alone commonly sells for 25 cents. There is also a green watermelon balloon, an airship balloon with a slow leak valve; when blown up and thrown in the air it sails around propelled by the escaping air. Also a sausage shaped squawker balloon. All extra heavy, strong rubber. The big balloon if blown up slowly, sometimes inflates to 26 inches in length by 18 inches in diameter, but we guarantee it for only 15x22 inches in diameter which is unusually large. Shpg. wt., 2 oz.
69F9136—Price **25c**

NOISEMAKER ASSORTMENT

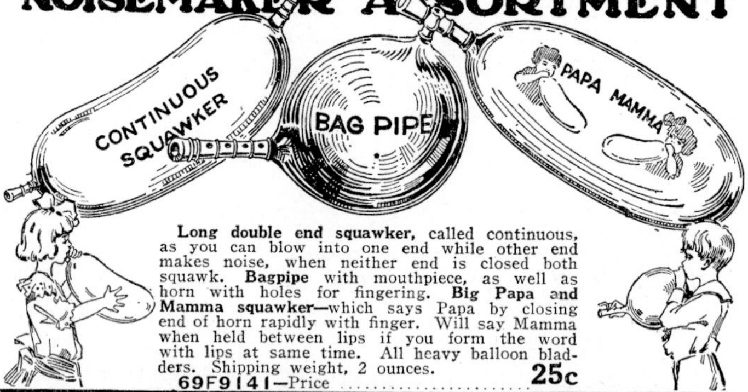

Long double end squawker, called continuous, as you can blow into one end while other end makes noise, when neither end is closed both squawk. **Bagpipe** with mouthpiece, as well as horn with holes for fingering. **Big Papa and Mamma squawker**—which says Papa by closing end of horn rapidly with finger. Will say Mamma when held between lips if you form the word with lips at same time. All heavy balloon bladders. Shipping weight, 2 ounces.
69F9141—Price **25c**

OUR MOST POPULAR MASQUERADE MASKS.

These masks are large enough to completely cover head.

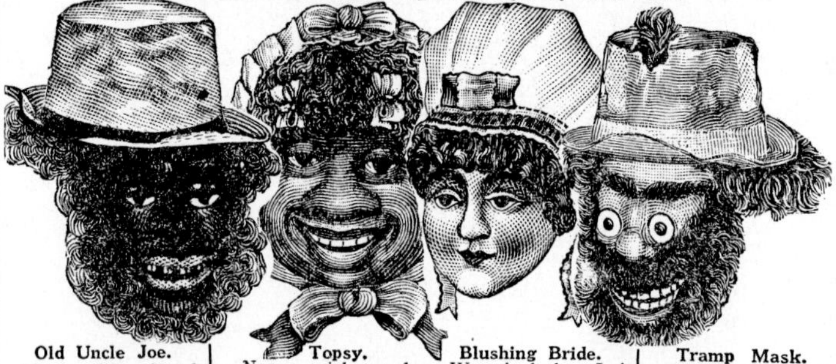

Old Uncle Joe.
Mask with cloth hat. Curled gray imitation beard and hair. Shipping wt., 10 oz.
49F4522 Price.......... **79c**

Topsy.
Negro girl mask. Waxed cloth. Has imitation hair bangs. Bonnet with streamers. Shpg. wt., 10 oz.
49F4523 Price.......... **67c**

Blushing Bride.
Waxed cloth. Imitation hair bangs and white bonnet with streamers. Shipping weight, 10 ounces.
49F4530 **59c**

Tramp Mask.
Waxed cloth. Imitation beard, eyebrows and hair. Shipping wt., 10 oz.
49F4527 Price **79c**

MASQUERADE SUITS.

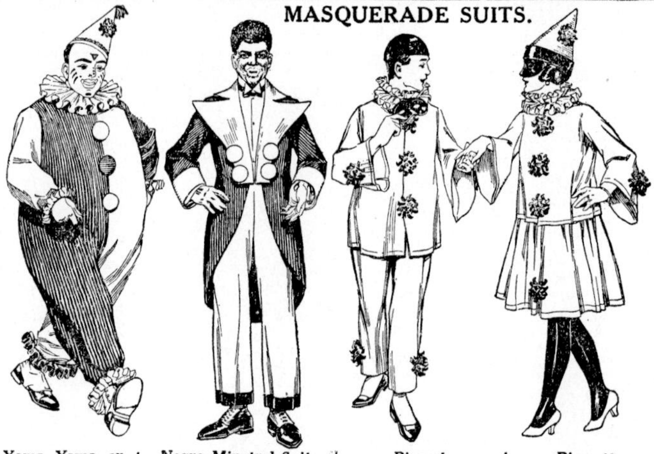

Yama Yama or Clown Suit.
A very snappy masquerade suit. Cloth. Yama Yama style. Complete with mask and peaked cloth hat to match. Suitable for men or women. Shipping weight, 1¾ pounds.
49F4533 Price....... **$3.98**

Negro Minstrel Suit.
Consists of yellow cloth trousers and black coat. Coat trimmed with broad yellow lapels and buttons. Cap style wig, made of curled horsehair on stiff cloth foundation, has kinky effect. Some black their faces. Mask sold separately. See below. Shpg. wt., 1¾ lbs.
49F4512 **$3.98** Price..........
Negro Mask to use with negro minstrel suit. Shipping wt., 1 oz.
49F4524 Price **39c**

Pierrot.
Made of white cloth with black rosettes, as shown. Ruffle at neck. Black cloth skull cap and black satin domino for eyes. Can be used alone or by a couple with companion Pierrette suit at right. Well made according to our own specifications. Shipping wt., 1 pound.
49F4515 Price **$3.98**

Pierrette.
Made of white cloth with black rosettes and trimming. Ruffled collar. Skirt can be let out. Peaked white cap with rosettes. Black satin domino. Can be used alone or by a couple with companion Pierrot suit at left. Made according to our own specifications and made right. Shipping wt., 1 pound.
49F4516 Price .. **$3.98**

Soft Pillow for Baby.

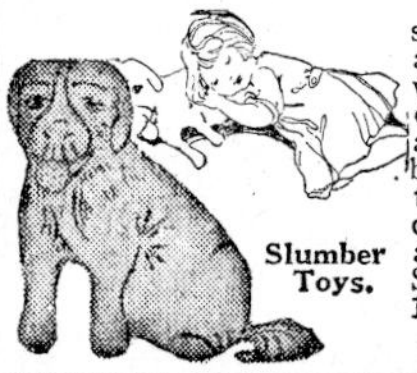

Stuffed with soft downy kapok and covered with washable crepe. Face of animal hand embroidered. A safe toy for babies' crib. Height, about 10¼ in. Shipping wt., 12 ounces.
Slumber Toys.
49F4005 Price ...**98c**

Glass Imitation Onyx Marbles.

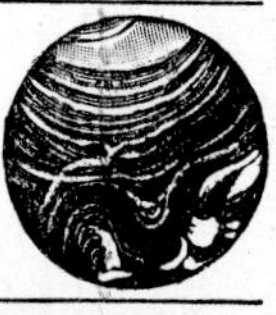

Twenty assorted green, blue and brown glass imitation onyx marbles. Exact size of illustration. Made of colored glass. Shpg. wt., 8 oz.
69F7740 Price, 20 for..... **28c**

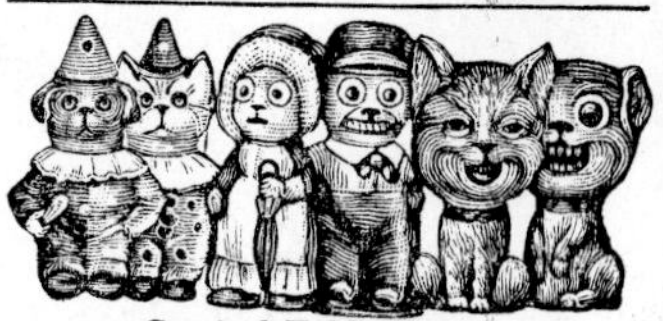

Comical Table Favors.
Little composition figures averaging about 3 inches high. Painted in attractive colors. Have removable heads for filling with candy, nuts, etc. Shpg. wt., 1 lb.
87F8607—Price, set of 6 **67c**

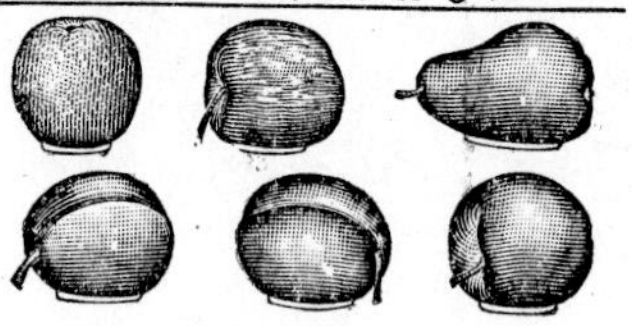

Assorted Fruit Candy Boxes.
One each papier mache orange, plum, pear, peach, green apple and red and green apple. May be filled with candy, nuts, etc. Shipping wt., 12 oz.
87F8605—Price for set of 6 **79c**

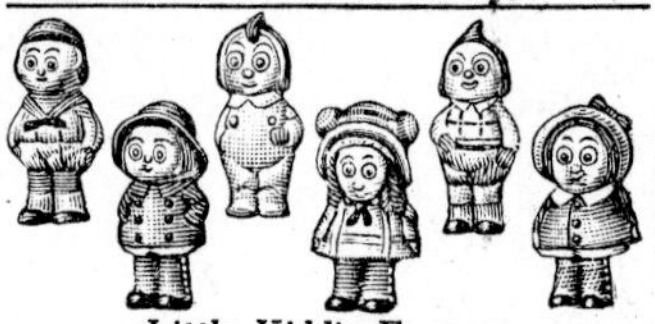

Little Kiddie Favors.
Dainty little composition figures, three boys and three girls, 2⅛ inches high, painted in bright, attractive colors. Shipping weight, 9 ounces.
87F8600—Price, for set of 6....**39c**

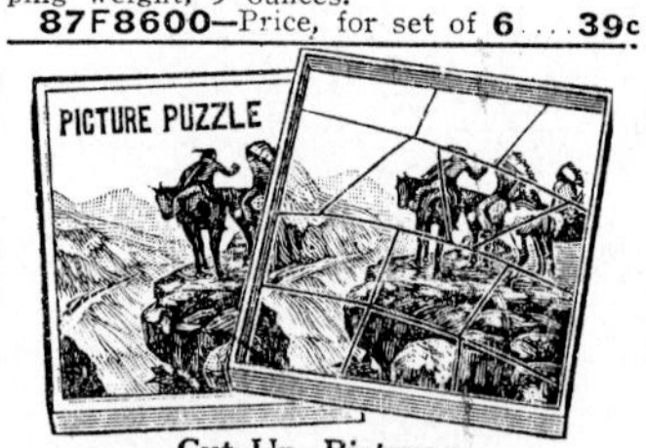

Cut-Up Pictures.
Two prettily colored reproductions of paintings, printed on heavy cardboard, then cut into odd shapes. Lots of fun for the children on rainy days building pictures from the mixed up pieces. Each picture about 7¼x9¾ inches. Shpg. wt., 8 oz.
49F3665—Price, 2 picture puzzles **39c**

Wood Alphabet Blocks.

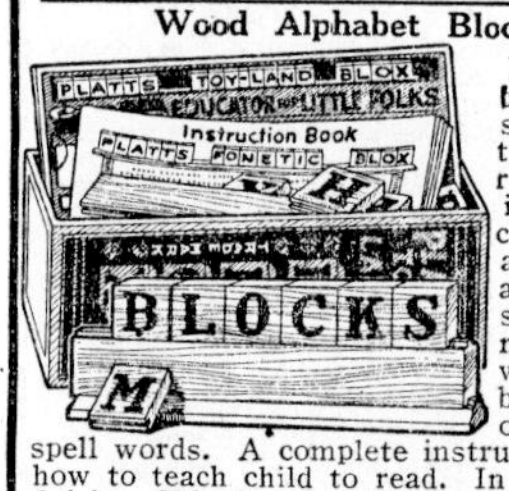

Educational blocks. Consist of thirty-six blocks representing two complete alphabets and two sets of numerals which can be arranged on bases to spell words. A complete instruction book, how to teach child to read. In box 9x3¼x3½ in. Shipping wt., 1½ lbs.
49F3619—Price, per set...... **47c**

Plush Sitting Cat.

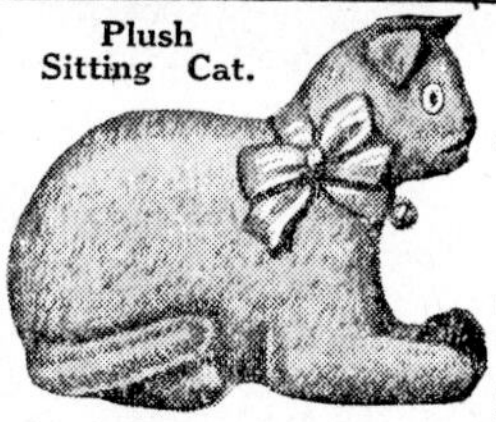

Made of good grade white plush. Well formed and finished throughout. Has natural looking glass eyes, ribbon with bell around neck, and colored yarn ball between front paws, 6¾ inches long and 4½ in. high. Shpg. wt., 1 lb.
49F4034—Price **59c**

FINE IMPORTED TOYS

This Monkey Turns Somersaults.

One of the cleverest little mechanical toys ever offered. Monkey really puts his little head down on the floor and turns somersaults one after another, or if hanging by hands from wire will "Skin the Cat." He is a very realistic looking little fellow, measuring about 9½ inches in height. Natural shaped head, glass eyes. Dressed in bright colors. No key to wind, simply turn arms backward, put on floor and he does the rest. Shipping weight, 9 ounces. **$1.39**
49F5770—Price ....

For High Grade Chessmen See Page 597

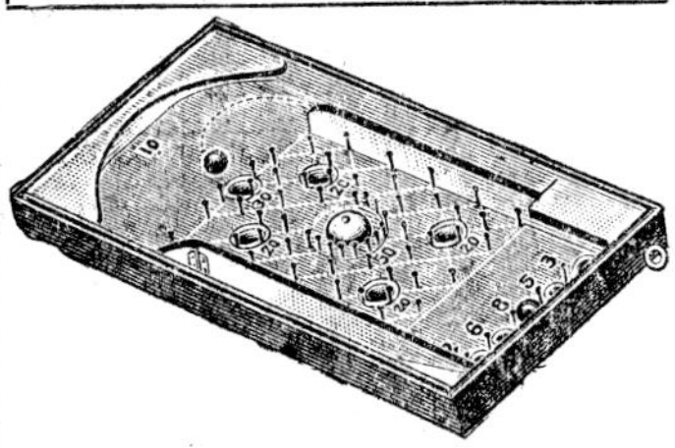

Bagatelle Board, Beautifully Finished.

Very handsome board, made of wood with bed of select maple varnished and highly polished. Also two alleys, one to use with spring shooter, the other to use with the 14½-inch tapered cue; one ball. Board measures 10¼x19½ inches and 1½ inches deep. Cups, bell and all guards are laid out with precision. A gameboard anyone can well be proud of. Shp'g. wt., 3½ lbs. **$1.67**
49F210—Price ....

Monkey Bicycle Rider.

This clever little monkey rides his bicycle almost as well as any little boy or girl. Simply wind up the spring, put on the floor and off he goes, busily pedaling and with an expression that seems to denote great satisfaction. Height over all, 9 inches. Very realistic, stuffed cloth head with glass eyes. Well made, substantial toy. Dressed in bright colors. Metal bicycle, rear wheels, about 4½ inches apart; length over all, about 6 inches. Shipping weight, 12 oz. **$1.39**
49F5777—Price ....

Our $1.98 Sewing Machine.

A nicely working Toy Sewing Machine. Simple in construction, no complicated parts. Worked easily by a child. Sews seam, with regular and tight stitch. Nicely finished, black enamel decorated with colored flowers and nickel plated trimming. Size, about 7½x4x7 inches. Shipping wt., 2¾ lbs. **$1.98**
49F5801—Price ....

For Imported Nine Pins See Page 598

Magic Lanterns to Entertain Your Friends.

Home picture shows are lots of fun. Hang a bed sheet on the wall, and with one of our magic lantern outfits you can have a picture show. Lanterns are light gauge sheet steel. Brass finished lens container and good quality lens. Equipped with kerosene lamp, lamp chimney, smoke stack and twelve glass lantern slides, with a number of pictures on each slide. (These machines do not project moving pictures.) Come in three sizes as listed below:

Our Best and Largest. 10⅝x11⅛x3⅝ inches. Has twelve slides, 7 inches long. Shipping weight, 4½ lbs.
69F9103 Price, each **$4.98**

Medium Size. 9¼x10¾x3⅝ inches. Has twelve 6¾-inch slides. Shipping wt., 3½ lbs.
69F9101 Price **$3.98**

Small Size. 7½x10⅛x3 inches. Has twelve 5⅝-inch slides. Shipping weight, 2⅜ pounds.
69F9100 Price **$2.98**

Fancy Decorated Metal Garage With Two Mechanical Autos.

98c

Here is a set every boy will want. It consists of a dandy metal garage and two mechanical automobiles with clockwork spring motors. The garage has a floor. It stands 4½ inches high by 8 inches wide. The two doors are hinged and have a latch on front to keep them closed. Windows are painted on sides and ends; also skylight on roof. There is one roadster, size 3x5½x3 inches, prettily painted in realistic way; and a limousine, size 3x5x3½ inches, with top, sides, etc., nicely finished and decorated. Both autos have strong clockwork motors. Autos will run straight or in a circle. Shipping weight, complete set, about 4½ pounds. **98c**
49F5796—Price ....

Every Little Child Wants a Walking Dog. Trots Behind You in a Very Lifelike Manner.

Yes, he will follow you. His little legs may have to trot along pretty fast, but they will keep up. Cute little dog, covered with imitation hair cloth, white with black spots. Has collar and lead string. Certain mechanism in legs causes them to move backward and forward when dog is pulled over floor. No spring and nothing to get out of order. Every little child will surely love this best of all toys. So natural looking and acting. Size of dog, 8 inches long including stubby tail and stands about 6½ inches high to tips of ears. Shipping weight, 1 pound.
69F9106 Price...... **$1.39**

Picture Block Cubes.

When properly put together all the blocks form a pretty childhood picture. As there are six sides to each block, six beautifully colored pictures can be formed. A set of colored pictures comes with each box of blocks to show how the pictures look when put together. The blocks are solid wood covered with paper, firmly glued on. Each set packed in strong wood case with hinged cover and latch. Pretty picture on cover. Three sizes.

49F3675—30 blocks. 1½-inch cubes in wood case. Size, 11⅛x9½ in. Shpg. wt., 1¾ lbs. Price **98c**

49F3676—20 blocks. About 1½-inch cubes in wood case. Size, 8⅞x7¼ inches. Shipping wt., 2¼ lbs....... **59c**

49F3677—12 blocks. 1⅜-inch cubes in wood case. Size, 6¾x5½ in. Shipping weight, 1¼ lbs. Price **39c**

Just Like a Real Street Roller.

Mechanical Street Roller with extra strong clockwork. A reproduction of the large steam rollers, with device on front roller for controlling direction. Movable piston rods. Water glass, steam gauge valves and cocks painted on side of boiler. (Not real.) Wind up the spring and see it move slowly over the floor. Finished in steel gray. Measures 9x5¼x3 inches. Shipping weight, 1½ pounds. **$1.39**
49F5763—Price ....

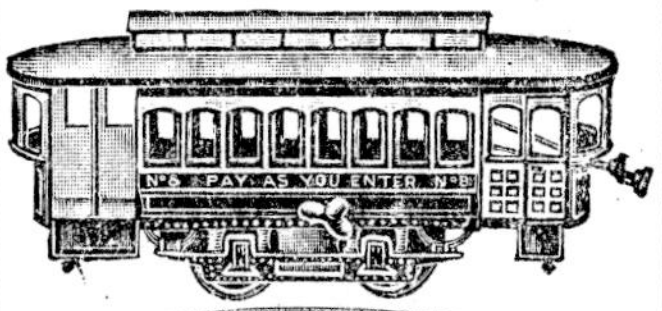

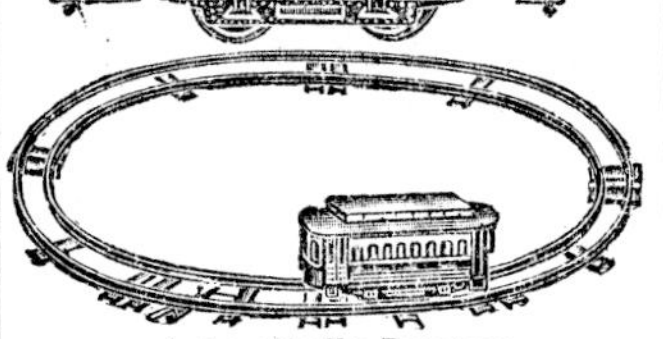

Automatically Reverses.

Mechanical street car, true in shape and coloring, on curved track. Eight sections of track, one with reversing switch device which allows child to stop or reverse car without touching it. Size of car, 8¼ inches long, 3½ inches high and 2¼ inches wide. Outside circumference of track when set up, about 6 feet 10 inches. Car is heavy enough to stay on track. Extra well made mechanism. One of our cleverest new imported toys. Shpg. wt., 1¼ lbs. **$1.67**
49F5750—Price ....

Blue Enamel Toy Sets.

All metal, absolutely unbreakable toy dishes, covered with rich dark turquoise blue enamel. A handsome set. Look like china. Will never leak nor break, and will please the little ones. The saucers are 2½ inches in diameter; cups, 1 inch high and 1½ inches in diameter; the teapot is 2⅛ inches high and 2½ inches in diameter, other pieces in proportion.

8-Piece Set, 59c. Two cups and saucers, creamer, sugar bowl, teapot, and cover. Shpg. wt., 1 lb.
49F1929 Price **59c**

12-Piece Set, 79c. Four cups and saucers, creamer, sugar bowl, teapot, and cover. Shpg. wt., 1¼ lbs.
49F1930 Price **79c**

16-Piece Set, 98c. Six cups and saucers, creamer, sugar bowl, teapot, and cover. Shpg. wt., 1½ lbs.
49F1931 Price **98c**

Finest White Enamel Toy Tea Sets.

Strong metal pieces, nicely shaped and covered with a heavy coat of white enamel which is then decorated in pretty design. Two colors baked on. Will not break, look like china and will not leak. The saucers are 3⅛ inches in diameter; cups, 1½ inches high; teapot, 2⅝ inches high and other pieces in proportion.

12-Piece Set, $2.98. 4 cups, 4 saucers, creamer, sugar bowl, teapot and cover. Shipping weight, 2¼ lbs.
49F1925 Price **$2.98**

16-Piece Set, $3.87. 6 cups, 6 saucers, creamer, sugar bowl, teapot and cover. Shipping weight, 2¾ lbs.
49F1926 Price **$3.87**

White Enameled Metal Tea Set.

Unbreakable. Look like china. Very pretty little white and blue enamel sets. Made of heavy metal, covered with heavy coat of enamel which is then decorated with pretty blue design and baked in oven. Saucers measure 2½ in. in diameter; cups are 1 inch high; teapot, 3 inches high, other pieces in proportion. Will not leak.

12 Pieces, 98c. 4 cups, 4 saucers, creamer, sugar bowl, teapot and cover. Shipping wt., 1¾ lbs.
49F1927 Price **98c**

16 Pieces, $1.33. 6 cups, 6 saucers, sugar bowl, creamer and cover. Shpg. wt. 2 lbs.
49F1928 Price **$1.33**

MISCELLANEOUS TOYS

Toy Bagpipe.

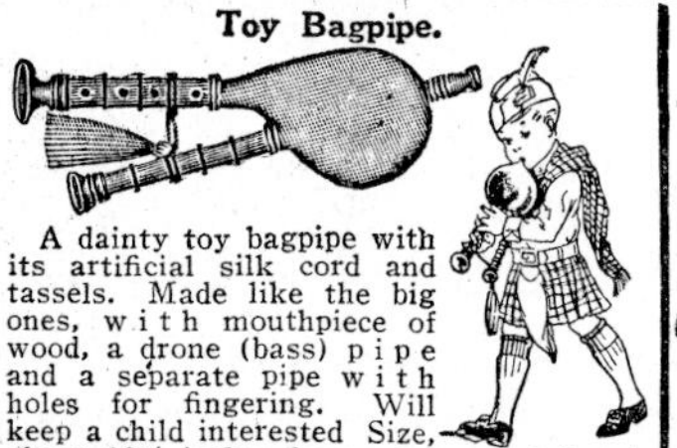

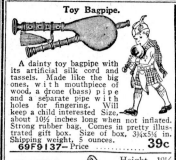

A dainty toy bagpipe with its artificial silk cord and tassels. Made like the big ones, with mouthpiece of wood, a drone (bass) pipe and a separate pipe with holes for fingering. Will keep a child interested Size, about 10½ inches long when not inflated. Strong rubber bag. Comes in pretty illustrated gift box. Size of box, 3¾x5¼ in. Shipping weight, 5 ounces.
69F9137—Price 39c

Big Wooden Goose.

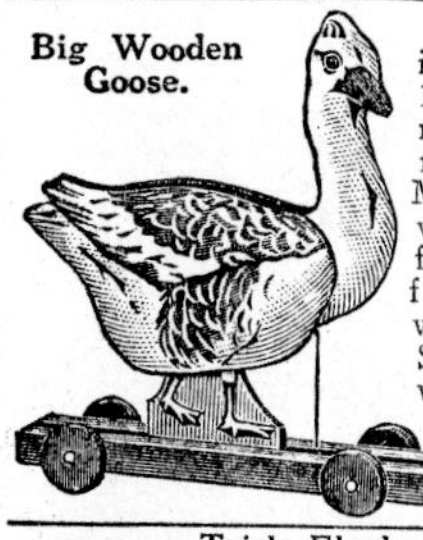

Height, 10½ inches; length, 10 in. Head nods as he rolls along. Mounted on wheeled platform. Nicely finished in white and gray. Shipping weight, 1½ lbs.
69F9150 Price, 47c

Trick Elephant.

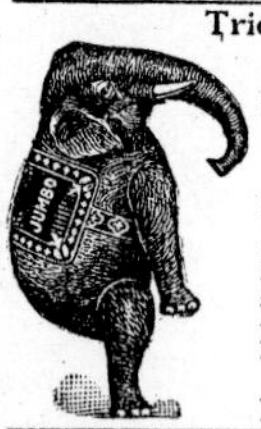

Wooden body finished in natural colors. Metal legs. This elephant will do stunts no circus elephant ever dreamed of. As he measures 8¼x7½ inches, the little folks can have lots of fun with him. Legs are movable. Shipping weight, 10 ounces.
49F5462 Price............. 25c

Dolly's Buggy Robes.

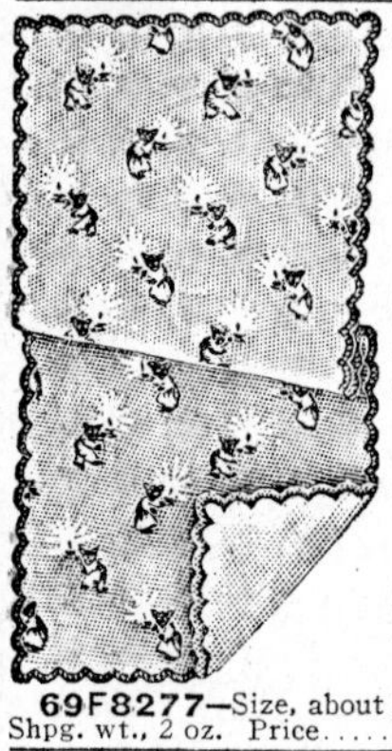

Made of heavy fleeced flannelette. Dainty colors with figures of kittens, Teddy bears, etc. Fancy bound edges. Some scalloped. Three sizes. Lined with white flannelette.
69F8275 Size, abt. 27½x16½ in. Shpg. wt., 4 oz. Price... 98c
69F8276 Size, abt. 20¼x13½ in. Shpg. wt., 3 oz. Price... 67c
69F8277—Size, about 17½x9 in. Shpg. wt., 2 oz. Price............. 47c

Dapple Gray Horse on Platform.

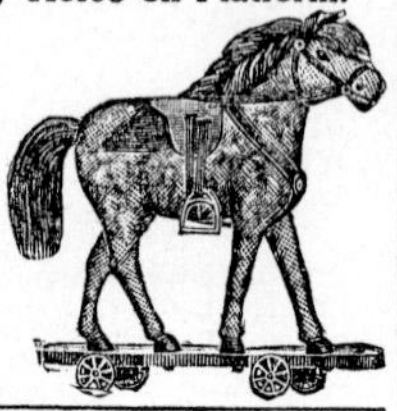

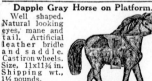

Well shaped. Natural looking eyes, mane and tail. Artificial leather bridle and saddle. Cast iron wheels. Size, 11x11¾ in. Shipping wt., 1½ pounds.
69F7616 Price, $1.39

Two Feet High.

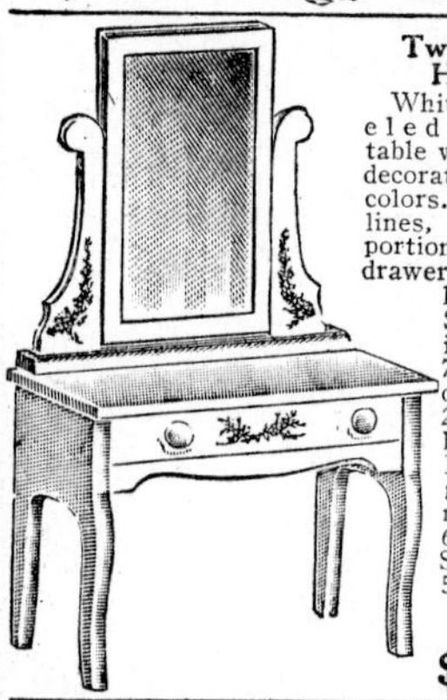

White enameled dressing table with fancy decorations in colors. Neat lines, well proportioned. One drawer with knobs. Size, 15¾ in. wide 7¾ inches deep and 24 inches high. Plate glass mirror is 6x10½ in. Shpg. wt., 5½ lbs.
79F8553¼ Price, $3.98

Horse and Bell Chimes, 79 Cents.

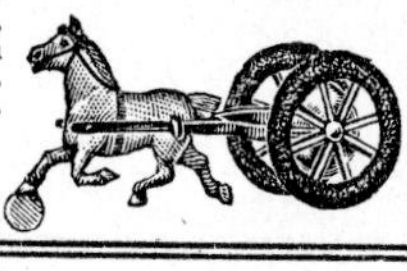

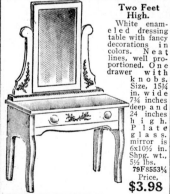

Horse with 2-inch bell. 3⅛-in. wheels with pads. Length, 9⅜ in. Shpg. wt., 1¾ lbs.
49F2356 Price, 79c

$1.00—Toy Assortment—$1.00

For Boy or Girl 4 to 12 Years Old.

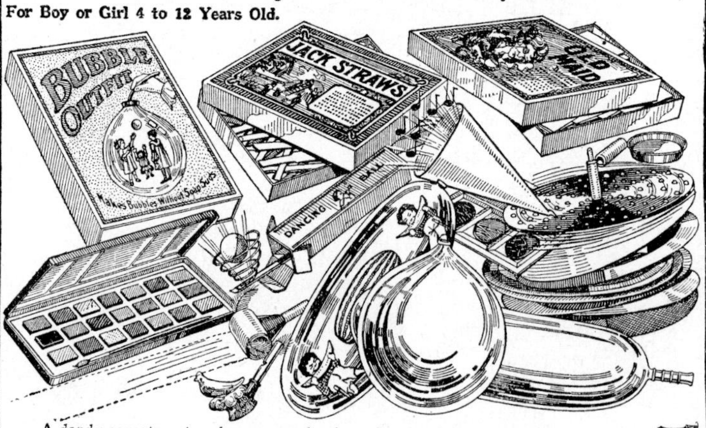

A dandy assortment and an unusual value. Consists of musical phonograph top, bubble blower, 21 water color paints in metal box, dancing ball, feather tickler blowout, canary bird whistle, a long watermelon balloon, a sausage squawker balloon and a large round balloon, a game of old maid and a game of jackstraws. Shipping weight, 1 pound.
69F9189—Price $1.00

$1.00 Toy Assortment for Babies.

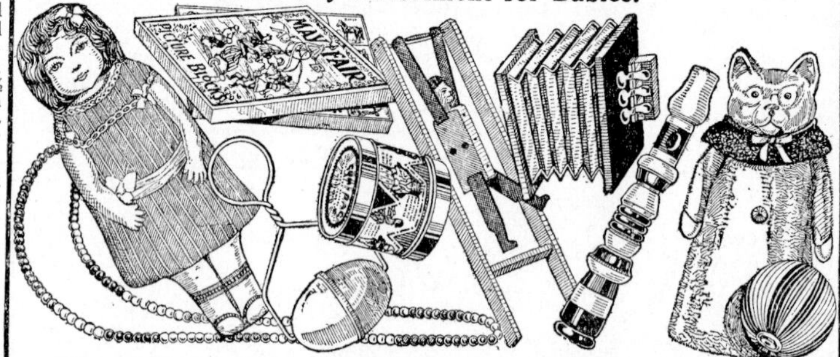

These are all toys that baby can use and enjoy. A stuffed cloth 10-inch doll that will not break. A little three-key accordion. A bright colored 7-inch wooden horn (assorted designs). A colored whistle rubber ball. A dandy egg shape, colored rattle. A 5-inch stuffed cloth animal (assorted designs). A cumbac toy—roll it away and it rolls back. A 40-inch length string of heavy, colored, ⅜-inch glass creeping beads, practically unbreakable. A good grade jumping jack and a box of A B C blocks. Shipping weight, 1 pound.
69F9190—Price $1.00

Tell Tomorrow's Weather.

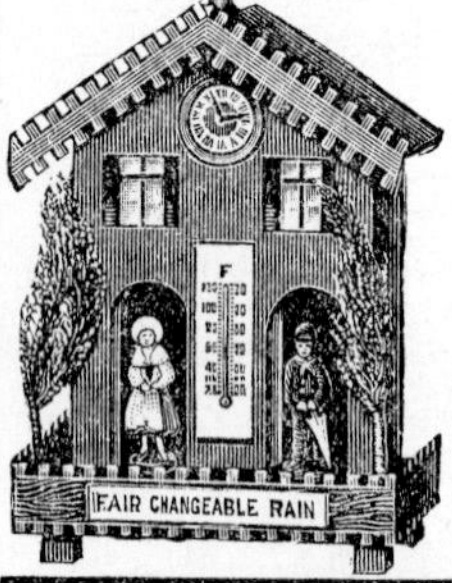

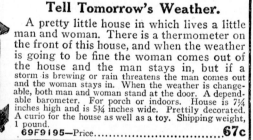

A pretty little house in which lives a little man and woman. There is a thermometer on the front of this house, and when the weather is going to be fine the woman comes out of the house and the man stays in, but if a storm is brewing or rain threatens the man comes out and the woman stays in. When the weather is changeable, both man and woman stand at the door. A dependable barometer. For porch or indoors. House is 7¼ inches high and is 5¾ inches wide. Prettily decorated. A curio for the house as well as a toy. Shipping weight, 1 pound.
69F9195—Price............................. 67c

Our Popular Decorated Tin Set—22 Pieces—$1.39.

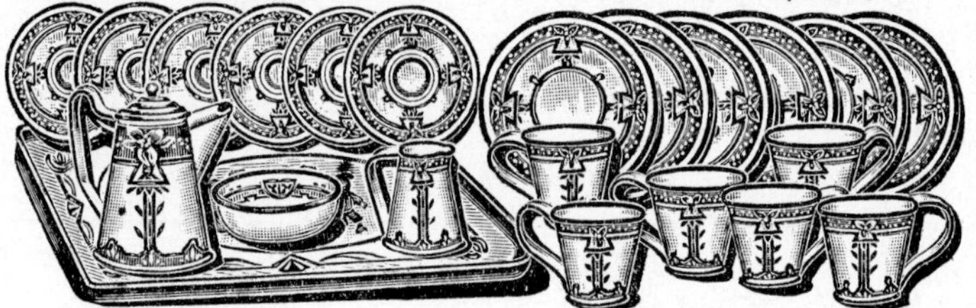

Made of heavy gauge metal, nicely lithographed in pretty colors and designs. Twenty-two pieces in all, consisting of tray, size 9x6¼ inches, six 1¾-inch cups, six 3-inch saucers, six 4⅛-inch plates, sugar bowl, 2½ inches in diameter, 2⅝-inch creamer, 3½-inch coffeepot and cover. We do not recommend this set for use with water, as any tin set may leak, but for sand or make believe tea parties it is ideal. Shipping wt., 1½ lbs.
49F1824—Price $1.39

Horse, Wagon and Auto.

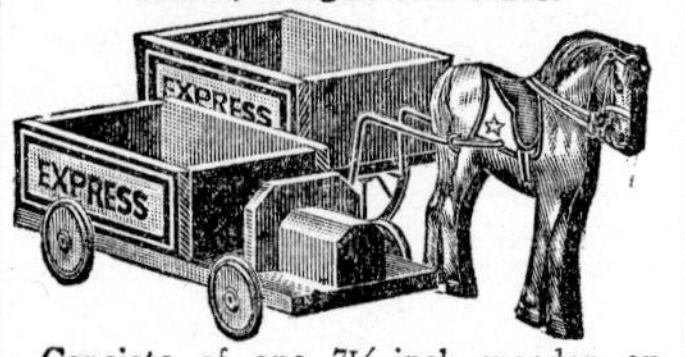

Consists of one 7½-inch wooden express auto and one wooden two-wheel cart with horse. Size over all, about 11½ inches. Made of wood with metal wheels. Shipping weight, per set, 14 ounces.
69F7606 Price, per set....... 29c

Imitation Cut Glass Toy Punch Set.

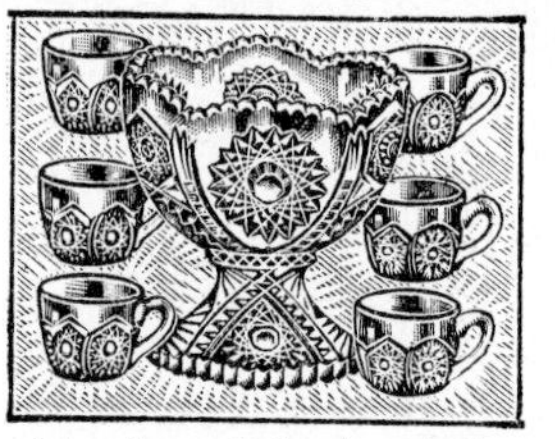

Consists of punch bowl and six cups. Punch bowl, diameter, 4⅜ inches; cups, size, 1¼ inches in diameter. Real heavy glass. Shpg. wt., 2¼ lbs.
49F1903—Price, per set........ 57c

Hippodrome Animated Circus.

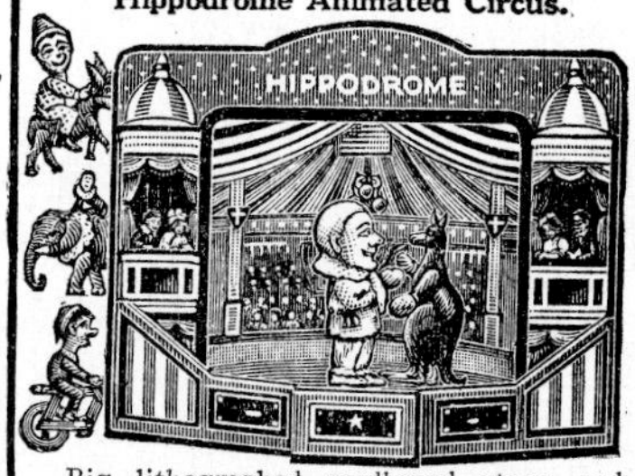

Big lithographed cardboard stage and four performing cardboard figures with movable joints. Stage and figures in bright colors. Four big circus acts. Elephant, with monkey rider. Tricky tramp bicycle rider (wheels revolve). Clown riding trick donkey, also clown boxing kangaroo. Lots of action. To all appearances figures come out from behind scenes, advance to front of stage and go through act. Size of stage, opened up, 11¼ inches wide, 9¼ inches high, 5 inches deep. Figures about 4¼ inches high. Av. shpg. wt., 1¼ lbs.
69F9185—Price............ 89c

Nine-Piece China Set, 98 Cents.

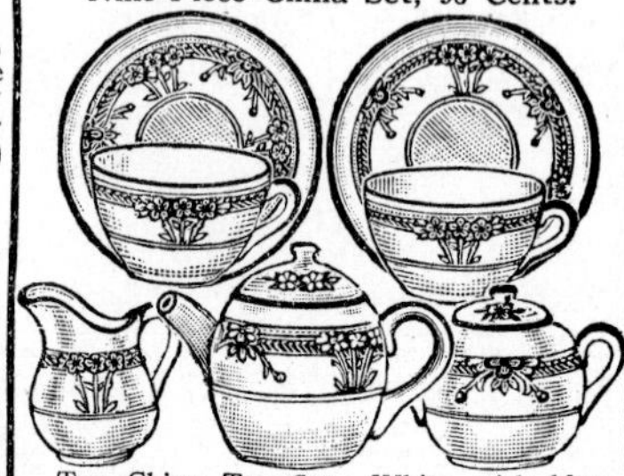

Toy China Tea Set. White with blue decorations. Two cups, 2⅞ inches diameter, 1½ inches high; two saucers, 4¼ in. diameter. Teapot with lid, 3⅝ inches high, 3 inches diameter. Other pieces in proportion. Shipping weight, 3⅛ lbs.
49F1612—Price 98c

Funny Folks Camera, 29 Cents.

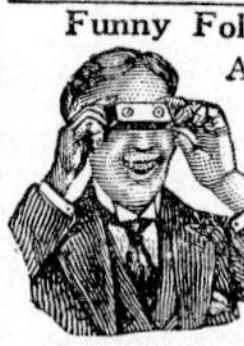

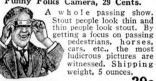

A whole passing show. Stout people look thin and thin people look stout. By getting a focus on passing pedestrians, horses, cars, etc., the most ludicrous pictures are witnessed. Shipping weight, 5 ounces.
49F6300—Price 29c

White Enameled Doll House Set.

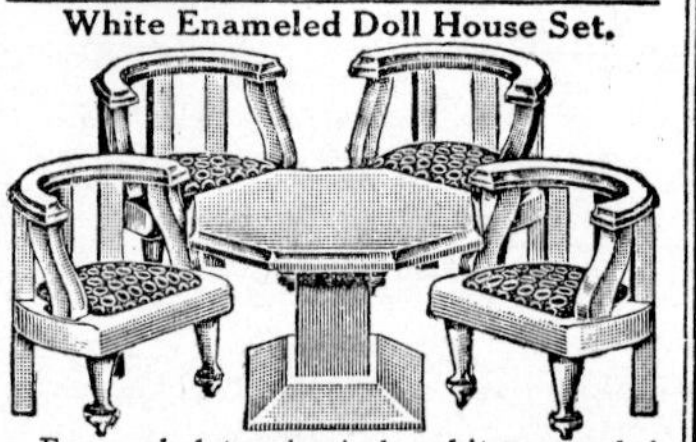

Four upholstered, nicely white enameled wood arm chairs and table to match. We especially recommend this set for strength and durability. Height of chairs, 2⅞ inches. Table, 3⅞ inches in diameter. Shipping weight, 12 ounces.
69F8542—Price............... 47c

Jumping Dog.

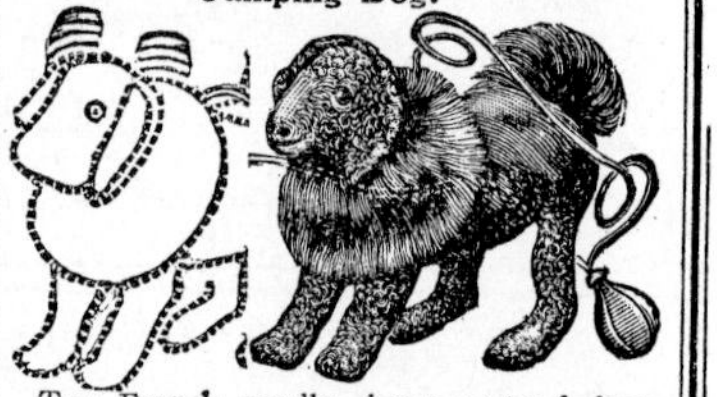

Toy French poodle, imported from France. Black cloth with fur neck and tail. Height, 4¾ inches. Length, about 6½ inches. Fitted with rubber bulb and tube. Slight pressure on bulb causes dog to jump. Baby will love him. A good little toy and very strong. Shipping weight, 6 ounces.
49F5772—Price.............. 47c

For Baby's Own Use.

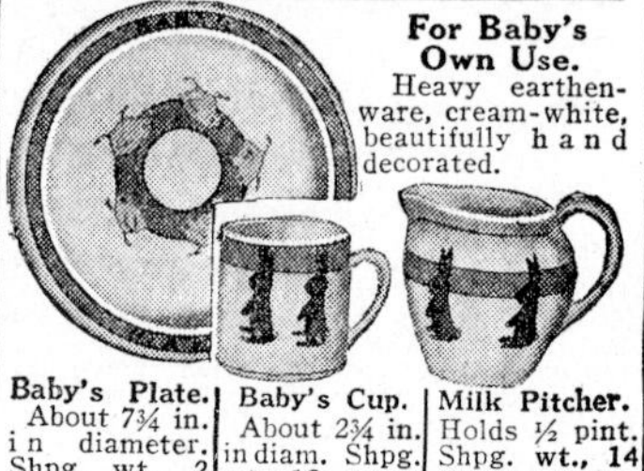

Heavy earthenware, cream-white, beautifully hand decorated.

Baby's Plate.	Baby's Cup.	Milk Pitcher.
About 7¾ in. in diameter. Shpg. wt., 2 lbs.	About 2¾ in. in diam. Shpg. wt., 12 oz.	Holds ½ pint. Shpg. wt., 14 ounces.
49F1600 Price 79c	49F1602 Price 39c	49F1603 Price 39c

Boys' Toys

Electric Moving Picture Machines.
Our Films Will Not Burn.

Excellent quality machines for the home. Made of steel, painted black. Absolutely safe. Uses ordinary electric light globes and current. Films will not burn. These outfits have the approval of the National Board of Fire Underwriters.

Machines use the professional type Geneva sprocket and star wheel for moving film. Powerful lenses, one for focusing. Plug, socket and 6 feet of cord for connecting with light fixtures. Instructions for operating sent with each machine. Tickets, posters, etc., for playing show. The films used with these machines have about twenty pictures to the foot. These machines all make good pictures; but of course the larger the machine the larger the light that can be used and the larger and clearer the picture.

SMALL.
Size, not including wire film holder, 5¾x8¾x10 in. Outfit includes 20 feet of film (our selection) and one slide. Nothing larger than ordinary home size electric light bulbs should be used with this size. Shipping wt., each in carton, 5 pounds.
79F6800¼—Price **$4.98**

MEDIUM.
Size, not including wire film holder, 6¾x12½x13 in. Outfit includes three slides, four 10-foot belts of film (our selection) and sheet of instructions. Has light adjuster. Shpg. wt., each in carton, 8½ lbs.
79F6801¼—Price............. **$8.95**

LARGE REWIND MODEL.
Will handle up to 100 feet of film. Size, not including film holder, 6¾x14¾x19 inches. Has three lenses. Light adjuster. Six slides. 100 feet of film (our selection) and simple instructions. Shipping weight, each in carton, 10½ pounds.
79F6802¼—Price............. **$12.67**

Safety Non-Inflammable Films. These Films Will Not Burn.
For moving picture machines listed above. About twenty pictures to the foot.

10-Foot Belts.
Shipping weight, 5 oz. Price, each......... **98c**
Charlie Chaplin.
49F6810—"The Kid."
49F6811—"Out for a Walk."
49F6812—"Fun in a Bake Shop."
49F6813—"Handle Rough."
Wm. S. Hart.
49F6814—"New Sheriff."
49F6815—"The Western Boss."
49F6816—Billy West. "Funny Musician."
49F6817—Fatty Arbuckle. "Fatty's Door."
49F6818—Mary Pickford. "Kindness."
49F6819—Ham and Bud. "Seltzer Bottle Bud."
49F6820—Mary Pickford. "Our Baby."

25-Foot Lengths.
Shipping weight, 6 oz. Price, each **$2.39**
49F6830—Wm. S. Hart. "The Western Outlaw."
49F6831—Tom Mix. "The Army Recruit."
49F6832—Charlie Chaplin. "Just for Fun."
49F6833—Charlie Chaplin. "The Clothing Store."
49F6838—Charlie Chaplin. "Easy Money."
49F6834—Western. "In the Hands of the Indians."
49F6835—Western. "Dick, the Baggage Boy."
49F6837—Ben Turpin. "The Store Keeper."
49F6836—Billy West. "The Prize Dancer."
49F6839—Billy West. "The Station Agent."

Chemistry Outfit.
For learning rudiments of chemistry in a decidedly interesting way. 9 chemicals in wooden boxes, 6 in bottles, necessary test tubes, mixing spatula, measures and litmus paper. An illustrated 75-page book of instructions included. Comes in fancy box, size 8½x12¼ in. Shpg. wt., 1½ lbs.
49F4750—Price **$2.39**

Electric Flying Airplane.
Has an electric motor which drives the airplane in circles around and around the center pole over which the wires travel to the electric batteries. Requires eight dry cells or transformer to run. Dry cells not included, but listed on page 1075 in this catalog. Sheet steel, nicely painted, 22x19½ in. Shipping weight, 7 pounds.
79F4755¼—Price **$3.98**

Six Large Size Balloons for 25 Cents.

Six permanently colored rubber balloons. The assortment consists of one round balloon, a large watermelon shape balloon, a bagpipe, an airship, a sausage squawker and one extra large size round balloon that can be inflated to about 15 inches in diameter. Shpg. wt., 2 ounces.
69F9120—Complete assortment of 6 balloons, as described..... **25c**

Shooflies, Hobby Horses and Kiddie Wheel Toys

$5⁸⁹

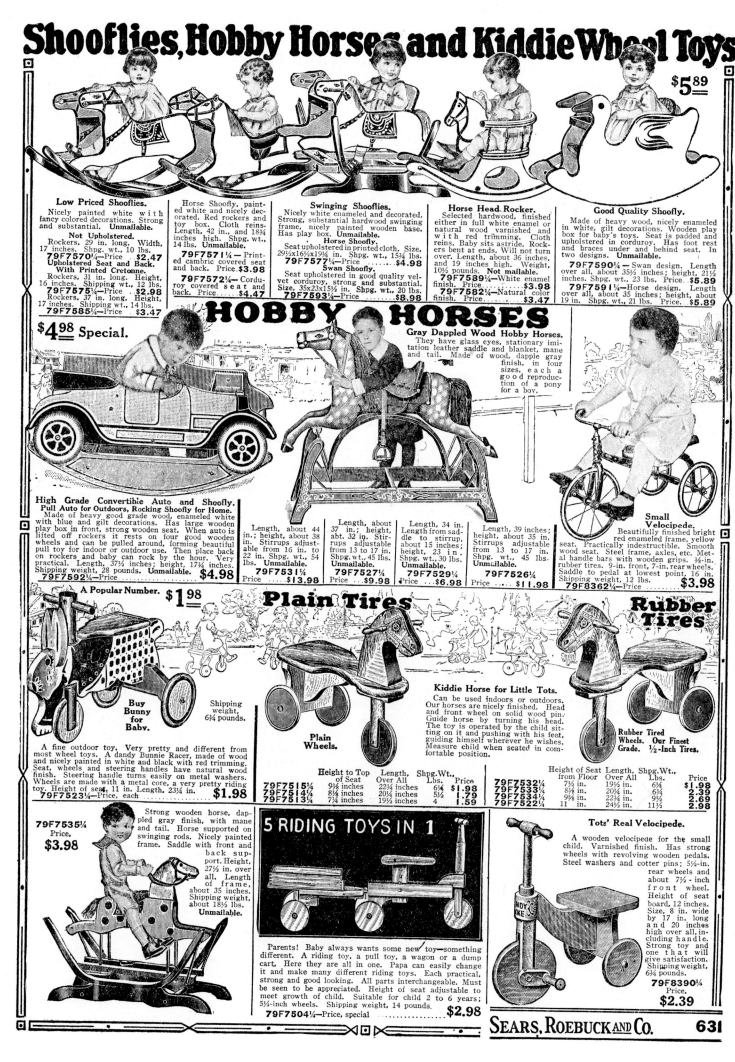

Low Priced Shooflies.
Nicely painted white with fancy colored decorations. Strong and substantial. **Unmailable.**
Not Upholstered.
Rockers, 29 in. long. Width, 17 inches. Shpg. wt., 10 lbs.
79F7570¼—Price . . . $2.47
Upholstered Seat and Back.
With Printed Cretonne.
Rockers, 31 in. long. Height, 16 inches. Shipping wt., 12 lbs.
79F7575¼—Price . . $2.98
Rockers, 37 in. long. Height, 17 inches. Shipping wt., 14 lbs.
79F7585¼—Price . . $3.47

Horse Shoofly, painted white and nicely decorated. Red rockers and toy box. Cloth reins. Length, 42 in., and 18¾ inches high. Shpg. wt., 14 lbs. **Unmailable.**
79F7571¼—Printed cambric covered seat and back. Price.$3.98
79F7572¼—Corduroy covered seat and back. Price. $4.47

Swinging Shooflies.
Nicely white enameled and decorated. Strong, substantial hardwood swinging frame, nicely painted wooden base. Has play box. **Unmailable.**
Horse Shoofly.
Seat upholstered in printed cloth. Size, 29½x16½x19¼ in. Shpg. wt., 15¾ lbs.
79F7577¼—Price $4.98
Swan Shoofly.
Seat upholstered in good quality velvet corduroy, strong and substantial. Size, 35x23x15½ in. Shpg. wt., 20 lbs.
79F7593¼—Price $8.98

Horse Head Rocker.
Selected hardwood, finished either in full white enamel or natural wood varnished and with red trimming. Cloth reins. Baby sits astride. Rockers bent at ends. Will not turn over. Length, about 36 inches, and 19 inches high. Weight, 10½ pounds. **Not mailable.**
79F7589¼—White enamel finish. Price. $3.98
79F7582¼—Natural color finish. Price. $3.47

Good Quality Shoofly.
Made of heavy wood, nicely enameled in white, gilt decorations. Wooden play box for baby's toys. Seat is padded and upholstered in corduroy. Has foot rest and braces under and behind seat. In two designs. **Unmailable.**
79F7590¼—Swan design. Length over all, about 35½ inches; height, 21½ inches. Shpg. wt., 23 lbs. Price. $5.89
79F7591¼—Horse design. Length over all, about 35 inches; height, about 19 in. Shpg. wt., 21 lbs. Price. $5.89

HOBBY HORSES

$4⁹⁸ Special.

Gray Dappled Wood Hobby Horses.
They have glass eyes, stationary imitation leather saddle and blanket, mane and tail. Made of wood, dapple gray finish, in four sizes, each a good reproduction of a pony for a boy.

High Grade Convertible Auto and Shoofly.
Pull Auto for Outdoors, Rocking Shoofly for Home.
Made of heavy good grade wood, enameled white with blue and gilt decorations. Has large wooden play box in front, strong wooden seat. When auto is lifted off rockers it rests on four good wooden wheels and can be pulled around, forming beautiful pull toy for indoor or outdoor use. Then place back on rockers and baby can rock by the hour. Very practical. Length, 37½ inches; height, 17¾ inches. Shipping weight, 28 pounds. **Unmailable.** $4.98
79F7592¼—Price. . . . .

Length, about 44 in.; height, about 38 in. Stirrups adjustable from 16 in. to 22 in. Shpg. wt., 54 lbs. **Unmailable.** 79F7531¼ Price . . . $13.98	Length, about 37 in.; height, abt. 32 in. Stirrups adjustable from 13 to 17 in. Shpg. wt., 45 lbs. **Unmailable.** 79F7527¼ Price . . $9.98	Length, 34 in. Length from saddle to stirrup, about 15 inches; height, 23 in. Shpg. wt., 30 lbs. **Unmailable.** 79F7529¼ Price . . $6.98	Length, 39 inches; height, about 35 in. Stirrups adjustable from 13 to 17 in. Shpg. wt., 45 lbs. **Unmailable.** 79F7526¼ Price . . . $11.98

Small Velocipede.
Beautifully finished bright red enameled frame, yellow seat. Practically indestructible. Smooth wood seat. Steel frame, axles, etc. Metal handle bars with wooden grips. ⅜-in. rubber tires. 9-in. front, 7-in. rear wheels. Saddle to pedal at lowest point, 16 in. Shipping weight, 12 lbs.
79F8362¼—Price $3.98

A Popular Number. $1⁹⁸

Plain Tires   Rubber Tires

Buy Bunny for Baby.
Shipping weight, 6¾ pounds.
A fine outdoor toy. Very pretty and different from most wheel toys. A dandy Bunnie Racer, made of wood and nicely painted in white and black with red trimming. Seat, wheels and steering handles have natural wood finish. Steering handle turns easily on metal washers. Wheels are made with a metal core, a very pretty riding toy. Height of seat, 11 in. Length, 23¾ in.
79F7523¼—Price, each $1.98

Plain Wheels.

	Height to Top of Seat	Length, Over All	Shpg.Wt., Lbs.	Price
79F7515¼	9⅝ inches	22¾ inches	6¼	$1.98
79F7514¼	8⅝ inches	20¼ inches	5½	1.79
79F7513¼	7¼ inches	19½ inches	4	1.59

Kiddie Horse for Little Tots.
Can be used indoors or outdoors. Our horses are nicely finished. Head and front wheel on solid wood pin. Guide horse by turning his head. The toy is operated by the child sitting on it and pushing with his feet, guiding himself wherever he wishes. Measure child when seated in comfortable position.

Rubber Tired Wheels. Our Finest Grade. ½-Inch Tires.

	Height of Seat from Floor	Length Over All	Shpg.Wt. Lbs.	Price
79F7532¼	7½ in.	19½ in.	6¼	$1.98
79F7533¼	8½ in.	20¼ in.	6¾	2.39
79F7534¼	9⅝ in.	22¾ in.	9½	2.69
79F7522¼	11 in.	24½ in.	11½	2.98

79F7535¼ Price, $3.98
Strong wooden horse, dappled gray finish, with mane and tail. Horse supported on swinging rods. Nicely painted frame. Saddle with front and back support. Height, 27½ in. over all. Length of frame, about 35 inches. Shipping weight, about 18½ lbs. **Unmailable.**

5 RIDING TOYS IN 1
Parents! Baby always wants some new toy—something different. A riding toy, a pull toy, a wagon or a dump cart. Here they are all in one. Papa can easily change it and make many different riding toys. Each practical, strong and good looking. All parts interchangeable. Must be seen to be appreciated. Height of seat adjustable to meet growth of child. Suitable for child 2 to 6 years; 5½-inch wheels. Shipping weight, 14 pounds.
79F7504¼—Price, special $2.98

Tots' Real Velocipede.
A wooden velocipede for the small child. Varnished finish. Has strong wheels with revolving wooden pedals. Steel washers and cotter pins; 5½-in. rear wheels and about 7½-inch front wheel. Height of seat board, 12 inches. Size, 8 in. wide by 17 in. long and 20 inches high over all, including handle. Strong toy and one that will give satisfaction. Shipping weight, 6¾ pounds.
79F8390¼—Price, $2.39

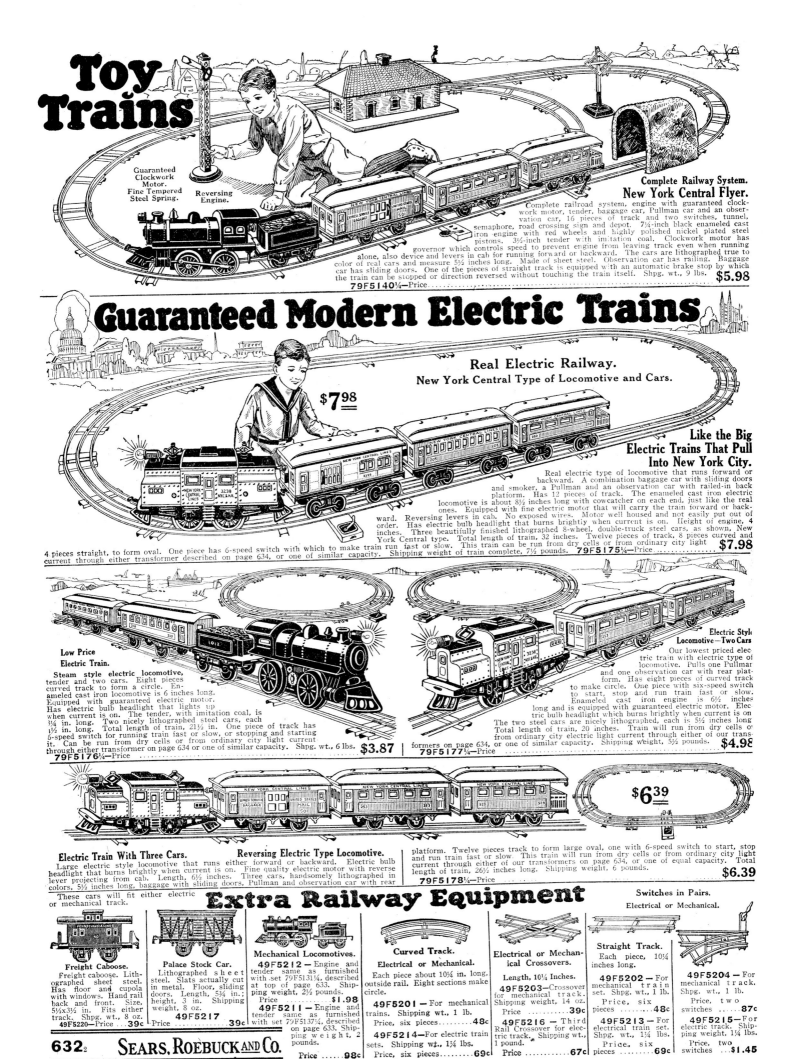

Toy Trains

Guaranteed Clockwork Motor. Fine Tempered Steel Spring. Reversing Engine.

Complete Railway System.
New York Central Flyer.

Complete railroad system, engine with guaranteed clockwork motor, tender, baggage car, Pullman car and an observation car, 16 pieces of track and two switches, tunnel, semaphore, road crossing sign and depot. 7¼-inch black enameled cast iron engine with red wheels and highly polished nickel plated steel pistons. 3½-inch tender with imitation coal. Clockwork motor has governor which controls speed to prevent engine from leaving track even when running alone, also device and levers in cab for running forward or backward. The cars are lithographed true to color of real cars and measure 5½ inches long. Made of sheet steel. Observation car has railing. Baggage car has sliding doors. One of the pieces of straight track is equipped with an automatic brake stop by which the train can be stopped or direction reversed without touching the train itself. Shpg. wt., 9 lbs.
79F5140¼—Price $5.98

Guaranteed Modern Electric Trains

Real Electric Railway.
New York Central Type of Locomotive and Cars.

$7.98

Like the Big Electric Trains That Pull Into New York City.

Real electric type of locomotive that runs forward or backward. A combination baggage car with sliding doors and smoker, a Pullman and an observation car with railed-in back platform. Has 12 pieces of track. The enameled cast iron locomotive is about 8½ inches long with cowcatcher on each end, just like the real ones. Equipped with fine electric motor that will carry the train forward or backward. Reversing levers in cab. No exposed wires. Motor well housed and not easily put out of order. Has electric bulb headlight that burns brightly when current is on. Height of engine, 4 inches. Three beautifully finished lithographed 8-wheel, double-truck steel cars, as shown, New York Central type. Total length of train, 32 inches. Twelve pieces of track, eight curved and four pieces straight, to form oval. One piece has 6-speed switch with which to make train run fast or slow. This train can be run from dry cells or from ordinary city light current through either transformer described on page 634, or one of similar capacity. Shipping weight of train complete, 7½ pounds. **79F5175¼—Price $7.98**

Low Price Electric Train.

Steam style electric locomotive, tender and two cars. Eight pieces curved track to form a circle. Enameled cast iron locomotive is 6 inches long. Equipped with guaranteed electric motor. Has electric bulb headlight that lights up when current is on. The tender, with imitation coal, is 3¼ in. long. Two nicely lithographed steel cars, each 1½ in. long. Total length of train, 21½ in. One piece of track has 6-speed switch for running train fast or slow, or stopping and starting it. Can be run from dry cells or from ordinary city light current through either transformer on page 634 or one of similar capacity. Shpg. wt., 6 lbs. **$3.87**
79F5176¼—Price ....

Electric Style Locomotive—Two Cars

Our lowest priced electric train with electric type of locomotive. Pulls one Pullman and one observation car with rear platform. Has eight pieces of curved track to make circle. One piece with six-speed switch to start, stop and run train fast or slow. Enameled cast iron engine is 6½ inches long and is equipped with guaranteed electric motor. Electric bulb headlight which burns brightly when current is on. The two steel cars are nicely lithographed. Total length of train, 20 inches. Train will run from dry cells or from ordinary city electric light current through either of our transformers on page 634, or one of similar capacity. Shipping weight, 5½ pounds. **$4.98**
79F5177¼—Price ....

Electric Train With Three Cars.
Reversing Electric Type Locomotive.

Large electric style locomotive that runs either forward or backward. Electric bulb headlight that burns brightly when current is on. Fine quality electric motor with reverse lever projecting from cab. Length, 6½ inches. Three cars, handsomely lithographed in colors, long one baggage with sliding doors, Pullman and observation car with rear platform. Twelve pieces track to form large oval, one with 6-speed switch to start, stop and run train fast or slow. This train will run from dry cells or from ordinary city light current through either of our transformers on page 634, or one of equal capacity. Total length of train, 26½ inches long. Shipping weight, 6 pounds. **$6.39**
79F5178¼—Price ....

These cars will fit either electric or mechanical track.

$6.39

Extra Railway Equipment

Freight Caboose.
Freight caboose. Lithographed sheet steel. Has floor and cupola with windows. Hand rail back and front. Size, 5½x3½ in. Fits either track. Shpg. wt., 8 oz.
49F5220—Price 39c

Palace Stock Car.
Lithographed sheet steel. Slats actually cut in metal. Floor, sliding doors. Length, 5¾ in.; height, 3 in. Shipping weight, 8 oz.
49F5217
Price 39c

Mechanical Locomotives.
49F5212—Engine and tender same as furnished with set 79F5131¼, described at top of page 633. Shipping weight, 2½ pounds.
Price **$1.98**
49F5211—Engine and tender same as furnished with set 79F5137¼, described on page 633. Shipping weight, 2 pounds.
Price **98c**

Curved Track.
Electrical or Mechanical.
Each piece about 10¼ in. long, outside rail. Eight sections make circle.
49F5201—For mechanical trains. Shipping wt., 1 lb.
Price, six pieces **48c**
49F5214—For electric train sets. Shipping wt., 1¼ lbs.
Price, six pieces **69c**

Electrical or Mechanical Crossovers.
Length, 10¼ Inches.
49F5203—Crossover for mechanical track. Shipping weight, 14 oz.
Price **39c**
49F5216—Third Rail Crossover for electric track. Shipping wt., 1 pound.
Price **67c**

Straight Track.
Each piece, 10¼ inches long.
49F5202—For mechanical train set. Shpg. wt., 1 lb.
Price, six pieces **48c**
49F5213—For electrical train set. Shpg. wt., 1¼ lbs.
Price, six pieces **69c**

Switches in Pairs.
Electrical or Mechanical.
49F5204—For mechanical track. Shpg. wt., 1 lb.
Price, two switches **87c**
49F5215—For electric track. Shipping weight, 1¼ lbs.
Price, two switches **$1.45**

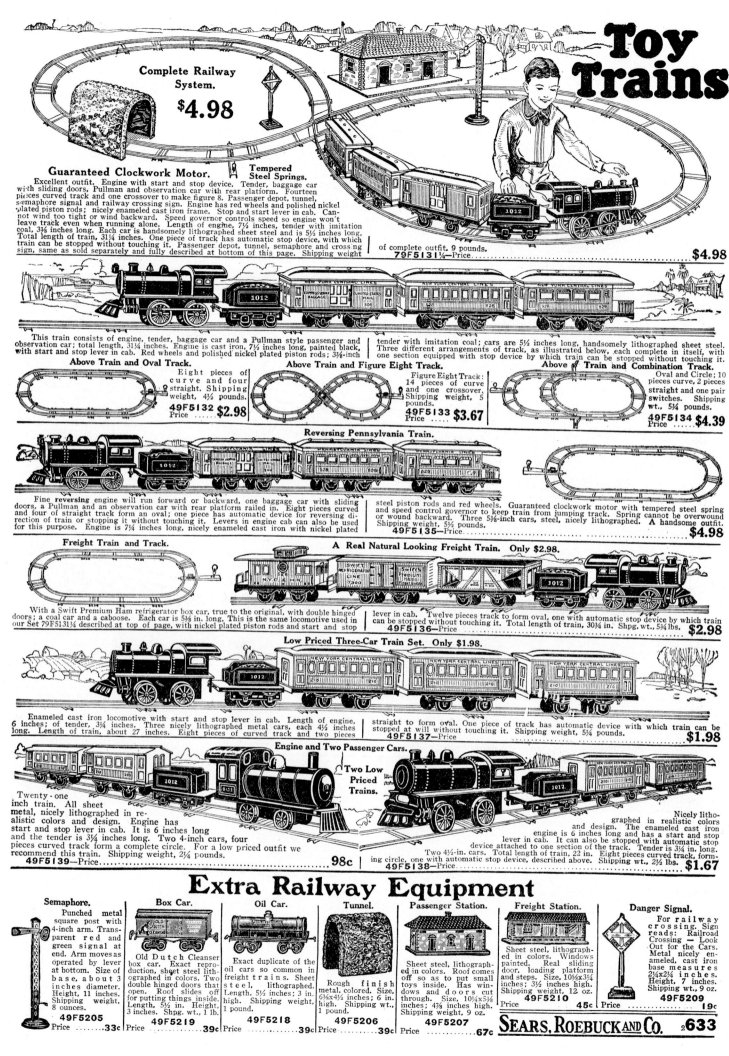

Toy Trains

Complete Railway System. $4.98

Guaranteed Clockwork Motor.   **Tempered Steel Springs.**

Excellent outfit. Engine with start and stop device. Tender, baggage car with sliding doors, Pullman and observation car with rear platform. Fourteen pieces curved track and one crossover to make figure 8. Passenger depot, tunnel, semaphore signal and railway crossing sign. Engine has red wheels and polished nickel plated piston rods; nicely enameled cast iron frame. Stop and start lever in cab. Cannot wind too tight or wind backward. Speed governor controls speed so engine won't leave track even when running alone. Length of engine, 7½ inches, tender with imitation coal, 3¾ inches long. Each car is handsomely lithographed sheet steel and is 5½ inches long. Total length of train, 31¼ inches. One piece of track has automatic stop device, with which train can be stopped without touching it. Passenger depot, tunnel, semaphore and crossing sign, same as sold separately and fully described at bottom of this page. Shipping weight of complete outfit, 9 pounds.

79F5131¼—Price...$4.98

This train consists of engine, tender, baggage car and a Pullman style passenger and observation car; total length, 31¼ inches. Engine is cast iron, 7½ inches long, painted black, with start and stop device; nicely enameled cast iron frame. Red wheels and polished nickel plated piston rods; 3⅜-inch tender with imitation coal; cars are 5½ inches long, handsomely lithographed sheet steel. Three different arrangements of track, as illustrated below, each complete in itself, with one section equipped with stop device by which train can be stopped without touching it.

Above Train and Oval Track.
Eight pieces of curve and four straight. Shipping weight, 4½ pounds.
49F5132 Price..... $2.98

Above Train and Figure Eight Track.
Figure Eight Track: 14 pieces of curve and one crossover. Shipping weight, 5 pounds.
49F5133 Price..... $3.67

Above Train and Combination Track.
Oval and Circle; 10 pieces curve, 2 pieces straight and one pair switches. Shipping wt., 5¾ pounds.
49F5134 Price..... $4.39

Reversing Pennsylvania Train.
Fine **reversing** engine will run forward or backward, one baggage car with sliding doors, a Pullman and an observation car with rear platform railed in. Eight pieces curved and four of straight track form an oval; one piece has automatic device for reversing direction of train or stopping it without touching it. Levers in engine cab can also be used for this purpose. Engine is 7¼ inches long, nicely enameled cast iron with nickel plated steel piston rods and red wheels. Guaranteed clockwork motor with tempered steel spring and speed control governor to keep train from jumping track. Spring cannot be overwound or wound backward. Three 5⅜-inch cars, steel, nicely lithographed. A handsome outfit. Shipping weight, 5½ pounds.
49F5135—Price...$4.98

Freight Train and Track.
A Real Natural Looking Freight Train. Only $2.98
With a Swift Premium Ham refrigerator box car, true to the original, with double hinged doors; a coal car and a caboose. Each car is 5½ in. long. This is the same locomotive used in our Set 79F5131¼ described at top of page, with nickel plated piston rods and start and stop lever in cab. Twelve pieces track to form oval, one with automatic stop device by which train can be stopped without touching it. Total length of train, 30¾ in. Shpg. wt., 5¾ lbs.
49F5136—Price...$2.98

Low Priced Three-Car Train Set. Only $1.98.
Enameled cast iron locomotive with start and stop lever in cab. Length of engine, 6 inches; of tender, 3¾ inches. Three nicely lithographed metal cars, each 4½ inches long. Length of train, about 27 inches. Eight pieces of curved track and two pieces straight to form oval. One piece of track has automatic device with which train can be stopped at will without touching it. Shipping weight, 5¼ pounds.
49F5137—Price...$1.98

Engine and Two Passenger Cars.
Two Low Priced Trains.

Twenty-one inch train. All sheet metal, nicely lithographed in realistic colors and design. Engine has start and stop lever in cab. It is 6 inches long and the tender is 3¾ inches long. Two 4-inch cars, four pieces curved track form a complete circle. For a low priced outfit we recommend this train. Shipping weight, 2¼ pounds.
49F5139—Price...98c

Nicely lithographed in realistic colors and design. The enameled cast iron engine is 6 inches long and has a start and stop lever in cab. It can also be stopped with automatic stop device attached to one section of the track. Tender is 3¾ in. long. Two 4½-in. cars. Total length of train, 22 in. Eight pieces curved track, forming circle, one with automatic stop device, described above. Shipping wt., 2¼ lbs.
49F5138—Price...$1.67

Extra Railway Equipment

Semaphore.
Punched metal square post with 4-inch arm. Transparent red and green signal at end. Arm moves as operated by lever at bottom. Size of base, about 3 inches diameter. Height, 11 inches. Shipping weight, 8 ounces.
49F5205
Price.....33c

Box Car.
Old Dutch Cleanser box car. Exact reproduction, sheet steel lithographed in colors. Two double hinged doors that open. Roof slides off for putting things inside. Length, 5½ in. Height, 3 inches. Shpg. wt., 1 lb.
49F5219
Price.....39c

Oil Car.
Exact duplicate of the oil cars so common in freight trains. Sheet steel, lithographed. Length, 5½ inches; 3 in. high. Shipping weight, 1 pound.
49F5218
Price.....39c

Tunnel.
Rough finish metal, colored. Size, 6⅛x4½ inches; 6 in. high. Shipping wt., 1 pound.
49F5206
Price.....39c

Passenger Station.
Sheet steel, lithographed in colors. Roof comes off so as to put small toys inside. Has windows and doors cut through. Size, 10¼x5⅝ inches; 4⅞ inches high. Shipping weight, 9 oz.
49F5207
Price.....67c

Freight Station.
Sheet steel, lithographed in colors. Windows painted. Real sliding door, loading platform and steps. Size, 10⅝x3¼ inches; 3½ inches high. Shipping weight, 12 oz.
49F5210
Price.....45c

Danger Signal.
For railway crossing. Sign reads: Railroad Crossing - Look Out for the Cars. Metal nicely enameled, cast iron base measures 2¼x2¼ inches. Height, 7 inches. Shipping wt., 9 oz.
49F5209
Price.....19c

SEARS, ROEBUCK AND CO. 633

BOYS' TOYS

Every Boy Wants This Gun

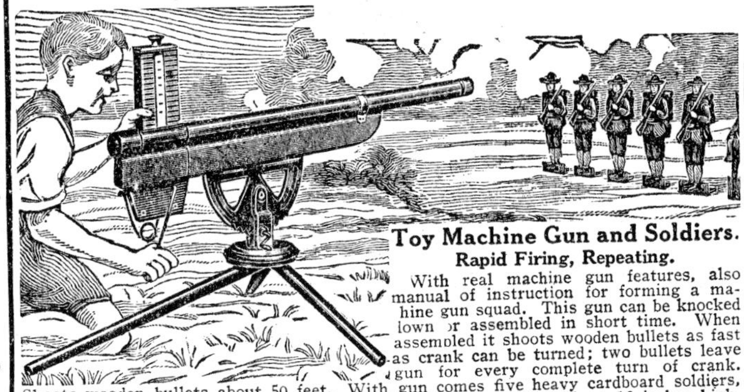

Toy Machine Gun and Soldiers.
Rapid Firing, Repeating.

With real machine gun features, also manual of instruction for forming a machine gun squad. This gun can be knocked down or assembled in short time. When assembled it shoots wooden bullets as fast as crank can be turned; two bullets leave gun for every complete turn of crank. Shoots wooden bullets about 50 feet. With gun comes five heavy cardboard soldiers, each 6¼ inches high, on wooden base. Gun stands, assembled, about 13 inches high, and from rear leg of tripod to front end of gun, about 2 feet. Steel barrel, enameled. Wood stock. Detachable magazine clip for 12 cartridges (wood bullets). Has firing crank with wood handle. Automatic traverse with elevating crank for raising and lowering aim; full circle swivel for turning gun completely around, if necessary. Two short wood forelegs and one long rear leg to form tripod. Strong shooting spring. Included is a manual of instruction for organizing machine gun squad which consists of eight soldiers (boys), and U. S. Army drill regulations for the conduct of the squad. Shipping weight, complete, 4 pounds.
49F5607—Price, complete....... **$2.98**
49F5605—Extra Wooden Bullets. Shipping weight, 2 ounces. Package of 12. Price....... **.25**

14-Inch Wood Target Set and Gun.

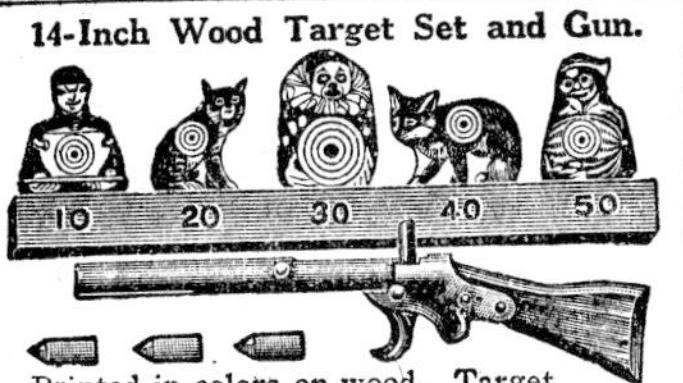

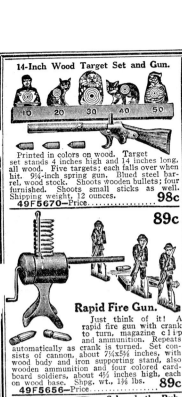

Printed in colors on wood. Target set stands 4 inches high and 14 inches long, all wood. Five targets; each falls over when hit. 9¼-inch spring gun. Blued steel barrel, wood stock. Shoots wooden bullets; four furnished. Shoots small sticks as well. Shipping weight, 12 ounces.
49F5670—Price....... **98c**

89c

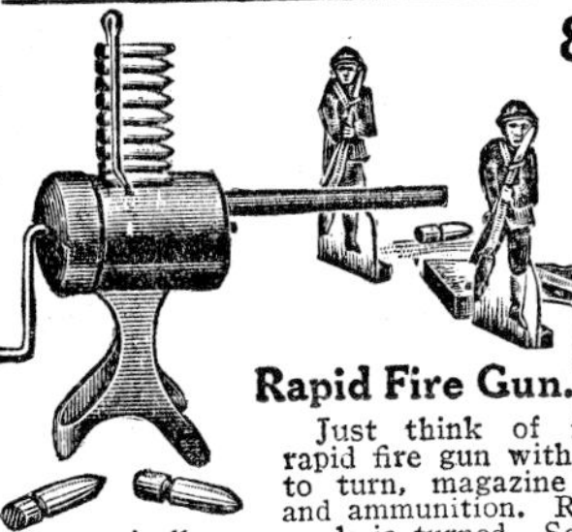

Rapid Fire Gun.

Just think of it! A rapid fire gun with crank to turn, magazine clip and ammunition. Repeats automatically as crank is turned. Set consists of cannon, about 7¼x5⅝ inches, with wood body and iron supporting stand, also wooden ammunition and four colored cardboard soldiers, about 4½ inches high, each on wood base. Shpg. wt., 1⅜ lbs.
49F5656—Price....... **89c**

Schoenhut's Rubber Ball Shooting Gallery.

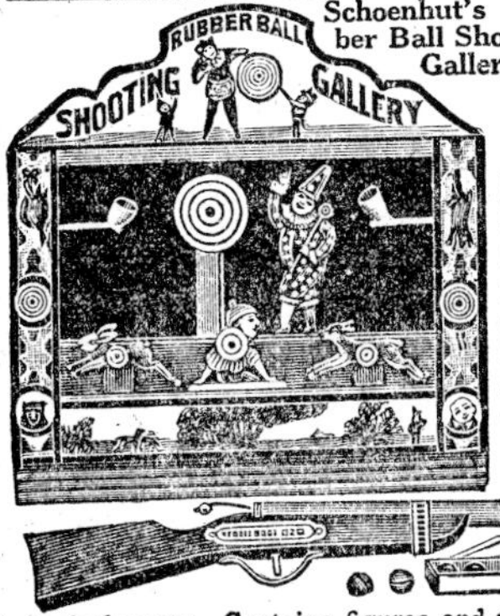

Made of light wood with cloth back. Front part of gallery covered with nicely lithographed paper. Contains figures and targets representing comic figures and animals, which fall down when hit. Comes with popgun, 15 inches long, over all, and 2 rubber balls and 2 corks. Size of target over all, 13x13¼x4½ in. Shpg. wt., 3 lbs.
49F5631—Price....... **$1.98**

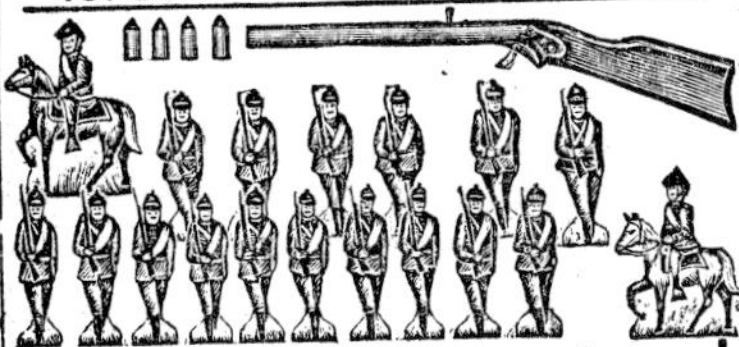

Boys, here is a dandy, just what you want. Consists of sixteen 3x1¼-inch lithographed tin soldiers on foot, two soldiers on horseback, 3¼x3⅛ inches, and 16½-inch gun that shoots wooden bullets. Good value for the money. Shpg. wt., about 1 lb.
49F5650—Price....... **98c**

Nine Intricate Puzzles.

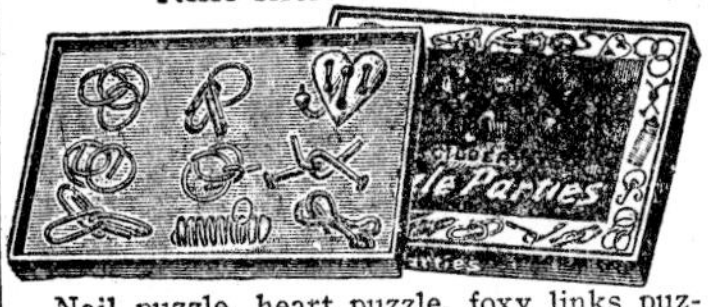

Nail puzzle, heart puzzle, foxy links puzzle, question puzzle, three-ring puzzle, etc. Most of them made of nickel plated wire. Nine in all. Directions in box. Test your skill. Shipping weight, 15 ounces.
49F6003—Price....... **67c**

Mammoth Trick Outfit.

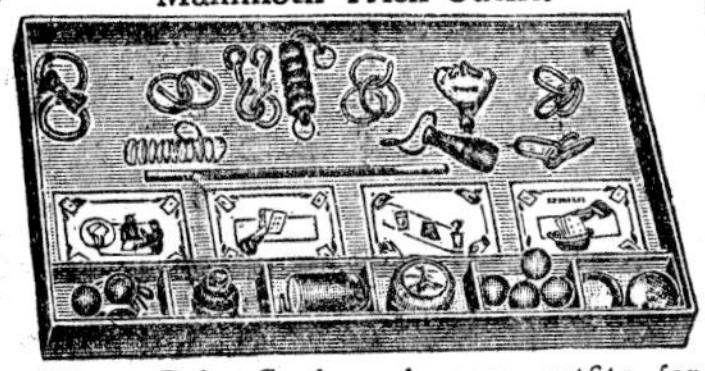

Three Fake Cards and seven outfits for other sleight of hand tricks. Also a booklet with full directions for doing other unusual tricks requiring no paraphernalia. Tricks include multiplying balls, disappearing money box, handkerchief trick, vanishing coin, etc. Also ten unusual mystifying puzzles. Shipping weight, 2¾ pounds.
49F6000—Price....... **$1.47**

Our Best Finished Toy Guns.

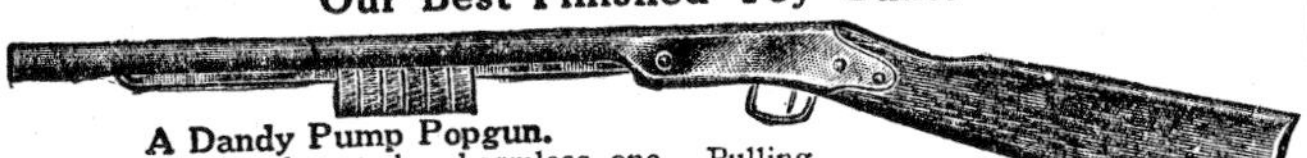

A Dandy Pump Popgun.

A dandy noisemaker and a harmless one. Pulling and pushing pump mechanism back and forth loads and shoots gun. Handsomely finished. Blued steel barrel and walnut stained and varnished wood stock. Measures about 27 inches long. Shipping weight, 1 pound.
49F5648—Price....... **98c**

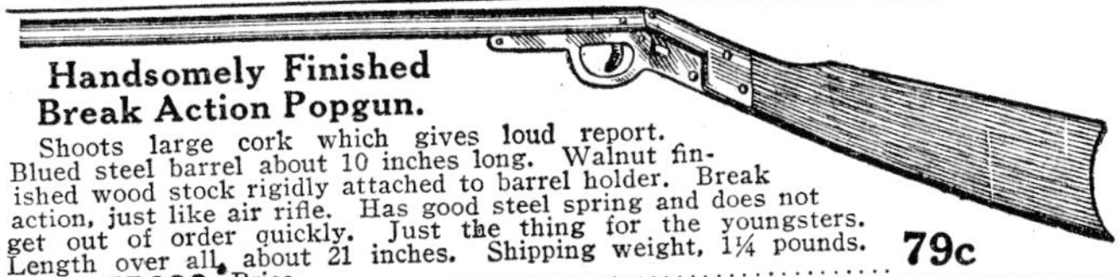

Handsomely Finished Break Action Popgun.

Shoots large cork which gives loud report. Blued steel barrel about 10 inches long. Walnut finished wood stock rigidly attached to barrel holder. Break action, just like air rifle. Has good steel spring and does not get out of order quickly. Just the thing for the youngsters. Length over all, about 21 inches. Shipping weight, 1¼ pounds.
49F5600—Price....... **79c**

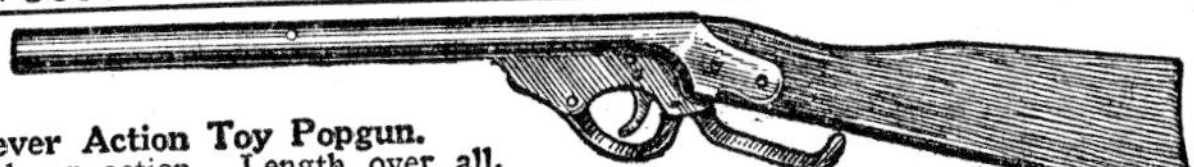

Lever Action Toy Popgun.

Has lever action. Length over all, about 16¼ inches. Shoots cork only, which is furnished. Barrel made of blued sheet steel, walnut stained wood stock. Popping report. Shipping weight, 11 ounces.
49F5647—Price....... **39c**

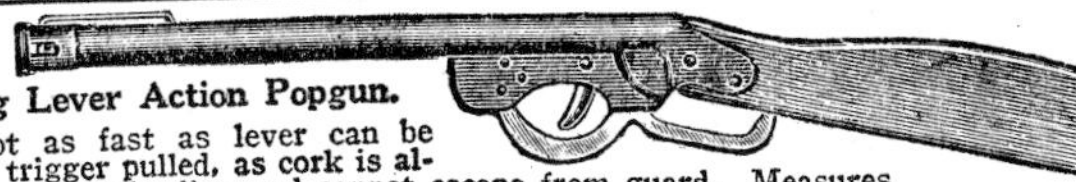

Repeating Lever Action Popgun.

Will shoot as fast as lever can be worked and trigger pulled, as cork is always in place for reloading and cannot escape from guard. Measures 16 inches over all. Stained wood stock, blued steel barrel. Average shipping weight, 11 ounces.
49F5632—Price....... **39c**

Toy Pistol and Belt With Wooden Bullets.

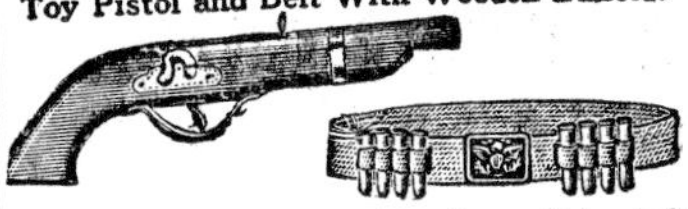

Toy pistol, about 10¼ in. long, 24-in. belt with wooden bullets. Pistol will shoot the little wooden cartridges but not hard enough to be dangerous. Belt for carrying cartridges included with this set. Shipping wt., 12 ounces.
49F5629—Price....... **67c**

Big Value Soldier Outfit.

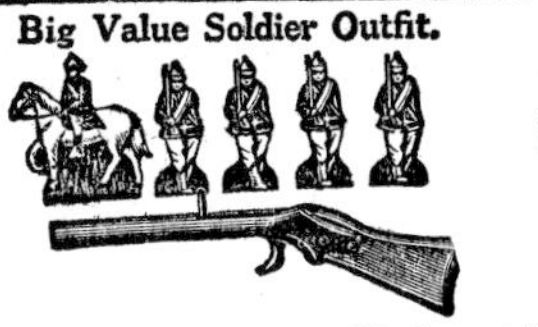

Set consists of four 2⅞-inch metal soldiers, one 3¼-inch cavalryman and 9¼-inch popgun. With cork. Shipping weight, 9 ounces.
49F5601—Price, per set....... **33c**

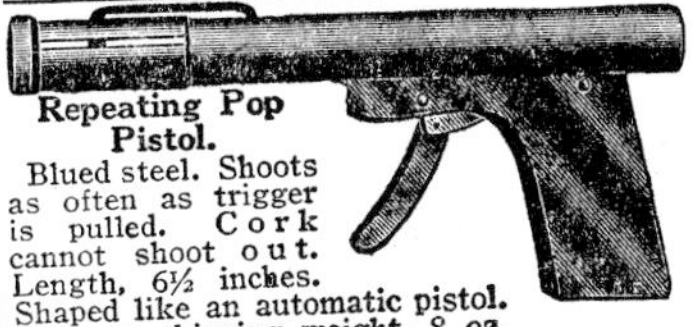

Repeating Pop Pistol.

Blued steel. Shoots as often as trigger is pulled. Cork cannot shoot out. Length, 6½ inches. Shaped like an automatic pistol. Average shipping weight, 8 oz.
49F5634
Price....... **39c**

Dandy 9¾-Inch Lever Action Pop Pistol.

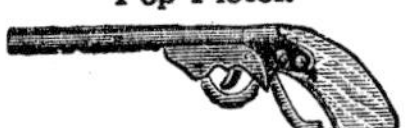

Well made pop pistol; wood handle; lever action. Sheet steel barrel. Complete with cork. Shipping weight, 8 ounces.
49F5603—Price....... **19c**

Dependable Water Pistols

Repeating Water Pistol.

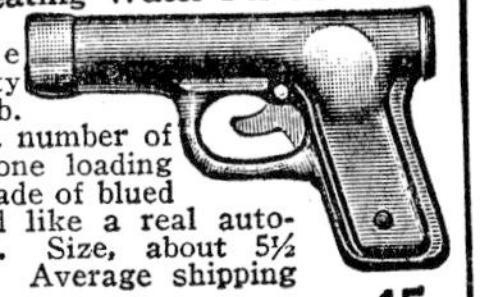

Has large good quality rubber bulb. Will shoot a number of times with one loading of water. Made of blued steel, shaped like a real automatic pistol. Size, about 5½ inches long. Average shipping weight, 8 ounces.
49F5633—Price....... **45c**

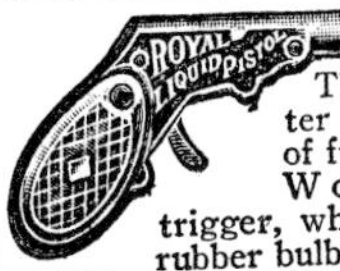

Water Pistol.

This 5-inch Tin Water Pistol affords lots of fun for the children. Works by pressing trigger, which acts against a rubber bulb. Will shoot water a fairly good distance. Shpg. wt., 8 oz.
49F5667—Price **25c**

Five 6¼-Inch Soldiers and Gun.

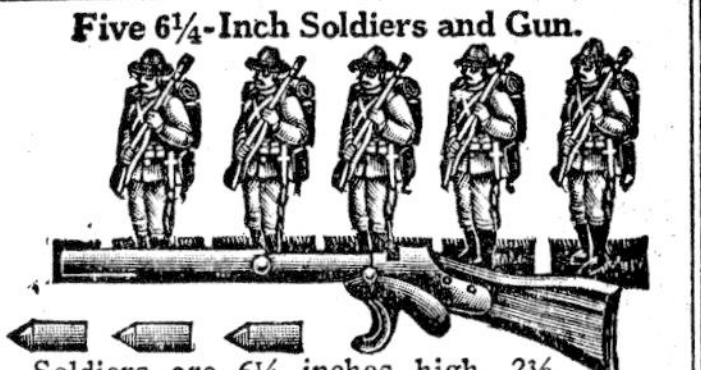

Soldiers are 6¼ inches high, 2⅜ inches wide, made of heavy cardboard printed in colors and varnished. Each on wooden base. Spring gun, 9¼ inches long. Blued steel barrel, stained wood stock. Shoots wooden bullets; four are furnished. Shoots small sticks as well. Shpg. wt., 12 oz.
49F5669—Price....... **67c**

Flying Airplane.

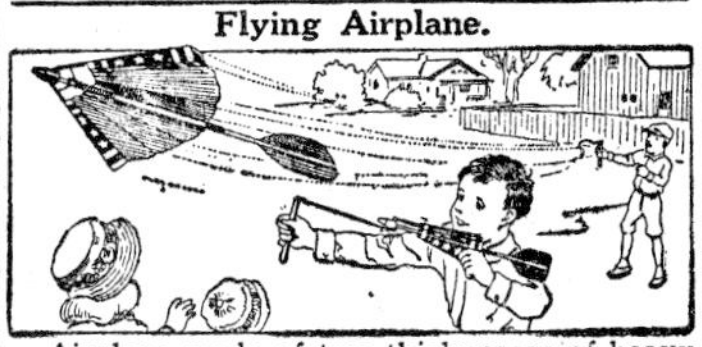

Airplane made of two thicknesses of heavy paper over wood frame. Shoot into air. At proper height spring opens up wings and it flies down. Strong rubber band launching attachment. When properly released will fly about 100 feet high or shoot about 200 feet in straight line. Shpg. wt., 8 oz.
69F9173—Price....... **39c**

Rise Off the Ground Type.

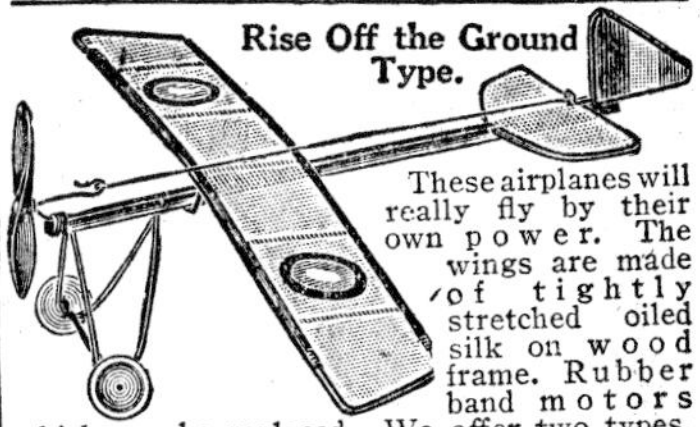

These airplanes will really fly by their own power. The wings are made of tightly stretched oiled silk on wood frame. Rubber band motors which can be replaced. We offer two types.

This model will rise off the ground. Equipped with landing gear and wheels. Wing spread, about 18 in. Length over all, about 18½ in.; 7½-in. carved wood propeller. Shipping weight, 1⅝ pounds.
69F9188
Price....... **$2.98**

Hand launching model. Has wing spread of about 16½ inches. Length, 17 in.; 7½-in. carved wood propeller. Shipping weight, 1¼ pounds.
69F9187
Price....... **$1.69**

12-Inch Wood Soldiers, With 16¼-Inch Gun.

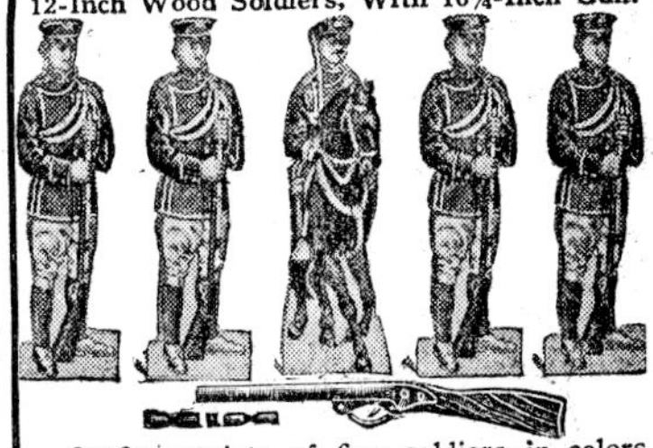

Outfit consists of five soldiers in colors on wood, about ¼-inch thick and standing about 12¾ inches high, each supported by a wooden base. Gun is about 16¼ inches long, with a blued steel barrel, walnut stained wood stock and shoots wooden bullets. Shipping weight, 2⅛ lbs.
49F5668—Price....... **98c**

Handsomely Hand Painted Lead Soldiers.

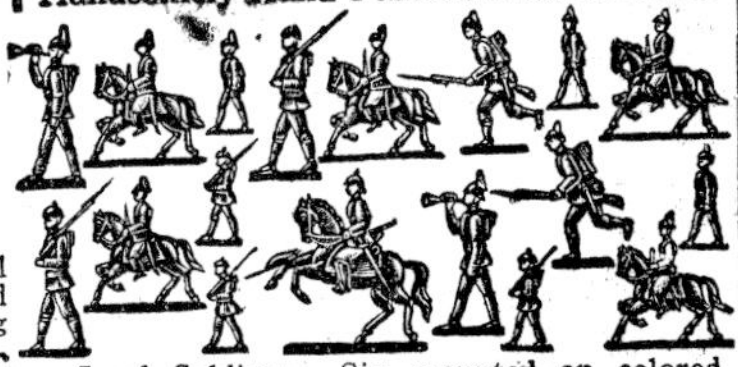

Lead Soldiers. Six mounted on colored horses, twelve infantry. Sizes range from 1⅞ to 2⅞ inches in height. Each on flat pedestal and will stand alone. Painted in a variety of colors. Shpg. wt., 2¼ lbs.
49F5663—Price, 18 soldiers....... **79c**

Big Value One-Car Special Train Set.

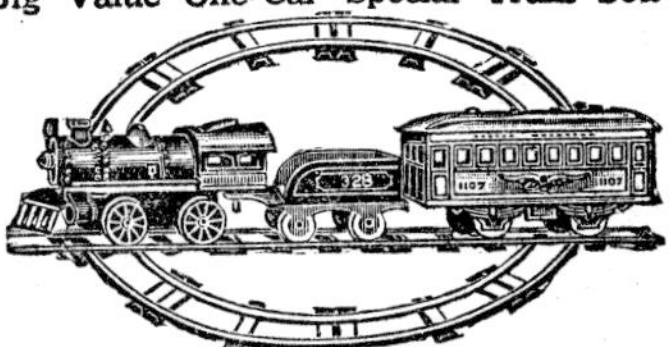

Nicely colored car, 5⅜ inches in length. Engine 6½ inches long, not including tender. Clockwork motor. Painted black, trimmed with gilt. No piston rods. Eight pieces of curved track form a circle nearly 7 feet in circumference. Runs forward only. Packed in strong box. Shpg. wt., 3¼ lbs.
79F5100¼—Price, complete....... **$1.67**

These should not be confused with the small cheap toy tool chests that serve no purpose at all except to make a display. We buy each of these tools separately and assemble them ourselves. The chests are made in our trunk factory under our own supervision. The tools are medium grade and not full size, being selected for their suitability for boys. Every boy, large or small, can find a suitable set of tools on this page—and every boy who is not already the possessor of a set should have one

Our Best Toy Tool Chest.

This is our best set of tools. It contains one wood handle saw with 16-inch steel blade, one 6-inch metal plane, one brace and two bits, different sizes; hammer, hatchet, one 12-inch spirit level, wood handle tri-square, coping saw with twelve blades, iron bench vise, steel chisel, wooden mallet, screwdriver, nail set, awl, 10-inch miter box, gimlet, dividers, pliers, 14-inch T square. 2-foot folding rule and a file. All are illustrated above.

Above Tools With Chest for $5.98.	Above Tools Without Chest for $4.47.
23 tools and 12 coping saw blades in good Mission finished hinged cover hardwood chest with tray. Size over all, 21½x9¼x6⅛ inches. Shipping weight, 15 pounds.	23 tools and 12 coping saw blades without chest. Boy can build his own chest. Packed in good shipping carton. Shipping weight, 9½ pounds.
79F7425¼—Price.......... **$5.98**	**79F7426¼** Price....................... **$4.47**

Our Lower Priced Tool Sets.

19 Tools and Chest, $4.98.
Set contains steel saw with 12-inch blade and iron handle, hammer, hatchet, 6-inch plane, brace and two bits assorted sizes, 12-inch spirit level, metal bench vise, screwdriver, steel chisel, wooden mallet, 14-inch T square, 10-inch miter box, nail set, wood handle tri-square, file, pliers and 2-foot folding rule. Packed in Mission finished hinged cover hardwood chest with tray. Size over all, 16½x8⅞x6 inches. This set illustrated above. Shipping weight, complete, 10½ pounds.
79F7429¼—Price............ **$4.98**

14 Tools and Chest, $3.98.
Set contains steel saw with 12-inch blade and iron handle, hammer, hatchet, 6-inch plane, brace and two bits, 12-inch spirit level, screwdriver, steel chisel, wood mallet, file, pliers, miter box. All packed in Mission finished hinged cover hardwood chest with tray. Size over all, 16½x8⅞x6 inches. Shipping weight, about 9¼ pounds.
79F7431¼—Price............ **$3.98**

Low Priced Outfits—8 Most Needed Tools.

These sets consist of steel saw with 12-inch blade and iron handle, hammer, brace and one bit, plane, steel chisel, mallet and miter box.

Packed in Chest.	Without Chest.
The 8 tools described above packed in Mission finish hinged cover hardwood chest with tray. Size, 16½x8⅞x6 inches. Shipping weight, 7¾ pounds.	The 8 tools described above packed in strong carton (without chest). Shipping weight, 3¼ pounds.
79F7433¼—Price **$2.98**	**79F7434¼**—Price............ **$1.87**

Endless pleasure for the boy that wants to build. Surely a great toy for the boy of 8 to 18 years of age. Nothing else quite takes its place.

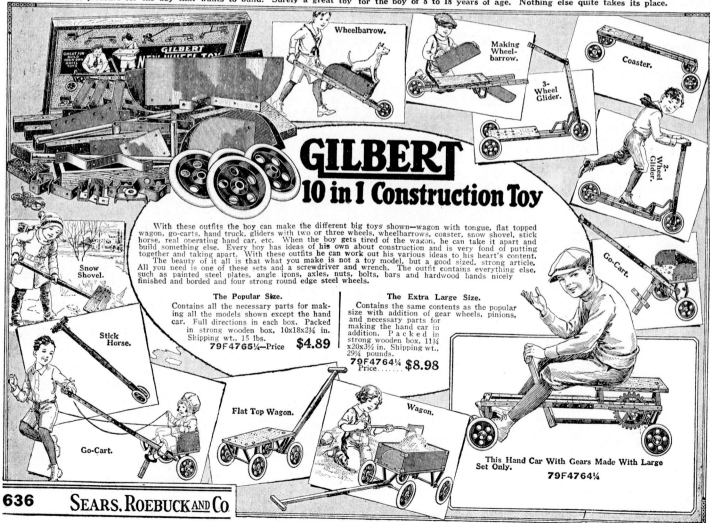

GILBERT 10 in 1 Construction Toy

With these outfits the boy can make the different big toys shown—wagon with tongue, flat topped wagon, go-carts, hand truck, gliders with two or three wheels, wheelbarrows, coaster, snow shovel, stick horse, real operating hand car, etc. When the boy gets tired of the wagon, he can take it apart and build something else. Every boy has ideas of his own about construction and is very fond of putting together and taking apart. With these outfits he can work out his various ideas to his heart's content. The beauty of it all is that what you make is not a toy model, but a good sized, strong article. All you need is one of these sets and a screwdriver and wrench. The outfit contains everything else, such as painted steel plates, angle irons, axles, nuts, bolts, bars and hardwood bands nicely finished and borded and four strong round edge steel wheels.

The Popular Size.
Contains all the necessary parts for making all the models shown except the hand car. Full directions in each box. Packed in strong wooden box, 10x18x2¾ in. Shipping wt., 15 lbs.
79F4765¼—Price **$4.89**

The Extra Large Size.
Contains the same contents as the popular size with addition of gear wheels, pinions, and necessary parts for making the hand car in addition. Packed in strong wooden box, 11¾ x20x3½ in. Shipping wt., 29¼ pounds.
79F4764¼ Price....... **$8.98**

This Hand Car With Gears Made With Large Set Only.
79F4764¼

636 SEARS, ROEBUCK AND CO

Construction Toys That Teach Elements of Science

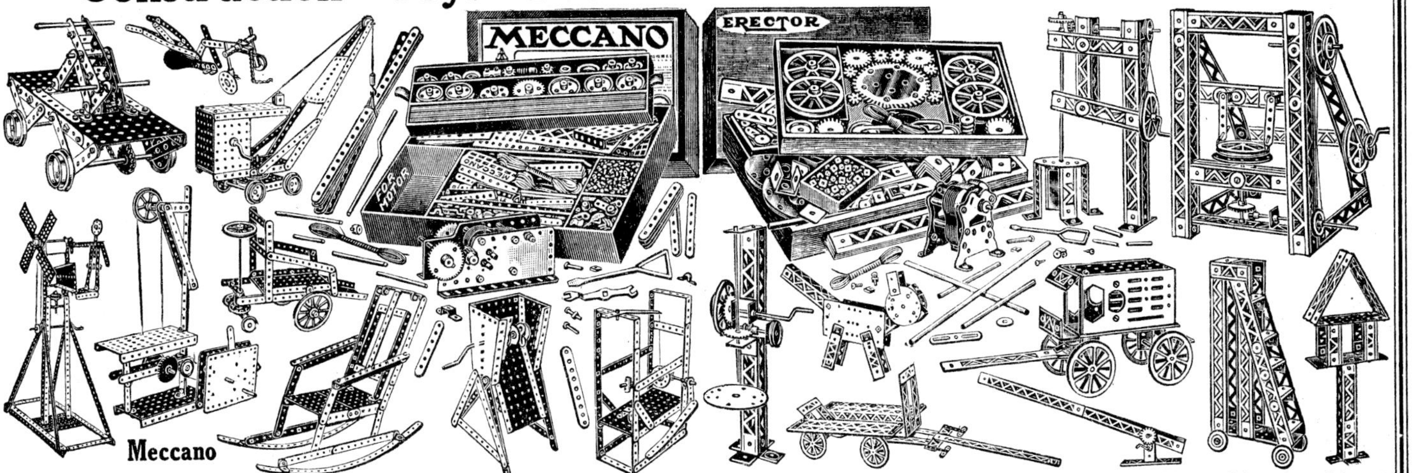

Parts are accurately matched for building models of machinery as well as structures. Gears, pulleys, bolts, etc., all furnished. Instruction manual with every set.

Our Leader Outfit. Good set with electric motor. Size of box, 12⅞x11⅛ inches. Sufficient parts for building about 105 models. Motor for running. Shipping weight, 4⅝ pounds.
49F4721—No. 1 X, with motor. Price........ **$4.98**

Meccano No. 2 X, with motor. Builds about 145 models. Box size, 10x13 inches. Shipping weight, 6½ pounds.
49F4722—Price **$7.89**

Meccano No. 3 X, with motor. Will build about 190 models. Box, 13¾x10⅜ inches. Shipping weight, 7¾ pounds.
79F4723¼—Price **$10.67**

Meccano No. 0. Contains enough parts to make about 78 models. Box, 13¼x9½ inches. Shipping weight, 2⅛ pounds.
49F4725—Price **$1.37**

Meccano No. 1. Will build about 105 models. Box size, 15¼x10¾ inches. Shipping weight, 3½ pounds.
49F4726—Price **$2.79**

Meccano No. 2. Will build about 145 models. Box size, 12⅞x9⅜ inches. Shipping weight, 5⅛ pounds.
49F4727—Price **$5.58**

Mecacano No. 4, With $2.00 Motor. Builds about 247 models. The best Meccano we list. Shipping wt., 11¼ pounds.
79F4738¼... **$13.85**

Accessory Outfits.

49F4731—No. 0A. Converts a No. 0 into a No. 1 outfit. Shipping wt., 1¾ lbs.
Price **$1.37**

49F4732—No. 1A. Converts a No. 1 into a No. 2 outfit. Shipping wt., 2½ lbs.
Price **$2.79**

49F4733—No. 2A. Converts a No. 2 into a No. 3. Shpg. wt., 2½ lbs... **$2.79**

49F4734—No. 3A. Converts a No. 3 into a No. 4, without motor. Shipping weight, 2½ lbs. Price.**$5.58**

A boy loves to build bridges, wagons and other working models and to elaborate on new ideas. A construction toy teaches him the principles of engineering and construction and **develops any ability** he may have along these lines. Hundreds of different models are shown in the instruction book which accompanies each set. The larger the set, the greater number of more intricate models can be built.

Erector.

Contains miniature steel girders, wheels, gears, etc. Particularly adapted for structural models.

Our Leader Erector.

Erector No. 4 Builds 278 models, medium complicated, with electric motor for running them. Outfit is packed in wooden box and is our most popular size. Shipping weight, 6¾ pounds.
79F4719¼—Our price.............................. **$4.47**

Builds About 410 Models.
Erector No. 7. A very complete set, with electric motor and reversible base. Packed in wooden hinged cover box. Shipping weight, 13½ pounds.
79F4716¼—Our price.... **$13.47**

Builds About 382 Models.
Erector No. 6. A very complete set. Has electric motor with reverse base. Packed in wooden box. Shipping weight, 7 pounds.
79F4720¼—Our price..... **$8.98**

Builds About 197 Models.
Erector No. 3. Nicely packed in neat box. Shipping wt., 5¼ lbs.
49F4715—Our price **$2.98**

Builds About 153 Models.
Erector No. 2. Nicely packed in neat box. Shipping wt., 2¾ lbs.
49F4718—Our price......... **$2.25**

Builds About 112 Models.
Erector No. 1. Nicely packed in neat box. Shipping wt., 1¾ lbs.
49F4717—Our price.............................. **$1.35**

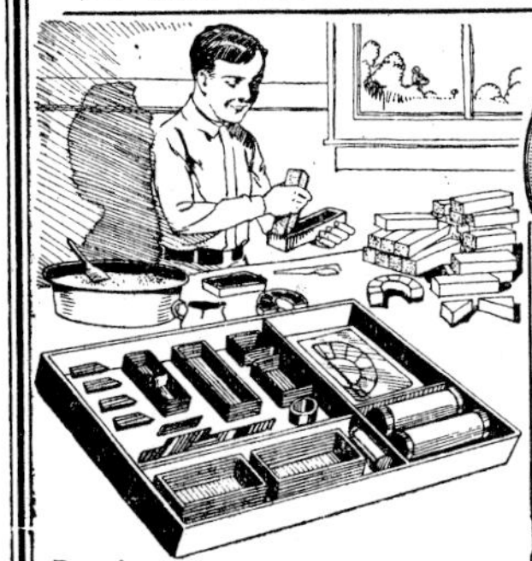

Boys!
Make Your Own Cement Blocks.
Miniature cement block plant. Actually teaches the correct method of making cement blocks, but on a small scale. Consists of 9 molds, 5 plates and 4 partitions. It is possible with these molds to make about 82 different kinds of toy cement blocks; also contains tools to make blocks, 2 boxes of cement mixture. Packed in box 13¾x11⅛ in. Shipping weight, 4 pounds.
49F4741
Price **89c**

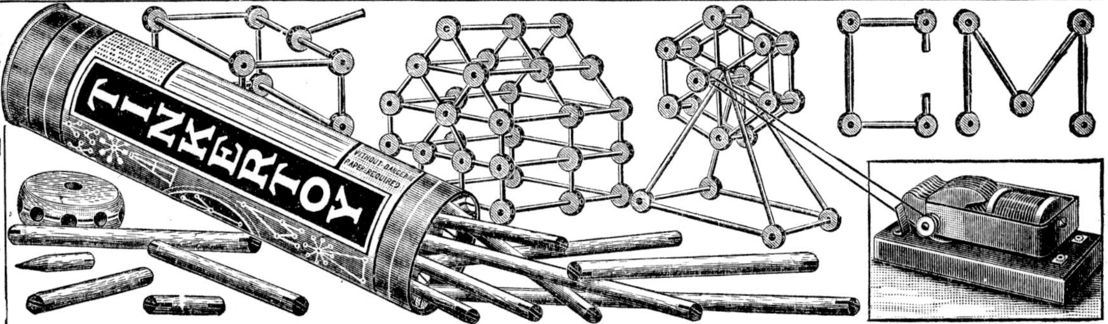

Famous Tinker Toy Model Builder.

Tinker Toy is the Wonder Builder. An educational, interesting and amusing toy for any child. With one or more sets you can build any of the toy models shown, together with many others. This toy is based on the old adage that "a stick and a spool will amuse a child." Each set consists of about seventy pieces of white wood, as illustrated. In building movable toys, such as windmill, Ferris wheel, merry-go-round, etc., if the motor listed at right is purchased all these models can be run by it. This motor will run on two dry cells. In order to enable a child to build large and more complicated models, two or three Tinker Toy sets should be purchased.

1 Set for 67c.
For building many simple models. Shipping weight, 1 pound.
49F4760
Price, per set............ **67c**

2 Sets for $1.33.
For building more complex or larger models. Shipping wt., 2¼ lbs.
49F4761—Price,
2 sets for **$1.33**

3 Sets for $1.98.
For building complicated as well as simple models. Shipping wt., 3¼ pounds.
49F4768—Price,
3 sets for **$1.98**

Buy This Motor
for Tinker Toy models and small toys. Two dry cells run it. Size over all, 1⅞x3⅝x2 inches. Mounted on wood base. Shipping weight, 9 ounces.
49F5938
Price................. **67c**

It Flies!

Electric Airplane BARGAIN

Was $9.45, Now $3.98.

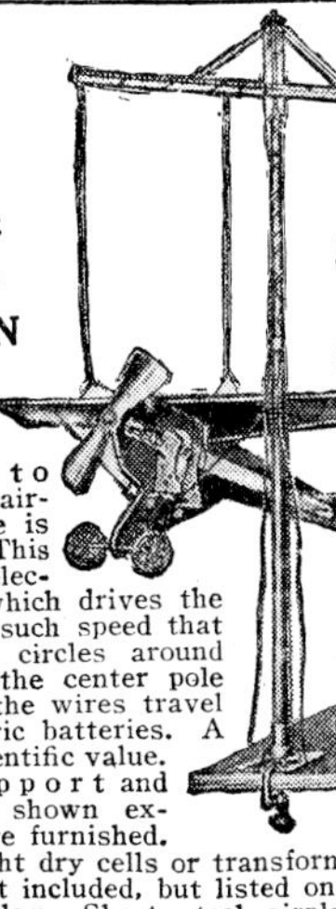

You boys who are craving an opportunity to study an airplane, here is your chance. This one has an electric motor which drives the propellor at such speed that the airplane circles around and around the center pole over which the wires travel to the electric batteries. A toy with scientific value. Vertical support and other parts shown except table are furnished. Requires eight dry cells or transformer to run. Dry cells not included, but listed on page 1075 in this catalog. Sheet steel airplane, nicely painted. Has electric motor, propeller, wheels and metal wings. Measures 22x19½ inches. A wonderful toy. Shpg. wt., 7 lbs.
79F4755¼—Price **$3.98**

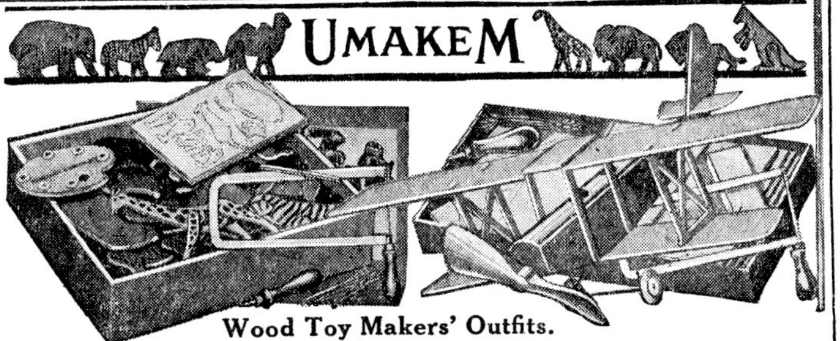

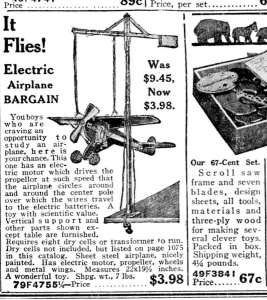

Wood Toy Makers' Outfits.

Our 67-Cent Set.
Scroll saw frame and seven blades, design sheets, all tools, materials and three-ply wood for making several clever toys. Packed in box. Shipping weight, 4¼ pounds.
49F3841
Price....... **67c**

Special for 38c.
Scroll saw and thirteen blades, awl, large number of washers. Palette about 7 inches long, with six water colors. Three-ply veneer boards and design sheets for making about twelve jointed animals. Shipping weight, 5 pounds.
49F3842
Price..... **98c**

Special Toy Making Outfit.
Makes an assortment of sixteen good size toys and animals. Set consists of scroll saw with a number of extra blades, an awl, sandpaper, water color paints, three-ply wood veneer and everything needed. Design sheets included. Shipping wt., about 9 lbs.
79F3846¼
Price, complete outfit.. **$2.98**

Boys Make This Airplane.
Design sheets, all materials and tools necessary. The wood furnished is imported from South America and is very light. Airplane has rubber motor, 26-inch wing spread. Aluminum cockpit. A valuable toy when finished. Shipping weight, 4 pounds.
79F3845¼
Price........ **$1.98**

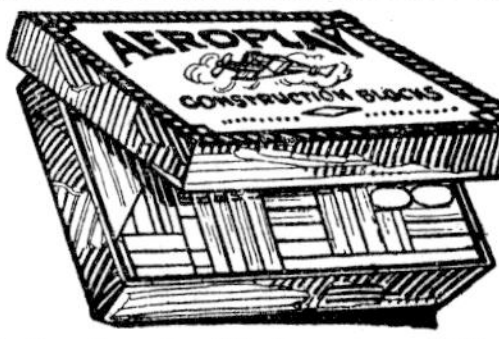

Wooden Aeroplay Blocks.

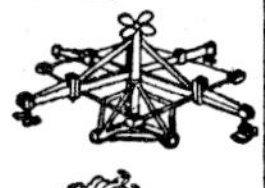

With this set of nicely turned wood blocks a child can build an airplane, houses, bridges, towers, etc. Possibilities of this set give child plenty of opportunity to exercise ability to build things. Makes an attractive airplane model with revolving propeller. Every child is interested in airplanes, particularly in building them. Packed in nice box, 12⅞x8⅛ inches. Shipping wt., 3 lbs.
49F4766—Price, per set **89c**

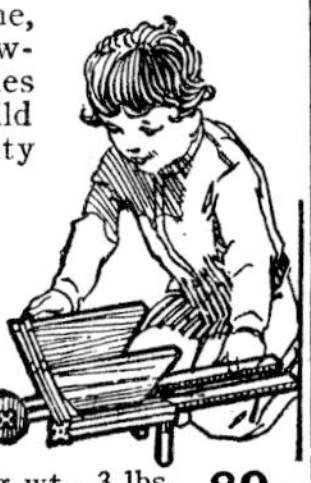

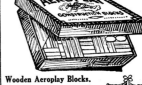

Automobiles

All Steel. Beautifully finished.
$9⁹⁸ and $7⁹⁸

Knuckle joints on front axles for steering like real auto. 10-inch wheels, with ½-inch rubber tires. Imitation starting crank makes loud noise. Hub caps. Rich maroon enameled yellow and black strip-

HOW TO ORDER—
In ordering one of these automobiles take measurement of boy from crotch to instep and compare with measurement given on each machine from seat to pedal extended to farthest point.

ing. Read paragraph "How to Order." See Sizes Below at Left.

All Steel Auto with Adjustable Wind Shield.
Reinforced steel frame. Knuckle jointed front axles to steer with like on real auto. 10-inch wire wheels, with ½-inch rubber tires. Bright metal hub caps. Crank in front with ratchet to make loud noise. Imitation radiator front. Enameled green with bright red hood. Read "How to Order" above. See Sizes Below at Right.

All Steel.
$10⁹⁸ and $8⁹⁸

Unmailable.

See description above.
This Auto $9.98.
Size, over all, 43 inches by 18 inches. Seat is upholstered with black imitation leather. Steel bumper. Measures 22 inches from center of seat to pedal at lowest point. Shipping weight, 33 lbs. Unmailable.
79F8923¼—Price.............. $9.98

This Auto $7.98.
Size, over all, 37 inches by 19 inches. All steel body. Measures 17 inches from center of seat to pedal at lowest point. Shipping weight, 28 pounds. Unmailable.
79F8914¼—Price............ $7.98

Dandy Car, Priced Low! With Wind Shield.

$9⁹⁸
$11⁹⁸

A medium priced car for the big boy or the small one. Comes in two sizes. Equipped with adjustable wind shield. Imitation gas tank. Imitation noisy crank starter. Hood, sides of tonneau, back of seat and sides of gas tank made of sheet steel. Wood frame. Front wheels on knuckle jointed axles for steering. Read "How to Order" in center above.

Medium Size Auto.
Measures 36 inches long; 19 inches wide; 25 inches to top of wind shield, 15 inches from center of seat to pedal at lowest point. Finished in bright colors. Number 6 stenciled on radiator. 10-inch rear wheels, 8-inch front wheels, with ⅜-inch rubber tires. Bright metal hub caps. Shipping wt., 38 lbs. Unmailable.
79F8915¼—Price.......... $9.98

Larger Size.
Measures 42 inches long; 19 inches wide; 27 inches to top of wind shield. 18 inches from center of seat to pedal at lowest point. 12-inch rear wheels; 10-inch front wheels, with ⅜-inch rubber tires. Beautifully finished in bright orange enamel, black striping and running gear. Bright metal hub caps. Shipping weight, 45 lbs. Unmailable.
79F8916¼—Price.......... $11.98

Bright Yellow Racers.

Built on same lines as a high powered racing model automobile. Striking looking hood, large and pretentious with three holes in each side for exhaust. Sheet steel hood, sides and back of seat. Painted bright yellow. Black trimming. Very snappy and attractive. Two sizes. Read "How to Order" above in center of page. Unmailable.

Large.
Measures 54 inches long, 27 inches high, 24 inches wide. Wood steering wheel. Imitation self starter in hood. Measures 21 inches from center of seat to pedal at lowest point. 12-in. wheels with ½-in. rubber tires. Nickel plated hub caps. Shipping wt., about 60 pounds.
79F8917¼—Price..... $14.95

Medium.
Metal steering wheel. Imitation crank starter in front. 12-inch rear wheels. 10-inch front wheels with ⅜-inch rubber tires. Nickel plated hub caps. Measures 42 inches long by 20 inches wide by 22½ inches high. 17½ inches from center of seat to pedal at lowest point. Shipping wt., about 45 lbs.
79F8921¼—Price.... $12.98

Our $10.98 Auto.
Sheet steel sides and seat. Steel frame and gears, steel bumpers. Seat is upholstered with black imitation leather. Steel dash and radiator, also radiator cap. Size, over all, 43¾ inches by 18½ inches. Measures 22 inches from center of seat to pedal at lowest point. Shpg. wt., 35 lbs. **$10.98**

Smaller Size.
Sheet steel sides and seat. Steel frame and gears, no bumper. Size, over all, 37 in. by 19 in. Measures 17 in. from center of seat to pedal at lowest point. Shpg. wt., 29 lbs. Unmailable.
79F8922¼—Price. $8.98

Our Low Priced Automobiles.
These autos are racy designs nicely finished in attractive colors with appropriate striping. They have metal steering wheels, ⅜-in. rubber tire wheels, steering knuckles, wood frame and seat bottom, steel hood and seat back. In two sizes. Unmailable. Read "How to Order" above in center of page.

36¼ Inches Over All, $6.98.
Nicely finished red body with black striping. Measures 36¼ x 18½ inches over all. Front wheels 8 inches, rear wheels 10 inches in diameter. Measures about 17½ inches from center of seat to pedal extended to farthest point. Shipping weight, 28 pounds.
79F8905¼—Price, each.... $6.98

42 Inches Over All, $8.98.
Painted dark green, orange striping. Measures 42x19¼ inches over all. Front wheels 10 inches, rear wheels 12 inches in diameter. Measures about 21½ inches from center of seat to pedal extended to farthest point. Shipping weight, 32 pounds.
79F8906¼—Price, each................... $8.98

A Beautiful Car.
Has All the Trimmings. Wind Shield, Fenders, Tank, Starters, Etc.

$13⁹⁸

Ball Bearing

Ball Bearing, for $13.98.
Rear axle only set in ball bearing hangers. Wind shield, fenders, upholstered seat and dummy tank. Painted brilliant red with black fenders and trimming. Frame is of wood, with hood, seat back, tank and fenders (not running board, which is wood) of sheet steel. Has imitation self starter which makes noise, and steering knuckles. Wheels have ⅜-inch rubber tires. Front wheels 10 inches, rear wheels 12 inches in diameter. Size over all, 44x19 inches. Measures 17½ inches from center of seat to pedal extended to farthest point. Shipping weight, 48 pounds. Unmailable. See "How to Order" at top of page.
79F8919¼—Price, each................... $13.98

Honk! Honk!!
Big Red Auto equipped with auto style practical wood steering wheel. Ball bearing crank hangers on rear axles. Bright red with black trimmings. 49½ inches long, 24½ inches wide, 27 inches to top of steering wheel. Wood frame, sheet steel hood and seat back. 12-inch wheels; ½-inch rubber tires. Front wheels on knuckle axles for steering.

Ball Bearing
$11⁹⁸

Imitation self starter. Seat upholstered. Measures 19½ inches from center of seat to pedal at lowest point. Read "How to Order" in center above. Shipping weight, 57 lbs. Unmailable.
79F8925¼—Price.... $11.98

WAGONS AND WHEELBARROWS FOR LITTLE FOLKS

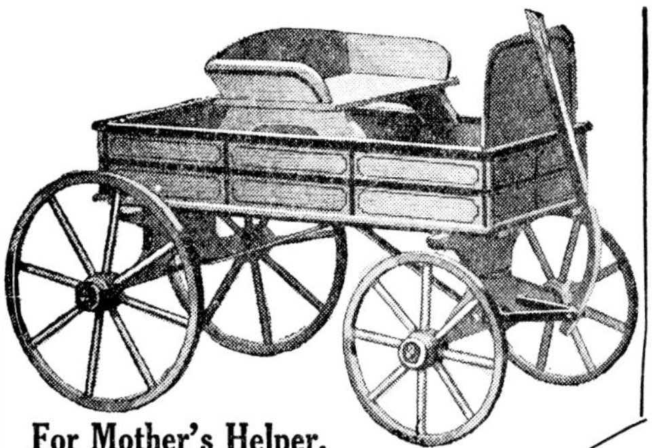

For Mother's Helper.
"YOUR BOY."

Get this low price big wagon for your boy to use for groceries, ice, etc.
Front wheels are 11 inches and back wheels about 14½ inches in diameter. Wood wheels with steel tires. Size of body, over all, 14x28 inches. Wood parts finished in natural wood color, varnished. Body, seat and dashboard nicely striped. Curved tongue for coasting. Dashboard comes off easily. Serviceable, removable seat. Shipping wt., 25 lbs.
79F7630¼—Price.......... **$3.98**

ONLY 6 INCHES HIGH.
Little Tots' Wagon.

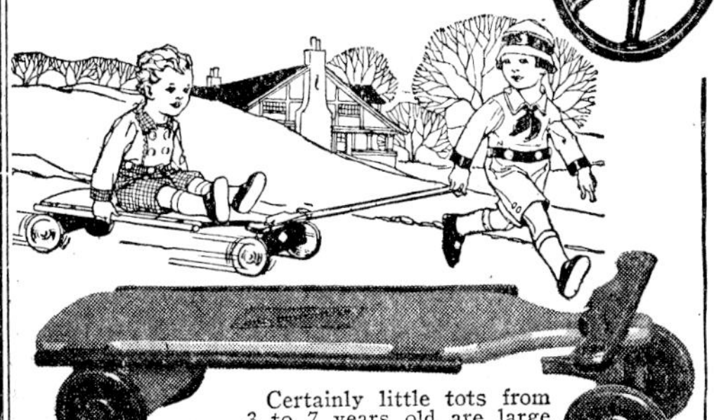

Certainly little tots from 3 to 7 years old are large enough for a coaster wagon. Let them get out on sunny days and coast back and forth along the sidewalk, in sight of mother, getting fresh air and strength for future growth. This coaster is built especially for children from 3 to 7 years—having flat top with side rails to hold on to. Low wheels, making top of wagon only 6 inches high from sidewalk, and having a steering handle in front for the hands when riding sled style, or for the feet when sitting up. This handle is bored with holes for a rope. A spring stabilizer underneath holds the front wheels straight when there is no guiding pressure. Prettily painted. Let the little fellows coast, too. Size, over all, 30x13 in. Shipping weight, 7½ lbs.
79F7636¼—Price.... **$2.67**

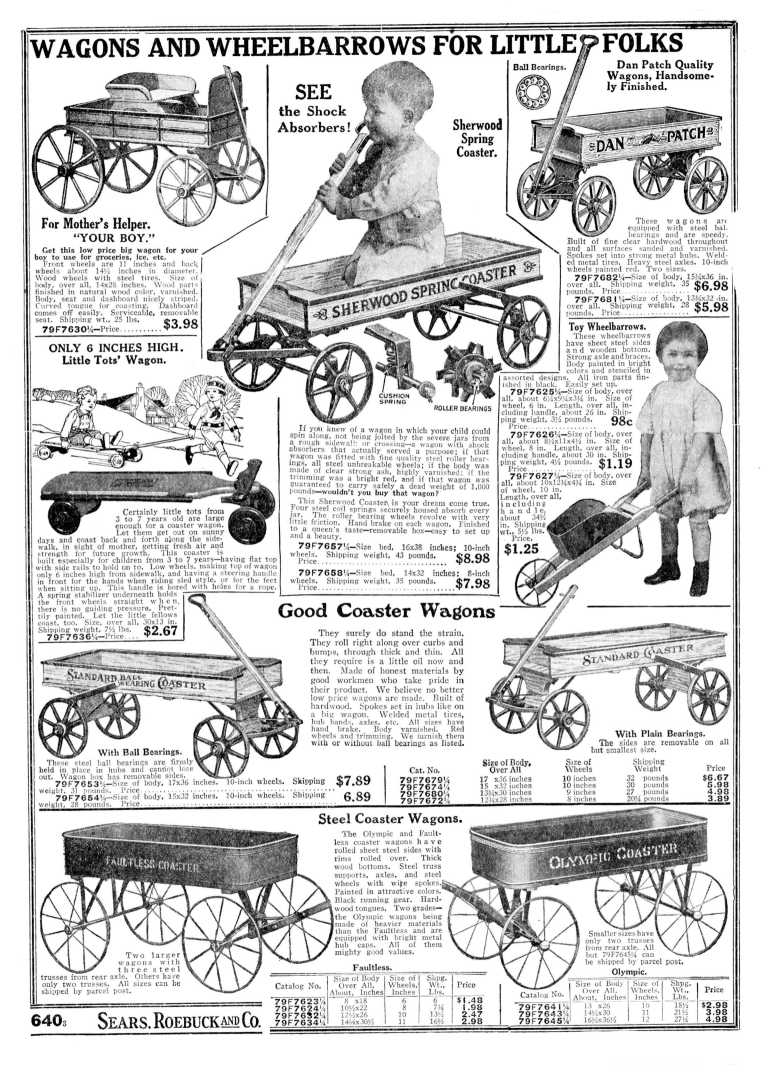

SEE the Shock Absorbers!

Sherwood Spring Coaster.

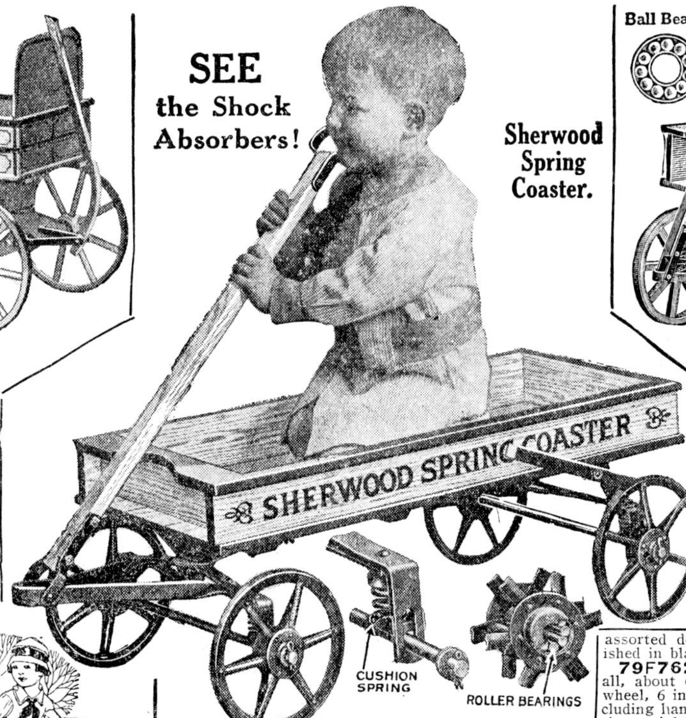

If you knew of a wagon in which your child could spin along, not being jolted by the severe jars from a rough sidewalk or crossing—a wagon with shock absorbers that actually served a purpose; if that wagon was fitted with fine quality steel roller bearings, all steel unbreakable wheels; if the body was made of clear strong ash, highly varnished; if the trimming was a bright red, and if that wagon was guaranteed to carry safely a dead weight of 1,000 pounds—**wouldn't you buy that wagon?**

This Sherwood Coaster is your dream come true. Four steel coil springs securely housed absorb every jar. The roller bearing wheels revolve with very little friction. Hand brake on each wagon. Finished to a queen's taste—removable box—easy to set up and a beauty.

79F7657¼—Size bed, 16x38 inches; 10-inch wheels. Shipping weight, 43 pounds. Price.............. **$8.98**

79F7658¼—Size bed, 14x32 inches; 8-inch wheels. Shipping weight, 35 pounds. Price.............. **$7.98**

Ball Bearings.

Dan Patch Quality Wagons, Handsomely Finished.

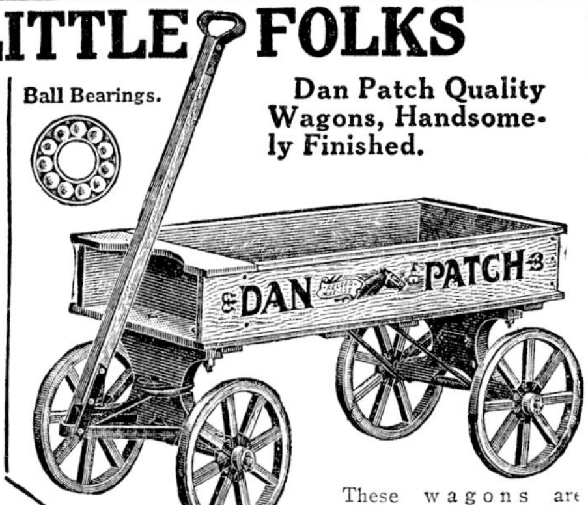

These wagons are equipped with steel ball bearings and are speedy. Built of fine clear hardwood throughout and all surfaces sanded and varnished. Spokes set into strong metal hubs. Welded metal tires. Heavy steel axles. 10-inch wheels painted red. Two sizes.
79F7682¼—Size of body, 15¾x36 in. over all. Shipping weight, 35 pounds. Price.................. **$6.98**
79F7681¼—Size of body, 13¾x32 in. over all. Shipping weight, 28 pounds. Price.................. **$5.98**

Toy Wheelbarrows.

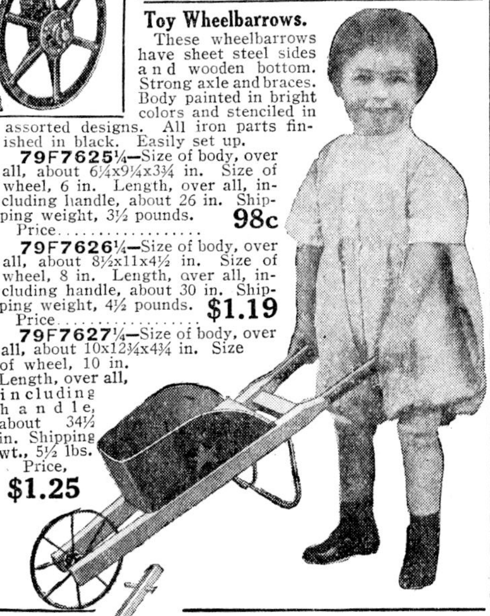

These wheelbarrows have sheet steel sides and wooden bottom. Strong axle and braces. Body painted in bright colors and stenciled in assorted designs. All iron parts finished in black. Easily set up.
79F7625¼—Size of body, over all, about 6¼x9¼x3¾ in. Size of wheel, 6 in. Length, over all, including handle, about 26 in. Shipping weight, 3½ pounds. Price.......... **98c**
79F7626¼—Size of body, over all, about 8½x11x4½ in. Size of wheel, 8 in. Length, over all, including handle, about 30 in. Shipping weight, 4½ pounds. Price.......... **$1.19**
79F7627¼—Size of body, over all, about 10x12¾x4¾ in. Size of wheel, 10 in. Length, over all, including handle, about 34½ in. Shipping wt., 5½ lbs. Price, **$1.25**

Good Coaster Wagons

They surely do stand the strain. They roll right along over curbs and bumps, through thick and thin. All they require is a little oil now and then. Made of honest materials by good workmen who take pride in their product. We believe no better low price wagons are made. Built of hardwood. Spokes set in hubs like on a big wagon. Welded metal tires, hub bands, axles, etc. All sizes have hand brake. Body varnished. Red wheels and trimming. We furnish them with or without ball bearings as listed.

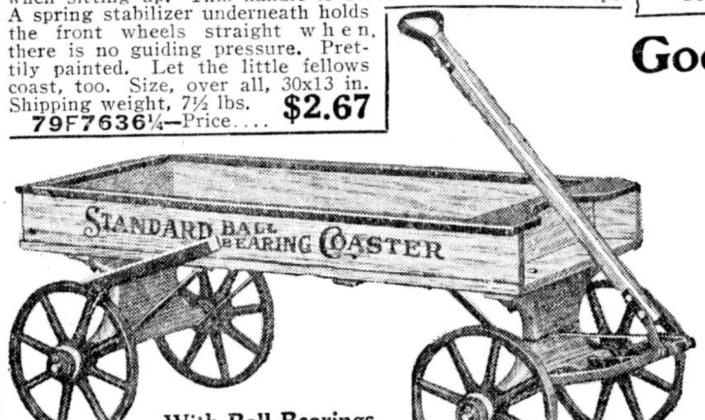

With Ball Bearings.

These steel ball bearings are firmly held in place in hubs and cannot lose out. Wagon box has removable sides.
79F7653¼—Size of body, 17x36 inches. 10-inch wheels. Shipping weight, 31 pounds. Price.............. **$7.89**
79F7654¼—Size of body, 15x32 inches. 10-inch wheels. Shipping weight, 28 pounds. Price.............. **6.89**

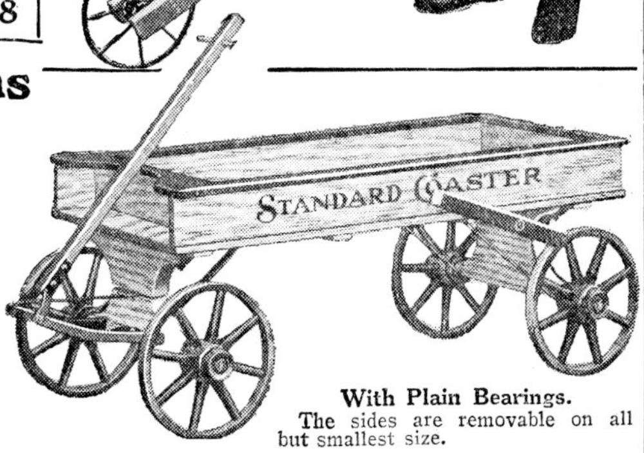

With Plain Bearings.

The sides are removable on all but smallest size.

Cat. No.	Size of Body, Over All	Size of Wheels	Shipping Weight	Price
79F7679¼	17 x36 inches	10 inches	32 pounds	$6.67
79F7674¼	15 x32 inches	10 inches	30 pounds	5.98
79F7680¼	13¾x30 inches	9 inches	27 pounds	4.98
79F7672¼	12¾x28 inches	8 inches	20¼ pounds	3.89

Steel Coaster Wagons.

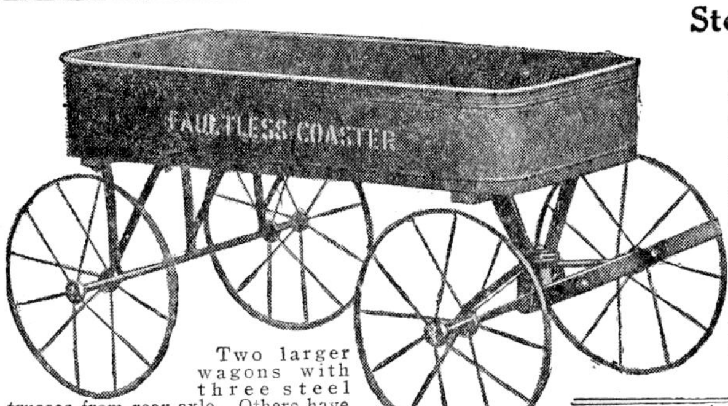

Two larger wagons with three steel trusses from rear axle. Others have only two trusses. All sizes can be shipped by parcel post.

The Olympic and Faultless coaster wagons have rolled sheet steel sides with rims rolled over. Thick wood bottoms. Steel truss supports, axles, and steel wheels with wire spokes. Painted in attractive colors. Black running gear. Hardwood tongues. Two grades—the Olympic wagons being made of heavier materials than the Faultless and are equipped with bright metal hub caps. All of them mighty good values.

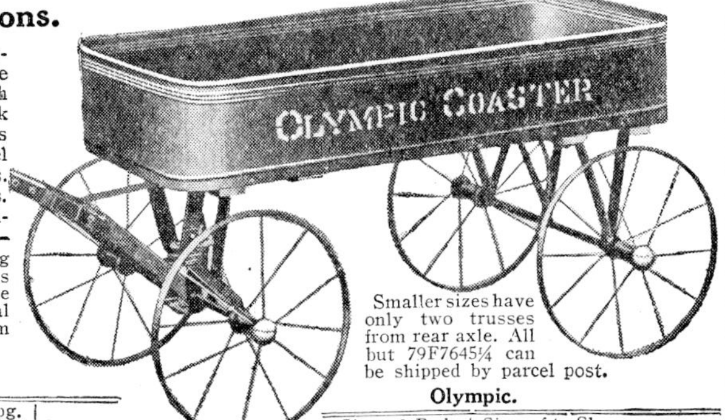

Smaller sizes have only two trusses from rear axle. All but 79F7645¼ can be shipped by parcel post.

Faultless.

Catalog No.	Size of Body Over All, About, Inches	Size of Wheels, Inches	Shpg. Wt., Lbs.	Price
79F7623¼	8 x18	6	6	$1.48
79F7624¼	10½x22	8	7¾	1.98
79F7632¼	12½x26	10	13½	2.47
79F7634¼	14⅛x30½	11	16½	2.98

Olympic.

Catalog No.	Size of Body Over All, About, Inches	Size of Wheels, Inches	Shpg. Wt., Lbs.	Price
79F7641¼	13 x26	10	18½	$2.98
79F7643¼	14½x30	11	21½	3.98
79F7645¼	16½x36½	12	27¼	4.98

BLOCKS

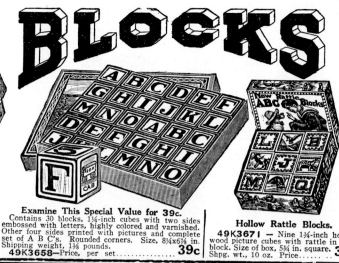

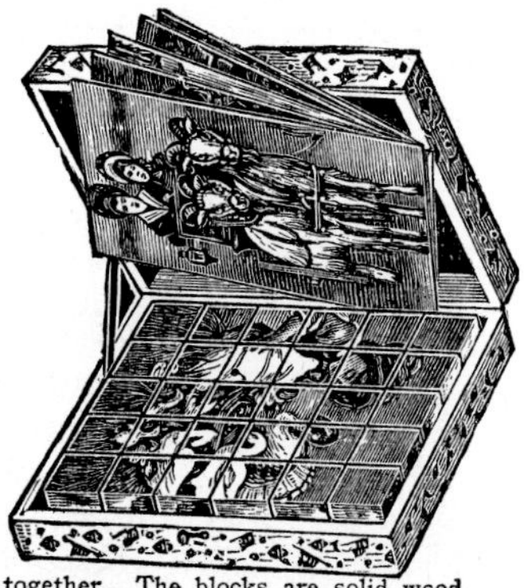

Imported Picture Block Cubes.
When properly put together all the blocks form a pretty picture. Six beautifully colored pictures can be formed. A set of colored pictures comes with each box of blocks as a guide to show how the pictures look when put together. The blocks are solid wood. Each set in strong wood case with hinged cover and latch. Pretty picture on cover.

49K3675—30 blocks. 1½-inch cubes in wood case. Size, 11⅛x9½ inches. Shpg. wt., 3¾ lbs. Price....**98c**

49K3676—20 blocks. About 1½-inch cubes in wood case. Size, 8⅞x7¼ in. Shpg. wt., 2¼ lbs. Price..**67c**

49K3677—12 blocks. 1⅝-inch cubes in wood case. Size, 6¾x5½ inches. Shpg. wt., 1¼ lbs. Price...**39c**

Examine This Special Value for 39c.
Contains 30 blocks, 1¼-inch cubes with two sides embossed with letters, highly colored and varnished. Other four sides printed with pictures and complete set of A B C's. Rounded corners. Size, 8¼x6⅞ in. Shipping weight, 1⅜ pounds.
49K3658—Price, per set..............**39c**

Hollow Rattle Blocks.
49K3671 — Nine 1¾-inch hollow wood picture cubes with rattle in each block. Size of box, 5¾ in. square. Shpg. wt., 10 oz. Price.......**39c**

Hollow Blocks.
49K3672 — Twelve 2⅜-inch hollow wood picture cubes. Size of box, 7¾x10½ in. Shpg. wt., 1¼ lbs. Price..**79c**

Imported Hollow Wood Picture A B C Blocks.
Beautifully lithographed hollow blocks, made of strong thin wood and covered with glossy colored pictures of children, familiar animals and the alphabet, all in bright colors. Each set in box with pretty picture on cover.

24 Animal A B C Blocks.
Solid wood blocks, 1⅞x1½ inches, ½ inch thick, with pictures of animals in colors on one side and letters of alphabet on the other. Very showy. Come in cardboard box, size 11⅝x6⅝ inches, with pretty colored picture cover. Shipping weight, 1¼ lbs.
49K3673—Price............**39c**

ROUND CORNERED BLOCKS

On two sides the letters are raised and colored with bright glossy enamel. The other four sides have letters, numerals and pictures in colors. Each block is a 1¾-inch cube.

36-Block Set, 98c.
49K3657 — Box, 10¾x10¾ in. Shipping wt., 4 lbs. Price **98c**

24-Block Set, 79c.
49K3656 — Box, 10¾x7⅜ inches. Shpg. wt., 2½ lbs. Price..........**79c**

18-Block Set, 59c.
49K3659 — Box, 10¾x5½ inches. Shpg. wt., 1⅞ lbs. Price..........**59c**

12-Block Set, 39c.
49K3652 — Box, 7¼x5½ inches. Shpg. wt., 1¼ lbs. Price..........**39c**

Wood Parquette Design Blocks.
Fine for kindergartens, schools and to keep the child amused. Made of white and red wood, smoothly finished, cut in triangles and squares. Hundreds of designs can be made with them. Design sheets in colors included. Average size of block, about 2 inches square. Two layers, each containing about 45 blocks. Packed in strong wood box with sliding cover. Size, 9¾x8½ in. Shpg. wt., 1¾ lbs.
49K3642—Price **59c**

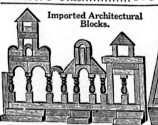

Imported Architectural Blocks. 
Every child loves to build. Enjoyment by the hour. Fine clear hardwood. Turned columns and odd shapes. Two layers of blocks, each set in wood box.

Our $4.79 Set.
79K3631¼
Size of box, 19½x12½ in. Shpg. wt., 15 lbs. Price ..$4.79

Our $2.39 Set.
79K3630¼
Size of box, 17¼x11¼ in. Shpg. wt., 11 lbs. Price..$2.39

Our $1.39 Set.
49K3629
Size of box, 12⅝x9½ in. Shpg. wt., 6¼ lbs. Price..$1.39

Our 69c Set.
49K3628
Size of box, 10¼x8 in. Shpg. wt., 4½ lbs. Price.....**69c**

3 Large Animal Puzzles.
Three large, beautiful animal puzzles in colors. Cut out of ⅝-inch wood with picture in colors. Size of each animal, 8½x11 inches. Horse, rooster and turkey. Colored pictures to guide child in assembling. Come in box, size 9x12 in., with colored label. Shipping weight, 1½ pounds.
49K3667—Price **98c**

Zoo Puzzles.
Animal Puzzle Pictures.
Eight puzzle pictures of animals and birds, beautifully lithographed in many colors. The pictures are on wood cut into puzzles to be assembled by the child. Mix them all up and several persons race to get one complete. Each puzzle picture, 4¼x4½ inches. Come in box, size, 9¼x10 inches, with picture cover. Shipping weight, 1¼ pounds.
49K3666—Price **67c**

Two Popular Toys, Both for Only 29c.
Picture puzzles and drawing slates are always sure to make a child happy. Here is a combination offer that is a winner. The slate is 7x7¾ inches with A B C wooden frame and frosted glass with pictures to put underneath. Use with pencil. The puzzle is a picture in colors on wood. Size of box and picture, 6½x7½ in. Shipping weight of the two, 1 pound.
49K3839—Price ..**29c**

PYRAMID BLOCKS

Telescope Pyramid Blocks.
Contains 8 pyramid blocks ranging in size up to 4x4x3½ in. Made strongly of wood—not paper—and come packed nested, one inside the other. Beautiful pictures of animals, birds, etc., in bright colors on all sides of blocks. When set up stands 25¾ in. high. Shpg. wt., 1 lb.
49K3674—Price..**39c**

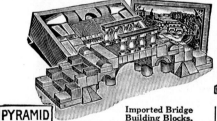

Imported Bridge Building Blocks.
All boys like to build bridges. Fine clear hardwood blocks in many new and attractive shapes. Particularly fine for building the most elaborate bridges over imaginary rivers. About 90 blocks in all, packed in two layers in a wooden box with slide cover. Size of box, 10¼x8 in. Shpg. wt., 4¾ lbs.
49K3641—Price **98c**

Big Wooden Letters.
Made of good grade, smooth white wood, carefully and firmly joined together. Each letter, 3⅞ in. high. Has full alphabet. They teach the letters quickly, as a young child is guided by the sense of touch. Packed in cardboard box, 26 pieces. Shipping weight, 2¾ lbs.
49K3614—Price **98c**

Cut Up U. S. Maps.
For teaching the shapes and location of states nothing better has been devised than these sets. States cut on state lines where possible. Principal cities, rivers, mountains and lakes shown. On opposite side world's flags in colors. Makes maps 20x14 inches.
49K3871—Our Best Map. Made of wood. Box, 15x9¼ in. Shpg. wt., 1⅝ lbs. Price..........**98c**
49K3870—Our Medium Priced. Made of heavy cardboard. Box, 9¾x8 inches. Shipping weight, 1⅛ pounds. Price......**45c**

Build Castles and Churches.
Blocks to build them! What boy ever built a house without a steeple? Here is a set that he will like, made of fine, smooth, clear hardwood. Steeples and fancy gables galore. A set with wonderful possibilities. Comes in wood box, size, 13⅝x8¾ inches with slide cover. Two layers of blocks, about 64 in all. Designs for different buildings included. Shipping weight, 6 pounds.
49K3640—Price **98c**

Konstructo Building Blocks.
Building blocks in different lengths. Interesting models of buildings, furniture, fences, etc., can be made. Book of instructions enclosed.
49K3633—Small Size Set, about 46 pieces. Shpg. wt., 1 lb. Price...**40c**
49K3634—Medium Size Set, about 95 pieces. Shpg. wt., 1¾ lbs. Price..**79c**
49K3635—Our Largest Set, about 175 pieces. Shpg. wt., 3 lbs. Price **$1.59**

Toys For The Baby

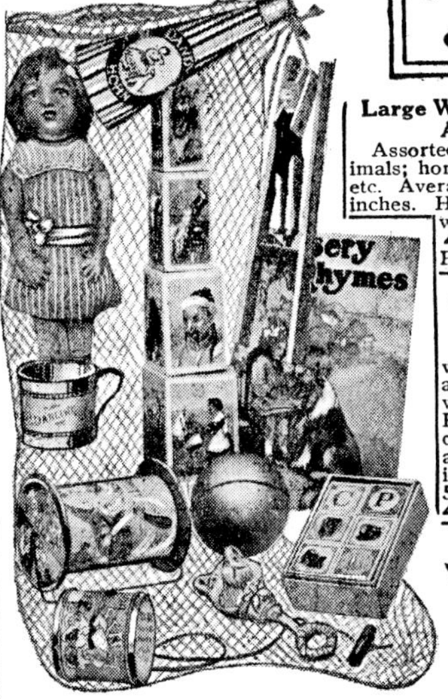

Our 98c Stocking for Baby.

Carefully Selected Playthings for Baby.

Rubber rattle to chew on and a pure red rubber (not painted) ball to play with. A "Cum-Bac" toy. Baby throws it away and it surprises him by rolling back to him. A beautiful light but strong chime for baby to pull around. Aluminum drinking cup; two sets of blocks; jumping jack in frame makes funny tricks when squeezed; a cute 10-inch stuffed dolly; a good grade horn and pretty colored picture book with nursery rhymes for mother to read to her darling. All with pretty net stocking. Shipping weight, 1½ pounds.
69K9914—Price............ **98c**

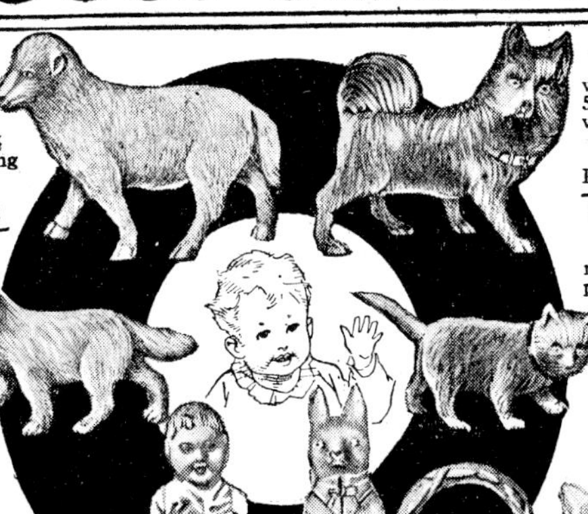

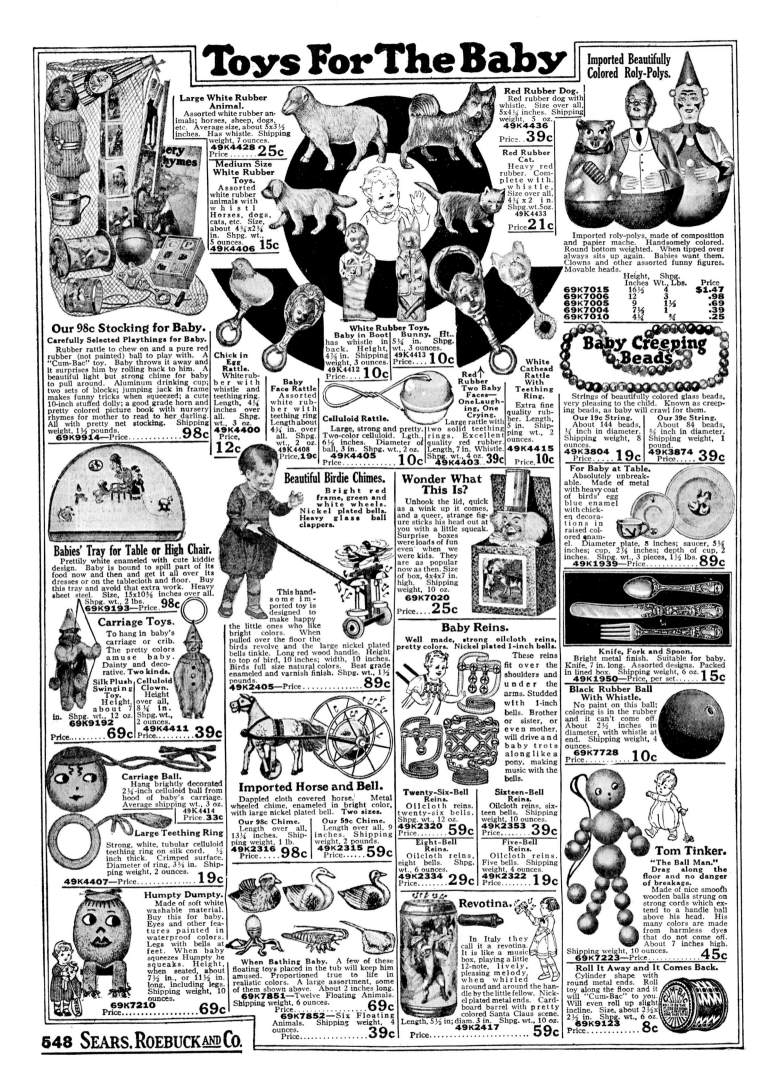

Large White Rubber Animal.
Assorted white rubber animals; horses, sheep, dogs, etc. Average size, about 5x3½ inches. Has whistle. Shipping weight, 7 ounces.
49K4428 Price....... **25c**

Medium Size White Rubber Toys.
Assorted white rubber animals with whistl Horses, dogs, cats, etc. Size, about 4¾x2¾ in. Shpg. wt., 5 ounces.
49K4406 **15c**

Red Rubber Dog.
Red rubber dog with whistle. Size over all, 5x4¼ inches. Shipping weight, 5 oz.
49K4436
Price.. **39c**

Red Rubber Cat.
Heavy red rubber. Complete with whistle, Size over all, 4¾ x 2 in. Shpg.wt.5oz.
49K4433
Price **21c**

White Rubber Toys. Baby in Boot has whistle in back. Height, 4⅝ in. Shipping weight, 3 ounces.
49K4412
Price.... **10c**

Bunny. Ht., 5¼ in. Shpg. wt., 3 ounces.
49K4413
Price.... **10c**

Chick in Egg Rattle.
White rubber with whistle and teething ring. Length, 4¼ inches over all. Shpg. wt., 3 oz.
49K4400
Price, **12c**

Baby Face Rattle
Assorted white rubber with teething ring Length about 4¾ in. over all. Shpg. wt., 2 oz.
49K4408
Price, **19c**

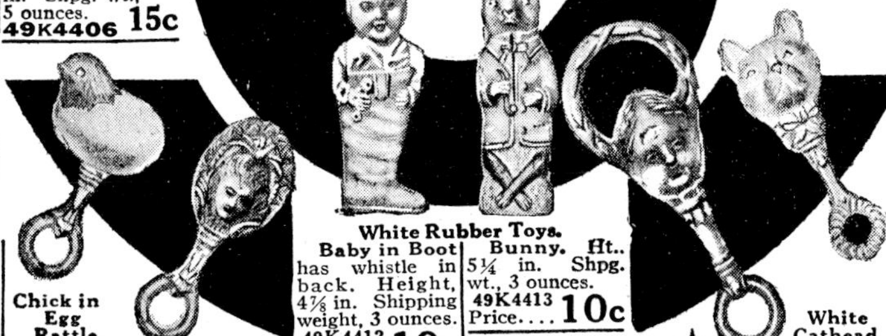

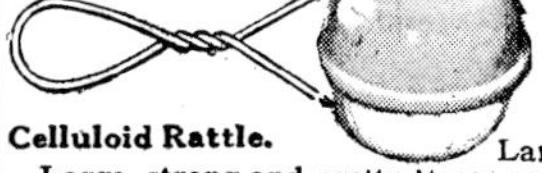

Celluloid Rattle.
Large, strong and pretty. Two-color celluloid. Lgth., 6½ inches. Diameter of ball, 3 in. Shpg. wt., 2 oz.
49K4405
Price............ **10c**

Red Rubber Two Baby Faces—One Laughing, One Crying.
Large rattle with two solid teething rings. Excellent quality red rubber. Length, 7 in. Whistle. Shpg. wt., 4 oz.
49K4403.. **39c**

White Cathead Rattle With Teething Ring.
Extra fine quality rubber. Length, 5 in. Shipping wt., 2 ounces.
49K4415
Price **10c**

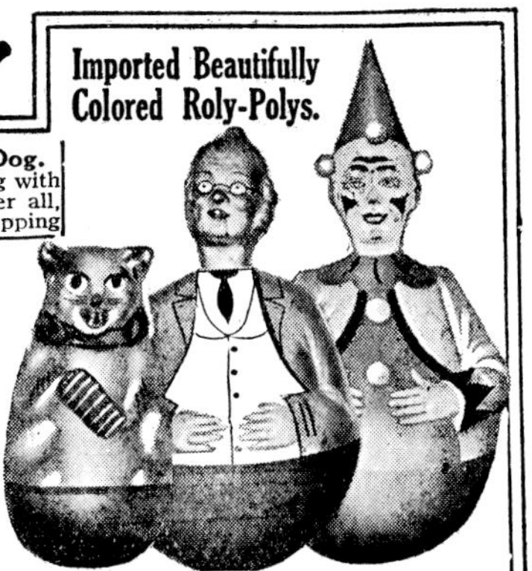

Imported Beautifully Colored Roly-Polys.

Imported roly-polys, made of composition and papier mache. Handsomely colored. Round bottom weighted. When tipped over always sits up again. Babies want them. Clowns and other assorted funny figures. Movable heads.

	Height, Inches	Shpg. Wt., Lbs.	Price
69K7015	16½	4	**$1.47**
69K7006	12	3	**.98**
69K7005	9	1½	**.69**
69K7004	7½	1	**.39**
69K7010	4¼	¾	**.25**

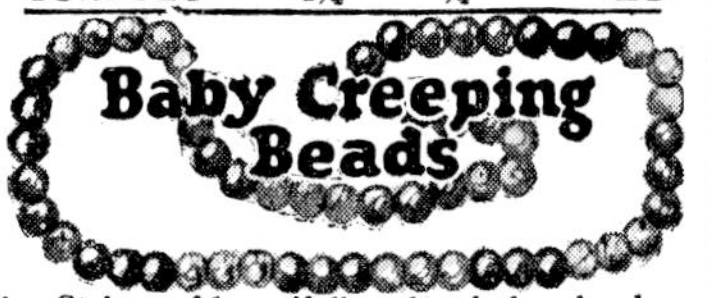

Baby Creeping Beads

Strings of beautifully colored glass beads, very pleasing to the child. Known as creeping beads, as baby will crawl for them.

Our 19c String.
About 144 beads, ¼ inch in diameter. Shipping weight, 8 ounces.
49K3804
Price..... **19c**

Our 39c String.
About 84 beads, ⅝ inch in diameter. Shipping weight, 1 pound.
49K3874
Price..... **39c**

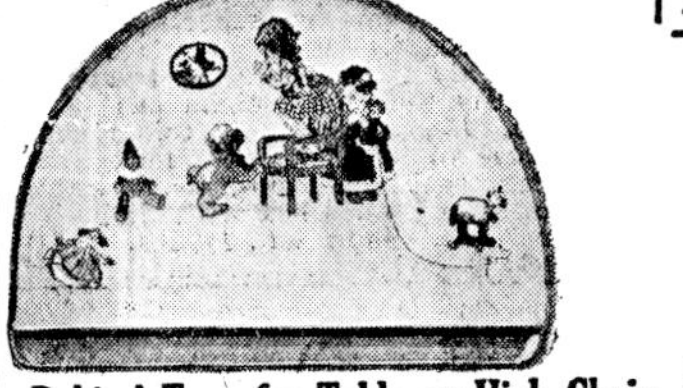

Babies' Tray for Table or High Chair.

Prettily white enameled with cute kiddie design. Baby is bound to spill part of its food now and then and get it all over its dresses or on the tablecloth and floor. Buy this tray and avoid that extra work. Heavy sheet steel. Size, 15x10⅜ inches over all. Shpg. wt., 2 lbs.
69K9193—Price. **98c**

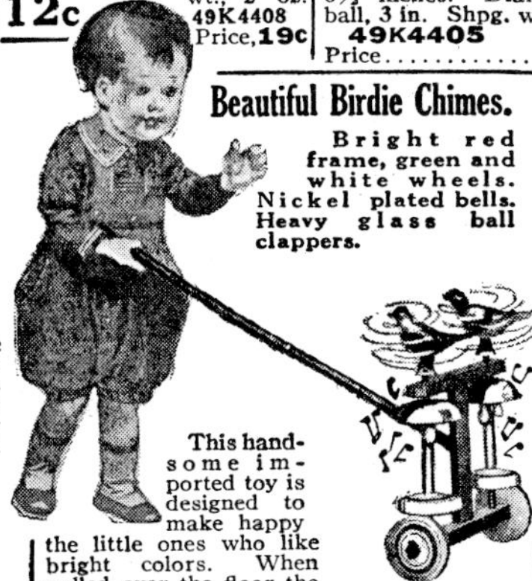

Beautiful Birdie Chimes.

Bright red frame, green and white wheels. Nickel plated bells. Heavy glass ball clappers.

This handsome imported toy is designed to make happy the little ones who like bright colors. When pulled over the floor the birds revolve and the large nickel plated bells tinkle. Long red wood handle. Height to top of bird, 10 inches; width, 10 inches. Birds full size natural colors. Best grade enameled and varnish finish. Shpg. wt., 1½ pounds.
49K2405—Price............ **89c**

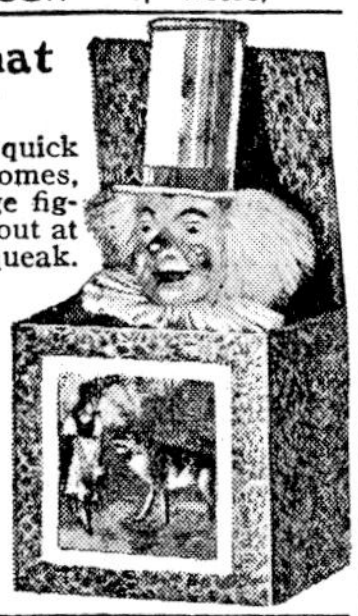

Wonder What This Is?

Unhook the lid, quick as a wink up it comes, and a queer, strange figure sticks his head out at you with a little squeak. Surprise boxes were loads of fun even when we were kids. They are as popular now as then. Size of box, 4x4x7 in. high. Shipping weight, 10 oz.
69K7020
Price.... **25c**

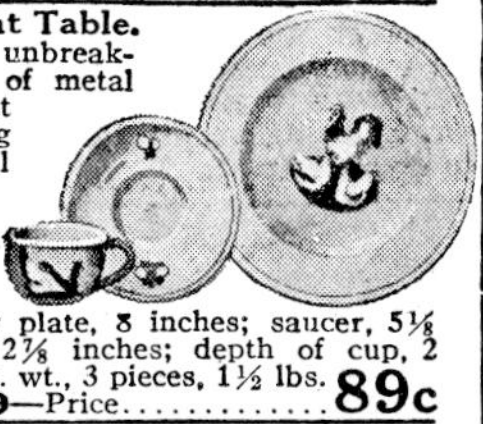

For Baby at Table.
Absolutely unbreakable. Made of metal with heavy coat of birds' egg blue enamel with chicken decorations in raised colored enamel. Diameter plate, 8 inches; saucer, 5⅛ inches; cup, 2⅞ inches; depth of cup, 2 inches. Shpg. wt., 3 pieces, 1½ lbs.
49K1939—Price............ **89c**

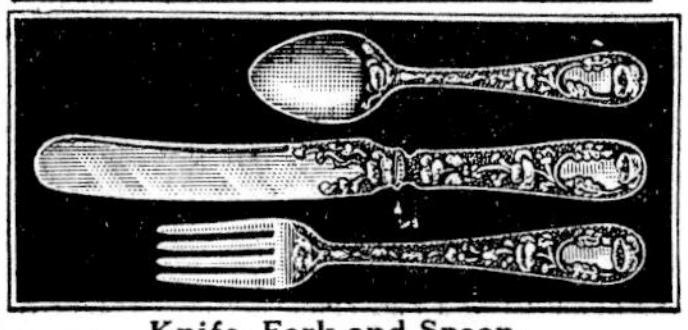

Knife, Fork and Spoon.
Bright metal finish. Suitable for baby. Knife, 7 in. long. Assorted designs. Packed in lined box. Shipping weight, 6 oz.
49K1950—Price, per set...... **15c**

Carriage Toys.

To hang in baby's carriage or crib. The pretty colors amuse baby. Dainty and decorative. **Two kinds.**

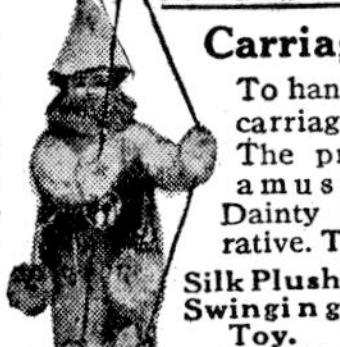

Silk Plush Swinging Toy.
Height, about 7 in. Shpg. wt., 12 oz.
69K9192
Price......... **69c**

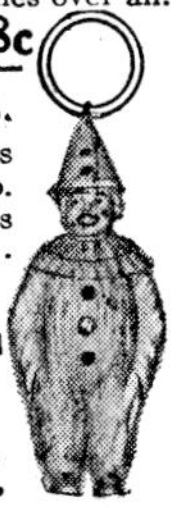

Celluloid Clown.
Height over all, 8¼ in. Shpg. wt., 2 ounces.
49K4411
Price......... **39c**

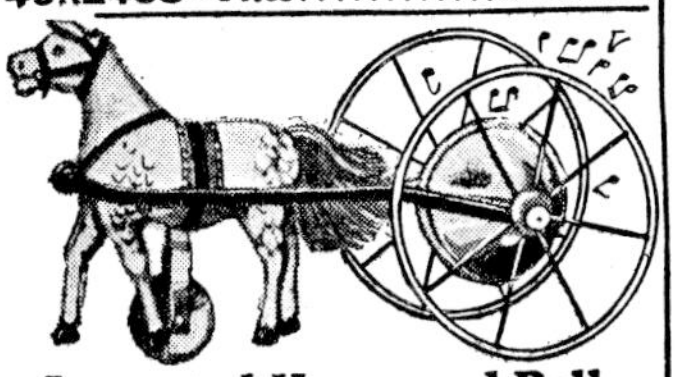

Imported Horse and Bell.

Dappled cloth covered horse. Metal wheeled chime, enameled in bright color, with large nickel plated bell. **Two sizes.**

Our 98c Chime.
Length over all, 13¾ inches. Shipping weight, 1 lb.
49K2316
Price..... **98c**

Our 59c Chime.
Length over all, 9 inches. Shipping weight, 2 pounds.
49K2315
Price...... **59c**

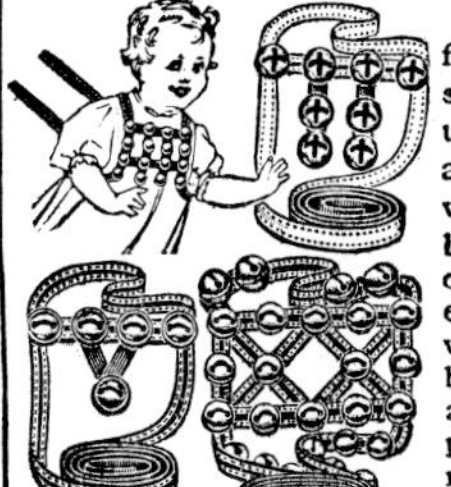

Baby Reins.

Well made, strong oilcloth reins, pretty colors. Nickel plated 1-inch bells.

These reins fit over the shoulders and under the arms. Studded with 1-inch bells. Brother or sister, or even mother, will drive and baby trots along like a pony, making music with the bells.

Twenty-Six-Bell Reins.
Oilcloth reins. twenty-six bells. Shpg. wt., 12 oz.
49K2320
Price......... **59c**

Sixteen-Bell Reins.
Oilcloth reins, sixteen bells. Shipping weight, 10 ounces.
49K2353
Price......... **39c**

Eight-Bell Reins.
Oilcloth reins, eight bells. Shpg. wt., 6 ounces.
49K2334
Price......... **29c**

Five-Bell Reins.
Oilcloth reins. Five bells. Shipping weight, 4 ounces.
49K2322
Price......... **19c**

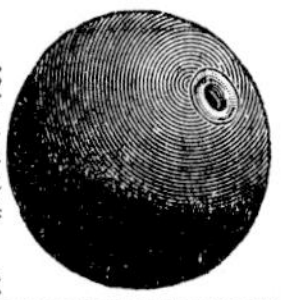

Black Rubber Ball With Whistle.
No paint on this ball; coloring is in the rubber and it can't come off. About 2½ inches in diameter, with whistle at end. Shipping weight, 4 ounces.
69K7728
Price............ **10c**

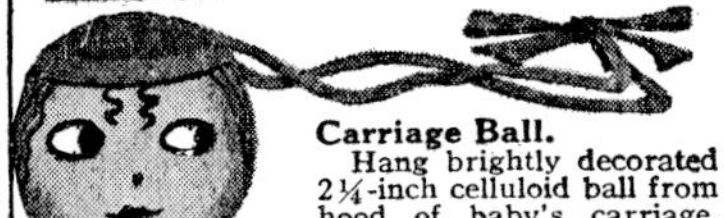

Carriage Ball.
Hang brightly decorated 2¼-inch celluloid ball from hood of baby's carriage. Average shipping wt., 3 oz.
49K4414
Price. **33c**

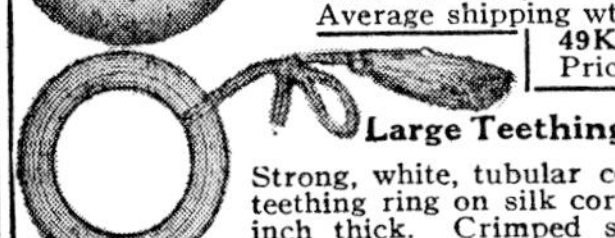

Large Teething Ring
Strong, white, tubular celluloid teething ring on silk cord. ½ inch thick. Crimped surface. Diameter of ring, 3⅜ in. Shipping weight, 2 ounces.
49K4407—Price............ **19c**

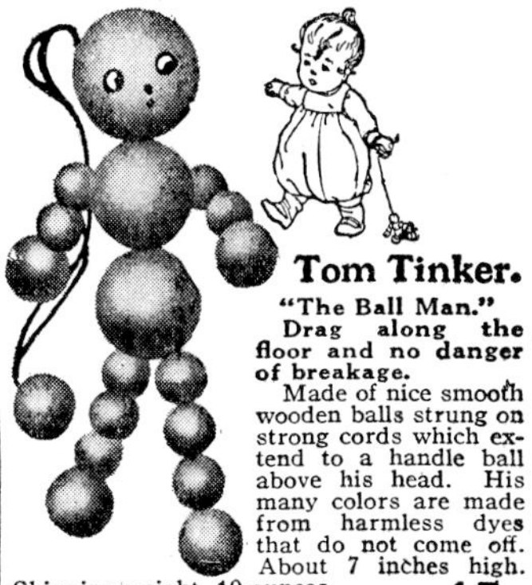

Tom Tinker.

"The Ball Man." Drag along the floor and no danger of breakage.
Made of nice smooth wooden balls strung on strong cords which extend to a handle ball above his head. His many colors are made from harmless dyes that do not come off. About 7 inches high. Shipping weight, 10 ounces.
69K7223—Price............ **45c**

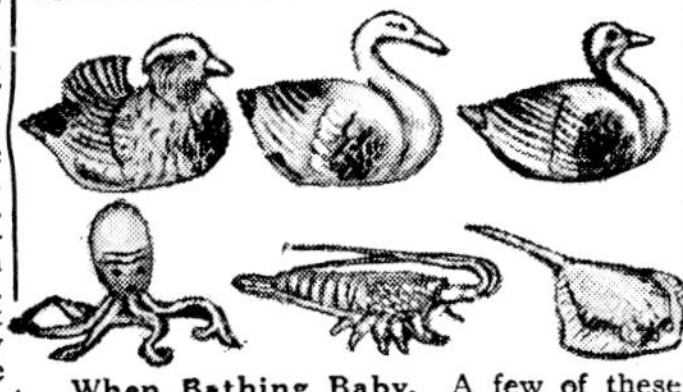

When Bathing Baby. A few of these floating toys placed in the tub will keep him amused. Proportioned true to life in realistic colors. A large assortment, some of them shown above. About 2 inches long.
69K7851—Twelve Floating Animals. Shipping weight, 6 ounces.
Price............ **69c**
69K7852—Six Floating Animals. Shipping weight, 4 ounces.
Price............ **39c**

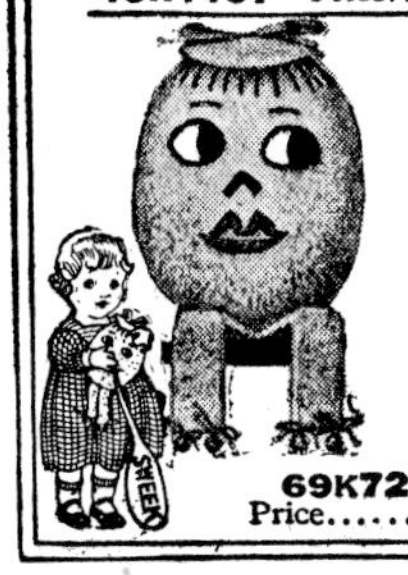

Humpty Dumpty.
Made of soft white washable material. Buy this for baby. Eyes and other features painted in waterproof colors. Legs with bells at feet. When baby squeezes Humpty he squeaks. Height, when seated, about 7½ in., or 11½ in. long, including legs. Shipping weight, 10 ounces.
69K7210
Price............ **69c**

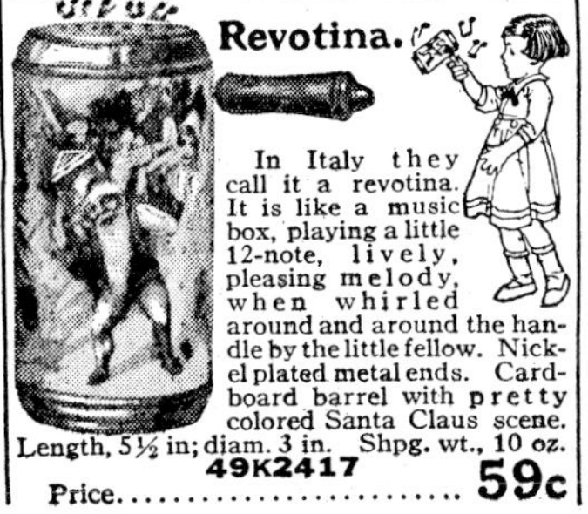

Revotina.

In Italy they call it a revotina. It is like a music box, playing a little 12-note, lively, pleasing melody, when whirled around and around the handle by the little fellow. Nickel plated metal ends. Cardboard barrel with pretty colored Santa Claus scene. Length, 5½ in; diam. 3 in. Shpg. wt., 10 oz.
49K2417
Price............ **59c**

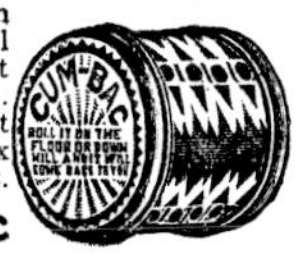

Roll It Away and It Comes Back.
Cylinder shape with round metal ends. Roll toy along the floor and it will "Cum-Bac" to you. Will even roll up slight incline. Size, about 2½x2½ in. Shpg. wt., 6 oz.
69K9123
Price............ **8c**

Furniture and Kitchen Cabinets

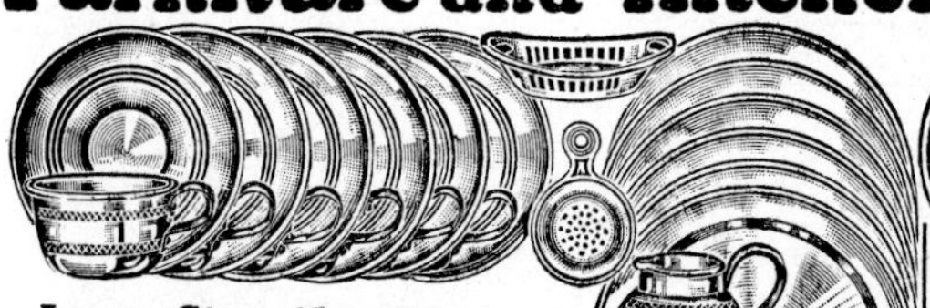

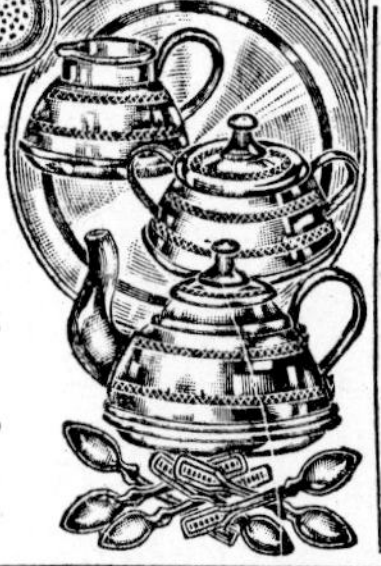

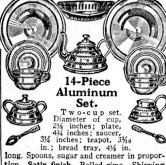

Large Size Aluminum Tea Sets.

Beautifully **satin finished** aluminum. Pot, 3½ inches diameter, not including spout. Height, 3 inches. 4¾-inch plates; 3¼-inch saucers; 2¼-inch diameter cups. Spoons, creamer and sugar bowl, bread tray and tea strainer in proportion. Rolled rims.

Our $1.67 Set. 49K1875—6-cup set; thirty-one pieces. Shipping weight, 1½ pounds. Price.... **$1.67**

Our $1.39 Set. 49K1874—4-cup set; twenty-three pieces. Shipping wt., 1 pound. Price.... **$1.39**

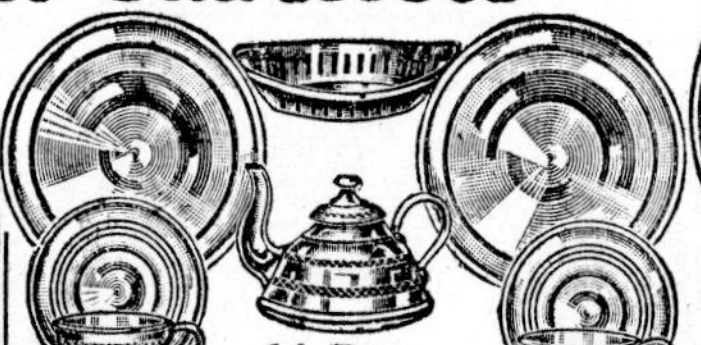

14-Piece Aluminum Set.

Two-cup set. Diameter of cup, 2⅛ inches; plate, 4¾ inches; saucer, 3¼ inches; teapot, 3 1/16 in.; bread tray, 4⅛ in. long. Spoons, sugar and creamer in proportion. **Satin finish.** Rolled rims. Shipping weight, 15 ounces.

49K1871—Price.............. **87c**

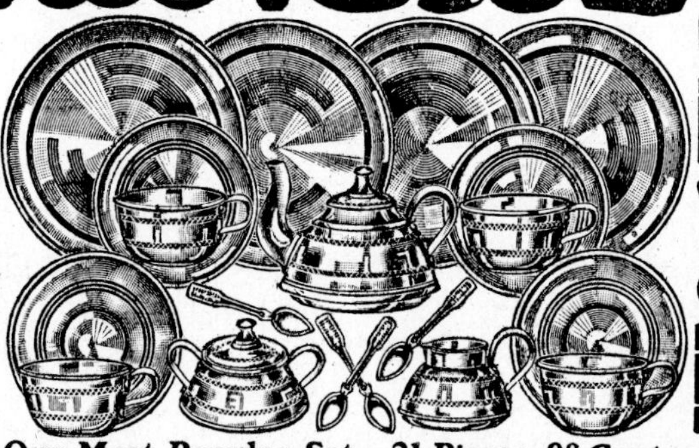

Our Most Popular Set. 21 Pieces, 98 Cents.

Beautiful **satin finish** aluminum tea set. Shaped teapot, 3 1/16-inch diameter base and 2 9/16 inches high; creamer, 2¼ inches in diameter; sugar bowl, 2⅜ inches in diameter; four plates, 4¾ inches in diameter; four saucers, 3¼ inches, and four cups, 2⅛ inches; four spoons in proportion. Very dainty and clean looking. Rolled rims, no sharp edges. Shipping weight, 1 pound.

49K1873—Price.............................. **98c**

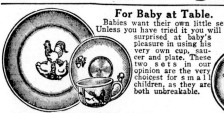

For Baby at Table.

Babies want their own little sets. Unless you have tried it you will be surprised at baby's pleasure in using his very own cup, saucer and plate. These two sets in our opinion are the very choicest for small children, as they are both unbreakable.

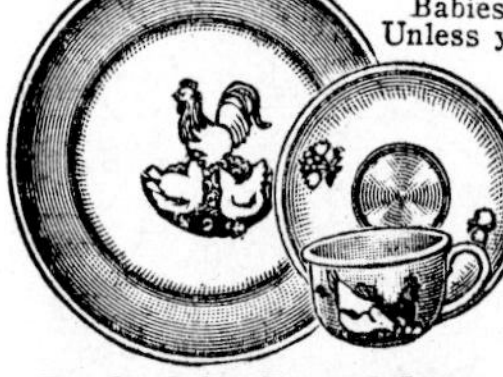

Bright Color Enamel Set, 89 Cents.

Absolutely unbreakable. Made of strong metal with an extra heavy coat of bird's egg blue enamel. Dainty and clean looking. The decorations are in white and colors. The little chicken group is in raised enamel. Plate, 8 in. in diameter; saucer, 5⅝ in. in diameter; cup, 2⅞ in. in diameter and 2 inches high. Shipping weight, three pieces in box, 1½ pounds.

49K1949—Price.............. **89c**

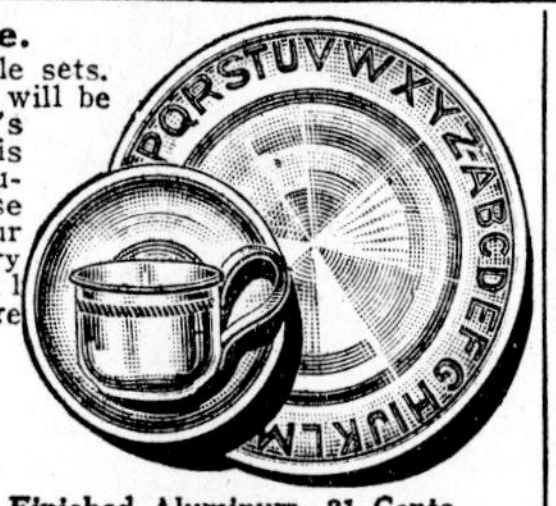

Satin Finished Aluminum, 21 Cents. ABC Set.

The **satin finish** is very pretty and has a gloss that only aluminum will take. ABC's around edge of plate. Plate, 6⅞ in. in diam.; saucer, 4⅛ in. in diam.; cup, 2⅜ in. in diam. This makes a most suitable present for tiny tots. Shipping weight, 10 ounces.

49K1859—Price.............. **21c**

17-Piece DeLuxe Dinner Set.

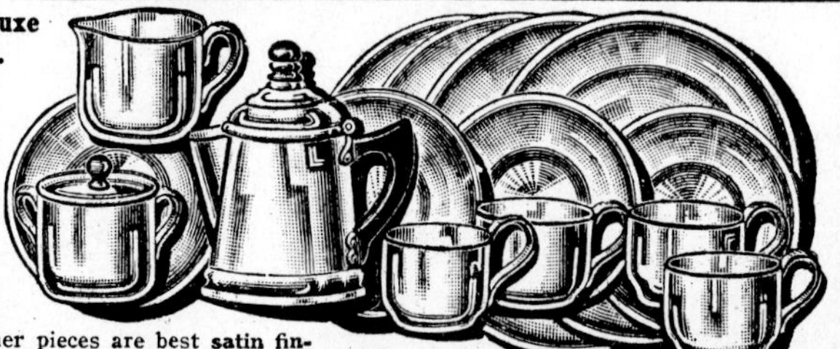

Our finest set, having a handsome mirror finish coffee pot, 5½ in. high, with ebonized wood handle. Capacity, 1 pint. Also a mirror finish two-handled sugar bowl and a creamer to match. Other pieces are best **satin finish.** Seventeen pieces, including two covers. Four 2 7/16-inch cups, with rolled edges; four 4-inch saucers; four 7-inch plates; sugar bowl with cover, 3½x3¼ in., and a 3⅛x2⅜ in. creamer. Packed in box. Shpg. wt., 1½ lbs.

49K1870—Price, per set.............................. **$2.79**

Imitation Cut Glass Sets.

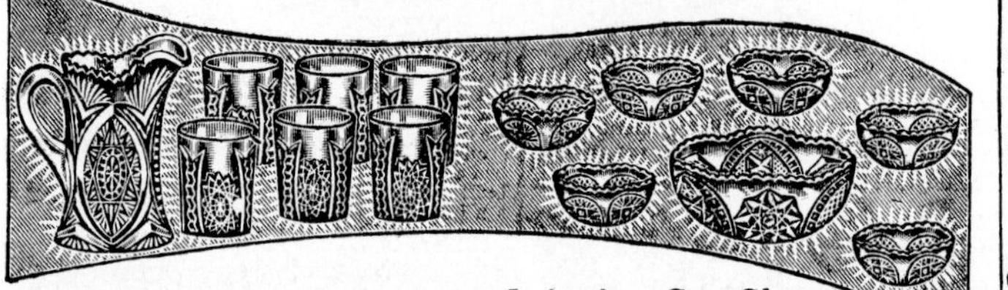

Imitation Cut Glass Water Set.

Seven pieces. Glass water pitcher, 4¾ inches high, and six glasses, each 2¼ inches high. Shipping weight, 2⅛ pounds.

49K1901—Price.............. **59c**

Imitation Cut Glass Toy Berry Set.

4¼-inch berry bowl and six small dishes, 2¼ in. in diam. Shpg. wt., 3 lbs.

49K1900—Price.............. **47c**

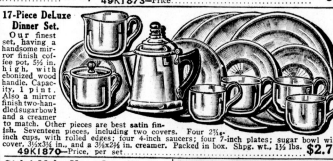

Girls! Make Your Own Waffles.

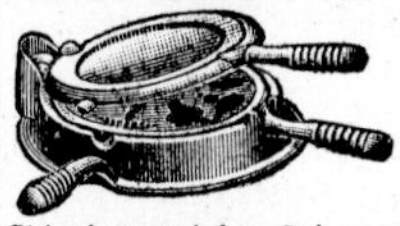

Real waffle iron with a ball joint just like a big one. Size of waffle will be about 3½ inches in diameter. Made of cast iron. Shipping weight, 1½ pounds.

69K9107—Price.............. **25c**

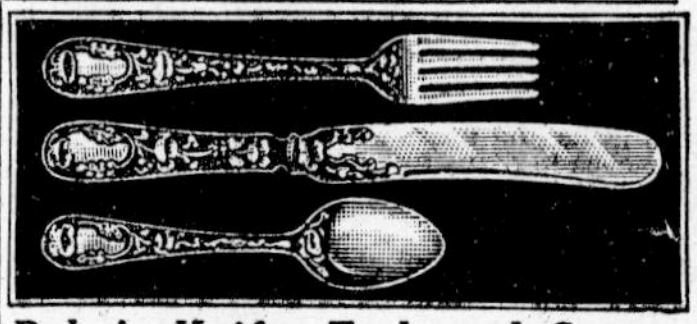

Baby's Knife, Fork and Spoon.

Bright polished white metal. Strong and durable. Flower embossed. Packed in neat white glazed box, with form to hold pieces in place. Knife, 7 in. long. Shpg. wt., 6 oz.

49K1960—Price, per set.......... **15c**

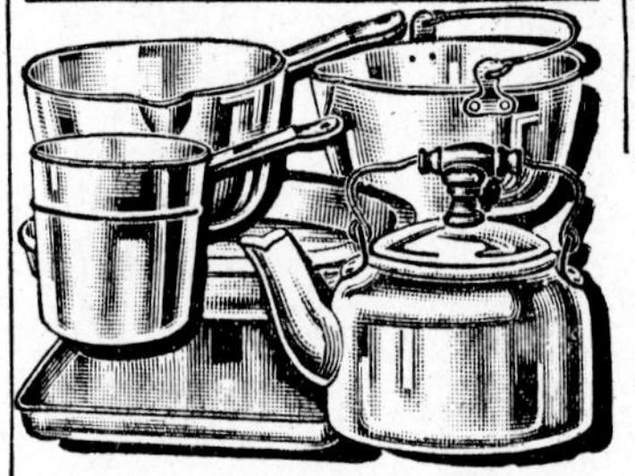

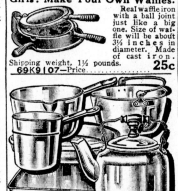

Aluminum Toy Domestic Science Set.

Girls Learn Cooking With This Set.

Consists of a 4¾-inch diameter teakettle, 1-pint lip saucepan, 1-pint preserving kettle, 7-inch cake pan, low biscuit pan, 6½x9¼ inches, and a ⅔-pint double boiler insert for teakettle. Heavier gauge metal. Shipping weight, 1½ pounds.

49K1865—Price, per set...... **$2.59**

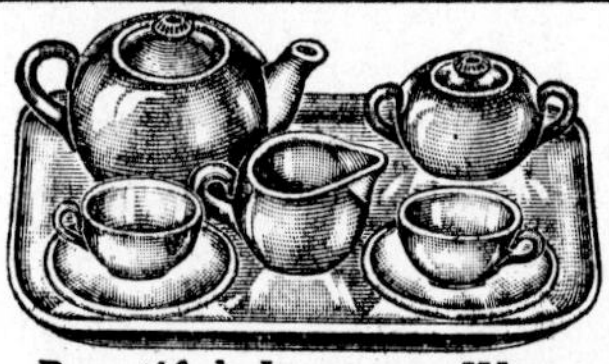

Beautiful Japanese Ware.

This tiny set is the same beautiful solid green color of the famous Japanese Owaji ware used for fashionable tea parties. Two cups and saucers, creamer, and sugar bowl and teapot with covers. Strong green fiber tray. Diameter of teapot, 1 9/16 inches; other pieces in proportion. Shipping wt., 1 pound.

49K1604—Price.............. **33c**

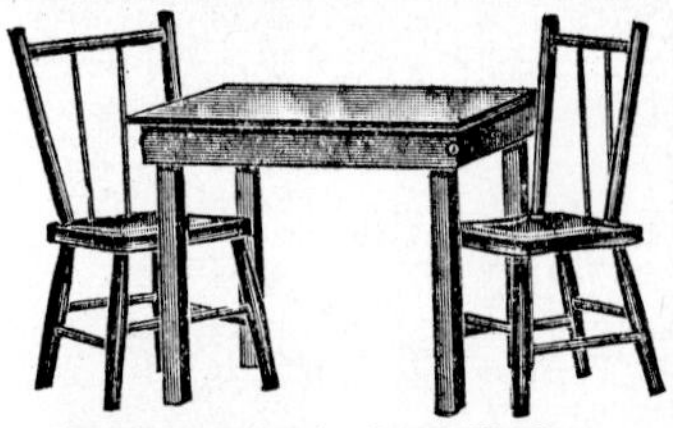

Red Dining Set for Small Children.

Nicely red finished wood dining set, consisting of two chairs, height, 17¾ inches over all; seats, 9x8½ inches, with yellow striping, and a table, top measuring 18x13 inches; height, about 14 inches. Big favorite with children. Practical for children's real and "make believe" tea parties. Shipping weight, about 8¾ pounds.

79K8543¼—Price, per set...... **$1.98**

Just Like at the Ice Cream Store.

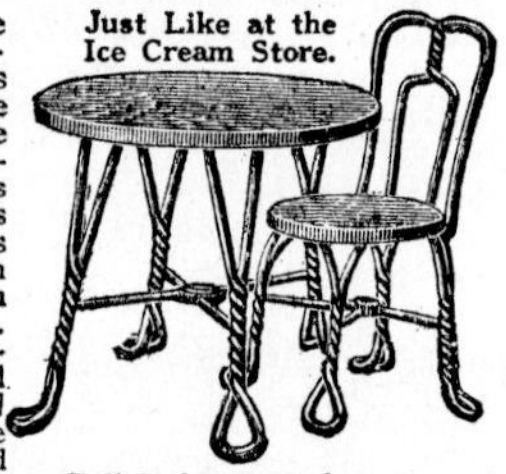

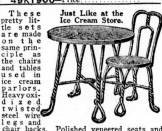

These pretty little sets are made on the same principle as the chairs and tables used in ice cream parlors. Heavy oxidized twisted steel wire legs and chair backs. Polished veneered seats and table top. Handsome and unusually strong, practically unbreakable. Height from floor to top of chair back, 20 inches. From floor to seat, 10 inches. Table top is 16 inches in diameter and is 17½ inches high.

79K8545¼—Chair. Shpg. wt., 4½ lbs. Each **$1.67**	79K8546¼—Table. Shpg. wt., 6¾ lbs. Each **$2.67**

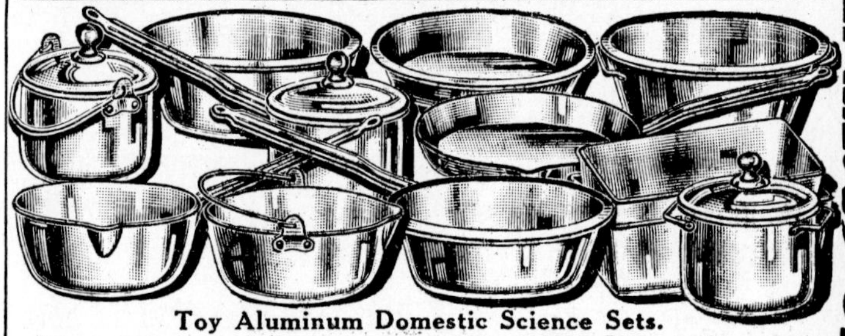

Toy Aluminum Domestic Science Sets.

Large enough for the little girl to use in practice cooking. Dish pan, 5 1/16 inches in diameter; other pieces in proportion.

Twelve-Piece Set. Illustrated. Shipping weight, 2¼ pounds. 49K1864 Price **$1.39**	**Eight-Piece Set.** Skillet, saucepan, stew pan, two kettles, pudding pan, dish pan and bread pan. Shipping weight, 2⅛ lbs. 49K1860—Price..... **98c**	**Four-Piece Set.** Skillet, pudding pan, preserving kettle and saucepan. Shipping weight, 1½ pounds. 49K1863—Price.... **47c**

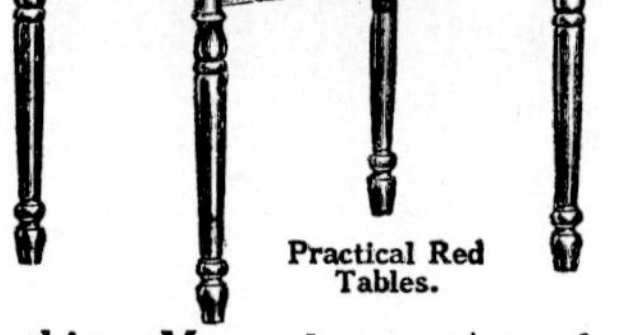

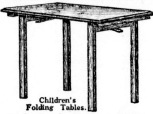

Practical Red Tables.

Nothing More Appropriate for the Girl Than a Red Table.

For outdoors or indoors. These are well made of seasoned lumber, nicely painted red and black striping. Each with a good size drawer.

79K8536¼—Size of top, 23x17 inches. Stands 19 inches high. Shipping weight, 12 pounds. Price...... **$2.48**	79K8535¼—Size of top, 21x15 inches. Stands 17 inches high. Shipping wt., 9 lbs. Price.... **$1.98**

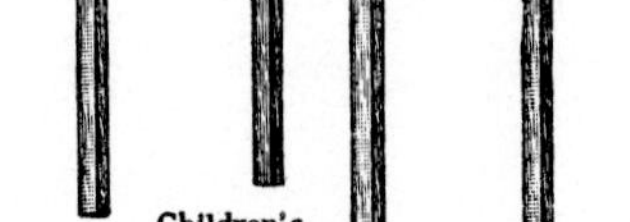

Children's Folding Tables.

High Grade Natural Finish Maple Top, Beveled Edge.

This table is strong and practical. When not in use can be folded up and stored in very small space. Made of birch and maple. Strongly braced. Will not collapse. Comes in two sizes as listed below.

79K8526¼ Size, 24x14 inches; stands 14 in. from floor. Shipping wt., 6¼ pounds. Price.... **$1.69**	79K8527¼ Size, 26x16 inches; stands 18½ in. from floor. Shipping wt., 8 pounds. Price.... **$2.39**

Aluminum Toy Cooking Set, 17 Pieces, 98 Cents.

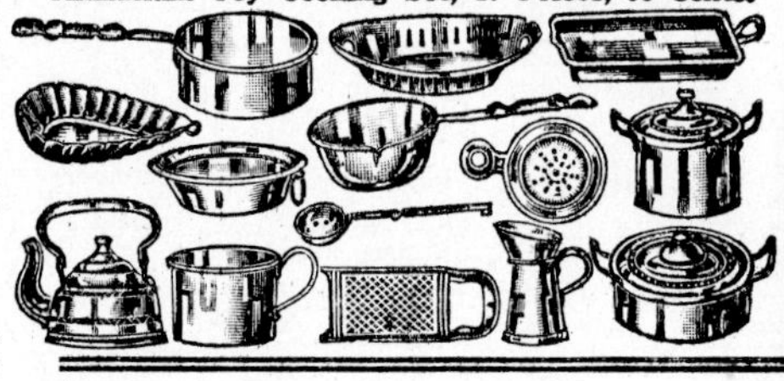

Rich **satin finish.** A variety of shapes. True proportions. Teakettle, 2⅞ inches high, other pieces in proportion. Two two-handle kettles with covers. Bread pan, tea strainer, pitcher, dipper, cup, grater, etc. This set is imported from Europe. They are such clever imitations of large pieces, with covers, bails, handles, etc., that they are immensely popular. Shpg. wt., of seventeen pieces (including three covers), 8 ounces.

49K1876—Price.. **98c**

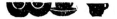

MUSICAL TOYS

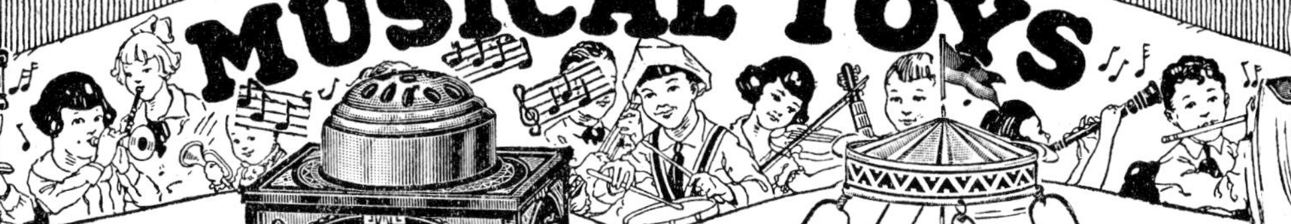

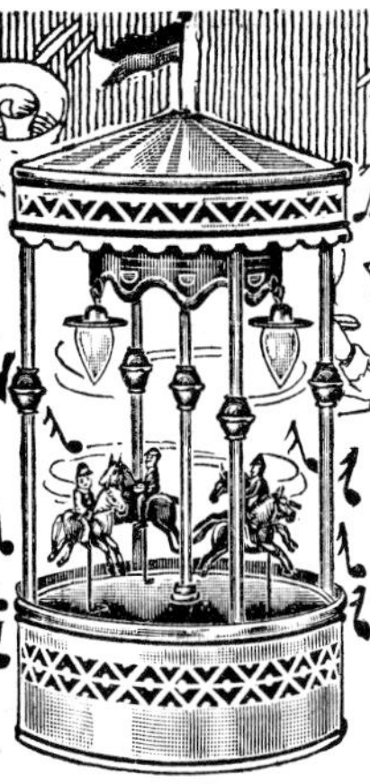

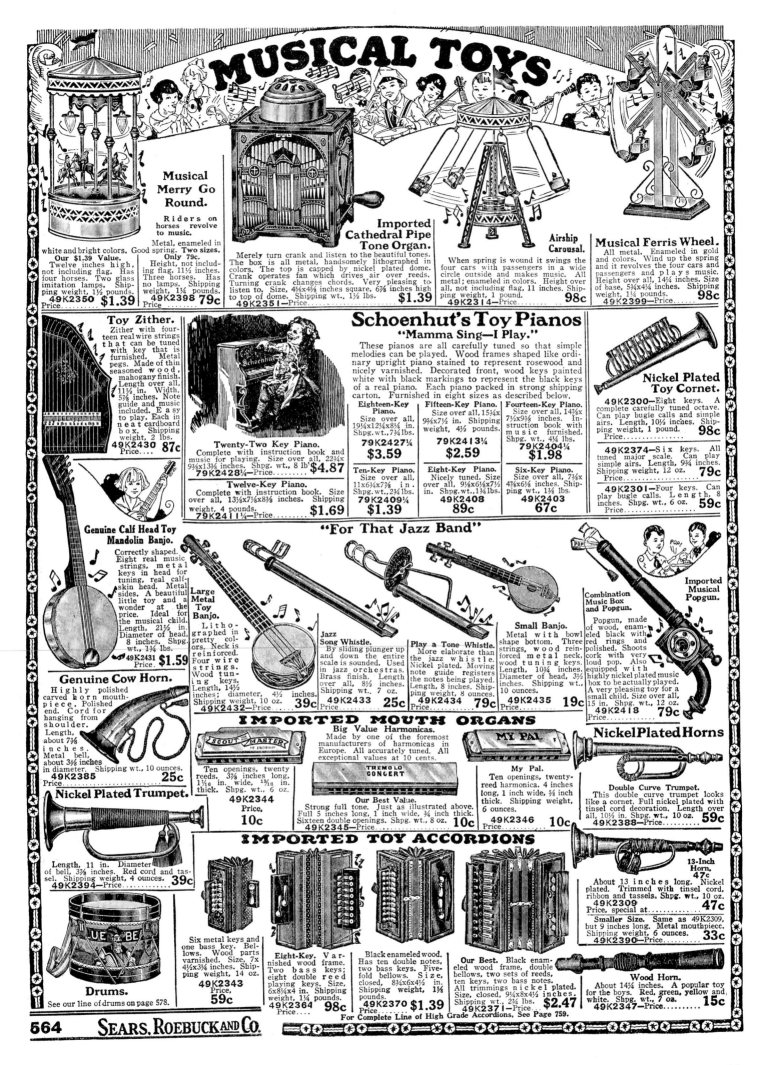

Musical Merry Go Round.

Riders on horses revolve to music.

Metal, enameled in white and bright colors. Good spring. Two sizes.

Our $1.39 Value. Twelve inches high, not including flag. Has four horses. Two glass imitation lamps. Shipping weight, 1½ pounds.
49K2350 Price.......... **$1.39**

Only 79c. Height, not including flag, 11½ inches. Three horses. Has no lamps. Shipping weight, 1¼ pounds.
49K2398 Price........ **79c**

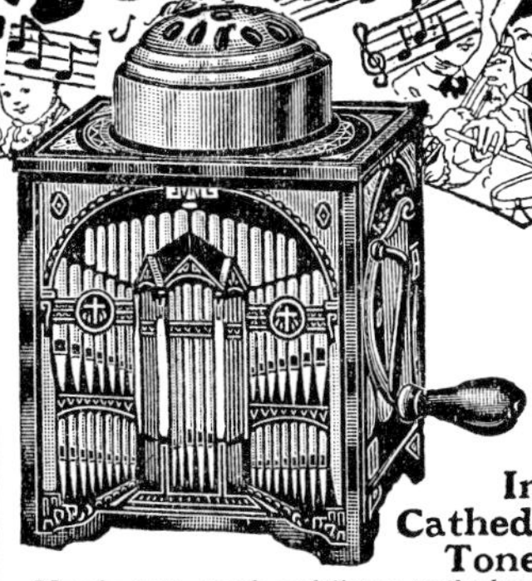

Imported Cathedral Pipe Tone Organ.

Merely turn crank and listen to the beautiful tones. The box is all metal, handsomely lithographed in colors. The top is capped by nickel plated dome. Crank operates fan which drives air over reeds. Turning crank changes chords. Very pleasing to listen to. Size, 4⅝x4⅝ inches square, 6⅞ inches high to top of dome. Shipping wt., 1½ lbs.
49K2351—Price.................. **$1.39**

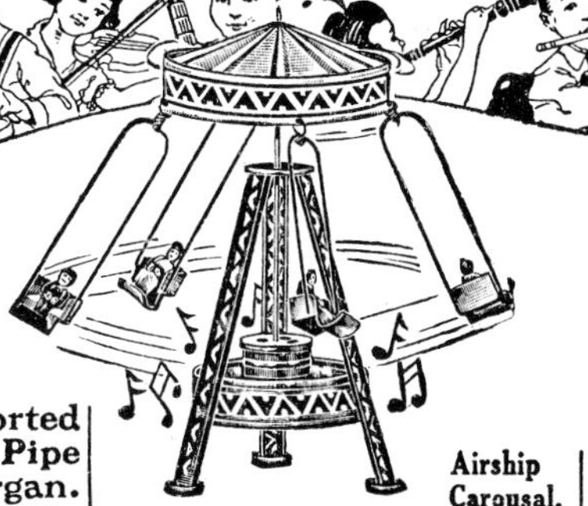

Airship Carousal.

When spring is wound it swings the four cars with passengers in a wide circle outside and makes music. All metal; enameled in colors. Height over all, not including flag, 11 inches. Shipping weight, 1 pound.
49K2314—Price.......... **98c**

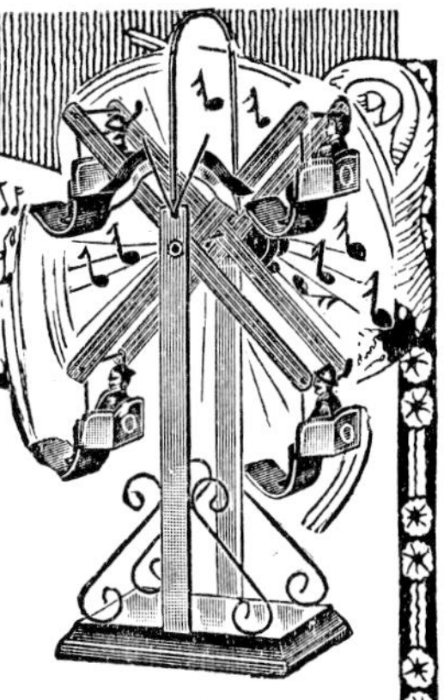

Musical Ferris Wheel.

All metal. Enameled in gold and colors. Wind up the spring and it revolves the four cars and passengers and plays music. Height over all, 14¼ inches. Size of base, 5¾x4¼ inches. Shipping weight, 1¼ pounds.
49K2399—Price........ **98c**

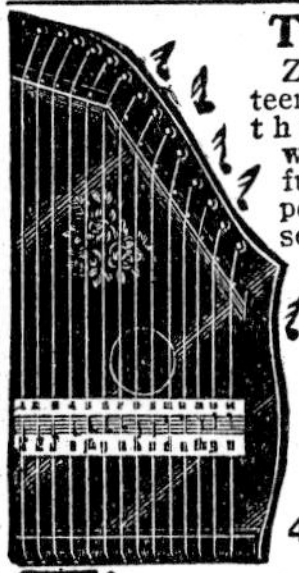

Toy Zither.

Zither with fourteen real wire strings that can be tuned with key that is furnished. Metal pegs. Made of thin seasoned wood, mahogany finish. Length over all, 11½ in. Width, 5⅞ inches. Note guide and music included. Easy to play. Each in neat cardboard box. Shipping weight, 2 lbs.
49K2430 Price.... **87c**

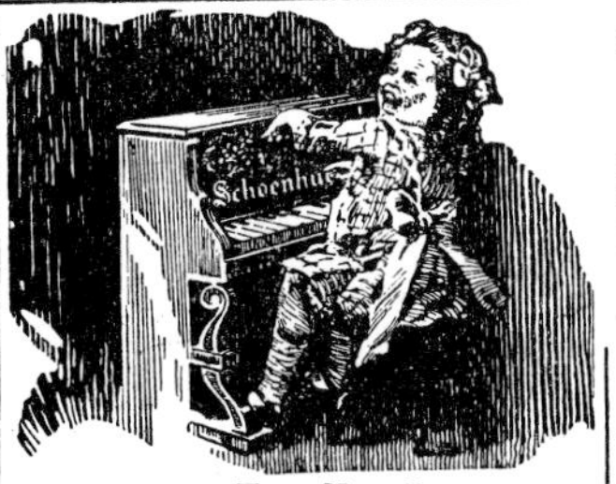

Schoenhut's Toy Pianos

"Mamma Sing—I Play."

These pianos are all carefully tuned so that simple melodies can be played. Wood frames shaped like ordinary upright piano stained to represent rosewood and nicely varnished. Decorated front, wood keys painted white with black markings to represent the black keys of a real piano. Each piano packed in strong shipping carton. Furnished in eight sizes as described below.

Twenty-Two Key Piano. Complete with instruction book and music for playing. Size over all, 22¾x9⅜x13⅜ inches. Shpg. wt., 8 lbs.
79K2428¼—Price.......... **$4.87**

Twelve-Key Piano. Complete with instruction book. Size over all, 13⅛x7⅛x8⅜ inches. Shipping weight, 4 pounds.
79K2411¼—Price.......... **$1.69**

Eighteen-Key Piano. Size over all, 19¼x12¼x8¼ in. Shpg. wt., 7¾ lbs.
79K2427¼ **$3.59**

Fifteen-Key Piano. Size over all, 15¾x9⅝x7¼ in. Shipping weight, 4½ pounds.
79K2413¼ **$2.59**

Fourteen-Key Piano. Size over all, 14⅞x7½x9⅜ inches. Instruction book with music furnished. Shpg. wt., 4¼ lbs.
79K2404¼ **$1.98**

Ten-Key Piano. Size over all, 11x6¾x7⅞ in. Shpg. wt., 2¾ lbs.
79K2409¼ **$1.39**

Eight-Key Piano. Nicely tuned. Size over all, 9⅛x6⅛x7½ in. Shpg. wt., 1¾ lbs.
49K2408 **89c**

Six-Key Piano. Size over all, 7⅜x4⅞x6⅛ inches. Shipping wt., 1⅜ lbs.
49K2403 **67c**

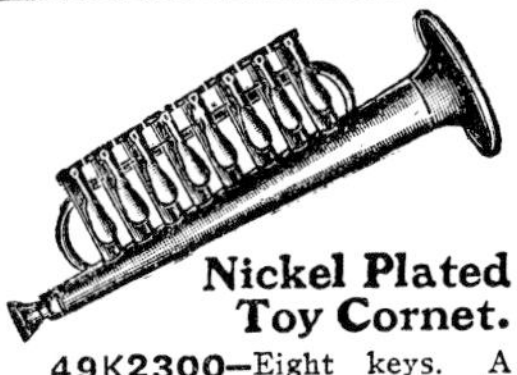

Nickel Plated Toy Cornet.

49K2300—Eight keys. A complete carefully tuned octave. Can play bugle calls and simple airs. Length, 10½ inches. Shipping weight, 1 pound.
Price.................. **98c**

49K2374—Six keys. All tuned major scale. Can play simple airs. Length, 9¾ inches. Shipping weight, 12 oz.
Price.................. **79c**

49K2301—Four keys. Can play bugle calls. Length, 8 inches. Shpg. wt., 6 oz.
Price.................. **59c**

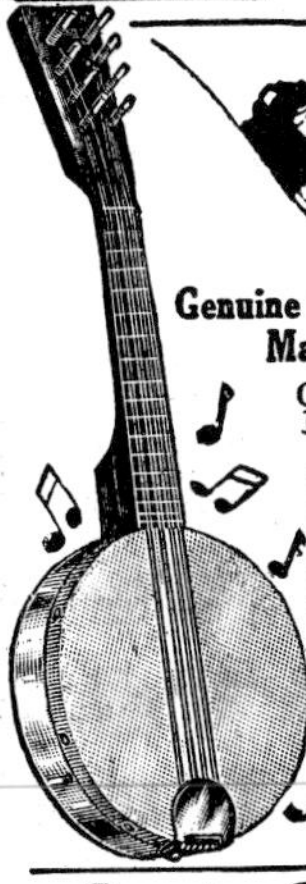

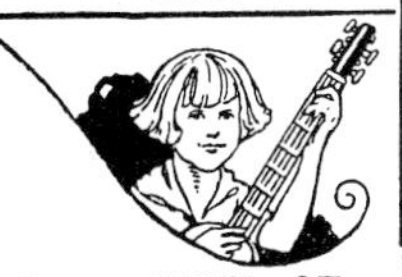

Genuine Calf Head Toy Mandolin Banjo.

Correctly shaped. Eight real music strings, metal keys in head for tuning, real calfskin head. Metal sides. A beautiful little toy and a wonder at the price. Ideal for the musical child. Length, 21½ in. Diameter of head, 8 inches. Shpg. wt., 1¾ lbs.
49K2431 Price. **$1.59**

"For That Jazz Band"

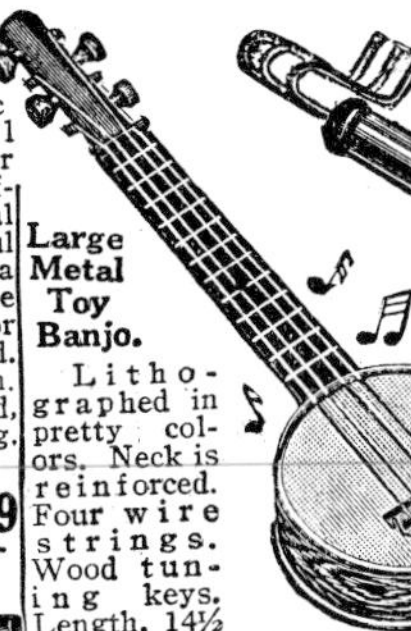

Large Metal Toy Banjo.

Lithographed in pretty colors. Neck is reinforced. Four wire strings. Wood tuning keys. Length, 14½ inches; diameter, 4½ inches. Shipping weight, 10 oz.
49K2432—Price.......... **39c**

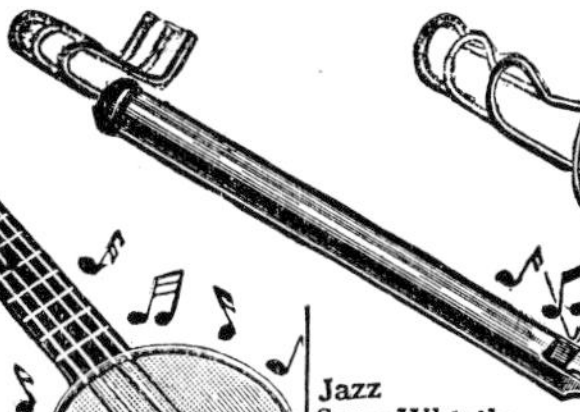

Jazz Song Whistle.

By sliding plunger up and down the entire scale is sounded. Used in jazz orchestras. Brass finish. Length over all, 8½ inches. Shipping wt., 7 oz.
49K2433 Price.......... **25c**

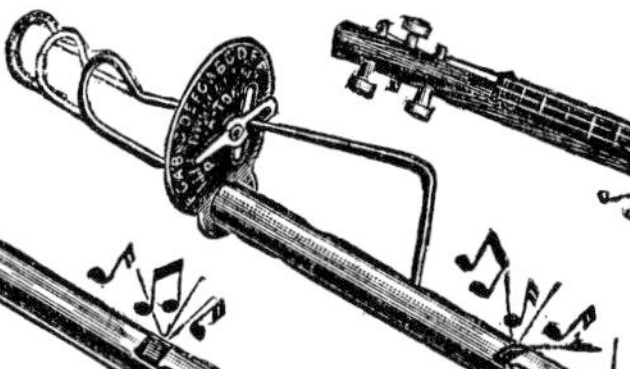

Play a Tone Whistle.

More elaborate than the jazz whistle. Nickel plated. Moving note guide registers the notes being played. Length, 8 inches. Shipping weight, 8 ounces.
49K2434 Price.......... **79c**

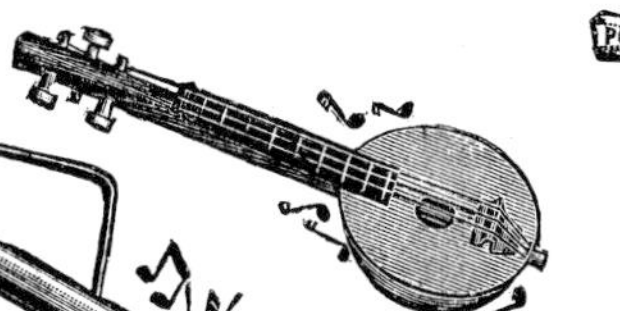

Small Banjo.

Metal with bowl shape bottom. Three strings, wood reinforced metal neck, wood tuning keys. Length, 10¾ inches. Diameter of head, 3½ inches. Shipping wt., 10 ounces.
49K2435 Price.......... **19c**

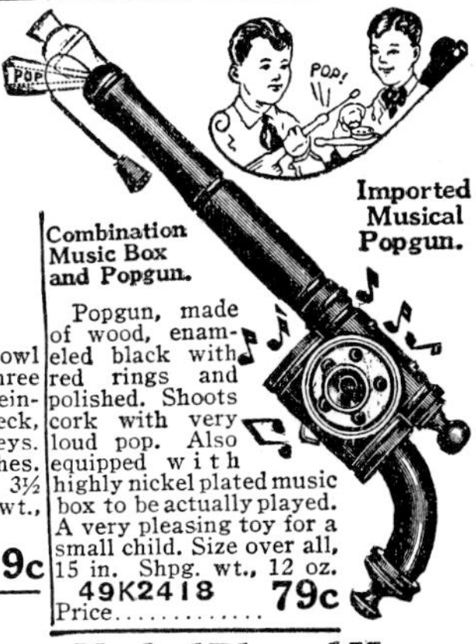

Combination Music Box and Popgun.

Imported Musical Popgun.

Popgun, made of wood, enameled black with red rings and polished. Shoots cork with very loud pop. Also equipped with highly nickel plated music box to be actually played. A very pleasing toy for a small child. Size over all, 15 in. Shpg. wt., 12 oz.
49K2418 Price.......... **79c**

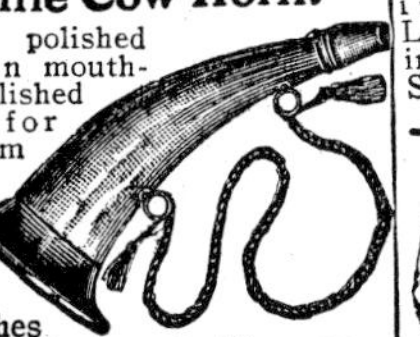

Genuine Cow Horn.

Highly polished carved horn mouthpiece. Polished end. Cord for hanging from shoulder. Length, about 7⅜ inches. Metal bell, about 3⅛ inches in diameter. Shipping wt., 10 ounces.
49K2385 Price.......... **25c**

IMPORTED MOUTH ORGANS

Big Value Harmonicas.

Made by one of the foremost manufacturers of harmonicas in Europe. All accurately tuned. All exceptional values at 10 cents.

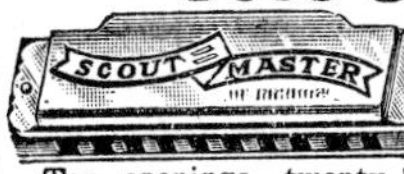

Ten openings, twenty reeds. 3⅞ inches long, 1⅛ in. wide, 1⁵⁄₁₆ in. thick. Shpg. wt., 6 oz.
49K2344 Price, **10c**

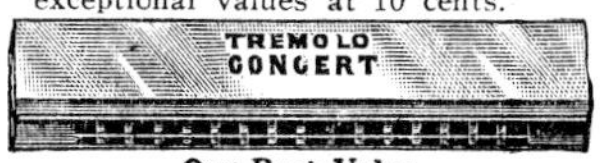

Our Best Value. Strong full tone. Just as illustrated above. Full 5 inches long, 1 inch wide, ¾ inch thick. Sixteen double openings. Shpg. wt., 8 oz.
49K2345—Price.......... **10c**

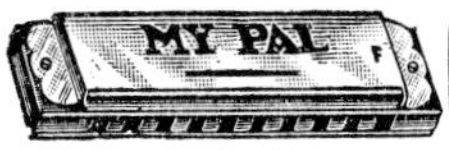

My Pal. Ten openings, twenty-reed harmonica. 4 inches long, 1 inch wide, ⅝ inch thick. Shipping weight, 6 ounces.
49K2346 Price.......... **10c**

Nickel Plated Horns

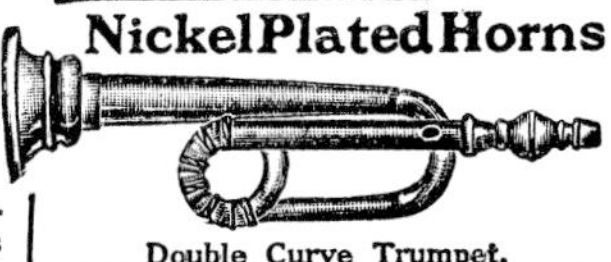

Double Curve Trumpet. This double curve trumpet looks like a cornet. Full nickel plated with tinsel cord decoration. Length over all, 10½ in. Shpg. wt., 10 oz.
49K2388—Price.......... **59c**

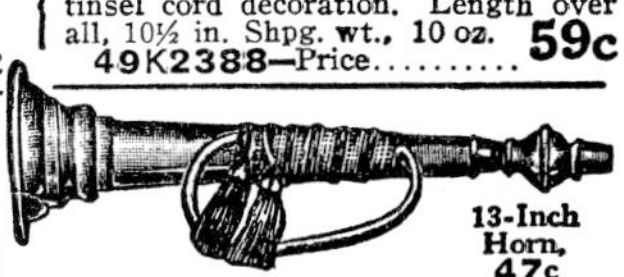

13-Inch Horn. 47c About 13 inches long. Nickel plated. Trimmed with tinsel cord, ribbon and tassels. Shpg. wt., 10 oz.
49K2309 Price, special at.......... **47c**

Smaller Size. Same as 49K2309, but 9 inches long. Metal mouthpiece. Shipping weight, 6 ounces.
49K2390—Price.......... **33c**

Nickel Plated Trumpet.

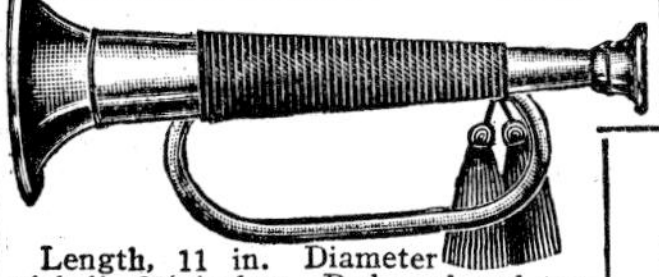

Length, 11 in. Diameter of bell, 3⅞ inches. Red cord and tassel. Shipping weight, 4 ounces.
49K2394—Price.......... **39c**

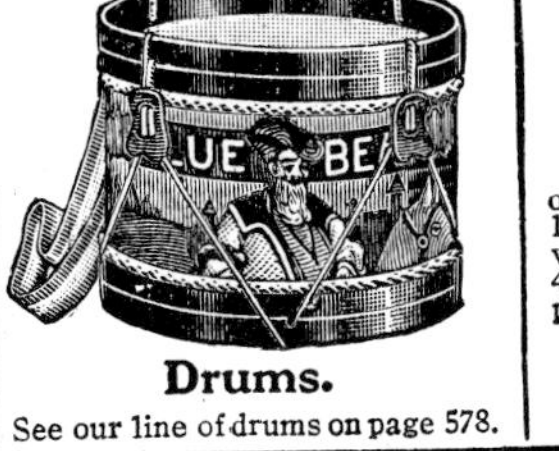

Drums.

See our line of drums on page 578.

IMPORTED TOY ACCORDIONS

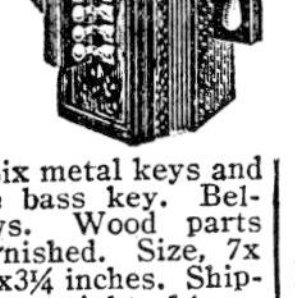

Six metal keys and one bass key. Bellows. Wood parts varnished. Size, 7x4½x3¼ inches. Shipping weight, 14 oz.
49K2343 Price, **59c**

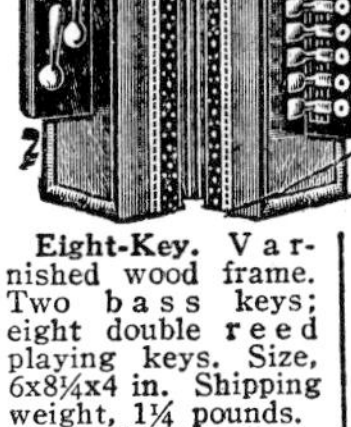

Eight-Key. Varnished wood frame. Two bass keys; eight double reed playing keys. Size, 6x8¾x4 in. Shipping weight, 1¼ pounds.
49K2364 Price.... **98c**

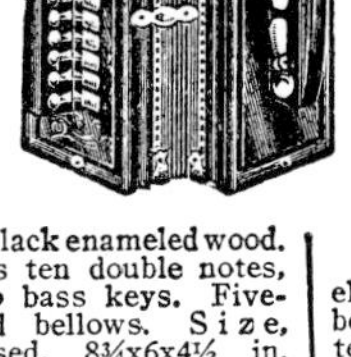

Black enameled wood. Has ten double notes, two bass keys. Fivefold bellows. Size, closed, 8¾x6x4½ in. Shipping weight, 1⅝ pounds.
49K2370 Price.... **$1.39**

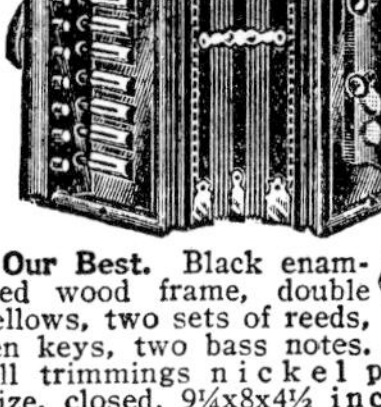

Our Best. Black enameled wood frame, double bellows, two sets of reeds, ten keys, two bass notes. All trimmings nickel plated. Size, closed, 9¼x8x4¼ inches. Shipping wt., 2¾ lbs.
49K2371—Price.... **$2.47**

For Complete Line of High Grade Accordions, See Page 759.

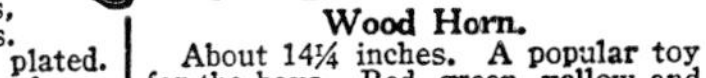

Wood Horn. About 14¼ inches. A popular toy for the boys. Red, green, yellow and white. Shpg. wt., 7 oz.
49K2347—Price.......... **15c**

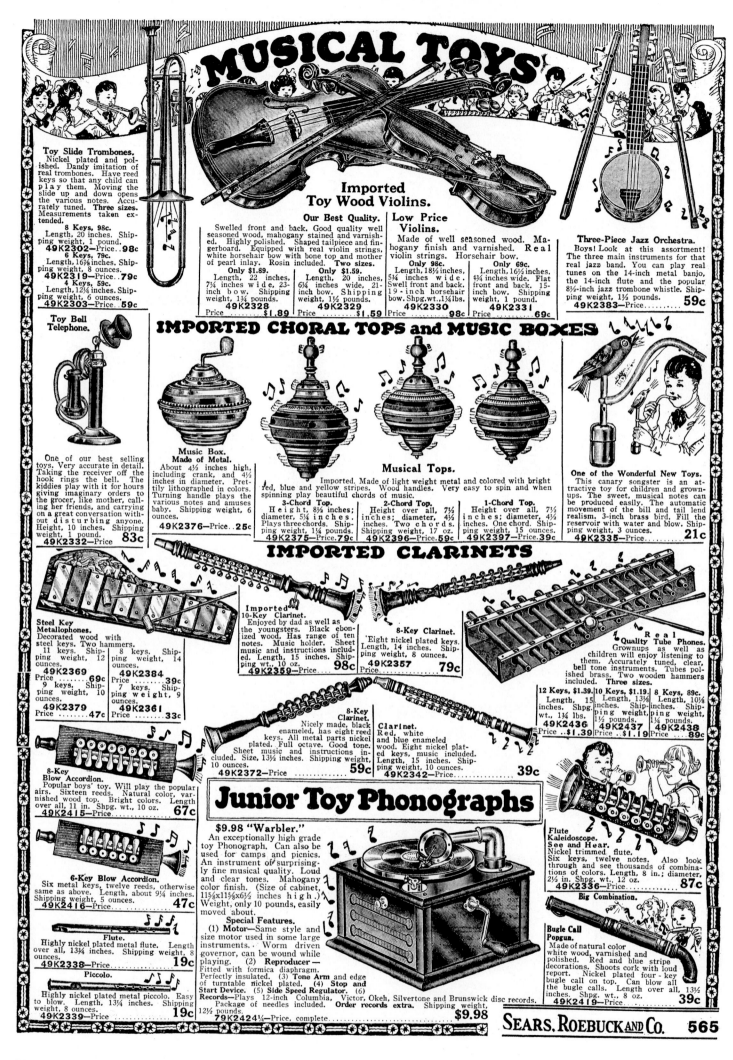

MUSICAL TOYS

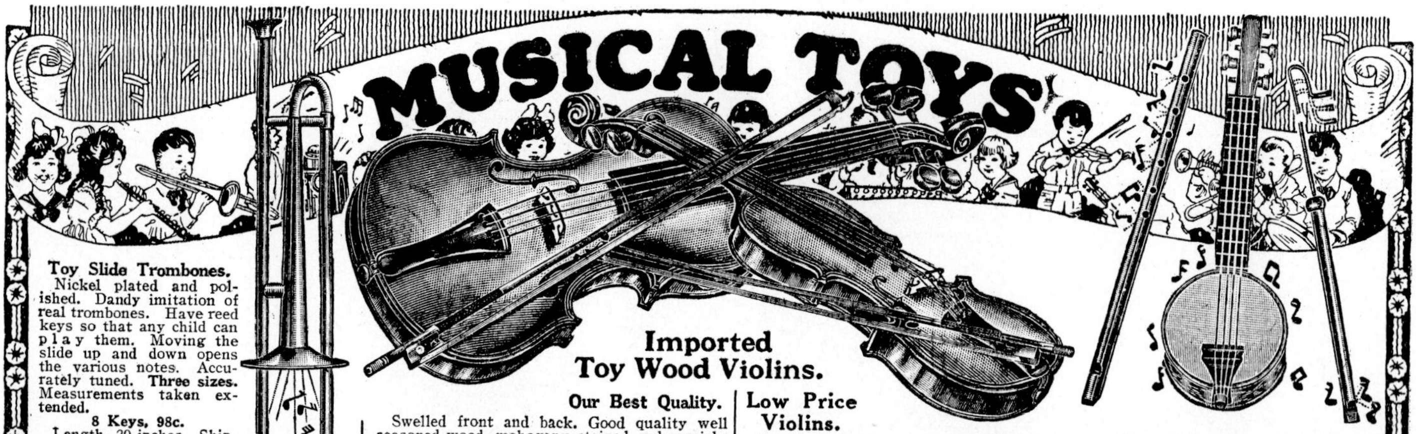

Toy Slide Trombones. Nickel plated and polished. Dandy imitation of real trombones. Have reed keys so that any child can play them. Moving the slide up and down opens the various notes. Accurately tuned. **Three sizes.** Measurements taken extended.

8 Keys, 98c. Length, 20 inches. Shipping weight, 1 pound.
49K2302—Price..98c

6 Keys, 79c. Length, 16⅞ inches. Shipping weight, 8 ounces.
49K2319—Price..79c

4 Keys, 59c. Length, 12¼ inches. Shipping weight, 6 ounces.
49K2303—Price..59c

Imported Toy Wood Violins.

Our Best Quality. Swelled front and back. Good quality well seasoned wood, mahogany stained and varnished. Highly polished. Shaped tailpiece and fingerboard. Equipped with real violin strings, white horsehair bow with bone top and mother of pearl inlay. Rosin included. **Two sizes.**

Only $1.89. Length, 22 inches, 7¼ inches wide, 23-inch bow. Shipping weight, 1¾ pounds.
49K2328
Price $1.89

Only $1.59. Length, 20 inches, 6¾ inches wide, 21-inch bow. Shipping weight, 1½ pounds.
49K2329
Price $1.59

Low Price Violins. Made of well seasoned wood. Mahogany finish and varnished. Real violin strings. Horsehair bow.

Only 98c. Length, 18½ inches, 5¾ inches wide. Swell front and back. 19-inch horsehair bow. Shpg.wt.,1¼lbs.
49K2330
Price 98c

Only 69c. Length, 16½ inches, 4¾ inches wide. Flat front and back. 15-inch bow. Shipping weight, 1 pound.
49K2331
Price 69c

Three-Piece Jazz Orchestra. Boys! Look at this assortment! The three main instruments for that real jazz band. You can play real tunes on the 14-inch metal banjo, the 14-inch flute and the popular 8½-inch jazz trombone whistle. Shipping weight, 1½ pounds.
49K2383—Price........ 59c

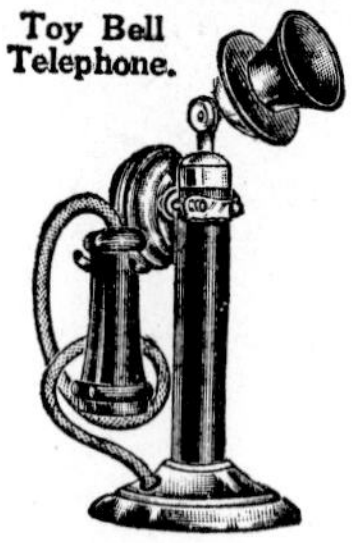

Toy Bell Telephone. One of our best selling toys. Very accurate in detail. Taking the receiver off the hook rings the bell. The kiddies play with it for hours giving imaginary orders to the grocer, like mother, calling her friends, and carrying on a great conversation without disturbing anyone. Height, 10 inches. Shipping weight, 1 pound.
49K2332—Price 83c

IMPORTED CHORAL TOPS and MUSIC BOXES

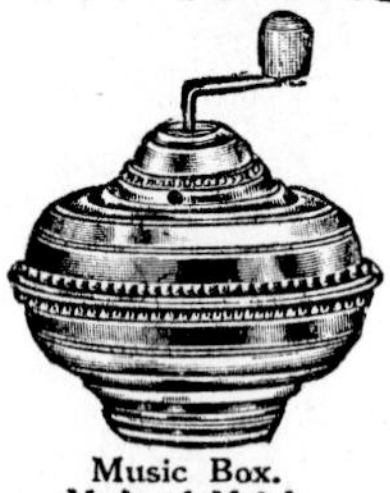

Music Box. Made of Metal. About 4½ inches high, including crank, and 4½ inches in diameter. Prettily lithographed in colors. Turning handle plays the various notes and amuses baby. Shipping weight, 6 ounces.
49K2376—Price..25c

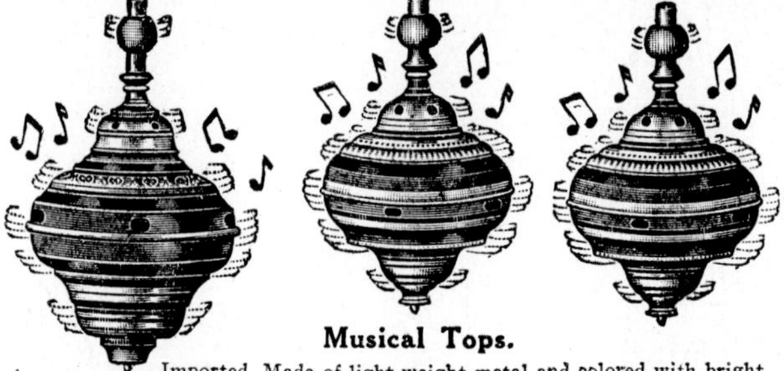

Musical Tops. Imported. Made of light weight metal and colored with bright red, blue and yellow stripes. Wood handles. Very easy to spin and when spinning play beautiful chords of music.

3-Chord Top. Height, 8½ inches; diameter, 5¼ inches. Plays three chords. Shipping weight, 1¼ pounds.
49K2375—Price.79c

2-Chord Top. Height over all, 7½ inches; diameter, 4½ inches. Two chords. Shipping weight, 17 oz.
49K2396—Price.59c

1-Chord Top. Height over all, 7½ inches; diameter, 4½ inches. One chord. Shipping weight, 15 ounces.
49K2397—Price.39c

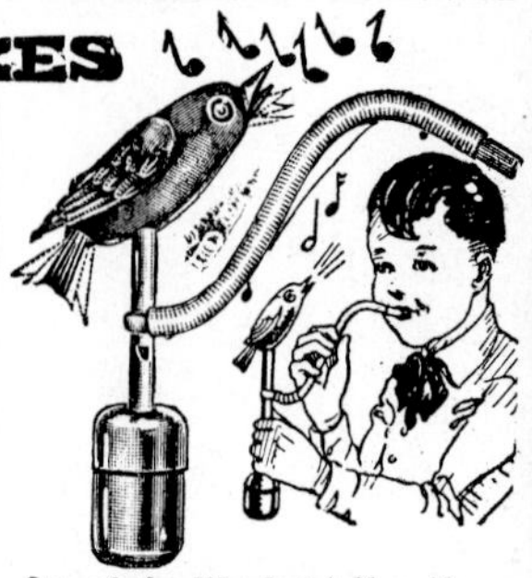

One of the Wonderful New Toys. This canary songster is an attractive toy for children and grownups. The sweet, musical notes can be produced easily. The automatic movement of the bill and tail lend realism. 3-inch brass bird. Fill the reservoir with water and blow. Shipping weight, 3 ounces.
49K2335—Price........ 21c

IMPORTED CLARINETS

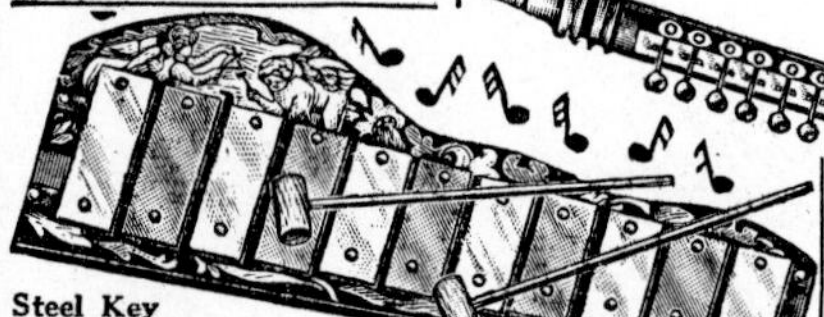

Steel Key Metallophones. Decorated wood with steel keys. Two hammers.

11 keys. Shipping weight, 12 ounces.
49K2369
Price 69c

8 keys. Shipping weight, 14 ounces.
49K2384
Price 39c

9 keys. Shipping weight, 10 ounces.
49K2379
Price 47c

7 keys. Shipping weight, 9 ounces.
49K2361
Price 33c

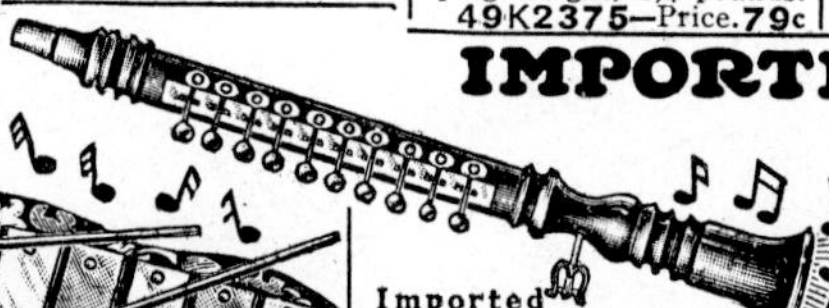

Imported 10-Key Clarinet. Enjoyed by dad as well as the youngsters. Black ebonized wood. Has range of ten notes. Music holder. Sheet music and instructions included. Length, 15 inches. Shipping wt., 10 oz.
49K2359—Price.... 98c

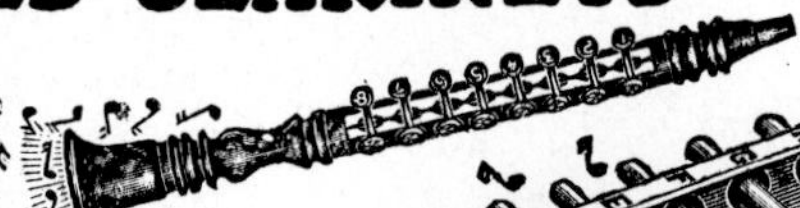

8-Key Clarinet. Eight nickel plated keys. Length, 14 inches. Shipping weight, 8 ounces.
49K2357
Price................ 79c

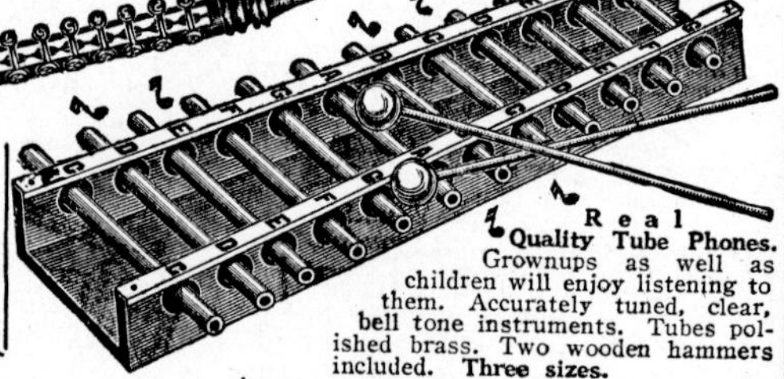

Real Quality Tube Phones. Grownups as well as children will enjoy listening to them. Accurately tuned, clear, bell tone instruments. Tubes polished brass. Two wooden hammers included. **Three sizes.**

12 Keys, $1.39.	10 Keys, $1.19.	8 Keys, 89c.
Length, 15 inches. Shpg. wt., 1¾ lbs.	Length, 13⅛ inches. Shipping weight, 1½ pounds.	Length, 10⅛ inches. Shipping weight, 1¼ pounds.
49K2436	49K2437	49K2438
Price ..$1.39	Price ..$1.19	Price 89c

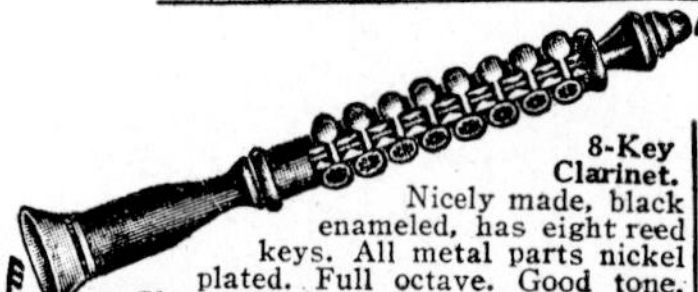

8-Key Clarinet. Nicely made, black enameled, has eight reed keys. All metal parts nickel plated. Full octave. Good tone. Sheet music and instructions included. Size, 13½ inches. Shipping weight, 10 ounces.
49K2372—Price 59c

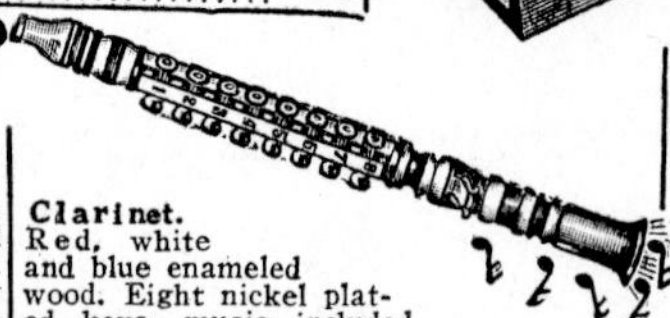

Clarinet. Red, white and blue enameled wood. Eight nickel plated keys, music included. Length, 15 inches. Shipping weight, 10 ounces.
49K2342—Price................ 39c

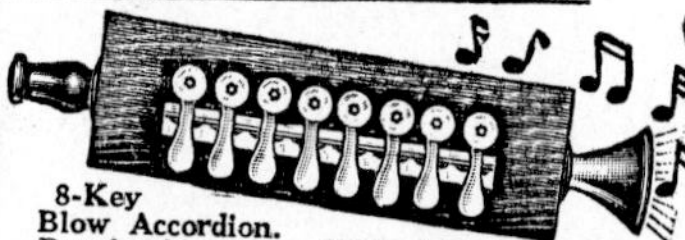

8-Key Blow Accordion. Popular boys' toy. Will play the popular airs. Sixteen reeds. Natural color, varnished wood top. Bright colors. Length over all, 11 in. Shpg. wt., 10 oz.
49K2415—Price.................. 67c

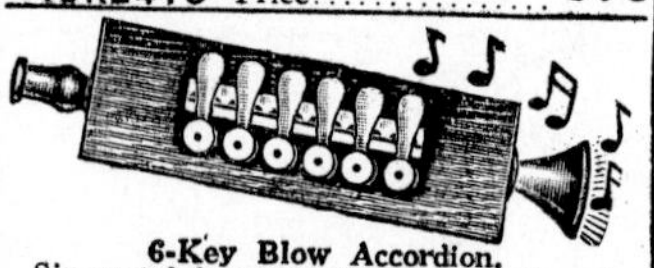

6-Key Blow Accordion. Six metal keys, twelve reeds, otherwise same as above. Length, about 9¼ inches. Shipping weight, 5 ounces.
49K2416—Price.................. 47c

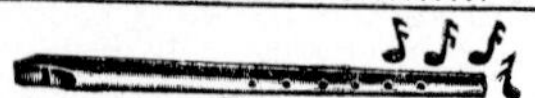

Flute. Highly nickel plated metal flute. Length over all, 13¾ inches. Shipping weight, 8 ounces.
49K2338—Price.................. 19c

Piccolo.

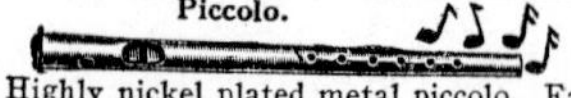

Highly nickel plated metal piccolo. Easy to blow. Length, 13¾ inches. Shipping weight, 8 ounces.
49K2339—Price.................. 19c

Junior Toy Phonographs

$9.98 "Warbler." An exceptionally high grade toy Phonograph. Can also be used for camps and picnics. An instrument of surprisingly fine musical quality. Loud and clear tones. Mahogany color finish. (Size of cabinet, 11⅝x11⅝x6½ inches high.) Weight, only 10 pounds, easily moved about.

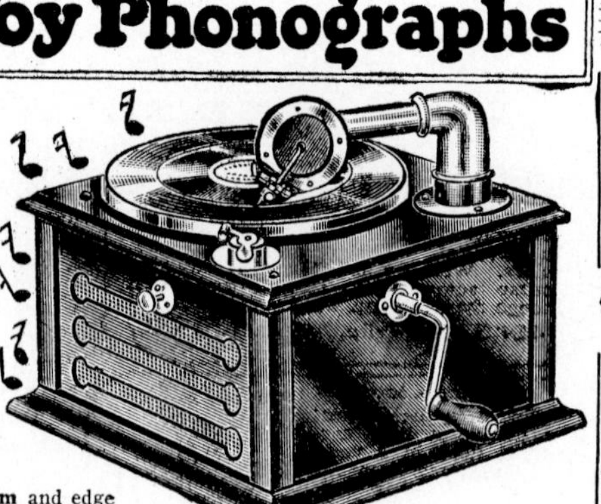

Special Features.
(1) **Motor**—Same style and size motor used in some large instruments. Worm driven governor, can be wound while playing. (2) **Reproducer**—Fitted with formica diaphragm. Perfectly insulated. (3) **Tone Arm** and edge of turntable nickel plated. (4) **Stop and Start Device.** (5) **Side Speed Regulator.** (6) **Records**—Plays 12-inch Columbia, Victor, Okeh, Silvertone and Brunswick disc records. Package of needles included. **Order records extra.** Shipping weight, 12½ pounds.
79K2424¼—Price, complete.................. $9.98

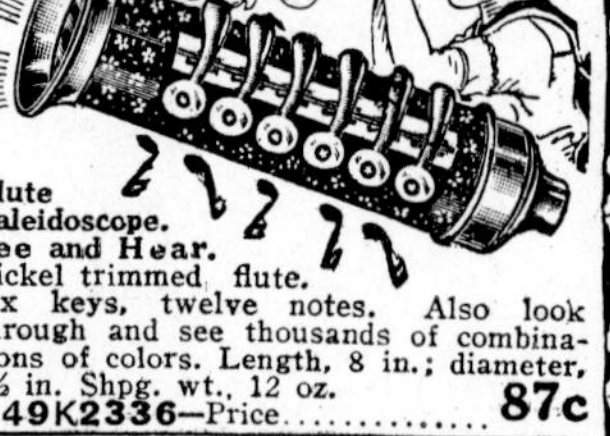

Flute Kaleidoscope. See and Hear. Nickel trimmed flute. Six keys, twelve notes. Also look through and see thousands of combinations of colors. Length, 8 in.; diameter, 2½ in. Shpg. wt., 12 oz.
49K2336—Price............ 87c

Big Combination.

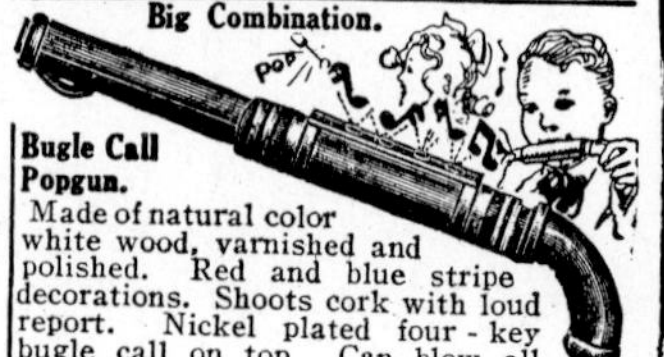

Bugle Call Popgun. Made of natural color white wood, varnished and polished. Red and blue stripe decorations. Shoots cork with loud report. Nickel plated four-key bugle call on top. Can blow all the bugle calls. Length over all, 13½ inches. Shpg. wt., 8 oz.
49K2419—Price............ 39c

Wonderful Mechanical Toys

Automatic Dumping Sandy.
No springs, no wheels, will run as long as sand is kept in hopper. See the sand car load up. When filled it swings around in a big circle and the little man dumps it in the can. All steel enameled. Bright colors. Size 13⅜x12 in. Shpg. wt., 3⅛ pounds.
79K5782¼—Price **$1.19**

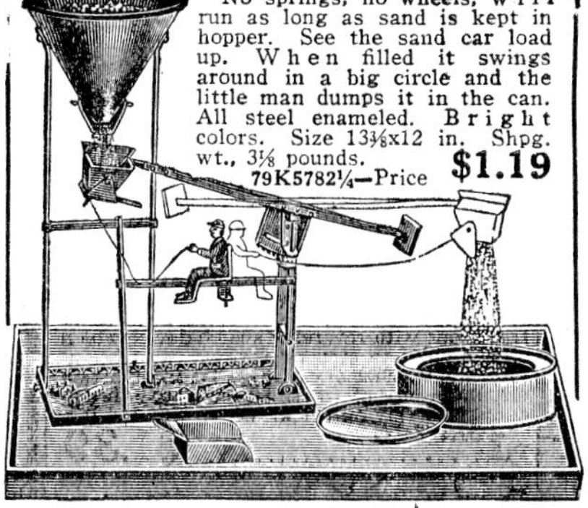

Imported Mechanical Locomotives.

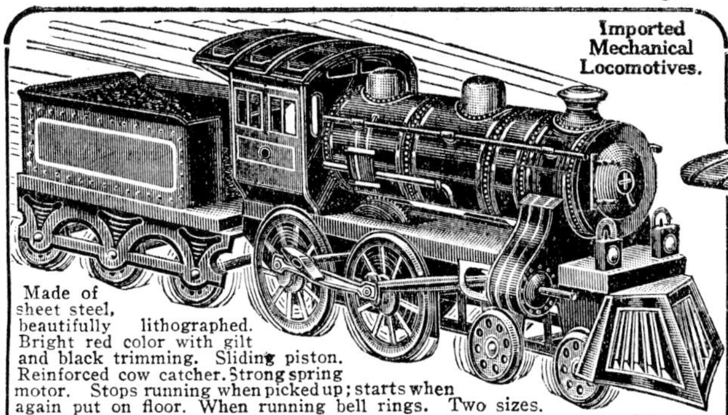

Made of sheet steel, beautifully lithographed. Bright red color with gilt and black trimming. Sliding piston. Reinforced cow catcher. Strong spring motor. Stops running when picked up; starts when again put on floor. When running bell rings. Two sizes.
49K5827—Small. 17¼ inches long. Shpg. wt., 3 lbs. Price **$0.98**
49K5828—Large. 21¼ inches long. Shpg. wt., 4 lbs. Price **1.39**

Mechanical Airplane.

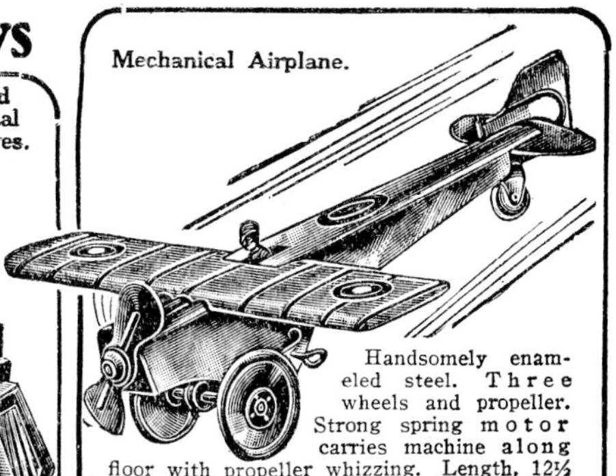

Handsomely enameled steel. Three wheels and propeller. Strong spring motor carries machine along floor with propeller whizzing. Length, 12½ inches. Wing spread, 9⅞ inches, and 3½ inches high. Man's head and shoulders extend from cockpit. Shipping weight, 1 pound.
49K5779—Price **79c**

The Loving Mother.

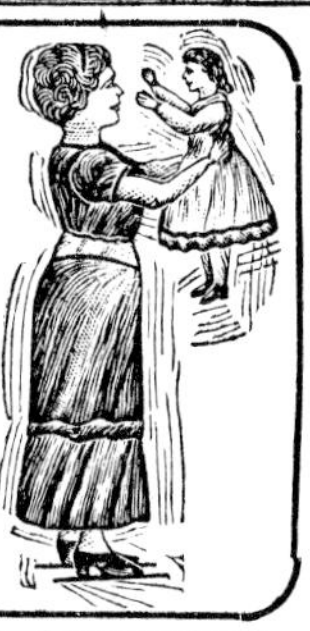

Just as a real mother in an excess of love catches up her little tot from the floor and tosses her in the air or dances around the room with her, so does this clever little metal toy. The only thing the manufacturer left out was the baby talk. Really pretty and has a tremendous appeal. Height over all, 7 inches. Simply wind up and stand on the floor. Shpg. wt., 8 oz.
49K5789 Price **59c**

Famous Alabama Coon Jigger.

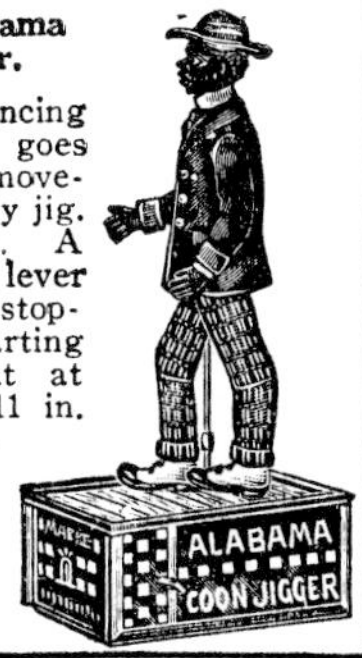

A realistic dancing negro who goes through the movements of a lively jig. Natural colors. A good spring. A lever at side permits stopping and starting the movement at will. Height, 11 in. Shipping weight, 13 ounces.
49K5730 Price, **59c**

Mechanical Pool Player.

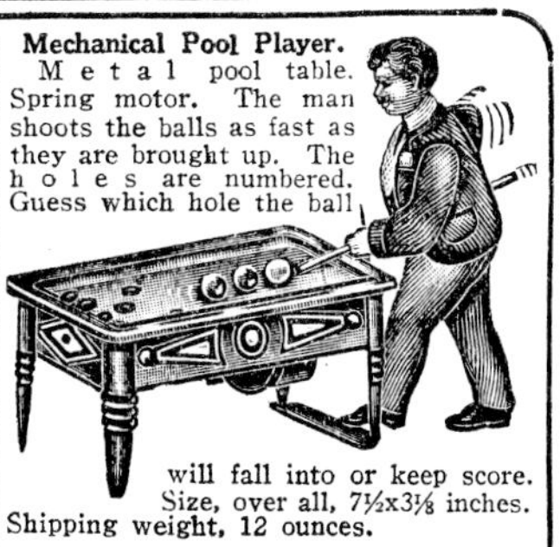

Metal pool table. Spring motor. The man shoots the balls as fast as they are brought up. The holes are numbered. Guess which hole the ball will fall into or keep score. Size, over all, 7½x3⅛ inches. Shipping weight, 12 ounces.
49K5722 Price **67c**

Balky Mule.

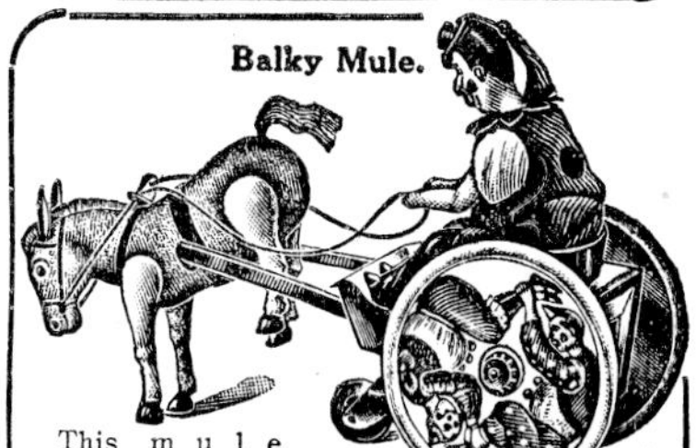

This mule balks, kicks up his heels, backs, whirls and the poor clown is nearly thrown out at every jump. Lifelike gray mule with ears laid back and tail in air. Metal cart decorated in colors, clown dressed in bright colored cloth. Length, 7½ inches; height, 5½ inches. Shpg. wt., 12 oz.
49K5747—Price **42c**

Somersaulting Monkey.

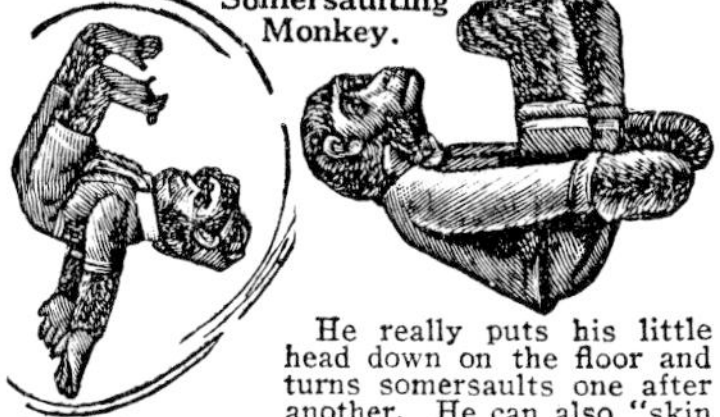

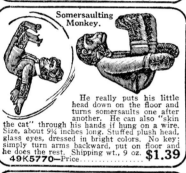

He really puts his little head down on the floor and turns somersaults one after another. He can also "skin the cat" through his hands if hung on a wire. Size, about 9¼ inches long. Stuffed plush head, glass eyes, dressed in bright colors. No key: simply turn arms backward, put on floor and he does the rest. Shipping wt., 9 oz.
49K5770—Price **$1.39**

The Colored Minstrel Boys. **Oh, What Music!**

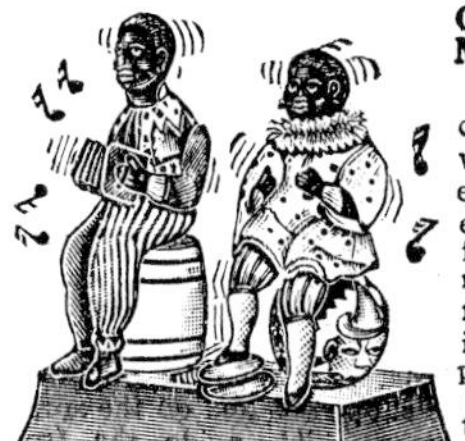

Two coons with the exaggerated head and foot movement of real darkies. One plays the accordion, the other pats time and beats a cymbal with his foot. The music comes from under the platform. Size of base, 8⅝x4½ inches; height, over all, 8¾ inches. Shipping weight, 1½ pounds.
49K5703—Price **$1.39**

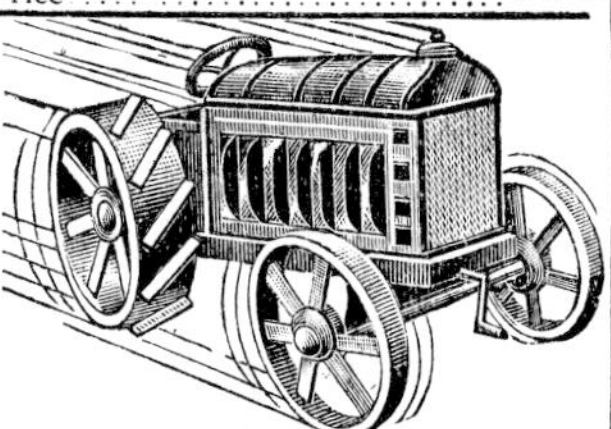

Mechanical Ford Tractor.
Miniature reproduction of the big tractor. Runs along just like a real Ford tractor. Extra strong spring motor. Size, about 5½ inches long over all. Made of metal, lithographed in true colors. Shipping weight, 2 pounds.
49K5752—Price **98c**

Climbing Monkey.

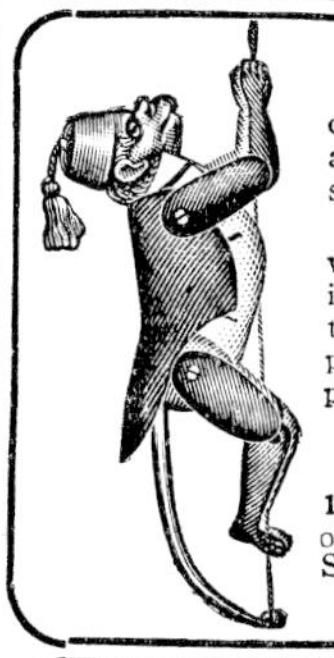

The popular monkey climbing string. Endless amusement. Made in two sizes.
Extra quality. The one we recommend, 9½x4½x2 inches. Red hat with real tassel, blue coat, yellow pants. Shipping weight, 1 pound.
49K5758—Price **21c**
Formerly 25c each—Now 10c. 7¾ inches long. The one formerly carried by us. Shpg. wt., 8 oz.
49K5706—Price **10c**

Kiddo Kar.

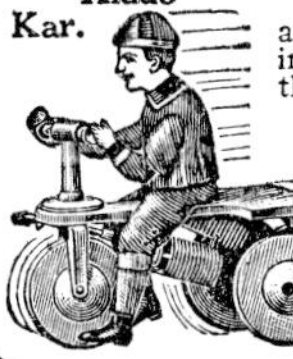

Little metal Kiddo Kar and boy rider. Lithographed in pretty colors. Wind up the strong spring motor and the little boy starts off, pushing the car along with his foot just as in real life. Length over all, 5½ inches; 6 inches high. Shipping weight, 12 ounces.
49K5736 Price **45c**

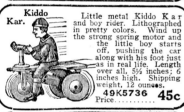

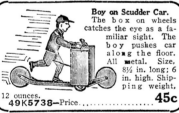

Mechanical Boats.
Actually Run Through Water.

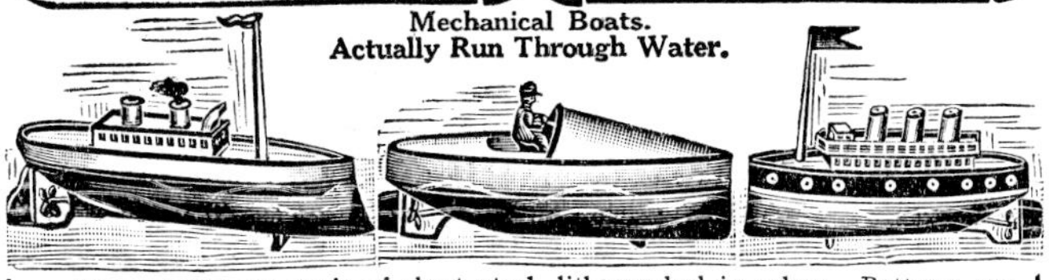

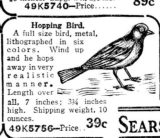

These boats are made of sheet steel, lithographed in colors. Bottoms are watertight.

Superior Quality. Ocean Liner. Guaranteed mechanism. Height to top of funnel, 3 inches; 8 inches long. Two passenger decks. Four-blade propeller. Shipping weight, 1½ pounds.
49K5744—Price **47c**

Large Motor Boat. Length, 10¼ inches. Height, 4 inches. Three-blade propeller. Shipping weight, 1½ pounds.
49K5745 Price **98c**

Big Ocean Liner. Three decks, 3 funnels, 3-blade propeller. Height to top of funnel, 4 in. Length, 8¼ in. Shpg. wt., 1 lb.
49K5743 Price **98c**

Hen and Chick.

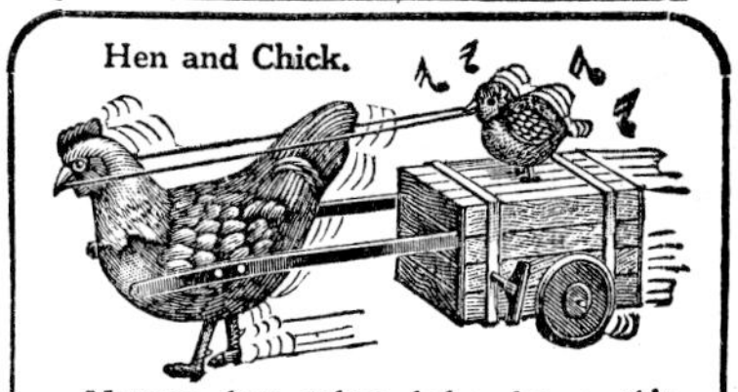

Mamma hen takes baby for a ride. Metal, lithographed in colors. The hen walks. Chick peeps and moves up and down. Length, 8¾ inches. Height, 4 inches. Shipping weight, 1 pound.
49K5718—Price **59c**

Boy on Scudder Car.

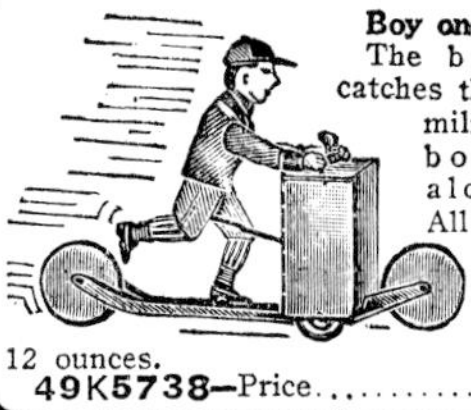

The box on wheels catches the eye as a familiar sight. The boy pushes car along the floor. All metal. Size, 8½ in. long; 6 in. high. Shipping weight, 12 ounces.
49K5738—Price **45c**

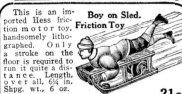

Boy on Sled. Friction Toy

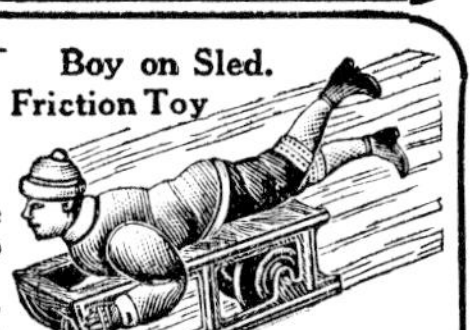

This is an imported Hess friction motor toy, handsomely lithographed. Only a stroke on the floor is required to run it quite a distance. Length, over all, 6¼ in. Shpg. wt., 6 oz.
49K5790—Price **21c**

Marble Conveyor.

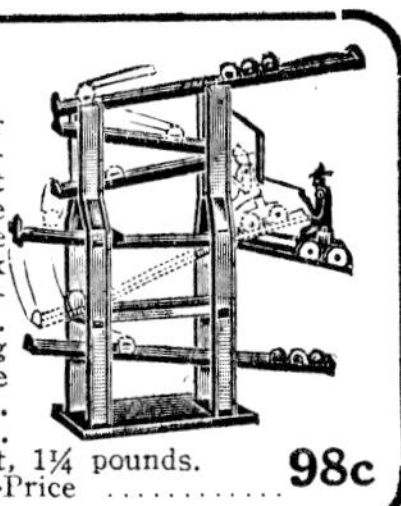

The conveyor carries the marbles down one at a time as the little man on the car drives back and forth opening the draw. Runs as long as marbles are kept in trough. Height, 12½ in. Shipping weight, 1¼ pounds.
49K5764—Price **98c**

Sand Man.

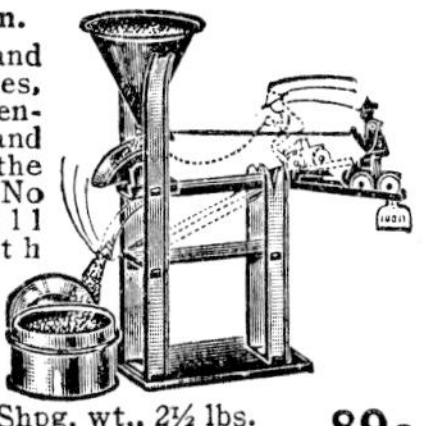

Back and forth he rides, always opening the sand hopper at the right time. No springs. Fill hopper with sand from box. Runs nearly three minutes. Ht., 13 inches. Shpg. wt., 2½ lbs.
49K5740—Price **89c**

Big Red Fire Engine.

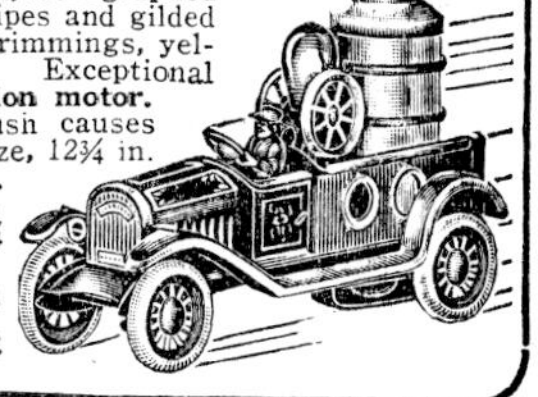

Sheet steel, lithographed red with stripes and gilded border and trimmings, yellow wheels. Exceptional **geared friction motor.** A slight push causes it to run. Size, 12¾ in. long; 8½ in. high. Shpg. weight, 2¼ pounds.
49K5734 Price, each **98c**

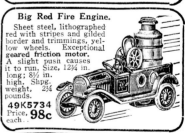

Ferris Wheel.

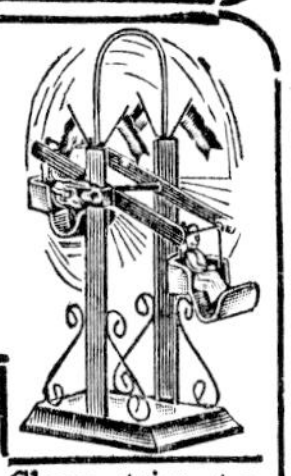

Sandy and his girl, one in each car, go for a ride. Very pretty colors, strong motor. Base, 5¾x4¼ in. Height, 12¾ in. Shpg. wt., 1 lb.
49K5720 Price **67c**

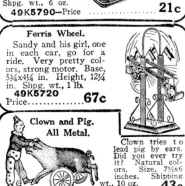

Clown and Pig. All Metal.

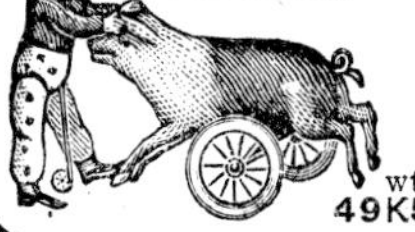

Clown tries to lead pig by ears. Did you ever try it? Natural colors. Size, 7½x6 inches. Shipping wt., 10 oz.
49K5776—Price **43c**

Cat With Fiery Eyes.

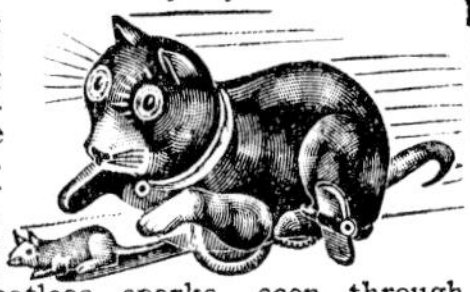

The cat with eyes flashing fire, chases the mouse. Mechanism inside cat's head causes heatless sparks, seen through transparent eyes. Sparks are inside metal head and are harmless. Length, over all, 9¼ inches. Shpg. wt., 12 oz.
49K5793—Price **79c**

Hopping Bird.

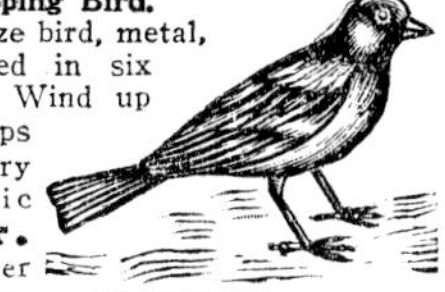

A full size bird, metal, lithographed in six colors. Wind up and he hops away in very realistic manner. Length over all, 7 inches; 3¼ inches high. Shipping weight, 10 ounces.
49K5756—Price **39c**

See Teddy Roller Skate.

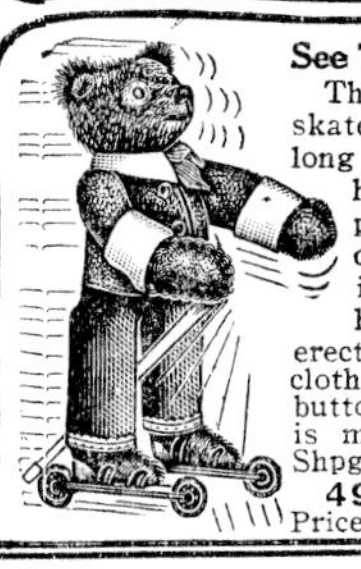

This little bear has roller skates on his feet and a long rubber tipped stick in his hand with which he pushes himself along over the floor. Teddy is about 8¾ inches high when he stands erect. He wears a cute cloth coat and pants, metal button and bow tie. He is made of brown plush. Shpg. wt., 12 oz.
49K5753 Price **$1.39**

Floor Toys for Girls and Boys

Every Child Enjoys Playing Fireman.

Three galloping horses with hook and ladder. Horses made of cast iron. Measure 5½x4⅛ inches over all, two are painted black and the third is white, nicely decorated. Two 10-inch wooden ladders, painted; cast iron cart, painted in four colors. Length over all, about 16 inches. Two men riders. Shipping weight, 4 pounds.
69K7602—Price.............89c

Friction Truck.

A new friction motor with gear connection gives this truck powerful speed. Just give it a push and away it goes. Entire motor encased underneath. Well made of heavy sheet steel and all sharp edges turned in. Prettily painted in attractive colors and trimmed with gilt. Size over all: Length, 13 inches; height, 6¼ inches; width, 4½ inches. Shipping weight, 3 pounds.
79K5825¼—Price.........$1.00

Butterfly on Wheels. Brilliantly Colored.

Lithographed in many pretty colors. Wings of butterfly move up and down as though flying; 9 inches wide. Made of metal; won't break easily. Twisted wire handle, about 20 inches long. Shipping weight, 1⅛ pounds.
49K5459—Price.........45c

Floor Auto.

21c For Baby to Pull.

This is a very substantially built car. Has no motor, but is to be pulled with string. Attractively finished in colors. Iron man included. 7½ inches long. Shipping weight, 1¼ pounds.
49K5001—Price.............21c

Friction Hook and Ladder.

A big outfit and a wonderful new motor. Only a slight push sends it along over the floor. Three detachable ladders. Handsomely lithographed in red with black stripes, gilt trimmed. Length, 12¾ inches, 6¼ inches high. Shipping weight, 2½ lbs.
49K5726—Price.............98c

Just Like a Real Street Roller.

Mechanical Street Roller with extra strong clockwork. Has device on front roller for controlling direction. Movable piston rods. Steam fittings lithographed on boiler. Wind up and see it move slowly over the floor. Steel gray. Measures 9x5x3 inches. Shipping weight, 1½ pounds.
49K5763—Price.........$1.39

Children's "Delight." A Stock Farm With Animals.

What sport for youngsters with this stock farm! They play for hours, opening and closing the sliding doors, putting the animals into the stalls and feeding them imaginary hay and grain. A box of toothpicks makes an ideal rail fence. Old spools, cut in half, and twigs inserted for fence posts and with mother's thread a fence can be built. The barn measures 13¼ inches long, 11⅜ inches high and 9⅜ inches wide over all. In it are nine wooden farm animals, each on small platform. The barn is made of good grade wood, nicely decorated. Roof detachable. Fence materials shown not included. Shipping weight, 7 pounds.
79K8120¼—Price.........98c

SEE THE CARS Pass Each Other.

Two Cars and Long Track. **Track 12 Feet in Circumference.**

Another wonderful imported toy. A long oval track with a siding. Wind up the two cars, place one on the siding and start the other in the opposite direction. It goes around, runs up on the siding and the waiting car starts off in the opposite direction. Automatic. Runs for a long time. Each car lithographed in natural colors. Size of car, 8¼x2⅜x4 inches high. Track, 12 feet in circumference. Shipping weight, complete, 6 pounds.
49K5746—Price....................$2.98

WONDER TRACKLESS TRAIN

With no track to guide it this train runs on the floor in five different figures as shown below.

Small circle, large circle, oval, a combination of figure eights and a number of small circles forming a large circle. Five small lugs, that can easily be slipped on and off the spring shaft by a child, guide the front wheels. Very simple. Engine has guaranteed clockwork motor. Length of engine tender and two cars, 20 in. Shipping weight, 2½ lbs.
49K5124—Price....$1.98

Toy Animals on Platforms See Page 549

$1.39

Every Little Child Wants a Walking Dog. Trots Behind You in a Very Lifelike Manner.

Yes, he will follow you. His little legs may have to trot along pretty fast, but they will keep up. Cute little dog, covered with imitation hair cloth, white with black spots. Has collar and lead string. Certain mechanism in legs causes them to move backward and forward when dog is pulled over floor. No spring and nothing to get out of order. Every little child will surely love this best of all toys. So natural looking and acting. Size of dog, 8 inches long, including stubby tail, and stands about 6½ inches high to tips of ears. Shipping weight, 1 pound.
69K9106 Price.........$1.39

Horses and Wagons.

These three toys will appeal to the child who wants a horse with a wagon large enough for toys and dolls. Wagons made of wood, painted red and varnished; metal wheels. Wood horses on all, 5⅛ inches long and have a wheel under front legs. They are decorated in colors and varnished. Very strong and dependable. Sure to be favorites.

Dray. Loaded with dummy food packages. Horse and dray, 14x5 inches. Shpg. wt., horse and dray, 1¼ lbs.
49K5460 Price.......47c

Dump Cart. Horse and cart, 12¾x5 inches. Shipping weight, horse and cart, 1 pound.
49K5464....35c

Milk Wagon. Loaded with four tin cans. Horse and wagon, 14x5 inches. Shipping weight, 1¼ lbs.
49K5461....59c

Automatically Reverses.

Mechanical street car, true in shape and coloring, on curved track. Eight sections of track, one with reversing switch device which allows child to stop or reverse car without touching it. Size of car, 8¼x3½ in. Outside circumference of track, 82 in. Car is heavy enough to stay on track. Shpg. wt., 1½ lbs.
49K5750—Price.............$1.39

Mechanical Street Car.

Nicely colored lithographed street car that runs around on circular track. Size of car, 6⅜x3⅜x2 inches. Good quality spring and a stop and start device on the side of car. Track measures over 4 feet in circumference. Shipping weight, 1 pound.
49K5735—Price.............69c

Jumping Dog.

Toy French poodle imported from France. Soft black fur. Height, 4¾ in. Length, about 6½ inches. Fitted with rubber bulb and tube. Slight pressure on bulb causes dog to jump. Baby will love him. A good little toy and very strong. Shpg. wt., 6 oz.
49K5772—Price.............59c

Low Priced Roller Chime.

Your baby wants this. A chime to pull over the floor and as it rolls along a continuous tinkling sound is heard. Diameter of wood wheel, 5 inches. Colored pictures on barrel, wire handle. Shpg. wt., 1 lb.
49K2406 Price, 39c

Open Door and Hear the Rooster Crow.

A dandy for parties or to amuse babies. Children will play for hours with this toy. Rooster substantially made to look like a real one with pretty feather on body and tail; red felt comb. Set on a platform with spring wire legs. Turn door latch and rooster will throw the door open, at the same time crow in a very natural manner, swinging back and forth on his wire legs. Cage is wood, about ¾ inch thick, well made and finished. Imitation tile roof and brick sides. Strong metal hinges. Fancy scroll at top. Size, 8⅝ inches high, 7¼ inches wide by 6⅝ inches deep. Shpg. wt., 1¼ lbs.
69K8111—Price.............79c

Wiggle Doggie.

A great big toy dog, made of wood, on wheels. Pull him along and see him wag his tail. Stained brown. Leather ears. Length over all, 22¾ inches. Decorated in colors. A big value. Shipping weight, 1¼ pounds.
49K5475—Price.............59c

All Steel Red Wagon.

Plenty big for the little toddler to pull his toys around. The front wheels turn under the wagon just like on larger wagons. Size of wagon bed, 10¼x6¼ inches. Enameled red. Twisted wire handle. Shipping weight 1¼ lbs.
49K5457 Price, 29c

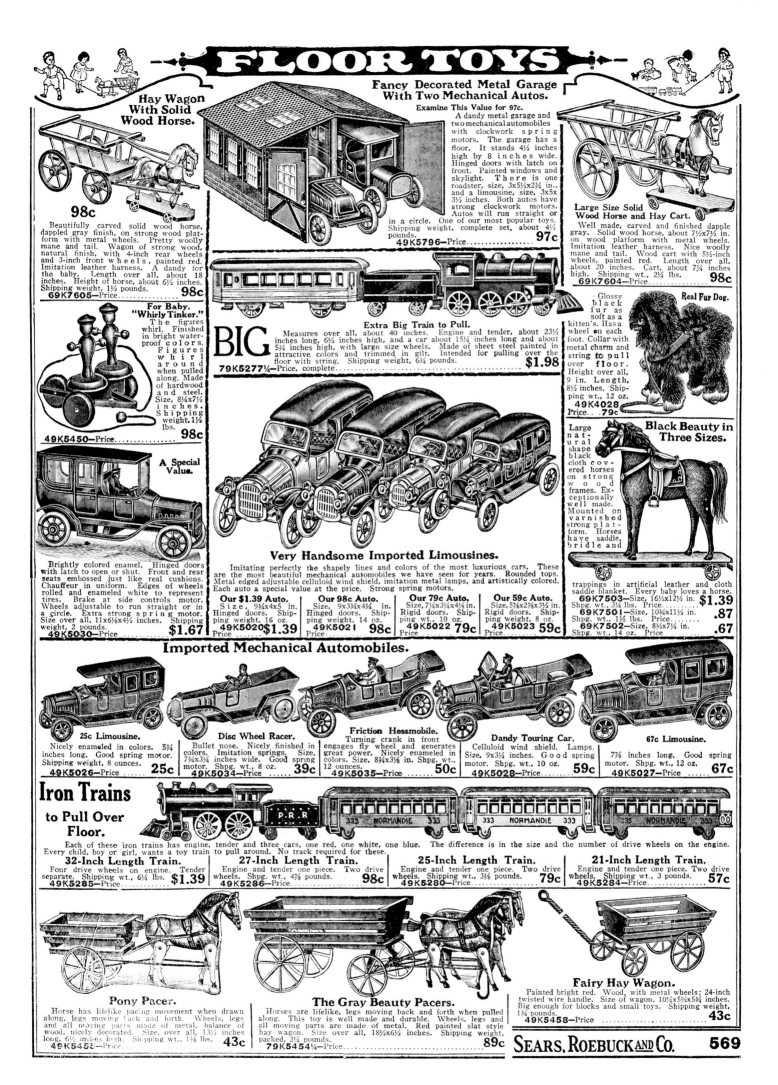

FLOOR TOYS

Hay Wagon With Solid Wood Horse.

98c

Beautifully carved solid wood horse, dappled gray finish, on strong wood platform with metal wheels. Pretty woolly mane and tail. Wagon of strong wood, natural finish, with 4-inch rear wheels and 3-inch front wheels, painted red. Imitation leather harness. A dandy for the baby. Length over all, about 18 inches. Height of horse, about 6½ inches. Shipping weight, 1½ pounds.
69K7605—Price................ **98c**

Fancy Decorated Metal Garage With Two Mechanical Autos.

Examine This Value for 97c.

A dandy metal garage and two mechanical automobiles with clockwork spring motors. The garage has a floor. It stands 4½ inches high by 8 inches wide. Hinged doors with latch on front. Painted windows and skylight. There is one roadster, size, 3x5½x2¾ in., and a limousine, size, 3x5x3½ inches. Both autos have strong clockwork motors. Autos will run straight or in a circle. One of our most popular toys. Shipping weight, complete set, about 4½ pounds.
49K5796—Price.................. **97c**

Large Size Solid Wood Horse and Hay Cart.

Well made, carved and finished dapple gray. Solid wood horse, about 7½x7½ in. on wood platform with metal wheels. Imitation leather harness. Nice woolly mane and tail. Wood cart with 5½-inch wheels, painted red. Length over all, about 20 inches. Cart, about 7¼ inches high. Shipping wt., 2¼ lbs.
69K7604—Price.................. **98c**

BIG Extra Big Train to Pull.

Measures over all, about 40 inches. Engine and tender, about 23½ inches long, 6½ inches high, and a car about 15¼ inches long and about 5¾ inches high, with large size wheels. Made of sheet steel painted in attractive colors and trimmed in gilt. Intended for pulling over the floor with string. Shipping weight, 6¾ pounds.
79K5277¼—Price, complete.. **$1.98**

Real Fur Dog.

Glossy black fur as soft as a kitten's. Has a wheel on each foot. Collar with metal charm and string to pull over floor. Height over all, 9 in. Length, 8½ inches. Shipping wt., 12 oz.
49K4028
Price.. **.79c**

For Baby. "Whirly Tinker."

The figures whirl. Finished in bright waterproof colors. Figures whirl around when pulled along. Made of hardwood and steel. Size, 8¾x7½ inches. Shipping weight, 1½ lbs.
49K5450—Price.................. **98c**

Very Handsome Imported Limousines.

Imitating perfectly the shapely lines and colors of the most luxurious cars. These are the most beautiful mechanical automobiles we have seen for years. Rounded tops. Metal edged adjustable celluloid wind shield, imitation metal lamps, and artistically colored. Each auto a special value at the price. Strong spring motors.

Our $1.39 Auto. Size, 9¾x4x5 in. Hinged doors. Shipping weight, 16 oz.
49K5020 Price **$1.39**

Our 98c Auto. Size, 9x3¾x4¾ in. Hinged doors. Shipping weight, 14 oz.
49K5021 Price **98c**

Our 79c Auto. Size, 7¼x3¼x4⅛ in. Rigid doors. Shipping wt., 10 oz.
49K5022 Price **79c**

Our 59c Auto. Size, 5⅞x2⅞x3½ in. Rigid doors. Shipping weight, 8 oz.
49K5023 Price **59c**

A Special Value.

Brightly colored enamel. Hinged doors with latch to open or shut. Front and rear seats embossed just like real cushions. Chauffeur in uniform. Edges of wheels rolled and enameled white to represent tires. Brake at side controls motor. Wheels adjustable to run straight or in a circle. Extra strong spring motor. Size over all, 11x6⅛x4½ inches. Shipping weight, 2 pounds.
49K5030—Price **$1.67**

Black Beauty in Three Sizes.

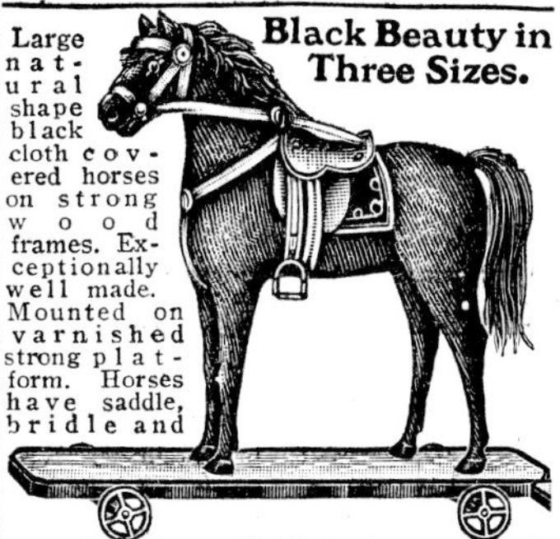

Large natural shape black cloth covered horses on strong wood frames. Exceptionally well made. Mounted on varnished strong platform. Horses have saddle, bridle and trappings in artificial leather and cloth saddle blanket. Every baby loves a horse.
69K7503—Size, 16½x12½ in. Shpg. wt., 3¼ lbs. Price......... **$1.39**
69K7501—Size, 10¾x11½ in. Shpg. wt., 1¾ lbs. Price......... **.87**
69K7502—Size, 8½x7½ in. Shpg. wt., 14 oz. Price......... **.67**

Imported Mechanical Automobiles.

25c Limousine.
Nicely enameled in colors. 5¾ inches long. Good spring motor. Shipping weight, 8 ounces.
49K5026—Price **25c**

Disc Wheel Racer.
Bullet nose. Nicely finished in colors. Imitation springs. Size, 7¾x3¼ inches wide. Good spring motor. Shpg. wt., 8 oz.
49K5034—Price **39c**

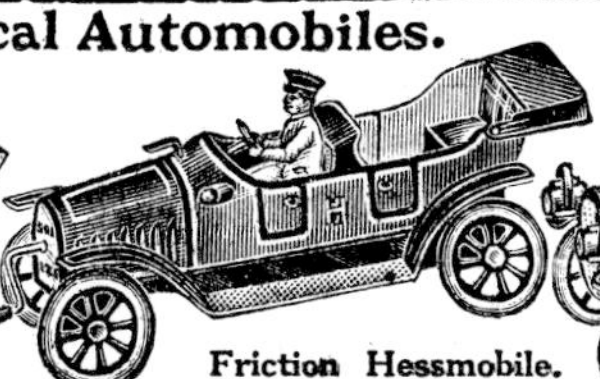

Friction Hessmobile.
Turning crank in front engages fly wheel and generates great power. Nicely enameled in colors. Size, 8¾x3⅛ in. Shpg. wt., 12 ounces.
49K5035—Price **50c**

Dandy Touring Car.
Celluloid wind shield. Lamps. Size, 9x3¼ inches. Good spring motor. Shpg. wt., 10 oz.
49K5028—Price......... **59c**

67c Limousine.
7⅞ inches long. Good spring motor. Shpg. wt., 12 oz.
49K5027—Price **67c**

Iron Trains to Pull Over Floor.

Each of these iron trains has engine, tender and three cars, one red, one white, one blue. The difference is in the size and the number of drive wheels on the engine. Every child, boy or girl, wants a toy train to pull around. No track required for these.

32-Inch Length Train.
Four drive wheels on engine. Tender separate. Shipping wt., 6¼ lbs.
49K5285—Price........ **$1.39**

27-Inch Length Train.
Engine and tender one piece. Two drive wheels. Shpg. wt., 4⅞ pounds.
49K5286—Price..................... **98c**

25-Inch Length Train.
Engine and tender one piece. Two drive wheels. Shipping wt., 3⅜ pounds.
49K5280—Price............................ **79c**

21-Inch Length Train.
Engine and tender one piece. Two drive wheels. Shipping wt., 3 pounds.
49K5284—Price........................ **57c**

Pony Pacer.

Horse has lifelike pacing movement when drawn along, legs moving back and forth. Wheels, legs and all moving parts made of metal, balance of wood, nicely decorated. Size, over all, 13½ inches long, 6½ inches high. Shipping wt., 1⅜ lbs.
49K5455—Price...... **43c**

The Gray Beauty Pacers.

Horses are lifelike, legs moving back and forth when pulled along. This toy is well made and durable. Wheels, legs and all moving parts are made of metal. Red painted slat style hay wagon. Size over all, 18½x6½ inches. Shipping weight, packed, 2¼ pounds.
79K5454¼—Price.. **89c**

Fairy Hay Wagon.

Painted bright red. Wood, with metal wheels; 24-inch twisted wire handle. Size of wagon, 10½x5½x5¾ inches. Big enough for blocks and small toys. Shipping weight, 1¾ pounds.
49K5458—Price **43c**

CONSTRUCTION TOYS

Erector

With only Erector can be built the sturdy square girders. The gears, pulleys, angle irons and other Erector parts are true models. The boy can build the framework of miniature skyscrapers, drawbridges and thousands of things too numerous to mention. Big illustrated book with each outfit.

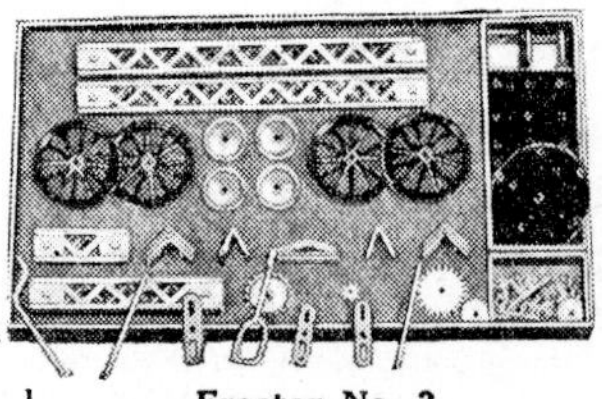

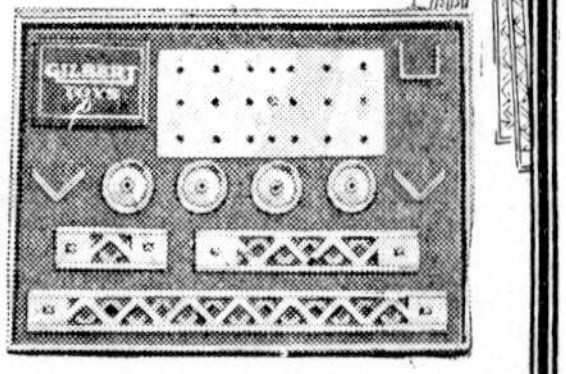

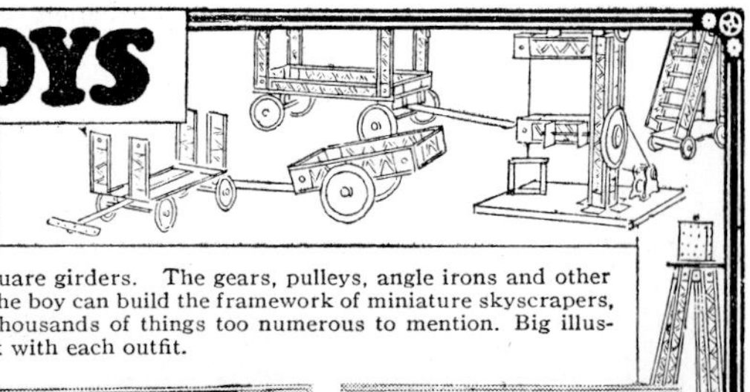

Erector No. 7.
Makes about 400 wonderful models and the many pieces furnished permit extended original work. This set includes an assembled electric motor with reversing and speed control attachments. Packed in stained wood cabinet with hinged cover and tray. Size, 17x10x3 inches. Shipping weight, about 11 pounds.
79K4716¼—Price........................ **$8.98**

$4.47, Was $8.98 Last Year.
This set was Erector No. 6 last year. It is now known as No. 4, and builds about 380 models. The set that made Erector famous. Packed with powerful electric motor, ready assembled in wood box. Size, 22x8¼x3 inches. Shipping weight, 7 pounds.
79K4720¼—Price.............. **$4.47**

Erector No. 3.
Builds about 200 models. Comes in strong sealed carton with cover illustrated in colors. Size of box, 18x10x1¼ inches. Shipping weight, 4 pounds.
49K4715—Price.... **$2.19**

Erector No. 1.
Builds more than 100 models. Comes in strong sealed carton with cover. Illustrated in colors. Size of box, 12¼x8½x1¼ inches. Shipping wt., 1 lb. 10 oz.
49K4717—Price.... **89c**

Meccano

Meccano parts are all standardized and interchangeable. The steel parts are heavily coated with nickel and the brass parts are finely finished and lacquered. With these parts any boy can build all the hundreds of models shown in the Meccano literature, and make them work, and this without previous knowledge or study. He can build cranes, wagons, bridges, towers, etc., using the same parts over and over again. A well illustrated book of instructions is furnished. No Meccano boy is content to build the models just as he finds them; he very soon commences to invent new models and designs. Knowing the value of this, The Meccano Company gives him encouragement by offering prizes for new models.

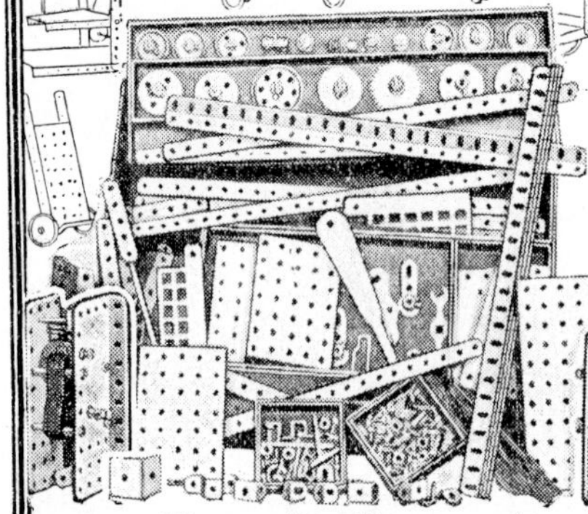

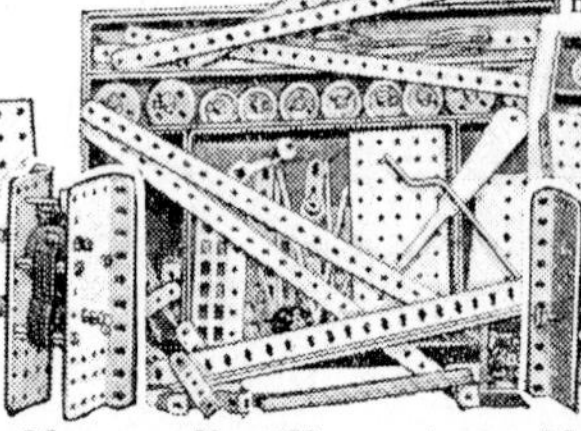

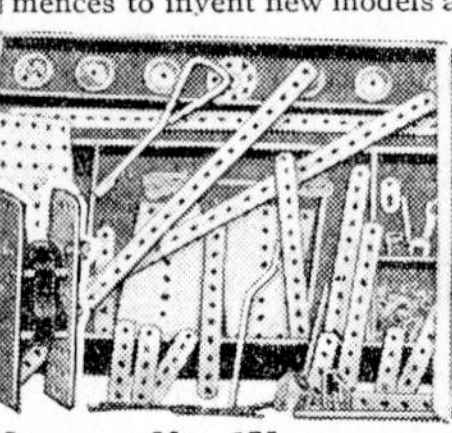

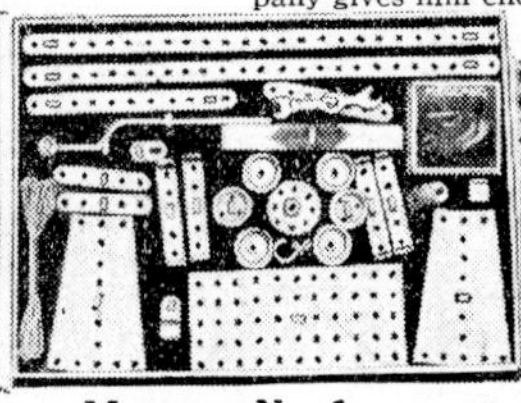

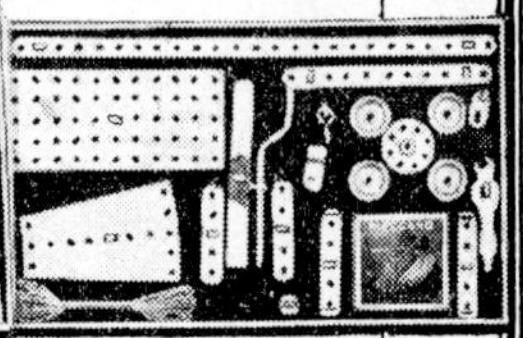

Meccano No. 3X.
With reversing electric motor. Builds 196 major models, including band saw, lawn swing, pile driver, etc. Box, 13⅜x10¾x2¼ in. Shpg. wt., 7¾ lbs.
79K4723¼—Price..... **$10.67**

Meccano No. 2X.
With reversing electric motor. Builds over 151 major models. Box, 13x9⅛x2¼ inches. Shipping weight, 6½ lbs.
49K4722—Price. **$7.89**

Meccano No. 1X.
Has one way electric motor. Otherwise same as No. 1 set. Box, 12⅞x9⅛x2¼ inches. Shipping weight, 4⅝ inches.
49K4721—Price. **$4.59**

Meccano No. 1.
Can make 105 major models. Box, 15¾x10¾x1 inch. Shipping weight, 3½ lbs.
49K4726—Price. **$2.79**

Meccano No. 0.
Builds 78 major models. Box, 13x8x1 inch. Shipping weight, 2⅛ pounds.
49K4725—Price. **$1.37**

Steel Engineering

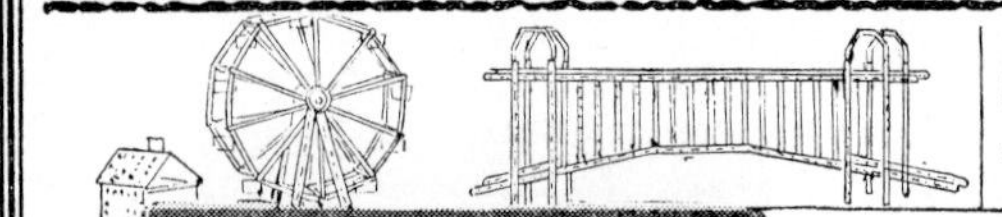

This is the new construction toy with black enameled steel strips and plates and nickel plated steel pulleys, angles, etc. The strips have round and oblong holes which permit of a very exact construction. Fine illustrated manual with each set. These outfits offered at remarkably low prices to introduce them.

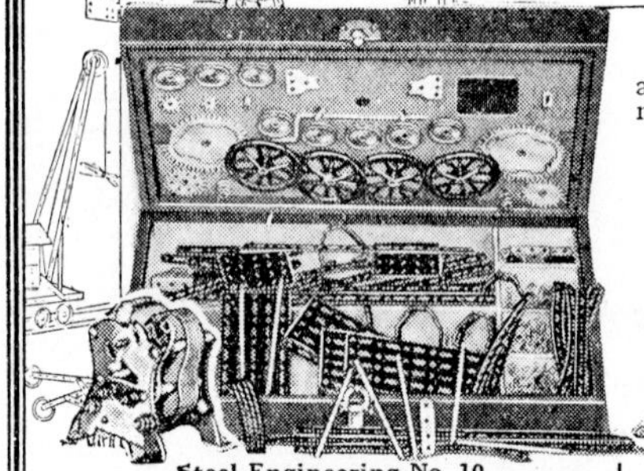

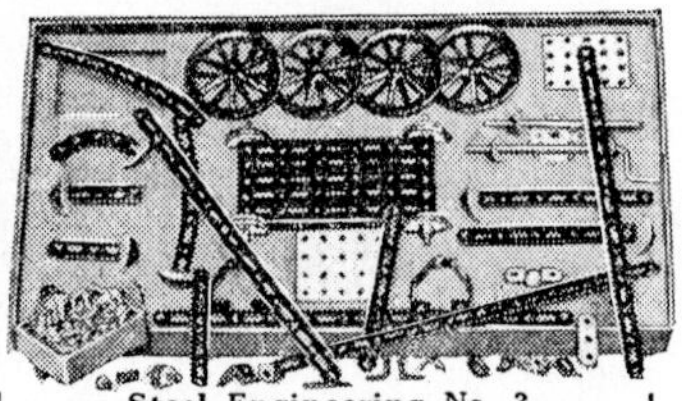

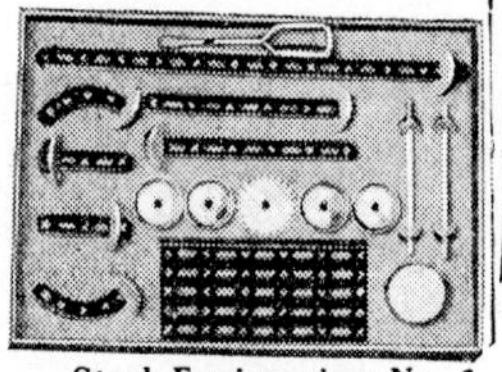

Steel Engineering No. 10.
Makes about 400 models. Equipped with electric motor with reversing base. Packed in stained wood cabinet with hinged cover. Size, 17x10x3 in. Shipping weight, 10½ pounds.
79K4703¼—Price............ **$8.98**

Steel Engineering No. 5.
Makes about 300 models. Equipped with electric motor which can be built right into the model. Size, 10x18x2½ inches. Shipping weight, about 5 pounds.
79K4702¼—Price........ **$4.47**

Steel Engineering No. 3
Has a nice assortment of small parts to make about 150 models. Size, 10x18x1⅜ in. Shpg. wt., 2¾ lbs.
49K4701—Price...... **$2.79**

Steel Engineering No. 1
Enough parts to make about 75 models. Manual of instructions included. Size, 8½x12x1⅛ inches. Shipping weight, 2 pounds.
49K4700—Price........ **89c**

Tinker Toy

The Popular Wood Construction Toy.

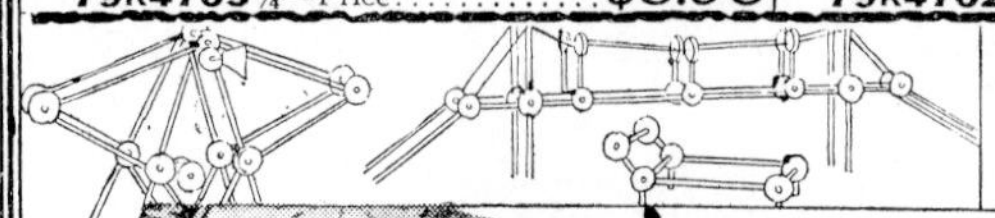

Tinker Toy is the Wonder Builder. An educational, interesting and amusing toy for any child. With one or more sets you can build any of the toy models shown, together with many others. This toy is based on the old adage that "a stick and a spool will amuse a child." Each set consists of about seventy pieces of white wood, as illustrated. In building movable toys, such as windmill, Ferris wheel, merry-go-round, etc., if the motor listed at right is purchased, all these models can be run by it. This motor will run on two dry cells.

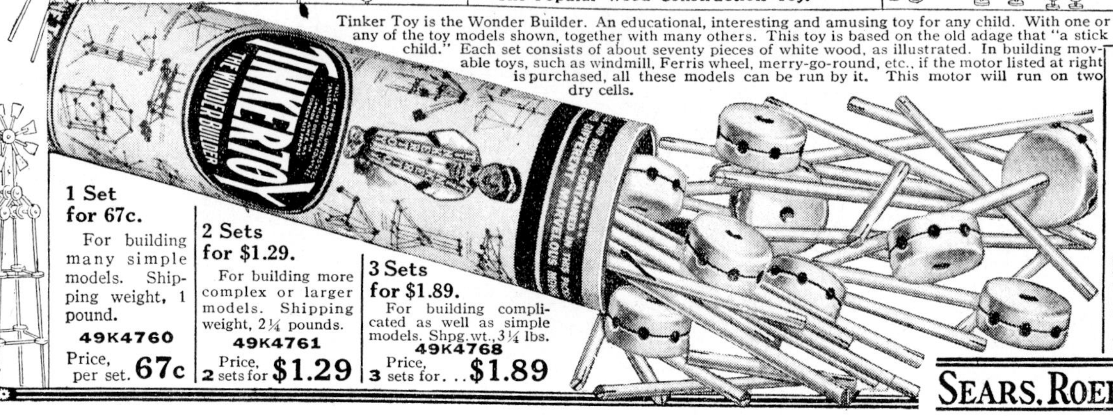

1 Set for 67c.
For building many simple models. Shipping weight, 1 pound.
49K4760
Price, per set. **67c**

2 Sets for $1.29.
For building more complex or larger models. Shipping weight, 2¼ pounds.
49K4761
Price, 2 sets for **$1.29**

3 Sets for $1.89.
For building complicated as well as simple models. Shpg. wt., 3¼ lbs.
49K4768
Price, 3 sets for... **$1.89**

Combination Horseshoe Magnet and Motor.

For Tinker Toy models and small toys. Will run on small flash light battery. Size, 3½ inches. Mounted on wood base. Shipping weight, 14 oz.
69K5939
Price............ **47c**

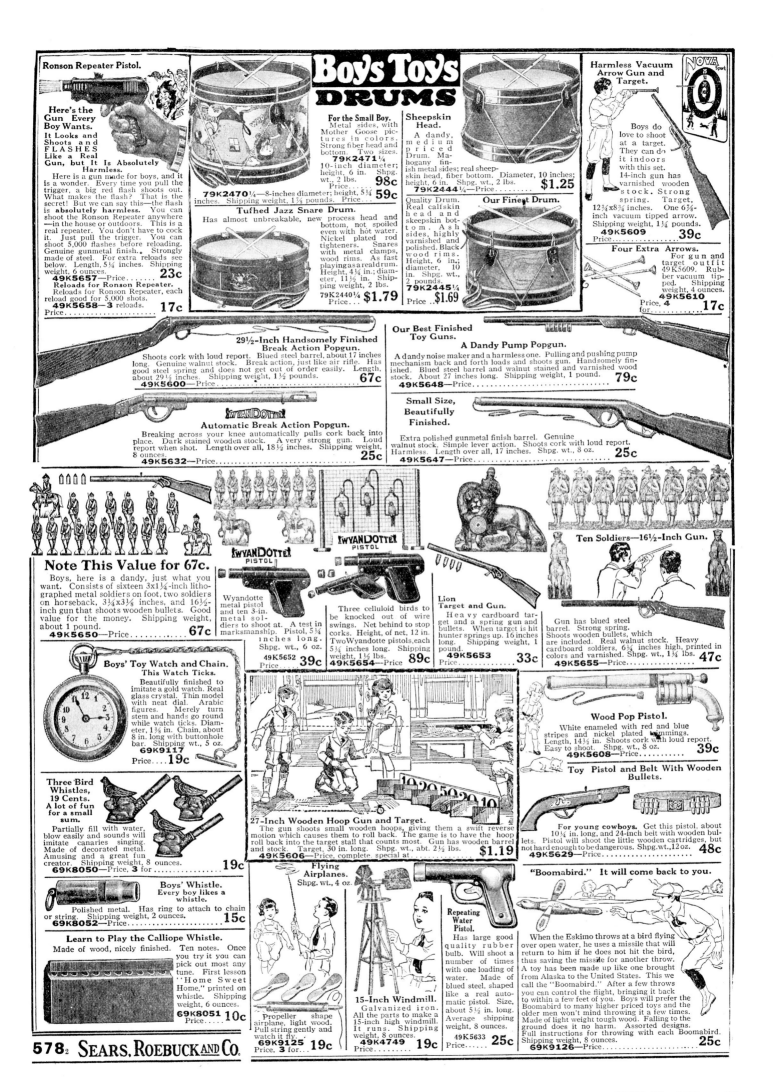

Boys Toys DRUMS

Ronson Repeater Pistol.

Here's the Gun Every Boy Wants. It Looks and Shoots and FLASHES Like a Real Gun, but It Is Absolutely Harmless.

Here is a gun made for boys, and it is a wonder. Every time you pull the trigger, a big red flash shoots out. What makes the flash? That is the secret! But we can say this—the flash is absolutely harmless. You can shoot the Ronson Repeater anywhere—in the house or outdoors. This is a real repeater. You don't have to cock it. Just pull the trigger. You can shoot 5,000 flashes before reloading. Genuine gunmetal finish. Strongly made of steel. For extra reloads see below. Length, 5¼ inches. Shipping weight, 6 ounces.

49K5657—Price. **23c**

Reloads for Ronson Repeater. Reloads for Ronson Repeater, each reload good for 5,000 shots.

49K5658—3 reloads. Price. **17c**

For the Small Boy.
Metal sides, with Mother Goose pictures in colors. Strong fiber head and bottom. Two sizes.

79K2471¼ 10-inch diameter; height, 6 in. Shpg. wt., 2 lbs. Price. **98c**

79K2470¼—8-inches diameter; height, 5¼ inches. Shipping weight, 1¾ pounds. Price. **59c**

Tufhed Jazz Snare Drum.
Has almost unbreakable, new process head and bottom, not spoiled even with hot water. Nickel plated rod tighteners. Snares with metal clamps, wood rims. As fast playing as a real drum. Height, 4¼ in.; diameter, 11½ in. Shipping weight, 2 lbs.

79K2440¼ Price. **$1.79**

Sheepskin Head.
A dandy, medium priced Drum. Mahogany finish metal sides; real sheepskin head, fiber bottom. Diameter, 10 inches; height, 6 in. Shpg. wt., 2 lbs.

79K2444¼—Price. **$1.25**

Our Finest Drum.
Quality Drum. Real calfskin head and skeepskin bottom. Ash sides, highly varnished and polished. Black wood rims. Height, 6 in.; diameter, 10 in. Shpg. wt., 2 pounds.

79K2445¼ Price. **$1.69**

Harmless Vacuum Arrow Gun and Target.

Boys do love to shoot at a target. They can do it indoors with this set. 14-inch gun has varnished wooden stock. Strong spring. Target, 12¾x8¾ inches. One 6⅞-inch vacuum tipped arrow. Shipping weight, 1¼ lbs.

49K5609 Price. **39c**

Four Extra Arrows.
For gun and target outfit 49K5609. Rubber vacuum tipped. Shipping weight, 4 ounces.

49K5610 Price, 4 for. **17c**

29½-Inch Handsomely Finished Break Action Popgun.
Shoots cork with loud report. Blued steel barrel, about 17 inches long. Genuine walnut stock. Break action, just like air rifle. Has good steel spring and does not get out of order easily. Length, about 29½ inches. Shipping weight, 1½ pounds.

49K5600—Price. **67c**

Automatic Break Action Popgun.
Breaking across your knee automatically pulls cork back into place. Dark stained wooden stock. A very strong gun. Loud report when shot. Length over all, 18½ inches. Shipping weight, 8 ounces.

49K5632—Price. **25c**

Our Best Finished Toy Guns.
A Dandy Pump Popgun.
A dandy noise maker and a harmless one. Pulling and pushing pump mechanism back and forth loads and shoots gun. Handsomely finished. Blued steel barrel and walnut stained and varnished wood stock. About 27 inches long. Shipping weight, 1 pound.

49K5648—Price. **79c**

Small Size, Beautifully Finished.
Extra polished gunmetal finish barrel. Genuine walnut stock. Simple lever action. Shoots cork with loud report. Harmless. Length over all, 17 inches. Shpg. wt., 8 oz.

49K5647—Price. **25c**

Note This Value for 67c.
Boys, here is a dandy, just what you want. Consists of sixteen 3x1¼-inch lithographed metal soldiers on foot, two soldiers on horseback, 3¼x3⅛ inches, and 16½-inch gun that shoots wooden bullets. Good value for the money. Shipping weight, about 1 pound.

49K5650—Price. **67c**

Wyandotte
metal pistol and ten 3-in. metal soldiers to shoot at. A test in marksmanship. Pistol, 5¼ inches long. Shpg. wt., 6 oz.

49K5652 Price. **39c**

Three celluloid birds to be knocked out of wire swings. Net behind to stop corks. Height, of net, 12 in. Two Wyandotte pistols, each 5¼ inches long. Shipping weight, 1½ lbs.

49K5654—Price **89c**

Lion Target and Gun.
Heavy cardboard target and a spring gun and bullets. When target is hit hunter springs up. 16 inches long. Shipping weight, 1 pound.

49K5653 Price. **33c**

Ten Soldiers—16½-Inch Gun.
Gun has blued steel barrel. Strong spring. Shoots wooden bullets, which are included. Real walnut stock. Heavy cardboard soldiers, 6¼ inches high, printed in colors and varnished. Shpg. wt., 1¼ lbs.

49K5655—Price. **47c**

Boys' Toy Watch and Chain.
This Watch Ticks.
Beautifully finished to imitate a gold watch. Real glass crystal. Thin model with neat dial. Arabic figures. Merely turn stem and hands go round while watch ticks. Diameter, 1¾ in. Chain, about 8 in. long with buttonhole bar. Shipping wt., 5 oz.

69K9117 Price. **19c**

Three Bird Whistles, 19 Cents. A lot of fun for a small sum.
Partially fill with water, blow easily and sounds will imitate canaries singing. Made of decorated metal. Amusing and a great fun creator. Shipping weight, 8 ounces.

69K8050—Price, 3 for. **19c**

Boys' Whistle.
Every boy likes a whistle.
Polished metal. Has ring to attach to chain or string. Shipping weight, 2 ounces.

69K8052—Price. **15c**

Learn to Play the Calliope Whistle.
Made of wood, nicely finished. Ten notes. Once you try it you can pick out most any tune. First lesson "Home Sweet Home," printed on whistle. Shipping weight, 6 ounces.

69K8051 Price. **10c**

27-Inch Wooden Hoop Gun and Target.
The gun shoots small wooden hoops, giving them a swift reverse motion which causes them to roll back. The game is to have the hoop roll back into the target stall that counts most. Gun has wooden barrel and stock. Target, 30 in. long. Shpg. wt., abt 2½ lbs.

49K5606—Price, complete, special at. **$1.19**

Flying Airplanes.
Shpg. wt., 4 oz.

69K9125 Price, 3 for. **19c**

15-Inch Windmill.
Galvanized iron. All the parts to make a 15-inch high windmill. It runs. Shipping weight, 8 ounces.

49K4749 Price. **19c**

Repeating Water Pistol.
Has large good quality rubber bulb. Will shoot a number of times with one loading of water. Made of blued steel, shaped like a real automatic pistol. Size, about 5½ in. long. Average shipping weight, 8 ounces.

49K5633 Price. **25c**

Wood Pop Pistol.
White enameled with red and blue stripes and nickel plated trimmings. Length, 14½ in. Shoots cork with loud report. Easy to shoot. Shpg. wt., 8 oz.

49K5608—Price. **39c**

Toy Pistol and Belt With Wooden Bullets.
For young cowboys. Get this pistol, about 10¼ in. long, and 24-inch belt with wooden bullets. Pistol will shoot the little wooden cartridges, but not hard enough to be dangerous. Shpg. wt., 12 oz.

49K5629—Price. **48c**

"Boomabird." It will come back to you.
When the Eskimo throws at a bird flying over open water, he uses a missile that will return to him if he does not hit the bird, thus saving the missile for another throw. A toy has been made up like one brought from Alaska to the United States. This we call the "Boomabird." After a few throws you can control the flight, bringing it back to within a few feet of you. Boys will prefer the Boomabird to many higher priced toys and the older men won't mind throwing it a few times. Made of light weight tough wood. Falling to the ground does it no harm. Assorted designs. Full instructions for throwing with each Boomabird. Shipping weight, 8 ounces.

69K9126—Price. **25c**

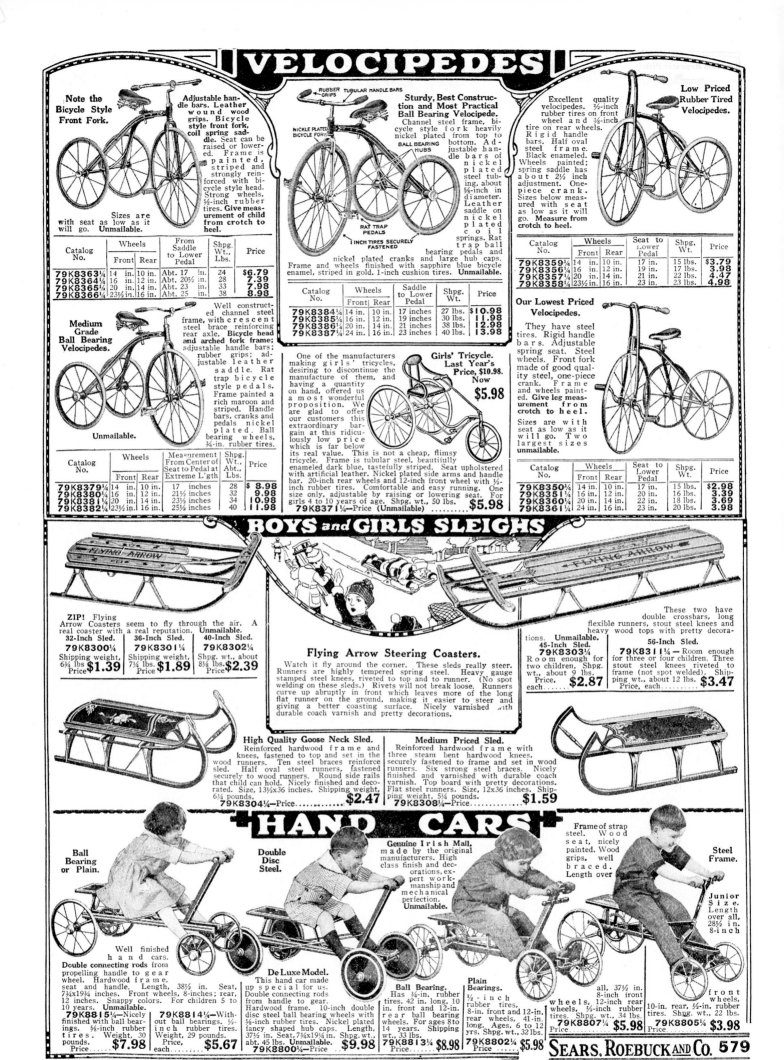

VELOCIPEDES

Note the Bicycle Style Front Fork. Adjustable handle bars. Leather wound wood grips. Bicycle style front fork, coil spring saddle. Seat can be raised or lowered. Frame is painted, striped and strongly reinforced with bicycle style head. Strong wheels. ⅝-inch rubber tires. Give measurement of child from crotch to heel. Unmailable. Sizes are with seat as low as it will go. Unmailable.

Catalog No.	Wheels		From Saddle to Lower Pedal	Shpg. Wt., Lbs.	Price
	Front	Rear			
79K8363¼	14 in.	10 in.	Abt. 17 in.	24	$6.79
79K8364¼	16 in.	12 in.	Abt. 20½ in.	28	7.39
79K8365¼	20 in.	14 in.	Abt. 23 in.	33	7.98
79K8366¼	23½ in.	16 in.	Abt. 25 in.	38	8.98

Sturdy, Best Construction and Most Practical Ball Bearing Velocipede. Channel steel frame, bicycle style fork heavily nickel plated from top to bottom. Adjustable handle bars of nickel plated steel tubing, about ⅝-inch in diameter. Leather saddle on nickel plated coil springs. Rat trap ball bearing pedals and nickel plated cranks and large hub caps. Frame and wheels finished with sapphire blue bicycle enamel, striped in gold. 1-inch cushion tires. Unmailable.

RUBBER TUBULAR HANDLE BARS. NICKLE PLATED BICYCLE FORK. BALL BEARING HUBS. RAT TRAP PEDALS. 1 INCH TIRES SECURELY FASTENED.

Catalog No.	Wheels		Saddle to Lower Pedal	Shpg. Wt.	Price
	Front	Rear			
79K8384¼	14 in.	10 in.	17 inches	27 lbs.	$10.98
79K8385¼	16 in.	12 in.	19 inches	30 lbs.	11.98
79K8386¼	20 in.	14 in.	21 inches	38 lbs.	12.98
79K8387¼	24 in.	16 in.	23 inches	40 lbs.	13.98

Excellent quality velocipedes. ½-inch rubber tires on front wheel and ⅜-inch tire on rear wheels. Rigid handle bars. Half oval steel frame. Black enameled. Wheels painted; spring saddle has about 2½ inch adjustment. One-piece crank. Sizes below measured with seat as low as it will go. Measure from crotch to heel.

Low Priced Rubber Tired Velocipedes.

Catalog No.	Wheels		Seat to Lower Pedal	Shpg. Wt.	Price
	Front	Rear			
79K8359¼	14 in.	10 in.	17 in.	15 lbs.	$3.79
79K8356¼	16 in.	12 in.	19 in.	17 lbs.	3.98
79K8357¼	20 in.	14 in.	21 in.	22 lbs.	4.47
79K8358¼	23½ in.	16 in.	23 in.	23 lbs.	4.98

Medium Grade Ball Bearing Velocipedes. Well constructed channel steel frame, with crescent steel brace reinforcing rear axle. Bicycle head and arched fork frame; adjustable handle bars; rubber grips; adjustable leather saddle. Rat trap bicycle style pedals. Frame painted a rich maroon and striped. Handle bars, cranks and pedals nickel plated. Ball bearing wheels. ¾-in. rubber tires. Unmailable.

Catalog No.	Wheels		Measurement From Center of Seat to Pedal at Extreme L'gth	Shpg. Wt. Abt. Lbs.	Price
	Front	Rear			
79K8379¼	14 in.	10 in.	17 inches	28	$8.98
79K8380¼	16 in.	12 in.	21½ inches	32	9.98
79K8381¼	20 in.	14 in.	23½ inches	34	10.98
79K8382¼	23½ in.	16 in.	25½ inches	40	11.98

Girls' Tricycle. Last Year's Price, $10.98. Now $5.98

One of the manufacturers making girls' tricycles, desiring to discontinue the manufacture of them, and having a quantity on hand, offered us a most wonderful proposition. We are glad to offer our customers this extraordinary bargain at this ridiculously low price which is far below its real value. This is not a cheap, flimsy tricycle. Frame is tubular steel, beautifully enameled dark blue, tastefully striped. Seat upholstered with artificial leather. Nickel plated side arms and handle bar. 20-inch rear wheels and 12-inch front wheel with ½-inch rubber tires. Comfortable and easy running. One size only, adjustable by raising or lowering seat. For girls 4 to 10 years of age. Shpg. wt., 50 lbs.
79K8371¼—Price (Unmailable) $5.98

Our Lowest Priced Velocipedes. They have steel tires. Rigid handle bars. Adjustable spring seat. Steel wheels. Front fork made of good quality steel, one-piece crank. Frame and wheels painted. Give leg measurement from crotch to heel. Sizes are with seat as low as it will go. Two largest sizes unmailable.

Catalog No.	Wheels		Seat to Lower Pedal	Shpg. Wt.	Price
	Front	Rear			
79K8350¼	14 in.	10 in.	17 in.	15 lbs.	$2.98
79K8351¼	16 in.	12 in.	20 in.	16 lbs.	3.39
79K8360¼	20 in.	14 in.	22 in.	18 lbs.	3.69
79K8361¼	24 in.	16 in.	23 in.	20 lbs.	3.98

BOYS and GIRLS SLEIGHS

ZIP! Flying Arrow Coasters seem to fly through the air. A real coaster with a real reputation. Unmailable.

32-Inch Sled.	36-Inch Sled.	40-Inch Sled.
79K8300¼	79K8301¼	79K8302¼
Shipping weight, 6¾ lbs. Price $1.39	Shipping weight, 7¼ lbs. Price $1.89	Shpg. wt., about 8½ lbs. Price $2.39

Flying Arrow Steering Coasters.

Watch it fly around the corner. These sleds really steer. Runners are highly tempered spring steel. Heavy gauge stamped steel knees, riveted to top and to runner. (No spot welding on these sleds.) Rivets will not break loose. Runners curve up abruptly in front which leaves more of the long flat runner on the ground, making it easier to steer and giving a better coasting surface. Nicely varnished with durable coach varnish and pretty decorations.

These two have double crossbars, long flexible runners, stout steel knees and heavy wood tops with pretty decorations. Unmailable.

45-Inch Sled. 79K8303¼	56-Inch Sled. 79K8311¼
Room enough for two children. Shpg. wt., about 9 lbs. Price, each...... $2.87	Room enough for three or four children. Three stout steel knees riveted to frame (not spot welded). Shipping wt., about 12 lbs. Price, each........... $3.47

High Quality Goose Neck Sled. Reinforced hardwood frame and knees, fastened to top and set in the wood runners. Half oval steel braces reinforce sled. Half oval steel runners, fastened securely to wood runners. Round side rails that child can hold. Nicely finished and decorated. Size, 13½x36 inches. Shipping weight, 6¾ pounds.
79K8304¼—Price............... $2.47

Medium Priced Sled. Reinforced hardwood frame with three steam bent hardwood knees, securely fastened to frame and set in wood runners. Six strong steel braces. Nicely finished and varnished with durable coach varnish. Top board with pretty decorations. Flat steel runners. Size, 12x36 inches. Shipping weight, 5¼ pounds.
79K8308¼—Price............. $1.59

HAND CARS

Ball Bearing or Plain. Well finished hand cars. Double connecting rods from propelling handle to gear wheel. Hardwood frame, seat and handle. Length, 38½ in. Seat, 7¾x19¾ inches. Front wheels, 8-inches; rear, 12 inches. Snappy colors. For children 5 to 10 years. Unmailable.
79K8815¼—Nicely finished with ball bearings. ⅝-inch rubber tires. Weight, 30 pounds. Price $7.98
79K8814¼—Without ball bearings. ½-inch rubber tires. Weight, 29 pounds. Price, each $5.67

Double Disc Steel. De Luxe Model. This hand car made up special for us. Double connecting rods from handle to gear. Hardwood frame. 10-inch double disc steel ball bearing wheels with ⅝-inch rubber tires. Nickel plated fancy shaped hub caps. Length, 37½ in. Seat, 7¾x19¾ in. Shpg. wt., abt. 45 lbs. Unmailable.
79K8800¼—Price $9.98

Genuine Irish Mail, made by the original manufacturers. High class finish and decorations, expert workmanship and mechanical perfection. Unmailable.

Ball Bearing. Has ¾-in. rubber tires. 42 in. long, 10 in. front and 12-in. rear ball bearing wheels. For ages 8 to 14 years. Shipping wt., 33 lbs.
79K8813¼—Price $8.98

Plain Bearings. ½-inch rubber tires, 8-in. front and 12-in. rear wheels, 41-in. long. Ages 6 to 12 yrs. Shpg. wt., 32 lbs.
79K8802¼—Price $5.98

Steel Frame. Frame of strap steel. Wood seat, nicely painted. Wood grips, well braced. Length over all, 37½ in. 8-inch front wheels, 12-inch rear wheels, ½-inch rubber tires. Shpg. wt., 34 lbs.
79K8807¼ Price $5.98

Junior Size. Length over all, 28½ in. 8-inch front wheels, 10-in. rear, ½-in. rubber tires. Shpg. wt., 22 lbs.
79K8805¼ Price $3.98

SEARS, ROEBUCK AND CO. 579

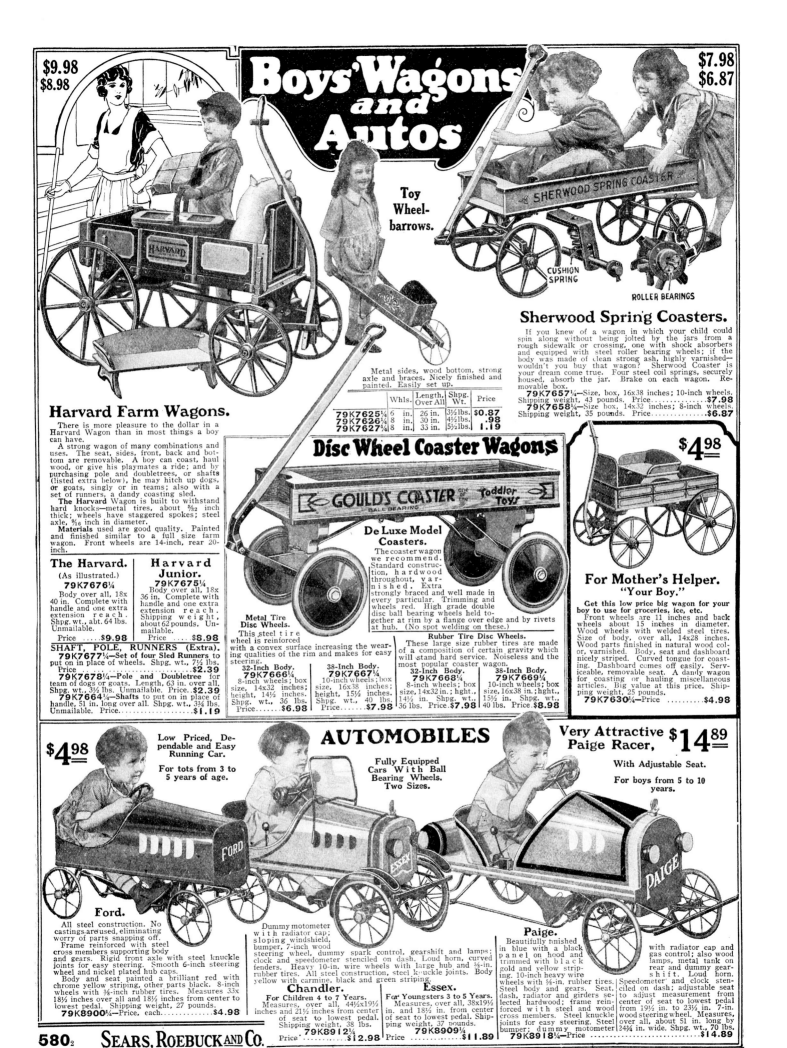

Boys' Wagons and Autos

HARVARD

$9.98
$8.98

Harvard Farm Wagons.

There is more pleasure to the dollar in a Harvard Wagon than in most things a boy can have.

A strong wagon of many combinations and uses. The seat, sides, front, back and bottom are removable. A boy can coast, haul wood, or give his playmates a ride; and by purchasing pole and doubletrees, or shafts (listed extra below), he may hitch up dogs, or goats, singly or in teams; also with a set of runners, a dandy coasting sled.

The Harvard Wagon is built to withstand hard knocks—metal tires, about 5/32 inch thick; wheels have staggered spokes; steel axle, 9/16 inch in diameter.

Materials used are good quality. Painted and finished similar to a full size farm wagon. Front wheels are 14-inch, rear 20-inch.

The Harvard. (As illustrated.) **79K7676¼** Body over all, 18x40 in. Complete with handle and one extra extension reach. Shpg. wt., abt. 64 lbs. Unmailable. Price **$9.98**

Harvard Junior. **79K7675¼** Body over all, 18x36 in. Complete with handle and one extra extension reach. Shipping weight, about 62 pounds. Unmailable. Price **$8.98**

SHAFT, POLE, RUNNERS (Extra).

79K7677¼—Set of four Sled Runners to put on in place of wheels. Shpg. wt., 7½ lbs. Price.....**$2.39**

79K7678¼—Pole and Doubletree for team of dogs or goats. Length, 63 in. over all. Shpg. wt., 3½ lbs. Unmailable. Price..**$2.39**

79K7664¼—Shafts to put on in place of handle, 51 in. long over all. Shpg. wt., 3¾ lbs. Unmailable. Price.....**$1.19**

Toy Wheel-barrows.

Metal sides, wood bottom, strong axle and braces. Nicely finished and painted. Easily set up.

	Whls.	Length, Over All	Shpg. Wt.	Price
79K7625¼	6 in.	26 in.	3½ lbs.	$0.87
79K7626¼	8 in.	30 in.	4½ lbs.	.98
79K7627¼	8 in.	33 in.	5½ lbs.	1.19

SHERWOOD SPRING COASTER
CUSHION SPRING
ROLLER BEARINGS

$7.98
$6.87

Sherwood Spring Coasters.

If you knew of a wagon in which your child could spin along without being jolted by the jars from a rough sidewalk or crossing, one with shock absorbers and equipped with steel roller bearing wheels; if the body was made of clean strong ash, highly varnished—wouldn't you buy that wagon? Sherwood Coaster is your dream come true. Four steel coil springs, securely housed, absorb the jar. Brake on each wagon. Removable box.

79K7657¼—Size, box, 16x38 inches; 10-inch wheels. Shipping weight, 43 pounds. Price.....**$7.98**

79K7658¼—Size box, 14x32 inches; 8-inch wheels. Shipping weight, 35 pounds. Price.....**$6.87**

Disc Wheel Coaster Wagons

GOULD'S COASTER
BALL BEARING
Toddler Toys

De Luxe Model Coasters.

The coaster wagon we recommend. Standard construction, hardwood throughout, varnished. Extra strongly braced and well made in every particular. Trimming and wheels red. High grade double disc ball bearing wheels held together at rim by a flange over edge and by rivets at hub. (No spot welding on these.)

Metal Tire Disc Wheels.

This steel tire wheel is reinforced with a convex surface increasing the wearing qualities of the rim and makes for easy steering.

32-Inch Body. **79K7666¼** 8-inch wheels; box size, 14x32 inches; height, 14½ inches. Shpg. wt., 36 lbs. Price.....**$6.98**

38-Inch Body. **79K7667¼** 10-inch wheels; box size, 16x38 inches; height, 15½ inches. Shpg. wt., 40 lbs. Price.....**$7.98**

Rubber Tire Disc Wheels.

These large size rubber tires are made of a composition of certain gravity which will stand hard service. Noiseless and the most popular coaster wagon.

32-Inch Body. **79K7668¼** 8-inch wheels; box size, 14x32 in.; hght., 14½ in. Shpg. wt., 36 lbs. Price.**$7.98**

38-Inch Body. **79K7669¼** 10-inch wheels; box size, 16x38 in.; hght., 15½ in. Shpg. wt., 40 lbs. Price.**$8.98**

$4.98

For Mother's Helper. "Your Boy."

Get this low price big wagon for your boy to use for groceries, ice, etc.

Front wheels are 11 inches and back wheels about 15 inches in diameter. Wood wheels with welded steel tires. Size of body, over all, 14x28 inches. Wood parts finished in natural wood color, varnished. Body, seat and dashboard nicely striped. Curved tongue for coasting. Dashboard comes off easily. Serviceable, removable seat. A dandy wagon for coasting or hauling miscellaneous articles. Big value at this price. Shipping weight, 25 pounds.

79K7630¼—Price **$4.98**

AUTOMOBILES

Fully Equipped Cars With Ball Bearing Wheels. Two Sizes.

$4.98 **Low Priced, Dependable and Easy Running Car.** **For tots from 3 to 5 years of age.**

Very Attractive Paige Racer, $14.89 **With Adjustable Seat.** **For boys from 5 to 10 years.**

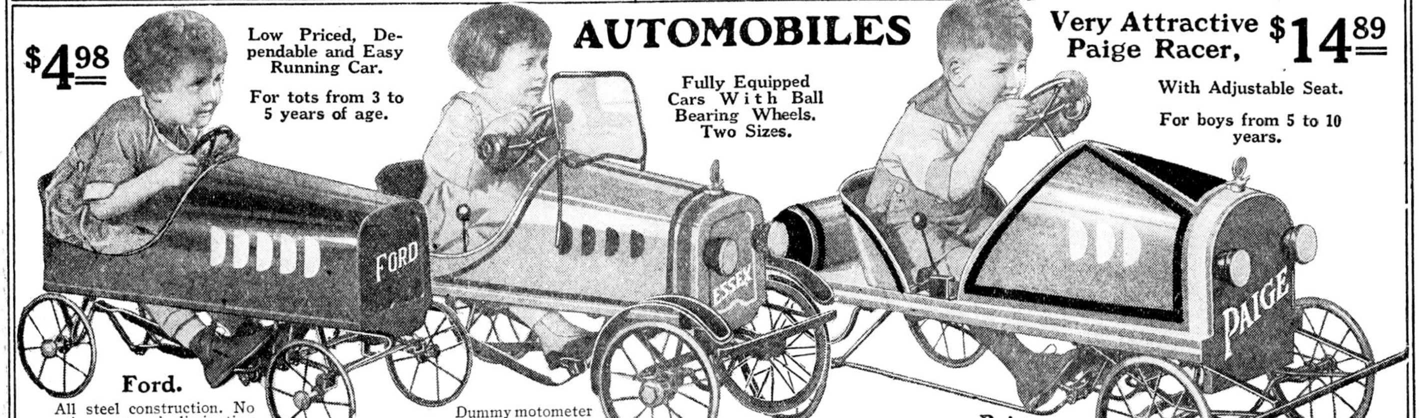

FORD
ESSEX
PAIGE

Ford.

All steel construction. No castings are used, eliminating worry of parts snapping off.

Frame reinforced with steel cross members supporting body and gears. Rigid front axle with steel knuckle joints for easy steering. Smooth 6-inch steering wheel and nickel plated hub caps.

Body and seat painted a brilliant red with chrome yellow striping, other parts black. 8-inch wheels with ⅜-inch rubber tires. Measures 33x18½ inches over all and 18½ inches from center to lowest pedal. Shipping weight, 27 pounds.

79K8900¼—Price, each.....**$4.98**

Dummy motometer with radiator cap; sloping windshield, bumper, 7-inch wood steering wheel, dummy spark control, gearshift and lamps; clock and speedometer stenciled on dash. Loud horn, curved fenders. Heavy 10-in. wire wheels with large hub and ⅝-in. rubber tires. All steel construction, steel knuckle joints. Body yellow with carmine, black and green striping.

Chandler.

For Children 4 to 7 Years.

Measures, over all, 44½x19½ inches and 21½ inches from center of seat to lowest pedal. Shipping weight, 38 lbs.

79K8912¼ Price.....**$12.98**

Essex.

For Youngsters 3 to 5 Years.

Measures, over all, 38x19½ in. and 18½ in. from center of seat to lowest pedal. Shipping weight, 37 pounds.

79K8909¼ Price.....**$11.89**

Paige.

Beautifully finished in blue with a black panel on hood and trimmed with black gold and yellow striping. 10-inch heavy wire wheels with ⅝-in. rubber tires. Steel body and gears. Seat, dash, radiator and girders selected hardwood; frame reinforced with steel and wood cross members. Steel knuckle joints for easy steering. Steel bumper; dummy motometer with radiator cap and gas control; also wood lamps, metal tank on rear and dummy gearshift. Loud horn. Speedometer and clock stenciled on dash; adjustable seat to adjust measurement from center of seat to lowest pedal from 19½ in. to 23½ in. 7-in. wood steering wheel. Measures, over all, about 51 in. long by 24¾ in. wide. Shpg. wt., 70 lbs.

79K8918¼—Price **$14.89**

For Health Giving Fun

$6.98

Sturdy Spoke Wheel Ball Bearing Wagons.

Made of dependable materials. Hardwood throughout, properly seasoned; heavy steel braces; steel axles, 9/16 inch in diameter. Rock maple ten pin shape spokes, set in rock elm felloe, steamed and bent in one piece. Heavy steel tire, set with hydraulic pressure and riveted to felloe in three places. Stamped steel hub with self contained ball bearings. 10-inch wheels and top rail painted a brilliant red. Steel parts enameled black. All other parts natural finish with two coats of varnish. Complete with brake and nickel plated hub caps. Two sizes.
79K7653¼—Body, 16x36 in. Shipping wt., 32 pounds. Price $6.98
79K7654¼—Body, 15x32 inches. Shipping wt., 28 lbs. Price $5.98

Scooter.

A great muscle developer for children 4 to 15 years of age. One foot on the platform and one on the sidewalk, and watch him go.

Will cover from 14 to 18 feet on good pavement with no more effort than an ordinary step. 10-inch heavy wire wheels with ½-inch rubber tires. All steel frame and fork, enameled bright red; foot board, 4¼x14¼ inches of rock maple selected stock, nicely varnished. Light running and high grade construction. Height, 30 in., length over all, 38 in. Shpg. wt., 18 lbs.
79K8801¼—Price $2.59

$7.98

Seat, Sides and Dash Are Removable.

Combination
Truck, Express and Coaster Wagon With Disc Steel Wheels.

Very Latest in Boys' Wagon.

Built for service as well as pleasure. Exceedingly attractive. It is something different and new. Out of the ordinary and every boy will want it. Make this a real Christmas for your boy. Standard construction, hardwood throughout, one-piece front and rear bolster; improved tongue support; new style combination king bolt and brace eliminating cotter pin or burr. Axles are held under bolster with eye bolts, avoiding holes in the axle and giving greater strength. Pressed steel fifth wheel. Disc steel wheels, with a heavy steel tire riveted to rim, patterned after those used on regular automobiles; with self contained type ball bearings swedged into the hub making the wheel one unit. This permits quick and easy assembling by the boy. All steel brake for stopping. Heavy steel axles and braces. Seat, dash and sides can be removed, making a dandy coaster wagon. Bottom of box finished natural and varnished. Seat, sides and wheels painted a beautiful brilliant red with black trimmings. Box measures, over all, 16x36 inches. Height to top of seat, 20 inches. Shipped knocked down in strong carton. Shpg. wt., 40 pounds.
79K7651¼—Price $7.98

Genuine "Waggie Toddlers"

Wagons for Little Tots.

Popular Disc Steel Wheel Wagons for the little tots. Baby really enjoys and loves a wagon. Same construction as our larger wagons; hardwood throughout, nicely finished natural with durable varnish; trimmings bright red. Two kinds.
Rubber Tires. Disc Wheels.
79K7613¼—Body, 8x18 inches. Wheels, 4 in. Height, 6⅞ in. Shpg. weight, 7 lbs. Price........$2.39
79K7614¼—Body, 10x23 inches. Wheels, 5 in. Height, 8½ in. Shipping weight, 11 lbs. Price...$2.98
Bright Red Wood Wheels.
Same as above, except solid hardwood wheels and metal bearings instead of red enamel.
79K7615¼—Body, 8x18 inches. Wheels, 4 inches. Height, 6⅞ in. Shpg. wt., 7 pounds. Price..$1.98

Steel Coaster Wagons

These wagons have rolled sheet steel sides with rims rolled over. Thick wood bottoms. Strong metal running gears. Steel truss supports, axles and wheels with heavy wire spokes. Strongly made and will stand hard use. Painted in attractive colors.

Parents: Please note these values and compare prices elsewhere on equal quality.

Faultless Wagons.
Lighter weight wagons, straight wooden tongue, and not so strongly made as our better grade Olympic wagons.

	Size of Wheels,		Shpg.	
	Body, In.	In.	Wt.	Lbs. Price
79K7623¼	8 x18	6	6	$1.39
79K7624¼	10½x22	8	7¾	1.69
79K7632¼	12½x26	10	13½	1.98

Olympic Wagons.
The strong, substantial metal wagons. Stronger bracing, better gears and wheels, curved handle bar and made to stand wear.

	Size of Wheels,		Shpg.	
	Body,In.	In.	Wt.	Lbs. Price
79K7641¼	12½x26¼	10	18½	$2.67
79K7643¼	14½x30	11	21½	2.98

AUTOMOBILES
These Snappy Models With Dummy Gearshift and Classy Equipment. Two Sizes.

Medium Priced Cars in Two Different Sizes.
These cars are of all steel construction, frame reinforced with steel cross members supporting body and gears. Steel knuckle joints for easy steering; steel bumper and wood imitation radiator cap. Strong twelve-spoke wire wheels with ½-inch rubber tires. Painted in snappy colors.

BOYS!
It's a Beauty!
For Boys From 4 to 7 Years.

A Special Value $9.98

Many features like on daddy's car. Dummy gearshift, lamps and cap, steel bumper. A loud horn; 7-inch wood rim steering wheel with dummy gas control; speedometer and clock stenciled on dashboard. Steel fenders fastened to all steel body. Frame reinforced with steel cross members. Steel knuckle joints for easy steering. 10-inch heavy wire wheels, ½-inch rubber tires. Body beautiful grotto blue with yellow and black striping.

Chevrolet.
For Girls or Boys From 4 to 7 Years of Age.
Wood steering wheel, with dummy gas or spark control. Body a brilliant red with yellow and black striping. Car measures, over all, 43½x18½ inches, and 21½ in. from center of seat to lowest pedal. Shpg. wt., 32 lbs.
79K8903¼—Price.$7.87

Overland.
For Smaller Tots From 3 to 5 Years of Age.
High back seat is safe and comfortable for the little ones. 6-inch metal steering wheel. Dummy gas control. Measures, over all, 37½x19¼ and 18½ inches from center of seat to lowest pedal. Shpg. wt., 29 lbs.
79K8901¼—Price.$6.39

Buick.
For Children From 4 to 7 Years. Car measures, over all, 43½x18¾ inches and from center of seat to lowest pedal, 21½ inches. Shipping weight, 35 pounds.
79K8907¼—Price $9.98

Dodge.
For Youngsters From 3 to 5 Years. Measures, over all, 38¼x18½ inches and from center of seat to lowest pedal, 18½ inches. Shipping weight, 33 pounds.
79K8902¼—Price $8.89

Jordan.
Equipped with 10-inch disc steel, ball bearing wheels with ½-inch rubber tires, enameled a brilliant red; black enameled sloping wind shield; dummy gearshift; steel bumper; 7-inch wood steering wheel with dummy gas control; speedometer and clock stenciled on dashboard. All steel body enameled a pretty coach green with carmine and yellow striping. Car measures, over all, about 44 inches in length and 19 inches in width. From center of seat to lowest pedal, 21½ inches. Shipping weight, 50 lbs.
79K8904¼—Price $9.98

SEARS, ROEBUCK AND CO.   581

Toys for the Growing Child

Genuine Toddler-Cars.

Disc Steel Wheels

Very Fine Quality. With ½-inch rubber tires. Sturdy construction; high grade materials throughout and high class workmanship. Finished a brilliant red and yellow and nicely varnished. Foot rest on front part of seat for child's feet for coasting.

	Ht. to Top of Seat, In.	Lgth., In.	Shpg. Wt., Lbs.	
79N7510—1 to 2 yrs.	8½	16¼	6	$2.59
79N7511—2 to 3 yrs.	10	18¼	8	2.87
79N7512—3 to 4 yrs.	11½	20	10	3.39

Bright Red Wood Wheels.

Baby's First Car.

These Toddler-Cars are well made and highly finished in snappy colors. The construction is the best and will bear the knocks to which a toy of this type is subjected. Has a foot rest for child's feet for coasting. Nickel plated hub caps.

Age, Years	Ht. to Top of Seat, In.	Lgth., Wt., In. Lbs.		
79N7546 1 to 2	8½	16¼	6	$1.79
79N7547 2 to 3	10	18¼	8	1.98
79N7548 3 to 4	11½	20	10	2.39

Horsie Toddlers

Disc Steel and Solid Wood Wheels.

Horse's head and front feet hinged for easy steering. Turns with wheels.

Its sturdy construction will bear every knock to which a toy of this type is subjected. Saddle shaped seats. Steel axles and nickel plated hub caps. Finished in 5 colors. Chip proof enamel.

Disc Steel, Rubber Tired Wheels.
79N7505—For children, 1 to 2 years. **$2.98** Shipping weight, 6 pounds.
79N7506—For children, 2 to 3 years. **3.59** Shipping weight, 8 pounds.

Solid Wood Wheels With Metal Bushings.
79N7519—For children, 1 to 2 years. **$2.39** Shipping weight, 6 pounds.
79N7520—For children, 2 to 3 years. **2.67** Shipping weight, 8 pounds.

Beautiful White Enamel Rocker or Chair.

Little girls must have a rocker to rock their dolly to sleep or a chair to complete their bedroom outfit. Made of sturdy lumber and beautifully enameled snow-white with dark blue knobs and a pretty bluebird stencil on back rest. Seat, 10x10 inches. Shipping weight, 6 pounds.
79N8569 **$1.59** 79N8568
Rocker. Chair.... **$1.39**

Two Big Values.

Little Tots' Velocipede With Disc Wheels, Only $2.98

Beautifully finished enamel frame and seat. Practically indestructible. Please note the full size comfortable seat. Steel frame, axles, etc. Metal handle bars with wooden grips. ½-inch rubber tires. 8-inch front. 6-inch rear wheels. Saddle at lowest point, 15 inches. Shipping weight, 12 pounds.
79N8362................**$2.98**

Kiddie's High Class Velocipede.

Disc Steel Ball Bearing Wheels.

An up to date improved small velocipede for youngsters. All steel construction with nicely finished wood seat and handle grips. Handle bars with nickel plated. 7-inch rear wheels with ⅝-inch rubber tires and 9-inch front wheel with ⅝-inch rubber tire. Nickel plated hub caps. Durable, almost indestructible. Shipping weight, 14 pounds.
79N8367................**$4.98**

Large Size Red Chair or Rocker.

Every little tot must have a rocker or chair. Hardwood with round back and arms. Painted bright red, yellow and black striping. Height, 22½ inches. Seat is about 11 inches from floor. Well constructed to withstand hard knocks and usage. Shipping weight, 7 pounds.
79N8565 **$1.79** 79N8566
Rocker. Chair... **$1.59**

GIRLS! Something New for Dolly.

You can now take dolly out for a walk in this safe walker. By tipping handle slightly forward Ma-Ma Dolls will talk.

TWO SIZES
For dolls up to 15 inches high. Shpg. wt., 1 lb.
69N9161
79c

For dolls from 16 to 30 inches high. Shipping weight, 1½ lbs.
69N9172 Special at...**$1.00**

Portable Slide for Youngsters.

The growing child needs plenty of exercise.
79N9147 .. **$12.98**

For indoors or out. Well seasoned hardwood just like the large ones. Aluminum finish steel pipe railing and 7-step ladder, about 3 feet high. Slide and side rails are selected maple, sanded natural finish; balance painted red. Length, 7½ feet over all. Shipping weight, 40 pounds.

Combination Teeter Totter and Merry-Go-Round. For Indoors as Well as Outdoors.

Board, 6 feet long, of selected lumber. Seats fitted with strong handles. Center post is iron piping; well braced with bolts. Two adjustments. Finished in snappy red. Shipping wt., 29 lbs.
79N9145................**$4.98**

Rocking Horse.

It's a Beauty.

$2.98

Note Long Sloping Rockers For Safety.

No effort has been spared in making this toy the leader in quality at an exceedingly low price. Selected materials and high class workmanship. Where is the youngster that doesn't love to have his own horse? Constructed entirely of wood with full shaped saddle. Dappled gray with red, yellow and black trimmings. Shpg. wt., 14 lbs.
79N7545 **$2.98**

Even Babies Like It.

High Class See-Saw for Little Tots.

Try this see-saw and see how they enjoy it. Board is 4 feet 6 inches long, made of selected 1-inch lumber and finished natural varnished. About 11 inches high to seat board when level. Shipping weight, 15 pounds.
79N9144..................**$3.98**

DADDY! THIS IS THE HORSE I WANT

Dappled Gray Wood Hobby Horse.

How tickled your youngster would be to receive this wonderful horse on Christmas morning or for his birthday. Natural looking eyes of glass. Hair mane and tail; imitation leather saddle and a cloth blanket with fringe. Strong, nicely shaped body and legs, dapple gray finish. Hardwood stand, strong metal braces. A good reproduction of a pony for a boy. Length, 34 inches. Height, 28 inches. Stirrups adjustable. Shipping weight, 30 pounds.
79N7530..................**$7.98**

A DANDY FOR LITTLE TOTS.

High Class Swinging Horse.

You cannot imagine how children enjoy riding a horse that has an even and gentle gallop. Here's one that will suit the youngster in every respect. Strong wood frame with metal swings. Quality horse finished in 5 snappy colors. Chip proof enamels. Height, 23¾ inches; length, 33 inches. Shipping weight, 17 pounds.
79N7544..................**$4.67**

Guaranteed Steam Engines

Horizontal Steam Engines With Brass Boilers.

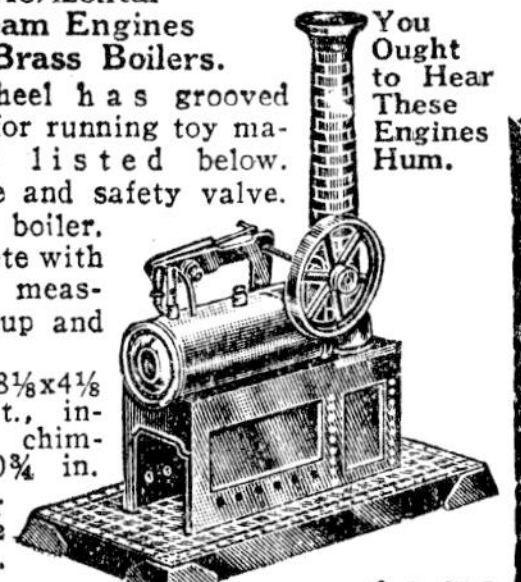
You Ought to Hear These Engines Hum.

Flywheel has grooved pulley for running toy machinery listed below. Whistle and safety valve. Brass boiler. Complete with burner, measuring cup and funnel. Base, 8⅛x4⅛ in. Ht., including chimney, 10¾ in. Shpg. wt., 1½ pounds.
49N5326 ..... $1.79
Size of base, 9⅝x4⅞ in. Ht., including chimney, 12¾ in. Shpg. wt., 7¾ lbs.
49N5327 ..... $2.67

Read This!

These beautifully finished Toy Engines are real quality and are such clever imitations of large engines, even in small details, that they take the eye of every boy.

Boys! This Is a Crackerjack Engine. Has Governor, Water Glass and Everything.

Just think, the double piston works from a real steam cylinder; dummy governor actually revolves. Has steam dome, safety valve, brass encased glass water gauge and whistle that blows loud enough for any boy. Big flywheel with pulley for running toys. Polished spun brass boiler. Painted cast iron base, 5¾x6 inches. Height over all, 5¾ inches. Shipping weight, 4⅝ pounds.
Large Size.
49N5330 ..... $3.98

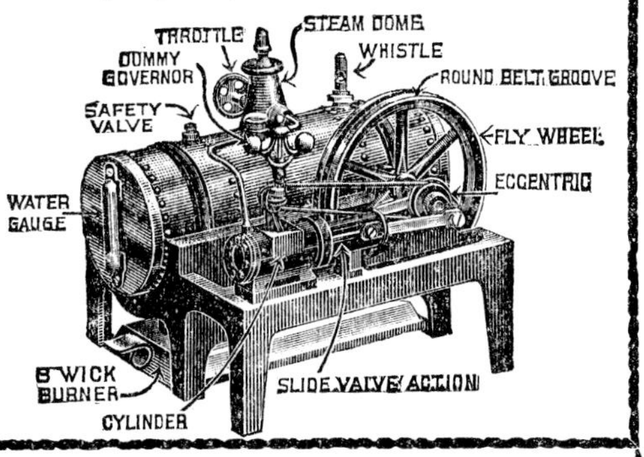
THROTTLE
DUMMY GOVERNOR
STEAM DOME
WHISTLE
ROUND BELT GROOVE
SAFETY VALVE
FLY WHEEL
ECCENTRIC
WATER GAUGE
WICK BURNER
SLIDE VALVE ACTION
CYLINDER

11-Inch Engine for $2.67.

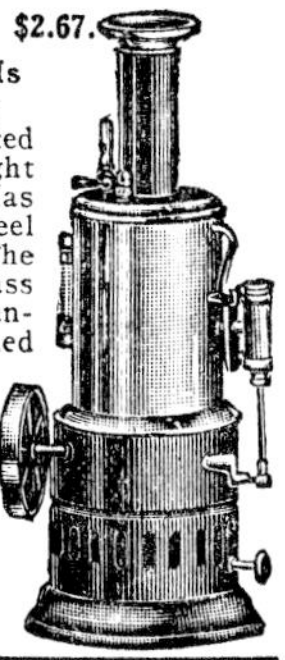

Boys! This Engine Is Surely Well Made.

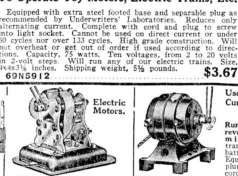

It has a finely fitted water gauge made tight by adjustable nuts. Has 2½-inch balance wheel and a real whistle. The boiler is polished brass and the base and running parts are finished in colors. The lamp and draft arrangement is especially adapted to both petroleum oil and alcohol as fuel. Full directions included. Shpg. wt., 3 lbs.
49N5308 $2.67

Horizontal Engines Are Very Popular.

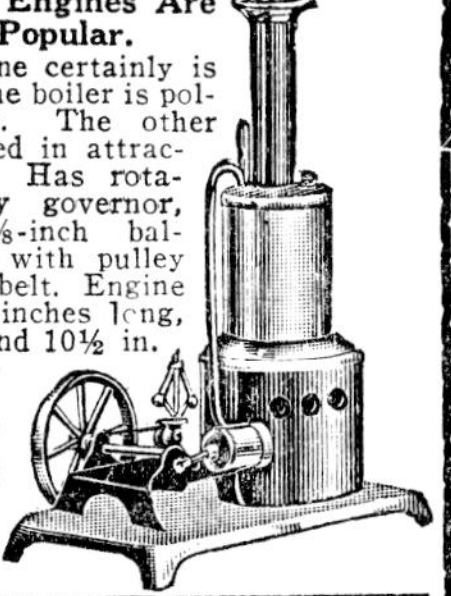

This engine certainly is a dandy. The boiler is polished brass. The other parts finished in attractive colors. Has rotating dummy governor, whistle, 2⅝-inch balance wheel with pulley for shafting belt. Engine measures 8 inches long, 4 in. wide and 10½ in. high. Complete instructions included. Shpg. wt., 2 pounds.
49N5313 $1.98

Boys! These Are Dandy Engines.

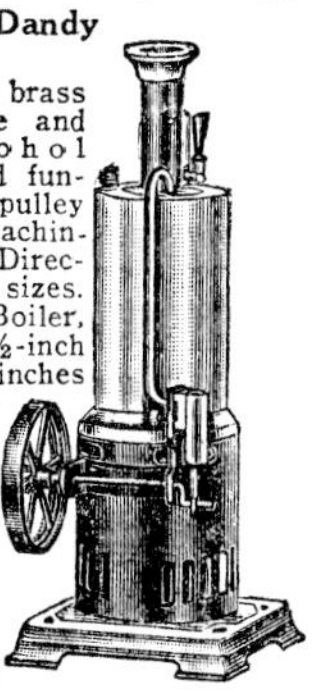

Seamless spun brass boiler, with whistle and safety valve, alcohol burner, measure and funnel. Flywheel has pulley for running toy machinery listed below. Directions included. Two sizes.
11 inches high. Boiler, 3½ inches high. 2½-inch flywheel. Base, 4¼ inches square. Shpg. wt., 3½ lbs.
49N5300 $1.98
8¾ inches high. Boiler, 2½ inches high. 1¾-inch flywheel. Base, 3¼ inches in diameter. Shipping weight, 2½ pounds.
49N5303 $1.00

Steam Tractors.

Just Like Dad's. They Move Under Their Own Power in Circle or Straight.

Our Finest Toy Tractor.
Accurate in detail and proportion. Brass boiler, handsome gunmetal finish. Flywheel has nickeled face. Chain drive. Boiler has wood handle drain cock, oil cup and safety valve. Alcohol burner; also measure and funnel and full directions. 9½ inches high and 7 in. long. Shpg. wt., 4 lbs.
49N5360 ..... $6.98

Medium Size Tractor.
Runs in a circle or straight. Spun brass boiler; alcohol lamp. Steam cylinder and pistons. Whistle. Safety valve, spring belt, 2¼-inch flywheel. Height, 7¾ inches; length, 5⅞ inches. Shpg. wt., 3 lbs.
49N5314 ... $3.98

Steam Roller That Reverses.
Runs forward or backward. Spun brass boiler, whistle and reverse lever. Solid 1⅞-inch flywheel. Coil spring belt. Cab for driver. Length, 6¾ inches; height, 5⅞ inches. Alcohol burner. Shipping weight, 4½ pounds.
49N5315 .... $4.67

The Busy Blacksmith.
When connected with toy engine the little man hammers on the anvil. Size, 5¼x2⅝ in. Height over all, 5⅝ inches. Shipping weight, 8 ounces.
49N5404 89c

Real Fountain.
Fill bowl with water and connect with toy engine. Diameter of bowl, 5¾ inches. Height over all, 4¼ in. Shpg. wt., 10 oz.
49N5402 89c

Set of Three Accessories for 69c.

Consists of small metal buzz saw, trip hammer and drill, all of which run with realistic movement. Each on polished wood base; size, 2⅝x2⅝ inches. Diameter of saw, 1½ inches; height, 3½ inches (absolutely harmless when running). Drill and trip hammer, 4¾ inches high. Shipping wt., 1 lb.
49N5401—Per set 69c

Windmill for Your Engine.

When attached to your engine its arms will fly around at a great rate. Made of metal, finished in attractive colors. Height over all, about 7 inches; width, 3 inches. Shipping weight, 12 ounces.
49N5405 39c

Electric Transformer

To Operate Toy Motors, Electric Trains, Etc.

Equipped with extra steel footed base and separable plug as recommended by Underwriters' Laboratories. Reduces only alternating current. Complete with cord and plug to screw into light socket. Cannot be used on direct current or under 60 cycles nor over 133 cycles. High grade construction. Will not overheat or get out of order if used according to directions. Capacity, 75 watts. Ten voltages, from 2 to 20 volts in 2-volt steps. Will run any of our electric trains. Size, 4x4x3⅛ inches. Shipping weight, 5½ pounds.
69N5912 ..... $3.67

Shafting.

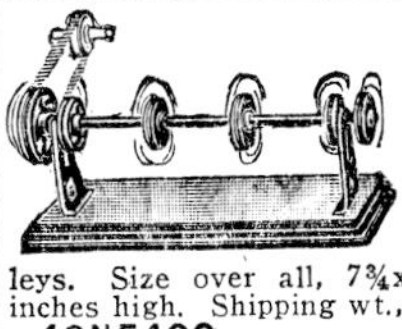

All metal. For use where more than one piece of toy machinery is to be operated at same time. Has six pulleys. Size over all, 7¾x3⅜ inches; 3 inches high. Shipping wt., 6 oz.
49N5400 48c

The Electric Thriller.

Mild or strong thrill, will not hurt anyone. The faster you turn the more thrills you get. Metal frame, wood base, 4⅜x3¼ inches. Shipping wt., 1½ lbs.
69N5903—Complete $1.39

Electric Motors.

Will operate Tinker Toy, Erector, etc. Latest type brushes. Mounted on steel base, size, 4x4 inches. Shpg. wt., 1 lb.
With Reverse Lever.
69N5940 ..... $1.79
Without Reverse Lever.
69N5941 ..... $1.39

Used on House Current of 110 Volts.

Runs about 8,000 revolutions per minute. No transformer or batteries needed. Equipped with plug and 6 feet of cord. Either direct or alternating current of 110 volts only. Black enameled steel base, measuring over all, 4x4 inches. Stands 3¾ inches high. Shaft, 4 inches long, has a detachable grooved pulley, about ⅝ inch in diameter. Shipping weight, 3 pounds.
69N5906 ..... $4.47

An Extra Large Motor for $2.39.

Shaft, about 4¾ in. long with a grooved pulley ⅜-inch in diameter. Will run Erector, Meccano and toy machine shops, etc. Our Toy Transformer will operate it, or attach to 4 to 8 dry cells. Height, about 4½ inches. Shpg. wt., 4¼ lbs.
69N5904 $2.39

Combination Motor and Magnet.

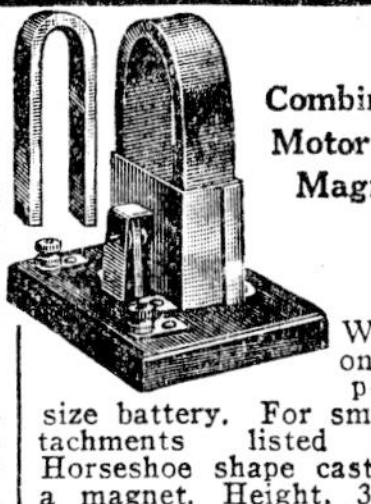

Will run on vest pocket size battery. For small attachments listed above. Horseshoe shape casting is a magnet. Height, 3¼ in. Wooden base. Shipping wt., 1 pound.
69N5947 ..... 39c

Electric Post Card Projector.

For projecting and enlarging post cards, etc.
Metal casing, well ventilated; seams curled to avoid use of solder. Throws a picture of 3 to 4½ feet in size depending on distance from screen. Has two adjustable post card holders, one holds picture in machine while the other is being changed. Equipped with two convex lenses, about 3 inches in diameter. Width, 9½ in.; height, 11 inches. Oxidized copper finish. Two top ventilators and bottom vents. Complete with two carbon lamps and cord and plug to attach to electric light socket, alternating current from 105 to 115 volts. Complete with full directions. Shpg. wt., 6¼ lbs.
79N6807 ..... $7.75

Children's Delight—Electric Magic Lanterns to Entertain Your Friends.

Hang a bed sheet on the wall and with one of our magic lantern outfits you can have a picture show. Lanterns are light gauge sheet steel. Brass finish, good grade lens container, and good quality lens. Equipped with cord and plug for electric light socket in your home. Twelve glass lantern slides, with a number of pictures on each. (These machines do not project moving pictures.) Come in three sizes as listed below. Extra slides listed at right.

Our Best and Largest. 10⅝x11⅛x3⅝ inches. Has twelve slides, 7 inches long and 2 inches wide. Shipping weight, 4½ pounds.
69N6877 $3.98

Medium Size. 9¼x10¾x3⅝ inches. Has twelve slides, 6¾ inches long and 1¾ inches wide. Shipping weight, 3½ lbs.
69N6876 .... $2.98

Small Size. 7½x10⅛x3 inches. Has twelve slides, 5⅛ inches long and 1 7/16 inches wide. Shipping wt., 2⅜ pounds.
69N6875 ... $1.79

Extra Slides to Fit Either Magic Lanterns or Movie Machines.

Popular assorted subjects to box.
For Small Machines. Slides Measure 5⅛x1 7/16 Inches.
69N6851—Box of 12 slides 48c
Shipping weight, 6 ounces.
For Medium Size Machines. Slides Measure 6¾x1¾ Inches.
69N6854—Box of 12 slides 98c
Shipping weight, 10 ounces.
For Large Machines. Slides Measure 7x2 Inches.
69N6857—Box of 12 slides $1.48
Shipping weight, 1 pound.

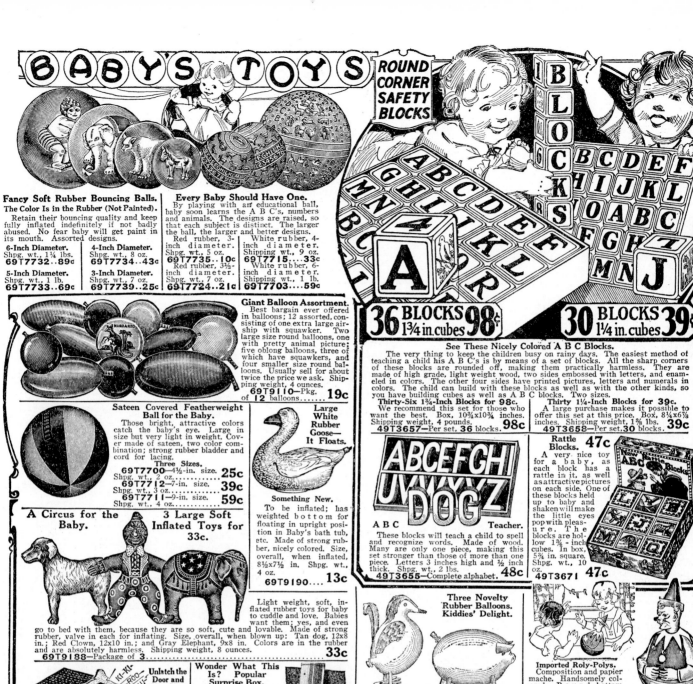

BABY'S TOYS

ROUND CORNER SAFETY BLOCKS

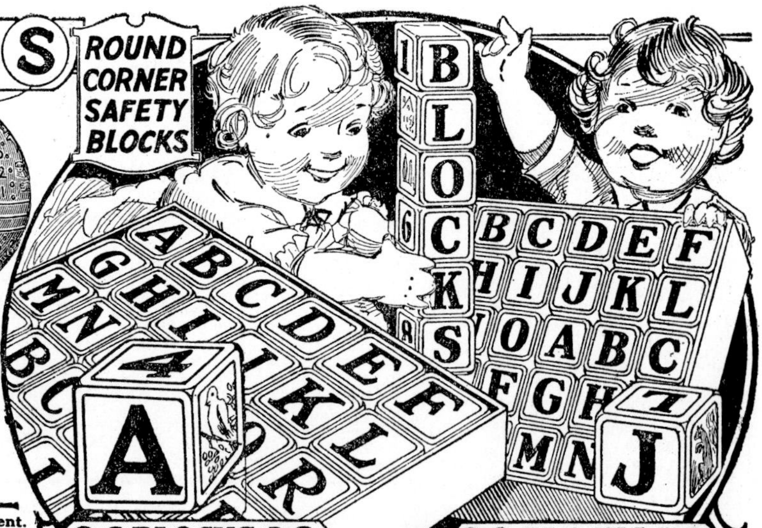

36 BLOCKS 1¾ in. cubes 98¢ — **30 BLOCKS 1¼ in. cubes 39¢**

Fancy Soft Rubber Bouncing Balls.
The Color Is in the Rubber (Not Painted).
Retain their bouncing quality and keep fully inflated indefinitely if not badly abused. No fear baby will get paint in its mouth. Assorted designs.

6-Inch Diameter. Shpg. wt., 1¼ lbs. 69T7732..89c
4-Inch Diameter. Shpg. wt., 8 oz. 69T7734..43c
5-Inch Diameter. Shpg. wt., 1 lb. 69T7733..69c
3-Inch Diameter. Shpg. wt., 7 oz. 69T7739..25c

Every Baby Should Have One.
By playing with an educational ball, baby soon learns the A B C's, numbers and animals. The designs are raised, so that each subject is distinct. The larger the ball, the larger and better designs.
Red rubber, 3-inch diameter. Shpg. wt., 5 oz. 69T7735..10c
White rubber, 4-inch diameter. Shipping wt., 9 oz. 69T7715....33c
Red rubber, 3½-inch diameter. Shpg. wt., 7 oz. 69T7724..21c
White rubber, 6-inch diameter. Shipping wt., 1 lb. 69T7703....59c

Giant Balloon Assortment.
Best bargain ever offered in balloons; 12 assorted, consisting of one extra large airship with squawker. Two large size round balloons, one with pretty animal picture; five oblong balloons, three of which have squawkers, and four smaller size round balloons. Usually sell for about twice the price we ask. Shipping weight, 4 ounces.
69T9110—Pkg. of 12 balloons....... 19c

See These Nicely Colored A B C Blocks.
The very thing to keep the children busy on rainy days. The easiest method of teaching a child his A B C's is by means of a set of blocks. All the sharp corners of these blocks are rounded off, making them practically harmless. They are made of high grade, light weight wood, two sides embossed with letters, and enameled in colors. The other four sides have printed pictures, letters and numerals in colors. The child can build with these blocks as well as with the other kinds, so you have building cubes as well as A B C blocks. Two sizes.

Thirty-Six 1¾-Inch Blocks for 98c.
We recommend this set for those who want the best. Box, 10¾x10¾ inches. Shipping weight, 4 pounds.
49T3657—Per set, 36 blocks. 98c

Thirty 1¼-Inch Blocks for 39c.
A large purchase makes it possible to offer this set at this price. Box, 8¼x6⅞ inches. Shipping weight, 1⅝ lbs.
49T3658—Per set, 30 blocks. 39c

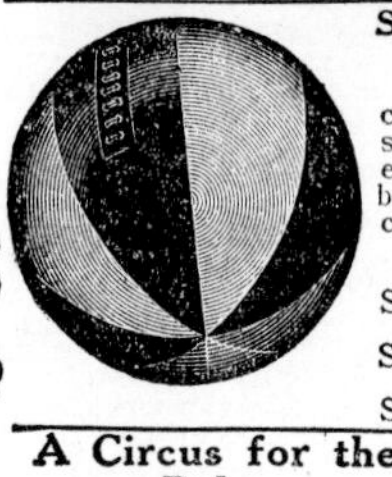

Sateen Covered Featherweight Ball for the Baby.
Those bright, attractive colors catch the baby's eye. Large in size but very light in weight. Cover made of sateen, two color combination; strong rubber bladder and cord for lacing.
Three Sizes.
69T7700—4½-in. size. Shpg. wt., 2 oz. 25c
69T7712—7-in. size. Shpg. wt., 3 oz. 39c
69T7711—9-in. size. Shpg. wt., 4 oz. 59c

Large White Rubber Goose—It Floats.
Something New.
To be inflated; has weighted bottom for floating in upright position in Baby's bath tub, etc. Made of strong rubber, nicely colored. Size, overall, when inflated, 8½x7½ in. Shpg. wt., 4 oz.
69T9190.... 13c

A B C Teacher.
These blocks will teach a child to spell and recognize words. Made of wood. Many are only one piece, making this set stronger than those of more than one piece. Letters 3 inches high and ½ inch thick. Shpg. wt., 2 lbs.
49T3655—Complete alphabet. 48c

Rattle Blocks. 47c
A very nice toy for a baby, as each block has a rattle in it, as well as attractive pictures on each side. One of these blocks held up to baby and shaken will make the little eyes pop with pleasure. The blocks are hollow 1¾-inch cubes. In box, 5¾ in. square. Shpg. wt., 10 oz.
49T3671 47c

A Circus for the Baby. **3 Large Soft Inflated Toys for 33c.**

Light weight, soft, inflated rubber toys for baby to cuddle and love. Babies want them; yes, and even go to bed with them, because they are so soft, cute and lovable. Made of strong rubber, valve in each for inflating. Size, overall, when blown up: Tan dog, 12x8 in.; Red Clown, 12x10 in.; and Gray Elephant, 9x8 in. Colors are in the rubber and are absolutely harmless. Shipping weight, 8 ounces.
69T9188—Package of 3..... 33c

Three Novelty Rubber Balloons. Kiddies' Delight.

Cute little squawker chick, with feathers attached. Natural looking squealing pig and Billy Whiskers. Babies will play with them by the hour. Shpg. wt., 4 oz.
69T9134—Per package of 3 balloons.......... 25c

Imported Roly-Polys.
Composition and papier mache. Handsomely colored. Round bottom weighted. When tipped over always sits up again. Babies want them. Clowns and other funny figures. The two large sizes have movable heads. Assorted subjects.

	Ht., In.	Shpg. Wt., Lbs.	Each
69T7006	11	3	98c
69T7005	9	1½	69c
69T7010	4½	¾	25c

Unlatch the Door and Hear Him Crow.
When door is unlatched, rooster will throw it open, and crow in a very natural manner. Cage is wood, finished. Imitation tile roof and brick sides. Metal hinges. Size, 8 in. high, 7½ in. wide and 5⅝ in. deep. Shipping weight, 1½ pounds.
69T8111....... 79c

Wonder What This Is? Popular Surprise Box.
Unhook the lid, quick as a wink up it comes, and a queer, strange figure sticks his head out at you with a funny squeak. Spring in tall hat. Wood box covered with pretty paper. Size, 7x4¼x4¼ inches when opened. Shipping weight, 10 ounces.
69T7020 29c

Cute Red Rubber Animals.

Fine for baby to play with and chew on. Fine quality red rubber. Each has whistle. Shipping weight, 5 ounces.
Pretty Dog for 39c.
49T4436—Size, 5x4½ inches.......... 39c
Cute Little Kitty for 21c.
49T4433—Size, 4¾x2 inches.......... 21c

Popular Baby Roly-Poly, 39c.
Enameled in bright snappy colors. Cute baby face; dress, bonnet and trimmings, beautiful harmonizing baby colors. Height, 6 inches. Shpg. wt., 1½ lbs.
69T7003.... 39c

Baby Will Enjoy This Music.
It is like a music box, playing a little 12-note, lively, pleasing melody, when whirled around and around the handle. Nickel plated metal ends. Length, 5½ inches; diameter, 3 inches. Shipping weight, 10 ounces.
49T2417.......... 39c

Let Baby Pull This Horsie Chime.
Gray iron horse pulling light gauge steel frame with nickel plated wheels. Bell clangs as toy is drawn along floor. A dandy toy for the little tot. Attractive and musical. Length, over all, 13 inches. Packed in box. Shipping weight, 2 pounds.
49T2426.......... 39c

Whistle Ball for Baby.
When squeezed it whistles. Just what baby enjoys. Good grade heavy weight rubber, in fancy checker design with a neat stripe around center. Diameter, 2¾ inches. Shipping weight, 4 oz.
69T7710.......... 10c

Baby Will Crawl After These.
A string of beautifully colored heavy glass beads in snappy colors which please even a crawling baby. Baby will crawl after them at a great rate. Beads thick enough so as not to break very readily. About 84 beads to string. ⅝ inch in diameter. Shpg. wt., 1 lb.
49T3825
39c

Ball for Carriage.

Brightly decorated 2¼-in. celluloid ball. Hang from hood of carriage. Shpg. wt., 3 oz. Regular 50c value.
49T4414
39c

Beautiful Enamel 3 pc. Set.

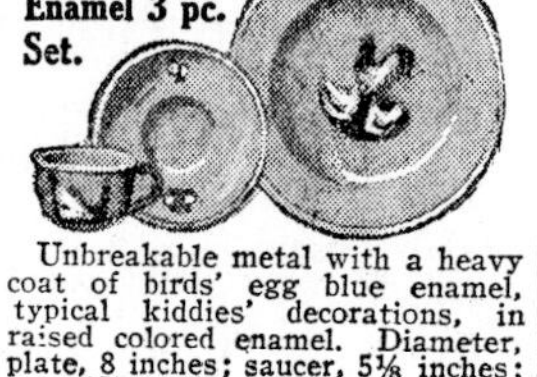

Unbreakable metal with a heavy coat of birds' egg blue enamel, typical kiddies' decorations, in raised colored enamel. Diameter, plate, 8 inches; saucer, 5⅛ inches; cup, 2⅞ inches. Shipping weight, 3 pieces, 1½ pounds.
49T1939—Per set...... 98c

Large Teething Ring.

Strong, white tubular celluloid teething ring on silk cord, ½ in. thick. Crimped surface. Diameter of ring, 3⅜ in. Shipping wt., 2 oz.
49T4407
19c

Roll It Away and It Rolls Back.

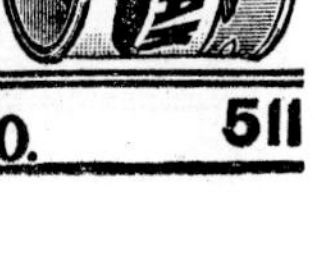

Cylinder shape with round metal ends. Roll toy along the floor and it will "Roll-back." Will even roll up slight incline. Will amuse babies for hours. Size, 2⅜x2⅜ in. Shpg. wt., 6 oz.
69T9123........ 8c

Let's Have a Party!

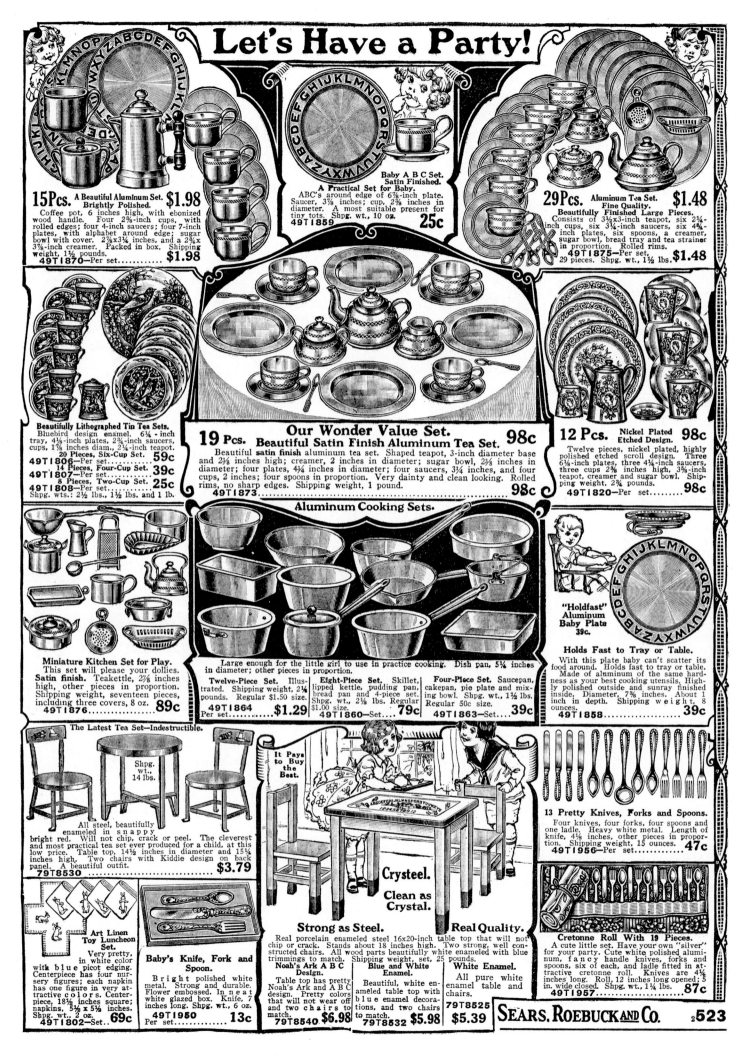

15 Pcs. **A Beautiful Aluminum Set. Brightly Polished.** **$1.98**

Coffee pot, 6 inches high, with ebonized wood handle. Four 2⅜-inch cups, with rolled edges; four 4-inch saucers; four 7-inch plates, with alphabet around edge; sugar bowl with cover. 2⅞x3¼ inches, and a 2¾x3⅞-inch creamer. Packed in box. Shipping weight, 1½ pounds.
49T1870—Per set........... **$1.98**

Baby A B C Set. Satin Finished.

A Practical Set for Baby.

ABC's around edge of 6⅞-inch plate. Saucer, 3⅞ inches; cup, 2⅜ inches in diameter. A most suitable present for tiny tots. Shpg. wt., 10 oz.
49T1859 **25c**

29 Pcs. **Aluminum Tea Set. Fine Quality.** **$1.48**

Beautifully Finished Large Pieces. Consists of 3½x3-inch teapot, six 2¼-inch cups, six 3¼-inch saucers, six 4⅝-inch plates, six spoons, a creamer, sugar bowl, bread tray and tea strainer in proportion. Rolled rims.
49T1875—Per set, 29 pieces. Shpg. wt., 1½ lbs. **$1.48**

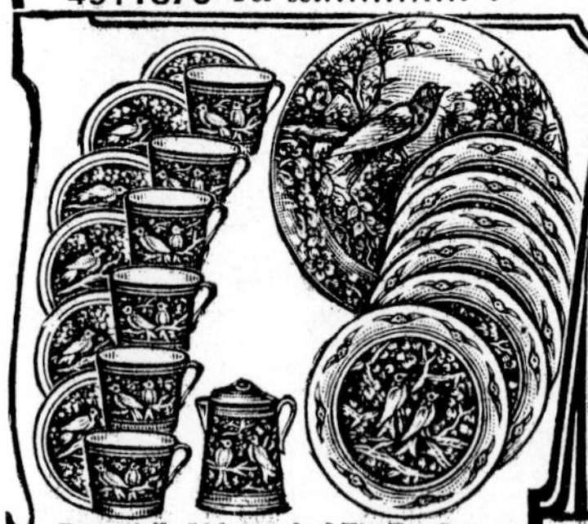

Beautifully Lithographed Tin Tea Sets.

Bluebird design enamel. 6¼-inch tray, 4⅛-inch plates, 2¾-inch saucers, cups, 1⅞ inches diam., 2¼-inch teapot.

20 Pieces, Six-Cup Set.
49T1806—Per set............ **59c**

14 Pieces, Four-Cup Set.
49T1807—Per set............ **39c**

8 Pieces, Two-Cup Set.
49T1808—Per set............ **25c**

Shpg. wts.: 2½ lbs., 1½ lbs. and 1 lb.

19 Pcs. Our Wonder Value Set. Beautiful Satin Finish Aluminum Tea Set. 98c

Beautiful **satin finish** aluminum tea set. Shaped teapot, 3-inch diameter base and 2⅜ inches high; creamer, 2 inches in diameter; sugar bowl, 2⅜ inches in diameter; four plates, 4¾ inches in diameter; four saucers, 3¼ inches, and four cups, 2 inches; four spoons in proportion. Very dainty and clean looking. Rolled rims, no sharp edges. Shipping weight, 1 pound.
49T1873.. **98c**

12 Pcs. **Nickel Plated Etched Design.** **98c**

Twelve pieces, nickel plated, highly polished etched scroll design. Three 6⅛-inch plates, three 4¼-inch saucers, three cups 2⅜ inches high, 3⅝-inch teapot, creamer and sugar bowl. Shipping weight, 2¾ pounds.
49T1820—Per set........ **98c**

Miniature Kitchen Set for Play.

This set will please your dollies. **Satin finish.** Teakettle, 2⅞ inches high, other pieces in proportion. Shipping weight, seventeen pieces, including three covers, 8 oz.
49T1876................ **89c**

Aluminum Cooking Sets.

Large enough for the little girl to use in practice cooking. Dish pan, 5¼ inches in diameter; other pieces in proportion.

Twelve-Piece Set. Illustrated. Shipping weight, 2¼ pounds. Regular $1.50 size.
49T1864
Per set........ **$1.29**

Eight-Piece Set. Skillet, lipped kettle, pudding pan, bread pan and 4-piece set. Shpg. wt., 2⅛ lbs. Regular $1.00 size.
49T1860—Set.... **79c**

Four-Piece Set. Saucepan, cakepan, pie plate and mixing bowl. Shpg. wt., 1½ lbs. Regular 50c size.
49T1863—Set.... **39c**

"Holdfast" Aluminum Baby Plate 39c.

Holds Fast to Tray or Table.

With this plate baby can't scatter its food around. Holds fast to tray or table. Made of aluminum of the same hardness as your best cooking utensils. Highly polished outside and sunray finished inside. Diameter, 7⅜ inches. About 1 inch in depth. Shipping weight, 8 ounces.
49T1858.................. **39c**

The Latest Tea Set—Indestructible.

Shpg. wt., 14 lbs.

All steel, beautifully enameled in snappy bright red. Will not chip, crack or peel. The cleverest and most practical tea set ever produced for a child, at this low price. Table top, 14½ inches in diameter and 15¼ inches high. Two chairs with Kiddie design on back panel. A beautiful outfit.
79T8530................................ **$3.79**

It Pays to Buy the Best.

Crysteel.

Clean as Crystal.

Strong as Steel. **Real Quality.**

Real porcelain enameled steel 16x20-inch table top that will not chip or crack. Stands about 18 inches high. Two strong, well constructed chairs. All wood parts beautifully white enameled with blue trimmings to match. Shipping weight, set, 25 pounds.

Noah's Ark A B C Design. Table top has pretty Noah's Ark and A B C design. Pretty colors that will not wear off and two chairs to match.
79T8540 **$6.98**

Blue and White Enamel. Beautiful, white enameled table top with blue enamel decorations, and two chairs to match.
79T8532 **$5.98**

White Enamel. All pure white enamel table and chairs.
79T8525 **$5.39**

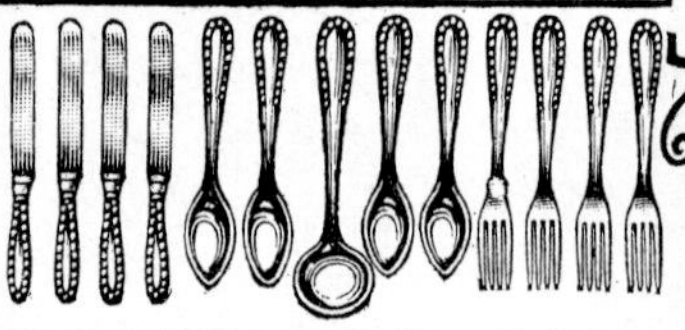

13 Pretty Knives, Forks and Spoons.

Four knives, four forks, four spoons and one ladle. Heavy white metal. Length of knife, 4⅛ inches, other pieces in proportion. Shipping weight, 15 ounces.
49T1956—Per set............ **47c**

Art Linen Toy Luncheon Set.

Very pretty, in white color with blue picot edging. Centerpiece has four nursery figures; each napkin has one figure in very attractive colors. Centerpiece, 18½ inches square; napkins, 5½ x 5½ inches. Shpg. wt., 2 oz.
49T1802—Set.. **69c**

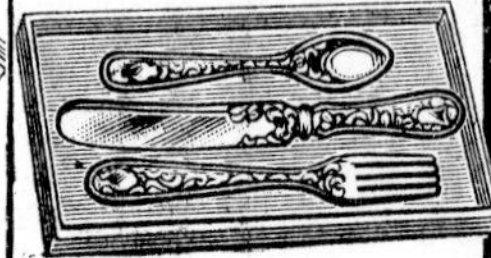

Baby's Knife, Fork and Spoon.

Bright polished white metal. Strong and durable. Flower embossed. In neat white glazed box. Knife, 7 inches long. Shpg. wt., 6 oz.
49T1950
Per set.......... **13c**

Cretonne Roll With 19 Pieces.

A cute little set. Have your own "silver" for your party. Cute white polished aluminum, fancy handle knives, forks and spoons, six of each, and ladle fitted in attractive cretonne roll. Knives are 4½ inches long. Roll, 12 inches long opened; 5 in. wide closed. Shpg. wt., 1¼ lbs.
49T1957................ **87c**

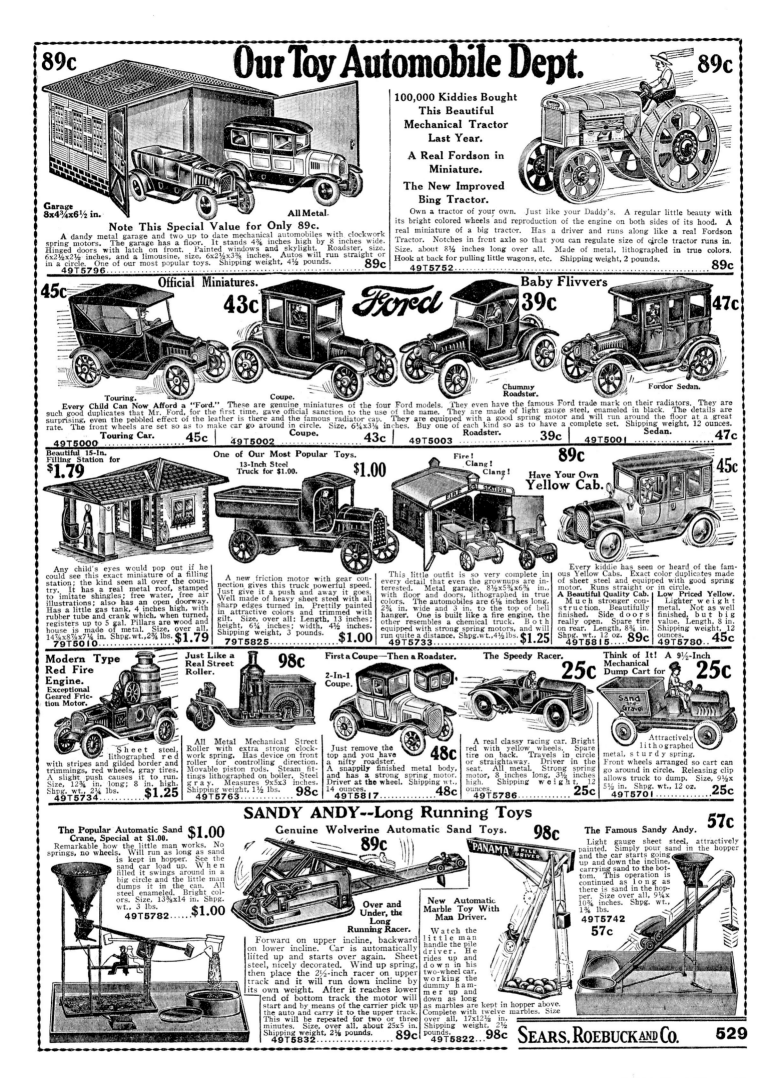

The Famous Buddy L All-Steel Playthings

The Finest Quality Floor Toys on the Market.

Boys! See these accurately proportioned miniatures of large trucks, steam shovels and tank trucks. Think of having a toy that will not break down or wear out! The trucks are ready to carry any load up to 150 pounds.

Every One a Real Job. 22-Gauge Steel.

The steam shovel is there to excavate for that new building you are planning to erect, and the tank truck is ready to keep the streets in your little toy town well flushed and clean. These toys are made of 22-gauge sheet steel, spot welded, riveted and with all edges carefully rounded to prevent cutting or scratching you. A year round toy; you can use them all summer, outside and all winter in your home.

22-Gauge Steel. Red Chassis.

22-Gauge Steel. Red Chassis.

Has Sprinkler Attachment.

$7.50 Dump Truck for $6.47.

$6.00 Steam Shovel for $4.98.

$8.50 Tank Truck for $6.98.

Exact miniature of Standard Dump Truck with real, working, steering knuckle, column and bumper. Solid aluminum disc wheels. The dumping device for hoisting and unloading is fitted with an automatic locking ratchet. All you have to do is turn the crank and it goes up or down. The back gate can be dropped down the same as on a big truck. The body is finished in shiny black auto enamel. Although this truck weighs only 9 pounds it will hold a grown man. Non-curling cotton pull cord included. Length over all, 24 inches. Height over all, 9¾ inches. Width, 8¾ inches. Shipping weight, 12 pounds.
79T5006.................$6.47

Every detail of a real big steam shovel. It will swing clear around to wherever you want it. Scoop the dirt, elevate it and unload it just like the big ones. All you have to do is work the crank. The carriage and roof are red and the other parts glossy black enamel. Cast iron wheels. Length over all, 25¼ in. Height, 13 in. Shpg. wt., 10½ lbs.
79T5008.................$4.98

Built on the same chassis as the dump truck. Has cab, 7½ inches high, with seat and steering wheel. Has 12-inch green enameled metal tank with filling cap on top and brass faucet in rear leading down into perforated sprinkler rail, with which you can run or shut off water. All finished in baked-on black auto enamel. Red disc aluminum wheels with rubber tire effect. Length, over all, 26 inches. Height, 12¼ inches. Width, 8¾ inches. Shipping weight, 12 pounds.
79T5007.................$6.98

BANKS

Three-Coin Bank.

Registers and adds nickels, dimes and quarters. Opens when $10 is deposited. Made of nicely lithographed sheet steel. Size, 5x5⅝x4 inches. Shpg. wt., 2¼ lbs.
69T8700.......$1.39

Home Savings Bank.

Nickel plated steel bank. Height, 2¼ in. Length, 3⅞ in. Opening for coins and paper money. Key furnished. Shipping weight, 10 oz.
69T8708 97c

Alabama Jigger Bank.

Popular Coon Dancing Toy Now on Bank. Children can be influenced to save while amused. Any size coin up to a quarter will make him jig until properly deposited. Height, 10½ in. Shpg. wt., 14 oz.
69T8720.......57c

Puppy Bank.

Popular with kiddies. Cast iron, nicely painted. Size, over all, about 4x2½ inches. Shpg. wt., 1½ lbs.
69T8715 21c

New Style 3-Coin Bank.

Will register and add pennies, nickels and dimes. Opens when $5.00 has been registered. Handsomely decorated in red, black and gold. Size, 5⅝x5½x4¼ inches. Shipping weight, 3 pounds.
69T8711 $1.79

Mail Box Bank.

Deposit coins like letters. Cast iron, painted bright red; gilt letters. Size, 5¼x3 inches. Shpg. wt., 1 lb.
69T8712 10c

Metal Telephone Bank With Bell.

Children enjoy telephones of any sort. Patterned after real telephone. Sheet steel, black enameled. Movable receiver rings bell. Size, over all, 9⅝x 4¼x2⅞ in. Shipping weight, 14 ounces.
69T9158.......29c

Boys! Here's a "Ready to Use" Crystal Radio Set for $6.45.

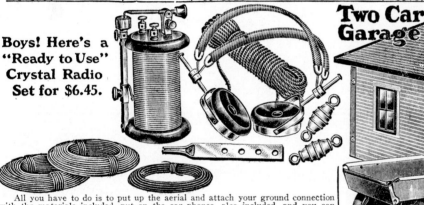

All you have to do is to put up the aerial and attach your ground connection with the materials included, put on the ear phones, also included, and you can hear voices or music within a radius of at least 25 miles, depending upon the power of the broadcasting station. This set will tune up to a wave length of 600 meters. No tubes or batteries necessary. Set is complete with crystal, aerial wire, insulators, phones and instructions for connecting set. Shipping weight, 5 pounds.
49T4712 ....$6.45

> For Tube Sets Write for Special Radio Catalog, 459T.

Radio Konstructor (Boys! Learn to Build Your Own Set.)

Most everybody would be interested in learning how to build a radio set of his own. This is just the thing. Enough materials to build a one or two-slide crystal set. Complete parts, plans and all the necessary tools to build a practical radio set included. Its complete manual of instructions explains the theory and practice of radio. It teaches the fundamentals and simplifies radio, and best of all, stimulates originality and invention. The kiddies are not the only ones to be entertained, for when completed this radio set will afford entertainment for the whole family. Assembled in neat box, 17½x14⅜x2⅜ inches. Shipping weight, 5½ pounds.
79T4704—Regular $5.00 set for............**$3.98**

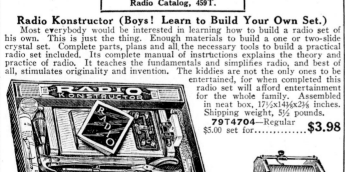

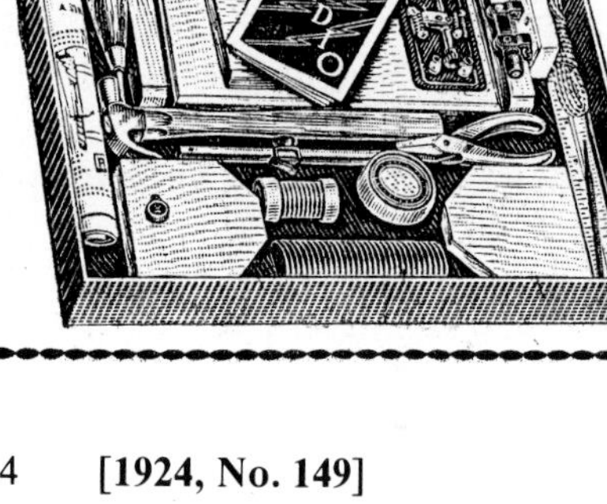

Two Car Garage — With Two Friction Autos

Kiddies! See This Great Big Garage and Autos With Real Rubber Tires.

All Metal.

Think of these two up to date autos and a 22-inch garage to play with. Every part is of the best quality heavy grade sheet steel, finished in high grade enamel. The garage measures 22x13½x16 inches. The doors swing on hinges like real doors. Comes in ten sections, knocked down. Simple enough to put together, but holding enough interest to give it the added feature of a construction toy. The autos are up to date models, made of heavy sheet steel, finished in beautiful deep automobile blue enamel and are equipped with yellow disc wheels, real rubber clincher tires, front bumpers, headlights and have the famous Hill Climber friction power motor. The truck has a red cab and a drop gate in back and measures 18⅜x5⅝x7⁷⁄₁₆ inches. The coupe has an extra wheel with tire and measures 17⅜x5⅝x7⅛ inches.
79T5836.............(Shipping weight, 17 pounds).....................$4.98

This Self Winding Doggie Runs 50 Feet. No Spring to Wind—Just Push Him Back and Forth.

The little tots' eyes will just pop out when they see this bow-wow. Nothing to break and even a small child can wind it up by simply pushing it back and forth 6 inches or so. Dog is of good grade velvet, stuffed with clean excelsior and has a movable head. He is mounted on a steel frame having 4 metal wheels like roller skate wheels. Length over all, 10⅝ in. Height, 8½ inches. Shipping weight, 3⅛ pounds.
49T4042.......$2.59

A Complete Toy Village.

To be used under Xmas tree or in child's play room. Twelve substantial cardboard houses, already set up and firmly glued. As illustrated, and artistically decorated in colors. Church, 3½ inches high, others in proportion. Shipping weight, 7 ounces.
69T9184.................25c

SEARS, ROEBUCK AND CO. 531

The World's Greatest Construction Toy

THE NEW ERECTOR

A New and Much Improved Erector.

Builds the Most Models—Has the Most Parts.

The Only Construction Toy With the Square Girder.

It has many new parts and consequently its flexibility is much greater than in the past and that is saying a great deal. Construction toys hold more possibilities for amusement and instruction than perhaps any other type of toy. Every boy loves to build bridges, machinery, wagons, etc., such as are shown in the very complete manual included in each set. Furthermore, he will like to elaborate on these models and create many according to his own imagination. This toy will teach him the fundamentals of engineering and construction and also help to develop any dormant ability he may have along those lines. The booklets included show hundreds of models that can be built with each size set. The possibilities of building other models are unlimited.

The gears, pulleys, angle irons and other parts are true models. With these any boy can build miniature skyscrapers, drawbridges and thousands of other things too numerous to mention.

Erector No. 7.

A new wonderful set. The new pieces, including the boiler, lend more reality to the models you can build. You can have an upright boiler for your steam shovel or a tank for your sprinkler wagon. You can build over 600 models with this set. Also has powerful Erector motor. Comes in strong stained wooden cabinet, about 21¾x8⅜x3¼ inches. Shpg. wt., 11 lbs.
79T4716........ **$8.98**

Erector No. 4.

Our most popular set, which will build over 450 models. This is the set that made Erector famous. Motor included. In strong box, 18x10¼x2¼ in. Shpg. wt., 6¼ lbs.
79T4720 **$4.47**

Erector No. 3.

Will build about 300 models. Comes in strong sealed carton with cover illustrated in colors. Very attractive. Box, 18x10x1⅜ in. Shpg. wt., 4 lbs.
49T4715 **$2.69**

Erector No. 1.

This new set will build more than 200 models. Packed in strong sealed carton with attractively lithographed cover. Box, 12½x8¾x¾ in. Shpg. wt., 1⅝ lbs.
49T4717 **89c**

Bilt-E-Z

"The BOY Builder"

As the Boy Builds the Toy, the Toy Builds the Boy.

As good for a girl as for the boy, however. Boys! Do you know that you not only can build skyscrapers and houses, but you can make accessories for your train sets, like stations, bridges, trestles, signal towers and hundreds of other structures, like castles, forts and garages to complete your play outfits.

Girls! Think of being able to build your own doll house, with as many stories or rooms as you like and with real windows and balconies, that will make your little friends envy you.

The buildings you make will not be flimsy and shaky, but will be structures you can lift and carry about. Still if you want to build something else, just take them apart in a jiffy and start building something else.

All Bilt-E-Z parts are interchangeable, so having one set is no barrier to purchasing another set. It will simply mean that you will have more parts and can build larger and more complex models. All parts are metal enameled in white and gray. We offer four different size sets. Each set comes in heavy cardboard box covered with neat looking imitation leather effect paper. Very attractive for gift purposes. In each set are floors, windows, walls, friction pieces, cornices and balconies in varying quantities, depending on the price of the set.

No. B—$5.00 Set for $4.47.

Wonderful models can be made with this set. You can build over 300 models. Has 331 parts. Heavy cardboard box, 13⅛x9¾x2¼ in. Shpg. wt., 6 pounds.
79T4707.. **$4.47**

No. D—$10.00 Set $8.98

Will build more than 400 models. Think of this. It has 695 parts. Wonderful models can be built with this big set. Double deck heavy cardboard box, 13⅛x9¾x4⅝ in. Shpg. wt., 13¼ lbs.
79T4708. **$8.98**

No. 00—$2.00 Set for $1.77.

Will build more than 200 models. Has 146 parts. Box, 9⅞x6¾x1¾ in. Shpg. wt., 2¾ lbs.
49T4706 **$1.77**

No. 0 Set, 89c.

Builds more than 100 models. There are 70 parts in this set. Size of box, 9¾ x 6⅞ x ⅞ in. Shpg.wt., 1⅝ lbs.
49T4705 **89c**

TINKER TOY

The Wonder Builder.

No toy is more educating or amusing to a child. This toy is based on the old adage that, "A stick and a spool will amuse a child." Each set consists of about seventy pieces. This toy is just as interesting to a girl as it is to a boy. The possibilities are unlimited. We sell it three ways: **1 Set for 63c.**

For building simple models. Shpg. wt., 1 lb.
49T4760—Per set.. **63c**

2 Sets for $1.21.

To build larger models. Shpg. wt., 2¼ lbs.
49T4761
2 sets for........ **$1.21**

3 Sets for $1.75.

For building the still more complicated models. Shpg.wt., 3¼ lbs.
49T4768
3 sets for........ **$1.75**

TYRO BLOCKS

Build Everything From Bridges to Bungalows.

After you have built something, you have a solid, actual object made of good smooth wood. A wren house, for instance, can be put up on a tree or pole, because it won't fall apart. Instruction book, full of models to copy.

$5.00 Set for $4.39.

Over 500 pieces. Will build an endless number of models, including large house shown. Box, 17x11x2¼ inches. Shipping Shpg. wt., 10¾ lbs.
79T4711........ **$4.39**

$2.00 Set for $1.69.

About 240 pieces. Builds many beautiful and complicated models. Box, 12¼x9x1⅞ in. Shipping weight, 4 pounds.
49T4710........ **$1.69**

$1.00 Set for 83c.

About 130 pieces. Will build loads of models. Box, 10½x7¼ inches. Shpg. wt., 2 lbs.
49T4709............ **83c**

$8.67 up

The Sturdy STUDEBAKER Farm Wagon

The Original Studebaker Junior Farm Wagon.

Boys! Here's a Perfect Miniature of Your Dad's Studebaker in Every Detail. The Best, Most Popular Wagon in the Country.

The sides and ends can be taken off, leaving bed and stakes, when lumber wagon is wanted. The gearing is made like that on large farm wagons with bent hounds and adjustable reach. All parts strongly ironed and braced; steel bushings in hub to take up wear; real steel tires 5/32 inch thick, welded together by hydraulic pressure; full 9/16-inch steel axles with each end threaded for a nut; strong hardwood staggered spokes with hub boxes and hub bands. All in all, built like a large farm wagon. Beautifully enameled in green and red, neatly striped and trimmed with black and yellow. All parts heavily varnished. Each complete with seat and tongue.

Studebaker Junior.

(As Illustrated.)

The one we recommend. An especially high class strong and substantial wagon. Well worth the difference in price over lower priced farm wagons. Body, 36x18 inches. Front wheels, 12 inches. Rear wheels, 18 inches. Strongly made throughout. Shipping weight, 75 pounds.

79T7685 .... $11.69

Harvard Farm Wagons.

Similar to the Studebaker Junior illustrated above, but with plainer gears and less trimming and details. Good, strong and substantial wagons. Will give good service and far superior to many cheaper made farm wagons sold at about the same price.

Large Size Harvard Farm Wagon. Body, 40x18 inches. Front wheels, 14 inches. Rear wheels, 20 inches. Shpg. wt., 75 lbs.

79T7676 .... $9.89

Harvard Junior. Body, 36x18 inches. Front wheels, 14 inches. Rear wheels, 20 inches. Shipping weight, 65 pounds.

79T7675 .... $8.67

Olympic Quality Steel Coaster Wagons.

Extra Strong Substantial Metal Wagons.

Stronger bracing, better gears and wheels, curved handle bar and made to withstand hard knocks. Rolled rim top reinforces body. Nickel plated hub caps. Body enameled a pretty blue and red; gears are black and handle natural.

79T7641—Size of body, 12½x26¼ inches; wheels, 10 inches. Shipping weight, 18½ pounds $2.98

79T7643—Size of body, 14½x30 inches; wheels, 11 inches. Shipping wt., 21½ lbs... 3.47

Faultless Steel Coaster Wagons.

The Smaller Size Metal Wagons.

Medium quality steel wagons. Rolled rim, sheet steel beaded body. Straight tongue and hardwood bottoms nicely finished, well braced throughout. Body enameled brilliant red outside; Euclid green inside; gilt stenciling. Gears and wheels black enameled.

Catalog No.	Size of Body, Inches	Wheels, Inches	Shpg. Wt., Lbs.	Each
79T7623	8 x18	6	6	$1.59
79T7624	10½x22	8	7¾	1.98
79T7632	12½x26	10	13½	2.59

It's a Sidway, Boys! Some Class!

The Beautiful Disc Wheel Steel Coasters.

High grade steel wagon throughout suitable for hauling and general utility. Extra strong sheet steel body beaded to reinforce sides and top rolled. Kiln dried wood bottom with four cross cleats. Strong heavy steel gears and fancy nickel plated hub caps. Body enameled blue and red.

Two Sizes.

Body, 26x12½. 10-inch double disc steel wheels with 5/8-inch rubber tires. Shipping weight, 20 pounds. 79T7644. $3.98

Body, 30x14½. 11-inch double disc steel wheels with ¾-inch rubber tires. Shipping weight, 25 pounds. 79T7645. $4.47

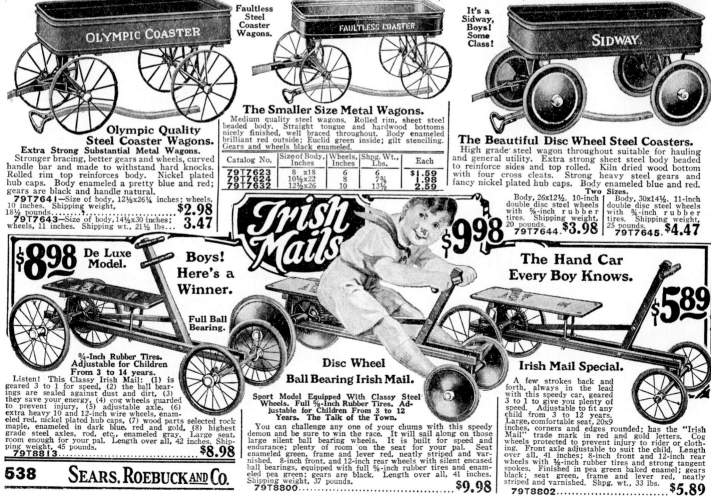

Irish Mails

$8.98 De Luxe Model.

Boys! Here's a Winner.

Full Ball Bearing.

¾-Inch Rubber Tires. Adjustable for Children From 3 to 14 years.

Listen! This Classy Irish Mail: (1) is geared 3 to 1 for speed, (2) the ball bearings are sealed against dust and dirt, (3) they save your energy, (4) cog wheels guarded to prevent injury, (5) adjustable axle, (6) extra heavy 10 and 12-inch wire wheels, enameled red, nickel plated hub caps, (7) wood parts selected rock maple, enameled in dark blue, red and gold, (8) highest grade steel axles, rod, etc., enameled gray. Large seat, room enough for your pal. Length over all, 42 inches. Shipping weight, 45 pounds.

79T8813 .... $8.98

$9.98

Disc Wheel Ball Bearing Irish Mail.

Sport Model Equipped With Classy Steel Wheels. Full 5/8-Inch Rubber Tires. Adjustable for Children From 3 to 12 Years. The Talk of the Town.

You can challenge any one of your chums with this speedy demon and be sure to win the race. It will sail along on those large silent ball bearing wheels. It is built for speed and endurance; plenty of room on the seat for your pal. Seat enameled green, frame and lever red, neatly striped and varnished. 8-inch front, and 12-inch rear wheels with silent encased ball bearings, equipped with full 5/8-inch rubber tires and enameled pea green; gears are black. Length over all, 41 inches. Shipping weight, 37 pounds.

79T8800 .... $9.98

The Hand Car Every Boy Knows.

$5.89

Irish Mail Special.

A few strokes back and forth, always in the lead with this speedy car, geared 3 to 1 to give you plenty of speed. Adjustable to fit any child from 3 to 12 years. Large, comfortable seat, 20x9 inches, corners and edges rounded; has the "Irish Mail" trade mark in red and gold letters. Cog wheels protected to prevent injury to rider or clothing. Front axle adjustable to suit the child. Length over all, 41 inches; 8-inch front and 12-inch rear wheels with ½-inch rubber tires and strong tangent spokes. Finished in pea green baked enamel; gears black; seat green, frame and lever red, neatly striped and varnished. Shpg. wt., 33 lbs.

79T8802 .... $5.89

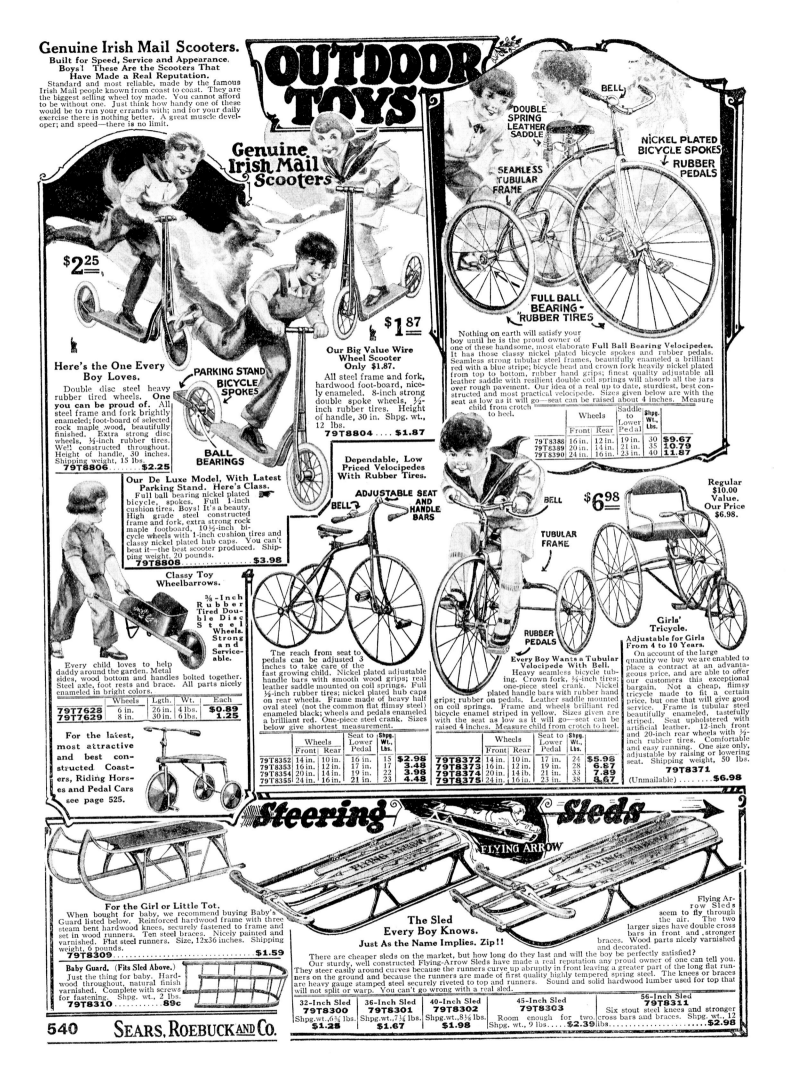

OUTDOOR TOYS

Genuine Irish Mail Scooters.

Built for Speed, Service and Appearance.
Boys! These Are the Scooters That Have Made a Real Reputation.

Standard and most reliable, made by the famous Irish Mail people known from coast to coast. They are the biggest selling wheel toy made. You cannot afford to be without one. Just think how handy one of these would be to run your errands with; and for your daily exercise there is nothing better. A great muscle developer; and speed—there is no limit.

Genuine Irish Mail Scooters

$2.25

Here's the One Every Boy Loves.

Double disc steel heavy rubber tired wheels. **One you can be proud of.** All steel frame and fork brightly enameled; foot-board of selected rock maple wood, beautifully finished. Extra strong disc wheels, ½-inch rubber tires. Well constructed throughout. Height of handle, 30 inches. Shipping weight, 15 lbs.
79T8806 . . . . $2.25

PARKING STAND
BICYCLE SPOKES
BALL BEARINGS

Our De Luxe Model, With Latest Parking Stand. Here's Class.

Full ball bearing nickel plated bicycle, spokes. Full 1-inch cushion tires. Boys! It's a beauty. High grade steel constructed frame and fork, extra strong rock maple footboard, 10½-inch bicycle wheels with 1-inch cushion tires and classy nickel plated hub caps. You can't beat it—the best scooter produced. Shipping weight, 20 pounds.
79T8808 . . . . $3.98

Classy Toy Wheelbarrows.

⅜-Inch Rubber Tired Double Disc Steel Wheels. Strong and Serviceable.

Every child loves to help daddy around the garden. Metal sides, wood bottom and handles bolted together. Steel axle, foot rests and brace. All parts nicely enameled in bright colors.

	Wheels	Lgth.	Wt.	Each
79T7628	6 in.	26 in.	4 lbs.	$0.89
79T7629	8 in.	30 in.	6 lbs.	1.25

For the latest, most attractive and best constructed Coasters, Riding Horses and Pedal Cars see page 525.

$1.87

Our Big Value Wire Wheel Scooter Only $1.87.

All steel frame and fork, hardwood foot-board, nicely enameled. 8-inch strong double spoke wheels, ½-inch rubber tires. Height of handle, 30 in. Shpg. wt., 12 lbs.
79T8804 . . . . $1.87

Dependable, Low Priced Velocipedes With Rubber Tires.

BELL
ADJUSTABLE SEAT AND HANDLE BARS

The reach from seat to pedals can be adjusted 3 inches to take care of the fast growing child. Nickel plated adjustable handle bars with smooth wood grips; real leather saddle mounted on coil springs. Full ½-inch rubber tires; nickel plated hub caps on rear wheels. Frame made of heavy half oval steel (not the common flat flimsy steel) enameled black; wheels and pedals enameled a brilliant red. One-piece steel crank. Sizes below give shortest measurement.

	Wheels		Seat to Lower Pedal	Shpg. Wt., Lbs.		
	Front	Rear				
79T8352	14 in.	10 in.	16 in.	15	$2.98	
79T8353	16 in.	12 in.	17 in.	17	3.48	
79T8354	20 in.	14 in.	19 in.	22	3.98	
79T8355	24 in.	16 in.	21 in.	23	4.48	

DOUBLE SPRING LEATHER SADDLE
SEAMLESS TUBULAR FRAME
BELL
NICKEL PLATED BICYCLE SPOKES
RUBBER PEDALS
FULL BALL BEARING RUBBER TIRES

Nothing on earth will satisfy your boy until he is the proud owner of one of these handsome, most elaborate **Full Ball Bearing Velocipedes.** It has those classy nickel plated bicycle spokes and rubber pedals. Seamless strong tubular steel frames, beautifully enameled a brilliant red with a blue stripe; bicycle head and crown fork heavily nickel plated from top to bottom, rubber hand grips; finest quality adjustable all leather saddle with resilient double coil springs will absorb all the jars over rough pavement. Our idea of a real up to date, sturdiest, best constructed and most practical velocipede. Sizes given below are with the seat as low as it will go—seat can be raised about 4 inches. Measure child from crotch to heel.

	Wheels		Saddle to Lower Pedal	Shpg. Wt. Lbs.	
	Front	Rear			
79T8388	16 in.	12 in.	19 in.	30	$9.67
79T8389	20 in.	14 in.	21 in.	35	10.79
79T8390	24 in.	16 in.	23 in.	40	11.87

$6.98

BELL
TUBULAR FRAME
RUBBER PEDALS

Every Boy Wants a Tubular Velocipede With Bell.

Heavy seamless bicycle tubing. Crown fork, ⅝-inch tires; one-piece steel crank. Nickel plated handle bars with rubber hand grips; rubber on pedals. Leather saddle mounted on coil springs. Frame and wheels brilliant red bicycle enamel striped in yellow. Sizes given with the seat as low as it will go—seat can be raised 4 inches. Measure child from crotch to heel.

	Wheels		Seat to Lower Pedal	Shpg. Wt., Lbs.	
	Front	Rear			
79T8372	14 in.	10 in.	17 in.	24	$5.98
79T8373	16 in.	12 in.	19 in.	28	6.87
79T8374	20 in.	14 in.	21 in.	33	7.89
79T8375	24 in.	16 in.	23 in.	38	8.67

Regular $10.00 Value. Our Price $6.98

Girls' Tricycle.

Adjustable for Girls From 4 to 10 Years.

On account of the large quantity we buy we are enabled to place a contract at an advantageous price, and are able to offer our customers this exceptional bargain. Not a cheap, flimsy tricycle made to fit a certain price, but one that will give good service. Frame is tubular steel beautifully enameled, tastefully striped. Seat upholstered with artificial leather. 12-inch front and 20-inch rear wheels with ½-inch rubber tires. Comfortable and easy running. One size only, adjustable by raising or lowering seat. Shipping weight, 50 lbs.
79T8371
(Unmailable) **$6.98**

Steering Sleds

FLYING ARROW

For the Girl or Little Tot.

When bought for baby, we recommend buying Baby's Guard listed below. Reinforced hardwood frame with three steam bent hardwood knees, securely fastened to frame and set in wood runners. Ten steel braces. Nicely painted and varnished. Flat steel runners. Size, 12x36 inches. Shipping weight, 6 pounds.
79T8309 . . . . $1.59

Baby Guard. (Fits Sled Above.)
Just the thing for baby. Hardwood throughout, natural finish varnished. Complete with screws for fastening. Shpg. wt., 2 lbs.
79T8310 . . . . 89c

The Sled Every Boy Knows.
Just As the Name Implies. Zip!!

There are cheaper sleds on the market, but how long do they last and will the boy be perfectly satisfied? Our sturdy, well constructed Flying-Arrow Sleds have made a real reputation any proud owner of one can tell you. They steer easily around curves because the runners curve up abruptly in front leaving a greater part of the long flat runners on the ground and because the runners are made of first quality highly tempered spring steel. The knees or braces are heavy gauge stamped steel securely riveted to top and runners. Sound and solid hardwood lumber used for top that will not split or warp. You can't go wrong with a real sled.

32-Inch Sled 79T8300	36-Inch Sled 79T8301	40-Inch Sled 79T8302	45-Inch Sled 79T8303	56-Inch Sled 79T8311
Shpg. wt., 6¾ lbs. $1.25	Shpg. wt., 7¼ lbs. $1.67	Shpg. wt., 8⅜ lbs. $1.98	Room enough for two. Shpg. wt., 9 lbs. . . . $2.39	Six stout steel knees and stronger cross bars and braces. Shpg. wt., 12 lbs. $2.98

Flying Arrow Sleds seem to fly through the air. The two larger sizes have double cross bars in front and stronger braces. Wood parts nicely varnished and decorated.

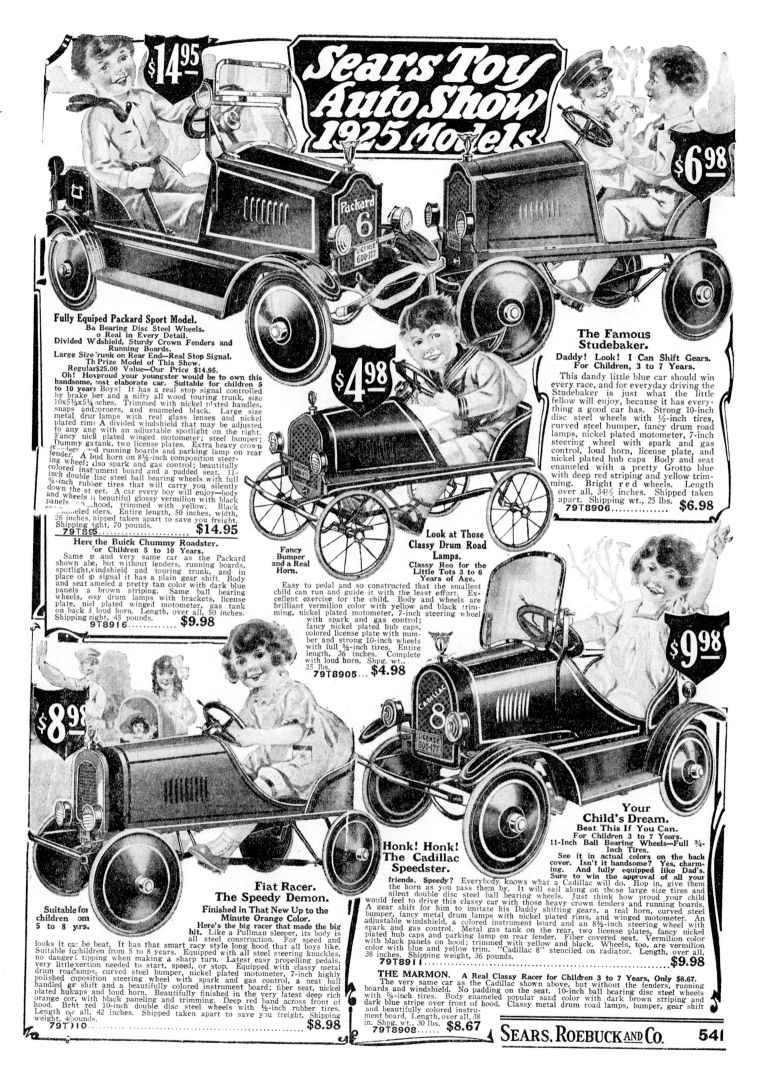

Sears Toy Auto Show 1925 Models

$14.95

$6.98

$4.98

$9.98

$8.98

Fully Equiped Packard Sport Model.

Ba Bearing Disc Steel Wheels.
o Real in Every Detail.
Divided Wdshield, Sturdy Crown Fenders and
Running Boards.
Large Size Trunk on Rear End—Real Stop Signal.
Th Prize Model of This Show.
Regular $25.00 Value—Our Price $14.95.

Oh! Ho proud your youngster would be to own this handsome, most elaborate car. Suitable for children 5 to 10 years. Boys! It has a real stop signal controlled by brake ler and a nifty all wood touring trunk, size 10x5½x5¼ inches. Trimmed with nickel plated handles, snaps and corners, and enameled black. Large size metal drur lamps with real glass lenses and nickel plated rim. A divided windshield that may be adjusted to any ang with an adjustable spotlight on the right. Fancy nicll plated winged motometer; steel bumper; Dummy ga tank, two license plates. Extra heavy crown fender. A loud horn on 8½-inch composition steering wheel; also spark and gas control; beautifully colored instrument board and a padded seat. 11-inch double disc steel ball bearing wheels with full ⅝-inch rubber tires that will carry you silently down the steet. A car every boy will enjoy—body and wheels in beautiful glossy vermilion with black panels on hood, trimmed with yellow. Black enameled iders. Entire length, 50 inches, width, 26 inches, hipped taken apart to save your freight. Shipping ight, 70 pounds.
79T895 . . . . $14.95

Here the Buick Chummy Roadster.
For Children 5 to 10 Years.

Same e and very same car as the Packard shown abe, but without fenders, running boards, spotlight, windshield and touring trunk, and in place of sp signal it has a plain gear shift. Body and seat ameled a pretty tan color with dark blue panels a brown striping. Same ball bearing wheels, ssy drum lamps with brackets, license plate, niel plated winged motometer, gas tank on back d loud horn. Length, over all, 50 inches. Shipping eight, 45 pounds.
9T8916 . . . . $9.98

The Famous Studebaker.

Daddy! Look! I Can Shift Gears.
For Children, 3 to 7 Years.

This dandy little blue car should win every race, and for everyday driving the Studebaker is just what the little fellow will enjoy, because it has everything a good car has. Strong 10-inch disc steel wheels with ½-inch tires, curved steel bumper, fancy drum road lamps, nickel plated motometer, 7-inch steering wheel with spark and gas control, loud horn, license plate, and nickel plated hub caps Body and seat enameled with a pretty Grotto blue with deep red striping and yellow trimming. Bright red wheels. Length over all, 34½ inches. Shipped taken apart. Shipping wt., 25 lbs.
79T8906 . . . . $6.98

Look at Those Classy Drum Road Lamps.

Classy Reo for the Little Tots 3 to 6 Years of Age.

Fancy Bumper and a Real Horn.

Easy to pedal and so constructed that the smallest child can run and guide it with the least effort. Excellent exercise for the child. Body and wheels are brilliant vermilion color with yellow and black trimming, nickel plated motometer, 7-inch steering wheel with spark and gas control; fancy nickel plated hub caps; colored license plate with number and strong 10-inch wheels with full ½-inch tires. Entire length, 36 inches. Complete with loud horn. Shpg. wt., 25 lbs.
79T8905 . . . $4.98

Fiat Racer.
The Speedy Demon.

Finished in That New Up to the Minute Orange Color.

Suitable for children om 5 to 8 yrs.

Here's the big racer that made the big hit. Like a Pullman sleeper, its body is all steel construction. For speed and looks it can be beat. It has that smart racy style long hood that all boys like. Suitable for children from 5 to 8 years. Equipped with all steel steering knuckles, no danger tipping when making a sharp turn. Latest easy propelling pedals, very little exertion needed to start, speed, or stop. Equipped with classy metal drum road lamps, curved steel bumper, nickel plated motometer, 7-inch highly polished omposition steering wheel with spark and gas control, a neat ball handled gar shift and a beautifully colored instrument board; fiber seat, nickel plated hubcaps and loud horn. Beautifully finished in the very latest deep rich orange cor, with black paneling and trimming. Deep red band across front of hood. Brht red 10-inch double disc steel wheels with ½-inch rubber tires. Length or all, 42 inches. Shipped taken apart to save you freight. Shipping weight, 4 pounds.
79T910 . . . . $8.98

Honk! Honk!
The Cadillac Speedster.

friends. Speedy? Everybody knows what a Cadillac will do. Hop in, give them the horn as you pass them by. It will sail along on these large size tires and silent double disc steel ball bearing wheels. Just think how proud your child would feel to drive this classy car with those heavy crown fenders and running boards. A gear shift for him to imitate his Daddy shifting gears, a real horn, curved steel bumper, fancy metal drum lamps with nickel plated rims, and winged motometer. An adjustable windshield, a colored instrument board and an 8½-inch steering wheel with spark and gas control. Metal gas tank on the rear, two license plates, fancy nickel plated hub caps and parking lamp on rear fender. Fiber covered seat. Vermilion color with black panels on hood; trimmed with yellow and black. Wheels, too, are vermilion color with blue and yellow trim. "Cadillac 8" stenciled on radiator. Length, over all, 38 inches. Shipping weight, 36 pounds.
79T8911 . . . . $9.98

Your Child's Dream.

Beat This If You Can.
For Children 3 to 7 Years.
11-Inch Ball Bearing Wheels—Full ¾-Inch Tires.

See it in actual colors on the back cover. Isn't it handsome? Yes, charming. And fully equipped like Dad's. Sure to win the approval of all your

THE MARMON.
A Real Classy Racer for Children 3 to 7 Years, Only $8.67.

The very same car as the Cadillac shown above, but without the fenders, running boards and windshield. No padding on the seat. 10-inch ball bearing disc steel wheels with ⅝-inch tires. Body enameled popular sand color with dark brown striping and dark blue stripe over front of hood. Classy metal drum road lamps, bumper, gear shift and beautifully colored instrument board. Length, over all, 38 in. Shpg. wt., 30 lbs.
79T8908 . . . . $8.67

Make Pals of Your Children

2 Boards in One **Aeroplane Race Game**

Metal checkerboard and aeroplane race. Brand new. Actual course of Round the World Flyers. Beautifully lithographed map of the world, flags of many nations, together with two spinners, on one side; 13-inch square checkerboard in black, red and white on other side. Four differently colored metal aeroplanes included. Turned edges, eliminating sharpness. Board, 16¾ in. square. Shipping wt., 2¾ lbs.
79D130.................. **89c**

79c **Barney Google and Spark Plug Game**

Two or four can play. Race between Spark Plug and Sassy Susie. Fun because of all the hazards and accidents. Beautifully lithographed, well bound playing board, 16½x16¼ inches. Two dice and 2 cups. Barney, Colonel Plop, Sparky and Sassy Susie are made of cardboard and mounted on wood blocks. Beautiful lithographed box, 17x8¾ in. Shipping weight, 2⅛ pounds.
49D170.................. **79c**

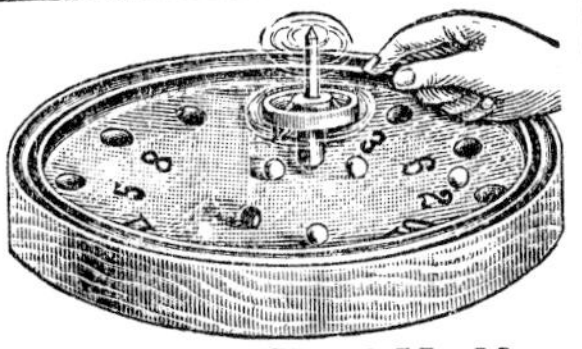

Watch Top Shoot Marbles Around

A Big $1.00 Retail Value for 69c

Highly polished hardwood bowl with overhanging lip. Numbered depression cups and square spindle top. Place balls in center and spin top, knocking balls in numbered holes. Largest score wins. Diameter, 7⅞ inches; 1 inch deep. Shipping weight, 2¼ pounds.
49D214.................. **69c**

Burrowes High Grade Home Pool Table

The Cleanest, Liveliest Indoor Entertainment

Inspires interest, develops skill and keeps the children at home. Encourages them to bring their friends in, thus enabling you to find out who their associates are. Burrowes tables are scaled down from the regulation size. Beds are smooth and level and covered with good quality cloth. The rubber cushions are live and give a quick accurate return. Four corner and two side pockets. Tables are of selected grain birchwood, mahogany finish. With each table is a complete outfit of 1⅞-inch balls, two 48-inch cues, triangle and chalk, also a Book of Rules.

This Fine Burrowes Table for $29.95

Size, 65x32½ inches between cushions. High grade. Has its own folding legs, rigidly braced and leveled by means of screw ball feet. These are collapsible so table can be put away. High grade rubber cushions covered with good quality green cloth. Shipping weight, 50 pounds. **Unmailable.**
79D481.................. **$29.95**

3 Popular Smaller Tables

Burrowes Pool Tables

These pool tables are unmailable

These three tables are characteristic Burrowes quality, but smaller in size. They are all made of the best materials, have good live cushions and good grade felt beds. With each table is a complete outfit of balls, two cues, triangle and chalk; also book of rules.

43½x23½ Inches With Folding Legs

Above are outside rail measurements. Comes with collapsible legs and looks like illustration above. Same quality as large size, but smaller throughout. Ht., 25½ in. Shpg. wt., 17 lbs.
79D477 **$8.59**

50x26½ Inches With Folding Legs Usually Retails for Around $18.00

One of our best selling sizes. Same as illustration above. Table measures 50x26½ inches outside rail, and when standing on its legs, 28 inches high. The stand is collapsible, permitting table to be put away. Pool balls, 1½ inches in diameter. Shipping weight, 25 pounds.
79D479.................. **$13.67**

43½x23½ Inches Without Legs

Outside rail measurements. No folding legs. Has 4 leveling blocks for table use. Shpg. wt., 15 lbs.
79D476 **$7.67**

79c **Toonin—A Real Radio Game**

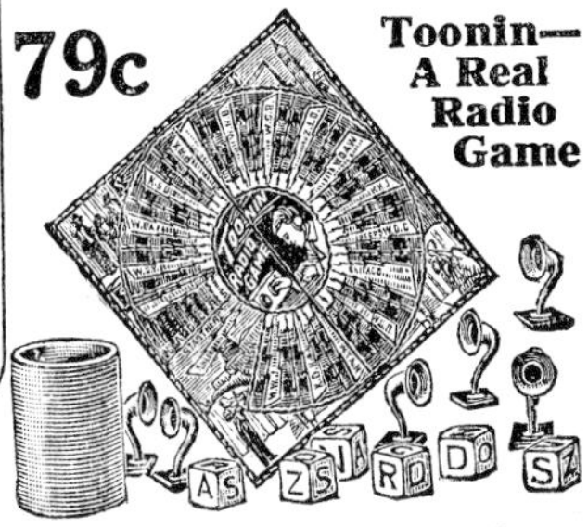

Very popular. Six can play. Interesting, thrilling race. Each player has a little metal loud speaker representing the six popular sets like Radiola, Crosley, Neutrodyne, etc. Large stations are represented on the beautifully lithographed playing board, 17x17½ inches. Loud speakers and wood dice included. Shipping weight, 1¼ pounds.
49D139.................. **79c**

Baseball and Football Games

Real Action More Popular Each Year

Only crack of the bat and the thud of the tackle missing. These games are sturdily built. Real action. Size, 13½x8⅞ in. Wood and steel frame. Shpg. wt., 2 lbs.

Baseball Game

Place player in batter's box, press lever; revolving drum and chart shows the result. Players run bases in regular fashion.
49D133.................. **$1.79**

Football Game

An exciting game where player can use judgment. Ball advances same as real game. Endorsed by college coaches.
49D132.................. **$1.79**

Special Auto Race Game for 39c

No more exciting game. Each kiddie has his own little metal racer. Spins the dial in his turn and advances or sets back his car on the attractively lithographed track according to his "break of luck." Big value for the price. Box, 11½ inches square. Shipping weight, 1¼ pounds.
49D144.................. **39c**

The Prettiest Ten-Pin Set We Have Ever Offered

Beautifully enameled ten pins in the shape of clowns finished in red, white, blue and black. Height, 5 inches, with a ⅝-inch base to make them stand up nicely. One red, one white and one blue ball. All in attractive box, 15⅛x5⅝ inches. Shpg. wt., 1⅝ lbs.
49D119.................. **98c**

Checkerboard in Case

Cloth covered portfolio case with a 14-inch flat cloth covered board and two sunken compartments holding composition checkers. When through just fasten snap on case and you have package only 14x7x½ inches. Shpg. wt., 1½ lbs.
49D114. **89c**

Backgammon and Checkerboard

Finished in red, gold and black. Book type, 15x15 inches, with set of checkers. Wood frame. Shpg. wt., 1½ lbs.
49D116. **43c**

4-Pole Magnetic Fish Pond

Pretty colored box, 9⅞x9⅞ inches. Folding pond, 6¾ inches square. Fish with the four poles, which are equipped with magnets. Twelve colored fish and other objects, like tin can, old shoes, etc. Shipping wt., 14 oz.
49D172 **39c**

Throw the Balls in the Basket

It isn't as easy as you think. Just try it. Lucky Pup is made of heavy fiber board with a metal frame support and is the creation of a famous illustrator in genuine, washable oil colors. Size, 13½x9⅛ in. Shpg. wt., 8 oz.
49D105 **39c**

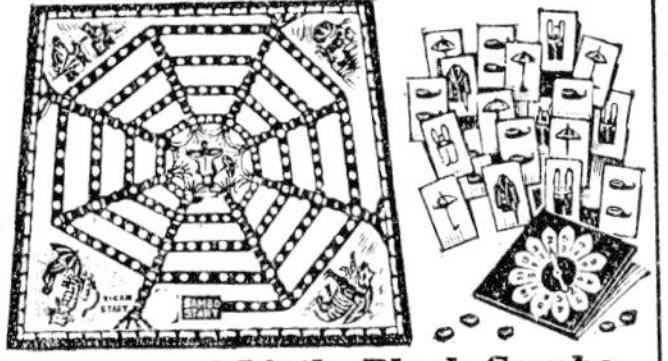

Game of Little Black Sambo

Retail 75c Game for 48c

Four ferocious tigers try to catch Sambo. When they catch him they take part of his clothes, just as in the story. Any tiger getting one each of the four articles of clothing wins. If Sambo gets around without being caught he wins. Five persons may play. Attractively lithographed, well bound playing board, 18x18 in. Shpg. wt., 1⅛ lbs.
49D180.................. **48c**

Shoot the Crows in the Corn

Four wood crows sit on wood rail fence with a funny farm scene on heavy cardboard as a background. When hit on the head crow falls over backward, but remains attached to the rail. 12-inch metal barrel pop-gun. Cork ammunition included. Attractive box, 12¾x11½ in. Shpg. wt., 2¼ lbs.
49D181.................. **79c**

19c

Three 10c Games in One Box, 19c

Nicely lithographed. Radio game printed on bottom of box. "Ocean to Ocean" and "Fire Fight" are the other two separate board games, measuring 11⅞x7¼ inches. Box, 12¼x7⅝ inches. Shipping weight, 1⅛ pounds.
49D122.................. **19c**

Donkey Party

Starched cloth sheet, 20 x 28½ in. With picture of donkey without tail, 23 loose tails to be attached. Blindfold everybody, give each a donkey tail and have him pin it on the donkey. Shipping weight, 5 oz.
49D135.................. **19c**

Playful Exercisers

Here's Value

$1.89

Genuine Toddler Cars

High Class

Riding Cars

Oh Boy—Sister is Winning

$2.25

$3.98

I Told you This was Some Bike

BICYCLE BELL

TUBULAR FRAME

BELL For Tots 2 to 5 Years

BALL BEARING WHEEL

Low broad wood seat with steel braces. 6-inch disc steel wheels with ⅜-inch rubber tires. Nicely enameled in red and black. Wood handle. A real bargain.

For Children from 1 to 3 Years

Height, to top of seat, 8¾ inches. Shipping weight, 7 pounds. **$1.89**
79D7516............$1.89

With Nickel Plated Bell— Rubber Pedals

For youngsters wanting pedal action. Extra strong double disc steel wheels. Practically indestructible. Seat, 15½ inches long and 7¼ inches wide. Steel frame and axles. Velocipede style steel handle bars with wooden grips, 8-inch front wheel with ⅝-inch rubber tire; 6-inch rear wheels with ½-inch tires and nickel plated hub caps. Beautifully enameled. Shpg. wt., 10 lbs. **$2.25**
79D8362.....$2.25

Kiddies' Velocipede

Adjustable seat can be raised 3 inches to allow for the fast growing child. Ball bearing double disc steel front wheel, full ¾-inch rubber tires and pedals. It is so easy to handle, parents need not worry about their child's safety. Up to date model, all steel construction. Wide comfortable wood seat. Nickel plated hub caps and velocipede style handle bars with smooth wood grips, 7½-in. rear wheels and 9½-in. front wheel. Enameled in rich snappy colors. Shpg. wt., 14 pounds. **$3.98**
79D8369.....$3.98

Disc Steel Wheels, with ½-inch rubber tires. Sturdy construction. Finished in brilliant red and yellow and nicely varnished. Foot rest for coasting.
79D7510—1 to 2 years. Height to top of seat, 8½ in. Length, 16¼ in. Shipping weight, 6 pounds. **$2.39**
79D7511—2 to 3 years. Height to top of seat, 10 in. Length, 18¼ in. Shpg. wt., 9 lbs....**$2.59**
79D7512—3 to 4 yrs. Ht. to top of seat, 11½ in. Lgth., 20 in. Shpg. wt., 10 lbs. **$2.79**

Baby's First Ride
$1.39

Little Brother Can Paddle *"Along and See the Whole Race"*

A Beautiful and Shiny Little Racer

for the Little Tot and Bright Gay Colors

Baby's first ride will be immensely enjoyed on this easy running paddle car. Nicely enameled wood seat, 4½-inch double disc steel wheels with ⅜-inch rubber tires. Shipping weight, 6 pounds. **$1.39**
79D7509............$1.39

And I'll Ride This Pony All the Way

Extra Fine Quality

Real Riding Horses

Horsie's head and front legs hinged for easy steering. Head turns with wheels. Hardwood reinforced with dowels, will withstand hard knocks and rough usage. Saddle shaped seat. Steel axles and nickel plated hub caps. Finished in chip proof enamel; red, green, gray and black.

Double Disc Steel Wheels—½-In. Rubber Tires

| 79D7506—For children 2 to 3 years. 5-in. wheels. Shpg. wt., 8½ lbs....**$2.98** | 79D7507—For children 3 to 4 years. 6-in. wheels. Shpg. wt., 11 lbs....**$3.48** |

Beautifully Ivory Cream Enameled Rocker
$1.98

Shpg. wt., 9½ lbs.

When dolly will not sleep just take her in your arms and rock her in this comfortable rocker. Well constructed, high grade in every respect. The long, flat arc rockers insure safety. Pretty transfer picture on back panel beautifully enameled in ivory-cream.
79D8563 **$1.98**

Height of seat from floor, 10¼ in. Seat, 10 in. square. Extreme height, 20⅝ in.

Baby's Giddap Horses

Usual $3.50 Retail Value **$2.47**

Da Da, Horsie

With This Pretty White Team of Horses Baby Can Keep Pace With the Rest of the Healthful Youngsters

The broad, flat arc of the rockers permits that gentle swaying motion so delightful to the little ones. Made of three-ply hardwood, beautifully enameled in white, red and black. Can be washed without injury to finish. Red enameled wood play box for baby's toys. All parts put together with strong wood screws. Has a wide comfortable seat and sanitary because it may be washed. Height, to tip of ears, 19¼ inches. Length, 36 inches. Width, about 12 inches. Shipping weight, 11 pounds. Unmailable.
79D7551............$2.47

Pretty Red Rockers

Round Bow Back Rocker

Made of strong hardwood. Painted bright red, neatly striped in black and yellow.

With Arm Rests

Seat, 10¾ in. from floor and is 11½ inches square. Height, 21½ in. Shipping weight, 6 pounds.
79D8565....**$1.69**

Without Arm Rests

Seat, 9½ in. from floor and measures 9x 10 in. Extreme height, 20 inches. Shpg. wt., 5½ lbs.
79D8559......**98c**

A Beauty Only $2.98

Gee! What a Swell Rocker

Oh Daddy BUY ME THIS BIG HORSE

This Beautiful Pony With Glass Eyes, Hair Mane and Tail

Only **$8.98**

Shpg. wt., 30 lbs.

Oh Boy This Is Some Galloper

$3.98

Shpg. wt., 17 lbs.

Shpg. wt., 13 lbs.

The broad platform and widely spaced rockers promote abundant stability. No effort has been spared in making this toy the leader in quality at an exceedingly low price. Selected materials and high class workmanship. Where is the youngster that doesn't love to have his own horse? Constructed entirely of wood with full shaped saddle. Dappled gray with red, yellow and black trimmings. Total height, 21½ inches. Height to saddle, 15 inches. Length of rockers, 37½ in. **$2.98**
79D7545—Unmailable..................$2.98

Dappled Gray Wood Hobby Horse

How tickled your youngster would be to receive this wonderful horse on Christmas morning or for his birthday. With one foot in the stirrup he grabs the reins and mounts his flying steed. Hair mane and tail; imitation leather saddle seat. Strong, nicely shaped body and legs, dapple gray finish. Natural looking glass eyes. Hardwood stand, strong metal braces. A good reproduction of a pony for a boy. Length, 38 in. Height, 29 in. Shaped metal stirrups. Unmailable.
79D7531............$8.98

High Class Swinging Horse

You cannot imagine how children enjoy riding a horse that has an even and gentle gallop. Here's one that will suit the youngster in every respect. Strong wood frame with metal swings. Quality horse finished in 5 snappy colors. Chip proof enamels. Height, 23¼ inches; length 33 inches. Unmailable.
79D7544............$3.98

This Is the Complete Gift Store

529

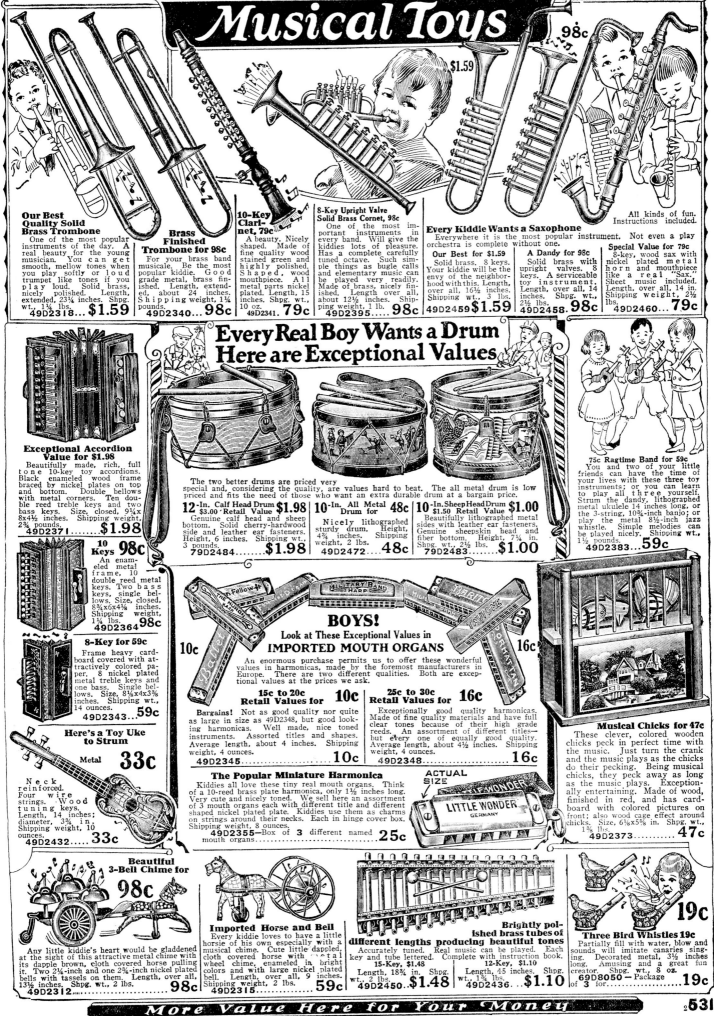

Musical Toys

Our Best Quality Solid Brass Trombone
One of the most popular instruments of the day. A real beauty for the young musician. You can get smooth, mellow tones when you play softly or loud trumpet like tones if you play loud. Solid brass, nicely polished. Length, extended, 23¼ inches. Shpg. wt., 1¼ lbs.
49D2318... **$1.59**

Brass Finished Trombone for 98c
For your brass band musicale. Be the most popular kiddie. Good grade metal, brass finished. Length, extended, about 24 inches. Shipping weight, 1¼ pounds.
49D2340... **98c**

10-Key Clarinet, 79c
A beauty. Nicely shaped. Made of fine quality wood stained green and highly polished. Shaped, wood mouthpiece. All metal parts nickel plated. Length, 15 inches. Shpg. wt., 10 oz.
49D2341. **79c**

8-Key Upright Valve Solid Brass Cornet, 98c
One of the most important instruments in every band. Will give the kiddies lots of pleasure. Has a complete carefully tuned octave. Such simple things as bugle calls and elementary music can be played very readily. Made of brass, nicely finished. Length over all, about 12½ inches. Shipping weight, 1 lb.
49D2395..... **98c**

Every Kiddie Wants a Saxophone
Everywhere it is the most popular instrument. Not even a play orchestra is complete without one.

All kinds of fun. Instructions included.

Our Best for $1.59
Solid brass. 8 keys. Your kiddie will be the envy of the neighborhood with this. Length, over all, 16½ inches. Shipping wt., 3 lbs.
49D2459 **$1.59**

A Dandy for 98c
Solid brass with upright valves. 8 keys. A serviceable toy instrument. Length, over all, 14 inches. Shpg. wt., 2½ lbs.
49D2458. **98c**

Special Value for 79c
8-key, wood sax with nickel plated metal horn and mouthpiece like a real "Sax." Sheet music included. Length, over all, 14 in. Shipping weight, 2½ lbs.
49D2460... **79c**

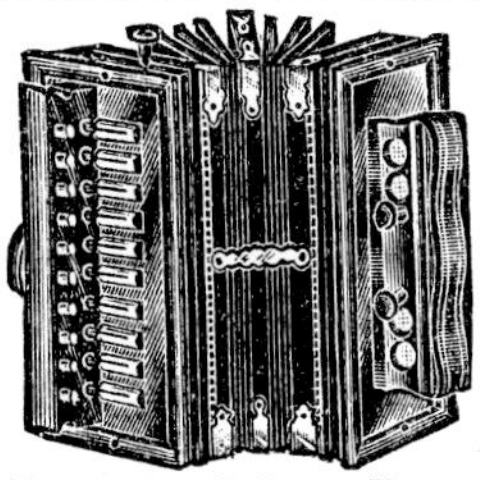

Exceptional Accordion Value for $1.98
Beautifully made, rich, full tone 10-key toy accordions. Black enameled wood frame braced by nickel plates on top and bottom. Double bellows with metal corners. Ten double reed treble keys and two bass keys. Size, closed, 9¼x8x4½ inches. Shipping weight, 2¾ pounds.
49D2371........ **$1.98**

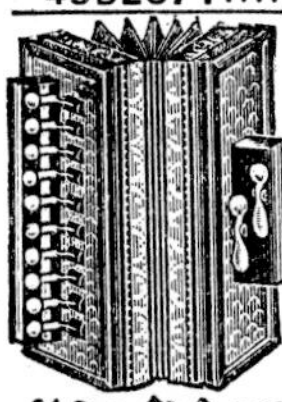

10 Keys 98c
An enameled metal frame, 10 double reed metal keys. Two bass keys, single bellows. Size, closed, 8¾x6x4⅛ inches. Shipping weight, 1¼ lbs.
49D2364 **98c**

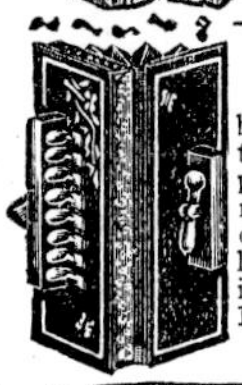

8-Key for 59c
Frame heavy cardboard covered with attractively colored paper. 8 nickel plated metal treble keys and one bass. Single bellows. Size, 8⅛x4x3⅜ inches. Shipping wt., 14 ounces.
49D2343... **59c**

Every Real Boy Wants a Drum
Here are Exceptional Values

The two better drums are priced very special and, considering the quality, are values hard to beat. The all metal drum is low priced and fits the need of those who want an extra durable drum at a bargain price.

12-In. Calf Head Drum $3.00 Retail Value $1.98
Genuine calf head and sheep bottom. Solid cherry-hardwood side and leather ear fasteners. Height, 6 inches. Shipping wt., 3 pounds.
79D2484........ **$1.98**

10-In. All Metal Drum for 48c
Nicely lithographed sturdy drum. Height, 4¾ inches. Shipping weight, 2 lbs.
49D2472.... **48c**

10-In. Sheep Head Drum $1.50 Retail Value $1.00
Beautifully lithographed metal sides with leather ear fasteners. Genuine sheepskin head and fiber bottom. Height, 7¼ in. Shpg. wt., 2½ lbs.
79D2483........ **$1.00**

75c Ragtime Band for 59c
You and two of your little friends can have the time of your lives with these three toy instruments; or you can learn to play all three yourself. Strum the dandy, lithographed metal ukulele 14 inches long, or the 3-string, 10¾-inch banjo; or play the metal 8½-inch jazz whistle. Simple melodies can be played nicely. Shipping wt., 1½ pounds.
49D2383... **59c**

10c

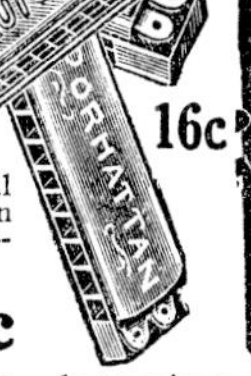

16c

BOYS!
Look at These Exceptional Values in IMPORTED MOUTH ORGANS

An enormous purchase permits us to offer these wonderful values in harmonicas, made by the foremost manufacturers in Europe. There are two different qualities. Both are exceptional values at the prices we ask.

15c to 20c Retail Values for 10c
Bargains! Not as good quality nor quite as large in size as 49D2348, but good looking harmonicas. Well made, nice toned instruments. Assorted titles and shapes. Average length, about 4 inches. Shipping weight, 4 ounces.
49D2345.............................. **10c**

25c to 30c Retail Values for 16c
Exceptionally good quality harmonicas. Made of fine quality materials and have full clear tones because of their high grade reeds. An assortment of different titles—but every one of equally good quality. Average length, about 4½ inches. Shipping weight, 4 ounces.
49D2348.............................. **16c**

Musical Chicks for 47c
These clever, colored wooden chicks peck in perfect time with the music. Just turn the crank and the music plays as the chicks do their pecking. Being musical chicks, they peck away as long as the music plays. Exceptionally entertaining. Made of wood, finished in red, and has cardboard with colored pictures on front; also wood cage effect around chicks. Size, 6⅛x5⅝ in. Shpg. wt., 1⅜ lbs.
49D2373.......... **47c**

Here's a Toy Uke to Strum
Metal **33c**

Neck reinforced. Four wire strings. Wood tuning keys. Length, 14 inches; diameter, 3¾ in. Shipping weight, 10 ounces.
49D2432..... **33c**

The Popular Miniature Harmonica
Kiddies all love these tiny real mouth organs. Think of a 10-reed brass plate harmonica, only 1½ inches long. Very cute and nicely toned. We sell here an assortment of 3 mouth organs each with different title and different shaped nickel plated plate. Kiddies use them as charms on strings around their necks. Each in hinge cover box. Shipping weight, 8 ounces.
49D2355—Box of 3 different named mouth organs........................ **25c**

ACTUAL SIZE

Beautiful 3-Bell Chime for 98c

Any little kiddie's heart would be gladdened at the sight of this attractive metal chime with its dapple brown, cloth covered horse pulling it. Two 2¼-inch and one 2¾-inch nickel plated bells with tassels on them. Length, over all, 13½ inches. Shpg. wt., 2 lbs.
49D2312.............................. **98c**

Imported Horse and Bell
Every kiddie loves to have a little horsie of his own especially with a musical chime. Cute little dappled, cloth covered horse with metal wheel chime, enameled in bright colors and with large nickel plated bell. Length, over all, 9 inches. Shipping weight, 2 lbs.
49D2315.............. **59c**

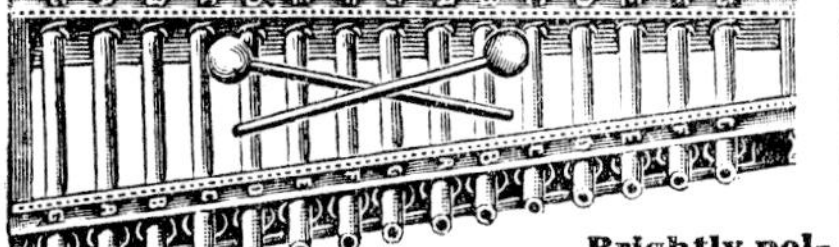

Brightly polished brass tubes of different lengths producing beautiful tones
Accurately tuned. Real music can be played. Each key and tube lettered. Complete with instruction book.

15-Key, $1.48
Length, 18¾ in. Shpg. wt., 2 lbs.
49D2450.. **$1.48**

12-Key, $1.10
Length, 15 inches. Shpg. wt., 1¾ lbs.
49D2436. .. **$1.10**

19c

Three Bird Whistles 19c
Partially fill with water, blow and sounds will imitate canaries singing. Decorated metal, 3½ inches long. Amusing and a great fun creator. Shpg. wt., 8 oz.
69D8050—Package of 3 for...................... **19c**

More Value Here for Your Money

Wind it up and watch Ham run his hands up and down the keyboard while Sam dances with his banjo in his hands. Snappy colors, with attractive decorations. Made of metal. Good spring. Size, 8x7½ inches. Has stop and start device. Shipping weight, 1½ pounds.
49D5788......................**89c**

Fluffy Jumping Rabbit
59c

Even a tiny baby's eyes will pop when he sees it. The size of a baby cottontail. Covered with real fur. Glass eyes. Press rubber bulb and rabbit jumps and moves its ears. A cuddling toy, as well. Size, over all, about 6 inches. Shipping weight, 10 ounces.
49D5769......................**59c**

Jazzbo Jim and His Fiddler
45c

While Jazzbo dances, his little friend Sambo fiddles away. Strong, substantial spring. A very clever toy and an exceptional value, far better than ever offered before. Made of metal, beautifully lithographed to represent a typical southern plantation cabin. Height, 11 inches; base, 4⅝ x 3⅛ inches. Shipping weight, 13 ounces.
49D5721..**45c**

New Automatic Marble Toy With Man Driver
98c

Watch the little man handle the pile driver. He rides up and down in his two-wheel car, working the dummy hammer up and down as long as marbles are kept in hopper above. Complete with twelve marbles. Size, over all, 16¼x12¼ inches. Shipping weight, 2½ lbs.
49D5822
98c

This Wild West Broncho Really Bucks
48c

A metal horse and cowboy rider. Lithographed in colors. Horse gallops, rears and plunges along over the floor. Good strong spring. Size, over all, 6¼ inches long and 6¼ inches high. Shipping weight, 12 oz.
49D5702.............**48c**

Looks Like a Real Mouse

It's just the size and color of a mouse and when it runs along the floor the girls climb onto the furniture. If you want to have fun, get one. Made of metal, friction motor. 2¾ in. long without tail. Shipping weight, 3 oz.
49D5716.................**19c**

89c

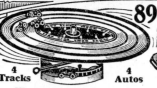

4 Tracks   4 Autos

These Autos Actually Race
Lots of Excitement for Old or Young

Another new mechanical toy hit. After motor is wound the cars sway round and round in their individual courses by the peculiar up and down revolving motion of the track which makes it very uncertain as to the progress of the racers, anyone being likely to win. Track, 11¾ inches in diameter made of metal, beautifully lithographed. Cars, 2⅛ inches long are made of metal and finished in snappy colors. Good spring motor. Height, over all, 3½ in. Shpg. wt., 1½ lbs.
49D5713......................**89c**

Over and Under, the Long Running Racer

Forward on upper incline, backward on lower incline. Then automatically up and over again. Sheet steel, nicely decorated. Wind up spring, then place the 2½-inch racer on upper track and it will run down incline. After it reaches lower end of bottom track the motor starts; carrier picks up auto and carries it to the upper track. Size, about 25x4 in. Shipping weight, 2⅛ pounds.
49D5832......................**89c**

Beam, 16 in.; Tower, 9¼ in.; Airplane, 8x6 in.

89c

The Most Realistic Airplane We Have Seen

One of the cleverest new toys of the season. Aluminum plane, 8x6 in. attached to the metal tower by metal arm and balanced by a weight on other end. Wind spring and airplane rises gradually off the floor until it flies at a level near top of tower. Then as motor dies down, it gets lower and lower until finally it gracefully lands on the floor again. Shpg. wt., 1½ lbs.
49D5703......................**89c**

Hee Haw—The Balky Mule
43c

A comical toy. Mule backs up when he should go forward and rears up on his hind legs so that the poor old driver doesn't know what to do. Metal, and finished in attractive natural colors. Assorted designs. Strong spring. Average length, about 9 inches; 6 in. high. Shipping weight, 12 ounces.
49D5747.................**43c**

Exceptional Value for **43c**

Every kiddie is interested in airplanes now and would be tickled to own one of these. Sheet steel and lithographed in attractive colors. Travels straight or in a circle. Adjustable rudder. A duplicate of a real plane. Size, 10x9¼x2¾ in. Shpg. wt., 1½ lbs.
49D5719......................**43c**

Watch Gobbling Goose Peck Away
43c

Goose all dressed up in his suit lithographed in bright colors on his body. Waddles along on his web feet, swaying his head up and down pecking at the ground. Durable metal and equipped with good spring. Measures, 9 inches long and 4½ in. high. Shpg. wt., 1 lb.
49D5712......................**43c**

The Famous Gidap Pony
21c

Length, over all, 7⅝ in.; height, 5 in. Shpg. wt., 10 oz.

Made entirely of metal, lithographed in attractive colors.

Pony trots around in a circle as clown driver moves in his seat.
49D5767......................**21c**

The Popular Automatic Sand Crane, Special at $1.00

Remarkable how the little man works. No springs, no wheels. Will run as long as sand is kept in hopper. See the sand car load up. When filled it swings around in a big circle and the little man dumps contents in the can. All steel enameled. Bright colors. Size, 13⅞x14 inches. Can of sand included. Shipping wt., 3 lbs.
49D5782...**$1.00**

The Famous Sandy Andy

Light gauge sheet steel, attractively painted. Simply pour sand in the hopper and the car starts going up and down the incline, carrying sand to the bottom. This operation is continued as long as there is sand in the hopper. Size over all, 9¼x10¾ inches. Can of sand included. Shipping wt., 1¾ lbs.
49D5742...**59c**

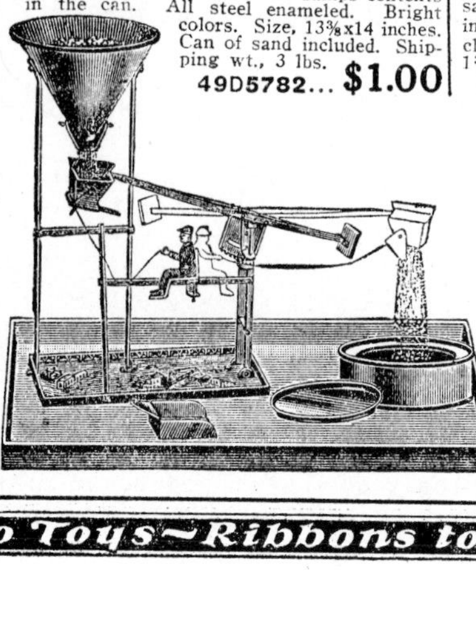

Greatest Mechanical Toy of the Year
89c

Ring-A-Ling Circus

Brand new; tremendous hit. When the spring is wound up the ringmaster goes round cracking his whip and making the animals and clown do their stunts. Monk climbs the pole, clown turns on the bar and lion and elephant rise up on the hind legs. Made of metal, lithographed in circus colors. Good spring motor. Width, 7¼ inches; height over all, 8½ inches. Shipping weight, 1½ pounds.
49D5717......................**89c**

Rap and Tap Boxers
43c

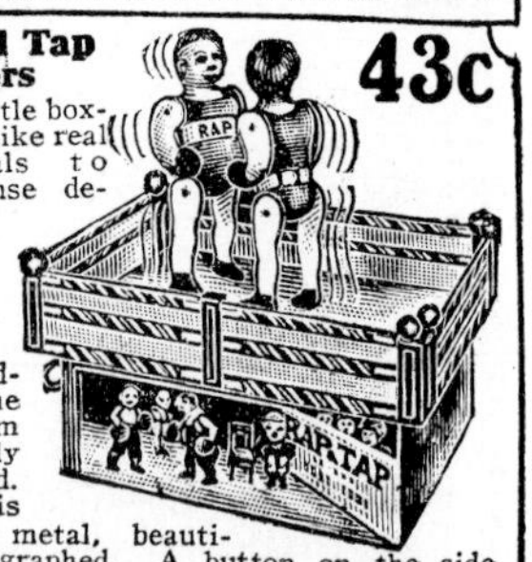

These little boxers battle like real professionals to the immense delight of the kiddies. The bout lasts over one minute for each winding. The mechanism is durably constructed. The toy is made of metal, beautifully lithographed. A button on the side stops the bout when you wish. 6½x6¼x5¾ inches. Shipping wt., 13 oz.
49D5761......................**43c**

The Famous Climbing Monkey
19c

Watch monk climb up and down the string. An ever popular toy and an endless run of pleasure for the kiddies. There are cheaper monkeys on the market, but they are not as satisfactory as this one. We offer large size, quality monk made of sheet metal lithographed in very attractive colors—just the kind to attract the child. A very good value, 9½ in. long and 3 in. wide. Shpg. wt., 1 lb.
49D5723.....**19c**

Famous Lehman Express
19c

An exceptionally good value. Man walks along naturally with his cart. A very popular toy with the kiddies. Made of metal lithographed in attractive colors. A very good spring motor. Has patented automatic brake which acts by itself, making it unnecessary to hold wheels while winding. 6¾ in. long, and 3¾ in. high.
49D5714—Shpg. wt., 1 lb.....**19c**

Playful Kitty

Runs around in real kittenlike manner. Realistically colored in black with decorative ribbon around neck. Brightly colored eyes. Durable metal; good spring. Size, 7¾ in. by 3¾ in. high.
49D5787—Shpg. wt., 8 oz...**23c**

See This Boat Spin Along the Water

Cranks like a racing auto. Friction motor spins propeller, thus driving boat through the water. Of sheet steel finished in red and white. Two rows of cabins. Two smokestacks. Two flags, one mast. 8⅝ in. long; height to top of stack, 3¾ inches. Shipping weight, 1½ pounds.
49D5743......................**59c**

For the Little Housekeeper

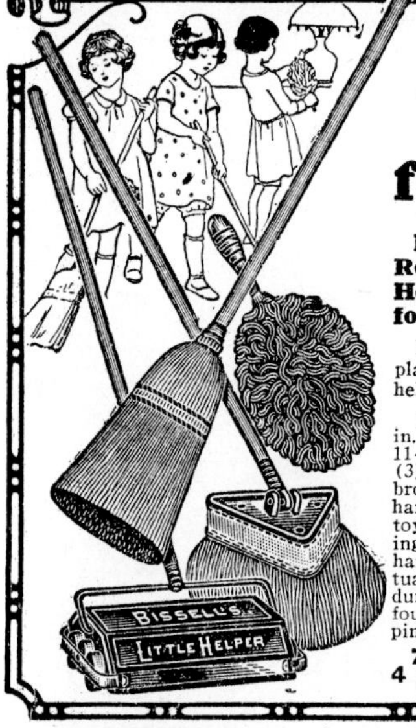

All 4 for 98c

Mothers! Here Is a Real Practical Toy House Cleaning Set for Little Girls.

Every little girl likes to play house, to sweep, and help mother with her work.

(1) A real mop with 24-in. round wood handle. (2) 11-in. cotton yarn duster. (3) A good grade 32-in. broom with varnished wood handle. (4) A real Bissell toy sweeper with revolving brush and round wood handle 24 in. long. It actually sweeps and has two dumping dust pans. All four packed in box. Shipping weight, 4 pounds.

79F9162—All 4 for........ 98c

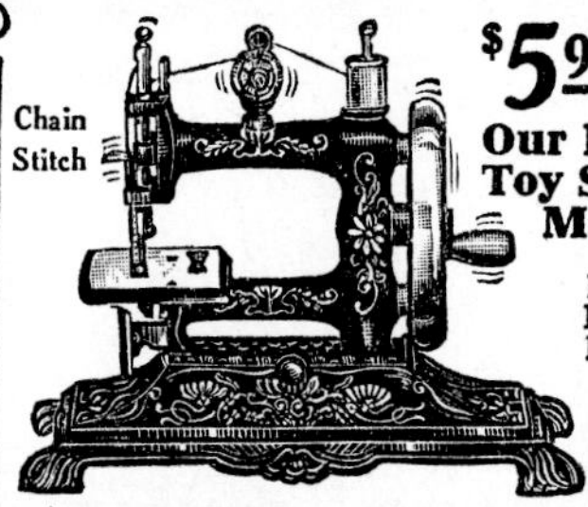

Chain Stitch

$5.98 Our Finest Toy Sewing Machine

Handy Little Machine for Around the House

Has many attachments for sewing. Can be used for many practical purposes. Very popular with travelers. All metal construction. Automatic tension, drop foot, shuttle, nickel plated sewing top, thread tension and heavy flywheel with handle. Base, black with gilt decoration. Size, 11x6½x8½ inches. Shipping weight, 13¾ pounds.

79F5810........................ $5.98

Remarkable Value for $3.47

$3.47

Chain Stitch

One of the best values we have ever offered for this price. For the smaller girl. Inexpensive but perfect in operation. All metal construction. Automatic tension. Chain stitch. Size, 7⅞x4½x6⅞ inches high. Shipping wt., 6 pounds.

49F5811........................ $3.47

Practical Toy Sewing Machine

$4.98

Chain Stitch

Sews easily and well. Fancy gilt decoration on black enamel; nickel plated wheel and trimmings. Made of heavy metal. Makes four chain stitches at each turn of the driving wheel. Size, 7⅞x5⅛x7¼ in. Shpg. wt., 6 lbs.

49F5800........................ $4.98

Every Little Girl Wants a Dresser Set These Are Hand Decorated. $2.69

Ivory Amber Set

This beautifully decorated set is sure to please. Made of grained ivory with amber edge. Filled pyralin mirror has beveled glass. Length of mirror, 8 inches. Brush and comb to match. Each set in cardboard display box. Shpg. wt., 2 lbs.

87F6131 $2.69

Hand Decorated Ivory Set

Attractive design toilet set made of white ivory filled celluloid. Mirror is 6¾ in. long and has a plain glass. Brush and comb to match. Each set in plain gift box. Shpg. wt., 1½ lbs.

87F6130 $1.39

Complete Sewing Box for Little Girls

98c

Here's an outfit every girl will enjoy. Made of bright red raffia interwoven with fancy straw braid. Hinged cover, and inside padded and covered with colored sateen. Six spools and two balls of colored thread, bodkin, thimble, celluloid tatting shuttle and three needles. Fancy snap for fastening. Size, 5½x3¾x2½ in. Neatly packed complete in box. Shipping weight, 1 pound.

69F9163........................ 98c

Girls' Octagon Shape Toy Wrist Watch

Every little girl loves to wear a wrist watch just like mother's. Ten pretty sparkling imitation diamonds set in around the dial; colored stone in stationary crown, heavy glass crystal; adjustable grosgrain ribbon wristlette with clasp for fastening. Shipping weight, 3 ounces.

69F9113........................ 25c

Popular Gift

$1.48

Chain Stitch

Black enamel metal. Nickel plated trimmings. A little machine that sews chain stitches smoothly. Size, 6x3½x6½ in. Each packed complete in box. Shpg. wt., 2½ lbs.

49F5802........ $1.48

Little Dandy

Chain Stitch

A Size Popular with Little Girls

$2.69

Solid and substantial. Made of heavy metal. Thread tension, raising foot. Makes fine stitches. Enameled black with gilt decorations. Nickel plated sewing top. Size, 6½x6x4 inches. Shipping weight, 4 lbs.

49F5809 $2.69

For the Doll's Laundry

Fancy Nickel Plated Stoves

Every little girl plays house and her first wish is to have a brightly nickel plated stove. Each stove has a fancy back with plate warmers, kettle, frying pan and lid lifter.

A Large Beauty for the Good Cook

As illustrated. Size, over all, 12x5¾ in. Total height, 11¼ in. Water reservoir and lined oven. Shipping wt., 8 lbs.

69F7321........ $2.59

Our $1.79 Stove

Size, over all, 11x5⅛ inches. Total height, 9½ in. Water reservoir, oven not lined. Shipping weight, 6 pounds.

69F7320........................ $1.79

For Baby Sister

Size of top, 6⅛x4 inches. Height, 6⅝ inches. No reservoir, coal scuttle or shovel. Oven is not lined. Shipping weight, 4 pounds.

69F7301........................ 98c

Beautiful Blue and White Enameled Toy Gas Ranges

Two lower ovens open on hinges and upper oven lifts up. Large size range has extra protector at top over cooking surface.

Here's a Dandy

Has two large size utensils. Height, 9¼ in.; width, 8⅝ in.; depth, 4⅞ in. Shpg. wt., 8 lbs.

69F7306........ $2.59

Our Special for $1.69

With two medium size utensils. Height, 8 inches; width, 7¾ in.; depth, 4 in. Shpg. wt., 5 lbs.

69F7305........................ $1.69

Everything for Dolly's Laundry

$1.98

Rubber Roll Wringers

10-Inch Metal Wash Tub

Glass Surface Wash-board

Usually retails for $2.50. Girls! When mamma does her washing you can do yours. 10-inch metal tub, finished in blue enamel with white enamel inside. Metal wringer with 3¾-inch rubber rollers which wring clothes. Wood frame, heavy glass surface washboard, 11x5⅛ inches, a collapsible clothes rack, wash basket, 11½x7 in., and 6 clothespins.

79F1701—Shipping weight, 4 pounds........ $1.98

Special Set $1.00

A dandy set for any little girl. Consists of a strong wood ironing board, 21¾x5⅝x13⅜ inches, a nickel plated sadiron, 4⅛x2½ inches, a basket, 11½x7¼ inches, 12 feet of clothesline, 2 iron pulleys, 6 tiny clothespins in bag, 6-inch metal tub and 7x3¾-inch metal washboard. Exceptional value. Shipping weight, 5¾ lbs.

79F1704 $1.00

Baby Betsy Ironing Boards

Will You Need a Toy Sadiron? See Them Below.

The One We Recommend

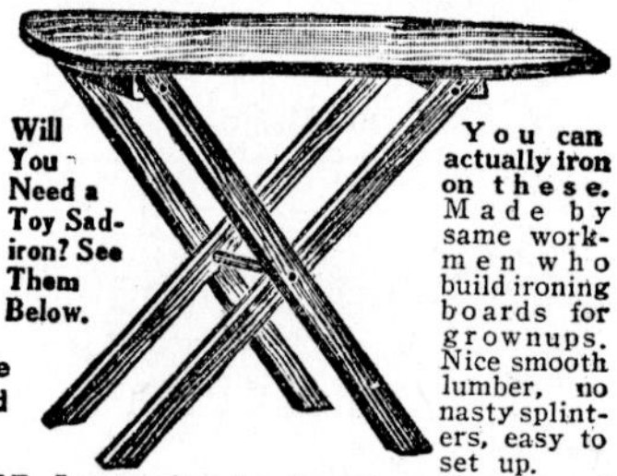

You can actually iron on these. Made by same workmen who build ironing boards for grownups. Nice smooth lumber, no nasty splinters, easy to set up.

79F1775—Large size for important business of ironing dolls' clothes, handkerchiefs, and lots of other things. Top is 35x10¾ in. Height, adjustable from 20 to 25 in. Shpg. wt., 5¾ lbs.... 98c

For the Tiny Tot

49F1777—Very strong. Looks just like mother's. Size, top, 21½x5½ in. About 13½ inches high. Shipping weight, 1½ pounds........ 39c

Nickel Plated Toy Sadirons

These actually iron. Like mamma's. Detach the bottom, heat and when hot attach handle and iron away. Polished wood handles. Two sizes.

Our Small Iron

4⅛x2½ in. Shpg. wt., 1 lb.

49F1797........................ 22c

Our Large Iron

4⅞x3½ inches. Shipping weight, 1¾ lbs.

49F1798........................ 45c

$2.98

Something Out of the Ordinary for the Little Girl

A Beautiful Sewing Cabinet

This handsome cabinet will be greatly appreciated by her. Made of wood, enameled in a pretty ivory and blue. Two hinged covers. Height, 20 in. Shpg. wt., 8 lbs.

79F9161. $2.98

48c

Four-Piece Metal Laundry Set, 48c

Every Girl Should Have This Washday Set

Consists of 6-in. diameter tub, 7-in. washboard, 5½x3¼-in. wash boiler and 3½x4½-in. water kettle. Like utensils mother uses. Shipping weight, 1¼ lbs.

49F1791 Per set........ 48c

9-Inch King Roadster for 25c

25c

A wonderful value. Complete with bumper, imitation headlights, motometer, disc wheels, extra wheel and a sport top. Made of metal, finished in snappy, bright colors. Good spring. Length, 9 inches; 3⅞ inches high.
49F5031—Shpg. wt., 12 oz....**25c**

Sand Crane and Dump Truck

48c

A big value, and a combination with lots of play value. Both items are made of metal, attractively decorated. Crane is reproduction of real crane. Just turn crank, and scoop will pick up dirt or sand and place it where you wish. Cab can be turned around on platform. Measures 8½x7¼ inches. The auto is a duplicate of a Mack Truck, has a driver, strong spring motor and will actually dump. Measures 9¾ inches long and 4¼ inches high. Shipping wt., 1½ lbs.
49F5028—Both for.........**48c**

See This Hand Car Fly Along

An attractively lithographed metal hand car with a man who bobs forward and backward as he pumps the handle up and down. Duplicate of what you see on the railroads. Strong spring motor. Length, 6 inches; height, 5¾ inches. Shipping weight, 8 oz. **23c**
49F5737.........................**23c**

The Whiz Airplanes

69c   **43c**

Patterned after monoplane that crossed the United States without a stop

Every kiddie is interested in an airplane, especially if it has action. When their strong spring motors are wound up these attractively lithographed airplanes run along the floor at a great speed. Two sizes:

Our Largest Airplane	Our Smallest One
Adjustable rudder runs it straight or in circle. 12½ in. long. 10 in. wide. Shpg. wt., 2 lbs. **49F5724. 69c**	No adjustable rudder. 10 inches wide, 9¼ inches long. Shipping weight, 1½ pounds. **49F5719. 43c**

89c

All Metal. Lithographed

Airplane, 9x6 in.
Tower, 10 in.
Beam, 13 in.

The Most Realistic Airplane on the Market

Plane is suspended from tower by long arm and balanced by dirigible balloon. When spring is wound up and released, airplane gradually rises until it flies at level near top of tower. As motor dies it glides gracefully to ground. Has globe on top.
49F5765—Shipping weight, 1½ pounds.........................**89c**

Brand New Funny Flivver

43c

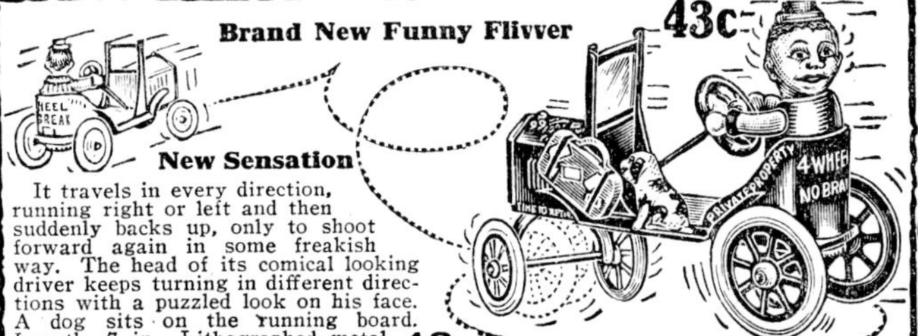

New Sensation

It travels in every direction, running right or left and then suddenly backs up, only to shoot forward again in some freakish way. The head of its comical looking driver keeps turning in different directions with a puzzled look on his face. A dog sits on the running board. Length, 7 in. Lithographed metal.
49F5026—Shpg. wt., 12 oz....**43c**

Four Marx Favorites

59c   **Famous Honeymoon Express**

One of the most popular mechanical toys. A miniature train travels along swiftly through three tunnels, while the flagman signals with his flag. Beautifully lithographed on metal in snappy colors. Lots of action and attractive in appearance. Strong spring motor. Diameter, 10 inches; height, 2¾ inches. Shipping weight, 1 pound.
49F5725.........................**59c**

Whole Circus in Itself

89c

Tremendous hit. When the spring is wound up the ringmaster goes round cracking his whip and making the animals and clown in their turn do their stunts. Monk climbs the pole, clown turns on the bar and lion and elephant rise up on their hind legs. Made of metal, lithographed in circus colors. Good spring motor. Diameter, base, 7⅞ inches; height, over all, 8 inches. Shipping weight, 1½ pounds.
49F5717.........................**89c**

Chicken Snatcher

45c

One of the new, most novel toys of the year. When the strong spring motor is wound up this scared looking negro shuffles along with a chicken dangling in his hand and a dog hanging on the seat of his pants. A very funny toy which will delight the kiddies. Snappily lithographed metal. Height, 9 inches. Shipping weight, 1 pound.
49F5728...............**45c**

Charleston Trio

45c

A toy right up to the minute. New this year. Very snappy action. When strong spring is wound up Charleston Charlie dances while the small negro fiddles and the dog nods his approval. Made of metal, lithographed in attractive colors. Length, 4⅝ inches; height, 9 inches. Shpg. wt., 1 lb.
49F5727...............**45c**

Spick and Span, the Comical Musicians

This toy certainly appeals to the kiddies because of its color and action. Made of metal, lithographed in very attractive colors. When strong spring motor is wound up Spic plays the bass drum, cymbal and trap drum while Span dances a jig as he rubs his bow on the violin. Length, 6¼ inches; height, 10 inches. Shipping weight, 13 ounces.
49F5726.....................**69c**

69c

Auto and Wrecker

48c

Here you have a wrecking car all ready to take care of your racer in case of breakdown. A popular combination. Both are lithographed in bright colors and have strong spring motors. Racer measures 8¼ inches long and the Wrecker, which has a crank that unwinds and winds up the cord holding the wrecking hook, measures 9¼ inches long. Shpg. wt., 1½ lbs.
49F5030—Both for.........**48c**

Home Run King

A real slugger. Stands with bat in hand, affixed to revolving platform 2½ in. in diameter. When strong spring motor is wound up and released the platform revolves, the player swings round with his bat and hits one of the wooden balls. Another ball automatically works up on pedestal. About 10 little balls included. Platform represents baseball diamond. 6¼x3½ inches. Height of toy, over all, about 6¾ inches. Metal, lithographed in attractive colors. Shipping weight, 12 ounces.
49F5749.....................**59c**

59c

10-Inch Motor Bus

47c

A duplicate of the type of bus that travels from city to city. Every kiddie who sees them will want one of his own. Made of metal, lithographed in attractive colors. Strong spring motor. Length, 10 inches; height, 3 inches. Shipping weight, 12 ounces.
49F5034.....................**47c**

Battling Boxers

45c

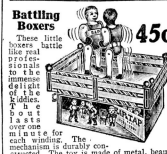

These little boxers battle like real professionals to the immense delight of the kiddies. The bout lasts over one minute for each winding. The mechanism is durably constructed. The toy is made of metal, beautifully lithographed. A button on the side stops the bout when you wish. Size, 6¼x5⅞x4¼ in. Shpg. wt., 13 oz.
49F5761.....................**45c**

4 Tracks   4 Autos

89c

Shpg. wt., 1½ lbs.

These Autos Actually Race

Lots of Excitement for Old or Young

After motor is wound the cars whirl round in their individual courses by the peculiar up and down rocking motion of the track which makes it very uncertain as to the progress of the racers, anyone being likely to win. Track, 13 inches in diameter, made of metal, beautifully lithographed. Cars, 2 inches long, are made of metal and finished in distinguishing snappy colors. Good spring motor.
49F5713—Height, over all, 3½ inches.....................**89c**

Hee Haw—The Balky Mule

43c

Real Action

He Balks
He Kicks

A comical toy. Uncanny how it operates. One of our most popular mechanical toys. Bigger and bigger hit each year. Mule backs up when he should go forward and rears up on his hind legs so that the poor driver doesn't know what to do. Metal, and finished in attractive natural colors. Assorted designs. Strong spring. Average length, about 9 inches; 5¾ inches high.
49F5747—Shipping weight, 12 ounces............**43c**

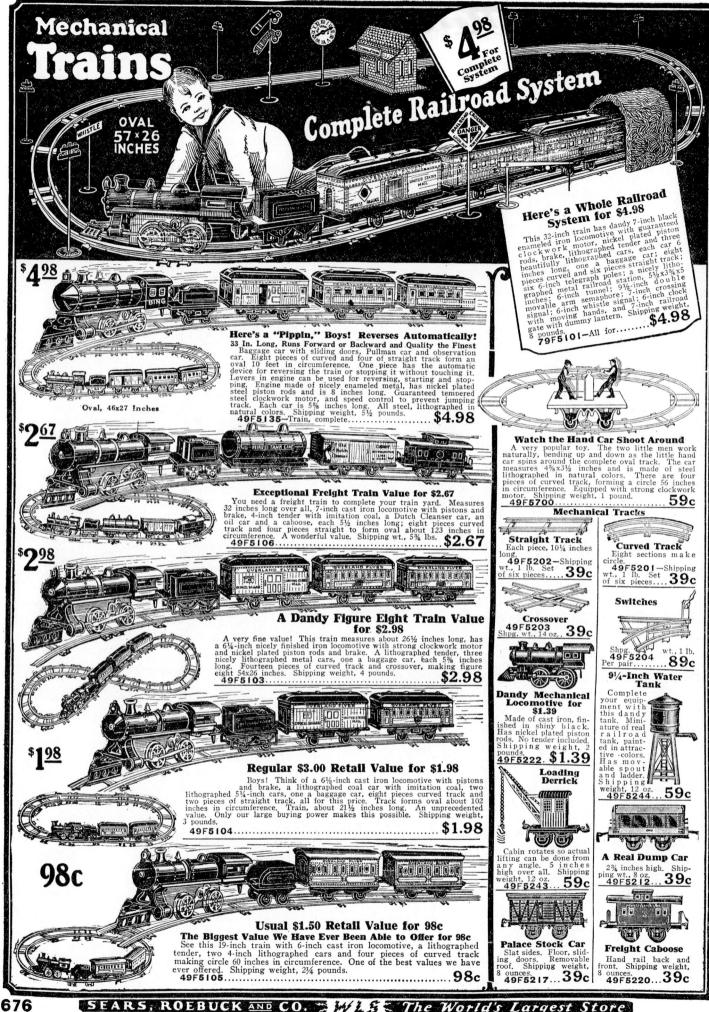

Mechanical Trains

OVAL 57×26 INCHES

WHISTLE

Complete Railroad System

$4.98 For Complete System

Oval, 46x27 Inches

$4.98

Here's a "Pippin," Boys! Reverses Automatically!

33 In. Long, Runs Forward or Backward and Quality the Finest Baggage car with sliding doors, Pullman car and observation car. Eight pieces of curved and four of straight track form an oval 10 feet in circumference. One piece has the automatic device for reversing the train or stopping it without touching it. Levers in engine can be used for reversing, starting and stopping. Engine made of nicely enameled metal, has nickel plated steel piston rods and is 8 inches long. Guaranteed tempered steel clockwork motor, and speed control to prevent jumping track. Each car is 5⅝ inches long. All steel, lithographed in natural colors. Shipping weight, 5½ pounds.

49F5135—Train, complete.....................$4.98

$2.67

Exceptional Freight Train Value for $2.67

You need a freight train to complete your train yard. Measures 32 inches long over all, 7-inch cast iron locomotive with pistons and brake, 4-inch tender with imitation coal, a Dutch Cleanser car, an oil car and a caboose, each 5½ inches long; eight pieces curved track and four pieces straight to form oval about 123 inches in circumference. A wonderful value. Shipping wt., 5¾ lbs.

49F5106.....................................$2.67

$2.98

A Dandy Figure Eight Train Value for $2.98

A very fine value! This train measures about 26½ inches long, has a 6¼-inch nicely finished iron locomotive with strong clockwork motor and nickel plated piston rods and brake. A lithographed tender, three nicely lithographed metal cars, one a baggage car, each 5⅝ inches long. Fourteen pieces of curved track and crossover, making figure eight 54x26 inches. Shipping weight, 4 pounds.

49F5103.....................................$2.98

$1.98

Regular $3.00 Retail Value for $1.98

Boys! Think of a 6½-inch cast iron locomotive with pistons and brake, a lithographed coal car with imitation coal, two lithographed 5¼-inch cars, one a baggage car, eight pieces curved track and two pieces of straight track, all for this price. Track forms oval about 102 inches in circumference. Train, about 21½ inches long. An unprecedented value. Only our large buying power makes this possible. Shipping weight, 3 pounds.

49F5104.....................................$1.98

98c

Usual $1.50 Retail Value for 98c

The Biggest Value We Have Ever Been Able to Offer for 98c

See this 19-inch train with 6-inch cast iron locomotive, a lithographed tender, two 4-inch lithographed cars and four pieces of curved track making circle 60 inches in circumference. One of the best values we have ever offered. Shipping weight, 2¼ pounds.

49F5105.....................................98c

Watch the Hand Car Shoot Around

A very popular toy. The two little men work naturally, bending up and down as the little hand car spins around the complete oval track. The car measures 4⅜x3½ inches and is made of steel lithographed in natural colors. There are four pieces of curved track, forming a circle 56 inches in circumference. Equipped with strong clockwork motor. Shipping weight, 1 pound.

49F5700.....................................59c

Mechanical Tracks

Straight Track
Each piece, 10¼ inches long.
49F5202—Shipping wt., 1 lb. Set of six pieces.....39c

Curved Track
Eight sections make circle.
49F5201—Shipping wt., 1 lb. Set of six pieces....39c

Crossover
49F5203
Shpg. wt., 14 oz......39c

Switches
Shpg. wt., 1 lb.
49F5204
Per pair.....89c

Dandy Mechanical Locomotive for $1.39

Made of cast iron, finished in shiny black. Has nickel plated piston rods. No tender included. Shipping weight, 2 pounds.
49F5222. $1.39

9¼-Inch Water Tank

Complete your equipment with this dandy tank. Miniature of real railroad tank, painted in attractive colors. Has movable spout and ladder. Shipping weight, 12 oz.
49F5244...59c

Loading Derrick

Cabin rotates so actual lifting can be done from any angle. 5 inches high over all. Shipping weight, 12 oz.
49F5243...59c

A Real Dump Car

2¾ inches high. Shipping wt., 8 oz.
49F5212...39c

Palace Stock Car

Slat sides. Floor, sliding doors. Removable roof. Shipping weight, 8 ounces.
49F5217...39c

Freight Caboose

Hand rail back and front. Shipping weight, 8 ounces.
49F5220...39c

Remarkable VELOCIPEDE Values

$9.87 UP

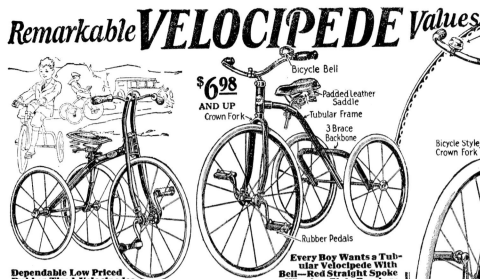

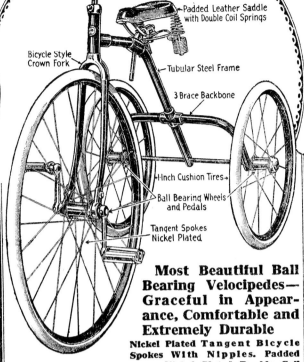

Bicycle Bell
Nickel Plated Adjustable Tubular Handles
Padded Leather Saddle with Double Coil Springs
Bicycle Style Crown Fork
Tubular Steel Frame
3 Brace Backbone
1-Inch Cushion Tires
Ball Bearing Wheels and Pedals
Tangent Spokes Nickel Plated

$6.98 AND UP — Crown Fork
Bicycle Bell
Padded Leather Saddle
Tubular Frame
3 Brace Backbone
Rubber Pedals

Dependable Low Priced Rubber Tired Velocipedes

Everything about this velocipede will please the youngster. Nicely curved, black enameled handle bars with enameled wood grips. Frame is wide and made of heavy half oval steel, enameled black. Wheels are equipped with ⅜-inch non-skid rubber tires and enameled bright red. One-piece steel crank. The nicely shaped seat is adjustable and may be raised 3 inches to take care of fast growing child. Sizes below give shortest measurements. **Two largest sizes unmailable.**

Catalog No.	Diam., Front Wheel	Seat to Lower Pedal	Shpg. Wt., Lbs.	Each
79F8342	14 in.	16 in.	17	$2.98
79F8343	16 in.	18 in.	18	3.48
79F8344	20 in.	20 in.	21	3.98
79F8345	24 in.	22 in.	27	4.48

Every Boy Wants a Tubular Velocipede With Bell—Red Straight Spoke Wheels—Plain Bearings

Heavy seamless bicycle tubing with three-brace backbone adding stability to the frame. Crown fork; ¾-inch rubber tires; nickel plated handle bars with rubber hand grips; rubber on pedals. Leather saddle mounted on coil springs. Frame and wheels finished in brilliant red bicycle enamel. Neatly striped. Sizes given are with seat as low as it will go. Seat can be raised 3½ inches. Measure child from crotch to heel. **Two largest sizes unmailable.**

Catalog No.	Diam., Front Wheel	Seat to Lower Pedal	Shpg. Wt., Lbs.	Each
79F8372	14 in.	17 in.	23	$6.98
79F8373	16 in.	19 in.	25	7.98
79F8374	20 in.	21 in.	27	8.98
79F8375	24 in.	23 in.	29	9.98

Most Beautiful Ball Bearing Velocipedes— Graceful in Appearance, Comfortable and Extremely Durable

Nickel Plated Tangent Bicycle Spokes With Nipples. Padded Motor-Bike Type Saddle on Nickel Plated Double-Coil Springs. 1-Inch Cushion Rubber Tires.

Can you picture your youngster when being presented with this classy velocipede? Built just like brother's large bicycle; sturdy, best constructed and most practical. Selected from many different types and, in our opinion, supreme in quality and up to date in every detail. Classy nickel plated tangent bicycle spokes with nipples for tightening. Ball bearing rubber pedals; large size rubber grips, fine quality leather padded seat with resilient nickel plated double coil springs. Enameled with glistening brilliant red enamel, neatly striped. Complete with bicycle bell. Sizes given below are shortest measurements. Measure child from crotch to heel. Seat may be raised 3½ inches. **Two largest sizes unmailable.**

Catalog No.	Diameter, Front Wheel	Seat to Lower Pedal	Shpg. Wt. Lbs.	Each
79F8388	16 inches	19 inches	25	$ 9.87
79F8389	20 inches	21 inches	29	10.98
79F8390	24 inches	23 inches	32	11.98

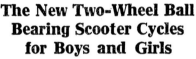

The New Two-Wheel Ball Bearing Scooter Cycles for Boys and Girls

Adjustable for Children from 5 to 10 Years

Biggest Hit This Year

Be Up to Date With One of These

Built just like the larger bicycles with high grade tubular steel frame finished in high gloss bicycle enamel; equipped with adjustable leather saddle mounted on coil springs; best grade adjustable bicycle roller chain; ball bearing sprocket axle and wheels; rubber pedals, and grips, parking stand, nickel plated spokes, hubs and trimmings. Length, over all, 41 inches; height to handle bars, 32 inches. Shipping weight, 31 pounds.

Nickle Plated Tubular Handles
Bicycle Bell
Motor Bike Style Saddle with Tool Bag
Extra Strong Tubular Steel Frame
Mud Guards
Foot Brake
Adjustable Sprocket Chain
Ball Bearing Wheels

Our De Luxe Model With Foot Brake and Mud Guards
(As Illustrated)

12-inch ball bearing wheels with 1⅛-inch balloon type rubber tires; leather tool bag on motorcycle type seat; nickel plated bell. Beautifully enameled green and striped in red; nickel plated trimmings.
79F8397 $14.98

Special Bargain Only $11.98

Same Scooter Cycle, but without brake, mud guards, bell and tool bag. Single coil springs on seat. Tires are 1 inch in diameter. Enameled bright red and striped in black; trimmings nickel plated.
79F8396 $11.98

FLYING ARROW SCOOTERS

Here's a Scooter

the Little Boys and Girls Can Handle With Ease

Beautiful in finish and construction, with 8-inch bright red enameled wheels and black enameled steel footboard. ½-inch rubber tires; steel parking stand on rear wheel. Strong steel frame and stand enameled bright red. A beauty at this price. Shipping weight, 14 pounds.
79F8819 $1.98

Stand
8 Inch Wheels
½ Inch Rubber Tires

Our De Luxe All Steel Scooter
The One We Recommend

$6.00 VALUE $3.98
Extra Strong Front Fork and Frame

Stand
Brake
Steel Footboard with Rubber Mat
12 Inch Roller Bearing Wheels
1⅛ Inch Balloon Type Tires

We searched the entire market for many months to be able to offer you this wonderful bargain, and it is a real bargain and we are proud of it. CLASSY—words cannot describe this beauty. Balloon tires, 1⅛ inches in diameter, high class 12-inch double disc steel red enameled gilt striped wheels with large steel roller bearings. Oh! how easy they run. Heavy rubber mat on steel footboard and a good brake for sudden stops. All steel strong frame and parking stand enameled red. Smooth wood handle. If you want quality—here it is. Shipping weight, 19 pounds.
79F8817... $3.98

$2.98
Stand
Brake
Steel Footboard
10 Inch Roller Bearing Wheels
1-Inch Balloon Type Rubber Tires

With Brake on Rear Wheel and Parking Stand

Your errands and daily exercise made a pleasure with this dandy all steel scooter. 10-inch double disc steel roller bearing wheels enameled red with gilt stripe, and equipped with full 1-inch balloon type rubber tires. Classy enameled steel footboard far superior to the common wood footboard because it will not crack, split or warp. The frame, fork and parking stand made from heavy gauge steel, beautifully enameled blue. Nicely varnished smooth wood handle. Quality in every respect. Shipping weight, 15 pounds.
79F8813 $2.98

Quality Autos at Money Saving Prices

$9.98

$17.98

Above illustration shows spring construction

DING! DONG! EVERYBODY STOP!

Look at This Classy All Steel Fire Chief, Only $9.98

Large Nickel Plated Bell—Headlights—Roller Bearing Wheels
Every Boy Enjoys Playing Fireman
For Children 3 to 6 Years

Made by makers of fine auto bodies. All parts made from heavy, stamped automobile steel. Body, hood and wheels enameled bright fire engine red with pretty striping. Other metal parts are black. The finish is baked-on enamel like on large cars. 10-inch roller bearing double disc steel wheels with ¾-inch rubber tires and nickel plated hub caps. A strong cord is attached to the large nickel plated bell. Size, over all, 36x22½ inches. Equipped with rubber pedals and colored instrument board. Shipping weight, 56 pounds. **Unmailable.** An extra special value.

79F8938.............$9.98

Steel Running Board

Boys!! Drive a Real Mack Jr. All Steel Truck With Regular Dumping Body and REAL TRUCK DESIGN STEEL SPRINGS

For Children From 5 to 10 Years

$22.00 to $25.00 Retail Value, Only **$15.98**

You can now haul ice, groceries, wood—anything up to 200 pounds—and drive yourself. Just like the big Mack truck on the street with the high sloping radiator front, seat and cowl. Frame of heavy channel steel. Absolutely no wood parts on this beautiful all steel original Mack Junior. Measures 50 inches in length, 21½ inches in width and the heavy, steel dumping body is 18x14¼x5 inches. Strong 10-inch double disc steel roller bearing wheels and ¾-inch rubber tires.

The steel hood, seat, body and wheels are enameled a bright red while the fenders, running board and entire gear are black. All baked-on enamel—not painted like on other inferior imitations. Complete with horn, nickel plated hub caps, rubber pedals and colored instrument board. Made strong enough so boy can stand on running board to get into seat.

79F8941— (Shpg. wt., 80 lbs.) Unmailable...........**$15.98**

BOYS! HERE'S CLASS AND PLEASURE

All Steel Construction

No Other Mail Order House Sells This Most Beautiful and Practical Toy Auto. Far Superior to the Ordinary Toy Autos Sold. There's No Comparison

Beautifully shaped sloping body. No wooden parts. Every part steel. Beautifully enameled in attractive colors.

$25.00 Retail Value for $17.98

For Children 5 to 10 Years

Made by manufacturers of high class large auto bodies. Every part is steel, same material as used in large cars. All enameled parts are hard baked in an oven like the finish on your daddy's car. The highly tempered steel springs make riding and driving a pleasure. 10-inch double disc steel roller bearing wheels with ¾-inch rubber tires. Body, hood and wheels enameled a pretty green and tastefully striped; fenders and other parts are black; classy lamps with real glass lenses, unbreakable wind shield with adjustable rear view mirror, nickel plated motometer and scuff plates, colored instrument board, spring bumper, padded seat, and horn. Size, over all: Length, 47½ inches; width, 23 inches. Shipping weight, 94 pounds. **Unmailable.**

79F8942.............$17.98

For Children 3 to 6 Years

This pretty, blue enameled racer will delight the heart of any little boy or girl. Easy to operate; has a comfortable high back seat. 10-inch double disc steel wheels enameled bright red with black striping; ½-inch rubber tires. Body, medium blue with panels and striping; gear, black enameled, 7-inch metal steering wheel with dummy gas control; curved steel bumper, fancy metal headlights with dimmers; a motometer, rubber pedals and nickel plated hub caps. Entire length, 34 inches. Shipping weight, 34 pounds.

The Moon Racer
Same as above, but without springs and imitation gear shift.
79F8931...............$7.39

Classy Jordan With Springs, Only $7.98

Unmailable

Jordan With Springs
79F8936..$7.98

DODGE

A Beautiful Car for the Little Tots

Don't Overlook This Big Value

Strong 10-inch wheels with ½-inch rubber tires; 7-inch metal steering wheel with dummy gas control. Up to date motometer and steel bumper; comfortable and roomy seat; nickel plated hub caps. Figure 5 stenciled on each side of hood just like on the big racers. Size, over all, 34x21½ inches. Bright red enameled body, seat and wheels with yellow striping and black enameled gear. **Unmailable.** Shipping weight, 30 pounds.

79F8925.................

$5.67

Bright Red Dodge Racer for Tots From 3 to 5 Years

$5.67

$11.98

All of your pals will stop and look at these wonderful cars. There's real class to them and it's a pleasure to drive them.

For Children 3 to 6 Years of Age

Made by makers of fine auto bodies for large cars. All parts are heavy stamped automobile steel, not to be compared with the light, sheet steel toy autos sold elsewhere at or about same prices. Wheels are of strong double disc steel with high grade rubber tires. Sides of hood perforated like on large autos. All steel frame, far superior to the old style wood frame. Heavy crown fenders and running boards; padded seat. Size, 38x22½ inches.

Fully Equipped Lincoln With Cushion Springs

(As illustrated.) With springs and 10-inch roller bearing wheels, ¾-inch rubber tires. Body, hood and wheels enameled a beautiful vermilion and striped in black and gilt; fenders and other parts are black. Fully equipped with wind shield, rear view mirror, motometer, lamps, bumper, tail lamp, colored instrument board, rubber pedals, horn and nickel plated hub caps. Shpg. wt., 85 lbs. **Unmailable.**
79F8940.............$11.98

Our $9.98 Special Beauty

Similar to Lincoln, but without tail lamp or mirror

Another beautiful car made by makers of fine, large auto bodies. All parts heavy stamped automobile steel, not the light sheet steel usually used in toy autos, but same kind as used in fenders of large high priced cars. 10-inch wheels with high grade plain bearings; ½-inch rubber tires. Heavy crowned fenders. Body, hood and wheels enameled in attractive colors and neatly striped. Shpg. wt., 60 lbs. **Unmailable.**
79F8939.............$9.98

Ten Million Satisfied Customers Buy Here

683

Hobo Train
45c

Real action! See the ferocious bulldog jerk at the coat tails and pull the scared, fleeing hobo back each time, while the car goes steadily on in a wide circle. 7½-inch metal box car, lithographed with scene showing hobos in box car. Fun galore. Size, over all, 7½x6⅝ in. Strong spring motor. Shipping weight, 1 pound.
49K5731............................**45c**

$1.00

Main Street 24 In. Long

The Newest Sensation—A Whole Town In Itself

Standard $1.50 Toy

One of the biggest mechanical toy sensations this year. A little town in itself. Just wind the strong spring motor, then release the brake, and see street cars, autos and trucks, hurry back and forth, some one way and some the other. Lithographed in attractive colors. Real enjoyment for the kiddies. Made of metal and measures 24x3¾x2¾ inches. Shipping weight, 2 pounds.
49K5732............................**$1.00**

See Circus Animals Do Their Tricks

Monk Climbs Pole

Clown Turns on Bar

87c

Wind spring; the ringmaster turns 'round, cracking his whip, making the animals and clown in their turn do their stunts. Made of metal, lithographed in circus colors. Good spring motor. Diameter, base, 7½ inches; height, over all, 8 inches. Shpg. wt., 1½ lbs.
49K5717............................**87c**

87c

These Autos Actually Race

Lots of Excitement for Young and Old

One of the Most Popular Toys Made

After motor is wound, the cars whirl round in their individual courses by the peculiar up and down rocking motion of the track, which makes it very uncertain as to the progress of the racers, any car being likely to win. Track, 13 in. in diameter, made of metal and beautifully lithographed. Cars, 2 inches long, are made of metal and finished in distinguishing snappy colors. Good spring motor. Height, over all, 3½ inches. Shipping weight, 1½ pounds.
49K5713............................**87c**

HeeHaw—The Balky Mule 42c

Real Action

He Balks He Kicks

Bigger and better hit each year. A comical toy. Uncanny how it operates. This mule has real pep and is some kicker. He backs up when he should go forward and rears up on his hind legs so that the poor driver doesn't know what to do. Metal, and finished in attractive natural colors. Assorted designs. Strong spring. Average length, about 9 inches; 5¾ inches high. Shipping weight, 1 pound.
49K5747............................**42c**

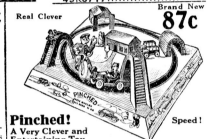

Real Clever

Brand New

87c

Pinched!
A Very Clever and Entertaining Toy

Speed!

See this speedy little roadster shoot round and round, through the bridges and tunnels, and all of a sudden, the motorcycle cop shoots out from behind the station, stops him and "pinches" him. When cop is pushed back behind station again, the auto starts away automatically, only to be "pinched" over and over again. Made of metal, lithographed in bright natural colors. Size, over all, 10 inches square, 3½ inches high. Shpg. wt., 1¼ lbs.
49K5738............................**87c**

Chicken Snatcher
45c

One of our most novel toys. When the strong spring motor is wound up the scared looking negro shuffles along with a chicken dangling in his hand and a dog hanging on the seat of his pants. Very funny action toy which will delight the kiddies. Nicely lithographed metal. Height, 8½ in. Shpg. wt., ¾ lb.
49K5728
45c

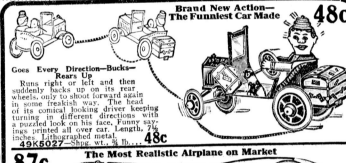

Brand New Action— The Funniest Car Made
48c

Goes Every Direction—Bucks— Rears Up

Runs right or left and then suddenly backs up on its rear wheels, only to shoot forward again in some freakish way. The head of its comical looking driver keeping turning in different directions with a puzzled look on his face. Funny sayings printed all over car. Length, 7½ inches. Lithographed metal.
49K5027—Shpg. wt., ¾ lb.......**48c**

The Famous Climbing Monkey, 19c

Watch monk climb up and down the string. There are cheaper monkeys on the market, but performance is not as satisfactory as this one. Large size, quality monk made of lithographed sheet metal. 9½ in. long and 3 in. wide. Shipping weight, 1 pound.
49K5723...**19c**

87c
The Most Realistic Airplane on Market

All Lithographed Metal

Tower 9 in. High

Beam 23 in.

Airplane 9x6 in. Strong Spring Motor

Plane Has Brake

SKY FLYER

When spring is wound up and starting lever on plane is released, it rises gradually from ground and circles a number of times around tower; as spring motor stops, the plane volplanes downward until it lands gracefully on ground. Parts all metal and lithographed in attractive colors. Shipping weight, 1½ pounds.
49K5765............................**87c**

New Two-Propeller Biplane

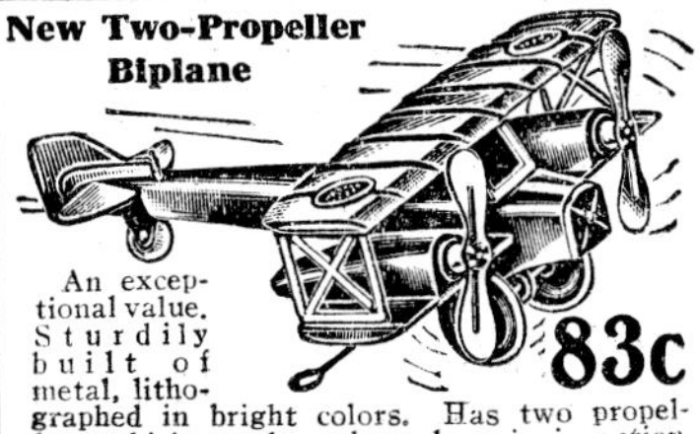

83c

An exceptional value. Sturdily built of metal, lithographed in bright colors. Has two propellers which revolve when plane is in action, and an adjustable rudder so plane can run straight or in circle. Man driver in cockpit. Just see it whiz along the floor. 12 inches long; a 9⅜-inch wing spread and 4½ inches high. Strong spring motor. Shipping weight, 2 pounds.
49K5739............................**83c**

Charleston Trio

45c

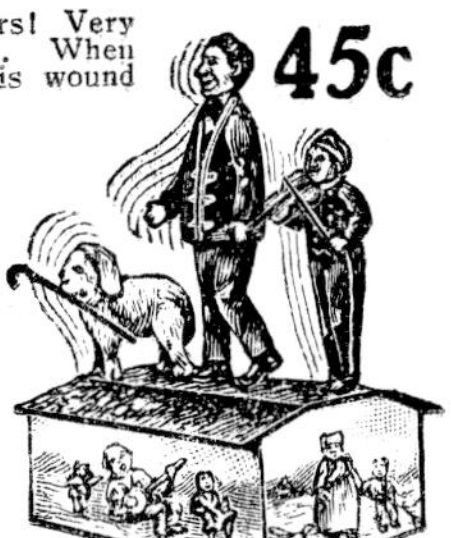

Some steppers! Very snappy action. When strong spring is wound up Charleston Charlie dances while the small negro fiddles and the animal nods his approval. Made of metal, lithographed in attractive colors. L'gth, 4⅝ inches; height, 9 in. Shipping wt., 1 pound.
49K5727
45c

49c
Famous Honeymoon Express, 49c

Every kiddie loves choo-choo trains

25c

One of the most popular mechanical toys ever brought out. Sells like hot cakes. After spring motor is wound up a miniature train travels round and round swiftly through three tunnels, while the flagman signals with his flag. Beautifully lithographed in snappy colors on metal. Lots of action and attractive in appearance. Diam., 9½ inches. Height, 2¾ inches. Shipping weight, 1 lb.
49K5725............................**49c**

The Biggest Value Ever Offered at 25c
See Limping Lizzie Shiver Along

The funniest motion in a car we have seen in years. Lots of fun to see it wobble and shiver as it runs along the floor, while driver in front seat holds on for dear life. Such sayings as: "Mrs. Often;" "99 44/100% pure tin;" "Thanks for the Buggy Ride;" "Four Wheels, No Brakes," and many other funny, popular remarks printed all over the car. Shipping weight, ¾ lb.
49K5009............................**25c**

Stop! Look! and Listen!

$1.00

Brand New and a Wonderful Toy

Really marvelous how this toy is timed to do what it does. The nicely lithographed train speeds along through the tunnel and by the station in order to keep on schedule. The racer, coming across a bridge is stopped by the crossing gate, thus permitting the train to go by, and avoid a collision. When train has passed, gate goes up and the auto goes on its way. This action is repeated time and again. Very interesting and amusing. Made of metal, lithographed in bright colors. Size, over all, 14x7½x3½ inches. Shipping weight, 1½ pounds.
49K5764............................**$1.00**

Features that make the Buddy "L" the finest in quality and detail

1. Made of twenty-two gauge automobile steel.
2. Strongly constructed—will hold 150 pounds.
3. Beautiful baked-on enamel finish.

Genuine Buddy "L" Toys

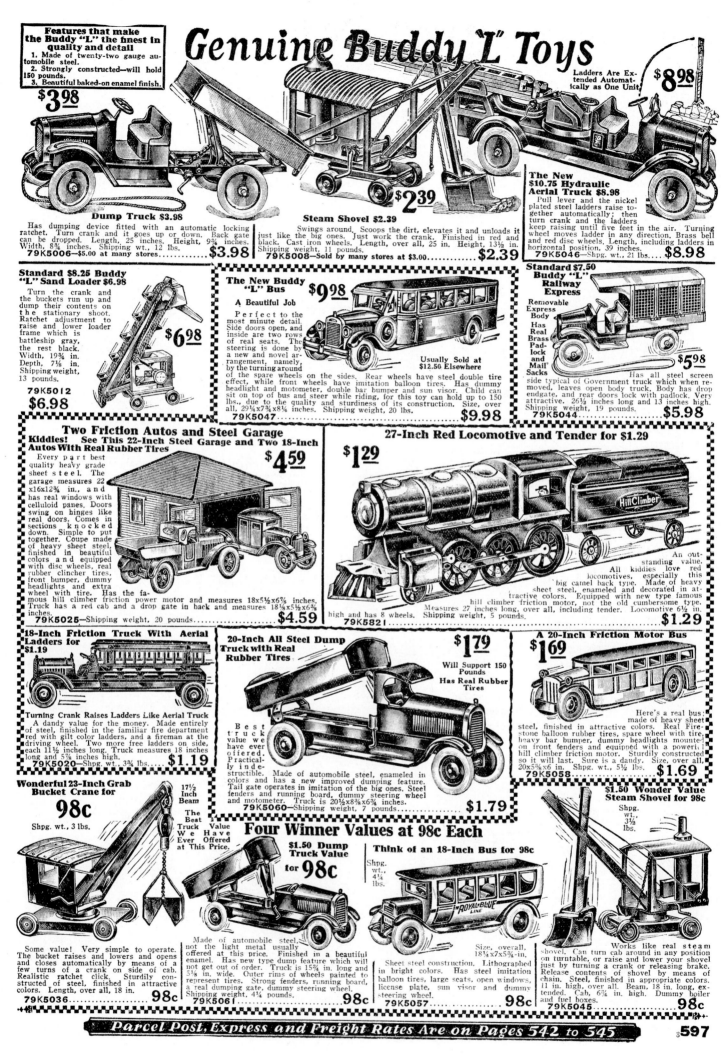

$3.98

$2.39

Ladders Are Extended Automatically as One Unit

$8.98

Dump Truck $3.98

Has dumping device fitted with an automatic locking ratchet. Turn crank and it goes up or down. Back gate can be dropped. Length, 25 inches. Height, 9¾ inches. Width, 8¾ inches. Shipping wt., 12 lbs.
79K5006—$5.00 at many stores............ **$3.98**

Steam Shovel $2.39

Swings around. Scoops the dirt, elevates it and unloads it just like the big ones. Just work the crank. Finished in red and black. Cast iron wheels. Length, over all, 25 in. Height, 13½ in. Shipping weight, 11 pounds.
79K5008—Sold by many stores at $3.00............ **$2.39**

The New $10.75 Hydraulic Aerial Truck $8.98

Pull lever and the nickel plated steel ladders raise together automatically; then turn crank and the ladders keep raising until five feet in the air. Turning wheel moves ladder in any direction. Brass bell and red disc wheels. Length, including ladders in horizontal position, 39 inches.
79K5046—Shpg. wt., 21 lbs.... **$8.98**

Standard $8.25 Buddy "L" Sand Loader $6.98

$6.98

Turn the crank and the buckets run up and dump their contents on the stationary shoot. Ratchet adjustment to raise and lower loader frame which is battleship gray, the rest black. Width, 19¾ in. Depth, 7⅛ in. Shipping weight, 13 pounds.
79K5012
$6.98

The New Buddy "L" Bus

$9.98

A Beautiful Job

Usually Sold at $12.50 Elsewhere

Perfect to the most minute detail. Side doors open, and inside are two rows of real seats. The steering is done by a new and novel arrangement, namely, by the turning around of the spare wheels on the sides. Rear wheels have steel double tire effect, while front wheels have imitation balloon tires. Has dummy headlight and motometer, double bar bumper and sun visor. Child can sit on top of bus and steer while riding, for this toy can hold up to 150 lbs., due to the quality and sturdiness of its construction. Size, over all, 29¼x7¾x8¼ inches. Shipping weight, 20 lbs.
79K5047.. **$9.98**

Standard $7.50 Buddy "L" Railway Express

Removable Express Body

Has Real Brass Padlock and Mail Sacks

$5.98

Has all steel screen side typical of Government truck which when removed, leaves open body truck. Body has drop endgate, and rear doors lock with padlock. Very attractive. 26½ inches long and 13 inches high. Shipping weight, 19 pounds.
79K5044...................... **$5.98**

Two Friction Autos and Steel Garage

Kiddies! See This 22-Inch Steel Garage and Two 18-Inch Autos With Real Rubber Tires

$4.59

Every part best quality heavy grade sheet steel. The garage measures 22 x16x12¾ in., and has real windows with celluloid panes. Doors swing on hinges like real doors. Comes in sections knocked down. Simple to put together. Coupe made of heavy sheet steel, finished in beautiful colors and equipped with disc wheels, real rubber clincher tires, front bumper, dummy headlights and extra wheel with tire. Has the famous hill climber friction power motor and measures 18x5½x6⅞ inches. Truck has a red cab and a drop gate in back and measures 18⅛x5½x6⅜ inches.
79K5025—Shipping weight, 20 pounds...................... **$4.59**

27-Inch Red Locomotive and Tender for $1.29

$1.29

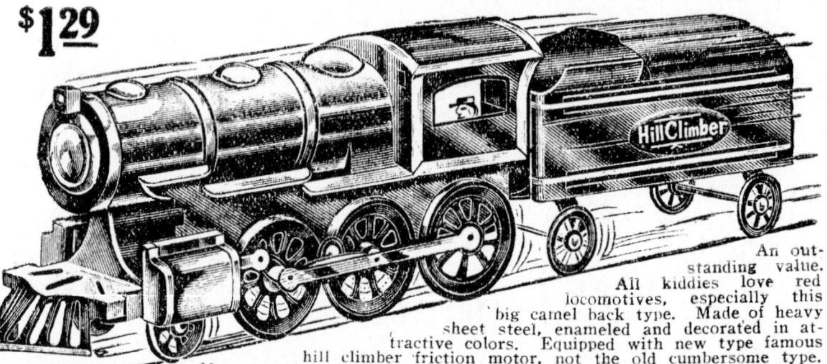

An outstanding value. All kiddies love red locomotives, especially this big camel back type. Made of heavy sheet steel, enameled and decorated in attractive colors. Equipped with new type famous hill climber friction motor, not the old cumbersome type. Measures 27 inches long, over all, including tender. Locomotive 6½ in. high and has 8 wheels. Shipping weight, 5 pounds.
79K5821.. **$1.29**

18-Inch Friction Truck With Aerial Ladders for $1.19

Turning Crank Raises Ladders Like Aerial Truck

A dandy value for the money. Made entirely of steel, finished in the familiar fire department red with gilt color ladders, and a fireman at the driving wheel. Two more free ladders on side, each 11½ inches long. Truck measures 18 inches long and 5⅞ inches high.
79K5020—Shpg. wt., 3¾ lbs..... **$1.19**

20-Inch All Steel Dump Truck with Real Rubber Tires

$1.79

Will Support 150 Pounds

Has Real Rubber Tires

Best truck value we have ever offered. Practically indestructible. Made of automobile steel, enameled in colors and has a new improved dumping feature. Tail gate operates in imitation of the big ones. Steel fenders and running board, dummy steering wheel and motometer. Truck is 20½x8⅜x6¾ inches.
79K5060—Shipping weight, 7 pounds................ **$1.79**

A 20-Inch Friction Motor Bus

$1.69

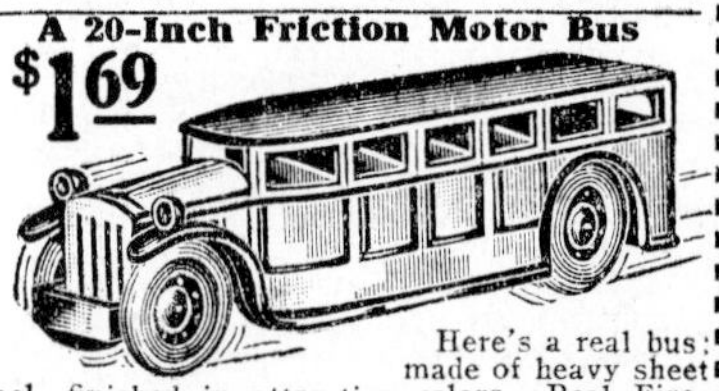

Here's a real bus; made of heavy sheet steel, finished in attractive colors. Real Firestone balloon rubber tires, spare wheel with tire, heavy bar bumper, dummy headlights mounted on front fenders and equipped with a powerful hill climber friction motor. Sturdily constructed so it will last. Sure is a dandy. Size, over all, 20x5⅝x6 in. Shpg. wt., 5½ lbs.
79K5058...................... **$1.69**

Wonderful 23-Inch Grab Bucket Crane for 98c

Shpg. wt., 3 lbs.

17½ Inch Beam

The Best Truck Value We Have Ever Offered at This Price.

Some value! Very simple to operate. The bucket raises and lowers and opens and closes automatically by means of a few turns of a crank on side of cab. Realistic ratchet click. Sturdily constructed of steel, finished in attractive colors. Length, over all, 18 in.
79K5036.................... **98c**

Four Winner Values at 98c Each

$1.50 Dump Truck Value for 98c

Made of automobile steel, not the light metal usually offered at this price. Finished in a beautiful enamel. Has new type dump feature which will not get out of order. Truck is 15¾ in. long and 5⅛ in. wide. Outer rims of wheels painted to represent tires. Strong fenders, running board, a real dumping gate, dummy steering wheel. Shipping weight, 4¼ pounds.
79K5061.......................... **98c**

Think of an 18-Inch Bus for 98c

Shpg. wt., 4¼ lbs.

Size, overall, 18¼x7x5¾-in.

Sheet steel construction. Lithographed in bright colors. Has steel imitation balloon tires, large seats, open windows, license plate, sun visor and dummy steering wheel.
79K5057................. **98c**

$1.50 Wonder Value Steam Shovel for 98c

Shpg. wt., 3½ lbs.

Works like real steam shovel. Can turn cab around in any position on turntable, or raise and lower your shovel just by turning a crank or releasing brake. Release contents of shovel by means of chain. Steel, finished in appropriate colors. 11 in. high, over all. Beam, 18 in. long, extended. Cab, 6¾ in. high. Dummy boiler and fuel boxes.
79K5045...................... **98c**

Parcel Post, Express and Freight Rates Are on Pages 542 to 545

The New ERECTOR

The Greatest Construction Toy in the World
Bigger Than Ever
Builds the Most Models—Has the Most Parts
The Only Construction Toy With the Square Girder

Build Models That Really Work

Erector is one of the most instructive as well as entertaining toys on the market. Each succeeding year brings improvements, refinements and new parts. The boys are convinced of the great flexibility of the Erector, which makes possible the building of an unlimited number of interesting as well as complicated models.

Every boy likes to tinker around and build things. With an Erector set he can satisfy this hankering. He can actually learn the fundamentals of engineering by studying carefully the complete book of instructions included.

Models built are true models, for the gears, pulleys, angle irons, etc., are duplicates of the real parts used in construction work. Bridges can be built, as can skyscrapers and thousands of other models.

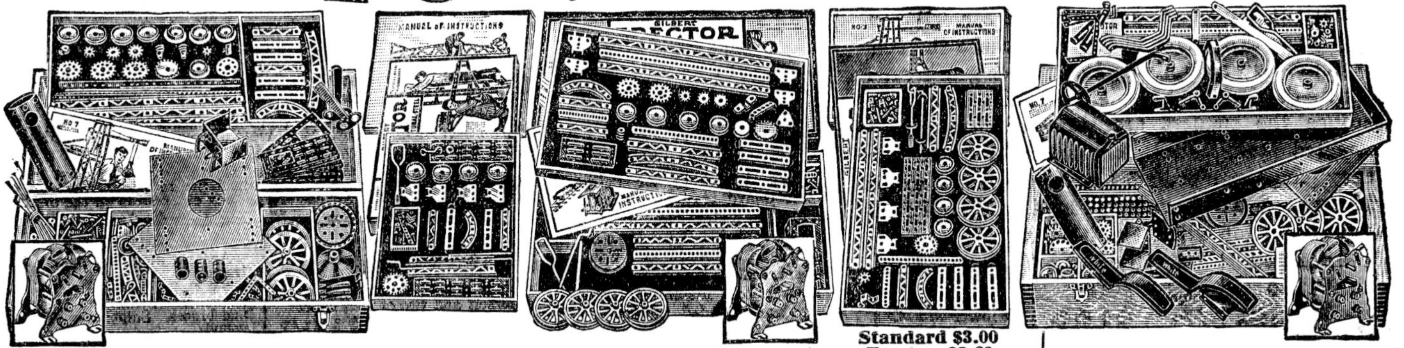

Standard $10.00 Erector, $8.98

473 Parts—Builds 533 Models

Here's a dandy set. It has a powerful, already assembled motor. Furthermore, it is assembled in a heavy, stained and varnished wood box with brass side grips and suitcase catches. It has many parts not in the smaller sets, which make it possible to build such models as a miniature steam engine, steam shovel, crane, derrick and Ferris wheel. A wonderful collection of girders, pulleys, boiler, digger, scoop, etc. Wood box, 21½ x 8¼ x 3¼ inches. Shipping weight, 13 pounds.
79K4716................**$8.98**

Standard $1.00 Erector Only 89c

104 Parts—Builds 278 Models

Just the set to start out with. Although it has less parts than the other sets, you can build many models with it. If you buy a larger size, just add these parts to your new set, for they are interchangeable. In attractive cardboard box, 12⅝ x 8⅝ x ¾ inches. Shipping wt., 1¾ pounds.
49K4717.......**89c**

Standard $5.00 Erector, With Motor, $4.47

235 Parts—Builds 500 Models

A very popular size which will make any boy happy. Builds bridges, airplanes, anything you wish. Then attach your model to the already assembled motor and watch it work. In attractive, strong cardboard box, 18 x 10 x 2½ inches. Shpg. weight, 6 pounds. **$4.47**
79K4720.

Standard $3.00 Erector, $2.69

169 Parts—Builds 380 Models

A barrel of fun to be had with this set. The square, girder-like structural steel enables you to build about 380 models. This is a dandy set, and any boy will find plenty of thrill in making all the models shown in the instruction book. In attractive, strong cardboard box, 18x10x1¼ inches. Shipping weight, 3 pounds. **$2.69**
49K4715.

Standard $15.00 Erector, $12.98 Motorized Erector Set With Chassis

627 Parts—Builds 554 Models.

Oh Boy! With this new set you can build all models shown on this page. A strong steel frame dump truck, hook and ladder, bus, steam boiler and also many other models that cannot be built with smaller sets. Included are rubber tired wheels, boiler plate, steering knuckle, bumper, fenders and electric motor. In strong wood box, stained and varnished, with hinged lid, brass side grips and snap catches. Size, over all, 21⅜x8¼x 4¾ inches. Shpg. wt., 20 lbs. **$12.98**
79K4718..............

TINKER TOY

Tinker Toy Wonder Builder

Will Build Operating Models

An ideal wood construction toy for the younger child. Very simple in principle, being based on the old adage, "A stick and a spool will amuse a child." Seventy pieces of different shapes packed in a neat cylindrical box. One set will build many models, but two or three will build more complicated and interesting models.

1 Set for 63c

For building simple models. Shipping weight, 1¼ pounds.
49K4760—Per set.........**63c**

2 Sets for $1.21

To build larger models. Shipping weight, 2½ pounds.
49K4761—2 sets for......**$1.21**

3 Sets for $1.75

For building still larger and more complicated models. Shipping weight, 3¾ pounds.
49K4768—3 sets for....**$1.75**

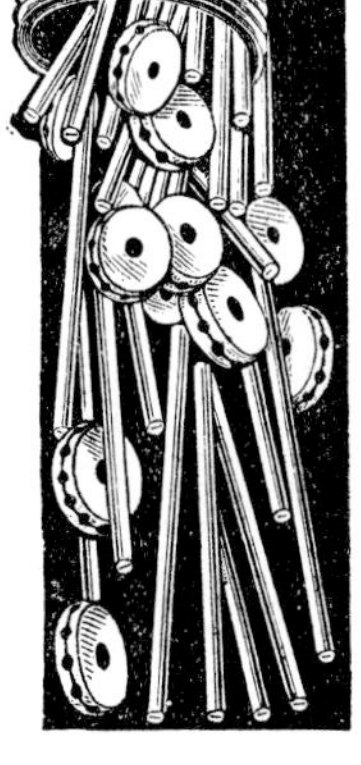

Polar Cub Motor
Biggest Selling Universal Motor in the World
For Direct or Alternating Current of 110 Volts

Runs about 2,700 revolutions per minute. With plug and 5 feet of cord. Black enameled iron base 2⅜x4 inches. Stands 4 inches high. Shaft, 4 inches long, has a detachable grooved pulley about ⅜ inch in diameter; bronze bearings. Shipping weight, 2¾ pounds.
69K5906......................**$4.59**

Powerful Battery Motors

Runs on 2 to 4 dry batteries. Book showing 48 experiments included with each motor. Will operate Tinker Toy, Erector and small accessories. Mounted on steel base; size, 4 x 4 inches.
With Reverse Lever
69K5940
Shpg. wt., 2 lbs.... **$1.79**
Without Reverse Lever and Metal Base
69K5942
Shpg. wt., 1¼ lbs.... **89c**

Bilt E-Z, the Popular Construction Toy

Bilt-EZ
"The BOY Builder"

Just as the Child Builds the Toy, So the Toy Builds the Child. For Both Boys and Girls.

Boys! Build beautiful skyscrapers or accessories for your train sets, such as stations, trestles and then forts, castles, etc., besides.

Girls! Think of the thrill of building your own doll house to order, with as many stories, rooms and porches as you want.

Complete models are not flimsy things, but substantial structures which you can carry about. When you tire of one building, pull it apart in a jiffy and start another.

All parts are interchangeable, buy as many sets as you like, for you just add that many more parts. All parts are sheet steel, enameled in white and gray. Each set in heavy cardboard box, covered with neat imitation leather effect paper. In each set are floors, windows, walls, friction pieces, cornices and balconies in varying quantities, depending on size of set. Four different sizes.

No. 0
Standard $1.00 Set 83c
Builds more than 100 models. 70 parts in this set. Size of box, 10x6¾x1⅞ in. Shpg. wt., 1¾ lbs. **83c**
49K4705.......

No. 00
Standard $2.00 Set $1.69
Builds more than 200 models. Has 146 parts. Box, 10¼x6¾x1½ inches. Shpg. wt., 2¾ lbs.
49K4706... **$1.69**

No. A
Standard $3.50 Set $2.95
With this set you can build about 300 models. Has 259 parts and comes packed in cardboard box, 10x7x2¼ inch. Shipping weight, 3½ pounds.
49K4703... **$2.95**

No. B
Standard $5.00 Set $4.35
Can build over 400 models with this popular set. Has 363 parts. Heavy cardboard box, 11x9x2¼ inch. Shpg. weight, 6 lbs.
49K4707... **$4.35**

To Find What You Want, See Index Pages 550 to 570

Marx Guaranteed Mechanical Toys

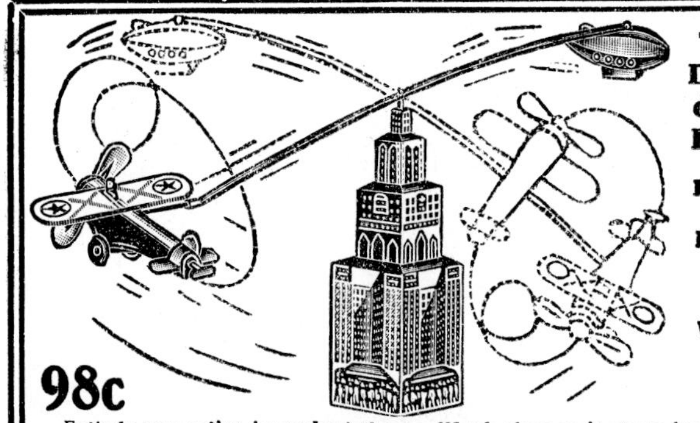

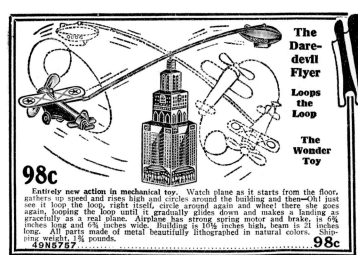

The Dare-devil Flyer

Loops the Loop

The Wonder Toy

98c

Entirely new action in mechanical toy. Watch plane as it starts from the floor, gathers up speed and rises high and circles around the building and then—Oh! just see it loop the loop, right itself, circle around again and whee! there she goes again, looping the loop until it gradually glides down and makes a landing as gracefully as a real plane. Airplane has strong spring motor and brake, is 6¾ inches long and 6¾ inches wide. Building is 10½ inches high, beam is 21 inches long. All parts made of metal beautifully lithographed in natural colors. Shipping weight, 1¾ pounds.

49N5757 .... 98c

Auto Race

One of the Most Popular Toys Made

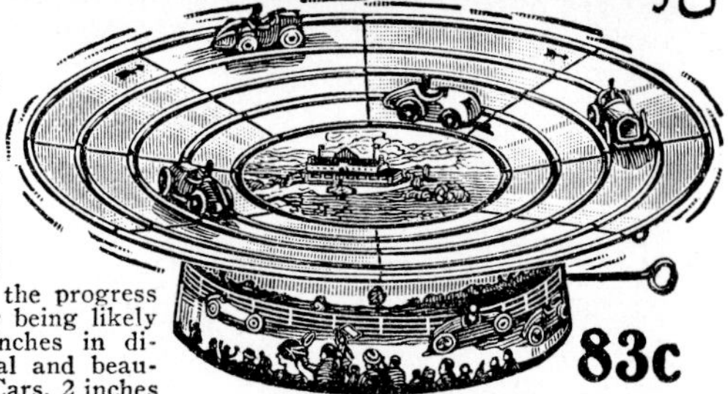

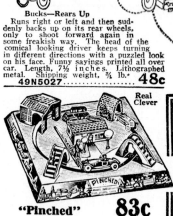

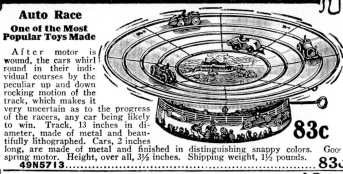

After motor is wound, the cars whirl round in their individual courses by the peculiar up and down rocking motion of the track, which makes it very uncertain as to the progress of the racers, any car being likely to win. Track, 13 inches in diameter, made of metal and beautifully lithographed. Cars, 2 inches long, are made of metal and finished in distinguishing snappy colors. Good spring motor. Height, over all, 3½ inches. Shipping weight, 1½ pounds.

83c

49N5713 .... 83c

The New "Big Parade"

The 1928 Mechanical Toy Hit, 98c

24 Inches Long

98c

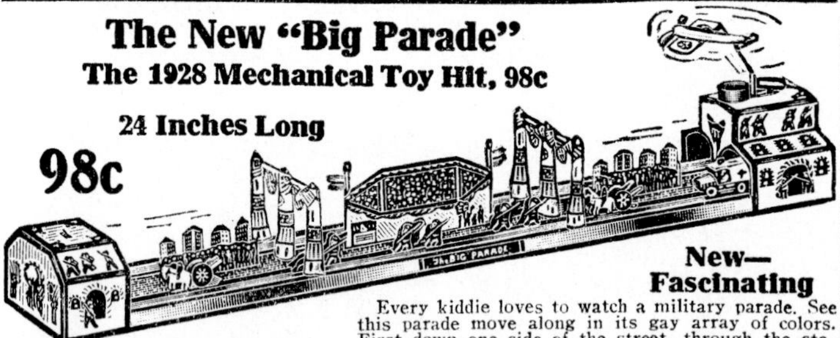

New—Fascinating

Every kiddie loves to watch a military parade. See this parade move along in its gay array of colors. First down one side of the street, through the station, and then up the other side of the street as the airplane flies around and around above. See the band, artillery, red cross and ambulance corps as they move in review before the highly colored crowded grand stand and under the flag decorated posts. A sight to thrill the heart of any child. Made of metal beautifully lithographed. Has typical Marx guaranteed spring. Size, over all, 24x3¾x2¾.

49N5758—Shipping weight, 2 pounds 98c

Hee Haw—The Balky Mule

42c

One of Our Most Popular Mechanical Toys Real Action

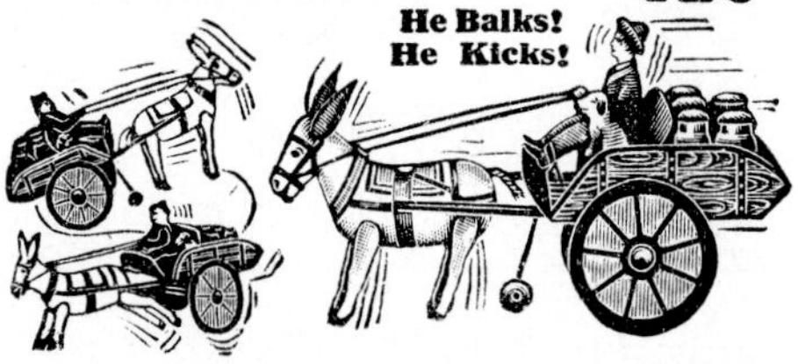

He Balks! He Kicks!

Bigger and better hit each year. A comical toy. Uncanny how it operates. This mule has real pep and is some kicker. He backs up when he should go forward, and rears up on his hind legs so that the poor driver doesn't know what to do. Metal, and finished in attractive natural colors. Assorted designs. Strong spring. Average length, about 9 inches; 5¾ inches high. Shipping weight, 1 pound.

49N5747 .... 42c

See "New York"

A Brand New Toy

Full of Action

42c

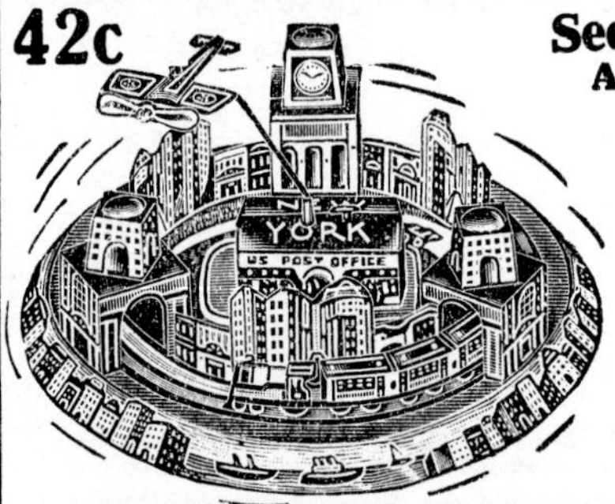

See the fast moving train dart around among the tall skyscrapers while the airplane circles around above them. Lots of action and color to attract the children. Made of metal, lithographed in bright natural colors. Has strong spring. Size, over all, 9½ inches diameter and 4½ inches high. Shipping wt., 1 pound.

49N5756 .... 42c

Hy & Lo—The 2-Auto Action Toy

48c

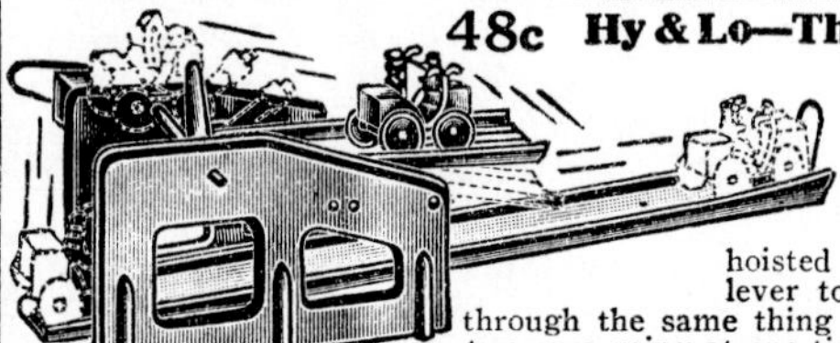

After spring is wound, set one of the 1¼-inch cars on upper track; see it roll down incline to lower track, then back along lower track only to be hoisted up again automatically by lever to upper track, and then go through the same thing over and over again. The two cars going at one time provide plenty of action. Made of metal, lithographed in colors. Has strong spring motor. Size, over all, 13½x4¼x3 inches. Shipping weight, 1½ lbs.

49N5705 .... 48c

Circus Tumbler

45c

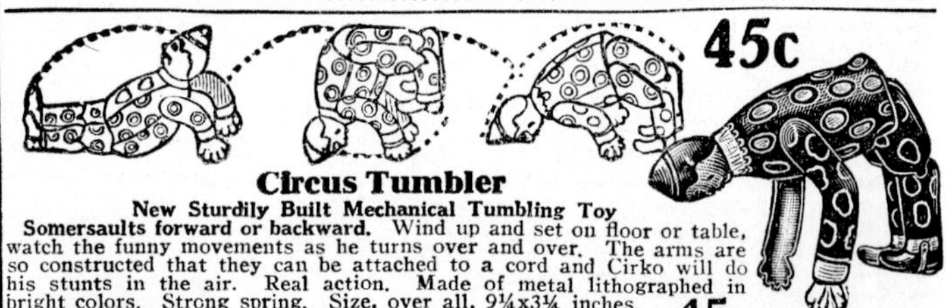

New Sturdily Built Mechanical Tumbling Toy

Somersaults forward or backward. Wind up and set on floor or table, watch the funny movements as he turns over and over. The arms are so constructed that they can be attached to a cord and Cirko will do his stunts in the air. Real action. Made of metal, lithographed in bright colors. Strong spring. Size, over all, 9¼x3¼ inches.

49N5706—Shipping weight, ¾ pound 45c

Mr. Crazy Driver

And His Bucking Funny Car Goes Every Direction

48c

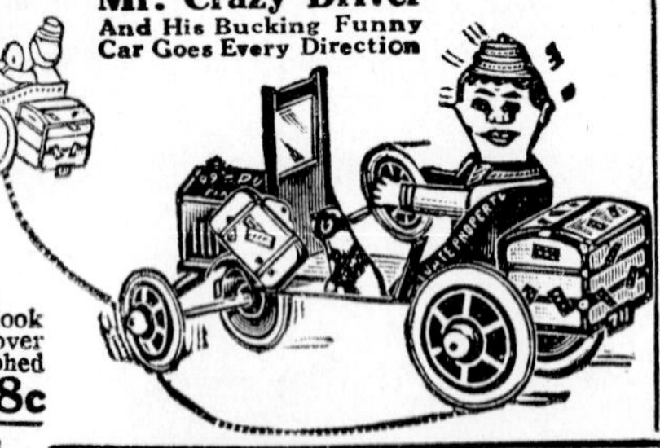

Bucks—Rears Up

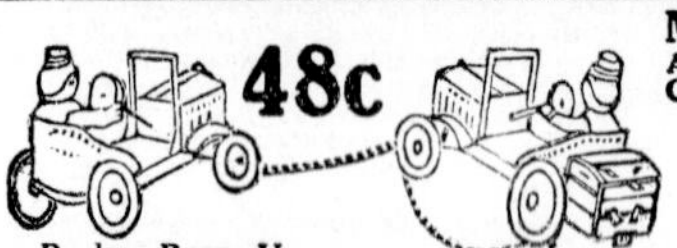

Runs right or left and then suddenly backs up on its rear wheels, only to shoot forward again in some freakish way. The head of the comical looking driver keeps turning in different directions with a puzzled look on his face. Funny sayings printed all over car. Length, 7½ inches. Lithographed metal. Shipping weight, ¾ lb.

49N5027 .... 48c

The New Loop the Loop

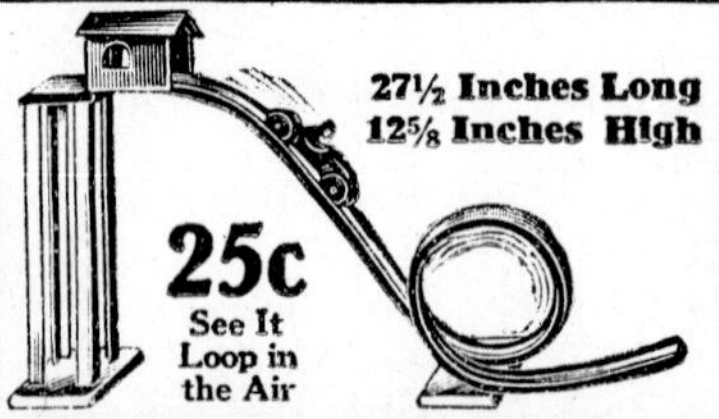

27½ Inches Long
12⅝ Inches High

25c

See It Loop in the Air

Put 2½x1½-inch metal auto in tower. Push to start it and see the auto shoot down the runway, follow up in the track making a loop, and spin on lower track to race off on to the floor. Made of metal attractively lithographed. 27½ inches long, 12⅝ inches high and 3 inches wide. Shipping wt., 1¼ pounds.

49N5055 .... 25c

Real Clever

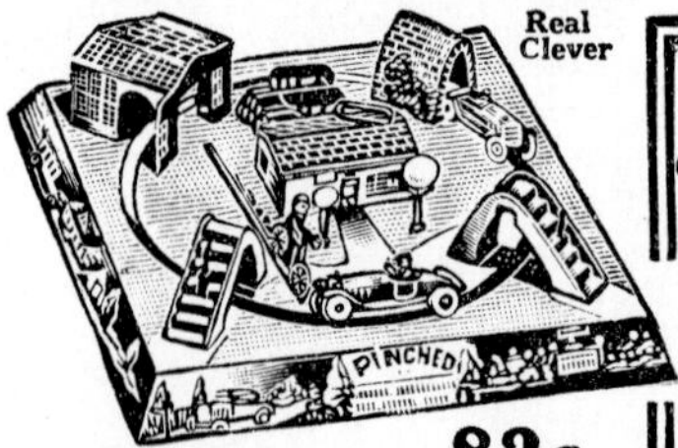

"Pinched"

83c

Very Realistic Entertaining Toy

See this chronic speeder shoot round and round, through the bridges and tunnels and, all of a sudden, the motorcycle cop shoots out from behind the station, stops him and "pinches" him. When cop is pushed back behind station again, the auto starts away automatically, only to be "pinched" over and over again. Made of metal, lithographed in bright natural colors. Size, over all, 10 inches square, 3½ inches high. Shpg. wt., 1¼ lbs.

49N5738 .... 83c

Lifelike Action Toys

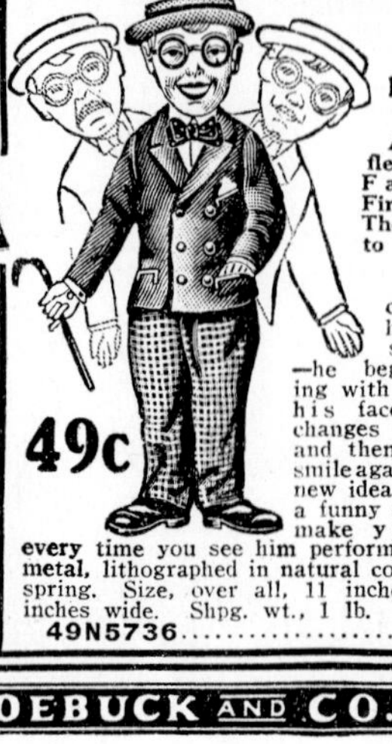

Funny Face

As He Shuffles Along His Face Shows First Joy—Then Changes to Gloom.

49c

New and clever. Wind him up and set him down—he begins walking with a smile on his face, which changes to a frown and then back to a smile again. A brand new idea, and surely a funny action. Will make you laugh every time you see him perform. Made of metal, lithographed in natural colors. Good spring. Size, over all, 11 inches tall, 4½ inches wide. Shpg. wt., 1 lb.

49N5736 .... 49c

Chicken Snatcher

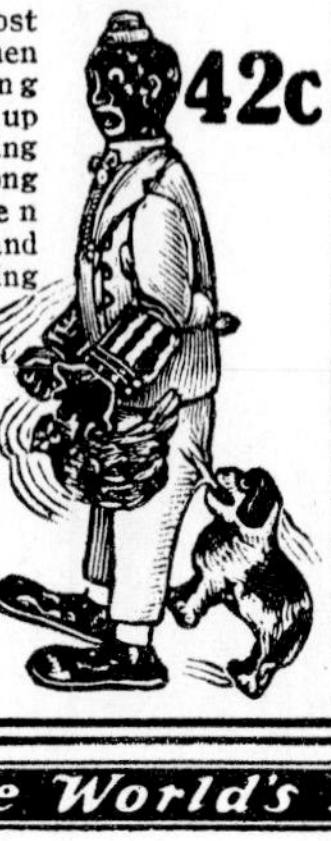

42c

One of our most novel toys. When the strong spring motor is wound up the scared looking negro shuffles along with a chicken dangling in his hand and a dog hanging on the seat of his pants. Very funny action toy which will delight the kiddies. Nicely lithographed metal. Height, 8½ in. Shpg. wt., ¾ lb.

49N5728

42c

Charleston Trio

42c

Some Steppers!

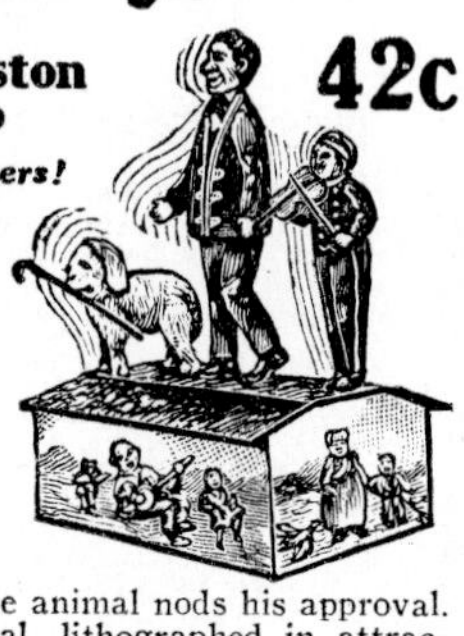

Very snappy action. When strong spring is wound up Charleston Charlie dances while the small negro fiddles and the animal nods his approval. Made of metal, lithographed in attractive colors. Length, 4⅝ inches; height, 9 inches. Shpg. wt., 1 lb.

49N5727 .... 42c

Velocipedes for Growing Youngsters

The Famous Fairy Velocipedes
Nationally Known for Almost 50 Years

Every father, mother and child knows the name Fairy on a child's Bike means that it is one of the best money can buy. It is so different from the common, ordinary type, there is no comparison. Our tremendous purchasing power has made it possible for us to offer this wonderful line at prices even lower than those usually asked for ordinary quality.

Points of superiority and Great Importance.
1—Frame of drawn steel tubing (not gas pipe).
2—All joints hand brazed, not just slipped in and riveted.
3—Tubular steel fork (not a casting).
4—Rustproof, heavily nickel plated bicycle spokes.
5—Enough spokes in each wheel to withstand jars.

← Famous Fairy
Full Tubular Ball Bearing Velocipede. With 1-Inch Cushion Rubber Tires and Rich Red Enamel. Baked-On Finish.

Fairy Aristocrat →
The Super Ball Bearing Velocipede With Mud Guard and large Corrugated Cushion Rubber Tires. Resemble Bicycle Tires. Finished in a pretty Blue Enamel. Tool Bag on Saddle.

Full 1-Inch Tires
All Ball Bearing Wheels and Pedals

Built just like brother's large bicycle; sturdy, best in construction and very practical. Heavy tubular steel frame and fork with nickel plated crown. Nickel plated bicycle spokes, cranks, adjustable handle bars, pedals and grips; padded leather seat with resilient nicked plated double coil springs and bicycle bell. Rims of wheels enameled red with black striping. Sizes given are shortest measurements. **Measure child from crotch to heel.** Seat may be raised 3½ inches. **Two largest sizes unmailable, and are shipped by freight or express.**

Catalog No.	Diam., Front Wheel	Seat to Lower Pedal	Shpg. Wt., Lbs.	Each
79N8357	14 in.	17 in.	24	$ 7.98
79N8358	16 in.	19 in.	25	8.98
79N8359	20 in.	21 in.	30	10.35
79N8360	24 in.	23 in.	35	11.98

New Joy-Toy Plain Bearing Tubular Bikes

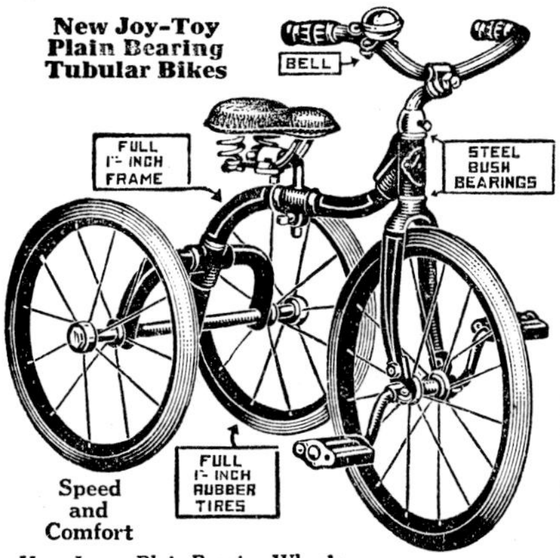

Speed and Comfort

Have Large Plain Bearing Wheels. **No Other Mail Order House Sells These New Type Bicycle Frame Velocipedes.**
They have all the latest features such as: (1) Full floating axle. (2) Full 1-inch tubular steel frame. (3) Three-brace back bone. (4) Full 1-inch cushion rubber tires. (5) Reinforced seat post. (6) Nickel plated bicycle bell. (7) Rubber pedals and grips. (8) Reversible handle bars. Wheels, frame and fork enameled red and striped in yellow, baked on finish. All shiny parts nickel plated. Two large sizes not mailable.

Catalog No.	Front Wheel	Rear Wheels	For Child	Shpg. Wt., Lbs.	Each
79N8325	12 in.	10 in.	2 to 3 yrs.	25	$6.79
79N8326	14 in.	12 in.	3 to 4 yrs.	28	7.87
79N8327	16 in.	14 in.	4 to 6 yrs.	29	8.79
79N8328	20 in.	16 in.	6 to 8 yrs.	36	9.95

Famous Ball Bearing Fairy Speed Bikes

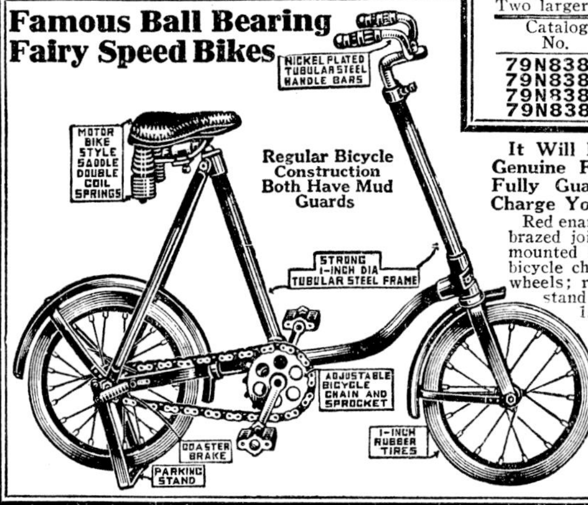

Regular Bicycle Construction Both Have Mud Guards

Red enameled tubular steel frame, with hand brazed joints, with adjustable leather saddle mounted on double coil springs; adjustable bicycle chain; ball bearing sprocket axle and wheels; rubber pedals and grips; parking stand with quick action spring. Wheels, 12 in. diameter. Rims striped in black. Length, over all, 41 in.; height to handle bars, 32 in. Shipping weight, 30 pounds.

De Luxe Model
With New Departure Coaster Brake.
79N8380...$14.98
Without Coaster Brake.
79N8379...$10.98

New Style JOY-TOY Velocipedes

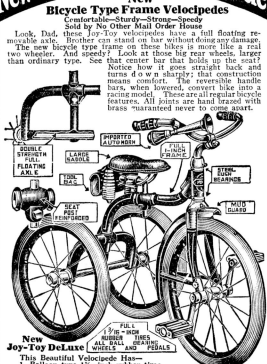

New Bicycle Type Frame Velocipedes
Comfortable—Sturdy—Strong—Speedy
Sold by No Other Mail Order House

Look, Dad, these Joy-Toy velocipedes have a full floating removable axle. Brother can stand on bar without doing any damage. The new bicycle type frame on these bikes is more like a real two wheeler. And speedy? Look at those big rear wheels, larger than ordinary type. See that center bar that holds up the seat? Notice how it goes straight back and turns down sharply; that construction means comfort. The reversible handle bars, when lowered, convert bike into a racing model. These are all regular bicycle features. All joints are hand brazed with brass guaranteed never to come apart.

New Joy-Toy DeLuxe

This Beautiful Velocipede Has—
1—Balloon type 1¾-inch rubber tires.
2—Full 1-inch tubular steel frame.
3—Extra large motor-bike type leather saddle with tool bag and nickel plated double coil springs.
4—Imported horn with rubber bulb.
5—Mud guard on front wheel.
6—Large rubber grips and pedals.
7—All wheels and pedals ball bearing.
8—Full floating axle.
9—Rustproof all weather nickel plated bicycle spokes with nipples.
10—Reinforced seat post.
Frame, fork and rims of wheels enameled black with gold striping (baked on). Nickel plated fork crown, handle bars and pedal arms. Two larger sizes not mailable.

Catalog No.	Front Wheel	Rear Wheel	For Child	Shpg. Wt., Lbs.	Each
79N8381	12 in.	10 in.	2 to 3 yrs.	29	$ 9.95
79N8382	14 in.	12 in.	3 to 4 yrs.	30	11.45
79N8383	16 in.	14 in.	4 to 6 yrs.	33	12.98
79N8384	20 in.	16 in.	6 to 8 yrs.	39	14.45

It Will Pay You to Buy One of These Genuine Fairy Speed Bikes—Every Part Fully Guaranteed. Other Stores Would Charge You Considerably More.

Fairy Aristocrat

Full 1⅛-Inch Rubber Tires
All Ball Bearing Wheels and Pedals

Built of same materials as finest bicycle; tubular steel fork with nickel plated crown. Ball bearing wheels and rubber pedals. Nickel plated bicycle style cranks and tangent spokes. Tubular steel frame, full 1 inch in diameter. Rims and frame enameled blue and gold. Motor bike type saddle and tool bag. Nickel plated tubular steel adjustable handle bars with nickel plated bell and rubber grips. Sizes given below are shortest measurements. Measure child from crotch to heel. Seat may be raised 3½ in. **Two largest sizes unmailable.**

Catalog No.	Diam., Front Wheel	Seat to Lower Pedal	Shpg. Wt., Lbs.	Each
79N8385	16 in.	19 in.	28	$10.95
79N8386	20 in.	21 in.	33	12.95
79N8387	24 in.	23 in.	39	13.95

New Joy-Toy Ball Bearing Tubular Bike

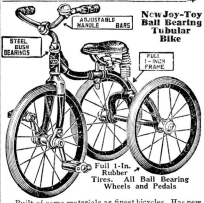

Full 1-In. Rubber Tires. All Ball Bearing Wheels and Pedals

Built of same materials as finest bicycles. Has new bicycle style frame. All joints are hand brazed with brass and guaranteed. Has following features: (1) Full tubular frame. (2) Full one-inch cushion rubber tires. (3) All wheels and pedals have case hardened steel ball bearings. (4) Bicycle type red leather saddle with double coil nickel plated springs. (5) Reversible nickel plated handle bars. (6) Large rubber grips and pedals. (7) Three-brace back bone frame. (8) Floating rear axle. Complete with bell and hub caps. Frame and fork enameled blue; rims of wheels are red, all baked on. Two larger sizes not mailable.

Catalog No.	Front Wheel	Rear Wh'ls	For Child Yrs.	Shpg. Wt., Lbs	Each
79N8329	12 in.	10 in.	2 to 3	27	$ 7.98
79N8330	14 in.	12 in.	3 to 4	29	9.45
79N8331	16 in.	14 in.	4 to 6	31	10.67
79N8341	20 in.	16 in.	6 to 8	37	12.50

Low Priced Sturdy Dependable Bikes

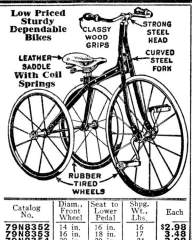

CLASSY WOOD GRIPS — STRONG STEEL HEAD — CURVED STEEL FORK — LEATHER SADDLE With Coil Springs — RUBBER TIRED WHEELS

Nicely curved, black enameled steel handle bars; wood grips. Frame made of heavy half oval steel, enameled black. Wheels are enameled bright red and equipped with ½-inch nonskid rubber tires. One piece steel crank and pedals enameled red. Leather seat (not fiber) is adjustable and may be raised 3 inches. Sizes given are shortest measurements. Measure child from crotch to heel. Largest size unmailable.

Catalog No.	Diam., Front Wheel	Seat to Lower Pedal	Shpg. Wt., Lbs.	Each
79N8352	14 in.	16 in.	16	$2.98
79N8353	16 in.	18 in.	17	3.48
79N8354	20 in.	20 in.	24	3.98

Order Blanks Are in Back of This Catalog

P **503**

AUTOMOBILES of the LATEST MODEL

Boys! This Is the Only Original Toy Mack Truck

Regular Dump Box

All Steel Autos

Pedals Adjustable to Three Sizes

Steel Springs

$14.98

Made from heavy gauge automobile steel. Not the ordinary lightweight sheet steel and wood construction. Every boy can now haul ice, groceries, wood, anything, and drive it himself. Just like the big Mack truck on the street. Frame of heavy channel steel.

The steel hood, seat, body and wheels are enameled a bright red, the fenders, running boards and undergearing are black. All baked-on enamel (not painted like inferior imitations). Complete with horn, rust proof hub caps which do not come off, and colored instrument board. Made strong enough so boy can stand on running board to get into seat.

Absolutely no wood parts on these.

Large Size Mack Jr.

Many stores sell this as high as $20.00. For Children 5 to 10 Years. (As illustrated).

Rear axle mounted on ball bearings. Has fenders, running boards and rubber pedals. Size, over all, 50x22 inches, with dump box 18¼x13¾x5 inches. Roller bearing 9½-in. double disc steel wheels with ¾-inch rubber tires. Shipping weight, 71 pounds.

79N8941—Unmailable. Shipped by freight or express only.... **$14.98**

Baby Mack

Sold as high as $12.00 elsewhere. For the Little Tots Up to 5 Years. (Not Illustrated.)

Similar to above, but without fenders and axle. Hood and seat, not as fancy as the one shown. Size, over all, 44½x19 inches. Dump box, 15x14x5 inches. Plain bearing 8½-inch disc steel wheels, ⅝-inch rubber tires. Shipping weight, 50 lbs.

79N8930—Unmailable—Shipped by freight or express only........ **$8.98**

"Spirit of St. Louis" Boys! Drive It Yourself

$12.98

All the Rage This Year. You'll Be Right in Style With One of These All Steel Planes. They're Fast and Easy to Propel. Speed Down the Street, and Watch Them All Make Way for You.

AIR MAIL

Made of heavy gauge automobile steel beautifully finished in gray baked enamel body with bright red striping and red enameled tail, propeller and double disc steel wheels. Large roomy cockpit for pilot; padded seat. Steering wheel has rod connected to rear wheel for easy steering.

Army Scout Plane

Sells Elsewhere for $12.00
For Children 3 to 7 Years

Metal wing, spread 28 inches; length, over all, 41½ inches. Front wheels, 10 inches in diameter. Rear wheel, 8 inches, all equipped with ½-inch rubber tires. Shipping weight, 35 pounds.

79N8907.......**$8.67**

"Spirit of St. Louis"

Sells Elsewhere Up to $18.00
For Children 5 to 10 Years

Has 30-inch metal wing and measures 57 inches long over all. Front wheels, 10 inches in diameter, with ¾-inch rubber tires; 8¼-in. roller bearing rear wheel with ⅝-inch rubber tire. Shipping weight, 85 lbs.

79N8909.......**$12.98**

Our Finest Toy Autos

With or Without High Speed Chain Drive

A New Achievement in Toy Autos

All shiny parts are finished with new process. Non-rusting utilite finish. Made from heavy gauge steel, not lightweight sheet steel as sold by others.

$16.98 And Up

All steel construction, made especially for us by makers of fine large size auto bodies and chassis. No other mail order house sells these. Beautifully finished and far superior to the ordinary Toy Autos sold. There's no comparison.

Adjustable pedals for children 5 to 10 years. Baked-on enameled parts. Highly tempered steel springs. 10⅝-inch double disc steel roller bearing wheels with ¾-inch rubber tires. Classy lamps with real glass lenses and colored side lights; unbreakable windshield with rear view mirror, nickel plated motometer and scuff plates, colored instrument board, spring bumper, horn and fiber covered seat. Size, over all: Length, 46¾ inches; width, 22 inches. Shipping weight, 95 pounds.

Lincoln De Luxe With High Speed Chain Drive Under Seat

Sold as high as $27.50 by many stores. Body, hood and wheels enameled red with cream and black striping; fenders and undergearing is black. Geared 2½ to 1, making driving and riding a real pleasure.

79N8946 .... **$18.95**

Lincoln Sport Model

Sold as high as $25.00 by many. Same as above, but without High Speed drive. Body and hood enameled green with orange color striping and orange color wheels with green striping.

79N8945 **$16.98**

New All Steel Cadillac Fully Equipped

With Cushion Springs and Ball Bearing Rear Axle

$9.98

Compare This With Other Cars Up to $15.00

The shiny parts will not tarnish or discolor because they are finished with new non-rusting process known as utilite finish. The enameled parts are hard baked in an oven. Will last long time. Made from heavy gauge automobile steel; not the thin, flimsy lightweight sheet steel usually used.

Child can stand on running board to get into seat.

Adjustable pedals to make riding more comfortable for children 3 to 6 years of age.

Classy, new style windshield, motometer, drum headlights and side lights, colored instrument board, horn, license plate and hub caps. Made by makers of fine auto bodies for large cars. All parts are heavy stamped automobile steel, not to be compared with the light sheet steel toy autos sold elsewhere at or about our price. Wheels are of strong double disc steel, 10 inches in diameter, with high grade ⅝-inch rubber tires. Sides of hood have vents like on large autos. All steel chassis, far superior to old style wood frame. Heavy steel crown fenders and running boards; fiber covered steel seat. Size, 37x20¼ inches. Body, hood and wheels enameled a bright red with orange color panels, black striping; fenders and other parts are black. Shipping weight, 61 pounds. **Unmailable. Shipped by freight or express.**

79N8903..................................**$9.98**

Snappy Whippet

For Children 3 to 5 Years

$5.79

A light step on the pedals and away you go. Another all steel beauty with a baked-on enamel finish, bright green color body with orange color striping. 8-inch double disc steel wheels, enameled orange color with green striping, ½-inch rubber tires. Length, over all, 29¼ in.; width, 20 in.

Complete with bumper, motometer, headlights and adjustable pedals. Shipping weight, 31 pounds.

79N8901......................**$5.79**

New Star Racer

$3.98

All Steel Practically Unbreakable

Regular $5.00 Value Elsewhere

A cute all steel speedy, easy running car for the little fellows 2 to 4 years of age. Built like a large racer with narrow racy hood of heavy gauge automobile steel and comfortable low seat. The smallest tot will be able to propel this new type auto with ease. Hood, seat and wheels finished in a baked-on glossy bright red color enamel with black striping; undergearing enameled black. 8-inch diameter, double disc steel wheels with ½-inch rubber tires. Length, over all, 30½ inches; width, 15¾ inches. Shpg. wt., 22 lbs.

79N8900....................**$3.98**

Hudson Sport Roadster

$7.98

Made Exclusively for Sears

You Can Give All of Your Friends a Run for Their Money With This Car

A delight to any boy or girl 3 to 6 years of age. Speedy and sturdy because it's all steel, not the ordinarily clumsy wood chassis construction offered by others. Baked-on green enamel finish on body and seat with orange color striping; drum headlights to match; black enameled sport fenders, undergearing and bumper. 10-inch diameter double disc steel wheels enameled orange color with green striping, equipped with ½-inch rubber tires. Complete with motometer, windshield and license plate. Length, over all, 38 in.; width, 20¾ in.

79N8902—Shpg. wt., 43 lbs... **$7.98**

BARN, 12¾x11¾x8½ In.

$1.00 Postpaid

27 In. Long

$1.00 POSTPAID

Your Play Farm Is Not Complete Without This 4-in-1 Tractor Set

Every child loves to play with a Tractor Set. We offer four pieces for only $1.00, Postpaid. Our biggest seller in a mechanical toy and one of our best values. Fits the wants of every child, because of its wonderful construction and play value. Just imagine the fun the kiddies will have hitching the different pieces behind the tractor to do the different jobs around your farm, just like Dad does with his big tractor. Our set consists of: Tractor with man driver, a four-wheel wagon, two-wheel rake and disc harrow. Tractor has strong spring motor. When all pieces are hooked together set measures 27 inches long over all. **Tractor is 7⅞ inches long, other three pieces in proportion.** Made of lithographed metal and has strong spring motor. **$1.00**

49T5748—Postpaid....................................

Our Latest Stock Farm Made Exclusively for Us

Have a Barn Just Like Daddy's
With Fourteen Beautifully Colored Animals
Seldom Has a Value Like This Ever Been Offered

This year we are offering our customers a larger value than ever before because of the nicely shaped beautifully colored animals included. Year after year the demand for these stock farms has been growing by leaps and bounds, and year after year we have been able to offer better values because of the tremendous quantities we purchase. This item gives loads of fun for very little money. Just think of all the fun the kiddies will have putting these animals into the barn and feeding them imaginary hay. This toy will keep the children amused for hours and hours because of the many different groupings in which these animals can be placed. The stalls are just the right size for the horses. A box of toothpicks, some old spools and a little bit of Mother's yarn will help make an ideal rail fence around your stock farm. **The barn measures 12¾ inches long and has two nicely shaped stalls with two oblong and one round troughs.** The barn is made of wood, nicely colored, and measures 11¾ inches high to tip of cupola. Width, across eaves, 8½ inches. Nicely decorated in yellow, white, black and red. Roof is pretty green color. Just think, you can buy all of this for—$1.00. **$1.00**

79T9149—Postpaid......................................

Gray Beauty Pacers

89¢ We Pay the Postage

Every child will enjoy playing with these lifelike horses. Pull them along and watch the legs move back and forth just like real horses. The beautiful red enameled slat style wood hay wagon on strong metal wheels, makes this toy most attractive to the youngsters. Size, over all, 19x6 inches. **89¢**

79T5454—Postpaid..............

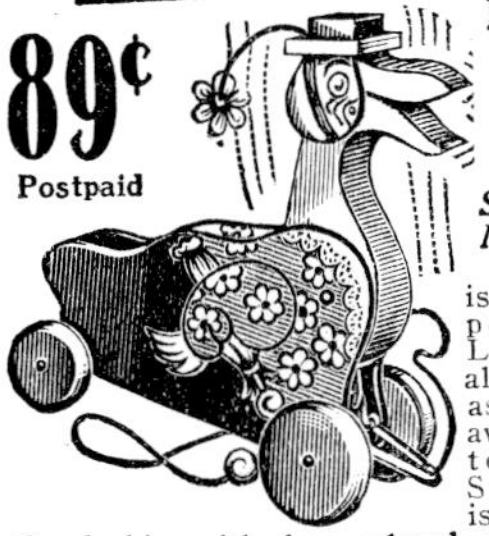

Proud Dolly Duck

89¢ Postpaid

Opens Mouth— Squawks— Nods Head

What fun it is to pull this peppy little Lady Duck along the floor as she squawks away like the town gossip. She certainly is a saucy little duckie with her colored outfit and a flower in her jaunty hat. Made of wood and strong cardboard, beautifully lithographed in many attractive colors. Rubber bands around front wheels to help give toy the lifelike action when pulled. Duck measures 9 inches high and 7 in. long. Complete with pull cord. **89¢**

49T5488—Postpaid............

Pony Pacer 45¢ Postpaid

When pulled along horse's legs move back and forth like a real pacer. Wheels, legs and all moving parts made of metal. Balance wood, beautifully decorated in colors. Size, 13½ in. long and 6½ in. high. **45¢**

49T5455—Postpaid............

Famous Humpty Dumpty Circus Figures With Movable Arms, Legs and Heads

Illustrated Booklet, Showing Endless Amount of Tricks, Included With Each Set

Every child should have a set of these well made figures of wood and leather strung with strong elastic, which can be set in an endless variety of positions producing the most fascinating and grotesque poses. Will perform innumerable balancing tricks. Elephant, 7x4½ inches; donkey, 8x6½ inches; nicely dressed 7-inch clown; chair ladder, tub and barrel in proportion. **$1.85**

49T9135—Postpaid..........

Our Big $1.00 Rubber Tired Steel Wagon

All Steel Wagon With Rubber Tires

An Outstanding Value
Sold Elsewhere for $1.50

Body, 17¼x8¾ Inches—5-Inch Wheels—½-Inch Rubber Tires.

This handsome, sturdy all steel play wagon for little tots is offered to you at a price hardly considered possible. Body is one-piece heavy gauge automobile steel (not tin), enameled blue (baked-on), strong double disc steel wheels, 5 inches in diameter and enameled blue. Steel bolsters and braces, enameled black; strong wood tongue, painted blue. **$1.00**

79T7601—Postpaid...............

30-Inch Steel Tractor Set $1.69 Postpaid

Dumping Gate

Fine Quality Tractor and Trailer

A pull toy every child would like to get. Made of sheet steel, finished in bright blue baked-on enamel, attractively trimmed. Tractor has dummy motor, gas tank, steering wheel and spring seat just like on large tractors. Driving wheels finished in bright red and measure 6¾ inches in diameter. Front wheels of tractor and wheels of trailer are 3½ inches in diameter and are painted to imitate balloon type tires. Trailer has dumping gate. Total length of toy, 30¼ inches, and 7¼ inches high. **$1.69**

79T5410—Postpaid..............

Every Kiddie Loves to Play He's Riding a Horse

One of Our Most Popular Toys

49¢ Postpaid

Youngsters will have lots of fun galloping along with this beautifully finished Stick Horsie. All kiddies want one. On account of the large quantity we buy we are able to offer an exceptional value. Beautifully enameled in many attractive colors. Pretty cutout horse's head made of wood finished and enameled in black and white with colorful decorations. Well made throughout. You can trot along, guiding the horse with the real tapelines. There is some class to this Stick Horsie. Complete with strong nicely blue enameled wood stick, and two 4-inch double disc red enamel steel wheels. **49¢**

49T9112—Postpaid......................

77¢ Postpaid

A Cracker Jack Three-Toy Assortment for 77c

Dandy Pull Toys. Will Attract Any Child

A clever 9-inch racer with realistic motor noise. See the little driver bob up and down as he speeds along. Kiddies choo-choo, 8x 3½x3½ in. Just hear it chug when pulled. A dandy rope jumper, 7¾x4x7¾ in. When pulled he skips his rope, following you wherever you go. All have wood bodies and metal bases. Finished in attractive colors. Pull cord attached to each one. **77¢**

49T5489—Postpaid.............

Merry-Go-Round

59¢ Postpaid

Usual 75c Value

10½ In. Long
6¾ In. High

You will be proud to play with this beautiful merry-go-round with three horses, which when pulled revolves, while the clown rings the bell by hitting it with his hammer. There is lots of action to this toy, which is made of metal, beautifully lithographed in many attractive colors. **59¢**

49T5484—Postpaid.............

Boy's Ticking Watch With Chain

Every boy wants a watch and chain like Daddy, and just think of it, this one has the mechanism which makes a ticking sound when you wind it. Beautifully finished to imitate silver watch with engraved back. Unbreakable crystal. Merely turn stem and hands go around, while mechanism inside makes watch tick. Diameter, 1¾ inches. Chain, about 8 inches long with buttonhole bar. **17¢**

49T9117—Postpaid.............

Games for All Ages

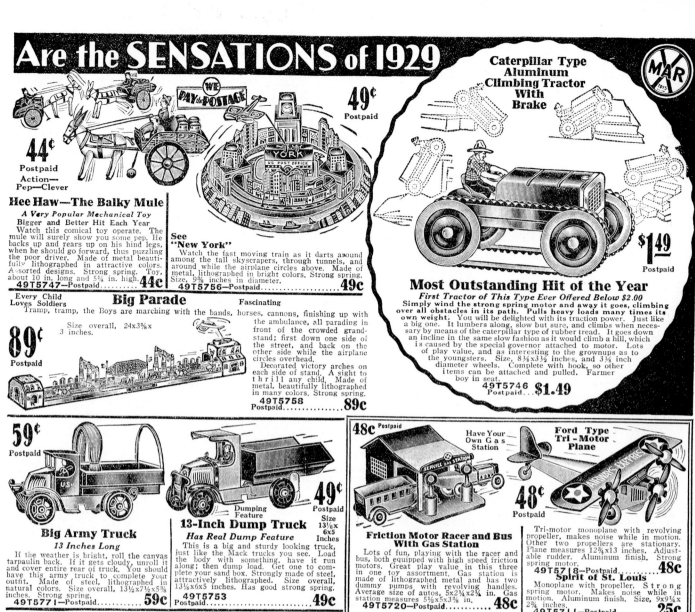

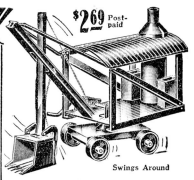

IDEAL AIRPLANE CONSTRUCTION SETS

WE PAY THE POSTAGE

FOR the YOUNG AVIATORS

METALCRAFT ZEPPELIN SETS

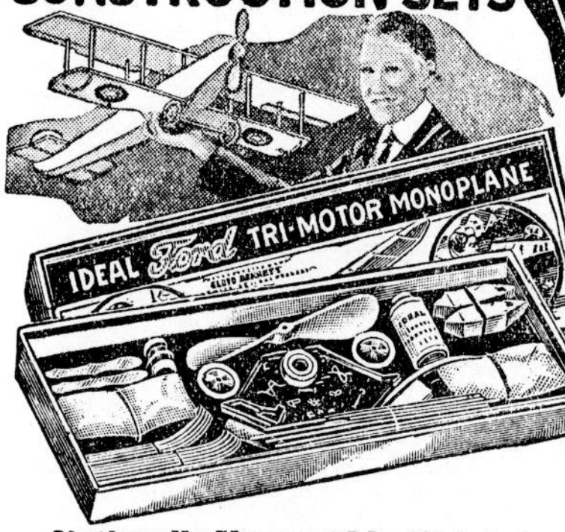

Nationally Known "Ideal" Sets

A Real Thrill to Build One of These Popular Planes, and Then Fly It

For many years "Ideal" has had the reputation of leading in offering construction sets to build planes true to actual models. "Ideal" planes are guaranteed to fly if properly constructed. All parts are accurately made. Three popular models at attractive prices.

Ford Tri-Motor Type Plane, $7.67
$8.50 Elsewhere
Exact Model of the 1929 Ford Plane

This is a dandy. Follow plans in assembling; test plane and get a record flight. All necessary parts in fancy box, 24¾x9⅛x2⅛ in.
49T4736—Postpaid............ **$7.67**

$6.00 Elsewhere. Every Boy's Model, $5.39
A Popular Monoplane Model

All parts packed in attractive box and comes complete with plans and instructions. Box, 24¾x9⅛x2 inches.
49T4735—Postpaid............ **$5.39**

$3.75 Elsewhere. Famous Cecil Peoli, $3.39
Pusher Type Racer Model

Has two propellers. Complete with necessary wood parts, propellers, varnish, Japanese rice paper, insignia, band motors, winder and full instructions. Packed in box, 24¾x3¼x1⅞ inches.
49T4734—Postpaid............ **$3.39**

FAMOUS "SPIRIT OF ST. LOUIS" CONSTRUCTION TOY

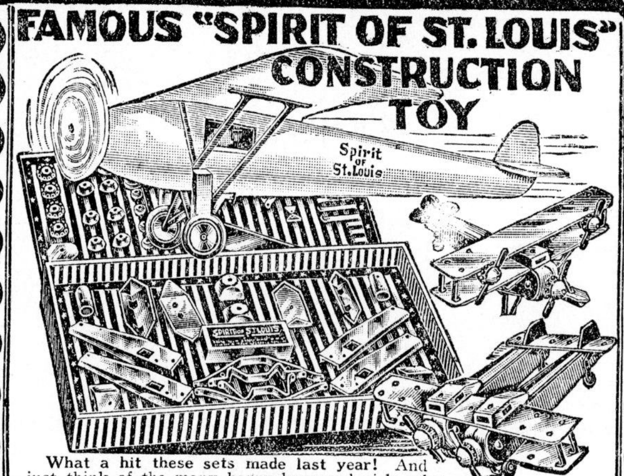

What a hit these sets made last year! And just think of the many happy boys and girls who received these model builders. If you didn't have one last year you can't be without one this year. Imagine! First the famous **Spirit of St. Louis**, then an **Army bomber**, and then a **seaplane**; all these wonderful models and many, many others to be constructed with this magnificent builder. All parts made of non-rusting metal. When constructed, models are lifelike reproductions, **not intended to fly.**

Our Most Popular Size
$5.00 Value Elsewhere. $4.48 Builds Over 250 Models

The well written instructions will be like a magnet to you. Takes you on a trip with a well known pilot, who explains all the tricks as he starts, loops, spins and stops. Set has 260 parts, and assembled completely in attractive box, 19½x13¼x1¹⁵⁄₁₆ in.
49T4727—Postpaid........................ **$4.48**

$3.00 Value Elsewhere, $2.59
Builds 100 Models

This will build plenty of models, with the 175 parts included. Full instructions. Packed in strong, attractive box.
49T4726—Postpaid.. **$2.59**

$1.50 Value Elsewhere, $1.34
Builds 25 Models

Builds plenty of models for the younger boy. Has 115 parts. Full instructions. Packed in strong box, 14x8¼x1½ inches.
49T4725—Postpaid.. **$1.34**

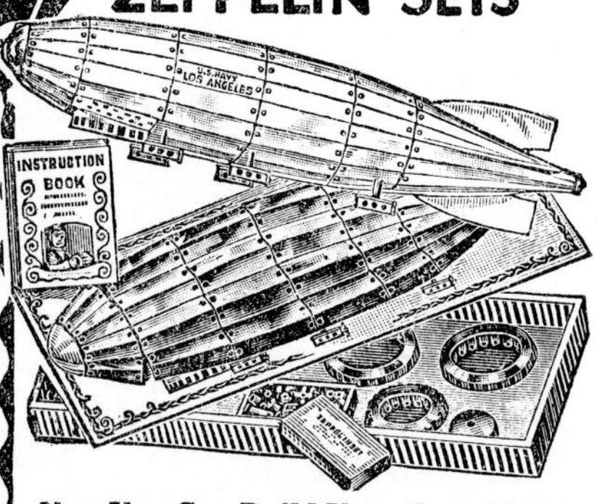

Now You Can Build Your Own Airship

Made by the Makers of the Famous "Spirit of St. Louis" Construction Sets

Would you like to construct a model of the Los Angeles, Graf Zeppelin, or the Italia? You can do it with these dandy all metal sets. All parts rustproof metal, and when assembled are so natural looking that you'll not be satisfied until you see them running on pulleys from one side of the room to the other. Do not fly.

Builds Zeppelin 27 Inches Long
$5.00 Value Elsewhere, $4.48.

Unlimited number of models can be built. What fun in reading up on balloons and dirigibles—and a complete story is included with the clear and simple instructions in this set. Has over 90 large parts and over 400 nuts and bolts. Design sheet with insignia included with set. In strong, attractive box, 27¾x10¼x2 in.
79T4730—Postpaid............ **$4.48**

$1.50 Value Elsewhere, $1.34. Builds over 20 models.

Has over 40 large parts and over 125 nuts and bolts. Complete instructions. In strong box, 13¾x10¼x1¼ inches.
49T4729—Postpaid............ **$1.34**

$1.00 Value Elsewhere, 87c. Builds 8 models.

We must not forget the little fellow. Set has about 178 pieces. Instructions included. In attractive box, 9⁹⁄₁₆x8¼x1 inches.
49T4728—Postpaid............ **87c**

Airplanes That Really Fly

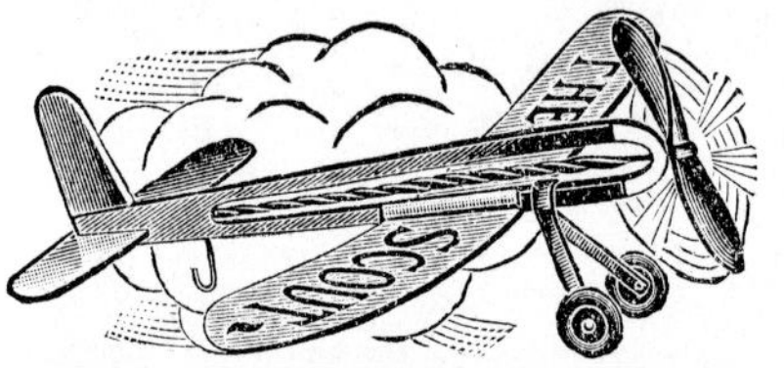

$1.00 "Scout", 87c

We believe this is best value on the market. A real flyer. 19 inches long; wing spread 21¾ inches. All made of balsawood. In attractive box.
49T4732—Postpaid...... **87c**

The "Pirate" 50c Value 42c

Constructed same as 49T4732, but with straight balsa fuselage. 14⅛ in. long; wing spread, 17¾ in.
49T4731—Postpaid...... **42c**

The "Thunderbolt" 21 Inches Long
Two-Propeller Pusher Type Racer

Wonderful new feature: Baked, bent wings; 23¾ inch spread; 21 inches long. Properly handled, will fly nearly 300 feet. All made of Balsa wood. Has improved hand winder. Packed in box, 21x11⅛x1¾ inches.
49T4733—Postpaid. **$1.79**

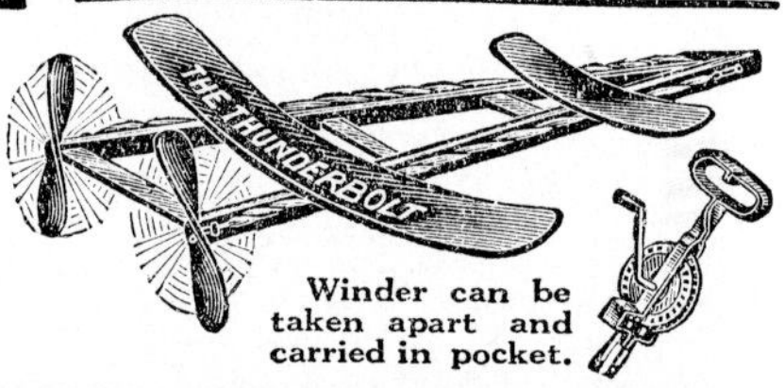

Winder can be taken apart and carried in pocket.

EVERY BOY WANTS a GUN!

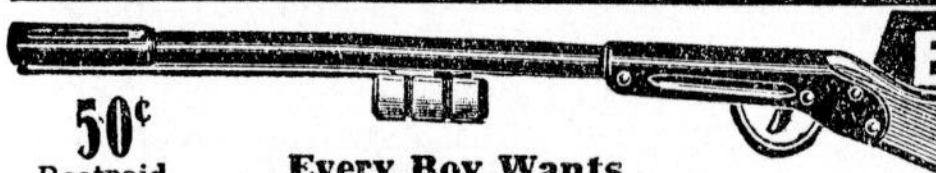

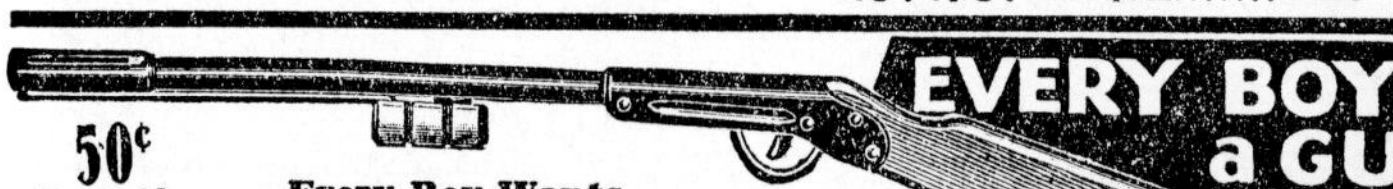

50¢ Postpaid

Every Boy Wants a Rapid Fire Pump Popgun

A gun every youngster should have. Operates like a big one. Pull back pump handle, release, and it falls back into place. Then pull trigger and—Bang! A loud report follows. Cork cannot be lost, because it remains encased in barrel. Gun measures 28 inches long; has polished black enamel steel barrel and varnished natural finish stock. A real dandy.
49T5649—Postpaid........................ **50c**

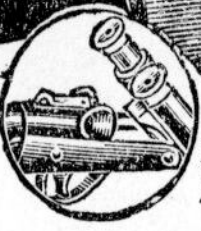

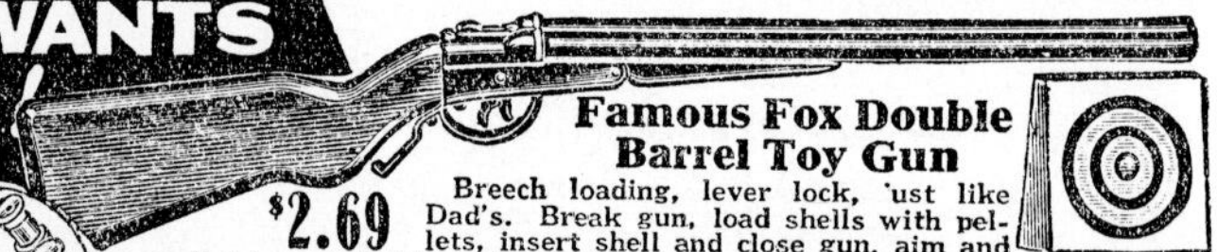

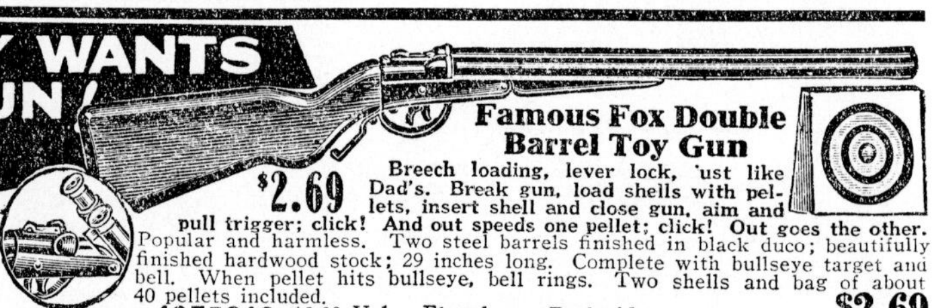

$2.69

Famous Fox Double Barrel Toy Gun

Breech loading, lever lock, just like Dad's. Break gun, load shells with pellets, insert shell and close gun, aim and pull trigger; click! And out speeds one pellet; click! Out goes the other. Popular and harmless. Two steel barrels finished in black duco; beautifully finished hardwood stock; 29 inches long. Complete with bullseye target and bell. When pellet hits bullseye, bell rings. Two shells and bag of about 40 pellets included.
49T5640—$3.00 Value Elsewhere. Postpaid.................. **$2.69**

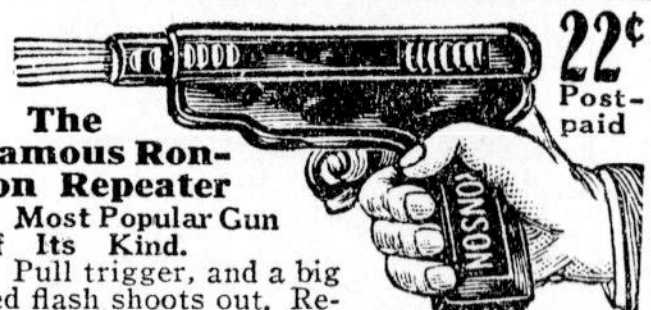

22¢ Postpaid

The Famous Ronson Repeater
Most Popular Gun of Its Kind.

Every Boy Wants One

Pull trigger, and a big red flash shoots out. Repeater action, just pull the trigger, which automatically goes back into original position. 5,000 flashes can be shot before reloading. Strong steel. Length, 4½ in. Extra reloads listed below.
49T5657—Postpaid.......... **22c**

Three reloads for Ronson Repeater. Each reload gives 5,000 shots.
49T5658—Postpaid.......... **10c**

42¢ We Pay the Postage

22¢ Postpaid

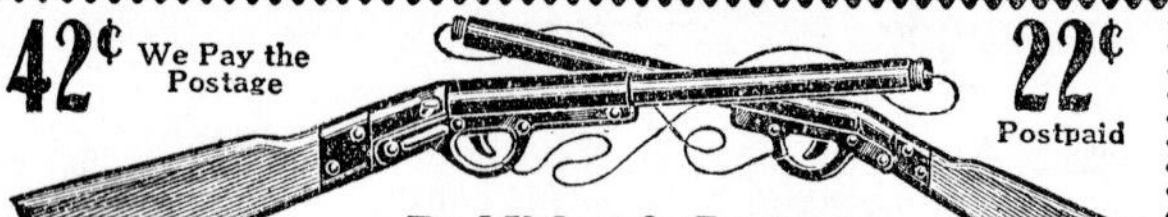

Real Values in Popguns

22-Inch Popgun for 42c

Dandy little gun for little money. Black enamel finish barrel and nicely varnished hardwood stock. Break action like air rifle. Has strong spring. Shoots cork with loud report. Cork tied onto gun to prevent losing.
49T5646—Postpaid........ **42c**

17-Inch Popgun for 22c

Shoots cork with loud report. Has black enameled finish barrel and nicely stained stock. Break action like the big ones. Strong spring. Cork fastened to string to prevent losing.
49T5647
Postpaid.................. **22c**

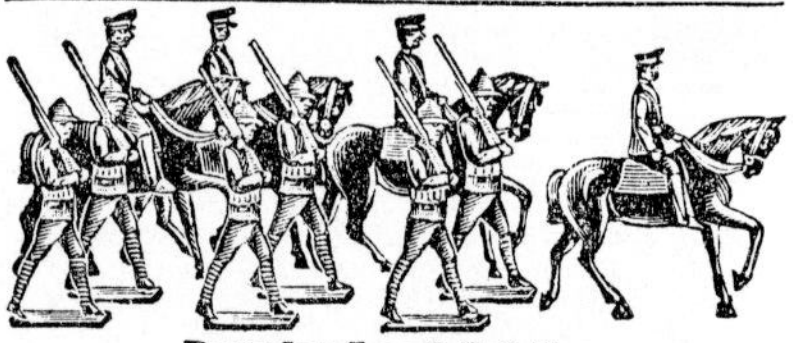

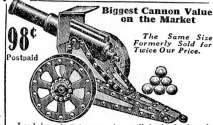

Popular Lead Soldiers

American Infantry and Cavalry set of four horsemen and six on foot, beautifully finished in army colors. Size of largest piece, 2¾ inches.
49T5611—Set of 10 pieces.
Our price, Postpaid.............................. **98c**

Indians

Four on horseback, and six on foot.
49T5613—10 pieces, Postpaid......... **98c**

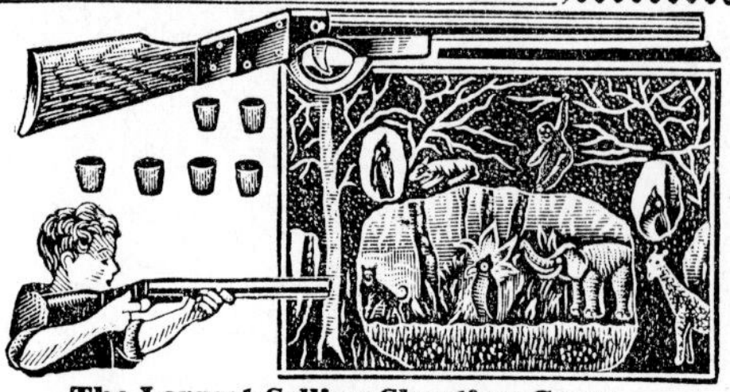

The Largest Selling Shooting Game

See if you can get a bigger score than Dad. Remember, it requires real skill and practice to shoot the pyralin birds from their perches. Target made of heavy cardboard. When set up, it represents a real Jungle in natural colors. **A 15¾-inch break action steel barrel popgun with cork ammunition.** Target measures 16 by 10⅜ inches.
49T5663—Postpaid........................ **79c**

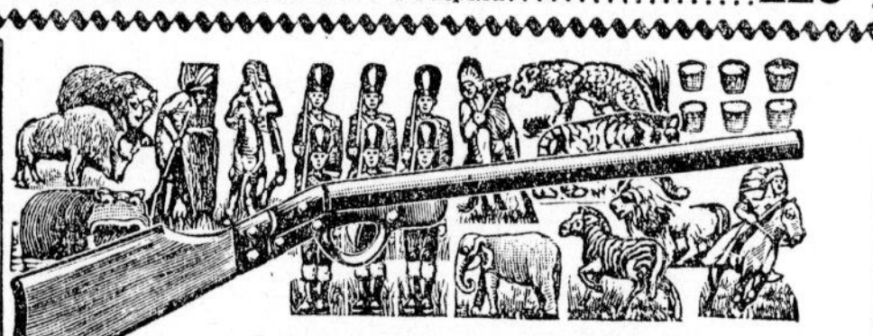

An Exceptional Shooting Game Value

Eighteen snappily colored figures, consisting of lion, tiger, bear, elephant, buffalo, zebra, hippopotamus, leopard, war painted Indians and soldiers, largest piece 6⅞ in. high. Line them all up for your Wild West Show; then see who is the crack shot. **The 17-inch steel barrel break action popgun,** well aimed, will do the rest. All figures of cardboard in natural colors. Shooting corks included.
49T5667—Postpaid.............................. **49c**

Biggest Cannon Value on the Market

98¢ Postpaid

The Same Size Formerly Sold for Twice Our Price.

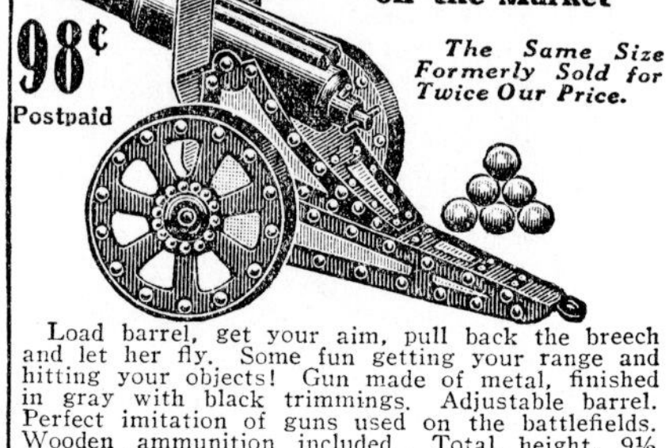

Load barrel, get your aim, pull back the breech and let her fly. Some fun getting your range and hitting your objects! Gun made of metal, finished in gray with black trimmings. Adjustable barrel. Perfect imitation of guns used on the battlefields. Wooden ammunition included. Total height, 9½ inches; length over all, 23 inches; diameter of wheels, about 5½ inches.
49T5610—Postpaid.................... **98c**

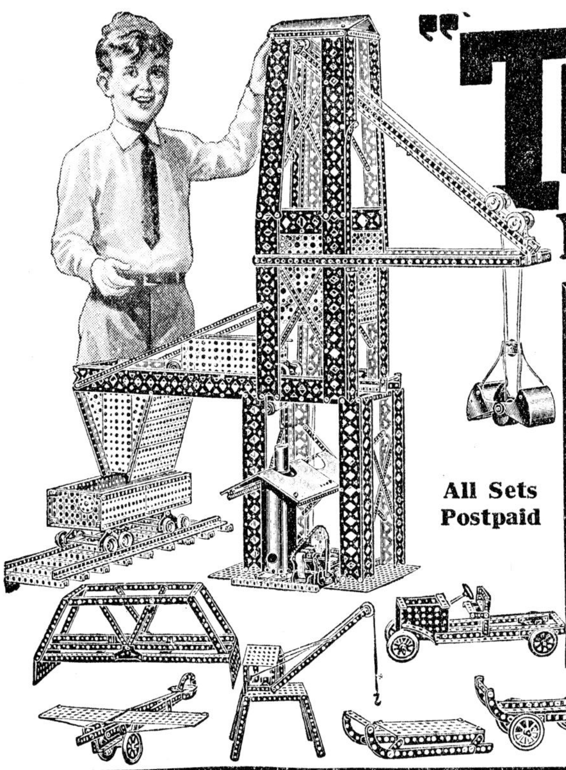

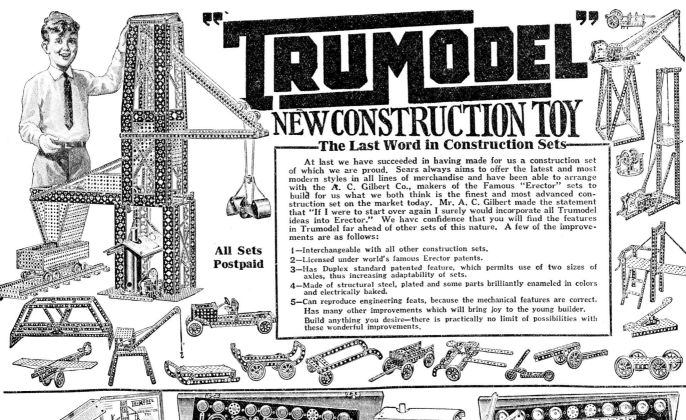

"TRUMODEL"

NEW CONSTRUCTION TOY

All Sets Postpaid

The Last Word in Construction Sets

At last we have succeeded in having made for us a construction set of which we are proud. Sears always aims to offer the latest and most modern styles in all lines of merchandise and have been able to arrange with the A. C. Gilbert Co., makers of the Famous "Erector" sets to build for us what we both think is the finest and most advanced construction set on the market today. Mr. A. C. Gilbert made the statement that "If I were to start over again I surely would incorporate all Trumodel ideas into Erector." We have confidence that you will find the features in Trumodel far ahead of other sets of this nature. A few of the improvements are as follows:

1—Interchangeable with all other construction sets.
2—Licensed under world's famous Erector patents.
3—Has Duplex standard patented feature, which permits use of two sizes of axles, thus increasing adaptability of sets.
4—Made of structural steel, plated and some parts brilliantly enameled in colors and electrically baked.
5—Can reproduce engineering feats, because the mechanical features are correct.
Has many other improvements which will bring joy to the young builder.
Build anything you desire—there is practically no limit of possibilities with these wonderful improvements.

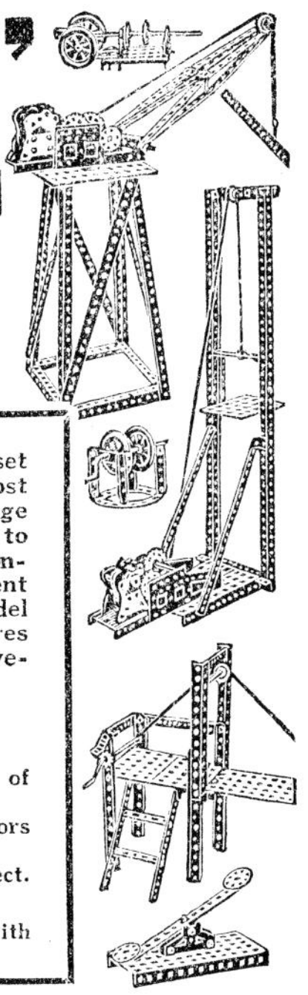

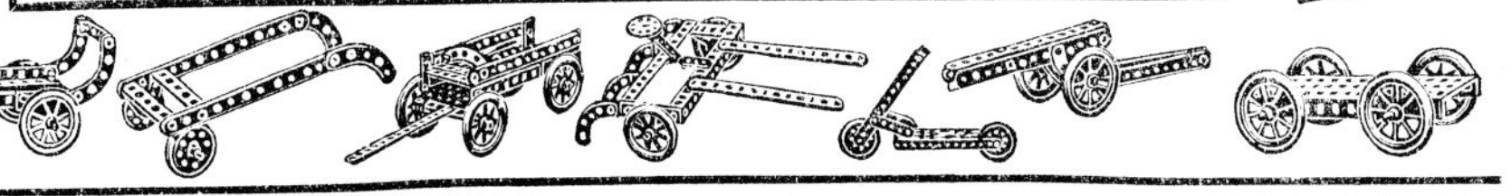

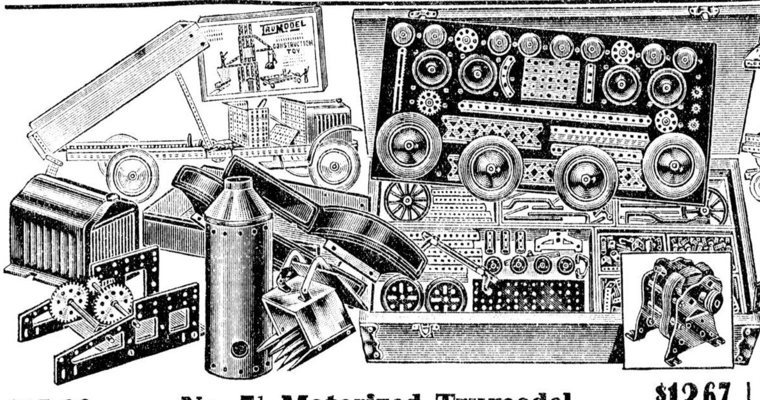

$15.00 Value

No. 7½ Motorized Trumodel

The Set That Builds the Chassis and Other Models

$13.67 Postpaid

This is the king of them all—and we know will give you the greatest thrill you ever had. Fun? Oh! Boy! It's the real thing, and has a thrill in each of its parts. **The completely assembled gear box, the building tray, 15-inch steel truck body, fenders, radiator hood, big red steel wheels with oversize balloon tires, springs, bumpers, steering wheel, heavy truck axles, cab top, boiler, digger scoop,** and all the rest of the parts will give you scientific thrills for every day in the year. Has big book of models and some "king pins too." Packed in large brass bound, red wooden chest, **with brass fittings and handle grips.** Size, over all, 22⅝x10¾x6 in.

79T4755—Postpaid........ **$13.67**

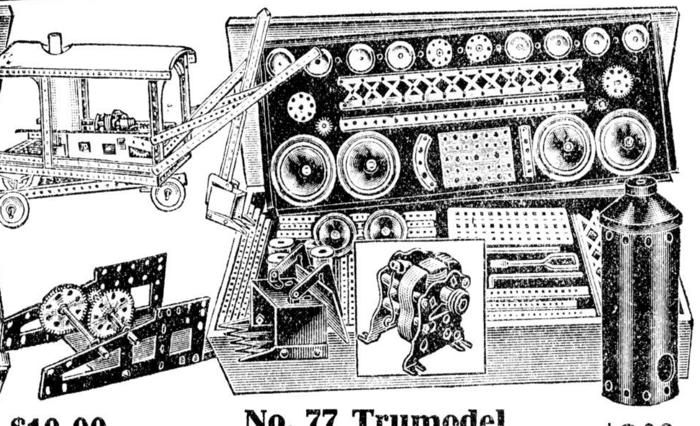

$10.00 Value

No. 77 Trumodel

The Set That Builds the Steam Shovel and Other Models

$8.98 Postpaid

Gee, fellows! With this set in which is a 6½-inch solid steel cab top, and a steam shovel digger scoop, you can make a big steam shovel and connect to the motor and assembled gear box, and actually operate it electrically. Everything, even to the big 20-inch solid steel building tray with which you can also build wagons, hoisting machinery, wheelbarrows, luggage trucks, some of which measure 2 and 3 feet long. The pieces in this set are very well constructed. Manual included in this set, has so many good models to make, that you will hardly be able to wait to build them one at a time. Packed in big red wooden box, with brass trimmings and with brass handle grips. Size, over all, 21⅞x8$\frac{3}{16}$x4⅞ inches.

79T4754—Postpaid........ **$8.98**

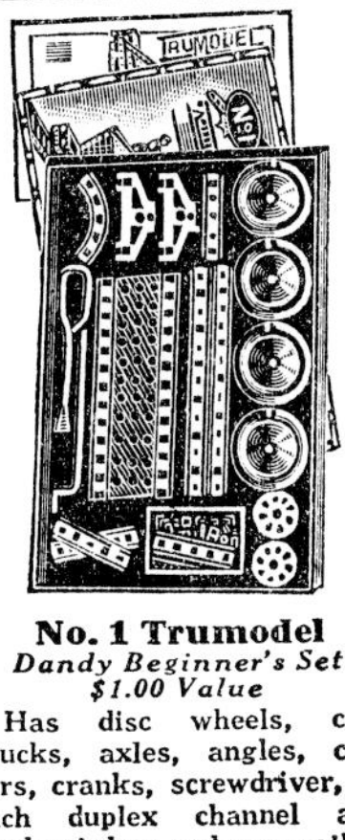

No. 1 Trumodel

Dandy Beginner's Set
$1.00 Value

Has disc wheels, car trucks, axles, angles, collars, cranks, screwdriver, **6-inch duplex channel and angle girders and many other parts.** Many of these pieces are in colors making models very attractive in appearance. Complete in attractive strong cardboard box, 12½x8¾x¾ inches. Has simply worded instruction and model book.

49T4750
Postpaid........ **89c**

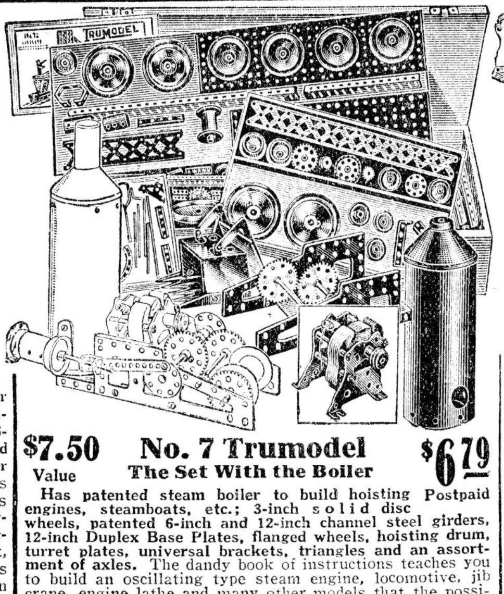

$7.50 Value

No. 7 Trumodel

The Set With the Boiler

$6.79 Postpaid

Has patented steam boiler to build hoisting engines, steamboats, etc.; 3-inch solid disc wheels, patented 6-inch and 12-inch channel steel girders, 12-inch Duplex Base Plates, flanged wheels, hoisting drum, turret plates, universal brackets, triangles and an assortment of axles. The dandy book of instructions teaches you to build an oscillating type steam engine, locomotive, jib crane, engine lathe and many other models that the possibilities are unlimited. Set put up in big red wooden box, brass trimmed. Size, over all, 21½x8¼x3¼ inches. **$6.79**

79T4753—Postpaid........

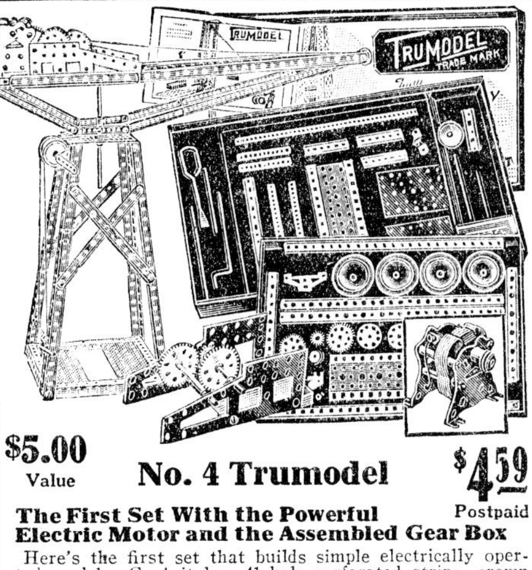

$5.00 Value

No. 4 Trumodel

The First Set With the Powerful Electric Motor and the Assembled Gear Box

$4.59 Postpaid

Here's the first set that builds simple electrically operated models. Gee! it has 41-hole perforated strips, crown gear, worm gear, couplings, the powerful motor which can be taken apart for experimental purposes, and a completely assembled gear box, adaptable to every possible gear combination. Instructions have directions for making all sorts of gear combinations and working possibilities. You can make loading derricks, cranes, automobiles, water wheels and many other models. Instruction book included. Box, 18x10⅛x1¼ inches. **$4.59**

79T4752—Postpaid........

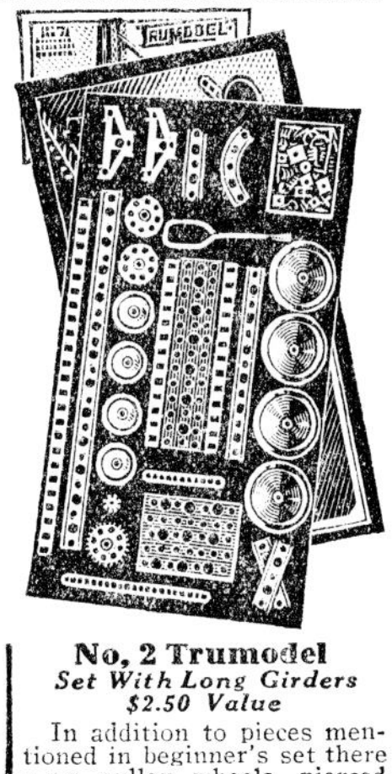

No. 2 Trumodel

Set With Long Girders
$2.50 Value

In addition to pieces mentioned in beginner's set there are pulley wheels, pierced discs, perforated strips, and, best of all, the 12-inch duplex channel girders and 12-inch angle girders. Builds larger models than No. 1 set. Complete instruction book. Packed in attractive cardboard box, 18x10½x1¼ inches.

49T4751 **$2.28**
Postpaid......

Do Your Christmas Shopping From This Catalog

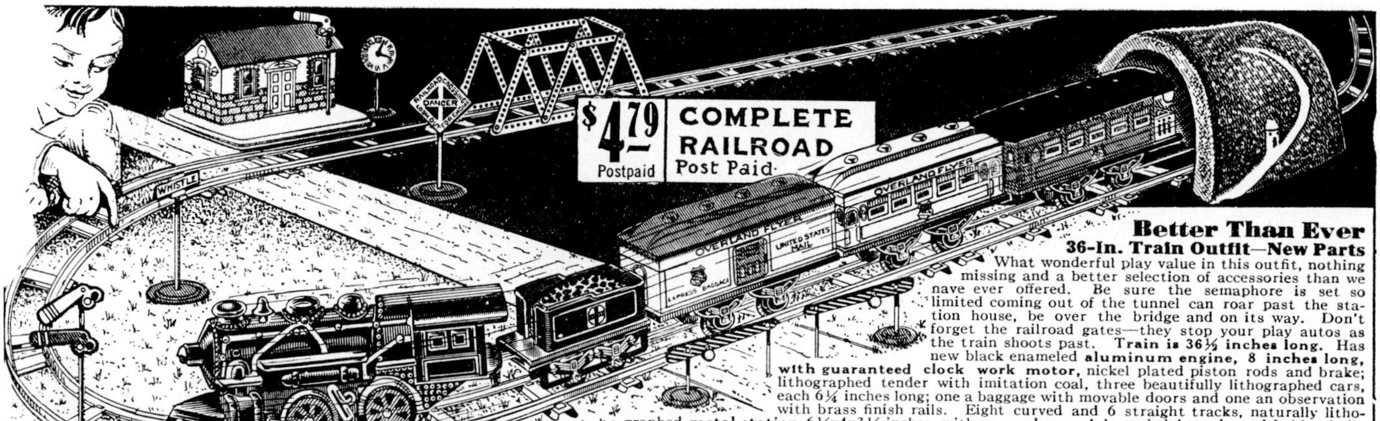

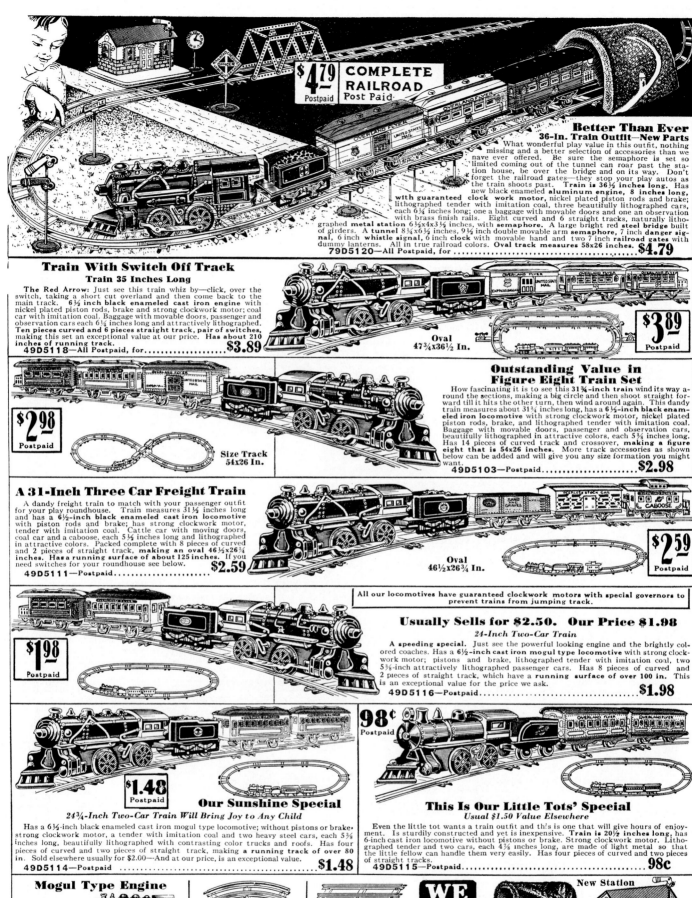

$4.79 Postpaid

COMPLETE RAILROAD Post Paid

Better Than Ever

36-In. Train Outfit—New Parts

What wonderful play value in this outfit, nothing missing and a better selection of accessories than we have ever offered. Be sure the semaphore is set so limited coming out of the tunnel can roar past the station house, be over the bridge and on its way. Don't forget the railroad gates—they stop your play autos as the train shoots past. **Train is 36½ inches long.** Has new black enameled **aluminum engine, 8 inches long, with guaranteed clock work motor,** nickel plated piston rods and brake; lithographed tender with imitation coal, three beautifully lithographed cars, each 6¼ inches long; one a baggage with movable doors and one an observation with brass finish rails. Eight curved and 6 straight tracks, naturally lithographed **metal station** 6½x4x3½ inches, with **semaphore.** A large bright red **steel bridge** built of girders. A **tunnel** 8¼x6½ inches, 9½ inch double movable arm **semaphore,** 7 inch **danger signal,** 6 inch **whistle signal,** 6 inch **clock** with movable hand and two 7 inch **railroad gates** with dummy lanterns. All in true railroad colors. **Oval track measures 58x26 inches.**

79D5120—All Postpaid, for **$4.79**

Train With Switch Off Track

Train 35 Inches Long

The Red Arrow: Just see this train whiz by—click, over the switch, taking a short cut overland and then come back to the main track. **6½ inch black enameled cast iron engine** with nickel plated piston rods, brake and strong clockwork motor; coal car with imitation coal. Baggage with movable doors, passenger and observation cars each 6¼ inches long and attractively lithographed. **Ten pieces curved and 6 pieces straight track, pair of switches,** making this set an exceptional value at our price. **Has about 210 inches of running track.**

49D5118—All Postpaid, for **$3.89**

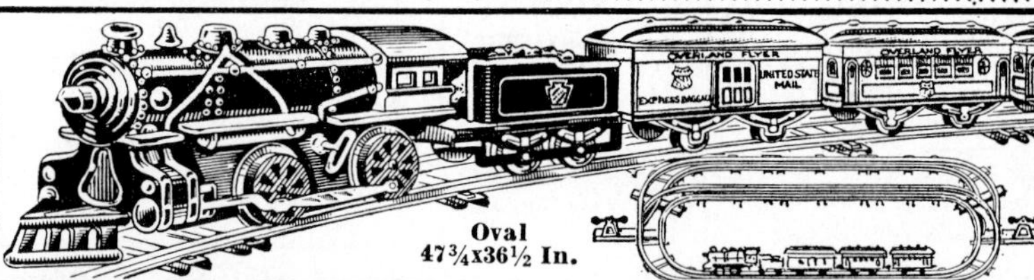

Oval 47¾x36½ In.

$3.89 Postpaid

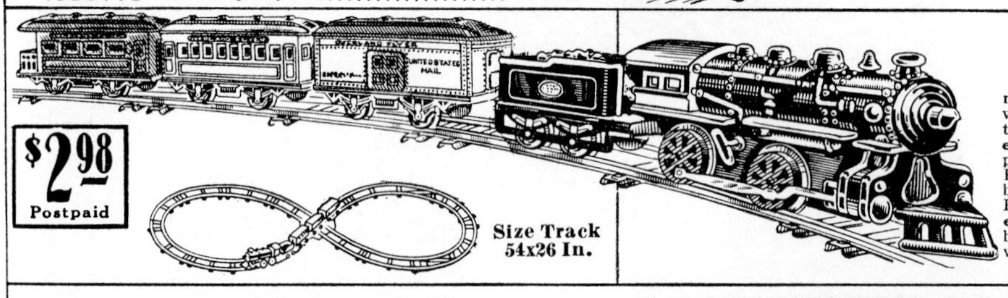

$2.98 Postpaid

Size Track 54x26 In.

Outstanding Value in Figure Eight Train Set

How fascinating it is to see this **31¾-inch train** wind its way around the sections, making a big circle and then shoot straight forward till it hits the other turn, then wind around again. This dandy train measures about 31¾ inches long, has a **6½-inch black enameled iron locomotive** with strong clockwork motor, nickel plated piston rods, brake, and lithographed tender with imitation coal. Baggage with movable doors, passenger and observation cars, beautifully lithographed in attractive colors, each 5⅜ inches long. Has 14 pieces of curved track and crossover, **making a figure eight that is 54x26 inches.** More track accessories as shown below can be added and will give you any size formation you might want.

49D5103—Postpaid **$2.98**

A 31-Inch Three Car Freight Train

A dandy freight train to match with your passenger outfit for your play roundhouse. Train measures 31½ inches long and has a **6½-inch black enameled cast iron locomotive** with piston rods and brake; has strong clockwork motor, tender with imitation coal. Cattle car with moving doors, coal car and a caboose, each 5½ inches long and lithographed in attractive colors. Packed complete with 8 pieces of curved and 2 pieces of straight track, **making an oval 46½x26¾ inches. Has a running surface of about 125 inches.** If you need switches for your roundhouse see below.

49D5111—Postpaid **$2.59**

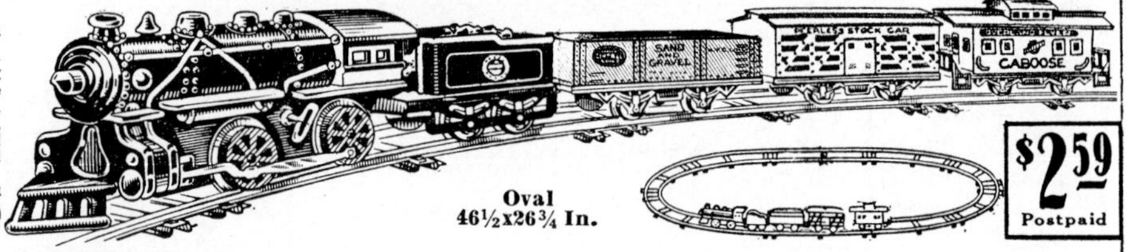

Oval 46½x26¾ In.

$2.59 Postpaid

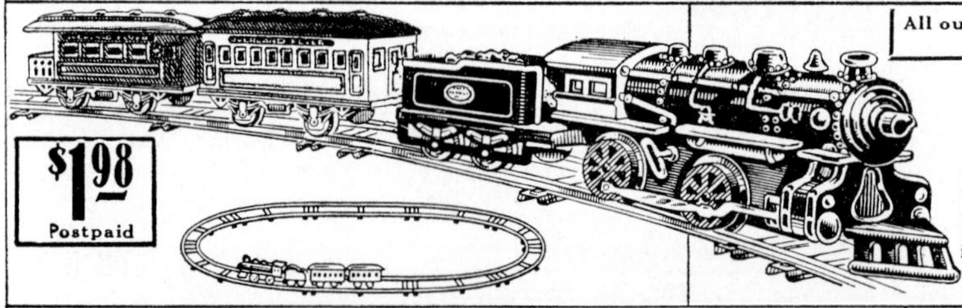

$1.98 Postpaid

All our locomotives have guaranteed clockwork motors with special governors to prevent trains from jumping track.

Usually Sells for $2.50. Our Price $1.98

24-Inch Two-Car Train

A speeding special. Just see the powerful looking engine and the brightly colored coaches. Has a **6½-inch cast iron mogul type locomotive** with strong clockwork motor; pistons and brake, lithographed tender with imitation coal, two 5⅜-inch attractively lithographed passenger cars. Has 8 pieces of curved and 2 pieces of straight track, which have a **running surface of over 100 in.** This is an exceptional value for the price we ask.

49D5116—Postpaid **$1.98**

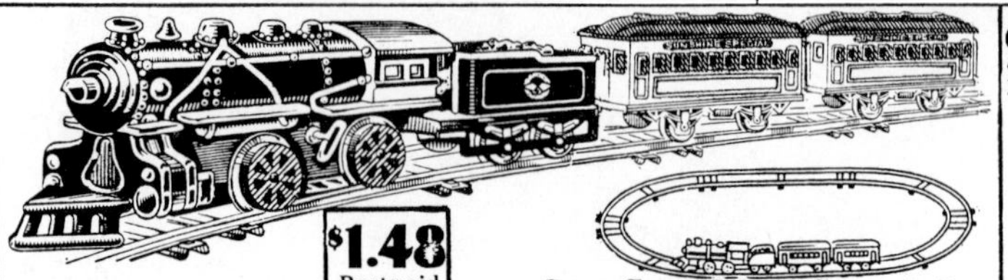

$1.48 Postpaid

Our Sunshine Special

24¾-Inch Two-Car Train Will Bring Joy to Any Child

Has a 6½-inch black enameled cast iron mogul type locomotive; without pistons or brake; strong clockwork motor, a tender with imitation coal and two heavy steel cars, each 5⅜ inches long, beautifully lithographed with contrasting color trucks and roofs. Has four pieces of curved and two pieces of straight track, making **a running track of over 80 in.** Sold elsewhere usually for $2.00—And at our price, is an exceptional value.

49D5114—Postpaid **$1.48**

98¢ Postpaid

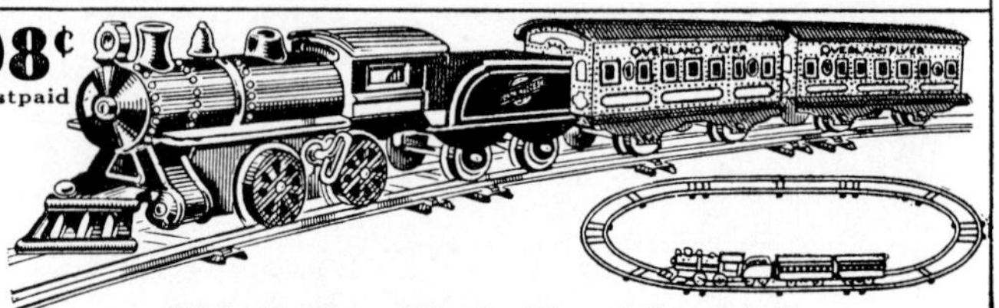

This Is Our Little Tots' Special

Usual $1.50 Value Elsewhere

Even the little tot wants a train outfit and this is one that will give hours of enjoyment. Is sturdily constructed and yet is inexpensive. **Train is 20½ inches long,** has 6-inch cast iron locomotive without pistons or brake. Strong clockwork motor. Lithographed tender and two cars, each 4⅞ inches long, are made of light metal so that the little fellow can handle them very easily. Has four pieces of curved and two pieces of straight tracks.

49D5115—Postpaid **98c**

Mogul Type Engine

Guaranteed Clockwork Motor

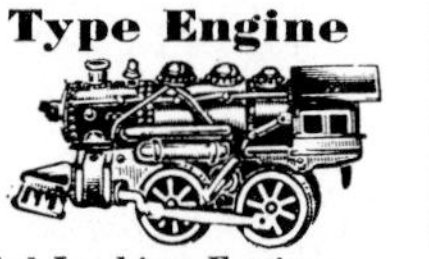

A Powerful Looking Engine

Is black enamel cast iron with nickel plated piston rods and brake. Size of engine 6½ inches long. **Tender not included.**

49D5222

Postpaid **$1.39**

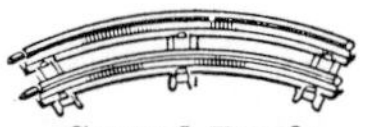

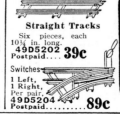

Curved Track

Eight sections make circle.

49D5201—6 Pieces.

Postpaid **39c**

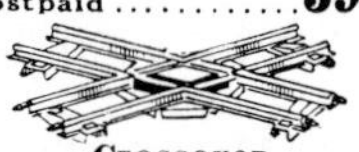

Crossover

49D5203

Postpaid **39c**

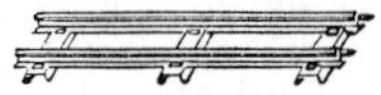

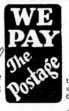

Straight Tracks

Six pieces, each 10¼ in. long.

49D5202

Postpaid.... **39c**

Switches—

1 Left, 1 Right, Per pair,

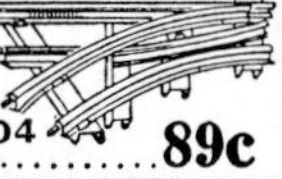

49D5204

Postpaid......... **89c**

WE PAY The Postage

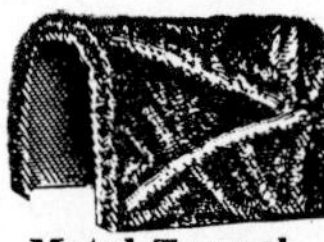

Metal Tunnel

All metal, very attractively finished to represent sides of a mountain. Size, 6¼x5½x5⅝ inches.

49D5206

Postpaid **35c**

New Station

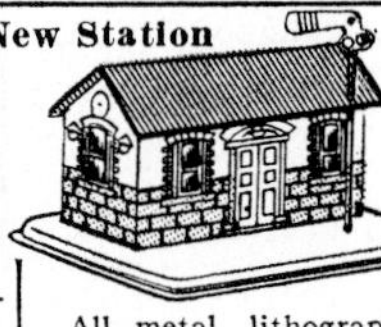

All metal, lithographed with semaphore. Size overall, 6½x4x3½ inches.

49D5208

Postpaid **39c**

660 C137P B-K-MN Items on These Pages Shipped POSTAGE PAID by Sears, Roebuck and CO.

[1930, No. 161] 73

$1.29 WE PAY THE POSTAGE EVERY CHILD WANTS A TRACTOR

98¢
83¢

A WONDERFUL CLIMBER
PULLS SEVERAL TIMES OWN WEIGHT
Size 8⅜x5½x3⅜

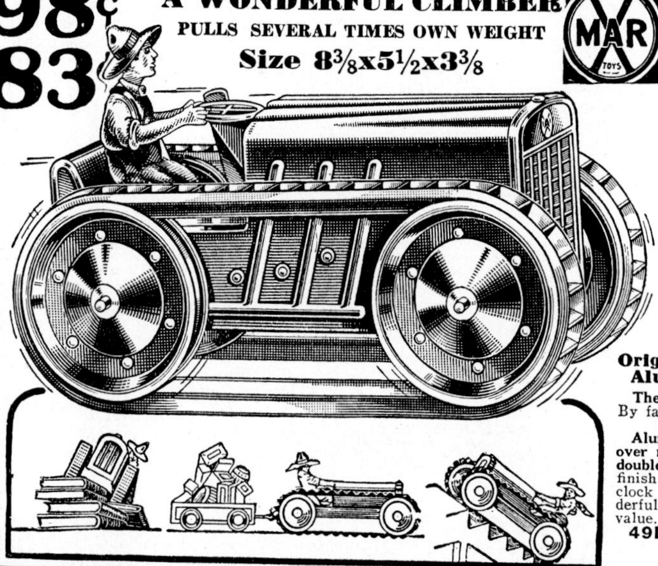

It Is Miniature, but Oh What Strength! Really Unbelievable.

It has been one of the most popular toys ever brought out. Kiddies entertain themselves for hours, either indoors or outdoors. As interesting to girls as it is to boys. Wind up the powerful Marx clock motor, release lever, and on with the show. Tractor can be started and stopped at will, just by throwing lever. Away goes the tractor pulling, pushing, climbing, nothing seems to stop its progress. Over obstacles, down dangerous curves and over everything in its path. Because it is constructed on the same mechanical principles as the large tractors, it is able to pull or push loads many times its own weight. It lumbers along slow but sure, climbing when necessary and goes down an incline without any change in its speed.

Outstanding Features Which Make This Toy the Sensational Hit It Is

1. **Has Marx guaranteed super strong powerful clock work motor** which cannot be overwound.
2. **Special governor on motor** to control the speed.
3. Scientifically constructed caterpillar type rubber tread.
4. **Lever to start and stop** tractor before spring is unwound.
5. **Pulls or pushes loads several times its own weight.**
6. **Climbs or goes down** steep hills at same slow speed.
7. **Powerful enough** to push aside small obstacles and has enough traction to climb over books, boxes, etc.
8. **Has hooks,** so other much heavier toys can be attached for pulling.
9. Sturdy construction and quality finish throughout.
10. Has farmer driver in seat.

We Offer Three Wonderful Tractor Values.

Original Marx DeLuxe Aluminum Tractor
The One We Recommend
By far the most popular toy sold in 1929. **Aluminum casing fitted over metal casing to insure double strength.** Its shiny finish is very popular. The clock work motor is a wonderful job. Regular $1.50 value. **Postpaid.**
49D5746 ... $1.29

Special Value Green Enameled Tractor
Clock work and construction similar to our DeLuxe model but has only one casing made of sheet metal, not aluminum, enameled in a beautiful green color. Farmer boy in seat. **Postpaid.**
49D5745
Special at **98c**

Regular $1.00 Value
To meet price competition we offer this sturdy well constructed tractor which is similar in appearance to our other tractors, but does not have as strong a spring. Made from lithographed metal. **Postpaid.**
49D5740 .... 83c

Play Bridge for Tractors see Cat. No. 49D5790

48¢ Postpaid

Two Friction Autos and Filling Station

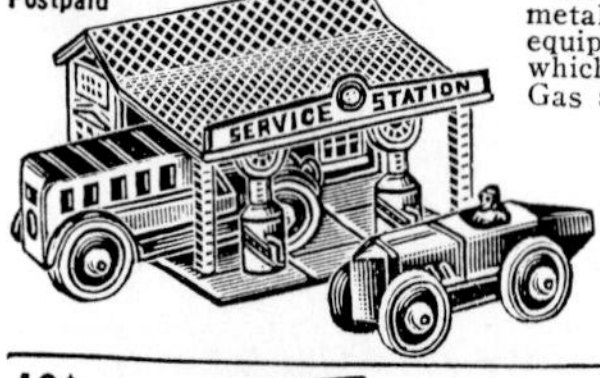

Lots of fun playing with the metal racer and bus, each equipped with friction motor, which makes them go very fast. Gas station made of metal prettily lithographed and has two dummy pumps with revolving handles. Average size of autos 5x2¼x2 inches. Gas Station measures 6x5¼x3¾ inches.
49D5720 Postpaid........... **48c**

49¢ Postpaid

13-Inch Real Dump Truck

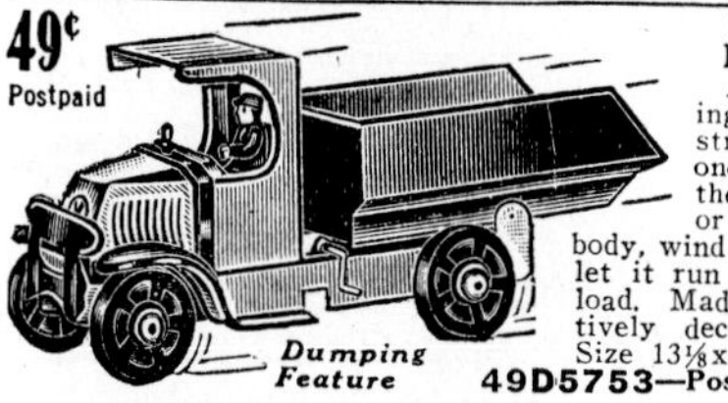

Dumping Feature

A handsome looking and sturdily constructed dump truck, one that will gladden the heart of any boy or girl. Load up the body, wind the strong spring, let it run along then dump load. Made of metal attractively decorated in colors. Size 13⅛x6x5 inches.
49D5753—Postpaid..... 49c

The Famous Whoopee Car Rider

49¢ Post-paid

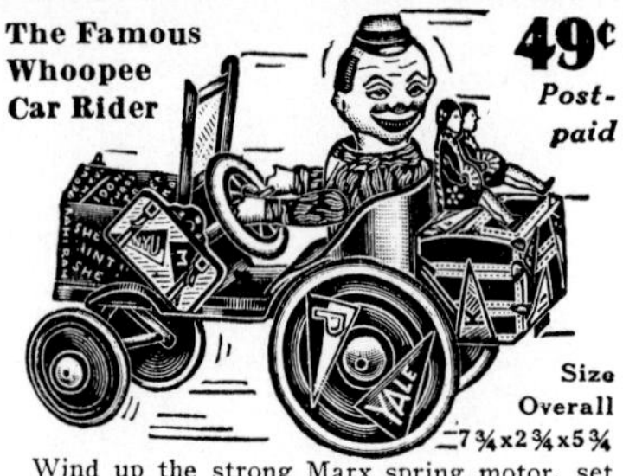

Size Overall 7¾x2¾x5¾

Wind up the strong Marx spring motor, set it down. **No telling which direction the car will go.** Not in a straight line but instead first one way, bucking up like a broncho, then again turning a different direction. The grotesque driver twirls his head as the car goes on, while his "girl friends" appear to be holding on for dear life. Made of metal in color lithography. Size overall 7¾x2¾x5¾ inches.
49D5778—Postpaid 49c

Play Castle and Bridge for Our Tractors and Tanks

49¢ Post-paid

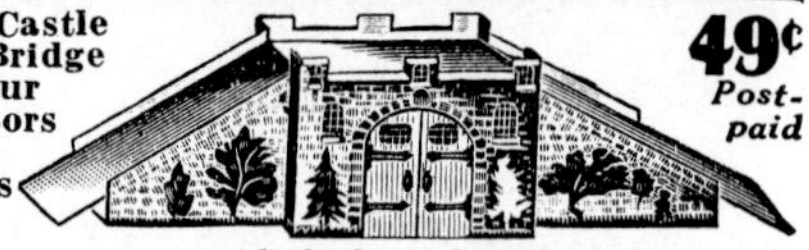

Have your tractor climb the incline, then down again on the other side, or use it as a fort along with your toy soldiers and turn-over tank. The double doors can be set so it can also be used as a garage for your toy autos. Amazing in how many new play combinations this can be used. Made of strong cardboard beautifully lithographed in attractive colors. **Easy to assemble and to take apart.** Size about 40 inches long by 10 inches high by 10¼ inches wide.
49D5790—Postpaid.......................... 49c

JOKE MOUSE

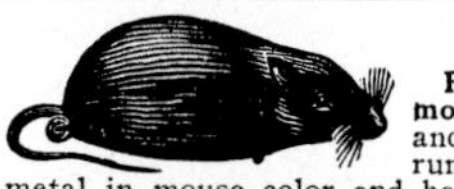

Perfect imitation of a real mouse. Hear the girls scream and see them jump when mouse runs along the floor. Made of metal in mouse color and has friction motor. Mouse 2¾ inches long, not including tail. **Action is just as realistic as that of a live mouse.**
49D5716—Postpaid...................... 21c

New Coast Defense Toy

Something entirely different.

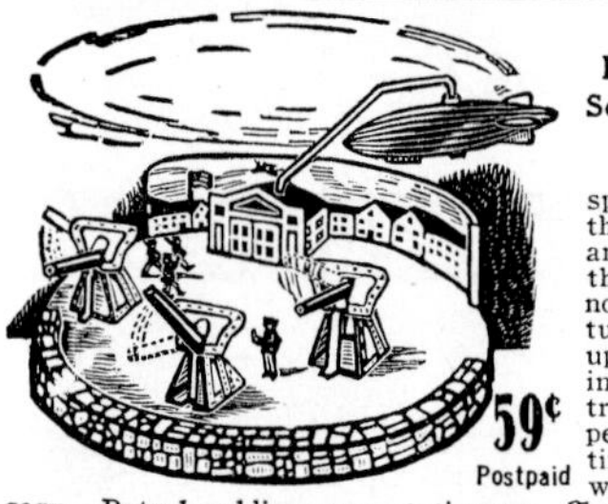

59¢ Postpaid

Wind the strong spring and watch the Zeppelin circle around fort while the three toy cannons move forward turning muzzles upward as if aiming, then again retreating. Toy repeats action several times before a rewinding is necessary. Patrol soldiers are stationary. Toy made of metal prettily lithographed in natural colors. Diameter of base about 9 inches, height in proportion.
49D5760—Postpaid 59c

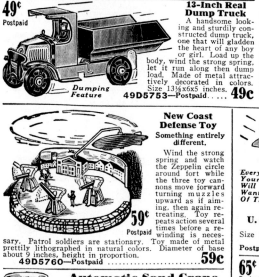

WE PAY POSTAGE

New Mechanical Monoplanes

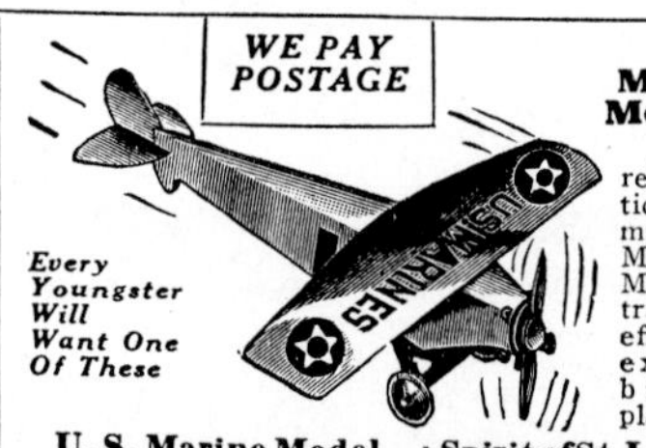

Every Youngster Will Want One Of These

As propeller revolves realistic noise is made. Strong Marx Spring. Metal in attractive color effect. Two exceptionally big value planes.

U. S. Marine Model (Illustrated)
Size 17⅝x17⅞ in.
49D5719 Postpaid.......... **48c**

Spirit of St. Louis Model
No army insignia on wings.
Size 12⅞x9⅜ in.
49D5714 Postpaid.......... **25c**

Big Three Triple Acrobat

89¢ Postpaid

Real Excitement and Fun for Youngsters.
Largest Trapeze Toy of its Kind ever Offered at our Exceptionally low price.

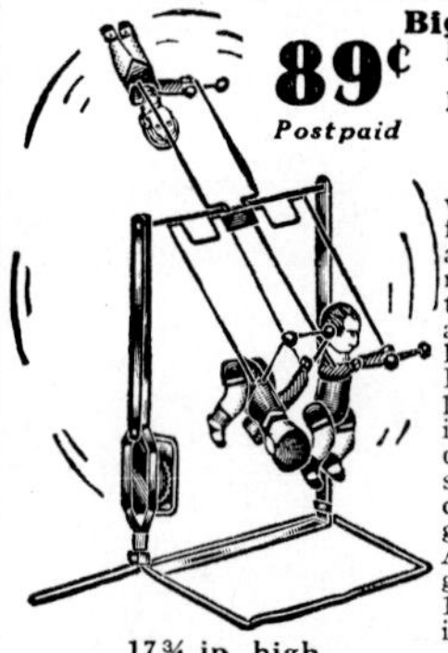

17¾ in. high
12½ in. wide

Just think of the fun, watching the acrobats perform innumerable stunts and always ready to perform more. All you have to do is to wind the strong spring and the performance starts, lasting for quite some time. Legs and arms of the two lower acrobats are free moving enabling them to reproduce acrobatic and trapeze stunts that thrill you at a circus. Toy made from light gauge steel highly finished. Acrobats made of metal lithographed in attractive colors. 17¾ inches high by 12½ inches wide.
49D5707 Postpaid........... **89c**

Automatic Sand Crane

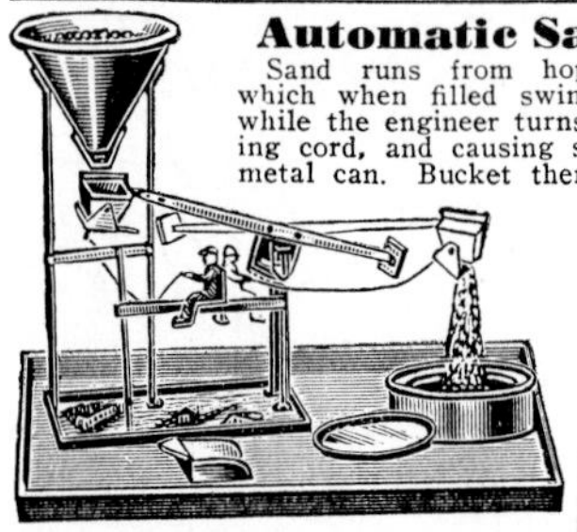

Sand runs from hopper into bucket, which when filled swings in half circle, while the engineer turns in his seat, pulling cord, and causing sand to dump into metal can. Bucket then swings back for another load. All steel, enameled in bright colors. Size 13¾x14 in. Scoop and can of sand included.
49D5782 Postpaid **$1.10**

65¢ Postpaid

Famous Sandy Andy

Automatic-Popular-Clever

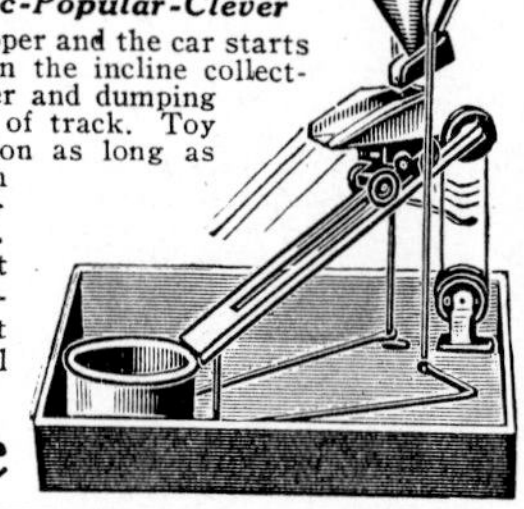

Pour sand into hopper and the car starts running up and down the incline collecting sand from hopper and dumping it in can at bottom of track. Toy can be kept in action as long as hopper is filled. Clean white sand in a friction lid can included. Made from light gauge sheet steel enameled in bright colors. Size overall 11x9¼ inches.
49D5742 Postpaid..... **65c**

The Giant King Racer

12 in. Long

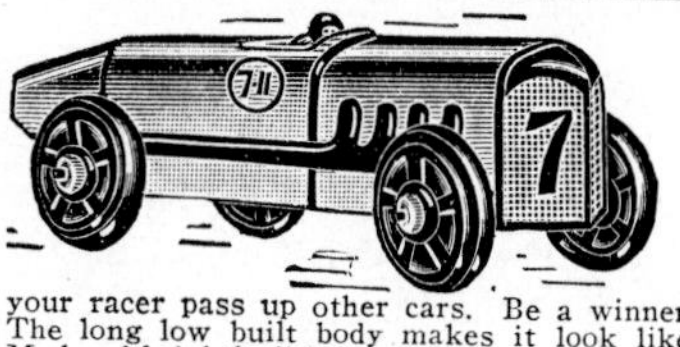

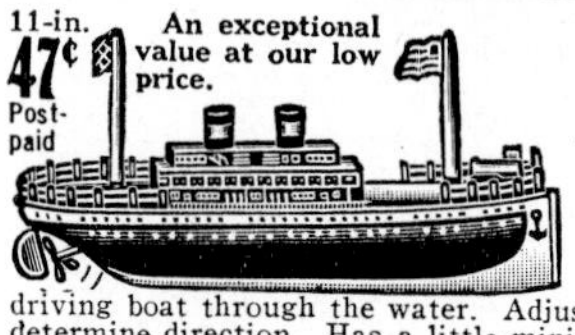

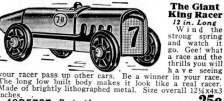

Wind the strong spring and watch it go. Gee! what a race and the thrills you will have seeing your racer pass up other cars. Be a winner in your race. The long low built body makes it look like a real racer. Made of brightly lithographed metal. Size overall 12¼x4x3 inches.
49D5737—Postpaid........................ 25c

Fluffy Real Fur Jumping Bunny

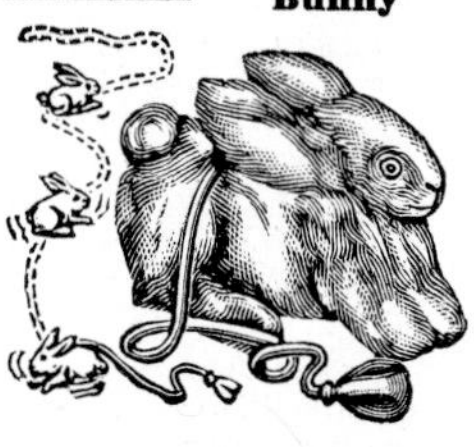

This little rabbit has a real fur coat and hops around wiggling his ears when bulb is pressed. A suitable toy for either little tots or older kiddies, because of the peppy action. Every youngster will love to cuddle this cute little fellow and will long remember this little playmate with the natural looking glass eyes. Size overall about 6 inches.
49D5769 Postpaid **45c**

11-in. 47¢ Post-paid

An exceptional value at our low price.

Mechanical Ocean Liner

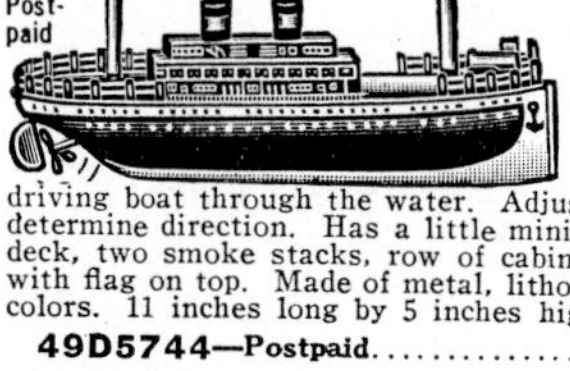

Any youngster will want one. Strongly constructed, powerful spring motor, when wound up spins propeller driving boat through the water. Adjust your rudder to determine direction. Has a little miniature airplane on deck, two smoke stacks, row of cabins and two masts with flag on top. Made of metal, lithographed in bright colors. 11 inches long by 5 inches high.
49D5744—Postpaid............................ 47c

Limping Lizzie

See It Shake and Shiver

25¢ Postpaid

A battered old "college" flivver has nothing on this car. Wind up the strong spring motor and see it ramble along as the driver holds on for dear life. Collegiate sayings such as: "It won't be long now," "Henry's old lady" and many others printed all over car. Made of metal attractively lithographed.

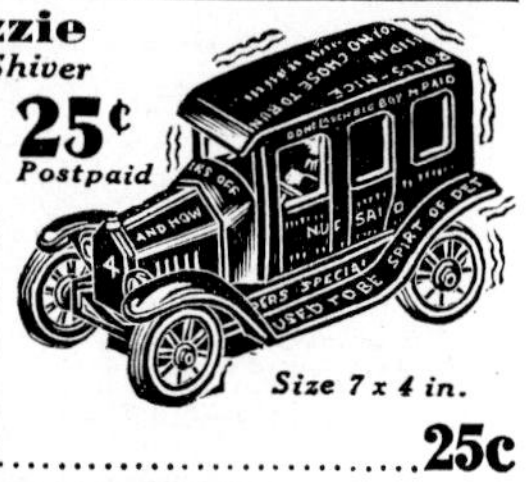

Size 7 x 4 in.

49D5709—Postpaid......................... 25c

Items on These Pages Shipped POSTAGE PAID by Sears, Roebuck and CO.

ORIGINAL and GENUINE *Amos 'n' Andy*

Um! Um! Aint Dis Sumpin!

Oh Sho-Sho-Check and Double Check

"Dat certainly am some propolition! Yessir, Andy, ah done think that's the finest little toy ah evah see. It's jest like the original taxi what beelong to the Fresh Air Taxicab Company of America Incorpulated. It could'n be realer. Jest wait til the Kingfish see dat. M-m!"

A toy that's been made famous by those two nationally known radio artists, Amos 'n' Andy. It's swept the country like wildfire. Popular with youngsters and oldsters, alike, because it is a good souvenir as well as a toy. And this is the **genuine reproduction of the Fresh Air Taxicab authorized by the creators** of Amos 'n' Andy—Freeman F. Gosden and Charles J. Correll. Just wind it up and watch its funny, side-splitting antics. The cab goes along a short distance, then suddenly stops, shakes and shivers as if it would fall apart, then just as suddenly starts up again and repeats this comical action until clock work motor unwinds. Made of metal lithographed in natural colors portraying the delapidation marks on tires and body, with the well known figures in their usual places. Amos and his beloved dog in the front seat and the lazy but so important Andy lolling in the back. The pictures on the four sides and ends of the carton in which the taxicab is packed are provided with tabs to make attractive cutouts. Length of taxi 8 inches, height 5 inches, width 3½ inches. **Postpaid.**

49D5762—Amos 'n' Andy Fresh Air Taxicab......95c

AMOS 'n' ANDY
FRESH AIR TAXICAB
The Famous Toy Sensation!

95¢ *Postpaid*

WE PAY THE POSTAGE

The Mechanical Toy Hit of 1930

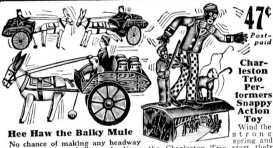

Hee Haw the Balky Mule

No chance of making any headway with this stubborn, balky mule. Very comical to watch him go backwards, rearing up on his hind legs when he should go forward, causing the driver lots of grief. Made of metal beautifully lithographed. Marx strong spring. Toy overall 10½ inches long by 5¼ inches high. **Postpaid.**
49D5747...............46c

47¢ *Postpaid*

Charleston Trio Performers Snappy Action Toy

Wind the strong spring and the Charleston Trio start their peppy act. Just watch the big fellow show you some real hot steps, while the negro boy fiddles and the dog rises up on his hind legs, keeping time. Made of metal beautifully lithographed. Toy overall 9½x5 inches. **47¢**
49D5727—Postpaid..47c

Genuine Original Amos 'n' Andy Walking Toys

Brand New—Also Authorized by Correll and Gosden. See America's Most Popular Team in Action—Watch Them Roll Their Eyes as They Shuffle Along on Their Big Feet.

The famous comedians and radio stars, Amos 'n' Andy impersonated in two separate clever ingenious walking toys. Andy, the important business man and Amos with his simple expression. A souvenir as well as a clever toy for youngsters. Just wind the strong spring and watch Amos 'n' Andy shuffle along rolling their eyes. Be among the first to own this clever pair. Made from metal lithographed in natural colors; about 11 in. high. Packed in novel display box with cutout feature forming theater background. **Postpaid.**

$1.39 *Postpaid*

49D5766—Both $1.39 Amos 'n' Andy......$1.39

Jumbo the Famous Climbing Monkey

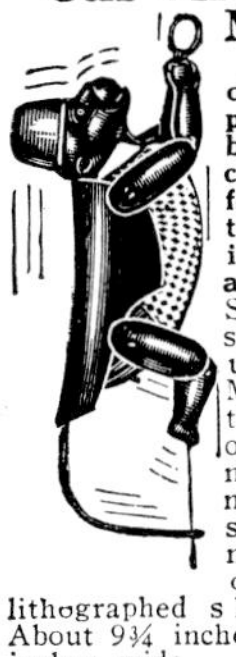

One of the oldest yet most popular toys because of the clever performance and the great fun it provides for any youngster. Step on the string and pull upper end. Monkey will then climb up on cord in most life-like manner. Large size, quality monk made of six color lithographed sheet metal. About 9¾ inches long and 4 inches wide. **Postpaid.**
49D5723....21c

The New Turnover Tank

$1.79 *Postpaid*

Runs on Caterpillar Type Rubber Tread
Real Clever Action

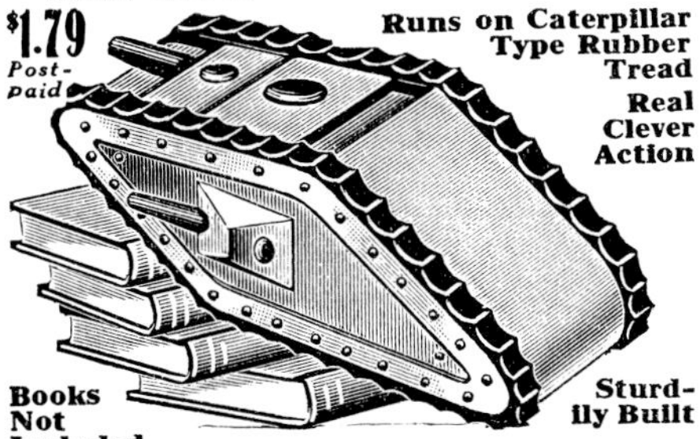

Books Not Included

Sturdily Built

Tank climbs on its top or on its bottom. No other tank does this. Tackles obstacles—if too high turns over on back and goes right back again. It never gives up. Wind up the strong motor and release it. Tank looks so powerful as it moves along climbing obstacles or steep inclines. It may fail to climb the obstacle and turn over on its back, however, it does not give up. No matter what position this tank gets into, it will keep on crawling, turning over in most any direction. If it falls sideways, will lumber along until it strikes other objects, again getting into its upright position. Interesting to the grownups as well as the youngsters because of the powerful action. Size about 9 inches long, 4 inches high and 4¾ inches wide.
49D5789—Postpaid.......................$1.79

3-Piece Artillery Set
Cannon—Caisson Covered Wagon

98¢ *Postpaid*

"Oh boy," this is a 10-inch cannon that actually shoots the four wood pellets included. There is also a 9-inch caisson with two lithographed metal soldiers and a 6½-inch typical army wagon with a standard army wagon cover. All parts made of metal in army colors. A splendid addition for your toy tank or tractor.
49D5704—Set of 3, Postpaid..........98c

This Goose Lays Golden Color Eggs

Plenty of Pep and Lots of Fun

Repeats action when rewound and eggs inserted.

Just wind the strong spring and watch it hop along bobbing its head up and down in the most realistic manner; at the same time laying golden colored wooden eggs as it hops along. Goose made of metal beautifully lithographed in gold with red and black details. Size about 9 inches long by 5 inches high.
49D5712—Postpaid........................45c

89¢ *Postpaid*

For Real Action and Fun

Popular Dutch Mill

Pour sand into hopper and set toy in motion. Runs a long time. Miller moves his arms turning the wheel, while sand pours into the separate metal container. Its fascinating action attracts the child's attention for a long time and banishes many idle hours. Toy made of metal beautifully lithographed. Complete with metal container and sack of sand. Size 4¾ inches square and 12 inches high.
49D5784 Postpaid............89c

Felix the Cat

Famous Cartoon and Movie Character

Beautifully lithographed metal mechanical toy designed by the originator of the comical and very famous cartoon and movie character, Felix. Wind the strong spring and watch how quickly Felix scoots away, always going in circles. Size overall, 8x6½ inches.

25¢ *Postpaid*

49D5765—Postpaid......................25c

Mechanical Tank With Dodging Sharp-Shooter

Watch Doughboy Pop In and Out

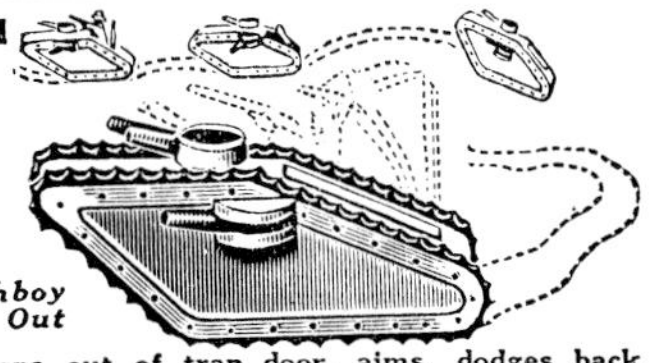

Doughboy pops out of trap door, aims, dodges back in again and door snaps back in place. This happens time and again as tank rambles along in fighting style after the strong spring is wound up and released. Runs a long time on one winding. The peppy and novel action will attract the child's attention for a long time. Made of metal attractively finished. Size about 9½ inches long by 4¼ inches high. **Postpaid.**
49D5763.........................95c

The Daredevil Flyer

Only Plane that rises on its own Power and Loops the Loop.

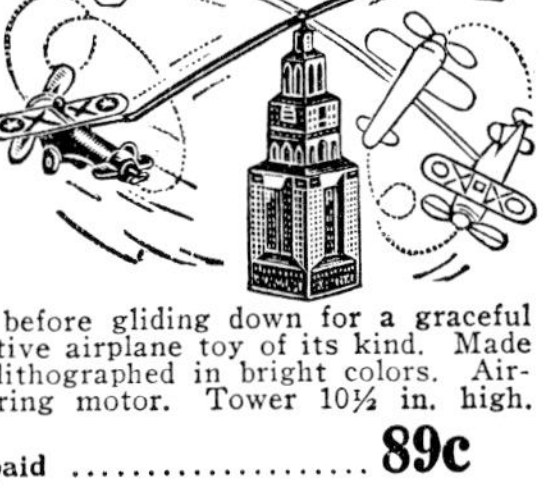

After winding spring, plane rises from the ground, circles the building and loops the loop in the air. Repeats action several times before gliding down for a graceful landing. Most attractive airplane toy of its kind. Made of metal beautifully lithographed in bright colors. Airplane has strong spring motor. Tower 10½ in. high. Beam 21 in. long.
49D5757—Postpaid 89c

15-Inch Filling Station

A clever duplication in miniature of a gasoline filling station with dummy pump that registers from one to five gallons when handle is turned.

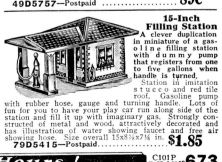

Station in imitation stucco and red tile roof. Gasoline pump with rubber hose, gauge and turning handle. Lots of fun for you to have your play car run along side of the station and fill it up with imaginary gas. Strongly constructed of metal and wood, attractively decorated and has illustration of water showing faucet and free air showing hose. Size overall 15x8⅞x7¼ in. **$1.85**
79D5415—Postpaid..................$1.85

WHILE THEY PLAY!

WAGON FILLED WITH BLOCKS

$1.98 Postpaid

A Wagon-load of Fun

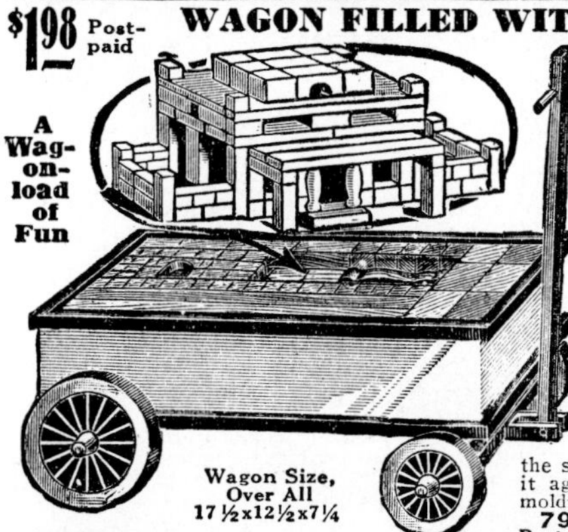

For Years—One of Our Biggest Sellers

Just imagine what fun the kiddies will have with one of these complete outfits. In a nicely colored sturdy wooden wagon with colored wheels, real turn-table and a detachable 15-inch tongue handle. The wheels are not just set in with nails, but have little axle dowels holding them in place, so that they revolve easily. Packed nicely in this wagon are about 156 nicely finished blocks. Many models of buildings, tunnels, bridges, and even furniture sets for sister's play house, can be constructed. When you are through building, pack the blocks into the wagon, detach the wheels and the handle, and put the set away until you are ready to use it again. Wagon has contrasting color molding. Building instructions included.

Wagon Size, Over All 17½x12½x7¼

79D3632 Postpaid **$1.98**

Imported Architectural Building Blocks

Make your own models of bridges, skyscrapers and steeples. 84 wood blocks which include pillars, arches, colored pieces, all nicely shaped and finished. Colors help make very attractive looking objects. Packed in 2 layers in slide cover wood box, 13½x10⅛x2 inches. Design sheet included.

49D3644—Postpaid ...**$1.39**

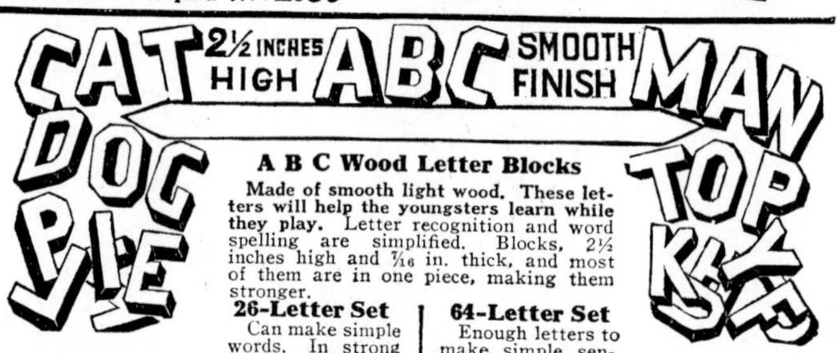

A B C Wood Letter Blocks

CAT 2½ INCHES HIGH ABC SMOOTH FINISH MAN DOG PIE TOP K S

Made of smooth light wood. These letters will help the youngsters learn while they play. Letter recognition and word spelling are simplified. Blocks, 2½ inches high and 7/16 in. thick, and most of them are in one piece, making them stronger.

26-Letter Set
Can make simple words. In strong cardboard box 13⅛ x7⅞x⅝ inches.
49D3655—Postpaid **45c**

64-Letter Set
Enough letters to make simple sentences. In strong cardboard box 16⅝x7¾x1 1/16 inches.
49D3656—Postpaid **89c**

Complete Train Building Set

What fun in building the engine, coal car, gondola, freight car with moving door, and the observation car out of these nicely finished pieces of wood!
Attach cord and pull this wonderful little train around. 27½ in. long. Packed in a lithographed box, 11¼x4⅜x3⅛ in.
49D3659—Postpaid **89c**

Little Village Builder

Enough smooth wood parts to build a church, home, school house, passenger and freight station all at one time without tearing one down to make the other. When parts assembled make complete village. Packed complete in lithographed box 16½x5⅞x2 inches.
49D3652—Postpaid **89c**

6 Large Picture Puzzles

What to do on bad days or when a fellow is ill. One of these sets is the answer. Race by having your friends try the others while you tackle one yourself. All in attractive box, 12½x10x1 in.
49D3648 Postpaid **83c**

Playtime Puzzle Box 3 Different Puzzles

Fascinating puzzle pictures. Puzzles, printed on heavy cardboard, each 12½x8⅞ in. when completed. Picture cover box, 12⅞x9⅞x⅞ in. An ideal racing game for the Kiddies.
49D3647—Postpaid **44c**

Picture Puzzle Blocks

6 Beautiful Pictures

Twenty 1⅜-inch cubes to make 6 complete pictures in attractive high gloss colors. Interest will never be lost. Key pictures included. In hinged wood box, 8½x6¾x2 in.
49D3677 Postpaid **98c**

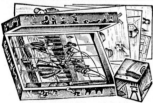

Quality Modeling Clay

Non-Greasy

8 strips each 6¼x1⅛x¼ inch in assorted colors. Six molding blocks, modeling stick and instructions. Does not harden.
49D3858—Postpaid **42c**
Extra Clay—1-lb. gray color. Postpaid.
49D3859—School quality..... **39c**

MAKE THESE

Big Value Painting Sets

Eight pans of semi-moist school paints in enameled metal box, 8x2 inches. Good camel's hair brush.
49D3884—Postpaid **39c**

For school work. These are the standard colors. Sixteen pans of semi-moist school paints in enameled metal box, 8x3¼ in. 2 good camel's hair brushes. **83c**
49D3885—Postpaid

An Outstanding Value

Fifteen tubes moist colors, 16 cakes dry paints, 2 two-section porcelain mixing trays, stick of sealing wax, and two camel's hair brushes.
In enameled metal box 9½x5 in.
49D3883—Postpaid **98c**

A 38-Cake Set for 49c

38 cakes dry colors, 2 porcelain mixing pans, metal rule and 2 brushes. Fine selection of colors and tints.
Hinged cover enamel metal box 9½x6¼ inches.
49D3882—Postpaid **49c**

De Luxe Paint Set

A Real Beauty! Eighteen ⅞-inch diameter cakes, four 1¼-inch diameter cakes of colors, 2 porcelain mixing cups, four section metal palette, 8 wax crayons, 2 camel's hair brushes, ten 8¼x5½ inch outline designs and color mixing guide. Attractively arranged in a beautiful hinge cover box, size 14¼x11¼x1½ inches, that will surprise you with its appeal and attractiveness.
49D3891—Postpaid **98c**

An Excellent Value for 33c

Eighteen cakes dry colors and 2 tubes of moist colors. 2 camel brushes in partitioned enameled metal box, 7⅝x3½ inches, brightly lithographed cover.
49D3881—Postpaid **33c**

18-Cake Set for 21c

18-Cake Set

Has 18 cakes of dry water colors in a neat black metal case, measuring 6¼x3 inches. A real bargain for this price. Brush included.
49D3880—Postpaid **21c**

HOME EDUCATOR-DESK AND BLACKBOARD

GIVE THE CHILD A DESK OF HIS OWN

CONTAINS 55 EDUCATIONAL CHARTS

CAN BE FOLDED FLAT AND OCCUPIES LITTLE SPACE WHEN NOT IN USE

$4.89

HAS SLATE SURFACE BLACKBOARD

Solid Oak Frame

ABCDEFGHIJKLM NOPQRSTUVWXYZ

APPROVED BY SCHOOL AUTHORITIES

We offer here, what is conceded to be the best constructed and most carefully planned blackboard now on the market. Our charts were devised and approved by Chicago educators. The kiddies surely can have loads of fun with these 55 charts (8 in colors), learning their A B C's, arithmetic, drawing, music, and many other subjects. There is something for kindergarten tots as well as the older kiddies. They can even do their "homework" on the blackboard. Writing surface is of the best, because it is not just painted, but is covered with slate paint put on with a trowel. More serviceable than real slate as it is unbreakable. The surface takes chalk easily and clearly and erases cleanly. Box of chalk and a good eraser included. Sturdy, braced, solid oak frame, finished with two coats of varnish. Lower the blackboard and you have a dandy desk with pigeonholes. **Blackboard folds flat, occupying little space.** Height, overall, 46 inches, and 21⅝ inches wide. Shipping weight, 17 pounds.
79DM3811—Shipped by freight or express only. Not Prepaid.... **$4.89**

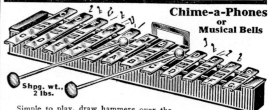

MARX Guaranteed
MECHANICAL TOYS
MANY NEW CLEVER ITEMS

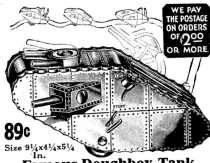

$1.39

89c

Size 9¼x4¼x5¼ In.

Famous Doughboy Tank

Sharpshooting American Soldier—Pops in and out

Wind up strong clock motor, release stop and start lever. Tank rumbles along in its zig zag course while doughboy pops out of trap door, aims and drops back again as trap door snaps back into place. This action occurs again and again as tank moves along. Will run a long time on one winding. Its powerful appearance and forceful action will keep any child happy and contented for a long time. Attractively colored and finished. All metal construction. Shpg. wt., 1¾ lbs.
49F5763 .... **89c**

Sandy, the Mechanical Walking Dog and Kennel

Cartoon character dog now a clever mechanical toy. He walks and carries metal basket in mouth. Lithographed in bright colors. Sandy measures 5x4¼x1½ in. Kennel of colored cardboard, overall, 8⅝x7x7¼ in.
49F5726 ...... **48c**
Shpg. wt., 1½ Lbs.

98c

Size 9x8x5¼ In.

Biggest 1931 Marx Hit

Famous Merrymakers—Startling Action—Very Unique

Just Think. A Mouse Orchestra. Surely a Merry Gang. Watch the little fellow on the piano direct the show and the fellow on the side drumming away while another one sits at the piano and the fourth one jigs showing us some clever dancing steps. Every one seeing this Mouse Orchestra will be startled at the clever mechanical action. Although there are no musical notes, the pantomime action of the individual characters makes this toy unique and entertaining. Mouse gang and piano made from metal lithographed in attractive contrasting colors.
49F5717—Shpg. wt., 1½ lbs. **98c**

Another New Sensation

Life-Like Mechanical Walking Horse and Milk Wagon

Has strong Marx clock work motor, and a stop and start brake. Horse's legs are jointed so that when walking the legs mechanically move in a very life-like manner, giving it a realistic appearance as if horse is pulling the milk wagon which is specially geared to run slowly. A driver sits in seat and holds driving reins. 5 features like
1—Strong Marx clock work motor. Powerful, cannot be over-wound.
2—Life-like action. Slow moving, runs a long time with one winding. Stop and start brake.
3—Realistic appearance. Looks like the regular horse and milk wagon you see on the streets.
4—Colorfully lithographed in bright colors.
5—Made of metal, size 16¼x8¼x4½ in. **$1.39**
49F5721—Shpg. wt., 3 lbs.........

11¾ In. Cadillac Coupe
25c

Here's a mechanical auto that will delight any youngster. Has strong spring motor with adjustable front wheels. Made of metal attractively lithographed. Dolled up with front and rear bumpers, also trunk rack.
49F5729—Shpg. wt., 1 lb. **25c**

47c

Size overall 9½x5 in.

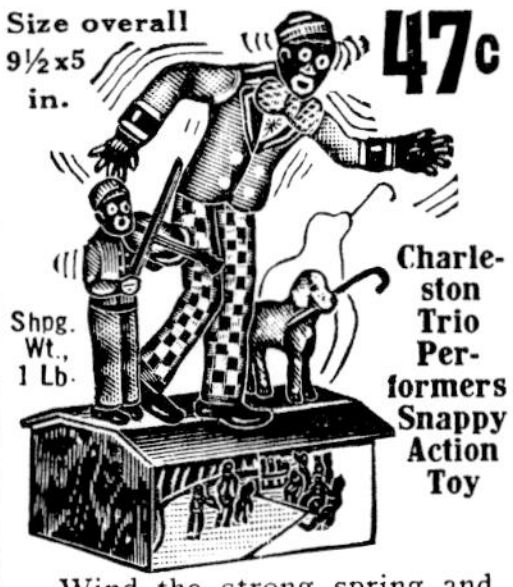

Shpg. Wt., 1 Lb.

Charleston Trio Performers Snappy Action Toy

Wind the strong spring and the Charleston trio start their snappy performance. How that big fellow can dance! Watch the little man fiddle away while the dog rises up on his hind legs keeping time. Toy is made of metal beautifully lithographed.
49F5727 .... **47c**

97c

4 Mechanical Toys in 1

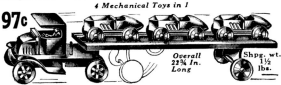

Overall 22¾ In. Long

Shpg. wt., 1½ lbs.

Auto Transport and Three Racers

With Mechanical Motors

Kiddies, the latest! Have your own, large auto transport as you see them on the road. There are four pieces to play with.
49F5735 .... **97c**

47c

10⅝-In. Modern Type Milk Truck

Size 10⅝x4½ x4¼ In.

Has milk case containing 12 wooden milk bottles each about 2 in. tall. Made of metal, handsomely colored. Assorted design decorations. Has Marx spring. Lots of play value.
49F5752—Shpg. wt., 1¾ lbs. **47c**

Cabin Type Plane
48c

International Air-Line Tri-Motor

This fine plane is driven by the famous Marx spring motor. All three propellers revolve. Plane is all metal finished in a beautiful crackled silver finish trimmed in contrasting colors. Exceptionally strong in construction. Length overall 17½ inches. Wing spread 17½ inches.
49F5730—Shpg. wt., 1¾ lbs. **48c**

Officer 666

He changes the expressions of his face from a happy smile to a frown, then cheers up again.

The funniest policeman you ever saw. Simply wind the strong Marx spring and watch this jolly fellow grinning from ear to ear through his big rim glasses, then cross as possible while he shuffles along with his arms swinging and his body swaying. Made of metal, lithographed. Ht. about 11 in. Shpg. wt., 1 lb.
49F5767 .... **48c**

Brand New Kiddie Cyclist

*Really Uncanny How It Works
Pedals Like a Real Kiddie*

Very natural looking, beautifully colored figure. Wind up strong Marx clock work motor and kiddie pedals away on his velocipede straight ahead or in circles, swaying from side to side in an easy natural looking way. New, novel, full of action. Lithographed in realistic colorful finishes. Size 8¾ in. high, 8 in. long, 4¾ in. wide. Shpg. wt., 1 lb.
49F5725 ..... **89c**

89c

Famous Cartoon Character Toys

ORPHAN ANNIE

25c
Size 8x6½x 3⅛ In.

Orphan Annie-Skipping Rope
New, Unique and Clever

When mechanism is wound Orphan Annie skips rope. If she falls she gets up herself to an upright position, never stopping her rope jumping, regardless of whether she falls on her back or on her face. This toy is just as full of pep and action as the Orphan Annie you see in the comics. Height about 5 in. Shpg. wt., 1 lb.
49F5776 .... **25c**

Felix, the Speedy Scooter Cat

Watch him Race Around in Circles.—More Popular than Ever.

This nationally known lovable movie and cartoon character made up into a clever mechanical toy. Wind the spring and away goes Felix scooting in wide circles. Toy made from metal, lithographed like Felix the movie cat. Shpg. wt., 1 lb.
49F5765 .... **25c**

The Funny Koo-Koo Car
59c

Unique—New—Clever

One of the most animated toys we have ever seen. Full of action. Simply wind the strong Marx motor and watch the funny fellow behind the wheel drive his car through some of the funniest kinds of antics. Forwards, backwards, in circles and all kinds of "curly cues" goes the car, then the man stands up with an excited expression, then falls back into his seat with front wheels high off the ground. Acts like a bucking bronco. Length, overall, 8 in. All metal attractively lithographed.
49F5773—Shpg. wt., ¾ lb. **59c**

Size 8x5x3½ In. Shpg. Wt., 1¼ Lbs.

48c

Only Original Amos 'n' Andy Fresh Air Taxicab at Low Price
Unique Mechanical Action Toy

Kiddies, what fun to watch the famous mechanical "Fresh Air Taxicab" which stops, shivers, shakes and performs many other funny side splitting antics with the famous comedians, Amos with his dog driving, and lazy Andy in the back seat. Strong Marx spring motor.
49F5762 .... **48c**

47c

Kitty Cat Playing Ball

New Easy Winding Toy for the Little Tots—Just Push Lever Down, Release, and Watch Kitty chase Ball.

New simplified mechanism to enable the tiniest tot to play with an action toy. Key is replaced by a lever which when pressed down winds the spring inside of toy. Action can be repeated continually by pressing down tail of cat. Toy made of metal attractively lithographed. Size 9x4½x4 in. Shpg. wt., 1 lb.
49F5731 .... **47c**

New Road Roller
48c

Size 8x4x 3½ In.

The Kind You See on the Road Every Day

Modern type steam road roller with driver. Lots of fun for kiddies to watch the slow rolling action when toy is wound and brake is released. Toy made from metal, lithographed in attractive life-like colors. Equipped with Marx strong mechanical spring. Shpg. wt., 1 lb.
49F5751 .... **48c**

44c

This Goose Lays Golden Color Eggs

Comical Action Will Be Enjoyed by the "Oldsters" as Well as the Youngsters

Wind the strong spring and watch Goosie wobbling along bobbing its head up and down, at the same time laying golden color wooden eggs. Very comical realistic action. Goose made of metal beautifully lithographed in gold color with red and black details. Size about 9 in. long by 4¼ in. high.
49F5712—Shpg. wt., ¾ lb....... **44c**

Do Your Christmas Shopping From This Catalog
P151B **1037**

LET'S ALL HAVE TEA

WE PAY THE POSTAGE ON ORDERS OF $2.00 OR MORE

23 Pcs. $2.48 Post Paid

32 Pcs. $1.59

Our Beautiful DeLuxe China Tea Set
Full Luster Large Size Quality China—A Wonderful Value

A fired-in design that Mother would select for her own set. Beautiful cream and blue full luster pieces with a soft lustrous attractive flower design with **orange and yellow** predominating. Handles on all pieces and the spout on teapot finished in blue luster. This same set in fancy display box would sell elsewhere for $4.00. Teapot, 5¾x3⁵⁄₁₆ inches. Has six 3-inch diameter cups; six 4⁵⁄₁₆-inch diameter saucers; six 5-inch diameter plates. Sugar, 4x2¾ inches. Creamer, 3¼x2¼ inches. Postpaid.
49F1655—COMPLETE 23-PC. SET **$2.48**

DeLuxe Set of Extra Large Pure Aluminum Pieces
Panelled Mirror Finish—In Display Box—Others Ask Up to $2.50

Bigger Value Than Ever—Teapot, 6x4⅛ inches, with a Tea Ball on chain. Six 5¹³⁄₁₆-inch plates, six 4-inch saucers, six 2¾-inch cups, **sugar, creamer,** 8-inch serving tray and 3¾-inch felt lined hot pad. All pieces paneled and mirror finished. Has six 3⁵⁄₁₆-inch spoons and a beautiful satin finish crumb set which has embossed figures and rhymes on it; size of tray, 6¼ inches by 3¼ inches, and the scraper is in proportion.
49F1882
Shpg. wt., 2½ lbs. COMPLETE 32-PC. SET FOR **$1.59**

23 Piece Set
Here's a Real China Set Value $1.59
A $2.00 Value Elsewhere

Decoration fired in and reglazed for a beautiful smooth finish with a finish glaze. Attractive decoration in bright colors, with background of **tan and cream** color luster. Quaint style teapot, 5¾x3¾ in. Has six 4½-inch plates, six 3¹¹⁄₁₆-in. saucers, six 2½-in. cups; sugar bowl and creamer in proportion. Shpg. wt., 3½ lbs.
49F1654—23-PC. SET FOR **$1.59**

New Embossed Design Tea and Coffee Set
30-Pc. Aluminum Set $1.00

Now we are offering the expensive Embossed Design pieces at no increase in price. Tea Pot is 4⅝x3¾ inches. **Coffee pot** is 4 inches tall by 2⅝-inch diameter base. Set has six 4⁹⁄₁₆-inch plates, six 3⅛-inch saucers, six 2½-inch cups, six 3⁵⁄₁₆-inch spoons and sugar and creamer in proportion. First you can serve coffee, then later tea. Shpg. weight 1½ lbs.
49F1872—30-PIECE SET **$1.00**

WE PAY THE POSTAGE ON ORDERS OF $2.00 OR MORE

23-Pc. Special Luster China Set $1.00
Sells Up to $1.50 Elsewhere

Shaped pieces made of good grade china. Design stenciled and painted on pieces before they are fired, fixing the design into the set, so they cannot wash off. All pieces are **blue** color luster finish, the borders and all edges in cream luster. Beautiful double flower design set off with green leaves. All handles and spout on teapot in glossy luster. Teapot, 5¾x3¾ inches; six 2¼-inch cups, six 3¼-inch saucers, six 4⁹⁄₁₆-inch plates, **sugar** and **creamer** in proportion. Shpg. wt., 3½ lbs.
49F1651—23-PIECE SET FOR **$1.00**

21-Pc. Pure Aluminum Set 79c
New Embossed Design—Mirror Finish

Offered for the first time in the more costly new embossed design. Pieces attractively polished to a mirror finish, the same as in our larger sets. Consists of Teapot, 4⅝x3¾ inches, four 4⁹⁄₁₆-inch plates, four 3⅛-inch saucers, four 2½-inch cups, four 3⅜-inch spoons, 3¾-inch diam. felt bottom table pad. **Sugar** and **creamer** in proportion. Shpg. wt., 1½ lbs.
49F1871—21-PIECE SET FOR **79c**

13-Pc. 49c Fired-in Design

Service for four with this fired-in design set (not just painted on). The pretty double flower washable design is set off with green stems and leaves on cream luster background. Pieces are highly glazed and finished with blue borders and bands. Teapot, 4½x3⅜ in. Four 3½-in. saucers, four 2¼-in. cups, **sugar** and **creamer** in proportion. Shpg. wt., 2½ lbs. **13-PC. SET** .....
49F1650—**49c**

16-Pc. $1.19 Turquoise Blue Enamel Set (Unbreakable)

Made of metal and coated with rich **turquoise blue** color enamel. Teapot is 4¼ inches wide; six saucers, each 2⁷⁄₁₆ inches in diameter, and **sugar** and **creamer** in proportion. Shpg. wt., 1¼ lbs.
49F1931
16-PIECE SET **$1.19**

65c

Imitation Cut Glass Water Set

How happy and p r o u d you will be when you serve your little guests with this water set. Looks just like mother's. Consists of four 2¼-inch high cut glass design glass tumblers. 7⅜-inch glass tray with beautiful cut glass style design and a 4⅝-inch heavy glass pitcher. Shpg. wt., 5 lbs.
49F1904—6-pc. Set ... **65c**

Lithographed Metal Tea Sets

NEW BO-PEEP DESIGN. Tray, 6⅛ in., Plates, 4¼ in., Saucers, 2⅝ in., Cups, 1⅞ in. Tea pot, 2⅛ in. tall.

Twenty Pieces Six-cup set. 49F1804 Shpg. wt., 1½ lbs...49c	Fourteen Pieces Four-cup set. 49F1805 Shpg. wt., 1½ lbs...39c

Practical Size Polished Pure Aluminum Cooking Sets

Many of these pieces are paneled and all are highly polished. These are all large pieces (not junior pieces) and are made by a manufacturer of the finest large size aluminum utensils. Size of tube cake pan, 4¾ inches; other pieces in proportion. Some have red handles.

15-Pc. Dandy Cooking Set for Only $1.39

Large beautiful roaster, 6 inches long by 2¹³⁄₁₆ inches high; latest style griddle, a cake turner, 3-piece household utility cooker, lipped saucepan, mixing bowl, preserving kettle, square cake pan, pudding pan, stew pan, bread pan, fry pan and tube cake pan.
49F1861—15-pc. Set. Shpg. wt., 2½ lbs..**$1.39**

8-Pc. BIG VALUE Set for Only 69c

Consists of new griddle and cake turner, fry pan, saucepan, layer cake pan, preserving kettle, graduated mixing bowl and a pie plate.
49F1860—8-pc. Set. Shpg. wt., 1½ lbs......... **69c**

1038 P151B

We Pay the Postage on Orders of $2.00 or More. Sears, Roebuck and Co.

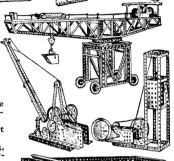

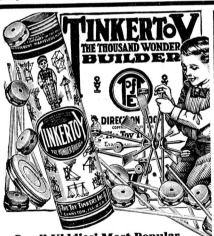

SEARS build them better and still save you money

Super Quality at a Thrift Price!

$5.98 *Postpaid*

Chromium Plated Curved Tubular Steel Tongue With Rubber Bumper

Body of Auto Steel Massive Rolls

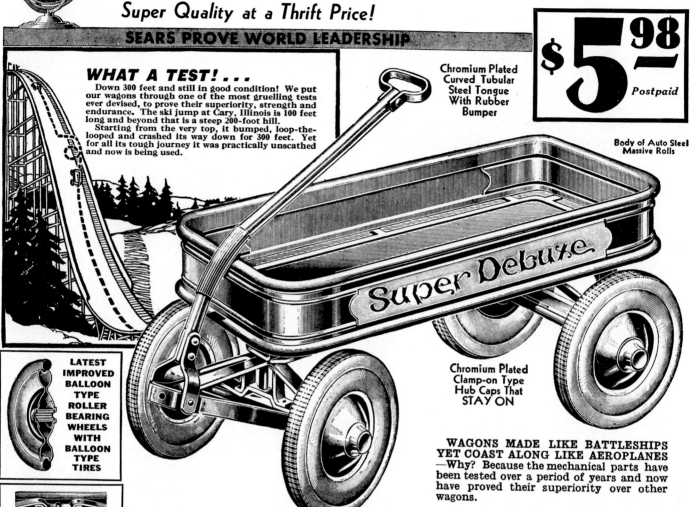

WHAT A TEST! . . .

Down 300 feet and still in good condition! We put our wagons through one of the most gruelling tests ever devised, to prove their superiority, strength and endurance. The ski jump at Cary, Illinois is 100 feet long and beyond that is a steep 200-foot hill.

Starting from the very top, it bumped, loop-the-looped and crashed its way down for 300 feet. Yet for all its tough journey it was practically unscathed and now is being used.

LATEST IMPROVED BALLOON TYPE ROLLER BEARING WHEELS WITH BALLOON TYPE TIRES

Chromium Plated Clamp-on Type Hub Caps That STAY ON

WAGONS MADE LIKE BATTLESHIPS YET COAST ALONG LIKE AEROPLANES —Why? Because the mechanical parts have been tested over a period of years and now have proved their superiority over other wagons.

Paramount Feature Front Bolster of Our New Super DeLuxe

America's Biggest Wagon Value!

BOYS! Buy Our New Super DeLuxe and Get the Best Money Can Buy $5.98 *Postpaid*

A Similar Wagon Would Cost $9.00 Elsewhere

Such a gruelling test as stated above unquestionably proves that to withstand such severe punishment without a break—all parts are just about mechanically perfect, and that these two wagons are thoroughbreds. Yet, for all this splendid sturdiness, rigidity and quality, our price on each is below what other stores ask for an inferior grade of wagons. The World's Largest Store always leads in value!

Our Right-o-way

Sells Elsewhere Up to $6.00 **$4.67** *Postpaid*

A WONDERFUL WAGON FOR THIS PRICE

Similar to our Super De Luxe and made in the same factory but not as sturdily constructed and with a less expensive front bolster construction, fine trimmings and details. Designed particularly for those who want a good wagon for less money than our Super De Luxe.

Body of 20-gauge steel throughout, enameled green, has large roll top and bottom, beaded sides and corrugations in bottom, also cream color enamel fancy panel in each side (baked-on finish). 10-inch giant size balloon type roller bearing wheels, ¾-in. gear tread rubber tires. Wide stamped channel steel undergearing and tubular steel tongue, enameled black. Chromium plated clamp on type caps that stay on. No rubber bumper. Beat this value if you can.

79F7609—$6.00 value elsewhere. Postpaid. **$4.67**

STRONGER AND MORE BEAUTIFUL THAN EVER

1 New Style Heavy Duty Wheels: Giant size balloon type 10¼-inch diameter beautifully shaped double disc steel roller bearing wheels of extra heavy steel.

2 Balloon Type Tires: Full 1-inch cushion-like auto tread rubber tires set in deep channel. New shape and enameling of wheels give effect of much larger tires.

3 Full Size body, 33½x14¾ in.,: Made of 20-gauge auto fender steel throughout. Beading in sides and bottom reinforces entire body. Double interlocking flange around entire bottom of wagon, this means fancy body of super-fine quality—no wrinkles—no sharp corners nor edges.

4 Large rolls: ⅝-inch diameter on top and bottom reinforces body; also raised panel in each side adds to its beauty.

5 Two-color finish: Body finished in a beautiful high gloss luster **red** enamel with rich **yellow** color panels. Baked-on in oven the same as fenders on large motor cars. Wheels finished to match body.

6 Undergearing: One of the best jobs of steel engineering ever built into a wagon. Long king bolt designed to stand excessive strain and severe jolts.

7 Steel Bolsters and Braces: 1 inch wide, also steel axles; ½-inch in diameter, enameled **black**.

8 Axles: No holes drilled through for braces which would weaken them.

9 Tongue: Chromium plated tubular steel with **red** rubber bumper.

10 Chromium Plated clamp-on type hub caps that stay on.

79F7618—Regular $9.00 value Elsewhere, Our Price, Postpaid............ **$5.98**

Watch 'Em Go!

Our Newest CADILLAC
With Balloon Style Wheels

$9.98

$15.00 Value Elsewhere

No Other Mail Order House Sells These All Steel Autos

PEDALS Adjustable to fit children from 3 to 6 years of age.

Our New Cadillac Now Equipped With 10-Inch Giant Size Balloon Type Roller Bearing Wheels With ¾-Inch Cushion Rubber Tires.

We defy competition to beat this exceptional value. Made of Auto Fender Steel. Ball Bearing Drive Shaft Makes it Easy to Propel. Tempered Carbon Steel Springs on Rear Axle Act as Shock Absorbers. Knuckle Steering Joints Mean Easy Driving.

Built like a battleship. Child can stand on running board to get into seat. **Strong enough to hold the weight of a man.** Pedal straps have three adjustments. Others would ask you at least $5.00 more for one similar but not exactly like it. No other mail order house sells this beautiful auto.

Body and seat enameled **black** with light **green** color panels on hood; **orange** color striping around panels and outlines. Wheels, aluminum finished edge with **green** bullseye and **orange** color parting stripe. A beautiful color combination. Cadmium finish (rust-proof) hub caps. New style sloping fenders; corrugated running boards, chassis, bumper, steering wheel, rod and windshield frame, enameled **black**. Windshield is adjustable to any angle. New style horizontal radiator enameled **green** color to match the panels on hood. Loud horn enameled **black**. Headlights with nickel plated lens. Colored license plate and instrument board. Fiber covered seat. Real propeller type ornament in place of motometer. Length, overall, 39¼ in.; width, 20¾-in. Unmailable. Shipped by freight or express. Not Prepaid.
79FM8920—Shipping weight, 49 pounds........................**$9.98**

LINCOLN DELUXE SPEEDSTER
$17.67

Others Ask Up To $25.00

FRENCH BULB HORN

GEARSHIFT

Look at This Beautiful Lincoln and Note Its Many Clever Features

For Children 5 to 10 Years

See the new dummy gearshift and spotlight. It has Closed Type Body, Enameled Green and Tan with Red Striping.

Chromium plated 8¾-in. metal steering wheel and radiator. Chromium plated classy spotlight attached to left running board and braced to body. Look at those large **giant** size balloon type 10¼-in. roller bearing wheels equipped with 1-in. auto tread rubber tires! Outer edge aluminum finish with **green** bullseye, red parting stripe. New, graceful sloping fenders, corrugated running boards, splash apron, also bumper, enameled **black**. Fiber covered seat. Nickel plated gear shift. French style bulb horn. Nickel plated adjustable windshield. Rear view mirror. Red and green parking lights. Fully nickel plated headlights. Bar between headlights holds colored license plate. Dummy tail light on left rear fender. Colored instrument board; nickel plated propeller type ornament in place of motometer. Pedals adjustable to 3 different positions. Length, overall, 45½ in.; width, 20 in. Unmailable. Shipped by express or freight. Not Prepaid.
79FM8923—Shpg. wt., 88 lbs.................................**$17.67**

Be the Fire Chief in Your Neighborhood

$7.89

CLANG CLANG ← Nickel Plated Brass Bell

For Children 3 to 6 Years

Sound the alarm! Jump into this beautiful red Fire Chief Roadster! Step on the pedals and away you go. Pull the bell cord! Everybody will clear the road when they hear the clang of the nickel plated brass bell.

You will gain plenty of speed because of the new extra wide hub, **plain bearing 10¼ inch diameter double disc steel wheels** but the auto will be silent because of the large cushion-like ¾-inch rubber tires.

Length, 38 inches; width, 20¾ inches. Body and wheels enameled a bright "fire engine red" with yellow striping. Dummy tank, steering wheel and rod, bell bracket, body of lamps and bumper enameled **black**. Rims of headlights nickel plated. Three adjustment pedal straps. License plate. Cadmium plated (rustproof finish) hub caps. Unmailable. Shipped by express or freight. Not Prepaid. Shpg. wt., 38 lbs.
79FM8919......................**$7.89**

$10.67

BULB HORN

SPOT LIGHT

$13.79

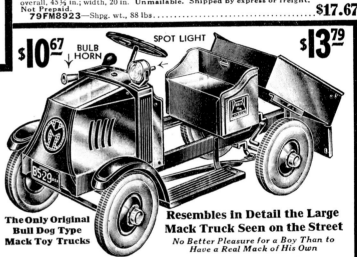

The Only Original Bull Dog Type Mack Toy Trucks

Resembles in Detail the Large Mack Truck Seen on the Street
No Better Pleasure for a Boy Than to Have a Real Mack of His Own

Giant size 10-inch diameter balloon type roller bearing wheels, aluminum finish edge, bullseye center matches body of truck; ¾-inch auto tread rubber tires. All parts made from heavy gauge automobile fender steel. No wood parts to crack. Frame of heavy channel steel. All baked-on enamel finish. Complete with French Style bulb horn, colored license plate, cadmium plated hub caps. 8¾-inch enameled steering wheel. Adjustable pedals. Both Are UNMAILABLE. Shipped by Express or Freight. Not Prepaid.

Baby Mack
For Children 3 to 5 Years
Similar to One Shown Above. Length, 44½ in.; width, 20 in. Dump box, 15¼ x 13¾x5 in. deep. Body seat and hood enameled in **red** with **cream** color panels. Neat striping. Fenders over front wheels but no running boards and no spotlight.
79FM8924—Shpg. wt., 49 lbs....**$10.67**

Large Size Mack (Illustrated)
For Children 5 to 7 Years
Length, 50 in.; width, 22½ in. Dump box, 18¼x13⅝x5 in. deep. Seat and hood enameled light **green** with dark **green** panels. Neat striping. Fenders over front wheels; strong running boards—hold the weight of man. Nickel plated spotlight.
79FM8925—Shpg. wt., 80 lbs....**$13.79**

$6.33 *Postpaid*

Extremely Low Price on This Beautiful Essex

Made from Auto Fender Steel

Adjustable pedals. For children 3 to 5 years. Has windshield, bumper, headlights, motometer, license plate. Total length, 32¼ in. Width, 17¾ in. 8¼-inch double disc steel plain bearing wheels, ⅝-inch rubber tires. Body and undergearing enameled **pea green**, **cream** striping. Wheels aluminum finish, **green** striping.
79F8908—Postpaid..............**$6.33**

All Steel Riding Planes
Baked on Enamel Finish—Front Axle in Ball Bearing Suspension

Each Has a Wing spread of 30 inches. All Three Sizes are Unmailable. Shipped by express or freight. Not Prepaid.

Just What the Kiddies Want

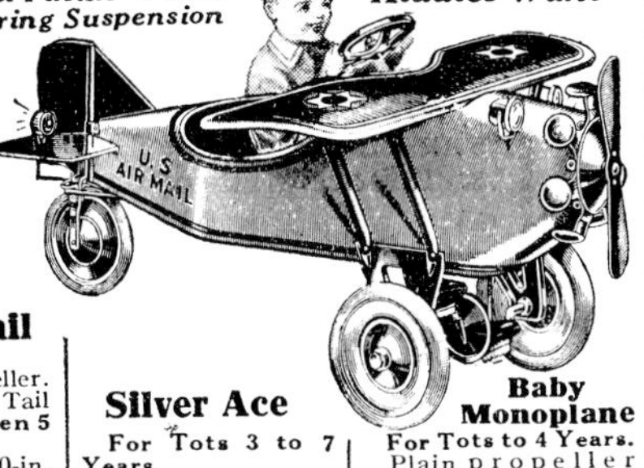

U. S. Airmail
(Illustrated)
Revolving Propeller. Dummy Spot and Tail Light. **For Children 5 to 10 years.** Balloon type 10-in. roller bearing front wheels; ¾-in. tires. 8-inch skid wheel. ⅝-inch rubber tire. Body, **gray, red** striping. Lgth, overall, 53½ in. Shpg. wt., 72 lbs.
79FM8922...**$15.45**

Silver Ace
For Tots 3 to 7 Years.
Similar to our 79FM8922. Skid wheel has ½-inch rubber tire. Lgth, overall, 43½ in. No struts. Shpg. wt., 34 lbs.
79FM8921...**$9.88**

Baby Monoplane
For Tots to 4 Years.
Plain propeller without dummy motor and struts. 8-inch plain front wheels, 6-inch rear. ⅝-inch rubber tires. Body, **red, gray** wing. Length, overall, 40 in. Shpg. wt., 30 lbs.
79FM8910...**$6.98**

$4.79 *Post Paid*

All Steel HUDSON

Daddy! Buy Me One of These!
Easy to Operate

Length, 31½ inches; width, 15½ inches. Has new style radiator and hood vents. 8-inch double disc steel plain bearing wheels; ½-inch rubber tires. Pedals adjustable to 3 different positions. **For Tots up to 4 years.** Body and wheels enameled in **red** and **yellow** striping. Large metal steering wheel and rod enameled **black**. Pedals and pedal rods enameled **tan**. Cadmium finish (rust-proof) motometer and hub caps.
79F8906—Postpaid..............**$4.79**

HEALTH BUILDERS for LITTLE TOTS

All Steel Coasters for Little Tots Who Want One Just Their Size

Lowest Prices in Our History

Same general construction as our larger size wagons. No sharp edges or corners. Body of one-piece heavy gauge automobile steel and tubular steel tongue have a high luster enamel finish which is baked-on, not just painted and air-dried like on most other wagons. Wheels are made of heavy gauge double disc steel and equipped with high grade rubber tires. Postpaid if part of $2 order.

95c
20⅞x10 IN. BODY

Little Tot's First Wagon
Some Value!
Body Size, 20⅞x10 Inches
6⅜-in. wheels, ½-in. rubber tires and nickel plated hub caps. Body and wheels enameled baby blue; under-gearing and tongue black.
79K7619—Shpg. wt., 11 lbs. . . **95c**

For the Little Fellow
Body Size, 24⅞x12 Inches
6¾-in. wheels, ⅝-in. rubber tires; Canary color body. Lettering, tongue and undergearing black. Wheels light green.
79K7635—Shpg. wt., 14 lbs. **$1.69**

$1.69
Seat 13⅝ In. High

A Rocking Horse Built for the Roughest Future Cowboy
Made of 5-ply veneer wood with four strong metal braces. Natural finish 29¼-inch horse, green and black decorations. Height, overall, 19½ in.; lgth. 35 in. Shpg. wt., 9 lbs.
79K7547—Postpaid if part of $2 order **$1.69**

6 Dandy Toys for Garden or Beach 89c
Keep Children Out of Doors
A steel pan wheelbarrow 24 in. overall. A 24-in. cart. Both have steel bodies. A four-wheel all steel wagon, front wheels turn, size, 10¼x6¼ in. All enameled in bright red. An 18½-in. steel tooth rake, 18½-in. hoe, a 19-in. steel spade. Postpaid if part of $2 order.
79K9136—Shpg. wt., 5 lbs. . . **89c**

$7.39 Natural Looking **$9.39**
Dapple Gray Ponies
Features—Nicely shaped wood head and legs—Natural looking glass eyes—Bushy hair mane and tail—Padded saddle—Decorated bridle and breastband—metal stirrups—hardwood stand enameled red.
Unmailable. Shpg. wt., large size, 35 lbs., small, 30 lbs. Shipped by express or freight, Not Prepaid.

$9.39

37-Inch Beauty
Genuine leather bridle, large high back saddle; colored cotton plush blanket. Height to saddle, 23¾ in.
79KM7576. . . . . **$9.39**

Smaller Horse for Tots
Length, 34 in. Height, overall, 29 in. Artificial leather small size saddle and trimmings. No blanket.
79KM7575. . . . . **$7.39**

Stand 34x14 Inches

MOST PRACTICAL TOY in Many Years
Developed and Sold Only by Sears
This Unique All Steel 2-In-1 Pedal Car and Dump Wagon at the Price of One. 32½ In. Long

Many playful hours will be spent riding and hauling. Youngster exercises while playing. FEATURES: 18x9 inch auto steel hinged dump box with steel handle may be raised almost straight up. Frames of ¾-in. steel tubing. Four 6-inch double disc steel rear wheels, 8¼-inch drive wheel with rubber pedals, ½-inch rubber tires. Adjustable steel seat; steel handle bars with rubber grips. Detachable trailer is fastened with bolt. Enameled in red and light green colors.
79K8366—Postpaid. **$2.39**

$2.39 *Detachable Postpaid Trailer*

Our De Luxe Model **$2.98**
Like a velocipede it has ⅞-in. tubular steel frame enameled green. Adjustable Troxel red saddle on nickel plated springs. Nickel plated handle bars; rubber grips and pedals. 10¾-in. ball bearing front wheel, 1-inch rubber tire; 8½-inch plain bearing rear wheels, ¾-inch rubber tires. Wheels enameled red.
79K8347
Post Paid. . **$2.98**

Ball Bearing Tubular Pedal Bikes
$4.00 VALUE

Exceptional Value **$2.00**
Easily Worth $3.00
Frame of ¾-in. steel tubing. Ball bearing 8½-in. front wheel; 6¾-in. rear wheels, all with ¾-in. gear tread rubber tires. Nickel plated hub caps. Adjustable steel seat. Enameled curved steel handle bars with rubber grips. Curved steel fork and one-piece steel pedal crank. Large rubber pedals. Enameled in red and green.
79K8346
Post Paid. . . . **$2.00**

$2.87 And Up Post Paid

Dapple Gray Riding Horses at Reduced Prices
What a Thrill for the Youngster to Ride His Own Horse!
Horsie's Head and Front Legs Hinged for Easy Steering. Hardwood reinforced with dowels. Saddle shape wood seat. Steel axles; nickel plated hub caps. Red, yellow, gray and black enamels. Red enameled double disc steel wheels, ½-inch rubber tires.

For Children 2 to 3 Years
Size, overall, length, 23½ in.; height, 16¾ in. Seat from floor, 11½ in. 5¼-inch wheels.
79K7506—Postpaid. **$2.87**

For Children 3 to 4 Years
Size, overall, length, 27½ in.; height, 19¼ in. Seat from floor 13¼ in. 6-inch wheels.
79K7507—Postpaid. **$3.48**

A Brand New, Well Made and Beautifully Colored All-in-1 Horse and Sulky
Picture your youngster with this new horse and sulky.
Dapple gray horse, 24 in. long overall of thick wood, nicely decorated; front part hinged for steering; steel springs right it after being turned. 6-inch double disc steel wheels, ½-inch rubber tires. Tape reins; green enameled wood seat, 11 inches from floor; wood shafts enameled red. Whip included.
79K7512—Postpaid. . . . **$3.98**

Full Length 38 Inches

TOY GUNS FOR BOY SHARPSHOOTERS

Brand New Dart Shooting Game
Target 10½x10½ In. **Gun** 7½ In.
Shpg. Wt. 2 Lbs.
Colorful target and an all steel revolver that shoots rubber tip suction cup dart. Gun shoots with accuracy and speed. Animals have numbers. Suction cup darts stick, making it easy to tell your score. Postpaid if part of $2 order.
49K5665. . . . . **49c**
49K5666—3 Extra Darts. **10c**

98c
Genuine Leather Double Holster Set With 2 Guns
Shpg. Wt., 2 Lbs.
You will be a real 2 gun cowboy with a right and left holster and these 2 guns. Belt 1-in. wide with nickel plated buckle and 6 dummy wooden bullets—2 dummy cast iron guns each 7 in. long. Holsters, 8¾x4⅞ in. Postpaid if part of $2 order.
49K5623—Complete Set. **98c**

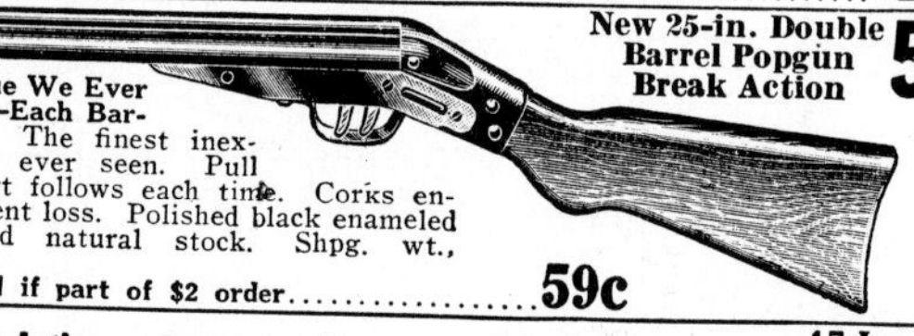

29 IN. LONG **$2.25** Post Paid

Fox Famous Double Barrel Breech Loading Play Gun
Bullseye target with bell to register a real hit and bag of extra ammunition included.
Every boy in America knows about this fine gun and wants one. Here is your opportunity to save money and how thrilled your boy will be when he gets it. A realistic reproduction of a real double barrel shotgun. Two triggers to enable you to shoot each barrel separately. Click! Out goes one pellet! Click! Out goes the other! The shells are removable as in the larger gun but uses a coil spring for power. Although it is harmless, it shoots a wooden ball with sufficient force and accuracy for real target practice. Well made with wearing parts hardened. Barrels finished in black enamel and stock of hardwood, walnut stained.
49K5640—Postpaid. **$2.25**

New 25-in. Double Barrel Break Action **59c**
Greatest Popgun Value We Ever Offered. Two Triggers—Each Barrel Shoots Separately. The finest inexpensive gun we have ever seen. Pull triggers and loud report follows each time. Corks enclosed in barrel to prevent loss. Polished black enameled steel barrel, varnished natural stock. Shpg. wt., 2 lbs. 4 oz.
49K5650—Postpaid if part of $2 order. **59c**

39c 22-In. Break Action Popgun With Loud Report
Looks and Works Like a Real Gun
Just the type gun a youngster should have. Black enamel finish barrel, nicely varnished hardwood stock. Cork attached to string. Postpaid if part of $2 order.
49K5646—Shpg. wt., 1 lb. . . **39c**

Easy to Operate
17-In. Break Action 21c Popgun—Makes Loud Report
Even little brother can shoot this one. Black enameled finish barrel. Bright red lacquered stock. Postpaid if part of $2 order. Shpg. wt., 12 oz.
49K5647. . . . . **21c**

Ronson Repeater
Shpg. Wt. 4 Oz.
Do not confuse this gun with cheaper imitations which do not operate as well and are easily put out of order. Shoots 5000 flashes with one loading. Pull trigger and red sparks shoot out. Black enameled steel. Lgth. 4½ in. Postpaid if part of $2 order. Shpg. wt., 4 oz.
49K5657. . . . . **21c**
Three extra reloads. Each gives 5000 flashes. Shpg. wt., 1 oz.
49K5658. . . . . **10c**

Wonderful Shooting Game Value
—30-in. all steel gun which shoots alternately 2 rubber bands with one loading.
—20 snappily colored cardboard figures with metal stands.
—6 rubber bands to shoot with.
Figures represent 6 doughboys, 6 Indians and 8 wild animals. Avg. size of animals, 2⅜x4¼ in. Soldiers and Indians avg., 5¾ in. high. Postpaid if part of $2 order. Shpg. wt., 2 lbs.
49K5668. . . . . **49c**

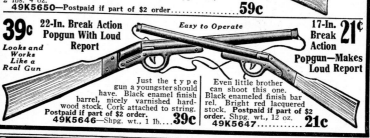

MARX GUARANTEED MECHANICAL TOYS

87c Famous Marx "Merrymakers"

Repeated Because of Last Year's Popularity

Every youngster will enjoy them as they are right up to the minute and full of pep. Just wind the strong spring motor and "on with the show." The mouse leader on the piano swings his baton, while another bangs the piano and a third one beats the trap drum. The fourth fellow dances merrily to keep in time. Although there are no musical notes every one who has seen this toy in operation marvels at the clever action. Made of metal, lithographed in attractive and contrasting colors. **Size overall, 9x9x5 inches.** Shipping weight, 1 lb. 8 oz.
49K5717 ....87c

OLD POP-EYE HIM-SELF
WE PAY THE POSTAGE ON ORDERS OF $2.00 OR MORE
AS EXPLAINED ON PAGE 1

Famous Popeye and His Dodging Parrot 59c

Brand New Famous Cartoon Character Toy

He is just "it" when he comes to strolling along pushing his wheelbarrow. No wonder they call him "Blow Me Down" Popeye. The happy go lucky expression and the famous pipe in his mouth portrays him very realistically. While he pushes his wheelbarrow the lid of the trunk opens and the famous parrot pops his head in and out from under his hiding place. This action is repeated many times with one winding. Every youngster will enjoy this distinctly different toy on account of its original action and the colorful portrayal of their famous cartoon character. Made from metal, lithographed. **Size, $7\frac{1}{4}$x$7\frac{1}{4}$x$3\frac{1}{4}$ in.**
49K5788—Shpg. wt., 1 lb. 12 oz...............59c

New Doughboy Tank

Military Flag Disappears When Soldier Pops Out to Aim

When strong spring is wound tank zig-zags along in real fighting fashion, turning its course every time the trap door opens, out of which a doughboy pops, aims, and dodges back again. Made from metal attractively lithographed. **Size overall, $9\frac{1}{4}$x$4\frac{1}{4}$x$5\frac{1}{4}$.** Shpg. wt., 1 lb. 12 oz.
49K5764 ....87c

MECHANICAL TOYS ALL 5 FOR $1.00

17 In. Long
TOYLANDS
MILK CREAM
FARM PRODUCTS
12 In. Long, 3 In. High
9¾ In. Long, 4½ In. High

SMITTY SCOOTER
7¾ In. High

6¾ In. High

Never Before Such A Value

All sturdily built from metal, attractively lithographed and equipped with strong spring motors. "Smitty" the well-known cartoon character scooting away in a zig-zag fashion; **the monkey on trapeze** who can show you some real acrobatic stunts, and when set on the floor can turn somersaults; the **Auto Transport with trailer** and three removable cars, the **Toyland Milkwagon** and **a racer which scoots out of the tower to the end of the runway and then returns.** Shpg. wt., 3 lbs.
49K5770........5 Mechanical Toys above, all for $1.00

59c New Monkey Cymbalist

Entirely new action toy to thrill every little youngster. Gee! That's a keen toy. Simply wind the strong spring and watch him hop lively along with the aid of his front feet and tail, all the while clapping his 2 cymbals together very realistically.
Made from metal, lithographed in lifelike colors. **Size overall, $8\frac{1}{4}$x6 in.** Shipping wt., 1 lb. 8 oz.
49K5710 ....59c

Electric Lighted Mechanical Auto

Has Real Head Lights and Red Tail Light

First One to Sell for Less Than $2.50

Heavy Gauge Steel Sport Coupe with real electric lights, strong clock work motor and balloon type rubber tired wheels.

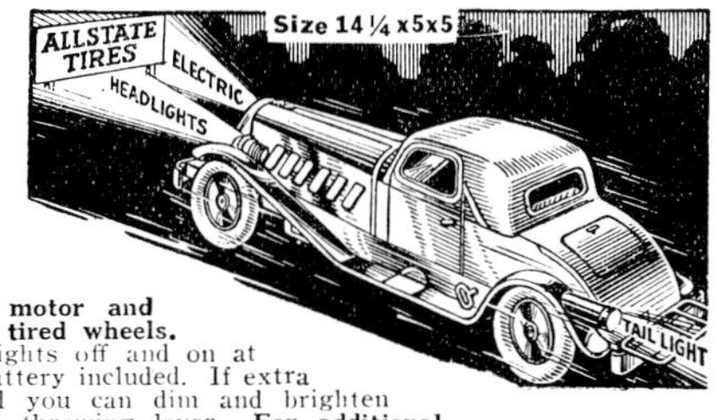

Size 14¼x5x5
ALLSTATE TIRES
ELECTRIC
HEADLIGHTS
TAIL LIGHT

Has lever to turn lights off and on at will. **One dry cell battery included. If extra battery** is purchased you can dim and brighten your head lights by throwing lever. **For additional batteries see, 20K1401, page 858.** Shipping wt., 3 lbs. 12 oz.
49K5713.....................................$1.00

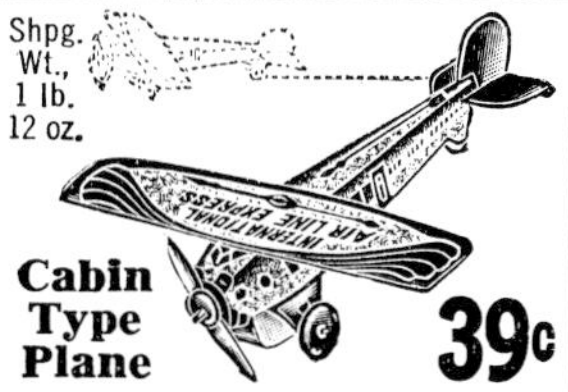

Cabin Type Plane 39c

Shpg. Wt., 1 lb. 12 oz.

Strong spring motor drives both plane and propeller. This fine, colorful lithographed metal **plane measures $17\frac{1}{2}$ in. long.** Wing spread of $17\frac{3}{8}$ in.
49K5732...............39c

Kiddy Cyclist

Biggest Selling Toy in America Last Year

Equipped with Marx strong spring motor. **The cutest most lifelike mechanical toy ever introduced.** The cute doll pedals along moving his legs in a very natural manner. He turns corners swaying his body from side to side, unexpectedly changing his direction. The cycle is metal attractively finished. **Size, $8\frac{3}{4}$ in. high, 8 in. long and $4\frac{1}{2}$ in. wide.**
49K5725 .....89c

89c
Shpg. Wt., 1 lb. 4 oz.

59c Whoopee Cowboy

Very Comical Action That Will Give You Real Thrills

Wind the strong Marx spring and watch him go—"Whoopee" Cowboy—that's what you will say when you see him drive his broncho-like car in side splitting antics. Forwards, backwards, in circles, and in all kinds of curly cues goes the car, while he bounces up and down in his seat just as if sitting on a bucking broncho. All metal attractively lithographed. **Size overall, 9x$6\frac{1}{2}$x3 in.**
49K5706—Shipping wt., 12 oz.....................59c

59c New Walking Horse With Rider

Every little kiddie loves a horsie. Here is an exceptionally fine pony which actually walks, moving its legs in the most life-like manner carrying its proud rider. Toy is made from metal attractively lithographed in contrasting colors and has a strong Marx spring. **Size overall, $8\frac{1}{2}$x8x$2\frac{1}{4}$ inches.**
49K5708—Shipping wt., 1 lb..............59c

59c 31-In. Long Brand New Mountain Climber Toy

A startling new mechanical development. Motor automatically starts and stops while in motion. Wind up the strong clock work motor in car and place at bottom of incline. Motor pulls car up incline then disengages while car scoots down on the other side of the incline, bumps the end and then comes back to the starting point on another path. Metal, prettily decorated. **Car is $3\frac{1}{8}$x$1\frac{1}{4}$x$1\frac{1}{2}$ in.**
49K5718—Shpg. wt., 1 lb. 8 oz.............59c

YOUR CHOICE—ANY 4 for Only $1.00

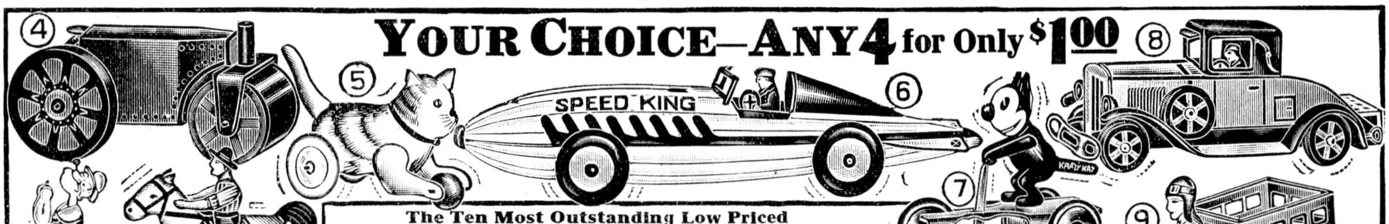

4
5
6
8
SPEED KING
KRAZY KAT
7

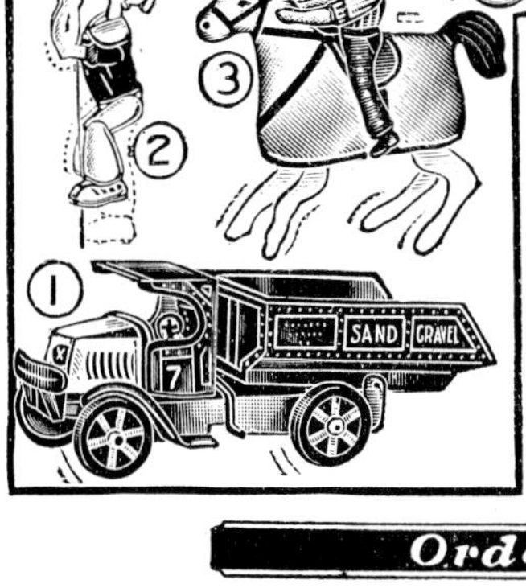

3
2
1
SAND GRAVEL
7

9
10

The Ten Most Outstanding Low Priced Mechanical Toys of the Year

All metal toys, prettily lithographed. Sturdily constructed and equipped with superior long lasting spring motors.

1—10-In. Dump Truck With Real Dumping Feature.
2—8-In. Climbing Popeye.
Stand on one end of the string, pull the upper end, and Popeye will climb up.
3—Bucking Broncho with Cowboy.
Clever action imitating a bucking broncho. **Size, $6\frac{1}{4}$x$2\frac{1}{4}$x$5\frac{1}{4}$ in.**
4—Mechanical Road Roller.
Has slow motion like the big road rollers. **Size, $8\frac{1}{4}$x$4\frac{1}{4}$x4 in.**
5—Kitty Cat Playing Ball.
New easy winding toy. Just push lever (tail) down, release and toy is in motion. **Size, 8x$3\frac{3}{4}$x$4\frac{1}{2}$ in.**
6—16-In. Speedy King Racer.
Painted exhaust pipes on sides.
7—Krazy Kat Scooter.
Watch him race around in circles. **Size, 8x$6\frac{1}{2}$x$3\frac{1}{8}$ in.**
8—12-Inch Cadillac Coupe.
Has bumper in front, bumperettes and trunk rack in rear.
9—10-In. Delivery Motorcycle.
A snappy toy with big play value.
10—Horse Pulling Lumber Wagon.
Front wheels turn to run wagon straight or in circles. **Size overall, 13x$4\frac{3}{4}$x4 inches.**

Give Numbers and names of the four toys you select.
49K5791—Average shpg. wt. of 4 toys, 3 lbs. 8 oz.....Any 4 for $1.00

Order Blanks Are in Back of This Catalog

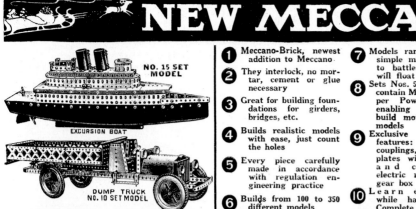

NEW MECCANO

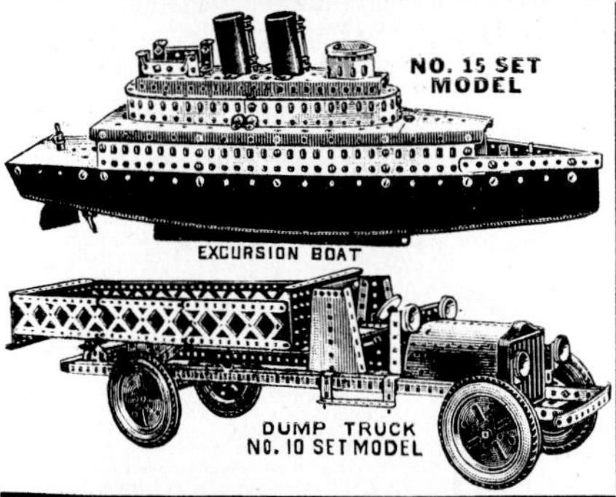

NO. 15 SET MODEL
EXCURSION BOAT
DUMP TRUCK
NO. 10 SET MODEL

1. Meccano-Brick, newest addition to Meccano
2. They interlock, no mortar, cement or glue necessary
3. Great for building foundations for girders, bridges, etc.
4. Builds realistic models with ease, just count the holes
5. Every piece carefully made in accordance with regulation engineering practice
6. Builds from 100 to 350 different models
7. Models range from simple moving toys to battleships that will float
8. Sets Nos. 5, 10 and 15 contain Meccano Super Power Motor enabling you to build motor driven models
9. Exclusive Meccano features: patented couplings, sector plates with flanges and combination electric motor and gear box
10. Learn engineering while having fun. Complete Manuals.

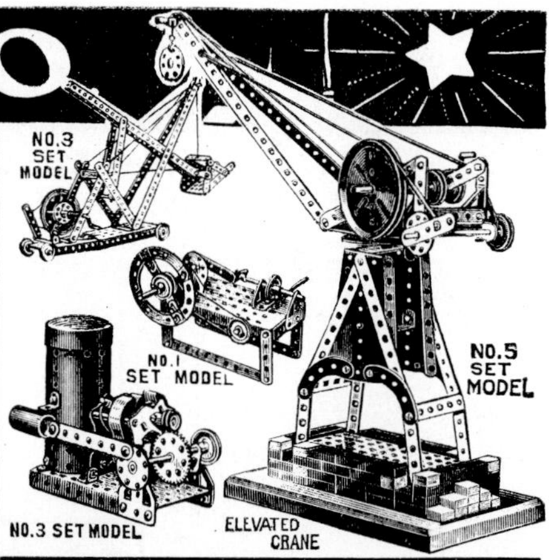

NO. 3 SET MODEL
NO. 1 SET MODEL
NO. 5 SET MODEL
NO. 3 SET MODEL
ELEVATED CRANE

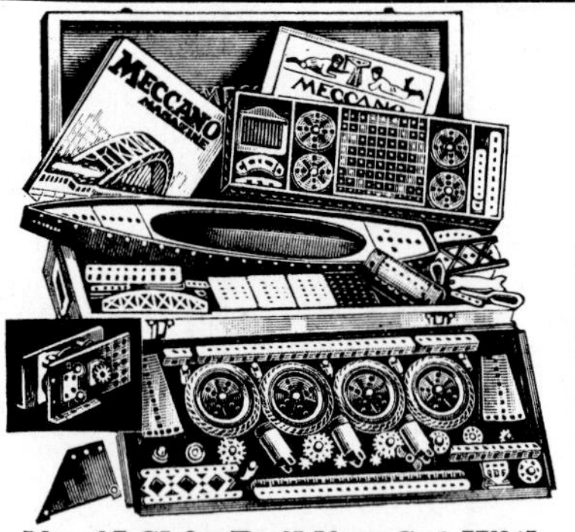

No. 15 Ship Building Set With New Meccano Brick

Builds 350 Models

Build steel ships that float and run under their own power. Also trucks, engines and many other models with Meccano natural looking composition bricks for building foundations. Also a powerful electric motor to bring your models to life. Green lacquered hinged wood chest with metal tray and manual of instructions. Size of chest $25\frac{3}{8}$x$10\frac{3}{4}$x$5\frac{1}{2}$ inches.

79K4777—$15.00 Set. Postpaid.. **$13.48**

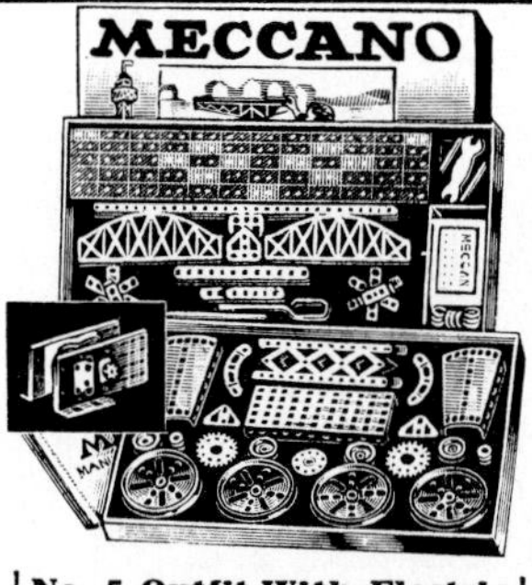

MECCANO

No. 5 Outfit With Electric Motor and New Meccano Brick

Over 300 models can be constructed with the **Meccano Super Power Unit,** combination 6-8 volt battery motor and gear box attached, enameled parts, large gears, pinions, worm gears, angle girders, etc. Then there are the natural looking Meccano bricks for foundations. **Beautifully lithographed box 18x10x$2\frac{1}{8}$ inches.** Postpaid.

49K4779—$5.00 Set. **$4.48**

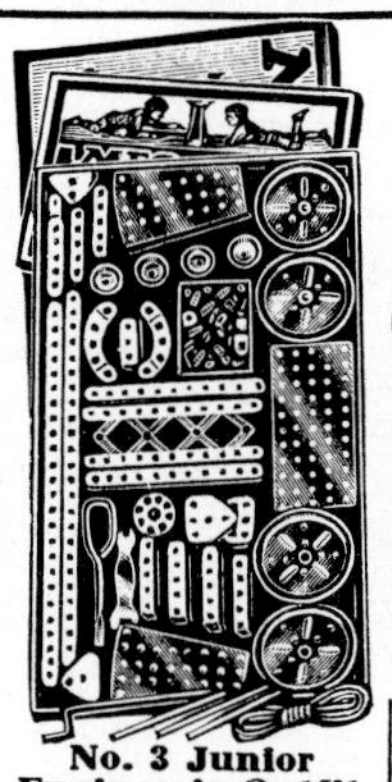

No. 3 Junior Engineer's Outfit

Builds over 200 models. Long beams, braced girders, disc wheels, gears, pulleys, pinions, etc. Enameled parts. **Lithographed box 18x10x$\frac{11}{16}$ in. Brick not included. Postpaid.**

49K4769 $3.00 Set..... **$2.69**

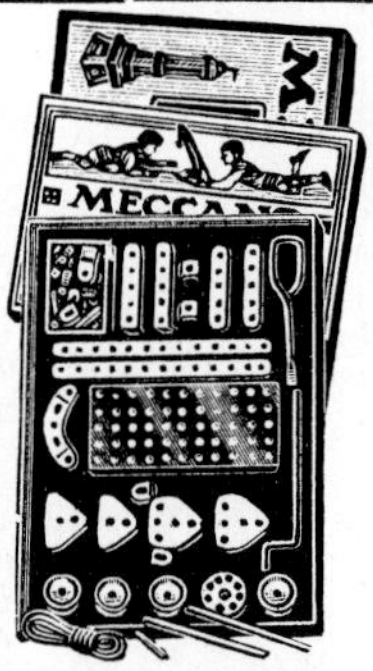

No. 1 Beginner's Meccano Outfit Builds Over 100 Models

Parts to build action models, some enameled. **Box $12\frac{3}{8}$x$8\frac{5}{8}$x$\frac{5}{8}$ in.** Bricks not included. **Shpg. wt., 2 lbs.**

49K4770 $1.00 Set..... **89c**

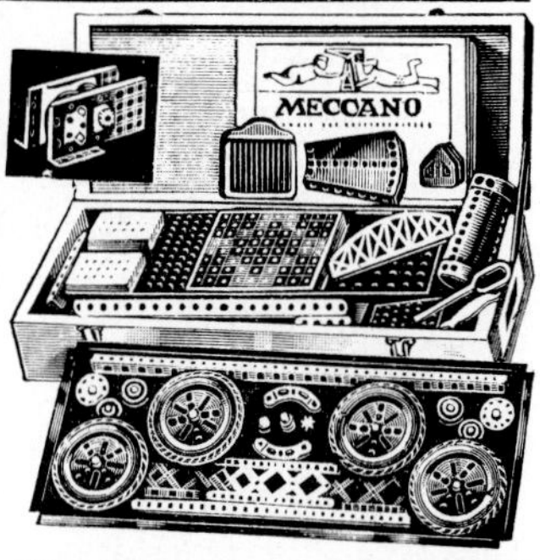

MECCANO

No. 10 Motor Car Set With Electric Motor—Also New Meccano Brick

Builds 325 models. Includes steel disc wheels, detachable Dunlap balloon tires, gears, pulleys, angle girders up to 18 in. long patented and improved. Electric motor operates on 2 dry cells or 110-volt house current transformer. **Green lacquered wood chest, size, $21\frac{1}{2}$x8x$4\frac{1}{2}$ in. Postpaid.**

79K4778—$10.00 Set. **$8.98**

TINKERTOY WONDER BUILDER

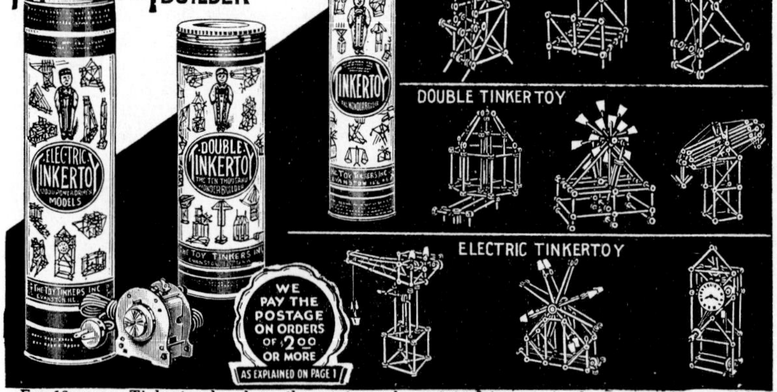

TINKERTOY
DOUBLE TINKER TOY
ELECTRIC TINKERTOY
ELECTRIC TINKERTOY
DOUBLE TINKERTOY
TINKERTOY
WE PAY THE POSTAGE ON ORDERS OF $2.00 OR MORE
AS EXPLAINED ON PAGE 1

For 18 years, Tinkertoy has been the most popular construction toy in the country for small kiddies. These are the finest playthings the Toy Tinkers have ever produced. There is no limit to the possible number of models.

Improved Popular Size Tinkertoy 69c

73 pieces made of smoothed and sanded white birch. Red enameled spools, colored cardboard wind blades. Instruction book. Mailing container 12x3 inches.

49K4760 Shpg. wt., 1 lb.......... **69c**

New Improved Double Set $1.37

Double the number of pieces in the single set and 10 additional pieces. Builds unlimited amount of constructive models. Instruction book. Packed in mailing container 4x12 in.

49K4762 Shpg. wt., 2 lbs..... **$1.37**

Electric Motorized Set $2.69

More pieces than double tinkertoy and powered by the new **Tinkertoy electric motor.** Motor runs on 60 cycle house current. Packed in mailing container 4x15 in. **Postpaid.**

49K4765 Motorized Set........ **$2.69**

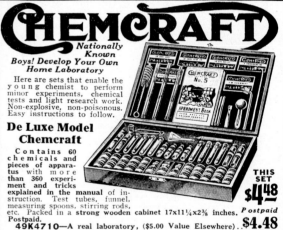

CHEMCRAFT

Nationally Known

Boys! Develop Your Own Home Laboratory

Here are sets that enable the young chemist to perform minor experiments, chemical tests and light research work. Non-explosive, non-poisonous. Easy instructions to follow.

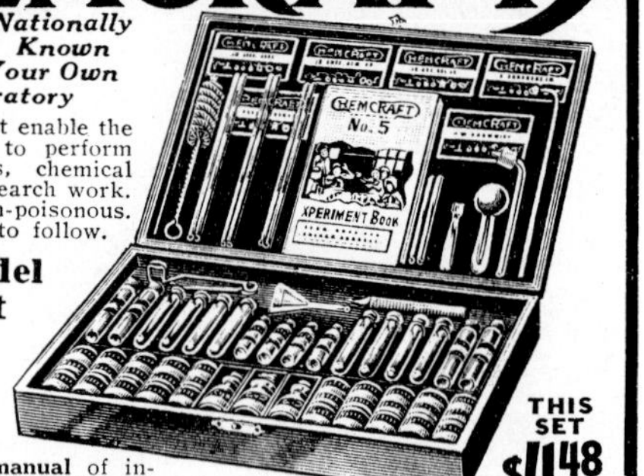

CHEMCRAFT
No. 5
EXPERIMENT BOOK

De Luxe Model Chemcraft

Contains 60 chemicals and pieces of apparatus with more than 360 experiment and tricks explained in the manual of instruction. Test tubes, funnel, measuring spoons, stirring rods, etc. Packed in a **strong wooden cabinet 17x$11\frac{1}{4}$x$2\frac{3}{8}$ inches.** Postpaid.

THIS SET $4.48 *Postpaid*

49K4710—A real laboratory, ($5.00 Value Elsewhere).. **$4.48**

Junior Model Chemcraft

Contains 43 different chemicals and pieces of apparatus such as glass test tubes, test tube holder, stirring rods, etc. and manual of instructions **to perform 265 experiments and tricks. Lithographed cardboard box $15\frac{1}{2}$x$10\frac{1}{2}$x$1\frac{1}{2}$ inches. Postpaid.**

49K4711—$3.50 Set. **$3.19**

Chemcraft for Beginners

A dandy set to start your chemical career. Contains **19 chemicals and pieces** of equipment. **Lithographed cardboard box, $12\frac{1}{2}$x$9\frac{1}{2}$x$1\frac{1}{2}$ inches. Perform 100 experiments or tricks.** Manual with instructions. **Shpg. wt., 1 lb. 4 oz.**

49K4712—Beginners $1.00 Set.................. **89c**

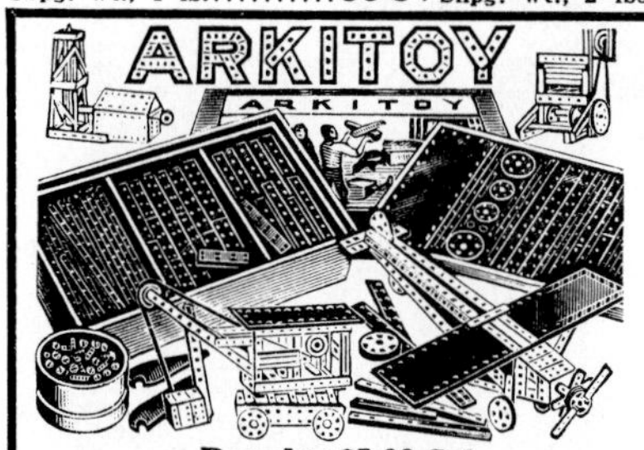

ARKITOY
ARKITOY

Regular $5.00 Set

40 page plan book. Builds many models. Box $20\frac{3}{4}$x10x$2\frac{3}{4}$ inches.

79K4748—Our Price. Postpaid.. **$4.48**

Arkitoy Wood Construction Sets

Arkitoy appeals to the child and parent alike. The cleverly designed colorful pieces of "play lumber" have such unlimited building flexibility that the average child never tires of it. Smooth beautifully lacquered prestwood materials; no sharp corners or edges. Complete with rust-proof machine screw bolts and nuts, wheels, etc. Plan book included in each set.

Regular $1.00 Set

40 different models. Box $18\frac{1}{4}$x$9\frac{3}{4}$x$\frac{3}{4}$ in.

49K4745—Shpg. wt., 2 lbs. 8 oz. Our Price.................. **89c**

Regular $2.00 Set

85 model size. Box $18\frac{1}{4}$x$9\frac{3}{4}$x$1\frac{3}{8}$ inches.

49K4746—Shpg. wt., 4 lbs. 8 oz. Our Price............... **$1.79**

Regular $3.50 Set

Builds trucks, steam shovels, etc. Box $20\frac{3}{4}$x10x$1\frac{3}{4}$ inches.

49K4747—Our Price. Postpaid... **$2.98**

Mold Your Own Toy Soldiers

Gilbert's Famous Electric Erector Kaster Kit

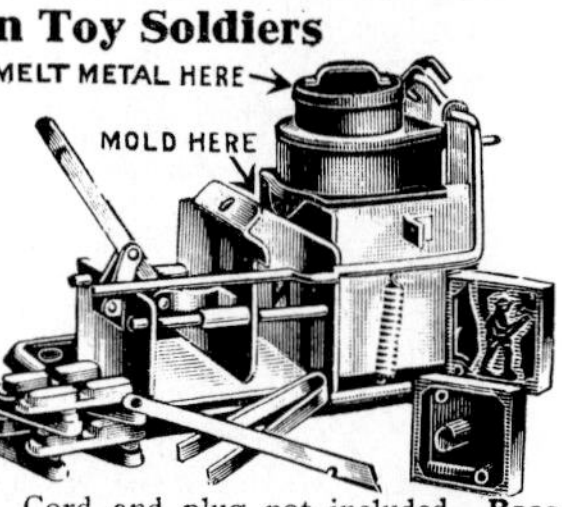

MELT METAL HERE
MOLD HERE

An electric casting outfit that molds toy soldiers. Every boy likes to play with lead soldiers. **Now he can have the added fun of making his own.** If they break, do not worry. You just drop them into the melting pot, attach to house current, melt them, pull lever and lead runs into the mold, then pull another lever and the toy drops out. **Operates on 110-volt 60 cycle house current.** Finished soldier is $1\frac{7}{8}$ in. tall. Complete with one set of molds, 8 pigs of metal, tweezers and scraper. Cord and plug not included. **Base measures $10\frac{7}{8}$x$5\frac{5}{8}$ in. and 6 in. high overall. Regular Price Elsewhere, $5.00.**

79K4713—Complete Kaster Kit. Postpaid............ **$4.59**

8 Extra Metal Bars

49K4702 Shpg. wt., 1 lb. 4 oz........ **23c**

Soldier on Horse Mold

49K4704 Shpg. wt., 1 lb.......... **89c**

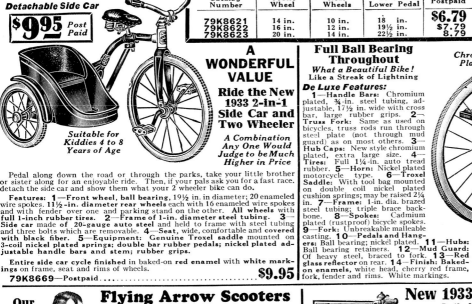

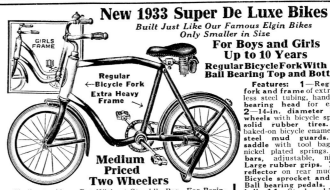

ALL STEEL BEAUTIES

$7.65 Post Paid

You've Heard of Bargains
—Here are Two Super Bargains

Buy one of these if you want the most for your money in a lower priced car.

Beautiful lines. New features.

These cars made of automobile steel and the finish is baked-on, same as the finish on bodies and fenders of large motor cars.

For Tots 2 to 5 years

1933 Willys-Knight

FEATURES: 1—Length, overall, 33 in.; width, 18½ in. 2—Has crown fenders. 3—Running boards will hold a man. 4—Unbreakable windshield. 5—Headlights. 6—9⅜-in. roller bearing double disc steel wheels; ¾-in. rubber tires, 7—Adjustable rubber pedals; steel bumper, motometer, license plate and loud horn.

Closed body type: Enameled green and canary color, black markings. Wheels with green bull's eye, fenders and bumper, black.

79K8931—Postpaid...**$7.65**

Latest Type Auburn

Similar to the one shown but no fenders or running boards.

Length, overall, 33 in.; width, 18 in., 8¼-in. double disc plain bearing wheels; ⅝-in. rubber tires. Has adjustable rubber pedals and adjustable windshield. Same headlights, bumper, motometer, license plate and horn. Body and hood enameled ivory and blue, black striping; wheels ivory color; striped. Bumper black.

79K8929—Postpaid.....**$5.95**

1933 ALL STEEL CADILLAC

$9.95

Not Only Looks Like a Real Auto But It's Made of Same Materials as Used in Large Motor Cars.

So Far Ahead of Any Toy Auto Value We Ever Offered. There Is No Comparison. Only 2 Years Ago, a Similar Car Sold Elsewhere for $20.00. This New Cadillac Is Even Better Built, Has Finer Lines and Many New Features.

FEATURES:
1—Length overall, 41 in.; width, 20¾ in.
2—10-in. roller bearing giant size balloon type wheels; full ¾-in. gear tread rubber tires.
3—New type chromium plated radiator and ornament.
4—Ball bearing rear axle.
5—New type, long, sloping, one piece fenders. Corrugated running boards; splash aprons.
6—Tempered carbon steel springs on rear axle absorb shocks.
7—Adjustable windshield.
8—Heavy channel steel chassis.
9—Adjustable rubber pedals.

Equipment consists of chromium plated head lights; a spot light, French type bulb horn, gear shift, fiber covered seat, colored instrument board, spring steel double bumper, colored license plate.

Body and hood enameled medium blue with ivory color panels and black striping. Fenders, running boards, splash aprons and undergearing enameled ivory. Wheels aluminum finish with blue bull's eye, black striping. One of the prettiest color combinations we have ever seen.

79KC8933—Shpg. wt., 56 lbs. Not Prepaid...**$9.95**

For Tots Up to 6 Years

$10.95
Unmailable Shipped by Freight or Express Not Prepaid

Rear Seat and Step ↓

REAL MACK DUMP TRUCK

New Improved All Steel Truck at New Low Price

The Only Original Bull Dog Type Mack Toy Truck. No Other Mail Order House Sells It. For Tots Up to 7 Years. Resembles in detail the large Mack seen on the street.

Made from heavy gauge automobile fender steel. No wood parts to crack. Frame of heavy channel steel. Finish is baked-on enamel like large auto bodies.

FEATURES:
1—Length overall, 47 in.; width, 21 in.
2—Roller bearing, 10-in. giant size balloon type wheels, ¾-in. rubber tires.
3—Fender over each front wheel and strong running boards braced to chassis. Strong enough to hold the weight of a man.
4—Dump box, 15x13¾x5 in. with crank so it may be raised or lowered.
5—Tempered carbon steel springs on rear axle.
6—Adjustable rubber pedals.

Equipped with chromium plated ⅞-in. tubular steel bumper; chromium plated spot light; black enameled head lights with chromium plated lens; nickel plated French type bulb horn. Hood, seat and dump box enameled red. Green panels on hood with ivory color markings. Wheels aluminum finish with red bull's eye, cream striping. Fenders, running boards and undergearing black.

79KC8935—Shpg. wt., 50 lbs. Not Prepaid...**$10.95**

Real Dump Box

$10.95

French Horn ↓

Balloon Type Wheels →

Chromium Plated Tubular Steel Bumper

Fully Equipped Mack Type Hook and Ladder

It not only looks like a real Hook and Ladder but it's built of automobile steel and the finish is baked-on enamel just like on the bodies of large motor cars. No other Mail Order House sells it. For Tots Up to 7 Years.

Clang the Bell and Race to the Rescue
Two Detachable Lanterns and Two Wood Ladders.

FEATURES:
1—Length, overall, 40½ in., width, 19¾ in.
2—Double seat, one for driver and the other in rear with steel step for your pal.
3—Carbon steel springs on rear axle.
4—Two wood ladders, 27 in. long, 6½-in. wide, finished natural, varnished.
5—Adjustable rubber pedals. 6—One each red and green detachable lanterns.
7—8¼-in. plain bearing double disc steel wheels, ⅝-in. rubber tires.

Equipment is nickel plated brass bell on front with cord fastened to steering wheel, chromium plated steel side rails, colored license plate in front.

Entire truck made of automobile steel. Hood, double seat and wheels enameled red with ivory color striping. Undergearing and step enameled black.

79KM8934—Shpg. wt., 63 lbs. Not Prepaid...**$10.95**

$5.65 Post Paid

Nickel Plated Brass Bell

Fire Chief
Clang! Clang! Clang!
Make Way for the "Fire Chief"

What fun dashing down the street clanging the big nickel plated bell! Heavy gauge automobile steel closed body type. Length, overall, 33 in.; width, 18 in. 8¼-in. double disc steel wheels, ⅝-in. rubber tires. Adjustable rubber pedals. Headlights with chromium plated lens, black enameled backs. Spring steel bumper. 3¼-in. nickel plated brass bell with strong cord fastened to steering wheel. License plate. Body and wheels enameled red, cream color markings.

For Children 2 to 5 Years

79K8928—Postpaid...**$5.65**

Improved Genuine Irish Mails

New Low Prices. New Colors For Speed, Action and Exercise.

Like rowing a boat. Lots of sport, plenty of exercise for the whole body.

Adjustable for boys and girls, 3 to 12 Years. Enameled in Bright Colors.

Length over all, 41 in.

DeLuxe Model With Roller Bearing Disc Steel Wheels
Full 1-in. gear tread rubber tires. 8¾-in. front and 13-in. rear wheels, on fully encased roller bearings.
79K8803—Postpaid...**$8.39**

The Irish Mail Special
Spoke wheels, 8-in. front and 12-in. rear, ½-in. rubber tires.
79K8802—Postpaid...**$5.39**

Every Child Wants to Help Daddy

79c
And Up

Buy Him One of These All Steel, Popular, Stylish Wheelbarrows

For indoors or outdoors. Their arms will develop while playing. The Finish is Baked-on Enamel—You'll Be Proud of it.

Brightly enameled heavy gauge automobile steel (not tin), body and strong tubular steel handles, are just what kiddies want. Each wheelbarrow has double disc steel wheel, steel axle, legs and braces.

Two Sizes.

For the Little Tots
Body, 14½x10½ in. Handles 26⅝ in. long. Five-in. steel wheel.
79K7625—Shpg. wt., 5 lbs...**79c**

For the Older Child
Heavier Gauge Steel Body, 18⅞x13½ in. Handles, 34½ in. long. 8-in. wheel, ⅝-in. rubber tire.
79K7627—Shpg. wt., 10 lbs...**$1.29**

Postpaid if part of $2 order.

$3.98 Post Paid

Motometer →

RED ACE

For Tots Up to 3 Years

Think of it!

The steel in this Little Ace is the same as that used in making large auto fenders and the beautiful high gloss finish is baked-on in the same oven in which large fenders are baked. Closed body type. Length, overall, 31 in.; width, 15¾ in. 8⅛-in. double disc steel wheels, ½-in. rubber tire. Enameled red, cream color striping.

79K8926—Postpaid...**$3.98**

Marx Guaranteed Mechanical Toys

59c

59c

Boys You'll Get a New Thrill Flying This New Crash-Proof Marx Airplane

Wind her up! Watch her go! Takes off from the ground after a run of a few feet. Up she goes! Under proper conditions this little ship will fly a surprising distance! Happy landings every time because when crashing or striking an obstruction the wings and the light weight metal under carriage detach themselves from the aluminum fuselage! Then you have the fun of putting the ship together again, for the plane is not harmed by the crash. Plane is 9½ inches long, has 11¾-inch wingspread yet weighs only one ounce. Boys! order Crash Proof Planes and Hold air races!
Equipped with strong strand gum-rubber motor.
Have the fellows in your neighborhood................**59c**

49 D 5755—Not Prepaid. Shpg. wt., 10 oz.

New Tricky Motorcycle
Entirely New Unique Action

Plenty of fun and laughs galore in watching the "Tipover" Motorcycle do stunts! When you wind the attached side keys and place this new toy on the floor it scoots off like a big motorcycle. But wait! Watch it fall over—first on one side—then on the other. Quick as a flash it rights itself—goes on its way —to fall over once more! What makes it perform so naturally? A new type of very fine clock spring motor. Lithographed metal construction. Size overall: 7¾x6x1⅞ in. Not Prepaid. Shpg. wt., 1 lb. 4 oz.
49 D 5750...................**59c**

UP AND AWAY TURNS OVER RIGHT   STARTS

UP AND AWAY   TURNS OVER LEFT

Watch Kitty Play Ball!

The tiniest tot can work it. Press down tail and away she goes. No key to wind or lose yet plenty of action. Metal lithographed. Size, 8x3¾x4½ in. Not Prepaid. Shpg. wt., 12 oz.
49 D 5731..........**25c**

16-In. Mechanical Racer

Modeled after latest type racing cars. A big toy, made entirely of metal. Colorfully lithographed. Strong spring sends it along at rapid speed. Not Prepaid. Shpg. wt., 1 lb. 6 oz.
49 D 5733.........**25c**

59c

Size 8¼x 5⅜x3⅜ inches

Run This Powerful Marx Climbing Tractor!

Climbs over obstacles and down steep grades—nothing seems to stop its progress. Will pull loads, lumbering along, like a big tractor. Suction cup type rubber treads. Strongly built of metal. Controlled speed, start and stop lever. Clock work motor. Not Prepaid.
49 D 5745—Shpg. wt., 1 lb. 10 oz...........**59c**
Cardboard play castle with incline for tractor to climb up or down. Size, 40x10x10 in. Not illustrated.
49 D 5790—Shpg. wt., 2 lbs. 12 oz........**33c**

Speedy Scooter Cat!

Watch Krazy Kat race in circles on his scooter. Wind the spring and away he goes! Immensely popular. Size, 8x6½x3⅛ in. Not Prepaid. Shpg. wt., 12 oz.
49 D 5765.......**19c**

"POPEYE" Walking Toy

Here's a toy-size model of Blow-Me-Down Popeye that walks when wound up. Very realistic walking action. Metal, nicely colored. 8¼ in. tall. Not Prepaid. Shpg. wt., 10 oz.
49 D 5715.......**25c**

Acrobatic Monkey!

Wind the spring—see monkey do lots of cute tricks. Lithographed metal. Toy, 6¾ in. high. Not Prepaid. Shpg. wt., 10 oz.
49 D 5722 **19c**

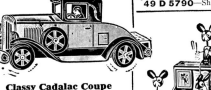

Classy Cadalac Coupe

A little beauty all dressed up in attractive colors on metal. Is 12 in. long, has a bumper on front, bumperettes and trunk rack on rear. The strong spring makes this snappy car spin right along. A real value at this low price. Not Prepaid.
49 D 5728—Shpg. wt., 1 lb. 6 oz........**25c**

59c

Famous Marx "Merrymakers"

Last year 87c— Now Only 59c

No wonder the youngsters like them! They are so full of pep! As soon as the powerful spring motor is wound, the show begins! The mouse leader and see mouse plays his violin— another mouse dances, one bangs the piano, a fourth beats a trap drum! Not a musical toy. Size, 9x9x5 in. All lithographed metal.
49 D 5717—Not Prepaid. Shpg. wt., 1 lb. 8 oz.**59c**

Comical Monkey Cyclist

Push down lever and see Jocko ride his cycle in realistic fashion. Monkey may be detached. Made of metal 5⅞ in. long. Not Prepaid. Shpg. wt., 10 oz.
49 D 5748.....**19c**

Whoopee Cowboy Driver

Watch this Whoopee Cowboy perform side-splitting antics with his broncho-like auto when spring is wound. Lithographed metal. Size, 9x6½x3 in. Not Prepaid. Shpg. wt., 1 lb.
49 D 5706........**47c**

$2²⁹

Murray Truck With Real Electric Lights!

Sit on the large steel saddle seat for coasting.
—steer with steel steering wheel like real truck— dump loads with hand dumping device—snap electric head lights on and off with switch. 2 batteries included. Auto fender 20-gauge steel. Disc wheels —rubber tires. Length, 25 in., width, 8 in. Not Prepaid.
79 D 5081—Shpg. wt., 11 lbs.....**$2.29**

DIGGING SWINGS AROUND DUMPING

$1⁰⁰

It's Fun to Run a Buddy "L" Digger!

Sit on the strong steel seat of this big 28-inch long "one boy-power" Digger—work the levers just like a steam shovel. Slides on runners to different locations. Seat and boom revolve. Strongly built of 20-gauge steel. Enameled in **black** and **red**. Length with boom extended, 38 in.; width, 10 in., height, 17 in. Not Prepaid.
79 D 5002—Shpg. wt., 5 lbs......**$1.00**

Buddy "L" Dump Truck With Electric Headlights

Will Hold a 200-lb. Man's Weight

$1⁰⁰

22 IN. LONG WHEN RAISED

The truck every kiddie wants now.
Lift dump body by pulling lever, which also opens end gate. No end of fun with this big toy. Chassis and cab **black**, dump body in **red** baked on enamel. One battery included gives dim light. For bright and dim lights see notice below.
79 D 5028—Not Prepaid. Shpg. wt., 6 lbs...........**$1.00**

20-Gauge Steel 24-In. Long

Buddy "L" Wrecking Car With Real Electric Lights

Lift heavy loads with lifting crane. One battery included makes dim lights. For bright and dim lights see below. Rubber wheels have balloon tire effect. White baked-on enamel body, red color wheels.
79 D 5017—Not Prepaid. Shpg. wt., 7 lbs...........**$1.00**

BUDDY "L" FIRE TRUCK
Red Electric Lights

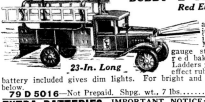

Has removable ladders adjustable to 25-inches high. Made of 20-gauge steel. Truck is **red** baked-on enamel. Ladders **yellow**. Soft tire effect rubber wheels. One battery included gives dim lights. For bright and dim lights see below.

23-In. Long

79 D 5016—Not Prepaid. Shpg. wt., 7 lbs...........**$1.00**

EXTRA BATTERIES **IMPORTANT NOTICE:** BUDDY L TRUCKS are built for two batteries which give bright as well as dim lights. The one battery included only gives dim lights. For bright lights use two batteries. For extra batteries for all Electric trucks See 20 D 1401—Page 716.

First Electric Lighted Dump Truck at This Low Price

15 in. long, rolls easily on its rubber tired wheels, dumps its load at touch of lever. Lights go on or off at turn of switch. Nicely enameled. Length, overall, 15 in. Complete with battery. Not Prepaid.
49 D 5406—Shpg. wt., 4 lbs...........**59c**

Tiny Tots

Can Ride This Big Steel Steam Roller

Just the right size to ride and play engineer! 16¾ in. long. Strong enough to hold a 150 lb. man. Steer it by means of smokestack. Baked-on enamel finish. One of our most popular steel toys. Not Prepaid.
49 D 5012—Shpg. wt., 6 lbs...........**95c**

Speedy, Busy Sandy Andy

The most popular sand toy ever designed. Every youngster loves to pour sand into the hopper, watch it flow into the little car and see car race down incline to dump load at bottom. Returns to top automatically after dumping load. Can of sand included. A big value at our low price. Size, 11x9¼ in. Made of metal, nicely decorated in color. Not Prepaid. Shpg. wt., 2 lbs.
49 D 5742
49c

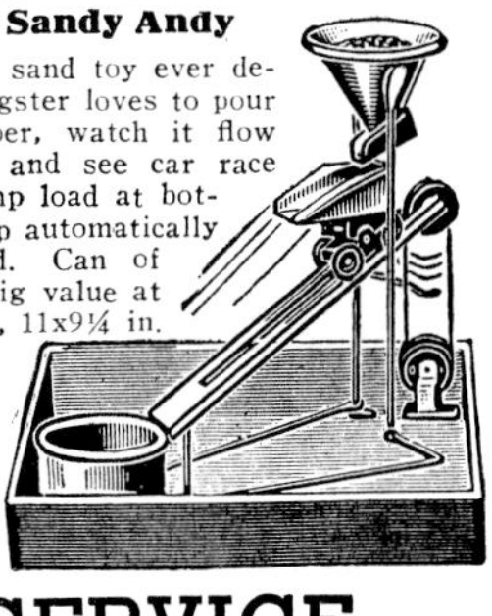

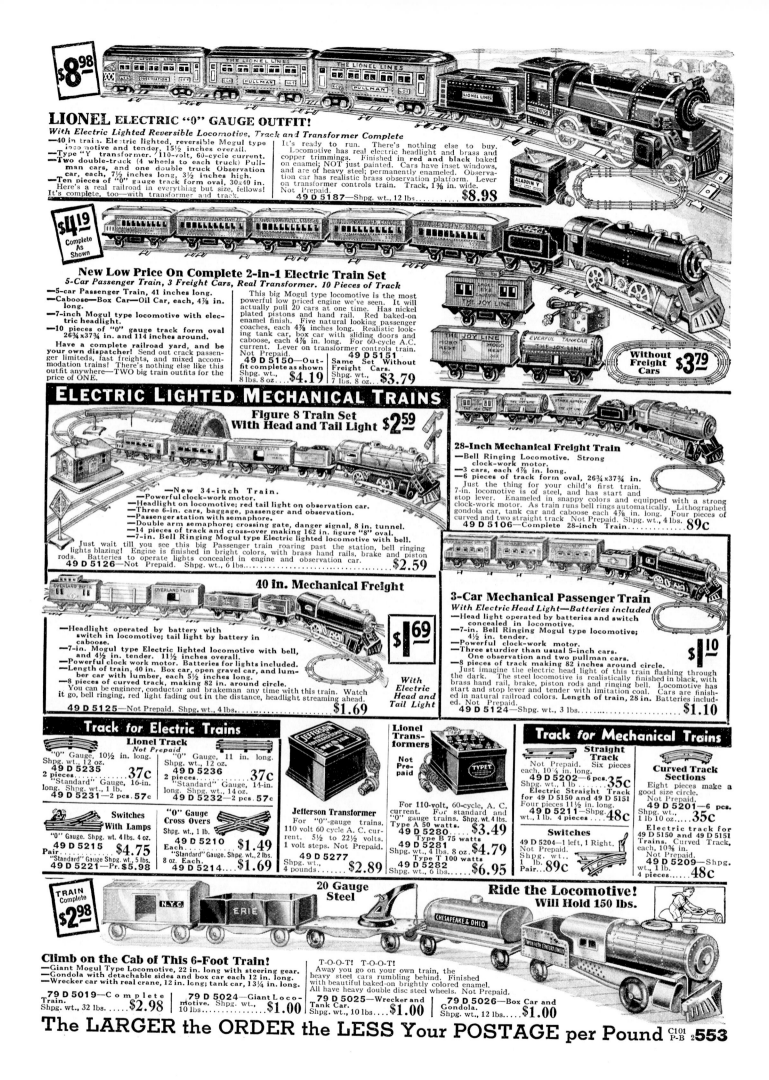

$8.98

LIONEL ELECTRIC "0" GAUGE OUTFIT!

With Electric Lighted Reversible Locomotive, Track and Transformer Complete

—40 in. train. Electric lighted, reversible Mogul type loco motive and tender, 15½ inches overall.
—Type "Y" transformer. 110-volt, 60-cycle current.
—Two double-track (4 wheels to each truck) Pullman cars, and one double truck Observation car, each, 7½ inches long, 3½ inches high.
—Ten pieces of "0" gauge track form oval, 30x40 in.
Here's a real railroad in everything but size, fellows! It's complete, too—with transformer and track.

It's ready to run. There's nothing else to buy. Locomotive has real electric headlight and brass and copper trimmings. Finished in red and black baked on enamel; NOT just painted. Cars have inset windows, and are of heavy steel; permanently enameled. Observation car has realistic brass observation platform. Lever on transformer controls train. Track, 1⅜ in. wide. Not Prepaid.

49 D 5187—Shpg. wt., 12 lbs............**$8.98**

$4.19 Complete As Shown

New Low Price On Complete 2-in-1 Electric Train Set

5-Car Passenger Train, 3 Freight Cars, Real Transformer. 10 Pieces of Track

—5-car Passenger Train, 41 inches long.
—Caboose—Box Car—Oil Car, each, 4⅞ in. long.
—7-inch Mogul type locomotive with electric headlight.
—10 pieces of "0" gauge track form oval 26¾x37¾ in. and 114 inches around.

Have a complete railroad yard, and be your own dispatcher! Send out crack passenger limiteds, fast freights, and mixed accommodation trains! There's nothing else like this outfit anywhere—TWO big train outfits for the price of ONE.

This big Mogul type locomotive is the most powerful low priced engine we've seen. It will actually pull 20 cars at one time. Has nickel plated pistons and hand rail. Red baked-on enamel finish. Five natural looking passenger coaches, each 4⅞ inches long. Realistic looking tank car, box car with sliding doors and caboose, each 4⅞ in. long. For 60-cycle A.C. current. Lever on transformer controls train. Not Prepaid.

49 D 5150—Outfit complete as shown Shpg. wt., 8 lbs. 8 oz....**$4.19**

49 D 5151 Same Set Without Freight Cars. Shpg. wt., 7 lbs. 8 oz....**$3.79**

Without Freight Cars $3.79

ELECTRIC LIGHTED MECHANICAL TRAINS

Figure 8 Train Set With Head and Tail Light $2.59

—New 34-inch Train.
—Powerful clock-work motor.
—Headlight on locomotive; red tail light on observation car.
—Three 6-in. cars, baggage, passenger and observation.
—Passenger station with semaphore.
—Double arm semaphore; crossing gate, danger signal, 8 in. tunnel.
—14 pieces of track and cross-over making 162 in. "figure 8" oval.
—7-in. Bell Ringing Mogul type Electric lighted locomotive with bell.

Just wait till you see this big Passenger train roaring past the station, bell ringing lights blazing! Engine is finished in bright colors, with brass hand rails, brake and piston rods. Batteries to operate lights concealed in engine and observation car.
49 D 5126—Not Prepaid. Shpg. wt., 6 lbs..............**$2.59**

40 in. Mechanical Freight

—Headlight operated by battery with switch in locomotive; tail light by battery in caboose.
—7-in. Mogul type Electric lighted locomotive with bell, and 4½ in. tender. 11½ inches overall.
—Powerful clock work motor. Batteries for lights included.
—Length of train, 40 in. Box car, open gravel car, and lumber car with lumber, each 5½ inches long.
—8 pieces of curved track, making 82 in. around circle.

You can be engineer, conductor and brakeman any time with this train. Watch it go, bell ringing, red light fading out in the distance, headlight streaming ahead.
49 D 5125—Not Prepaid. Shpg. wt., 4 lbs..............**$1.69**

$1.69 With Electric Head and Tail Light

28-Inch Mechanical Freight Train

—Bell Ringing Locomotive. Strong clock-work motor.
—3 cars, each 4⅞ in. long.
—6 pieces of track form oval, 26¾x37¾ in.

Just the thing for your child's first train. 7-in. locomotive is of sheet steel, and has start and stop lever. Enameled in snappy colors and equipped with a strong clock-work motor. As train runs bell rings automatically. Lithographed gondola car, tank car and caboose each 4⅞ in. long. Four pieces of curved and two straight track Not Prepaid. Shpg. wt., 4 lbs.
49 D 5106—Complete 28-inch Train..............**89c**

3-Car Mechanical Passenger Train

With Electric Head Light—Batteries included

—Head light operated by batteries and switch concealed in locomotive.
—7-in. Bell Ringing Mogul type locomotive; 4½ in. tender.
—Powerful clock-work motor.
—Three sturdier than usual 5-inch cars. One observation and two pullman cars.
—8 pieces of track making 82 inches around circle.

Just imagine the electric head light of this train flashing through the dark. The steel locomotive is realistically finished in black, with brass hand rail, brake, piston rods and ringing bell. Locomotive has start and stop lever and tender with imitation coal. Cars are finished in natural railroad colors. Length of train, 28 in. Batteries included. Not Prepaid.
49 D 5124—Shpg. wt., 3 lbs..............**$1.10**

$1.10

Track for Electric Trains

Lionel Track
Not Prepaid
"0" Gauge, 10½ in. long. Shpg. wt., 12 oz.
49 D 5235 2 pieces.............**37c**

"0" Gauge, 11 in. long. Shpg. wt., 12 oz.
49 D 5236 2 pieces.............**37c**

"Standard" Gauge, 16-in. long. Shpg. wt., 12 oz.
49 D 5231—2 pcs.**57c**

"Standard" Gauge, 14-in. long. Shpg. wt., 14 oz.
49 D 5232—2 pcs.**57c**

Switches With Lamps
"0" Gauge. Shpg. wt. 4 lbs. 4 oz.
49 D 5215 Pair.............**$4.75**
"Standard" Gauge Shpg. wt., 5 lbs.
49 D 5221—Pr.**$5.98**

"0" Gauge Cross Overs Shpg. wt., 1 lb.
49 D 5210 Each.............**$1.49**
"Standard" Gauge. Shpg. wt., 2 lbs. 8 oz. Each.
49 D 5214.............**$1.69**

Jefferson Transformer
For "0"-gauge trains. 110 volt 60 cycle A. C. current. 5½ to 22½ volts. 1 volt steps. Not Prepaid.
49 D 5277 Shpg. wt., 4 pounds......**$2.89**

Lionel Transformers
Not Prepaid
For 110-volt, 60-cycle, A. C. current. For standard and "0" gauge trains. Shpg. wt., 4 lbs.
Type A 50 watts
49 D 5280.............**$3.49**
Type B 75 watts
49 D 5281 Shpg. wt., 4 lbs. 8 oz.**$4.79**
Type T 100 watts
49 D 5282 Shpg. wt., 6 lbs......**$6.95**

Track for Mechanical Trains

Straight Track
Not Prepaid. Six pieces each, 10¼ in. long.
49 D 5202—6 pcs.**35c** Shpg. wt., 1 lb.

Electric Straight Track for 49 D 5150 and 49 D 5151 Four pieces 11½ in. long.
49 D 5211—Shpg. wt., 1 lb. 4 pieces.....**48c**

Switches
49 D 5204—1 left, 1 Right. Not Prepaid. Shpg. wt., 1 lb. Pair.**89c**

Curved Track Sections
Eight pieces make a good size circle. Shpg. wt., 1 lb 10 oz.....**35c**
49 D 5201—6 pcs.

Electric track for 49 D 5150 and 49 D 5151 Trains. Curved Track, each, 10⅜ in. Not Prepaid.
49 D 5209—Shpg. wt., 1 lb. 4 pieces.....**48c**

TRAIN Complete $2.98

Climb on the Cab of This 6-Foot Train!

—Giant Mogul Type Locomotive, 22 in. long with steering gear.
—Gondola with detachable sides and box car each 12 in. long.
—Wrecker car with real crane, 12 in. long; tank car, 13¼ in. long.

79 D 5019—Complete Train. Shpg. wt., 32 lbs.....**$2.98**

20 Gauge Steel

Ride the Locomotive! Will Hold 150 lbs.

T-O-O-T! T-O-O-T!
Away you go on your own train, the heavy steel cars rumbling behind. Finished with beautiful baked-on brightly colored enamel. All have heavy double disc steel wheels. Not Prepaid.

79 D 5024—Giant Locomotive. Shpg. wt., 10 lbs.....**$1.00**

79 D 5025—Wrecker and Tank Car. Shpg. wt., 10 lbs.....**$1.00**

79 D 5026—Box Car and Gondola. Shpg. wt., 12 lbs.....**$1.00**

The LARGER the ORDER the LESS Your POSTAGE per Pound

C101 P-B 2 **553**

NEWEST ELECTRIC LIGHTED TOYS

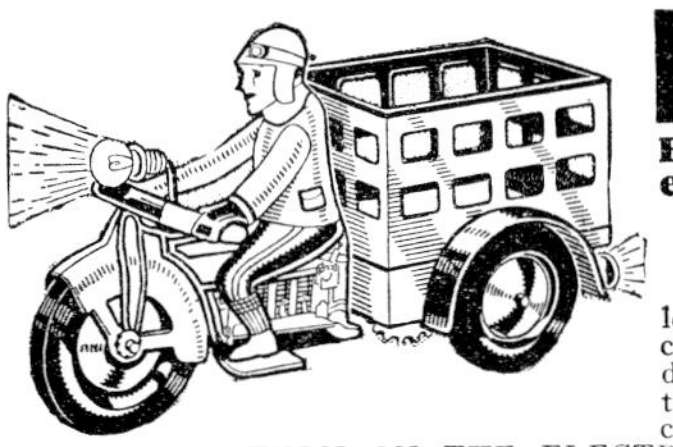

Electric Lighted Mechanical Delivery Motorcycle

Boys! Here's lots of fun! You can load up the delivery box of this dandy motorcycle, wind up the strong spring, TURN ON THE ELECTRIC HEAD AND TAIL LIGHTS, and away she goes! Yes-siree! REAL electric lights. Turn 'em on and off with a switch. **We include two one-inch diameter batteries.** All metal. Strong spiral spring. Nicely decorated. **Length, 10 in.,** height, 5⅝ in. Not Prepaid. Shpg. wt., 1 lb. 8 oz.
49 D 5724—Complete with lights and 2 Batteries 59c

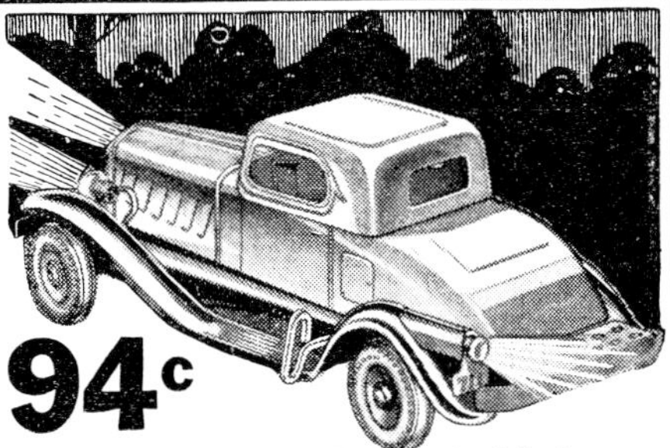

94c

Electric Lighted Mechanical Auto With Two 1⅜-In. Diameter Batteries

Has Brake, Bell and Newest Accessories!

Lights can be switched from dim to bright. Has real Headlights and Red Taillight!

One of the most amazingly popular toys ever designed, and a value that broke all previous records. Has front and rear bumpers and trunk rack. Front axle turns so coupe can be steered. You start and stop auto with brake! When in motion a bell rings! Push the switch one way front lights and tail lights come on dim, push it the other way and the lights become very bright. Strong clockwork motor. Balloon type rubber tired wheels. Beautifully decorated in baked enamel finish. What a coupe. Not Prepaid. Shpg. wt., 3 lbs. 12 oz. Size, 14¼x5x5 in.
49 D 5713 .... 94c

For Extra Batteries For All Electric Headlight Toys, See Flashlight Batteries on Page 716.

Electric Lighted Speed Boat

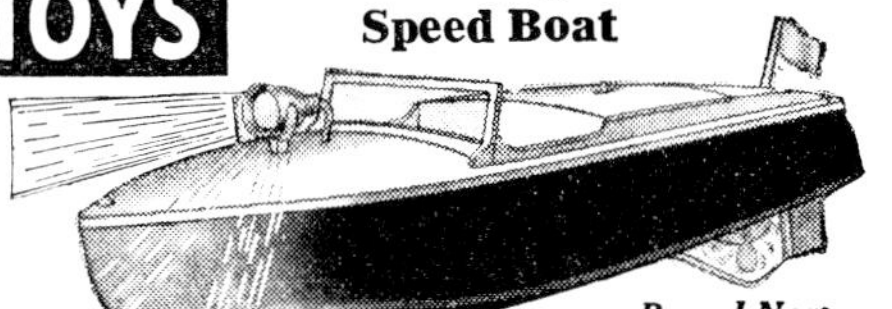

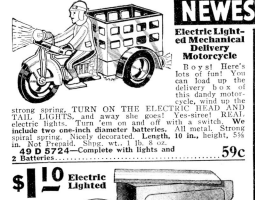

Brand New

Here comes the big 17-inch ELECTRIC LIGHTED speed boat! Here she comes! There she goes! Fast because of its strong super spring motor. All lighted up with its powerful electric searchlight. Turn it on and off with a switch also swing it to either side. Gee whiz! 20-gauge enameled steel hull. **Complete ready to operate, with one 1⅜ in. diameter battery.**
49 D 5794—Not Prepaid. Shpg. wt., 3 lbs. $1.39

$1.10 Electric Lighted

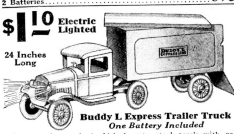

24 Inches Long

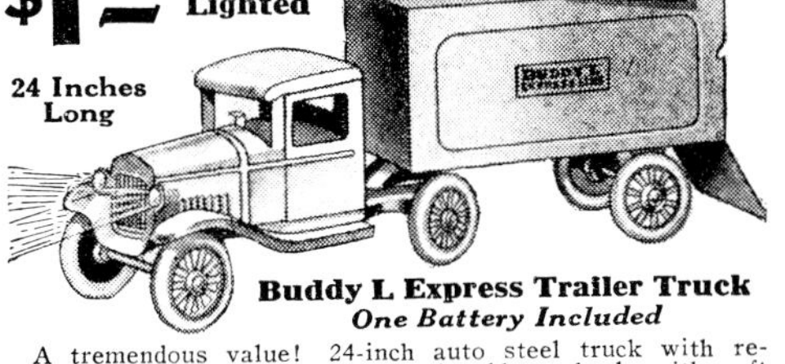

Buddy L Express Trailer Truck

One Battery Included

A tremendous value! 24-inch auto steel truck with removable top, hinged end gate and rubber wheels with soft tire effect. **The 1⅜ in. diameter battery included gives dim light only.** For extra battery to give both dim and bright lights see page 716. Not Prepaid.
79 D 5029—Shpg. wt., 9 lbs. $1.10

89c

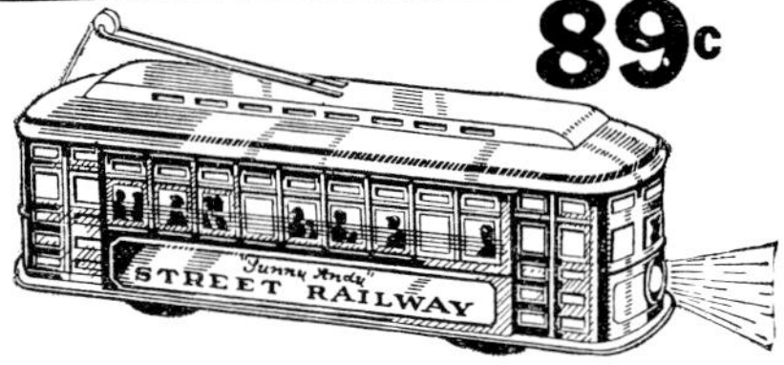

Electric Lighted Trolley Car with Bell!

This popular toy now is going to travel at night, because it's Electrically LIGHTED. Won't the children love to pull it along with its headlight flashing, its bell ringing. "Ding! Ding! Look Out! Here She Comes." Beautifully made, realistic design, no sharp corners to catch little hands. **Complete with one 1⅜ in. diameter battery.** Size, 13¾x4½x4 in.
49 D 5487—Not Prepaid. Shpg. wt., 2 lbs. 8 oz. 89c

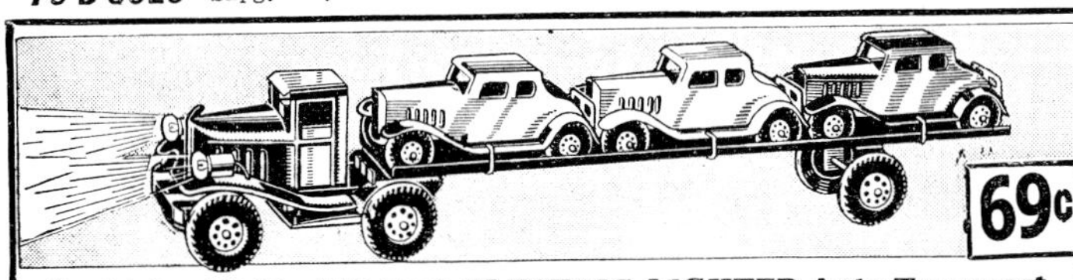

69c

Look! An All-Steel 22-Inch ELECTRIC LIGHTED Auto Transport

You can have more fun with this toy. **It's really 5 separate toys in one—and it is now equipped with real headlights which you can switch from bright to dim.** Think of that Boys! A big, husky hauler with detachable trailer and three cars—HAULER HAS 2 STRONG ELECTRIC HEADLIGHTS! Cars are modern sport coupes. Hauler and trailer have balloon type rubber tired wheels. **Two 1-inch diameter batteries included operate the electric lights.** Heavy gauge constuction. **Length, overall, 22 inches.** Each coupe, 5⅞x2¾x2½ in.
49 D 5408—Not Prepaid. Shpg. wt., 4 lbs. 69c

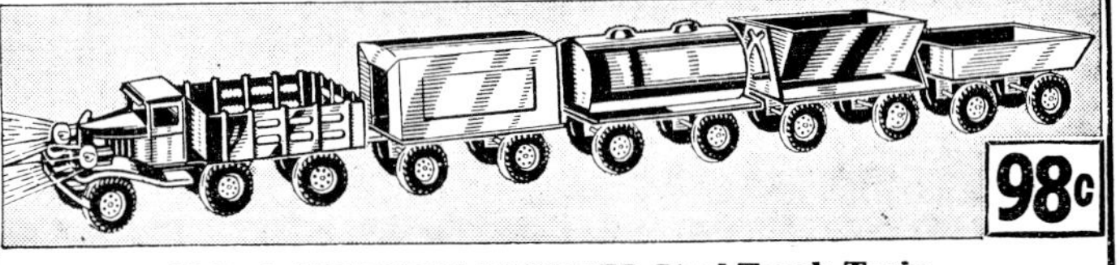

98c

41-Inch ELECTRIC LIGHTED Steel Truck Train

And what's more, every car in this big truck train is mounted on easy-rolling rubber-tired wheels. But best of all, the hauler is equipped with 2 strong headlights which you can turn on and off and change from dim to bright by moving switch! Train comes **complete with two 1-inch diameter dry cell batteries** to light these headlights. All made from heavy gauge steel, beautifully colored. Includes hauler, gravel car, stake trailer, dump truck, oil car and van. Trailers average, 5½x3½x4 in. Hauler is 7x4x4½ in.
49 D 5416—Not Prepaid. Shpg. wt., 6 lbs. 4 oz. 98c

NEW GENUINE MICKEY MOUSE GIFTS

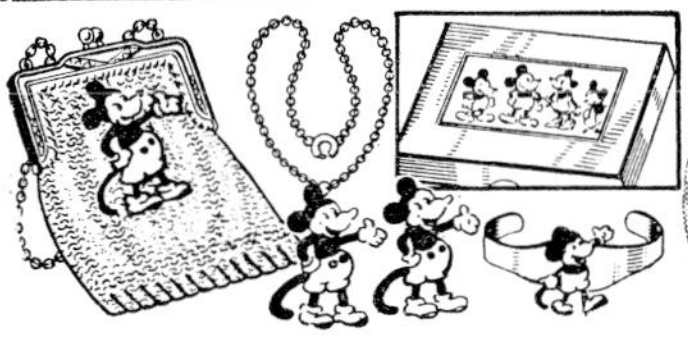

Mickey Mouse Jewelry Set

Girls! Here's a Mickey Mouse Jewelry set that's just too cute for words! A nice mesh bag. Metal Mickeys also adorn the necklace, bracelet and pin. All in neat presentation box. Not Prepaid. Shpg. wt., 4 oz.
4 D 4450—All 4 pieces for 98c

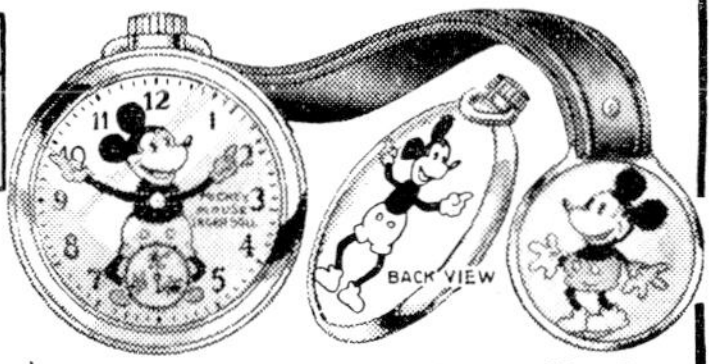

Boys! Own a Mickey Mouse Watch

Yessiree! It's a genuine Ingersoll watch that keeps fine time. On the dial is a picture of Mickey himself, and he tells you the time with his hands. A dandy fob with Mickey on that too! Unbreakable crystal. Not Prepaid.
4 D 1620—Shpg. wt., 6 oz. 98c

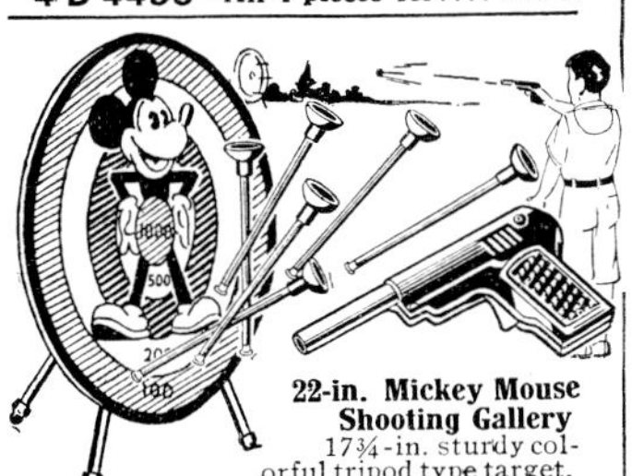

22-in. Mickey Mouse Shooting Gallery

17¾-in. sturdy colorful tripod type target. 6 rubber tipped vacuum cup darts! 7⅝ in. gun enameled steel with powerful spring. Shpg. wt., 3 lbs. 8 oz.
49 D 5669—Not Prepaid. 89c

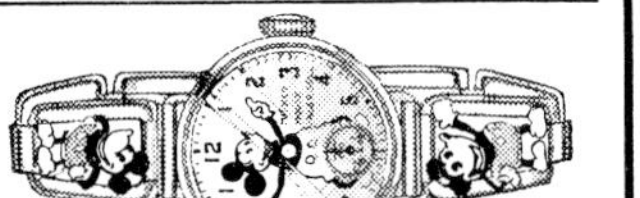

Ingersoll — **A $2.50 Value Elsewhere**

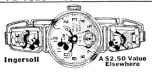

Mickey Mouse Wrist Watch $2.29

The cutest thing you ever saw in a wrist watch! Mickey on the dial tells you the time with his hands. Enameled metal Mickeys on the open link band. Non-breakable crystal. Guaranteed by Ingersoll and Sears. Not Prepaid. Shpg. wt., 6 oz.
4 D 920—With metal band $2.29
4 D 921—With leather strap $2.29

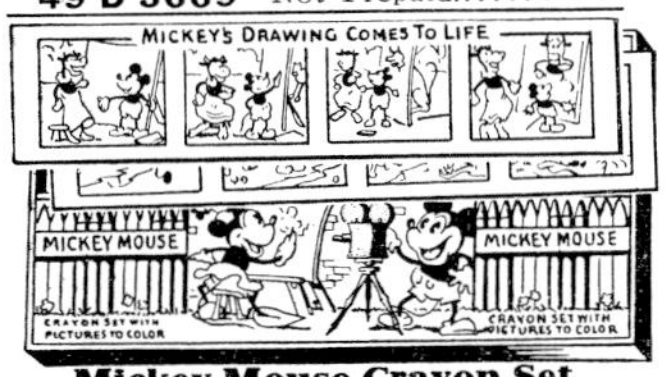

Mickey Mouse Crayon Set

What a thrill little "Tots" will get when they see this Mickey Mouse Crayon set! 12 non-poisonous colored crayons, 2 sets of pictures to color. In neat box, size, 15x8 in. Not Prepaid.
49 D 3853—Shpg. wt., 8 oz. 23c

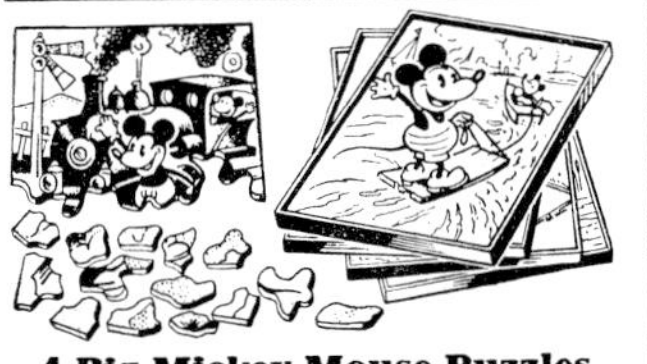

4 Big Mickey Mouse Puzzles

Lots of fun to solve these cut-up Puzzles. Each puzzle in separate tray. Subjects: Mickey Mouse as **"The Engineer," Canoeist, Surf Rider and at the Picnic.** Packed in 12x10 in. box. Not Prepaid. Shpg. wt., 2 lbs.
49 D 3845 ...... 4 Puzzles for 45c

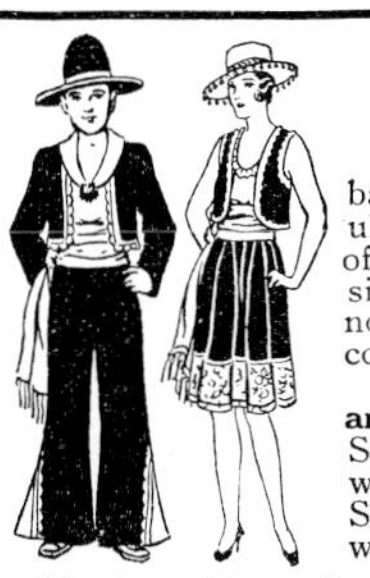

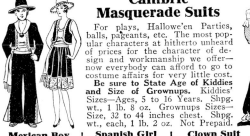

Cambric Masquerade Suits

For plays, Hallowe'en Parties, balls, pageants, etc. The most popular characters at hitherto unheard of prices for the character of design and workmanship we offer—now everybody can afford to go to costume affairs for very little cost. **Be sure to State Age of Kiddies and Size of Grownups.** Kiddies' Sizes—Ages, 5 to 16 Years. Shpg. wt., 1 lb. 8 oz. Grownups Sizes—Size, 32 to 44 inches chest. Shpg. wt., each, 1 lb. 2 oz. Not Prepaid.

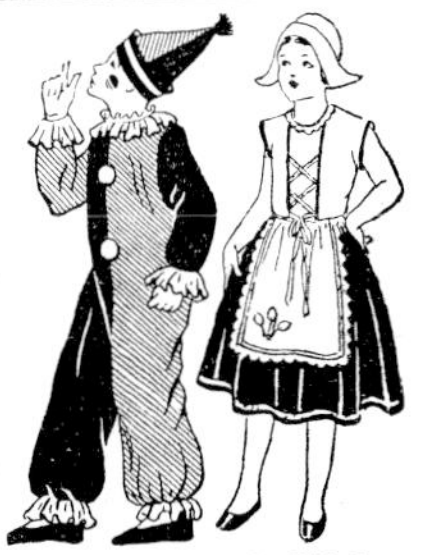

Mexican Boy
Consists of jaunty sombrero with tassels and braid flared bottom trousers, vest and white collared blouse with fringed sash.
Adults' Sizes 49 D 4554 **$1.69**
Kiddies' Sizes 49 D 4550 **98c**

Spanish Girl
Here's a snappy "Senorita" costume from Old Spain that always makes a hit. Hat is ball fringed. Blouse is bolero type.
Adults' Sizes 49 D 4535 **$1.69**
Kiddies' Sizes 49 D 4555 **98c**

Clown Suit
Go as a clown and have a riot of fun! 2-piece contrasting color cambric costume. Cut big and full. Trimmed with gold colored tinsel braid.
Adults' Sizes 49 D 4563 **$1.69**
Kiddies' Sizes 49 D 4562 **98c**

Dutch Girl
Typical Dutch type skirt and blouse with apron trimmed with dainty lace. Bonnet is made of white cambric.
Adults' Sizes 49 D 4561 **$1.69**
Kiddies' Sizes 49 D 4560 **98c**

LOW PRICED COSTUMES FOR THE KIDDIES

Same characters as above, but not so well made, as edges are not finished. Big value for the price. Not Prepaid. Shpg. wt., each, 10 oz.

Mexican Boy	Spanish Girl	Clown Suit	Dutch Girl
49 D 4564	49 D 4565	49 D 4566	49 D 4567
69c	69c	69c	69c

Sears Grab Bag of Joy Toys!

Chock-full of Toys for Girls and Boys Age 2 to 6 Years

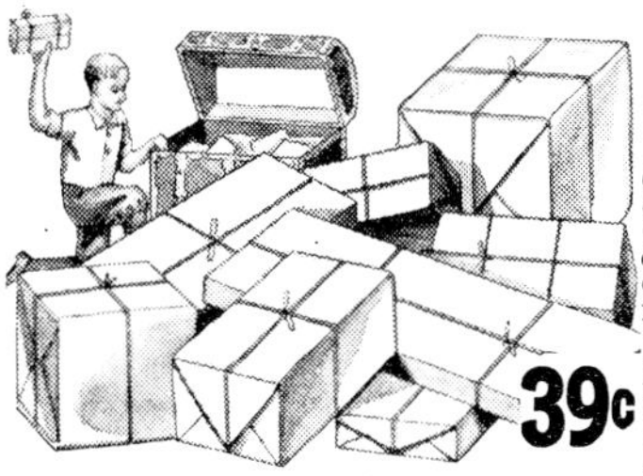

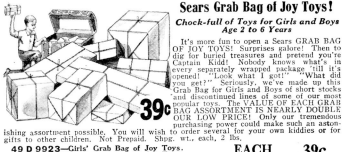

39c

It's more fun to open a Sears GRAB BAG OF JOY TOYS! Surprises galore! Then to dig for buried treasures and pretend you're Captain Kidd! Nobody knows what's in every separately wrapped package 'till it's opened! "Look what I got!" "What did you get?" Seriously, we've made up this Grab Bag for Girls and Boys of short stocks and discontinued lines of some of our most popular toys. The VALUE OF EACH GRAB BAG ASSORTMENT IS NEARLY DOUBLE OUR LOW PRICE! Only our tremendous purchasing power could make such an astonishing assortment possible. You will wish to order several for your own kiddies or for gifts to other children. Not Prepaid. Shpg. wt., each, 2 lbs.
49 D 9923—Girls' Grab Bag of Joy Toys.
49 D 9924—Boys' Grab Bag of Joy Toys .... EACH 39c

We Return the Difference if You Send Us Too Much Postage C101P-B3 **557**

Have a GOOD TIME!

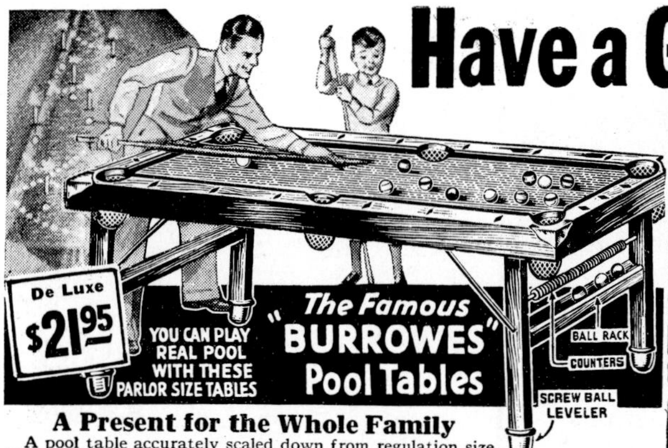
De Luxe
$21.95
YOU CAN PLAY REAL POOL WITH THESE PARLOR SIZE TABLES
The Famous "BURROWES" Pool Tables
BALL RACK
COUNTERS
SCREW BALL LEVELER

A Present for the Whole Family

A pool table accurately scaled down from regulation size. Mahogany color finish. Beds are of hard composition board fastened to the hardwood frame. Will not warp. Screw ball leveling feet, folding legs securely braced. Ball racks and counters. Diamond markers. Felt covered live rubber cushions. Unmailable.

De Luxe Parlor Set
71x37¾x32 In.
Fifteen 1¾-in. numbered balls, one cue ball, triangle, two 48-in. two prong cues, chalk and rule book. A very popular size. Shpg. wt., 80 lbs.
79 FM 492.......$21.95

Junior Apartment Set
60x31x30 In.
Fifteen 1½-in. **balls,** one cue ball, two **42-in. cues,** triangle, chalk and rule book. Nice size for small rooms, apartments, etc.
Shpg. wt., 35 lbs.
79 FM 493.......... $11.67

Juvenile Pool Tables (Not Illustrated)
Fiber board bed reinforced by four V-shaped steel girders. Fifteen numbered balls, and one cue ball. Wood triangle, **two 40-in. cues,** chalk and rule book. Green colored live rubber cushions.

Size, 55x29x28 Inches
1½-Inch Balls
79 FM 497
Shpg. wt., 26 lbs.. $8.95

Size, 50x28x26 Inches
1¼-Inch Balls
79 FM 495
Shpg. wt., 20 lbs.. $6.95

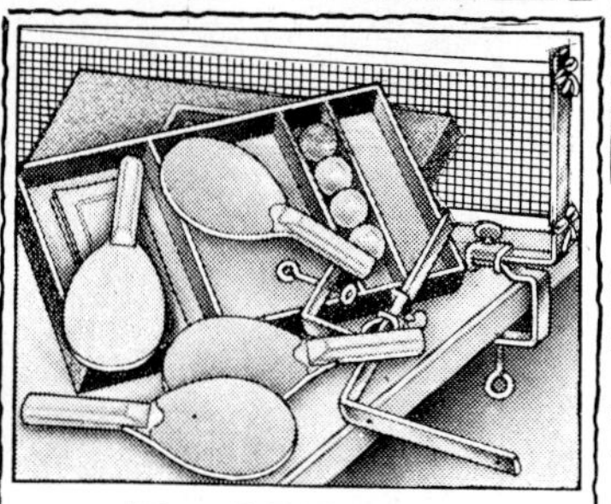

DeLuxe Table Tennis Set
3-ply bats, stained handles. Four bats 2 sanded and 2 rubber faced both sides. 66-in. net, 2 adjustable metal uprights, 8 English Balls. Instructions.
49 F 426—Shpg. wt., 2 lbs. 8 oz.................... $1.39

4-Bat Regular Table Tennis Set
66-in. net, 3-ply wood bats. 2 cork faced and 2 sanded on both sides. Adjustable metal uprights. 4 English balls.
49 F 425—Shpg. wt., 2 lbs. 4 oz 98c

4-Bat Low Priced Table Tennis Set
One side sanded. 60-in. net, metal uprights, 2 English Balls, Instructions.
49 F 424—Shpg. wt., 1 lb. 14 oz. 59c

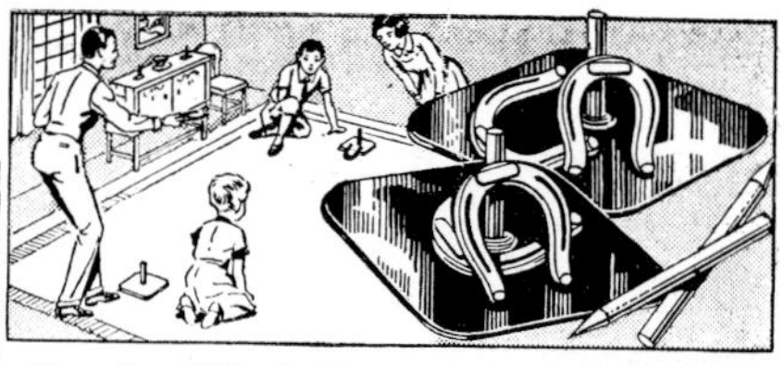

Popular "Pitch 'Em" Horse Shoe Game
How are you at pitching horseshoes? Try it with this set, indoors or out. Rubber horseshoes are 5⅜ inches long and reinforced with steel. Two wood pegs to use when playing out doors; nickel plated pegs in metal plates for indoors.
49 F 127—Shpg. wt., 3 lbs. 4 oz.......... 89c

Low Priced Horse Shoe Game: Similar to above but shoes are not reinforced. No outdoor pegs.
49 F 119—Shpg. wt., 2 lbs. 10 oz.......... 63c

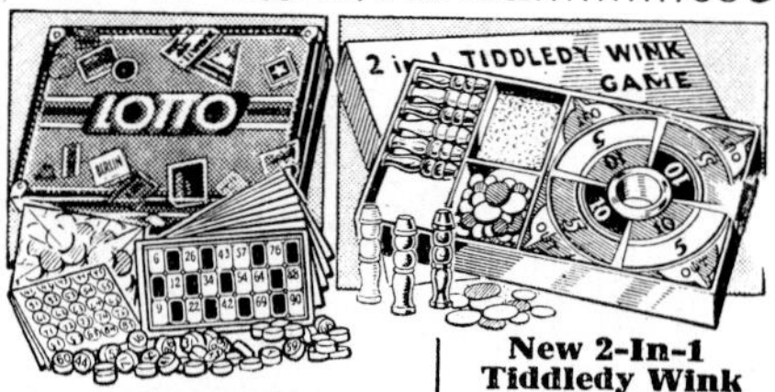
LOTTO
2 in 1 TIDDLEDY WINK GAME

Play Lotto
⅞-in. embossed wood discs. Trunk style box, 12x8½ in. 24 cards, 7x3⅞ in.
49 F 178—Shpg. wt., 1 lb. 14 oz....... 42c

Low Priced Lotto
⅝-in. wood discs, box, 8½x5¼ in. 24 cards, 7x3⅞ in.
49 F 176
Shpg. wt., 1 lb. 6 oz.. 22c

New 2-In-1 Tiddledy Wink Game
Ideal for Children's Parties. Snap the winks into the glass cup or knock down the **10 wooden Tiddledy Tots.** 3 felt pads. 12 colored winks. 3 can play. Lithographed box. 11½x6½ in. Shpg. wt., 1 lb.
49 F 206.... 29c

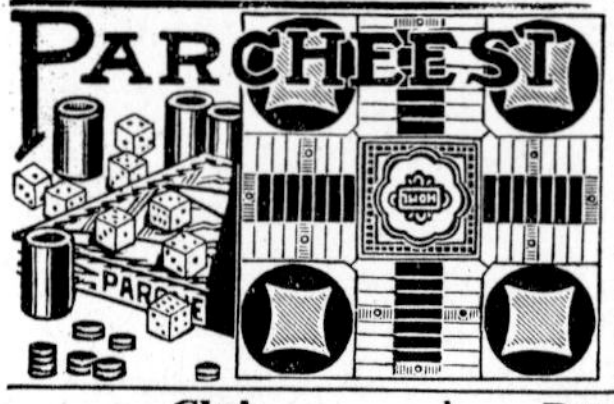
PARCHEESI

New Improved Parcheesi
America's Favorite Game for Half a Century
Folding board, **15⅝ in. square.** 4 dice cups, playing pieces and directions. Box, 16⅛x8$\frac{5}{16}$ in. Shpg. wt., 2 lbs.
49 F 101 89c

Club Parcheesi
Folding board **15½ in. sq.** Beautifully finished playing pieces. An extra heavy complete set for the expert. Regular $1.50 value. Shpg. wt., 1 lb. 12 oz.
49 F 109... $1.39

Parcheesi and Backgammon
Folding board **15¾ in. sq.** Playing surfaces on opposite sides. Playing pieces included. A game of real quality. A dandy gift. Shpg. wt., 2 lbs. 2 oz.
49 F 103..... $1.79

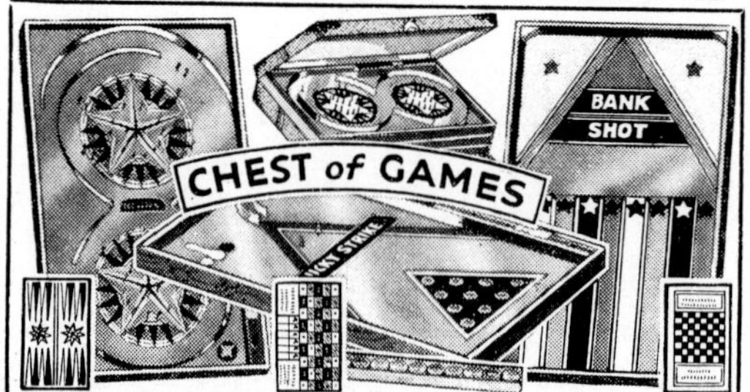
CHEST of GAMES
BANK SHOT

One of season's big hits! No end of fun with these six games. One game on each side of each board. **Bank Shot** and **Checkers** on one; **Lucky Strike and Horse Race game** on another; and **Bagatelle and Backgammon** on a third. Sizes of each, **15¼x9½ inches.** Mahogany colored metal rims. **Included are black and red checkers, marbles, spring shooter, pins, dice, betting chart and wire to adjust position.** Packed in gold color drop-front chest with hinged cover and snap lock.
49 F 122—Shpg. wt., 5 lbs. 4 oz.............. $1.19

Staunton Pattern French Chess Men
Varnished and Waxed
Finest grade clear white boxwood. Beautifully cut and finished. Imported from France.

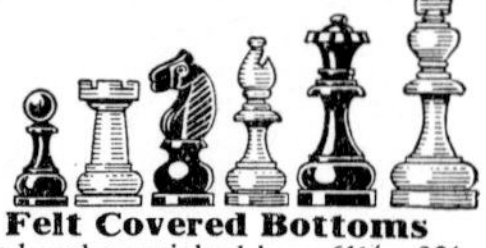

Weighted and Felt Covered Bottoms
In slide cover stained and varnished box, 6$\frac{11}{16}$x3¾x2⅝ in. **King 2⅞ in. high.**
49 F 204—Shpg. wt., 1 lb. 6 oz.......... $2.69

Without Weighted Bottoms
King 2½ in. tall. Otherwise same as 49 F 204. Shpg. wt., 1 lb.
49 F 203—Plain wood box............. $1.29

Hinged Chess and Checker Board
Flat folding board. Made of heavy pressed cardboard. Manila hinge. Shpg. wt., 1 lb. 6 oz.
49 F 201—**Size open, 16 in. sq**........... 25c

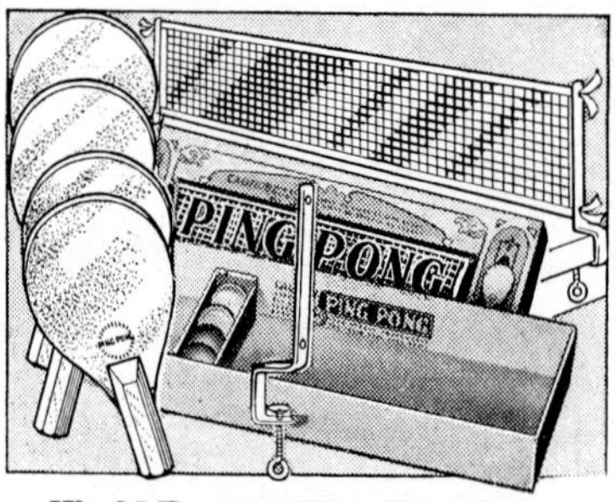
PING PONG
PING PONG

World Famous Ping Pong Sets
Everybody's Playing Ping Pong!

Regular Size
Set consists of four **3-ply veneer rackets both sides sanded;** 11¾x5¼ in. 60 in. net and 9-in. metal uprights. 4 English balls, 2 red and 2 white. Shpg. wt., 2 lbs. 2 oz.
49 F 435. $2.19

Junior Size
Set consists of **two bats, 3-ply veneer,** plain faced, size, 11½x5¼ inches. 2 white English balls; 60-inch net and with metal uprights. Shpg. wt., 1 lb. 8 oz.
49 F 434. $1.00

Genuine English Ping Pong Balls
49 F 436
Shpg. wt., 2 oz. 4 **White Balls**......... 36c

The Rage of the Nation

Sold by Mail Only at Sears

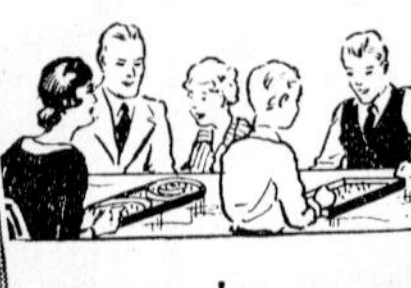

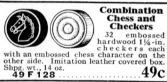

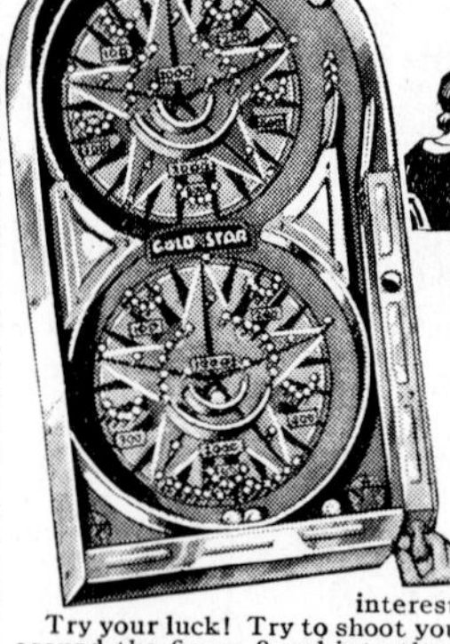
GOLD STAR

Famous Gold Star Bagatelle
$1.00
A very interesting game.
Try your luck! Try to shoot your marbles around the figure 8 and into the high number traps—then add up your score! Any number can play. Mahogany finished steel frame on ply-wood base. Highly polished. Strong spring releases one marble at a time. **23½x14 in.** Shpg. wt., 5 lbs.
79 F 236................. $1.00

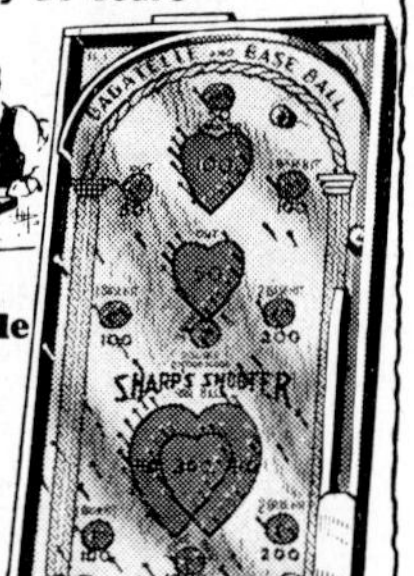
BAGATELLE AND BASE BALL
SHARP'S SHOOTER

Bagatelle and Base-ball Game
59c
Hi, baseball fans! See what kind of a score you make in this game! Shoot the marbles past the hazards into the high scores. 3-ply wood veneer; frame stained walnut color. **Size, 20½x11 in.** 5 marbles. Highly polished base. Shipping weight, 1 lb. 14 oz.
49 F 117........... 59c

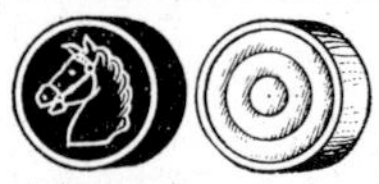

Combination Chess and Checkers
32 embossed hardwood 1¼-in. checkers each with an embossed chess character on the other side. Imitation leather covered box. Shpg. wt., 14 oz.
49 F 128.................. 49c

Backgammon and Checker Boards
Box Style
With each board we include equipment for playing checkers as well as backgammon.

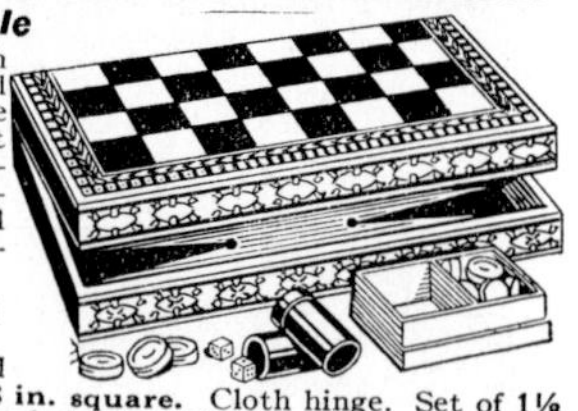

Our Best Board
Wood frame. **18 in. square.** Cloth hinge. Set of 1⅛ in. embossed checkers; 2 dice cups, 2 wood dice; rules. Shpg. wt., 1 lb. 14 oz.
49 F 194......................... 67c

Popular Priced Board
Box style folding **board, 15½x14¾ in.** with cardboard frame. Checkers 1 in. in diam. Cup and 2 wood dice. Not illustrated.
49 F 193—Shpg. wt., 1 lb. 2 oz..... 29c

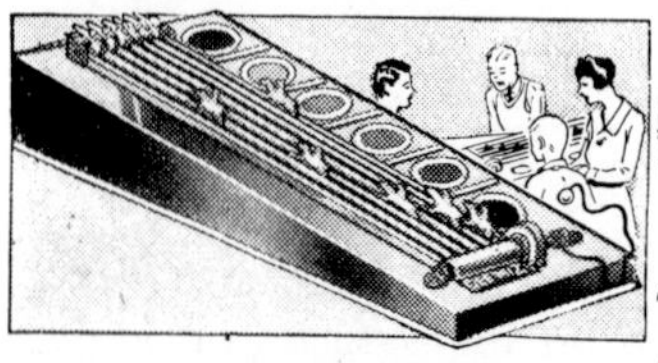

Gee Wiz Horse Race Game
Pick your horse! Watch him race down the stretch and come in a winner. Here's entertainment for a whole crowd—grown-ups or children. Every horse has the same chance. No two races alike. Just spin the axle like a top. Directions for five different forms of play included. Heavy gauge metal with a heavy coat of baked-on enamel Revolving parts of game are accurately machined. Can stand the abuse of a crowd. Everybody likes to "play the races"—this way. **Size, 15x6¾-in.** Shipping weight, 2 lbs. 12 oz.
49 F 107................ $1.79

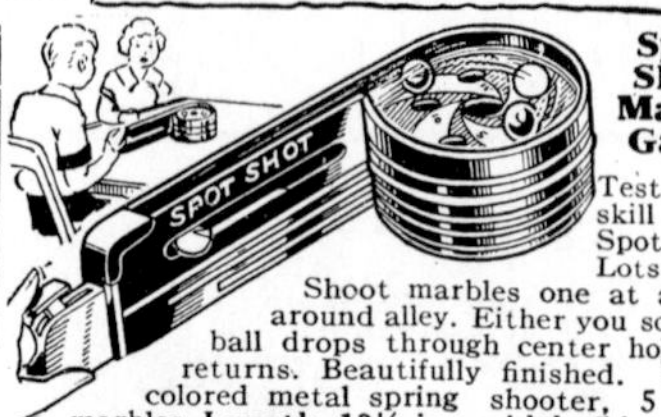
SPOT SHOT

Spot Shot Marble Game
Test your skill with Spot Shot! Lots of fun! Shoot marbles one at a time around alley. Either you score or ball drops through center hole and returns. Beautifully finished. Bright colored metal spring shooter, 5 glass marbles. **Length, 13½ in.; width, 5 in.**
49 F 212—Shpg. wt., 1 lb. 4 oz..... 45c

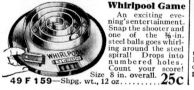

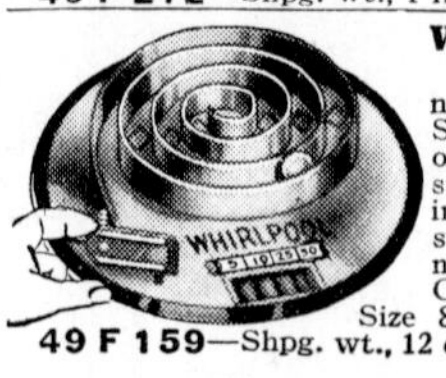
WHIRLPOOL

Whirlpool Game
An exciting evening's entertainment. Snap the shooter and one of the ⅜-in. steel balls goes whirling around the steel spiral! Drops into numbered holes. Count your score! Size 8 in. overall.
49 F 159—Shpg. wt., 12 oz......... 25c

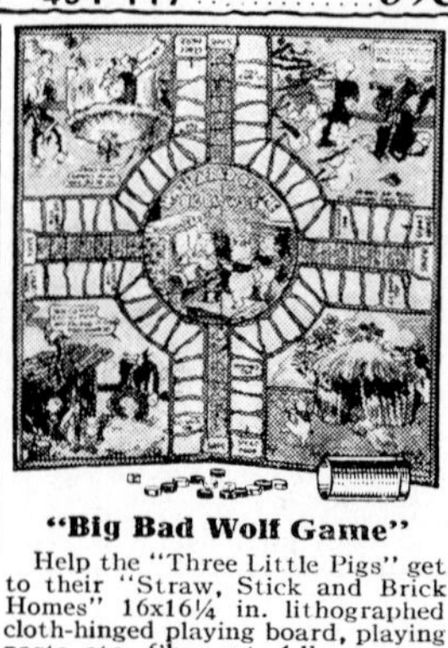

"Big Bad Wolf Game"
Help the "Three Little Pigs" get to their "Straw, Stick and Brick Homes" 16x16¼ in. lithographed cloth-hinged playing board, playing parts, etc. Shpg. wt. 1 lb.
49 F 129............. 45c

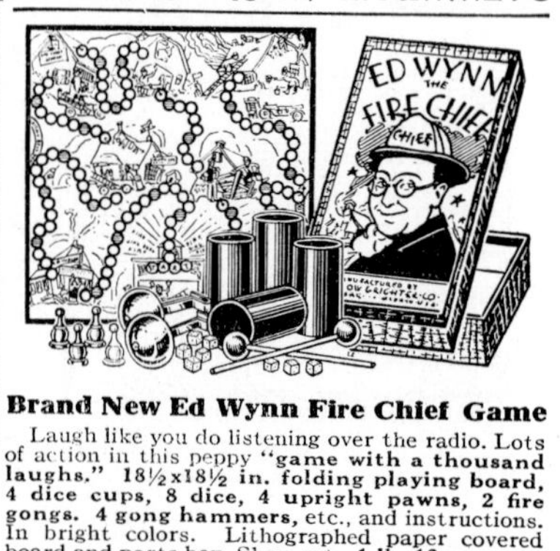

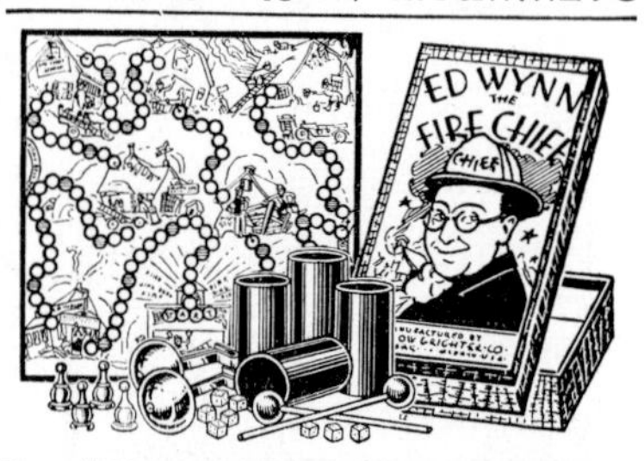
ED WYNN THE FIRE CHIEF
CHIEF

Brand New Ed Wynn Fire Chief Game
Laugh like you do listening over the radio. Lots of action in this peppy **"game with a thousand laughs." 18½x18½ in. folding playing board, 4 dice cups, 8 dice, 4 upright pawns, 2 fire gongs. 4 gong hammers,** etc., and instructions. In bright colors. Lithographed paper covered board and parts box. Shpg. wt., 1 lb. 12 oz.
49 F 207......................... 89c

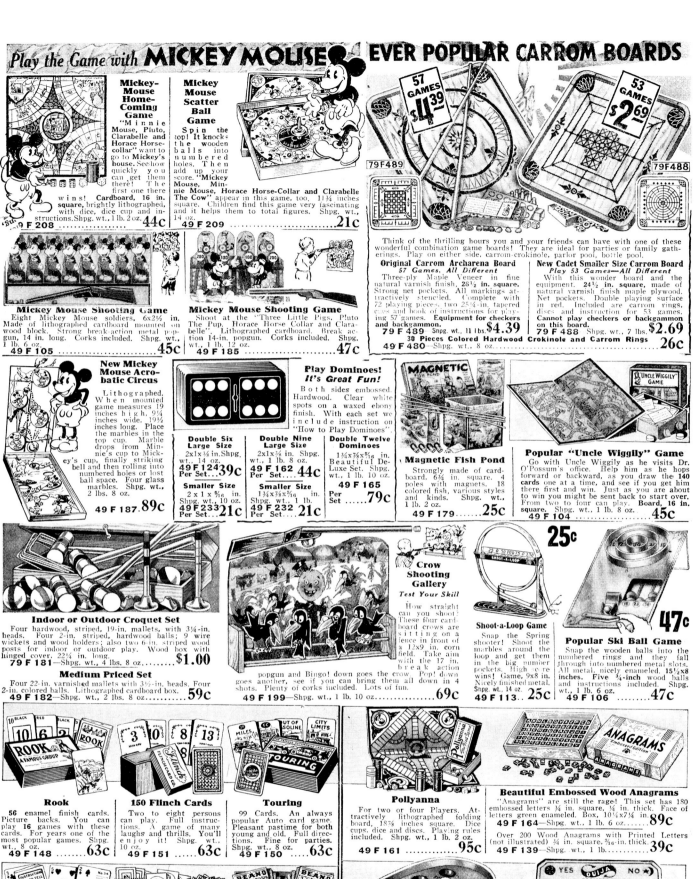

Play the Game with MICKEY MOUSE

EVER POPULAR CARROM BOARDS

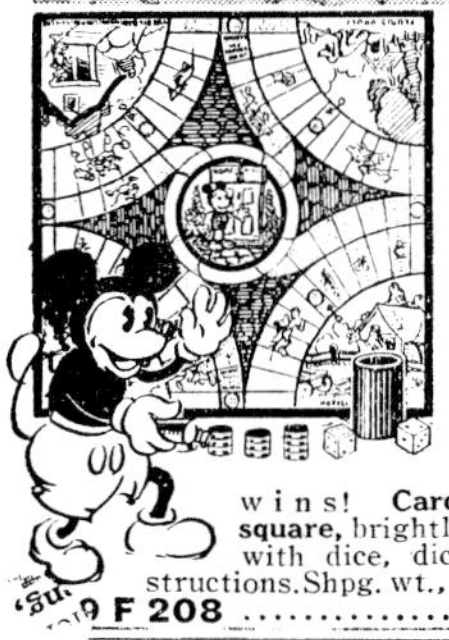

Mickey-Mouse Home-Coming Game

"Minnie Mouse, Pluto, Clarabelle and Horace Horse-collar" want to go to Mickey's house. See how quickly you can get them there! The first one there wins! **Cardboard, 16 in. square,** brightly lithographed, with dice, dice cup and instructions. Shpg. wt., 1 lb. 2 oz.
49 F 208 .... **44c**

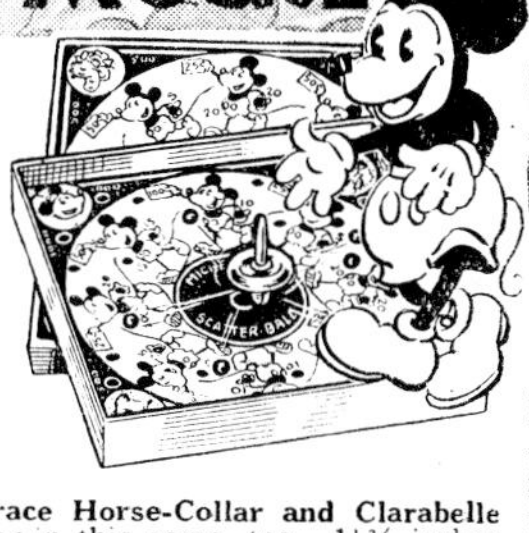

Mickey Mouse Scatter Ball Game

Spin the top! It knocks the wooden balls into numbered holes. Then add up your score. "Mickey Mouse, Minnie Mouse, Horace Horse-Collar and Clarabelle The Cow" appear in this game, too. 11¾ inches square. Children find this game very fascinating and it helps them to total figures. Shpg. wt., 14 oz.
49 F 209 .... **21c**

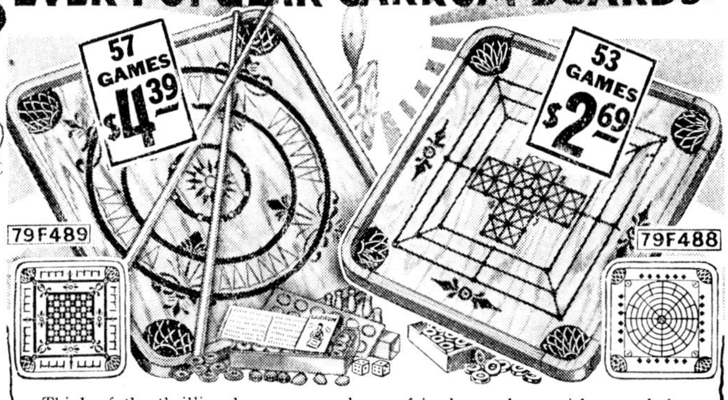

Think of the thrilling hours you and your friends can have with one of these wonderful combination game boards! They are ideal for parties or family gatherings. Play on either side, carrom-crokinole, parlor pool, bottle pool.

Original Carrom Archarena Board
57 Games, All Different

Three-ply Maple Veneer in fine natural varnish finish, 28½ **in. square.** Strong net pockets. All markings attractively stenciled. Complete with 72 playing pieces, two 25¼-in. tapered cues and book of instructions for playing 57 games. **Equipment for checkers and backgammon.**
79 F 489—Shpg. wt., 11 lbs. **$4.39**

New Cadet Smaller Size Carrom Board
Play 53 Games—All Different

With this wonder board and the equipment. 24½ **in. square,** made of natural varnish finish maple plywood. Net pockets. Double playing surface in red. Included are carrom rings, discs and instruction for 53 games. **Cannot play checkers or backgammon on this board.**
79 F 488 Shpg. wt., 7 lbs. **$2.69**

30 Pieces Colored Hardwood Crokinole and Carrom Rings
49 F 480—Shpg. wt., 8 oz. **26c**

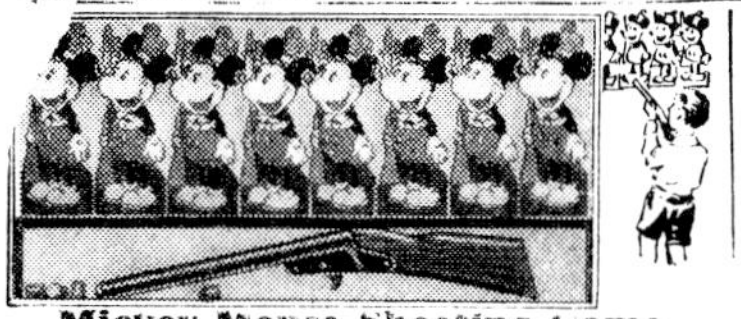

Mickey Mouse Shooting Game

Eight Mickey Mouse soldiers, 6x2½ in. Made of lithographed cardboard mounted on wood block. Strong break-action metal popgun, 14 in. long. Corks included. Shpg. wt., 1 lb. 6 oz.
49 F 105 .... **45c**

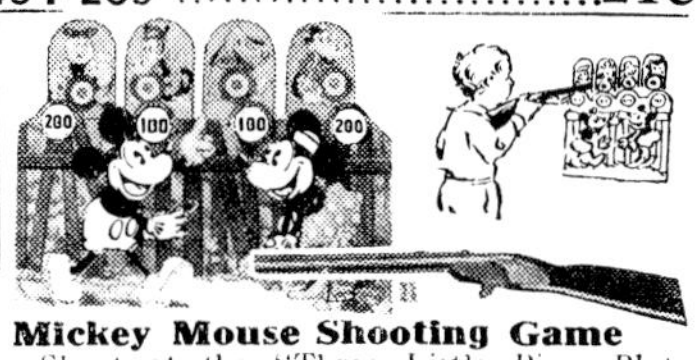

Mickey Mouse Shooting Game

Shoot at the "Three Little Pigs, Pluto The Pup, Horace Horse Collar and Clarabelle". Lithographed cardboard. Break action 14-in. popgun. Corks included. Shpg. wt., 1 lb. 12 oz.
49 F 185 .... **47c**

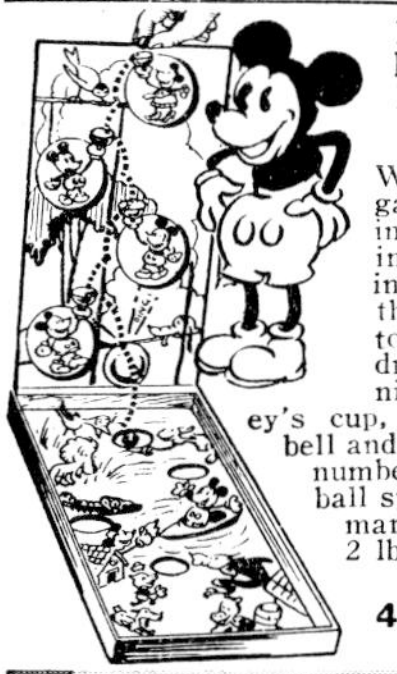

New Mickey Mouse Acrobatic Circus

Lithographed. When mounted game measures 19 inches high, 9¼ inches wide, 19½ inches long. Place the marbles in the top cup. Marble drops from Minnie's cup to Mickey's cup, finally striking bell and then rolling into numbered holes or lost ball space. Four glass marbles. Shpg. wt., 2 lbs. 8 oz.
49 F 187 **89c**

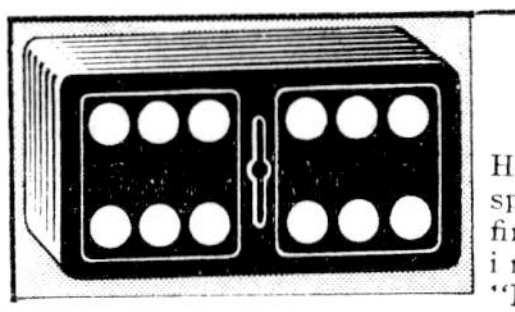

Play Dominoes! *It's Great Fun!*

Both sides embossed. Hardwood. Clear white spots on a waxed ebony finish. With each set we include instruction on "How to Play Dominoes".

Double Six Large Size
2x1x¼ in. Shpg. wt., 14 oz.
49 F 124 Per Set... **39c**

Smaller Size
2x1x5/16 in. Shpg. wt., 10 oz.
49 F 233 Per Set... **21c**

Double Nine Large Size
2x1x¼ in. Shpg. wt., 1 lb. 8 oz.
49 F 162 Per Set... **44c**

Smaller Size
1¾x⅞x5/16 in. Shpg. wt., 1 lb.
49 F 232 Per Set... **21c**

Double Twelve Dominoes
1¾x⅞x5/16 in. Beautiful De-Luxe Set. Shpg. wt., 1 lb. 10 oz.
49 F 165 Per Set **79c**

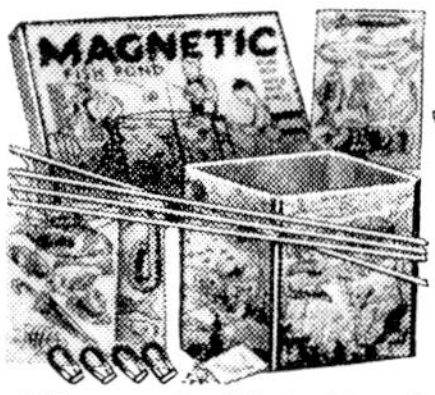

Magnetic Fish Pond

Strongly made of cardboard. 6¾ in. square. 4 poles with magnets. 18 colored fish, various styles and kinds. Shpg. wt., 1 lb. 2 oz.
49 F 179 ...... **25c**

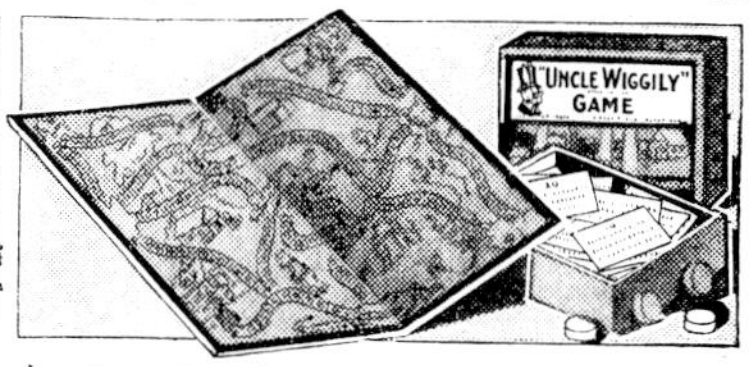

Popular "Uncle Wiggily" Game

Go with Uncle Wiggily as he visits Dr. O'Possum's office. Help him as he hops forward or backward, as you draw the **140 cards** one at a time, and see if you get him there first and win. Just as you are about to win you might be sent back to start over. From two to four can play. **Board, 16 in. square.** Shpg. wt., 1 lb. 8 oz.
49 F 104 .... **45c**

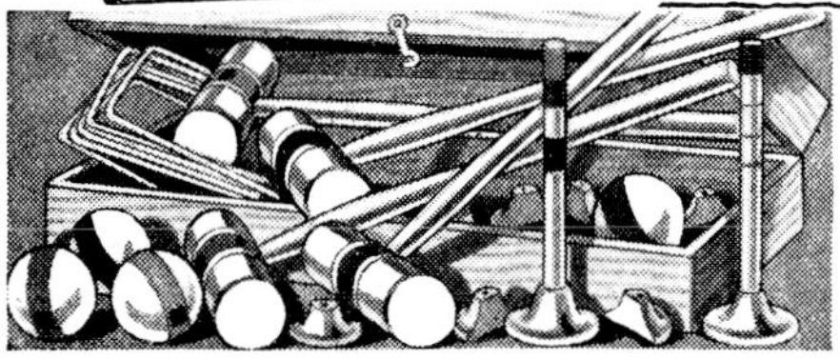

Indoor or Outdoor Croquet Set

Four hardwood, striped, 19-in. mallets, with 3¼-in. heads. Four 2-in. striped, hardwood balls; 9 wire wickets and wood holders; also two 6-in. striped wood posts for indoor or outdoor play. Wood box with hinged cover, 22¼ in. long.
79 F 181—Shpg. wt., 4 lbs. 8 oz......... **$1.00**

Medium Priced Set

Four 22-in. varnished mallets with 3½-in. heads. Four 2-in. colored balls. Lithographed cardboard box.
49 F 182—Shpg. wt., 2 lbs. 8 oz............ **59c**

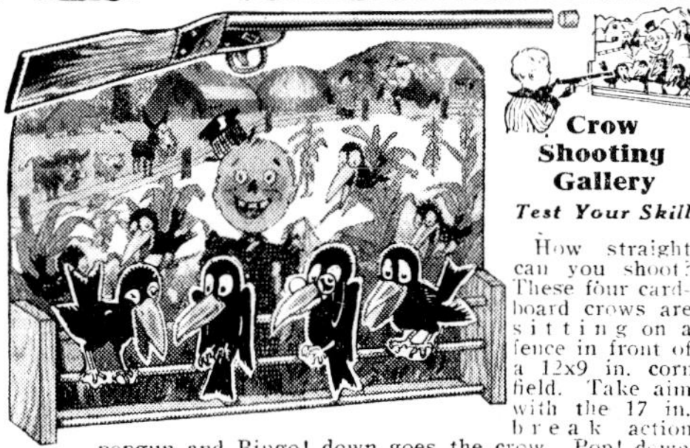

Crow Shooting Gallery
Test Your Skill

How straight can you shoot? These four cardboard crows are sitting on a fence in front of a 12x9 in. corn field. Take aim with the 17 in. break action popgun and Bingo! down goes the crow. Pop! down goes another, see if you can bring them all down in 4 shots. Plenty of corks included. Lots of fun.
49 F 199—Shpg. wt., 1 lb. 10 oz................ **69c**

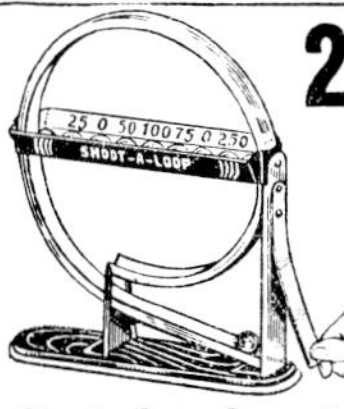

25c

Shoot-a-Loop Game

Snap the Spring shooter! Shoot the marbles around the loop and get them in the big number pockets. High score wins! Game, 9x8 in. Nicely finished metal. Shpg. wt., 14 oz.
49 F 113.. **25c**

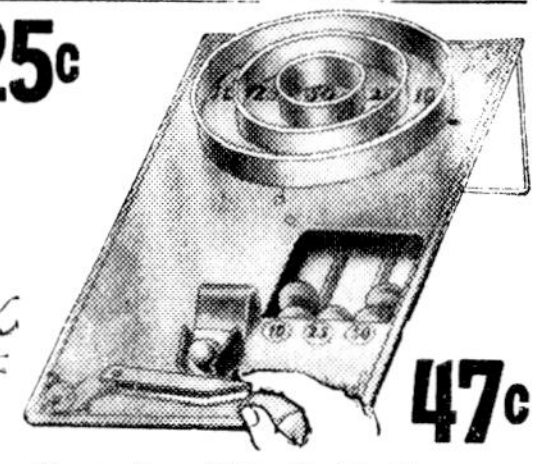

47c

Popular Ski Ball Game

Snap the wooden balls into the numbered rings and they fall through into numbered metal slots. All metal, nicely enameled. **15½x8 inches. Five ¾-inch** wood balls and instructions included. Shpg. wt., 1 lb. 6 oz.
49 F 106 .... **47c**

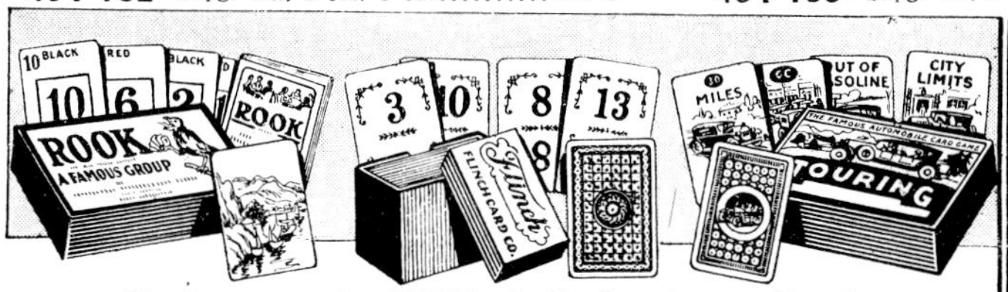

Rook

56 enamel finish cards. Picture backs. You can play **16** games with these cards. For years one of the most popular games. Shpg. wt., 8 oz.
49 F 148 .... **63c**

150 Flinch Cards

Two to eight persons can play. Full instructions. A game of many laughs and thrills. You'll enjoy it! Shpg. wt., 10 oz.
49 F 151 ...... **63c**

Touring

99 Cards. An always popular Auto card game. Pleasant pastime for both young and old. Full directions. Fine for parties. Shpg. wt., 8 oz.
49 F 150 ...... **63c**

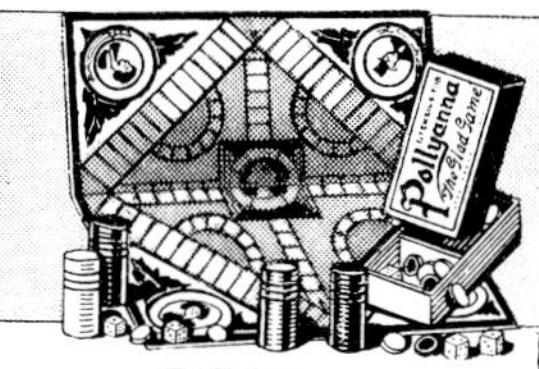

Pollyanna

For two or four Players. Attractively lithographed folding board, 18¾ inches square. Dice cups, dice and discs. Playing rules included. Shpg. wt., 1 lb. 2 oz.
49 F 161 .... **95c**

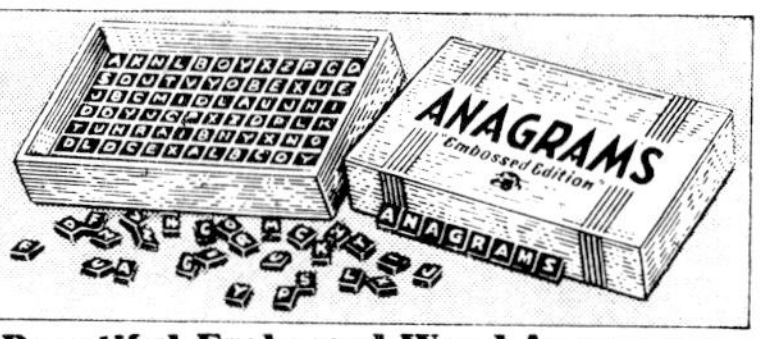

Beautiful Embossed Wood Anagrams

"Anagrams" are still the rage! This set has 180 embossed letters ¾ in. square, ¼ in. thick. Face of letters green enameled. Box, 10¼x7¼ in.
49 F 164—Shpg. wt., 1 lb. 6 oz....... **89c**

Over 200 Wood Anagrams with Printed Letters (not illustrated) ¾ in. square, 3/16-in. thick.
49 F 139—Shpg. wt., 1 lb............ **39c**

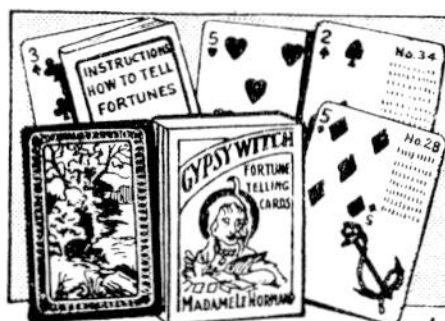

Gypsy Witch Fortune Telling Cards

Very easy to tell fortunes. Learn how with this full deck of cards. Complete instructions. Will give you hours of fun. Shpg. wt., 4 oz.
49 F 153...... **53c**

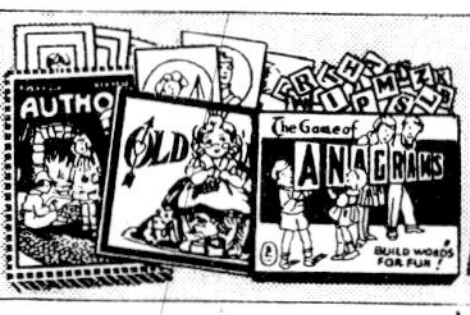

3-Game Assortment

Authors and Old Maid each with 31 white, round cornered cards in bright colors. **Anagrams, with 215** cardboard letters ¾ in. square. In colorful boxes, 6½x5⅛ in. Shpg. wt., 10 oz.
49 F 198—**3** for **21c**

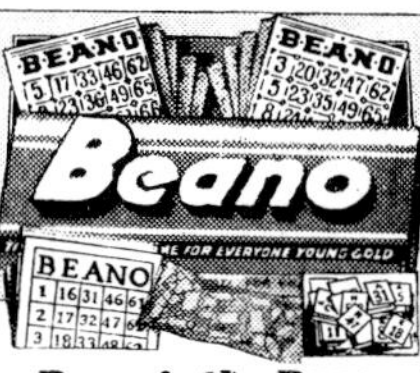

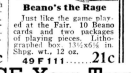

Beano's the Rage

Just like the game played at the Fair. 10 Beano cards and two packages of playing pieces. Lithographed box. 13½x6⅛ in. Shpg. wt., 12 oz.
49 F 111 .... **21c**

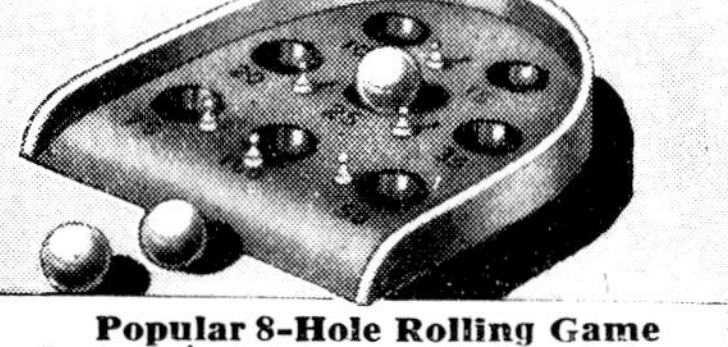

Popular 8-Hole Rolling Game

Looks easy, but just try it! Your ball may hit one of the obstacles and prevent a score. Cherry color wood. **14⅜x13½x⅞ in. Three 2-in.** hardwood balls.
49 F 170—Shpg. wt., 4 lbs........ **79c**

All Steel, 8-Holes, No Obstacles. Size 12x11⅝ in. Finished in 2 colors. Three 2-in. wood balls.
49 F 174—Shpg. wt., 3 lbs........ **47c**

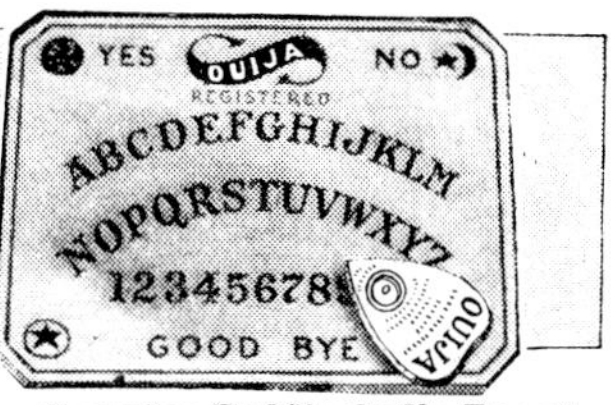

Genuine Fuld's Ouija Board

Apparently answers questions concerning spirit world, past, present, and future. Has Fuld's patented transparent indicator. Selected plywood. Natural varnish finish. **15x22 in.** Shpg. wt., 3 lbs. 4 oz.
49 F 112 .... **$1.19**

Larger Orders REDUCE Your Transportation Cost per Pound

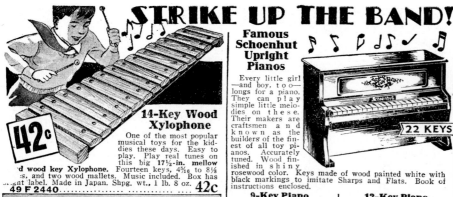

STRIKE UP THE BAND!

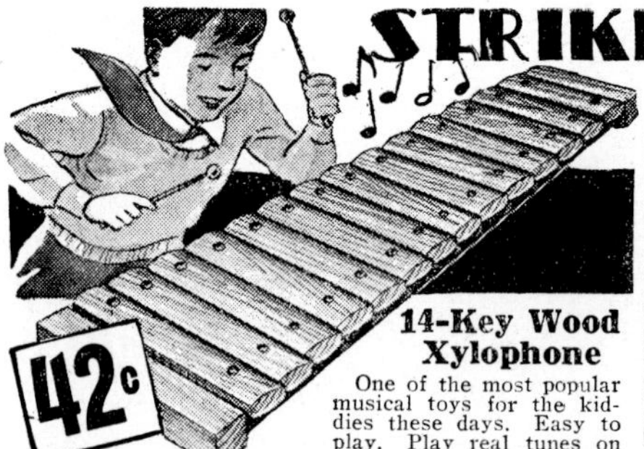

14-Key Wood Xylophone

One of the most popular musical toys for the kiddies these days. Easy to play. Play real tunes on this big 17½-in. mellow ...d wood key Xylophone. Fourteen keys, 4 5/16 to 8⅛ ...s, and two wood mallets. Music included. Box has ...gnt label. Made in Japan. Shpg. wt., 1 lb. 8 oz.
49 F 2440 .... **42c**

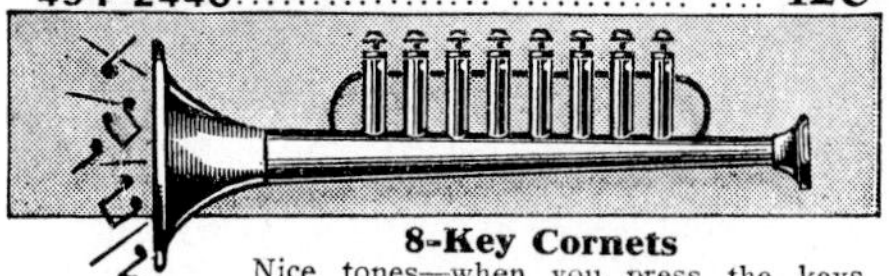

8-Key Cornets

Nice tones—when you press the keys and blow! Modeled after latest orchestra cornets. Gold color finish metal. Produces accurate tones. **16½ in. long, with 4¼-in. bell.** Music included. Metal mouthpiece. Made in Czechoslovakia. Shpg. wt., 1 lb. 8 oz.
49 F 2391 .... **$1.19**

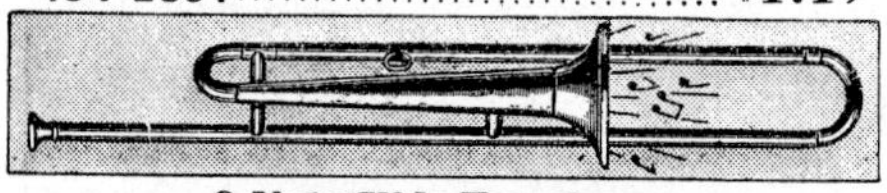

8-Note Slide Trombone

Music included. **28¾ in. long extended.** Gold color finish metal. Accurately tuned. Made in Czechoslovakia.
49 F 2317—Shpg. wt., 1 lb. 12 oz. **$1.00**

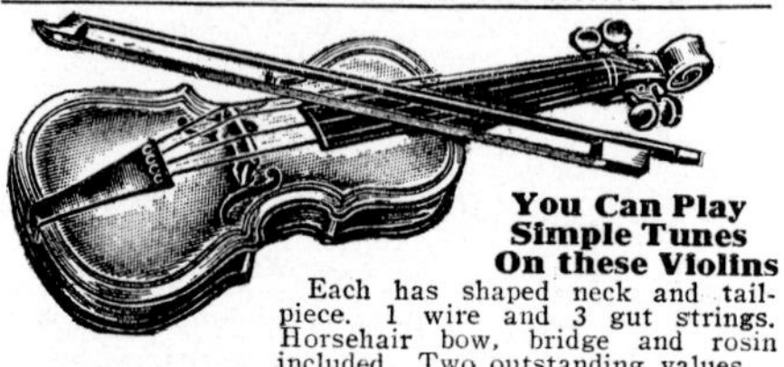

You Can Play Simple Tunes On these Violins

Each has shaped neck and tailpiece. 1 wire and 3 gut strings. Horsehair bow, bridge and rosin included. Two outstanding values.

Wood Violin
18¾ in. long. 5¾ in. wide. Cherry color. Kiln dried wood. Has 17½-in. adjustable horsehair bow. Made in Germany. Shpg. wt., 1 lb. 8 oz.
49 F 2331 .. **$2.29**

Metal Violin
17 in. long. 5½ in. wide. Cherry colored. 15¾-in. adjustable horsehair bow. Made in Czechoslovakia. Shpg. wt., 1 lb. 12 oz.
49 F 2334 .. **$1.00**

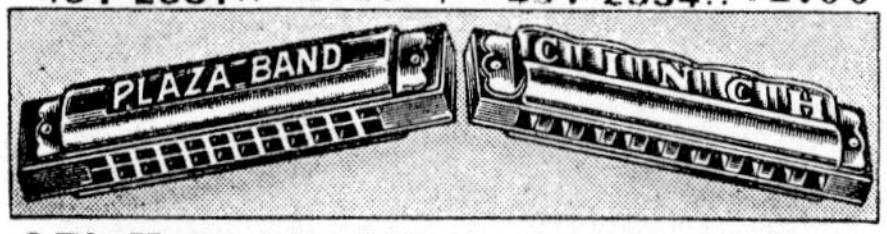

PLAZA BAND

2 Big Harmonica Values—Accurately Tuned

Good construction. Beautiful nickel plated finishes. **Assorted styles.** Accurately tuned. Made in Germany.

24 Brassed Reed Harmonica
Tremola. Length, about 4½ in. Shpg. wt., 4 oz.
49 F 2348 .... **20c**

18-Reed Harmonica
Length, about 4 in. Easy to blow. Shpg. wt., 4 oz.
49 F 2345 .... **14c**

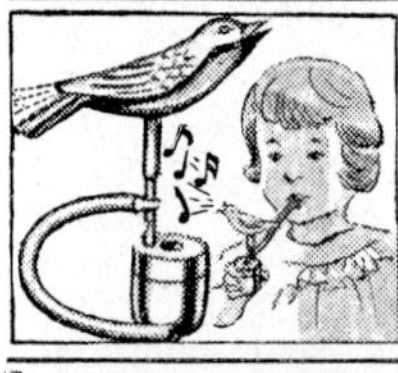

Warbling Bird Whistler

Surprising what you can do with these warbling canaries. Place a little water in bottom of brassed songster—blow—and you'll hear a sound like a warbling canary! Tots love them. Brass finish; 4 in. high. Shpg. wt., 4 oz.
49 F 2490—**2** for **23c**

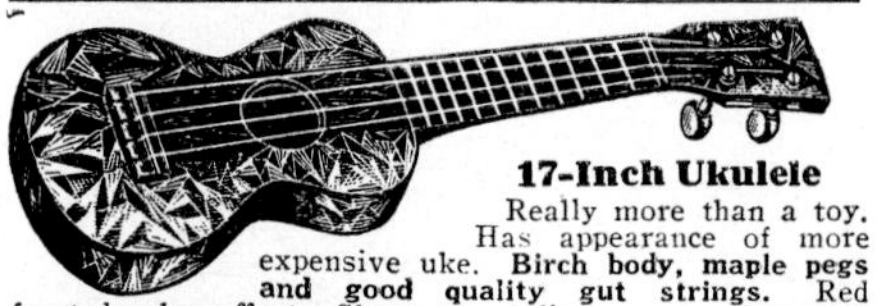

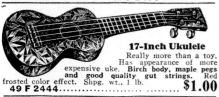

17-Inch Ukulele

Really more than a toy. Has appearance of more expensive uke. **Birch body, maple pegs and good quality gut strings.** Red frosted color effect. Shpg. wt., 1 lb.
49 F 2444 .... **$1.00**

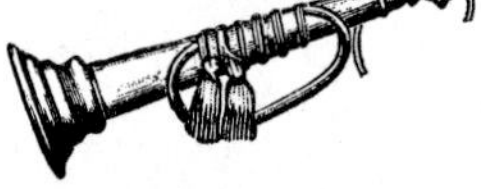

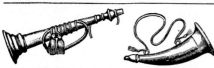

Nickel Plated Trumpet

All metal. **Has 2 notes.** Gilt trimmed chenille cord with 2 tassels. **Length, 12 in. 3½-in. bell.** Metal grip. Made in Czechoslovakia. Shpg. wt., 12 oz.
49 F 2390 .... **29c**

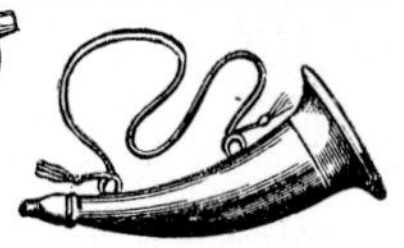

Little Boy Blue Horn

Enameled metal with cord for hanging over shoulder. **Has 2 notes. 8¼ in. long, 2¾ in. diam. bell. Wood mouthpiece.** Made in Germany. Shpg. wt., 6 oz.
49 F 2385 .... **29c**

Famous Schoenhut Upright Pianos

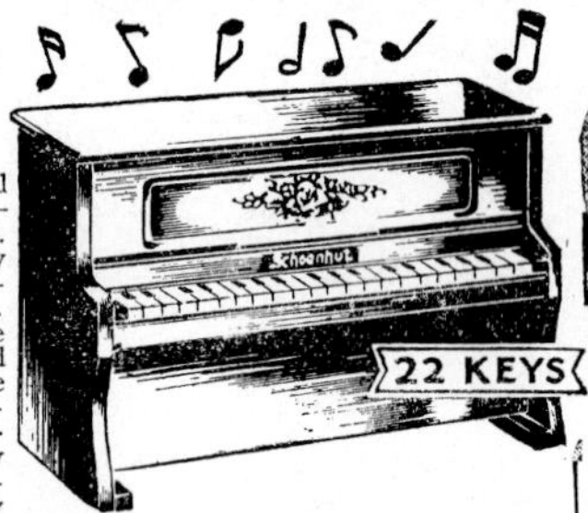

Schoenhut
22 KEYS

Every little girl—and boy, too—longs for a piano. They can play simple little melodies on these. Their makers are craftsmen and known as the builders of the finest of all toy pianos. Accurately tuned. Wood finished in shiny rosewood color. Keys made of wood painted white with black markings to imitate Sharps and Flats. Book of instructions enclosed.

9-Key Piano
49 F 2402 — Length, 10½ inches; Height, 6¾ inches; Depth, 5 inches. Shpg. wt., 3 lbs. 8 oz. **95c**

12-Key Piano
49 F 2403 — Length, 13¼ inches; Height, 8¼ inches; Depth, 6½ inches. Shpg. wt., 4 lbs. 8 oz. **$1.49**

14-Key Piano
79 F 2404 — Length, 15 inches; Height, 9½ inches; Depth, 6½ inches. Shpg. wt., 6 lbs. 8 oz. **$1.98**

22-Key Piano
79 F 2405 — Length, 23¼ inches; Height 13⅛ inches; Depth, 9¼ inches. Shpg. wt., 19 lbs. **$4.59**

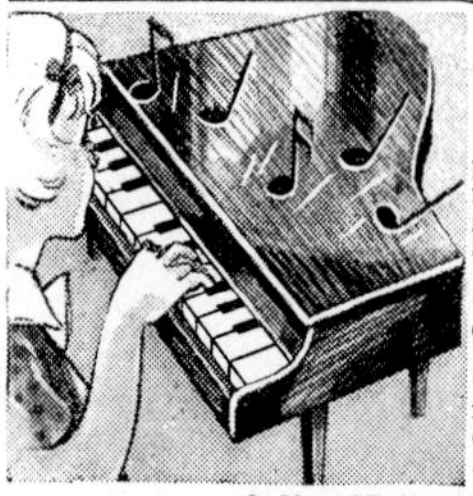

New Mello-Tone Pianos

They'll love these new pianos. A new development in piano making that gives a new Mello-tone—a chime-like sound. Wood finished in shiny rosewood color; keys made of wood, painted to look like natural sharps and flats. Book of instructions included. Simple melodies can be played on them. Accurately tuned.

8-Key Mello-Tone Piano
Size, 9⅛ in. wide, 10 in. deep, 5¾ in. high.
49 F 2414—Shpg. wt., 3 lbs. 8 oz. **$1.10**

12-Key Mello-Tone Piano
5¾ in. high, 12⅞ in. wide, 12¼ in. deep.
49 F 2415—Shpg. wt., 4 lbs. 8 oz. **$1.79**

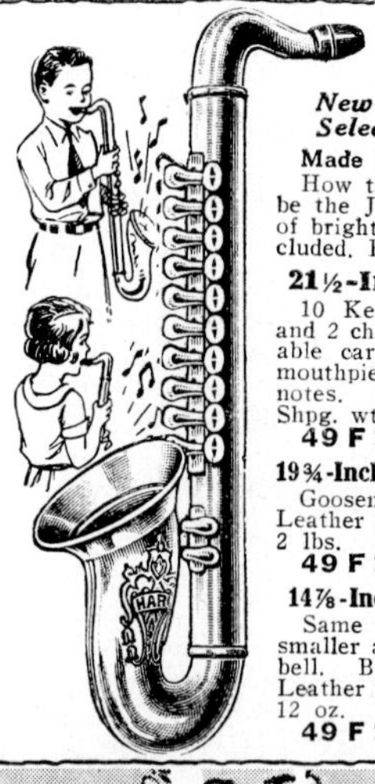

Toy Saxophones

New Gold Color Finish
Selected Tuned Reeds

Made in Czechoslovakia.
How this sax can play! You'll be the Jazz King with this one of bright metal. Sheet music included. Exceptional quality.

21½-Inch Sax—20 Notes
10 Keys that play 20 notes, and 2 chord bass notes. Adjustable carrying cord. Has wood mouthpiece. Accurately tuned notes. Leather padded keys. Shpg. wt., 3 lbs.
49 F 2478 .... **$1.89**

19¾-Inch Sax—10 Notes, 2 Bass
Gooseneck. Wood mouthpiece. Leather padded keys. Shpg. wt., 2 lbs.
49 F 2472 .... **$1.00**

14⅞-Inch Sax—8 Note—8 Key
Same quality materials but smaller and fewer notes. 2½ in. bell. Black wood mouthpiece. Leather padded keys. Shpg. wt., 12 oz.
49 F 2473 .... **69c**

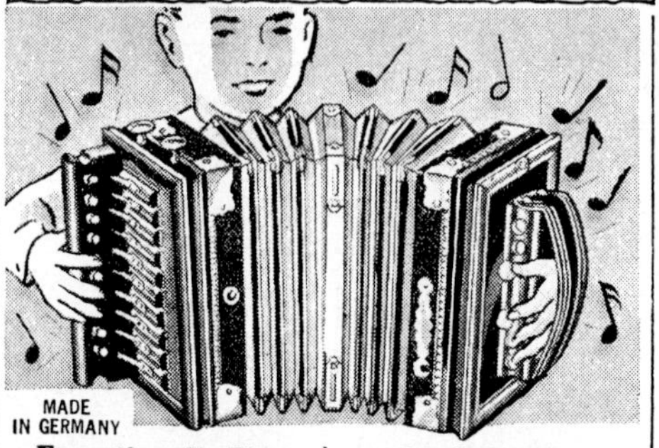

MADE IN GERMANY

Exceptionally Fine Quality Toy Accordion

Pleasing tone, neat workmanship and fine finish. Accurately tuned. Black enameled wood frame. Double bellows. Plays **20 treble notes and 2 bass harmony notes. Size closed, 9¼x8x4½ in.** Shpg. wt., 3 lbs. 8 oz. Made in Germany.
49 F 2371 .... **$2.59**

Good Quality 20-Note Accordion

10 double reed metal keys, 20 notes, 2 bass. Enameled metal frame. Accurately tuned. Nicely finished. Size closed, 9⅞x4 11/16 in. Made in Germany. Shipping weight, 1 pound 14 ounces.
49 F 2367 .... **$1.39**

Low Priced 16-Note Accordion

8-treble keys plays 16 notes, also has 1 bass key. Sturdily constructed. Accurately tuned. **Size closed, 10x4½ in.** Made in Germany. Shpg. wt., 1 lb.
49 F 2355 .... **79c**

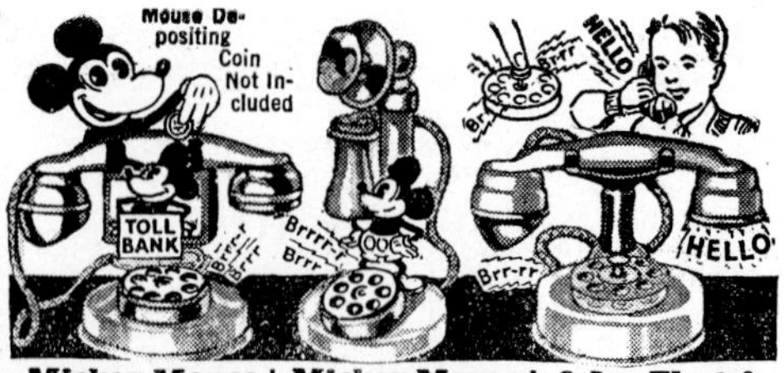

Mouse Depositing Coin Not included
TOLL BANK
HELLO

Mickey Mouse Bank Phone

A bell rings when you dial numbers. Enameled metal. It's a 3-coin bank, too! Nickeled bell receiver and mouthpiece. **8½-in. long.**
49 F 2456
Shpg. wt., 1 lb. 8 oz. **59c**

Mickey Mouse Upright Phone

Dial your number and hear the phone ring! Nickel plated dial, mouthpiece and receiver hook; wood receiver; enameled base. **Height, 8 inches.**
49 F 2455
Shpg. wt., 8 oz. **29c**

8-In. Electric Dial Phone

With battery and electric bell which produces sound of real telephone bell. When receiver is placed to ear, the patented voice says "Hello."
49 F 2458
Shpg. wt., 1 lb. 8 oz. **89c**

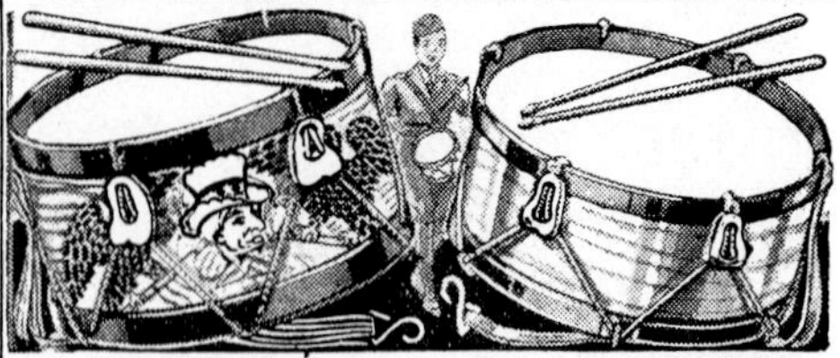

13-Inch Low Priced Drum

Drum a march on it. This drum has two metal hoops, 2 processed fabric heads which give a nice drum-like tone and are exceptionally tough and strong, inside snare, leather ears, pair of drum sticks. Diameter, **13 in.** Shpg. wt., 2 lbs.
79 F 2485 .... **98c**

12-In. Real Calfskin Head Drum

Real cherry wood drum with real calfskin head and bottom. Heavy web carrying strap, and 2 drum sticks. Black enameled hoops; 3 inside snares. Leather ears control the tension.
Shpg. wt., 2 lbs.
79 F 2486 **$1.98**

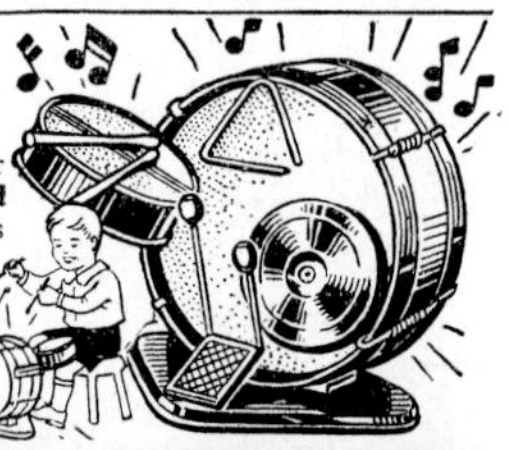

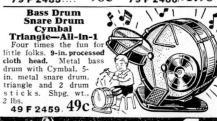

Bass Drum Snare Drum Cymbal Triangle—All-in-1

Four times the fun for little folks. **9-in. processed cloth head.** Metal bass drum with Cymbal, 5-in. metal snare drum, triangle and 2 drum sticks. Shpg. wt., 2 lbs.
49 F 2459 **49c**

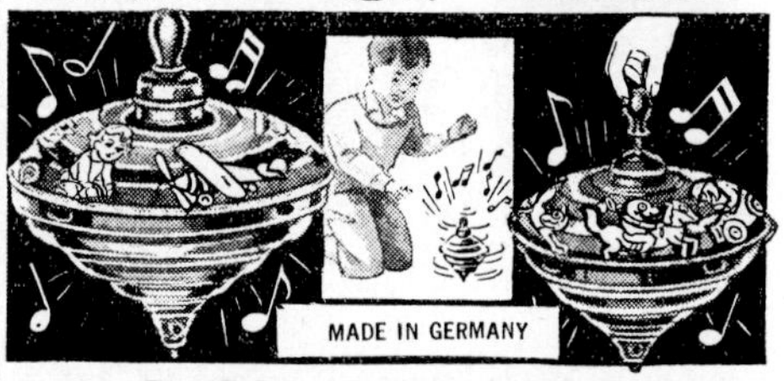

MADE IN GERMANY

Gay Colored Musical Metal Tops

Large Size
Makes music while it spins! One musical chord. Metal, lithographed in juvenile pictures. Spin it by pulling up handle and pushing down several times. **9 in. high, 8¼ in. across.** Shpg. wt., 1 lb.
49 F 2375 .... **59c**

Smaller Size
So easy to spin! No string or spring! Just pull up handle and push down several times. Spins with a musical sound. One chord. Juvenile lithograph pictures on metal. **7¼ in. high; 6¼ in. in** diameter. Shipping weight, 12 oz.
49 F 2376 ... **33c**

Musical Chimes

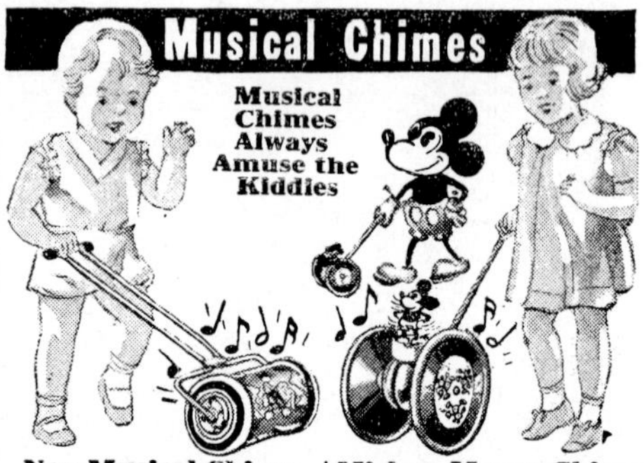

Musical Chimes Always Amuse the Kiddies

New Musical Chime

Just the thing for baby. Color and noise. Pull it along and hear the metal chimes! Bright scenic designs lithographed on metal. Made in Germany.
24 inches long, including handle; 7½ inches wide. Shpg. wt., 1 lb.
49 F 2420 .... **47c**

Mickey Mouse Chime

All Kiddies like Mickey Mouse Toys. Hear the tinkly chime as you wheel it along. Mickey Mouse rides on top of the bell ornament. Red enameled metal; 3-in. nickel plated bell. **21 in. long overall.** 8 in. high. Shpg. wt., 1 lb. 8 oz.
49 F 2434 ... **33c**

BE SURE to Include Sufficient POSTAGE With Your Order

FOR THE LITTLE HOUSEKEEPER

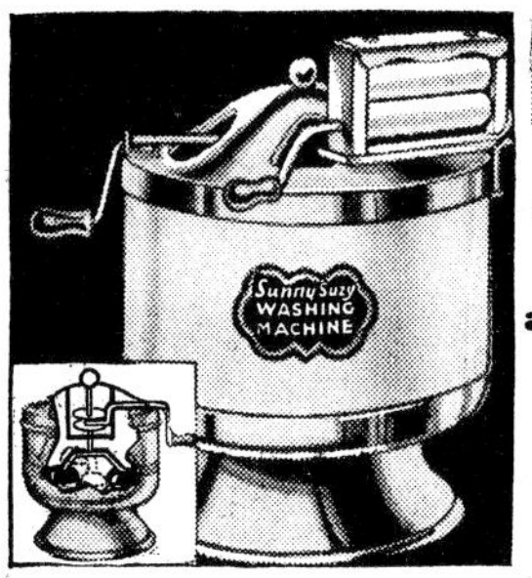

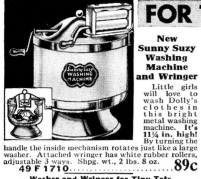

New Sunny Suzy Washing Machine and Wringer

Little girls will love to wash Dolly's clothes in this bright metal washing machine. **It's 11¼ in. high!** By turning the handle the inside mechanism rotates just like a large washer. Attached wringer has white rubber rollers, adjustable 3 ways. Shpg. wt., 2 lbs. 8 oz.
49 F 1710.................. **89c**

Washer and Wringer for Tiny Tots
Same as above. 8¾ in. high by 7 in. wide.
49 F 1708—Shpg. wt., 2 lbs. 6 oz.... **59c**

Household Outfit
6 Big Pieces for Only
$1.00

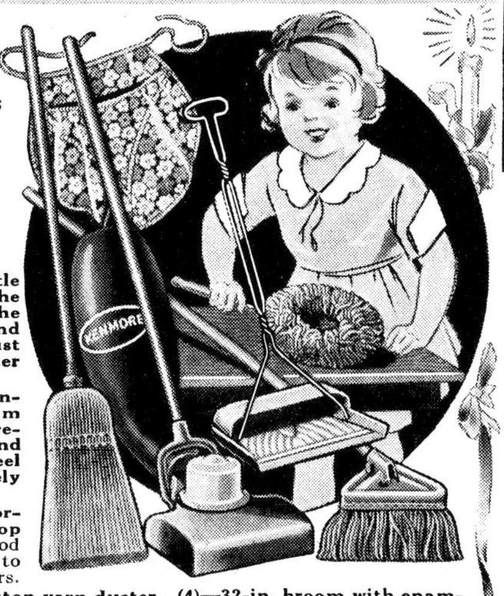

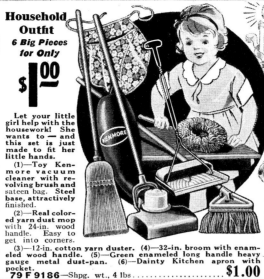

Let your little girl help with the housework! She wants to — and this set is just made to fit her little hands.

(1)—**Toy Kenmore vacuum cleaner with revolving brush and sateen bag. Steel base, attractively** finished.
(2)—**Real colored yarn dust mop** with 24-in. wood handle. Easy to get into corners.
(3)—**12-in. cotton yarn duster.** (4)—**32-in. broom with enameled wood handle.** (5)—**Green enameled long handle heavy gauge metal dust-pan.** (6)—**Dainty Kitchen apron with pocket.**
79 F 9186—Shpg. wt., 4 lbs.................. **$1.00**

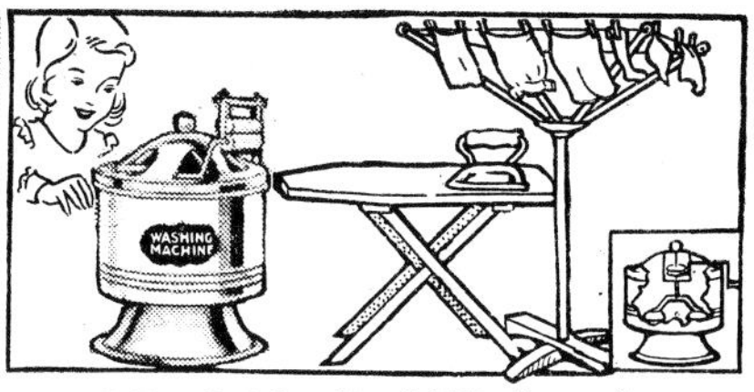

5-Pc. Set for the Little Laundress **$1.00**
It's fun to wash for Dolly! Here's a nice washing machine outfit just like mother's! **The metal washer is 8¾ in. high and 7 in. wide.** Turn the handle and the inside mechanism operates just like a big washer. 3-position wringer has rubber rollers. **Ironing board 16 in. long; wood clothes rack 13½ in. tall.** Other pieces in proportion.
79 F 1707—Shpg. wt., 3 lbs........ **$1.00**

Laundry Set for the Tiny Miss
9-in. Ironing Board, 6¼-in. washboard, wash bench, nickeled iron, metal tub, clothes dryer in proportion, also clothes pins. Not illustrated.
49 F 1711—Shpg. wt., 1 lb. 12 oz....... **59c**

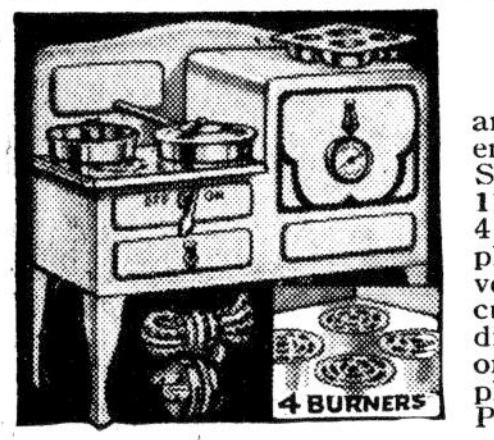

Electric Stove With Switch
Yes, it really cooks and bakes! White enameled **all** steel. Size, overall, **12½x11⅛x5⅝ inches**; 4½-foot cord with plug. For 105 to 120 volt A.C. or D.C. current. Heat indicator, and switch on oven. Nickel-plated cooking top. Pans included.
49 F 7319—Shpg. wt., 7 lbs. 8 oz... **$2.98**

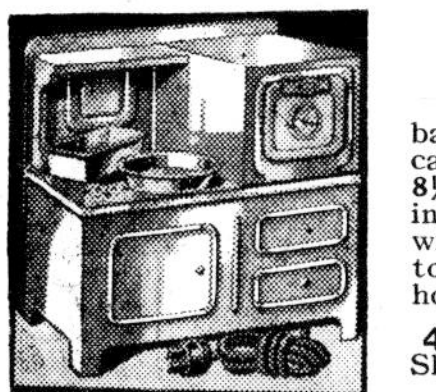

Cabinet Style Electric Stove
Actually cooks and bakes. Real heat indicator. Size, overall, 9⅞x8½x5⅝ inches. 2 pans included. 4½-foot cord with plug. For any 110 to 120-volt A.C. or D.C. house current.
49 F 7314 Shpg. wt., 5 lbs. **$1.00**

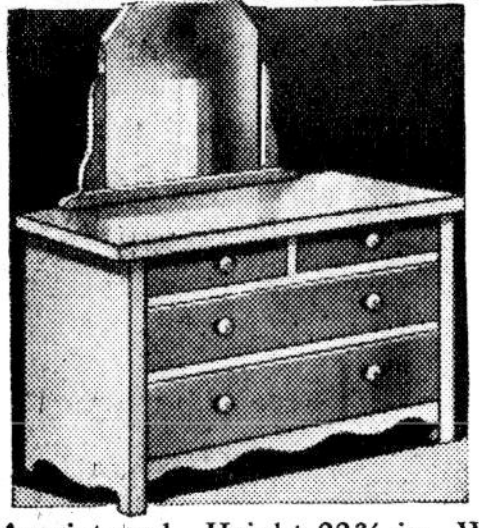

Enameled Wood Dressers
Every little mother wants her Dolly to have a real dresser of her own! These have a fancy mirror with beveled edge set in wood frame. The front of drawers and mirror frame are enameled **light green;** the rest of the dresser is **cream** color.
79 F 7157
As pictured. Height 22¾ in. Width, 19⅝ in. Shpg. wt., 13 lbs.......... **$2.98**
79 F 7156—Ht., 18⅝ in. Width, 15⅝ in. 3 large drawers; Shpg. wt., 7 lbs......... **$1.98**
79 F 7155—Height, 13⅞ in.; width, 12 in.; 2 large drawers; 1 knob on each. Shpg. wt., 4 lbs.......................... **$1.00**

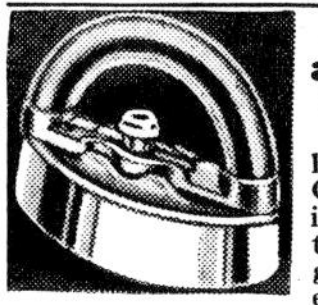

Sadiron and Stand
Mrs. Potts Style
She can really iron with it! Cast iron; 4¾ in. long. Detachable green enameled handle.
49 F 1788
Shpg. wt., 1 lb. 8 oz......... **45c**

Sadiron for the Tiny Miss
Similar to above, but iron is 4 in. long and has yellow handle.
Shpg. wt., 12 oz.
49 F 1789.............. **23c**

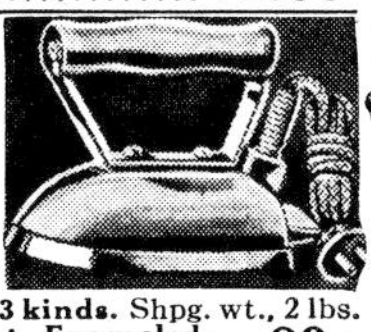

Toy Electric Irons
Nickeled ironing surface. Use on 110-volt, 60-cycle current. **3 kinds.** Shpg. wt., 2 lbs.
Low heat, Enameled.
49 F 1793........ **89c**
For Older Girls
High heat, Nickeled.
49 F 1794......... **89c**
Low Priced Special
49 F 1792
Shpg. wt., 1 lb.......... **59c**

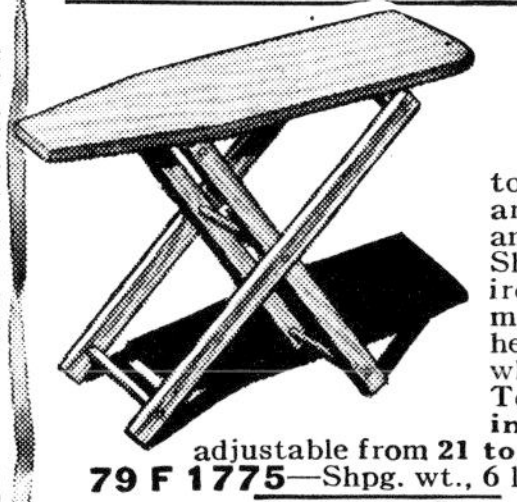

Toy Ironing Boards
All edges; top and legs are rounded and smooth. She'll do her ironing when mother does hers. Of clear white wood. Top, 34¾x9⅞ in. Height adjustable from 21 to 25 in.
79 F 1775—Shpg. wt., 6 lbs.... **69c**
For Little Girls
Same finish as above. Top, 21x5 in. Adjustable from 13 to 15 in.
49 F 1777
Shpg. wt., 1 lb. 12 oz............. **27c**

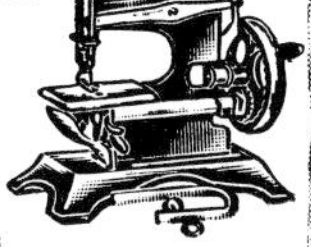

Sew Like Mother
Every little girl loves to sew. What fun to make Dolly's clothes! It teaches girls to be handy at an early age because it actually sews! Size, 7½x7⅜x3¾ in. Has drop-foot thread tension and heavy flywheel. Green enamel steel. Shpg. wt., 2 lbs. 4 oz.
49 F 5803 **$1.00**

Nickel Plated Cast Iron Stoves

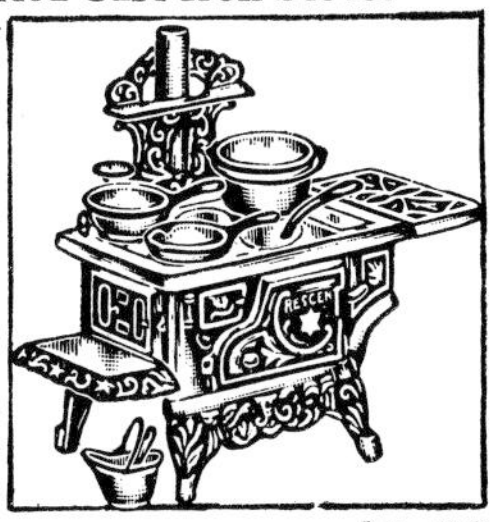

Fancy back; removable lids and aprons; hinged oven door.
Has All Features As Pictured
Four 2¼-in. lids. Size, overall, 13¼x11¾ in.
49 F 7321
Shpg. wt., 12 lbs... **$2.19**

For Young Cooks
Four 1½-in. lids. Size, overall, 10½x10¼ in. only 2 utensils.
49 F 7320—Shpg. wt., 6 lbs......... **$1.39**

For Baby Cooks
Four 1½-in. lids; size, **overall**, 6¼x4⅜x6⅜ in. only skillet and lid lifter included.
49 F 7315—Shpg. wt., 2 lbs. 8 oz...... **45c**

Girls' Wrist Watch

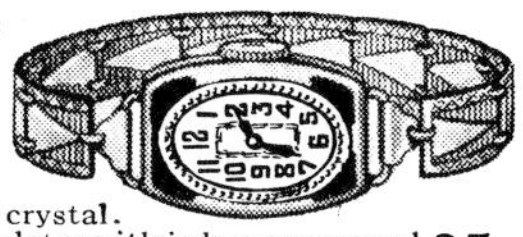

She'll "make believe" tell the time. Work stem winder and hands move. Size, overall, 6¾ in. Unbreakable crystal. Gold color metal plates with jade green enamel.
49 F 9109—Shpg. wt., 4 oz........... **25c**

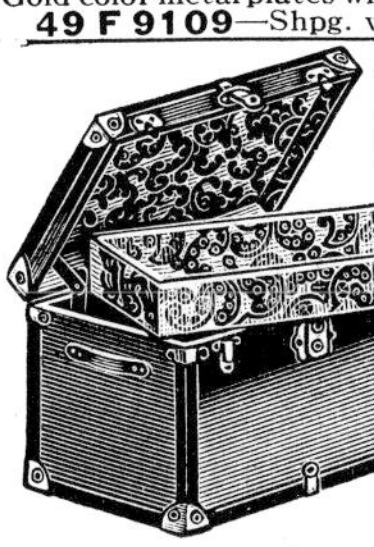

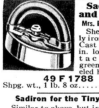

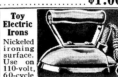

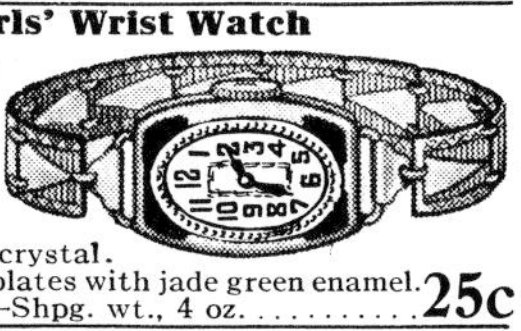

Quality Doll Trunks
Colored metal covering. Leather handles and metal bound edges. Real Lock and Key. Inside Tray. **Size, 18⅝x10¾x11 in.**
79 F 8419
Shpg. wt., 12 lbs... **$2.49**

14-Inch Trunk
(Not Illustrated)
Covered with **colored embossed material.** Size, 14x7¾x7½ in. Lock and key. Inside tray.
79 F 8403—Shpg. wt., 5 lbs....... **$1.19**

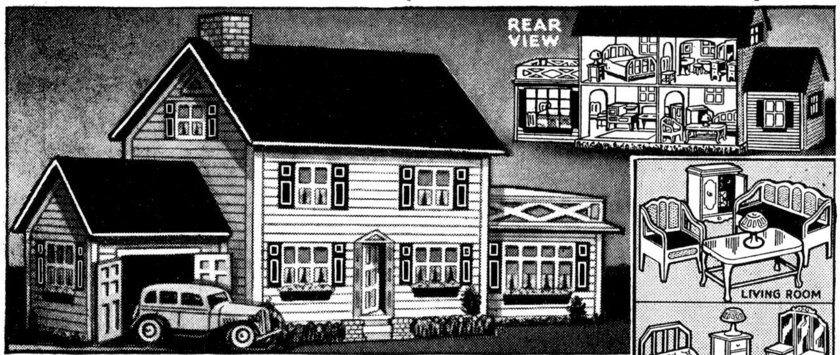

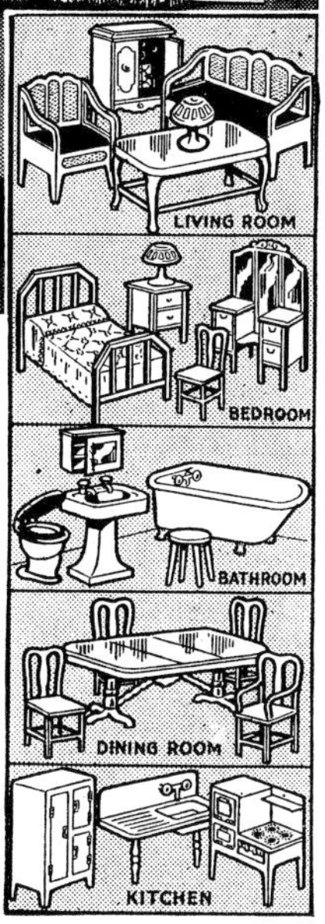

27 Piece COMPLETE DOLL HOUSE SET $1.79

5-Room House—Breakfast Porch—Garage Sedan Car and 23 Pieces of Metal Furniture

Size, overall, 28½ inches; height 15⅝ inches

What little girl wouldn't love Santa if he brought her this adorable house—**all furnished!** A great big white and green fiber-board colonial house. A front door, that opens. And printed flowers all around base, and in the window boxes! Of course the back is open, so she can rearrange the furniture! Five rooms, besides the **7½x7½ inch breakfast porch!** The garage, **7½ inches square,** holds a shiny-bright blue-enameled metal sedan, 4 inches long! There are 23 pieces of practically unbreakable furniture! See what you get for the living room . . . gilt finish settee (3½x2 inches), oblong table, chair, and table lamp; also mahogany-finish radio. The bedroom set is in pink enamel. 3⅜-inch bed, triple mirror vanity, night table, lamp and chair. The dining table (3⅜ inches) long arm chair and three side chairs are finished walnut. A white kitchen—3½-inch sink, 2-inch icebox; and range. Orchid enameled 3⅜-in. bath tub, toilet with movable seat, wash stand, medicine chest and stool. It's a set to delight the heart of any little girl!

49 F 7149—House, breakfast porch, and garage with 23 pieces of metal furniture and sedan.
Shpg. wt., 5 lbs. 8 oz.... **$1.79**

49 F 7134—House with Breakfast Porch and Garage. No furniture or sedan included with this set.
Shpg. wt., 3 lbs. 8 oz......... **59c**

Doll Furniture only, 49 F 7130—
Shpg. wt., 2 lbs. 8 oz.............................. **23** Pieces for **$1.29**

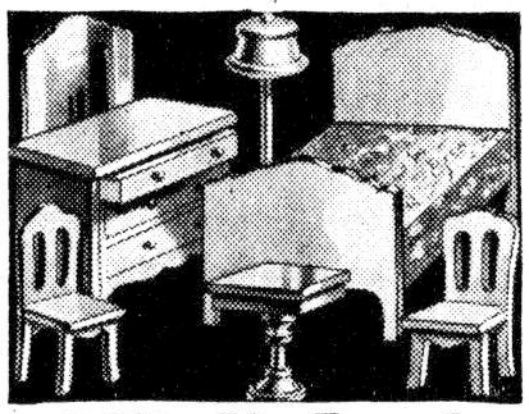

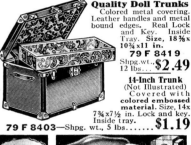

6 Piece Blue Enamel Wood Bedroom Set
3⅞-in. wood bed with colored paper spread. 3¼-inch dresser, with metal mirror and movable top drawer. Two chairs, floor lamp, night table in proportion. Shpg. wt., 12 oz.
49 F 7172.......... **43c**

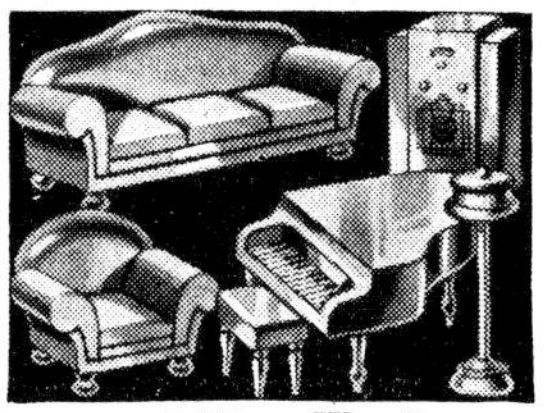

6 Piece Wood Parlor Set
Red 4¹⁵⁄₁₆-inch settee and 2⁹⁄₁₆-inch chair. Walnut color radio 2⁹⁄₁₆-inch high. A green-enameled Baby Grand piano and bench, also silvery finish floor lamp. Shpg. wt., 12 oz.
49 F 7170........... **43c**

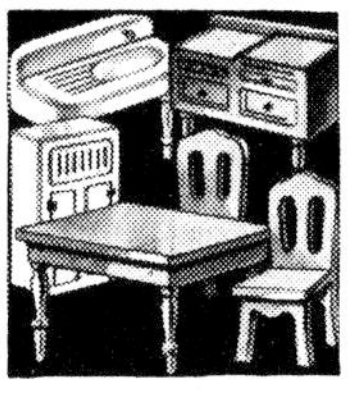

6 Piece Wood Kitchen Set
2⅜-inch stove; two, 2⅝-inch chairs, and a table, all enameled a pretty green! White enameled, 3½-in. sink and 2¾-inch refrigerator. Shipping weight, 12 ounces.
49 F 7173. **43c**

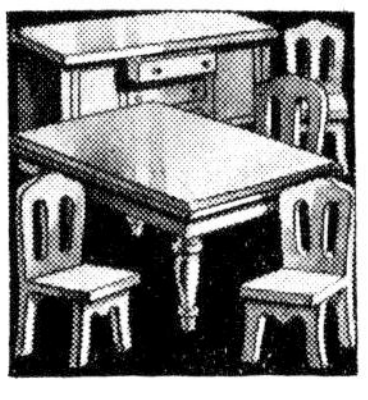

6 Pc. Buff Enamel Dining Set
Made of Wood
Table top, 3¾x2⅜ in. nicely beveled; turned wood legs. 3⅝x1⁹⁄₁₆ inch buffet with movable top drawer. Four, 2⅝-in. chairs. Shipping weight, 12 ounces.
49 F 7171. **43c**

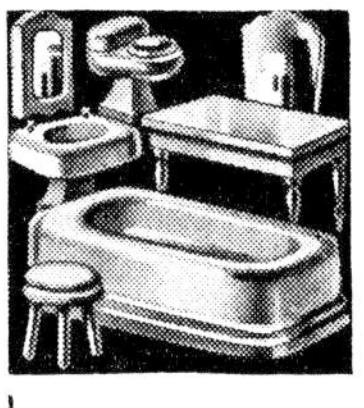

6 Piece Wood Bathroom Set
Modern! 3½-inch bathtub. 3¼-in. dressing table with metal mirror, medicine cabinet with metal mirror. Washstand, toilet and stool. **Orchid color.** Shpg. wt., 12 oz.
49 F 7174. **43c**

 QUALITY First—QUALITY Always—at Sears

LET'S PLAY STORE

COMIC CHARACTER *Ingersoll* Watches

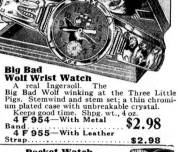

Uncle Sam's 3-Coin Registering Bank
Country's outstanding bank. Baked-on enamel, heavy steel. **Registers nickels, dimes and quarters; rings bell.** Locks itself and opens when $10.00 is deposited. Size, 6⅛ x 4½ x 5¼ in. Shpg. wt., 2 lbs. 8 oz.
49 F 9193 **$1.98**

3-Coin Banks
Lithographed metal. Register nickels, dimes and quarters. Banks open when deposits reach $10.00. Bell rings once for nickels, twice for dimes and five times for quarters. Size, 4x4x2½-in. Shipping weight, 12 ounces.
49 F 9172....47c

Cash Register Big Value
Press a key! Bell rings. Drawer opens, amount registers. Has toy money. Black enameled steel. Size, 4¾x5x4⅝-in.
49 F 9192 Shipping weight, 1 pound 10 ounces. **89c**

Mickey Mouse Wrist Watch
Mickey on the dial tells you the time with his hands. Enameled metal Mickeys on the open link band. Non-breakable crystal. Real Timekeeping Wrist Watch. Guaranteed by Ingersoll and *Sears*. Shpg. wt., 4 oz.
4 F 920—With metal band.......... $2.98
4 F 921—With leather strap $2.98

Big Bad Wolf Wrist Watch
A real Ingersoll. The Big Bad Wolf winking at the Three Little Pigs. Stemwind and stem set; a thin chromium plated case with unbreakable crystal. Keeps good time. Shpg. wt., 4 oz.
4 F 954—With Metal Band.......... $2.98
4 F 955—With Leather Strap.......... $2.98

New Uncle Sam Budget Bank
Save for 4 different purposes in same bank. 4 compartments. Two locks. Slots for coins up to 50 cents—holes for depositing paper money. Heavy gauge metal crystaline finish. Size, 5¼x4½x1⅞ in. Shpg. wt., 1 lb.
49 F 9189.......69c

Let's Play Store! 55 Play Pieces
Fill orders! Make change! 15x12 in. cardboard shelves, 12-in. metal and wood front counter, metal scale, paper holder with paper, 25 empty food containers, 25 pieces of toy money. Shpg. wt., 2 lbs 10 oz.
49 F 9159 **98c**

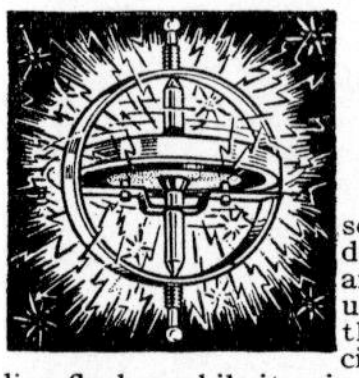

Unbreakable Crystal

Boys! Own a Mickey Mouse Watch
It's a genuine Ingersoll watch that keeps correct time. Mickey Mouse is on the dial. A dandy fob, too! Shpg. wt., 6 oz.
4 F 1620.......... **$1.39**

Pocket Watch
What boy doesn't crave an Ingersoll? With every tick, the Big Bad Wolf winks at the prancing little Pigs, colored dial. Thin nickel plated case; and fob. Stem wind; stem set. Black leather strap. Shpg. wt., 6 oz.
4 F 1653 **$1.39**

Ingersoll Alarm Clock
Let Mickey Mouse wake you in the morning and point to the time all day long. **Red** or **green** case. State color. 4⅜ in. high. 30-hour movement.
5 F 8518 Shpg. wt., 1 lb. 10 oz. **$1.39**

Ingersoll Alarm
The Big Bad Wolf tells the time, opens and closes his hungry jaws, and wakes you in the morning. Bright red, 3⅝-inch dial and 4⅜-inch case.
5 F 8519 Shpg. wt., 1 lb. 10 oz. **$1.39**

New Sparkling Gyroscope Top
An unusual scientific wonder top. Balances at unusual angles throwing fascinating sparkling flashes while it spins. Lots of fun on 4th of July, especially at night, to let this sparkling top spin and do tricks.
49 F 9754—Shpg. wt., 6 ounces.................. **25c**

3-In-1 Disguise Outfit
1—Red paper nose with glasses. 2—Mustache and beard. 3—Sailor beard.
49 F 4501—Shpg. wt., 8 oz.... **25c**

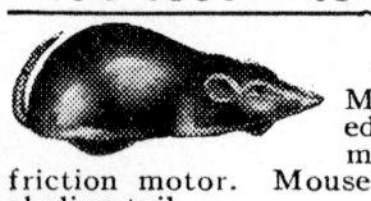

Joke Mouse
Watch him scoot! Made of lithographed metal, in life-like mouse color. Has friction motor. Mouse about 3 in. not including tail.
49 F 5719—Shpg. wt., 4 oz... **10c**

Mickey Mouse Jewelry Set
Girls! Here's a Mickey Mouse Jewelry set that's just too cute for words! A nice mesh bag. Metal Mickeys also adorn the Necklace, bracelet and pin. All in neat presentation box. Shpg. wt., 8 oz.
4 F 4450......All **4** pieces for...... **98c**

This Watch Ticks **19c**
Boys! What fun to own your own watch! Wind up and release lever. Hands move making ticking sound. Unbreakable crystal. Watch 1¾ in. in diam. Shipping weight, 2 oz.
49 F 9117.......19c

Play Store Scale **59c**
This computing scale weighs anything up to 16 oz.; figures the cost of items 5c to 40c a pound. Platform, 5¾x3⅛ in. Made of metal, in gay colors. Shpg. wt., 1 lb. 4 oz.
49 F 9123...59c

"Blow-Me Down" Popeye
All children love Popeye. Push lever, he'll drum away! Lever always springs back. Made of metal, in gay colors. 7 in. high. Shpg. wt., 8 oz.
49 F 9133...19c

10 Cartoon Characters In Natural Colors
Orphan Annie, Fire Chief, Betty Boop, Red Riding Hood, Bear, Moon Mullins and Kayo. 8½ to 10⅛ in. tall on wooden stands. Sandy, Pop-eye, Mouse. Heads, arms, legs move.
49 F 9131—Made of composition board. Shpg. wt., 1 lb. 10 oz. **10** figures for.. **98c**

Make Your Own Movie Show
Famous Scrappy Movie Paint Set. Three paper films (Scrappy goes Fishing, to the Picnic and Hunting). Mounted on wood rollers with cardboard stage. Paint them (with the 14 colors, paint brush and water pan included. 9¹⁵⁄₁₆x7⅛x2½ in. Shpg. wt., 1 lb. 8 oz.
49 F 3887.................. **49c**

MASQUERADE SUITS for Grownups and Kiddies

Be a Mexican Boy! A Dutch Girl or a Spanish girl! A clown! Gay—Brilliant—Colorful cambric. Cheaper than making your own. Wear them to plays, Halloween parties, balls, pageants. The most popular characters at holiday or costume affairs for very little cost. **Be sure to state Age of Kiddies' size of Grownups. Kiddies' Sizes**—Ages, 5 to 16 years. Shpg. wt., 1 lb. 2 oz. Grownups' Sizes—32 to 44 inches chest. Shpg. wt., each, 1 lb. 8 oz.

Train This Magic Tabby
Mystify your friends! You can make Tabby wag his tail, lie down, get up, do everything but talk because his legs, tail and neck are flexible. Just read the simple directions. No motors or springs—nothing to get out of order. Wood. Stands almost six in. high. Finished in three colors. Shpg. wt., 8 oz.
49 F 9134.................. **23c**

Make Them Act
A squawking Wolf, others are cartoon characters of enameled wood, jointed with elastic cord so you can pose them anyway you wish. Av. size, 5 in. Shpg. wt., 1 lb. 8 oz.
49 F 9132 6 for.. **59c**

Mexican Boy	Spanish Girl	Clown Suit	Dutch Girl	Mickey Mouse and Minnie Mouse Stiff Cloth
Consists of jaunty sombrero, flared bottom trousers, vest with metallic braid, sash trimmed with fringe.	Here's a snappy "Senorita" costume from Old Spain that always makes a hit. Blouse is bolero type, trimmed with Gold or silver color metallic braid. Sombrero type hat. Fringed sash, etc.	Go as a clown and have a riot of fun! 2-piece contrasting color cambric costume. Cut big and full. Trimmed with fluffy pompons and gold colored tinsel braid. Cut big and roomy.	Typical Dutch type skirt and blouse with apron panel effect trimmed with gold colored metallic braid. Trimmed with dainty lace. Blouse front has laced effect. Bonnet is of white cambric. Shipping wt., 12 oz.	mask; cambric waist and pants or skirt. Felt gloves. Pants or skirt have a long black rubber tail attached. Shipping wt., 12 oz.
Adults' Sizes 49 F 4554 **$1.69**	**Adults' Sizes** 49 F 4535 **$1.69**	**Adults' Sizes** 49 F 4563 **$1.69**	**Adults' Sizes** 49 F 4561 **$1.69**	**Mickey Mouse** 49 F 4502 **$1.49**
Kiddies' Sizes 49 F 4550 **98c**	**Kiddies' Sizes** 49 F 4555 **98c**	**Kiddies' Sizes** 49 F 4562 **98c**	**Kiddies' Sizes** 49 F 4560 **98c**	**Minnie Mouse** 49 F 4503 **$1.49**

Mickey Mouse Band
Minnie poses with her violin, Mickey a Sax, a little mouse with accordian, another with a mandolin. Minnie and Mickey 5½ inches tall, little mice in proportion. Colored porcelain. Shpg. wt., 1 lb. 4 oz.
49 F 9110 4 for **29c**

Play By the Hour
4 cute toys, just as you see them, 3½ in. bisque doll, other pieces enameled wood, metal and composition board. Hichair 5¹⁄₁₆ inches, other pieces in proportion. Shpg. wt., 12 oz.
49 F 9135 4 for **39c**

7 Tricky Nail Puzzles
Loads of fun! New nickelplated nail puzzles. Booklet with explanation for each puzzle included. Shpg. wt., 1 lb.
49 F 6004 **25c**

We Return the Difference if You Send Us Too Much Postage SLA ₂**521**

ACTION! And Plenty of It!
MARX FAMOUS MECHANICAL TOYS

59c **A Great Thrill! Crash-Proof Airplane**

Hold horizontal in hand, launch against the wind, let it go and watch it sail. When striking an obstruction or crashing, the wings and the lightweight metal under-carriage detach themselves from the aluminum fuselage. Then you have the fun of putting the plane together again, as its not harmed by the crash. It will fly a long way under proper conditions. Equipped with a strong strand gum-rubber which you wind. **Plane is 9½ inches long, has 11¾-inch wing spread yet weighs only one ounce.** This is one of the newest toys and will give lots of pleasure to the average child.

Boys! Have the fellows in your neighborhood order Crash Proof Planes and hold air races! Free directions in each box.
49 F 5755—Shpg. wt., 10 oz. **59c**

"Tipover" Motorcycle **59c**

Off to a good start! But look! Over it falls on its side. Quick as a flash it rights itself—goes on its way—to fall over once more! Plenty of fun and laughs galore watching the "Tipover" Motorcycle do stunts. What makes it perform so naturally? A new type of very fine clock spring motor. Wind the attached side keys and place this new toy on the floor and watch it scoot off like a big motorcycle. In bright colors—both the motorcycle and the uniformed rider. Lithographed metal. Has start and stop lever. Will afford hours of amusement for the children. Size overall, 8½x6 in. **59c**
49 F 5750—Shpg. wt., 14 oz. ....

New—Different Clever

59c Climb! Fireman! Climb!

To the rescue! Up climbs the fireman, rung by rung! He looks like a real fireman—and acts like one, too. Just wind up the clockwork spring and start him on his way. Stops at top. Metal, lithographed true to life fireman. Ladder, **about 23 in.** high, set on base. Fireman 7¾ in. tall. Shpg. wt., 1 lb.
49 F 5768 **59c**

Racer

There it goes! A real racer! Big toy. **16 inches long,** made entirely of metal, colorfully lithographed. Strong, spring motor. Shpg. wt., 1 lb. 6 oz.
49 F 5733 .... **25c**

Speedy Scooter Cat!

Round and round goes this funny cat on his scooter! Wind up the strong spring and away he goes. Lithographed metal, 7¾ inches long. Shpg. wt., 12 oz.
49 F 5766 .... **19c**

9½-In. Trolley With Motor, Bell, Headlight

Here it comes! Bell ringing! Headlight streaming ahead! Lithographed metal in realistic colors; strong spiral spring motor. 10c battery included. Runs in straight line or circle. Shpg. wt., 1 lb.
49 F 5736—With Battery **33c**

Acrobatic Monkey!

Watch him do tricks, turn somersaults. Just wind the spring! Colorfully lithographed metal. Toy 6¾ in. high. Shpg. wt., 10 oz.
49 F 5722 **25c**

Honeymoon Express
Off roars this express thru the three tunnels after you wind the spring. Toy, 9¼ in. diam. Colorfully lithographed metal. Shpg. wt., 1 lb.
49 F 5758 .... **29c**

MARX Powerful Climbing TRACTOR

8½ Inches Long **59c** **Nothing Seems to Stop It**

Over obstacles! Up or down over steep grades. Will pull loads lumbering along like a big tractor. Load your play things into a truck—this tractor will move them for you! It's lots of fun winding it up, starting it, stopping it with the start and stop lever. The sturdy rubber treads give it traction power and the speed governor causes it to lumber along like a real tractor. Strongly built of metal. Powerful clockwork motor.
49 F 5745—Size, 8½ **59c**

x5⅜x3⅜ inches. Shpg. wt., 1 lb. 10 oz. ....

Cardboard Play Castle
Incline for Tractor to climb up or down. Size, 40x10x10 in. Not Illustrated. Shpg. wt., 2 lbs. 12 oz.
49 F 5790 .... **39c**

89c 3 Pieces

Powerful Climbing Tractor with Plow and Wagon
Attach accessories, wind the powerful clockwork motor and off it goes, pushing or pulling along up or down steep grades. Has speed governor and sturdy rubber treads to give it traction power. Start and stop lever. Heavy gauge metal, enameled. Hitched up it is 17¼ in. long. Tractor alone 8½ in. Shpg. wt., 2 lbs. 8 oz.
49 F 5759—Tractor, wagon and plow for **89c**

Whoopee! Cowboy Driver

This auto acts like a broncho when it's wound up! Watch this Whoopee Cowboy perform side-splitting antics. Twists, Turns, Bucks, Balks, Jumps. Does everything but throw him. There's plenty of action. The unique and cleverly constructed motor causes the car to do most anything to produce a riot of laughter and fun. Indeed for many years, one of the finest mechanical toys made. Lithographed metal. Strong spring. Size, 9x7x3 in. **59c**
49 F 5706—Shpg. wt., 1 lb. ....

All For $1.00

The Electric Lighted "LINCOLN HIGHWAY"
Complete with 3 Batteries
Electric Lighted Filling Station, Traffic Signal and Automobile.
Turn on the lights in the filling station! Change the traffic lights from red to green! Wind the strong spring and put on the head lights in the mechanical coupe! And, watch it go! All realistically lithographed metal. Filling station, with two dummy pumps, hose and oil display, has two lamps, one on each pump just like real ones! Coupe is 8-in. long, 3¼ in. wide and 3 in high and operates on one battery for headlights. There also is a battery for the 7-inch Traffic Light. Filling Station, 9¼ in. long, 3¼ in. deep and 6 in. high, also has battery. Complete outfit as illustrated including batteries. Shpg. wt., 2 lbs.
49 F 5793—Complete with 3 10c batteries for **$1.00**

Electric Lighted Speed Boat
Brilliant electric adjustable search light shows the way! Here comes the big **18-inch ELECTRIC LIGHTED** Speed boat! Here she comes! Cutting the waves gracefully. There she goes! Fast because of its strong super clock work motor. All lighted up with its powerful electric searchlight. Turn it off and on with a switch also swing it to either side. Has adjustable Rudder! Heavy-gauge enameled steel hull. Shpg. wt., 3 lbs. 8 oz.
49 F 5794
Ready to Operate, complete with 10c 1⅜ in. diameter battery **$1.39**
For Extra Batteries for all Electric Headlight Toys, See Opposite Page.

8-Inch Electric Lighted Coupe
Turn on the lights with a switch, wind the strong spiral spring and let her go—Oh boy, what fun. Has keen looking bumper and radiator front. Complete with 10c battery. Shpg. wt., 12 oz.
49 F 5734 .... **33c**

Comical Animal Cyclist

Just push down lever and see Jocko ride his cycle in realistic fashion. So simple a little tot can work it. Animal may be detached. Made of metal 5⅞ in. long.
49 F 5748—Shpg. wt., 10 oz. **23c**

"Blow-Me-Down" Popeye
Wind him up! Off he'll trundle with an old style trunk on his wheel-barrow, the same Popeye you see in the Daily Papers. Pipe in mouth! The parrot is here, too! **Height of Popeye, 8¼ inches.** Shpg. wt., 1 lb. 2 oz.
49 F 5788 **59c**

New Police Car With Siren
Clear the way Here comes a green and black police car, its siren screeching! Now it's backing up. Has friction motor—a slight pressure when pushing it on floor winds it up. Size, 8x3½x3 inches. Shpg. wt., 10 oz.
49 F 5771 .... **25c**

Colorful Darky Dancer
Does a Lifelike Buck and Wing **29c** 
He doesn't need music! Just wind the spring and start him off and this happy darky just can't keep from dancing! He seems to like it, too. All dressed up in bright colors on a darky-cabin base. All of bright lithographed metal 10 in. high. Shpg. wt., 10 oz.
49 F 5738 ..... **29c**

Electric Lighted Mechanical Delivery Motorcycle
Load the delivery box! Wind up the metal spiral spring! TURN ON THE ELECTRIC HEAD AND TAIL LIGHTS, and away she goes! Yes-Siree! REAL electric lights. Turn 'em on and off. We include two 10c one-inch diameter batteries. All metal. Nicely decorated. Length, 9¾ in., ht., 5¾ in.
49 F 5724—Shpg. wt., 1 lb. 6 oz. **59c**
Complete with lights and batteries.

THINGS that GO and GO!

AWR-R-R SIREN—

Super DeLuxe Fire Chief with Loud Siren

$**1**59
10c Battery Included

—Electric lights.
—Super clock work motor.
—Loud Siren.

Wind it up and send it off, head lights streaming ahead, the loud siren clearing the way, just like a Fire Chief's car. **15 inches long.** Lithographed strong metal in bright red with attractive lettering. Oversize balloon rubber wheels with shiny metal discs. Front wheels adjustable to run in straight line or circle. Equipped with headlights and one 10c battery. Sturdy long running clockwork motor, and brake to start and stop. Shpg. wt., 3 lbs. 10 oz.
49 F 5799—Fire Chief and 10c Battery for.................. **$1.59**

New Playboy Machine Gun

98c

—Shoots bright Flashes.—Makes noise like a real one.

Take aim! Pull the release in the handle! Just hear the rat-tat-tat machine gun noise that the winding spring motor makes. See the bright flashes shooting out! And how grand they look, especially in a darkened room. No bullets, but a revolving flint. Made after a modern type machine gun of strong metal and decorated to look like it. Swings easily on the swivel tripod. About, 23 in. long. Give your boy a modern, up to the minute toy. Has 2 flints, one inserted ready to shoot.

Brand New Flash-Shooting Machine Gun Complete with 2 Flints	3 Extra Flints
Shpg. wt., 1 lb 14 oz. 49 F 5792.............. **98c**	Shpg. wt., 2 oz. 49 F 5787— **3** Flints for **10c**

DIGGING · SWINGS AROUND · DUMPING

It's Fun to Run a Buddy "L" Digger!

$100
20-gauge steel

Sit on the strong steel seat of this big 28-inch long "one boy-power" Digger—work the levers just like a steam shovel. Slides on runners to different locations. Seat and boom revolve. Strongly built of 20-gauge steel. Enameled in black and red. Length with boom extended, 38 inches; width, 10 inches; height, 17 inches. Shpg. wt., 5 lbs.
79 F 5002.............. **$1.00**

IT'S MECHANICAL · · · has SIREN and ELECTRIC LIGHTS

AWR-R-R SIREN—

$159
With 2 10c Batteries

4 Electric Lights—Siren—2 Ladders—Dummy Hose
You can switch lights from bright to dim

Off to the fire! Siren shrieking! Headlights lighting the way. Adjustable searchlight and tail light blazing. Now unwind the hose! Hook the two 8-inch ladders together and erect them on the truck. Then the rescue! A big truck, 14⅜x5⅛ inches, of heavy-gauge steel in bright red baked-on enamel. Oversize rubber balloon tires with metal discs. Front wheels will adjust to run toy in a straight line or circle. Strong clockwork motor that sends the engine a long distance with one winding. Shpg. wt., 4 lbs.
49 F 5796—Fire Truck and Two 10c Batteries........ **$1.59**

New AIRFLOW CHRYSLER
14¼ Inches Long

Electric Lighted Up-to-the-Minute Model
Brand New

98c
Battery Included

Give him a New Airflow Chrysler of sturdy steel. The car of the minute! New streamlines just like the real Chrysler. Bright nickel plated radiator, front and rear bumpers. License plate. All bright colors! Electric headlights stream ahead at the touch of a switch. Red electric tail light, too. 1 battery included. Wind it up—and off it zooms! Balloon type solid rubber wheels; painted disc. Powerful clock spring Kingsbury motor. Shpg. wt., 3 lbs.
49 F 5712—With Battery **98c**

24-Inch Electric Lighted Buddy "L" Wrecker Truck
20-Gauge Steel

$100
Battery Included

Answer distress calls! Go out and bring in broken-down autos and wagons. Attach the hook, wind up the crane and lift heavy loads! Body is enameled white with red derrick and wheels; black tires. Equipped with headlights and one battery. 24 in. long. 8¾ in. to top of crane. Shpg. wt., 6 lbs.
79 F 5008—Wrecker and One Battery. **$1.00**

21½ Inches Long

Buddy "L" Dump Truck with Electric Headlights

$100
Battery Included

Heavy 20-gauge steel.

Just a touch of the lever and it dumps its load! Back again, and it's ready for another. You can carry toys, blocks, sand —almost anything in this strong dump truck. It will hold a 200 pound weight! The bright electric headlights turn on and off with a switch. One battery included. Great fun to play with. And a big bargain! 21½ inches from tip to tip when it's raised: 9¼ inches high! Width 6½ inches. Body is bright red with yellow chassis, black rubber tires. Shpg. wt., 6 lbs.
79 F 5005—Truck and One Battery... **$1.00**

25-Inch Dump Truck with Electric Lights!
Two Toys in One

$198
With 2 Batteries

Sit on the large steel saddle seat for coasting—steer like a real truck—dump loads with hand dumping device—snap electric headlights on and off with switch. 2 batteries included. Made of auto fender 20-gauge steel. Has disc wheels and rubber tires. Length, 25 in., width, 8 in. Shpg. wt., 11 lbs.
79 F 5081—Truck and 2 Batteries. **$1.98**

22⅞-Inch Electric Lighted Buddy "L" Ladder Fire Truck
With Red Lights

$100
Battery Included

Be a fireman! Switch on the headlights! Adjust the ladders to 25⅜ inches! It's a dandy. Red body and wheels, yellow ladders and black tires. 20-gauge steel, 22⅞x6½x6½ inches. Shpg. wt., 6 lbs.
79 F 5006—Fire Truck and One Battery. **$1.00**

EXTRA BATTERIES

IMPORTANT NOTICE: BUDDY "L" TRUCKS are built for two regular unit cell batteries which give bright as well as dim lights. The one battery included only gives dim lights. For bright lights use two batteries. Compare with 10c batteries. Shpg. wt., 4 oz.
20 F 1401—Regular Unit Cell. Each...... **4c**

19-Inch Electric Lighted Buddy "L" Baggage Truck

$100
With Battery

This truck is **19 inches long**, 6½ inches wide. Made of 20-gauge steel and has a separate 6½x3 inch black hand truck. Truck has yellow body, green cab and chassis with red wheels and black tires. Equipped with headlights. One battery included.
79 F 5007—Shpg. wt., 6 lbs....... **$1.00**

ELECTRIC LIGHTS YOU CAN SWITCH FROM BRIGHT TO DIM

22 IN. TRANSPORT

89c
2-10c Batteries Included

Look! An All-Steel 22-Inch Electric Lighted *Auto Transport—Turn Lights, Dim or Bright

You can have more fun with this toy. It's really 5 separate toys in one—and it is now equipped with real headlights which you can switch from bright to dim. Think of that Boys! A big, husky hauler with detachable trailer and three cars—HAULER HAS 2 STRONG ELECTRIC HEADLIGHTS! Cars are modern sport coupes in assorted colors. Hauler and trailer have balloon type rubber wheels. Two 10c baby cell batteries included to operate the electric lights. Heavy gauge construction. Length, overall, 22 inches. Each coupe, 5⅞x2¾x2½ in. Shpg. wt., 4 lbs.
49 F 5408—Transport and two 10 cent Batteries..................**89c**

DING-A-LING · 30 IN. TRAIN SET-WITH ELECTRIC HEADLIGHT

69c
2-10c Batteries Included

This Pull Toy Will Gladden the Heart of Any Youngster

Now the little fellow gets a break! A dandy 30-inch train of heavy-gauge steel with shiny steel wheels. Has a bright baked-on enamel finish locomotive 8¾ inches long, with real electric headlight you can switch off and on. Two 10c regular unit cell batteries included. Ding-aling-a-ling goes the bell as the engine is pulled along. Coal tender, 6½ inches long. Gondola you can load up with sand or blocks measures 7¼ inches long. And a passenger car in proportion. The little tot will have hours of fun with this fine train. Shpg. wt., 4 lbs.
49 F 5418—Train with two 10 cent Batteries..................**69c**

AS 2**529**

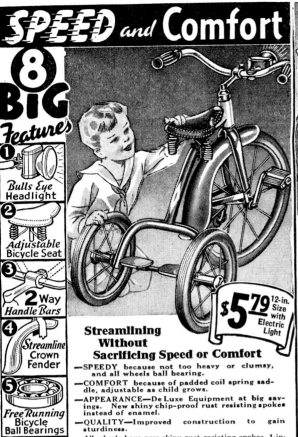

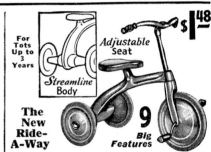

The LATEST IN WAGONS
ALL STEEL STREAMLINE COASTER WAGON
BOY CRAFT 3-IN-1 TRUCK
STREAK-O-LITE
Six Wheel 40-Inch Truck $6.98
Equipped With Electric Headlights $4.79

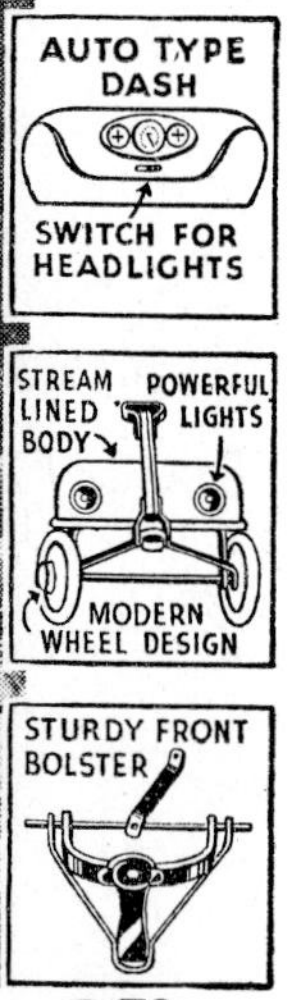
AUTO TYPE DASH
SWITCH FOR HEADLIGHTS
STREAM LINED BODY
POWERFUL LIGHTS
MODERN WHEEL DESIGN
STURDY FRONT BOLSTER

Three Wagons in One!

Three Times the Fun!

Big 3-in-1 Truck! Six wheels, just like a big motor truck. Use it as a regular coaster wagon. Then take off the sides and use it as a coaster and for hauling wood. Or put on its stake body and haul milk cans in it. All three models in one.

1—**Body, size, overall; Length, 40 in.; width, 17½ in.**
2—**Slip the staked sides and ends into the strong steel supports to haul newspapers, groceries or two milk cans.**
3—**Red enameled 11-inch double disc steel roller bearing wheels; 1⅛-inch rubber tires.**
4—**Curved tubular steel tongue makes coasting easy.**
5—**Four wheels on rear axle and two in front.**

Body of kiln dried hardwood, natural finish varnished reinforced with two steel rods. Removable wood staked sides and ends enameled green. Channel steel bolsters and steel braces enameled black. ½-in. steel axles. Metal grip tongue. Snap-on type nickeled hub caps.
79 F 7685—Shpg. wt., 61 lbs........................ **$6.98**

Hardwood Shafts for Goat or Dog
Length, overall, 42⅝ in. Enameled in red.
79 F 7699—Shpg. wt., 6 lbs........................ **$1.39**

1. As a coaster
2. As a milk wagon
3. As a lumber wagon

New Streak-o-Lite

Full Size Streamline Coaster

Be the first with a Modern full sized Streamline all steel coaster. Look at its large auto-like hubs and large fancy nickeled caps—its colorful instrument panel on the dashboard; powerful beacon headlights. Roller bearings are pressure greased at the factory to insure life-long lubrication.

Body: 33½x15x5 in. of 20-gauge auto steel rolled edges; reinforced bottom.

Without Headlights $3.79

Wheels: 9⅜-inch roller bearing, double disc steel. ¾-inch rubber tires. Finish baked-on red enamel. Glossy black undergearing and tubular steel handle. **No batteries included.** See 20 F 1401 on page 529.

With Headlights 79 F 7611	**Without Headlights 79 F 7610**
Shpg. wt., 34 lbs...... **$4.79**	Shpg. wt., 34 lbs....... **$3.79**

The ACE of ALL STEEL WAGONS
$5.98
NEW STYLE WHEELS
SPEE-DEE DE LUXE

Our Spee-Dee De Luxe

Tested and proved! Looks like a powerful wagon and is! Engineers say it's the most powerful wagon ever built. They spent months perfecting it! And—fast? It goes like the wind!

Check These 8 Points of Superiority

1—**Wheels; New artillery balloon type 10¼-in. with roller bearings.**
2—**Tires; Large 1-in. cushion like auto tread rubber.**
3—**Body: 33½x15 in.** of 20-gauge auto fender steel throughout.
4—**Tongue: Chromium plated tubular steel with rubber bumper.**
5—**Body Finish** a beautiful high gloss luster red enamel finish.
6—**Undergearing:** One of the best steel jobs ever built into a wagon.
7—**Steel bolsters, braces.** Also ½-in. steel axles enameled black.
8—**Hub caps:** 3½-inch bell shaped, chromium plated.

79 F 7648—Shpg. wt., 40 lbs........................ **$5.98**

Our New Flyaway Coaster—Body, 33½x15 Inches
Similar to above but with less expensive undergearing; has 9⅜ in. roller bearing plain double steel disc wheels; ¾-inch rubber tires. **Body 33½x15 inches** of auto fender steel. Baked-on red enamel finish. **Channel steel bolsters;** heavy, steel braces; tubular steel handle; no bumper.
79 F 7605—Shpg. wt., 35 lbs........................ **$2.98**

Olympic Junior Red Steel Wagon for the Little Fellow
Body: 28½x12¼-in.; 8¼-in. plain double disc steel wheels, ⅝-in. rubber tires.
79 F 7607—Shpg. wt., 25 lbs........................ **$2.48**

MODERN BEAVER-TAIL BACK
REAL ELECTRIC HEADLIGHT
Scamp
Bright Red Enameled $3.39

New Improved Scamp Wagon!

Designed Like The New Motor Cars and Airplanes

Here comes the speedy Scamp! Airplane fenders! Beavertail back! Bright red enameled! Size overall, 31½ in. long; 16 in. wide; 10¼ in. high. Be the first of your gang to have a new low-slung coaster. Headlight built into body ready to operate. **Just insert battery. (Not included; see page 529.)** Body of heavy auto body steel; green enameled steel handle has rubber bumper. 6½-inch double disc steel wheels; ⅝-inch clincher type rubber tires.
79 F 7670—Shpg. wt., 21 lbs........................ **$3.39**

Three Super Values

Speed—Exercise

Sold by Mail only at Sears
$6.25 38½-In.
THE NEWEST MODELS
$2.87

Stream-Lined Irish Mails

Get the newest model! Nicely enameled streamlined wood body. Adjustable. **For children 5 to 10 years. 47 in. long overall.** Ball bearing, 10½-inch tangent spoke wire wheels; 1-inch rubber tires.
79 F 8810—Shpg. wt., 40 lbs.. **$9.98**
Similar to above. Length 38½-in.; 8½-in. plain bearing wheels.
79 F 8806—Shpg. wt., 27 lbs.. **$6.25**

Irish Mail For Children
3 to 7 Years

Push! Pull! And away it goes with you on the seat. It's fun—and good exercise, too. **Blue enameled** steel frame. **Red enameled saddle shaped** wood seat. **Red enameled 8½-in. wire wheels with** ⁹⁄₁₆-in. **rubber tires. Black** wood pull handle. Leg reach adjustable. **Size, overall, 33½ inches long, 16½ inches wide.** Nickel plated hub caps. Shpg. wt., 12 lbs.
79 F 8804.............. **$2.87**

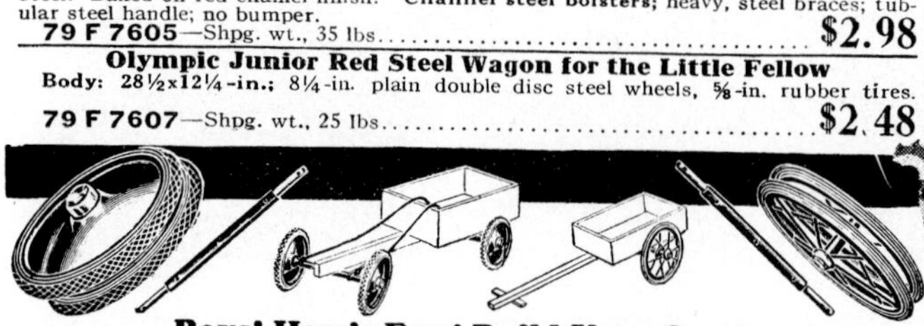

Boys! Here's Fun! Build Your Own!

Red enameled wheels with rubber tires, ½-in square steel axle, 18½-in. long, rounded at ends, drilled for cotter pins and for fastening. Each set has washers, cotter pins and two nickel plated hub caps.

Roller Bearing Disc Wheels
79 F 7649—Two Roller Bearing 9½-inch **Double Disc Steel Wheels with** ¾-in. **rubber tires and One Axle.** Shpg. wt., 8 lbs...... **98c**

Strong Wire Spoke Wheels
79 F 7647—Two 10-in. **Wire Spoke Wheels with** ½-inch **rubber tires and one Axle.** Shpg. wt., 5 lbs........ **69c**

All Steel Wheelbarrows

Two Sizes

$1.00
14½x10½ Inches

Finished in hard baked-on enamel. Double disc wheel, steel axle, legs and braces.

For Little Tots
14½ x 10½ in. Body. 26⅝-in. handles. 5-in. steel wheel. Shpg. wt., 6 lbs.
79 F 7625.......... **$1.00**

For the Older Child
Body, 19x13½ in. 34½-in. handles 8-in. wheel. ⅝-in. rubber tire. Shpg. wt., 9 lbs.
79 F 7627.......... **$1.49**

Roller Bearing Scooters

De Luxe Model
Has bicycle bell, brake, parking stand and rear mudguard. **Length, overall, 40 in. 10½ in.** New Artillery type wheels. 1³⁄₁₆ in. rubber tires. **Enameled in red, yellow and black.**
79 F 8826 Shpg. wt., 20 lbs. **$3.98**

A Rare Bargain
Length, 38 in. 10-in. wheels, 1-in. tires. No bell or fender. **Enameled green and black.**
79 F 8828 Shpg. wt., 16 lbs.... **$2.98**

One-Piece Steel Footboard with Rubber Mat
New Style Wheels

For Little Tots
Length, 32-in.; 8½-in. wheels, ¾-in. rubber tires, no brake, fender or bell. **Enameled red and green.**
79 F 8829—Shpg. wt., 13 lbs.... **$1.98**

Larger Orders REDUCE Your Transportation Cost per Pound

New Streamline Pedal Bike

98c

For Tots Up to 3 Years.
Built to sell for $1.25. It's the latest! First with step plates. Larger and stronger than most others. Frame of 20-gauge auto body steel is neatly shaped, forming beavertail back with stamped out step plates over rear axle. Length, 22½ inches. Rubber grips and pedals. 8-inch front wheel, ½-in. rubber tires.
79 K 8375—Shipping weight, 9 pounds........ **98c**

New Baby STREAK-O-LITE Wagon

95c

Auto Body Steel—For Tots Up to 3 Years
Only low priced wagon made of same sturdy steel used for big brother's wagon. Selected for lasting quality rather than show. Not just a pull toy. Red baked-on enamel finish. There's a front bumper and large double-disc rubber-tired steel wheels. Smooth rolled edges. Heavy steel under-gearing. Body, 17½x8¾ in.
79 K 7612—Shipping weight, 7 pounds........ **95c**

New Tot's Bike Is Streamlined, Too

$2.29

For Tots 2 to 4 Years
Streamlined from the handlebars to the step plates in the back. Even the adjustable steel spring saddle and rubber grips and pedals are streamlined. Bright red with shiny spokes on the large rubber-tired wheels. 10-inch front wheel; seat to lower pedal, 15½ inches.
79 K 8606—Shpg. wt., 10 pounds... **$2.29**

$1.15
79 K 7503

Tots Love to Ride Buddie Bikes

Just right for tots up to three years. Tinkling nickel plated bell. Enameled, shaped wood seat; double-disc steel wheels; ½-in. rubber tires.
79 K 7503—For tots up to 3. Ht. to seat, 8¼ in. 5-in. wheels. Shpg. wt., 5 lbs.. **$1.15**
79 K 7504—For tots up to 3. Ht. to seat, 9¼ in. 6-in. wheels. Shpg. wt., 6 lbs.. **$1.49**

Life-like Teddy Bears — Medium Long Pile Alpaca Plush

(A) American Made! Don't confuse with lower priced imported cheaper quality short-pile bears. Cute faces—glass eyes; deep brown medium long pile. Movable arms, legs, head, with large double washer joints, not nailed or wired as on cheaper bears. Each has squeaker voice.

12-In. Size	15-In. Size	18-In. Size
49 K 4330	49 K 4331	49 K 4332
Shpg. wt., 10 oz.... **59c**	Shpg. wt., 15 oz.... **79c**	Shpg. wt., 1 lb. 5 oz. **$1.00**

(B) Big 14-In. Soft Cuddly Finer Quality Bear
Prettier, more shapely, softer! Soft, lustrous, dark brown alpaca longer pile plush bear stuffed with cotton. Squeaker voice. Glass eyes. Movable head, arms, legs on double washer joints.
49 K 4333—Shipping weight, 1 pound.. **$1.00**

Baby Will Enjoy This Team

$1.98

Easily worth ¼ more than we ask. The best shoofly value we have ever offered. Large in size, still our usual standard of quality. A smooth, safe ride! Baby is sure to like its smooth, rocking motion. Brightly colored horse shoofly. With large swinging play box. It's safe, too, because it has a foot rest and guard rail so baby can't slip out. Solid sides of heavy 3-ply wood all in one piece put together with screws (not nailed). Beautifully decorated in bright attractive colors. Length overall, 32⅝ inches. Height, 15¾ inches. Shipping wt., 10 lbs. **$1.98**
79 K 7561 .... **$1.98**

$1.00

A Bouncing Horse Regular $1.50 Value

Lots of fun and the proper exercise, too! Bright enameled sturdy wood base is braced and fastened with bolts. Large saddle shaped wood seat, securely fastened to wood bar. Height overall, 21 in. Length, 23¾ in. Has a strong dependable safety coil spring mechanism. Shipping weight, 12 lbs. **$1.00**
79 K 7502........ **$1.00**

Little Ones Can Ride Him

Holds 200 lbs. Brilliant, harmless lacquer on solid wood. Bright red wooden saddle and reins. Horse is 17½ inches tall. Seat is about 11 inches off the floor. Shpg. wt., 2 lbs. 14 oz.
49 K 5475 .... **79c**

New! Halsam Improved Safety Blocks

45c
1⁵⁄₁₆-In.

36 blocks, choice of two sizes! Brilliant non-poisonous enamel in 4 colors. Tots soon find letters, numbers, fairy tales characters, designs and animals. Round corners and edges that can't hurt Baby. Each block has 2 enameled, 2 embossed and 2 etched surfaces.

49 K 3676	49 K 3677
Shipping wt., 3 lbs. 8 oz.	Shipping wt., 1 lb. 12 oz.
36 1¾-inch Blocks.... **89c**	36 1⁵⁄₁₆-inch Blocks.... **45c**

New 23-in. Mickey Mouse Wagon and Team

98c

The very latest! Every little tot wants a wagon like this—it's sure to please him. Two gaily colored horses pull the bright, colorful wooden wagon with Mickey Mouse pictured on one side in colors to delight the little tot. There's room for lots of things in the wagon. Well made and of all wood; wagon has big wheels. With pull cord. Shipping weight, 4 lbs. 4 oz.
49 K 5473 .... **98c**

Rubber Puppy

7-in. White. Unbreakable and washable. Nicely tinted; fast colors. Metal voice. Shpg. wt., 8 oz.
49 K 4420 ... **20c**

Roly Poly

9½-in. Musical. Knock him down; he gets up again, chimes tinkling. Colorful papier mache. Assorted styles. Made in Germany. Shpg. wt., 1 lb. 2 oz.
49 K 9162.... **37c**

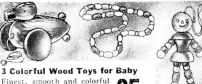

Infant's Chamber

Colorful embossed enameled unbreakable steel. Practical size, 6⅞-in. top. Made in Germany. Shpg. wt., 1 lb. 12 oz.
49 K 1944 **59c**

Musical Ball

4½-inch. With bell inside. Made of rubber and air filled. Assorted glossy marbleized finish. Shpg. wt., 10 oz.
49 K 7710 **20c**

Scottie Ball

3-inch. Made of rubber and air filled. Bright cheerful colors. Attractively designed. Lively, but soft so it can't hurt baby. Shpg. wt., 7 oz.
49 K 7724 .. **10c**

27-Inch Wooden "Choo Choo"

With 5-inch engine, a tender and four wooden cars in proportion; painted in bright colors like a real train and you can couple them together! Every little tot will love to push or pull it along the floor on the easy rolling, smooth finish wooden wheels. Shipping weight, 12 oz.
49 K 5498 .... **49c**

Electric Lighted Streamline Street Car

Brand New! Pull it along, hear the bell ring! Yes, it's electric lighted. Just turn on the headlight and see it flash! Modern silvery colored lithographed metal. The car itself is 17 inches long and there's a pull-cord attached. Battery included. Shpg. wt., 2 lbs. 9 oz.
49 K 5489—Shipping wt., 2 lbs. 9 oz. **89c**

White Washable Rubber Toys

29c

We prefer to offer sanitary white rubber toys. Red rubber toys around this price are usually only coated red. 5½-inch cat and dog with whistles, and handled teething ring. Shipping weight, 8 ounces.
49 K 4416—All 3 for.................. **29c**

Rubber Chick-in-Egg Rattle

Sanitary. For teething babies 4¼ in. long. Whistles. Shpg. wt., 2 oz.
49 K 4400 .. **13c**

Unbreakable Dishes

Beautifully colored and embossed; enameled steel. Made in Germany.
49 K 1941—3-in. Mug ... **25c**
Shpg. wt., 6 oz.
49 K 1943—Mug and Plate Set ... **89c**
Non-tip 8⅝-in. plate; 3-in. mug. Shpg. wt., 1 lb. 9 oz.

3 Colorful Wood Toys for Baby

25c

Finest, smooth and colorful wood playthings to amuse and keep baby busy for hours. A 32-inch string of beads, a 3¾-inch ducky that waddles and a 6-inch bead doll. Shipping wt., 10 oz.
49 K 9169—All 3 for **25c**

You pay only the actual amount of postage   **727**

The Most Popular Mickey Mouse Toys for Little Tots

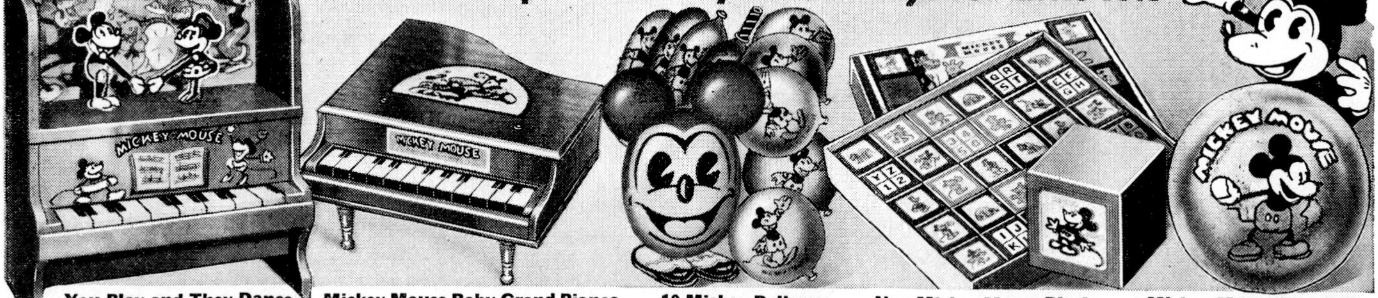

You Play and They Dance

Brand new 10-in. red enameled wood piano. **$1.00** Cardboard Mickey and Minnie Mouse, famous movie characters, are so attached that they dance when the 8 accurately tuned keys are played. The Big Bad Wolf and Three Little Pigs are lithographed on the background. Shipping weight, 1 pound 14 ounces.

49 K 2421 ....$1.00

Mickey Mouse Baby Grand Pianos

Sold by Mail Only by Sears. Accurately tuned chime-like sounding notes. Dark oak hardwood case. Enameled black and white keys look like natural flats and sharps. **98c** 9-Key

9-Keys, Size 10¼x7¾ in.
49 K 2423—Shpg. wt., 3 lbs. 98c
12-Keys, Size 10⅞x10⅛ in.
49 K 2424—Shipping weight, 3 pounds 5 ounces............$1.49

10 Mickey Balloons

Big value. You can inflate Mickey to 8 inches tall and he has cardboard feet, too. Long ones inflate to 15 in., round shapes to about 9 in. diam. One has squawker. Shipping weight, 4 ounces. **19c**

49 K 9114
10 Balloons for.......19c

New Mickey Mouse Blocks

Non-poisonous Hal-sam enameled round cornered safety blocks. Embossed with colorful genuine characters. **45c** 15 Pcs.

30—1¾-in. Blocks
49 K 3674—Shipping wt., 3 lbs. 89c
15—1¾-in. Blocks
49 K 3675—Shipping wt., 1 lb. 9 oz. 45c

Mickey Mouse Play Balls

Newest thing. Inflated rubber in colors. Design is in rubber, not just stenciled. **10c** 3-in.

49 K 7715—4½-in. Diam. Shpg. wt., 8 oz. 22c
49 K 7731—6-in. Diam. Shpg. wt., 1 lb. 5 oz. 47c
Solid Sponge Rubber
49 K 7701—3-in. Diam. Shpg. wt., 1 lb. 12 oz. 10c

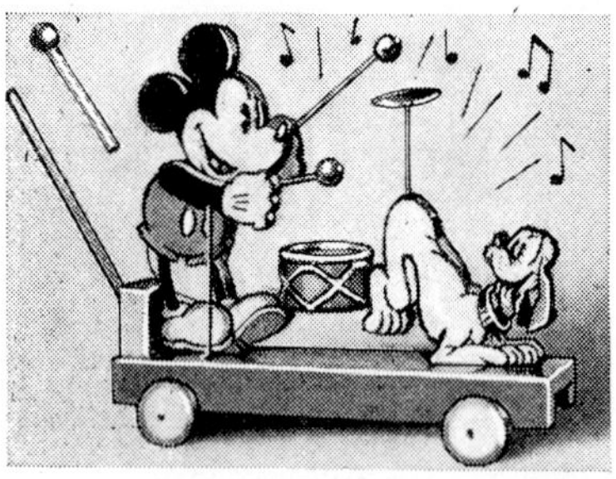

Brand New Mickey Mouse Band

Push it or pull it . . . and Mickey's one arm beats the metal drum; with the other he strikes the metal cymbal on Pluto's tail. It's a picnic. The cutest wood toy you've ever seen, brightly colored, 12 in. long. 16-in. Push handle. **89c**

49 K 5430—Shpg. wt., 2 lbs. 4 oz....89c

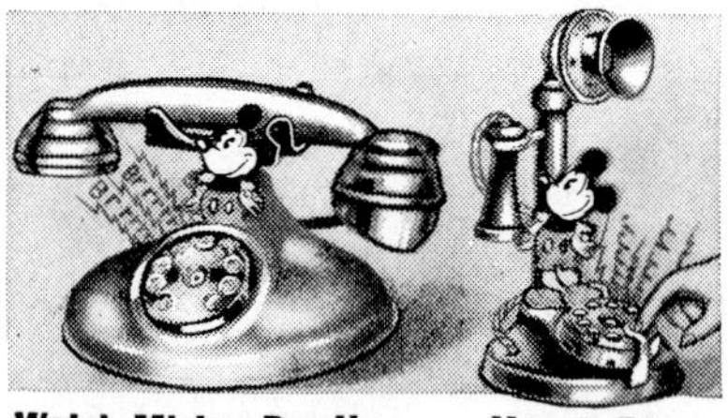

Watch Mickey Pop Up

Lift the receiver—Mickey jumps up big as life. Dial your number—phone rings. A big 8⅜-in. French type phone enameled bright red, with nickeled trim and felt base, size 6³⁄₁₆ in. Green cord attached to metal receiver and mouth piece. Looks just like a regular phone. Shipping weight, 1 pound 9 ounces.

49 K 2457.......49c

Hear it Ring

Mickey grins at you as you dial your number and the bell rings. Nickel plated dial, mouthpiece and receiver hook; enameled metal base. Height, 8 in. Wood receiver. Shpg. wt., 14 oz.

49 K 2455..25c

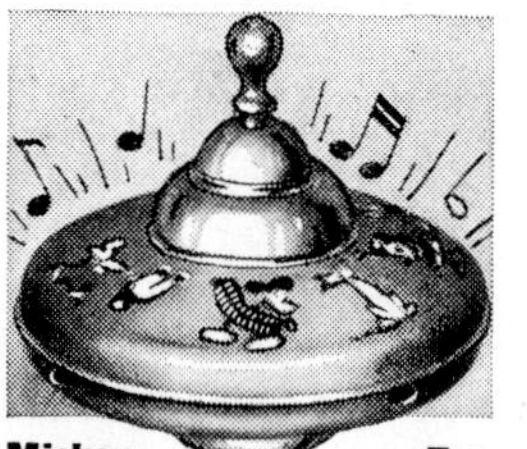

Mickey Mouse Tops — **Easy to Spin**

Brightly lithographed Mickey, Minnie and Pluto figures. One musical chord. Just pull up bright red knob and push down.

Large 8-In. Size
49 K 2378—Shpg. wt., 1 lb. 10 oz. 47c
Junior 6½-In. Size
49 K 2377—Shipping weight, 1 pound 2 ounces...........23c

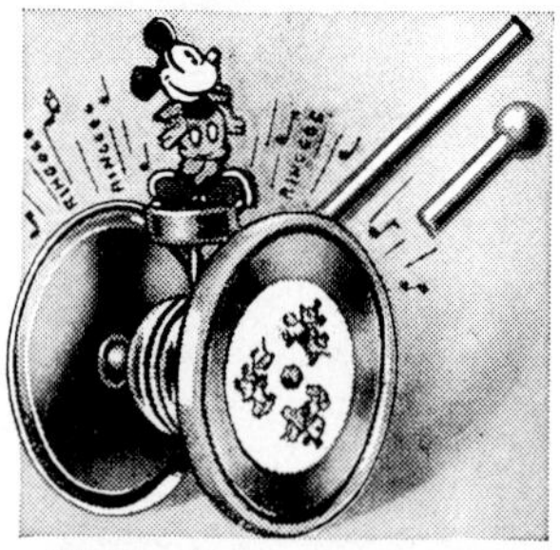

Mickey Mouse Rolling Chime

There is Mickey Mouse—big as life on top of the nickel plated bell. Lots of fun for little tots. Red enameled metal. 21 in. long, 8 in. high. Shpg. wt., 1 lb. 8 oz. **29c**

49 K 2434 ....29c

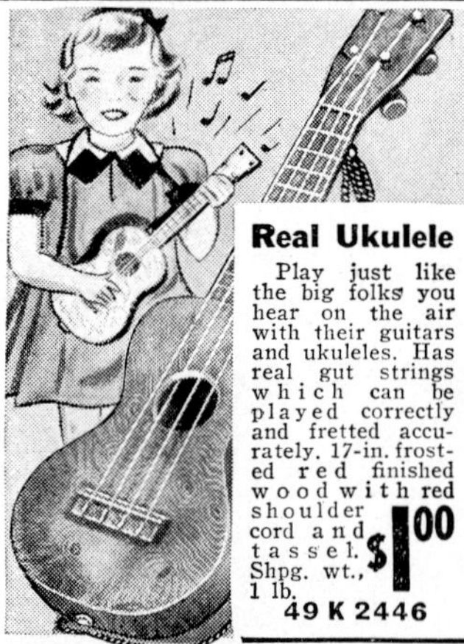

Real Ukulele

Play just like the big folks you hear on the air with their guitars and ukuleles. Has real gut strings which can be played correctly and fretted accurately. 17-in. frosted red finished wood with red shoulder cord and tassel. Shpg. wt., 1 lb. **$1.00**

49 K 2446

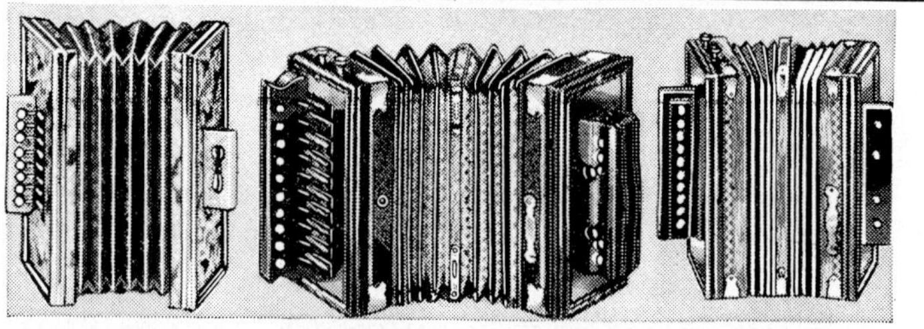

Accordions That Really Play

Specially Priced

8 treble keys, plays 16 notes; 1 bass key. Easy to play. Accurately tuned. Well made. Size closed, 10x4½ inches. Made in Germany. Shipping weight, 1 pound 2 ounces. **69c**

49 K 2355.

Our De Luxe Quality

20 treble notes and 2 bass. Accurately tuned. A real instrument except small in size. Fine workmanship and finish. Double bellows. Black enameled wood frame. Size closed, 9¼x8x4½ in. Made in Germany. Shipping wt., 3 lbs. 1 oz. **$2.59**

49 K 2371.......

Unusual Value

10 double reed metal keys. 20 notes, 2 bass. Nickel plated trimmed metal frame. Accurate deep tone. Nicely finished. Size 9⅝x6¾ in. Shipping weight, 1 lb. 12 oz. **$1.00**

49 K 2368.

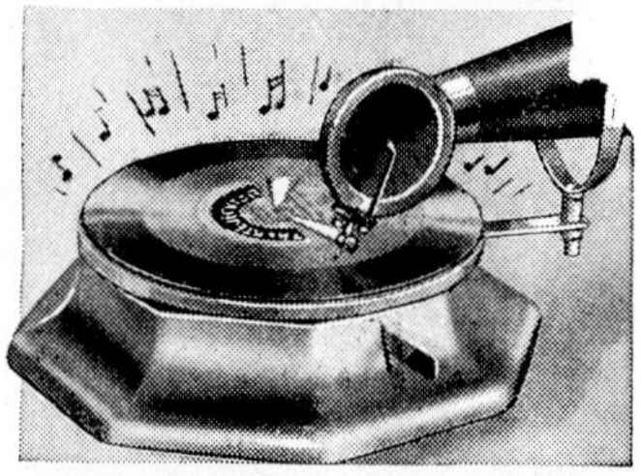

Real Phonograph—New Low Price

Sold by Mail Only by Sears. Plays up to 10-in. records. Wind up clock-work motor. 14-inch two-color steel base. Reproducer and fiber horn. Shpg. wt., 2 lbs. 7 oz.

49 K 2435..........98c

6-Inch Double Faced Non breakable Records 15c ea.

Assorted titles—Shpg. wt., each, 5 oz.
49K2362—Old King Cole and Piper's Son
49K2363—Cat & Fiddle and Ding Dong Bell
49K2364—Mary's Lamb and Little Boy Blue

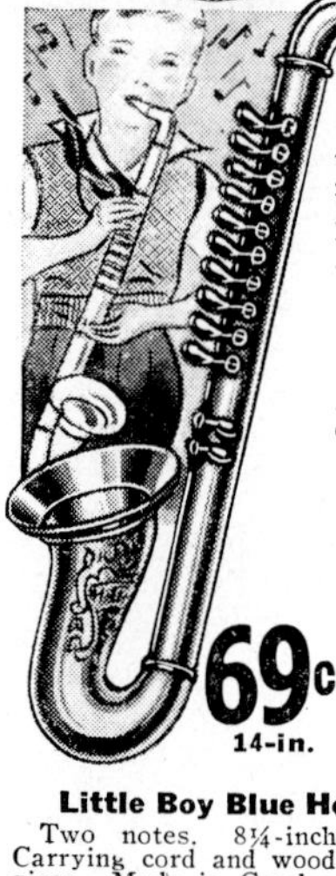

Gold Color Saxophones

You'll be the Jazz King with these toy saxophones of bright metal. Sheet music included. Leather padded keys, sanitary wood mouthpiece. Accurately tuned reeds. Made in Czechoslovakia.

23-Inch Sax—20 Notes
10 keys that play 20 notes and 2 chord bass notes. Adjustable cord. Shpg. wt., 1 lb. 12 oz.
49 K 2487..........$1.89

19-Inch Sax—10 Notes
2 Bass. Shpg. wt., 1 lb. 7 oz.
49 K 2472 ....$1.00

14-Inch Sax—10 Notes
Shpg. wt., 14 oz.
49 K 2479 ....69c

69c 14-in.

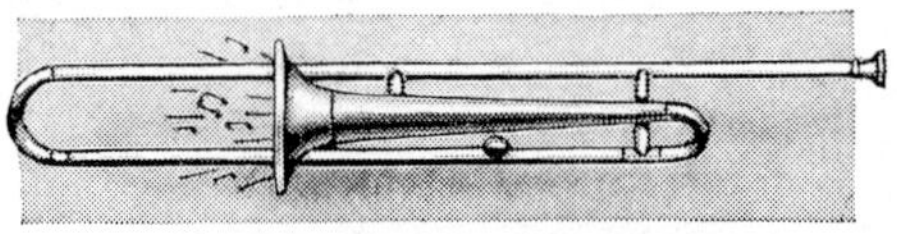

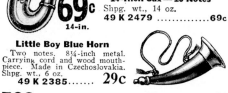

8-Note Gold Color Trombone

You can really play simple melodies on this accurately tuned metal slide trombone. 28¾ inches long, extended. Lots of real fun. Music included. Made in Czechoslovakia. **$1.00**

49 K 2317—Shipping weight, 1 lb. 7 oz.

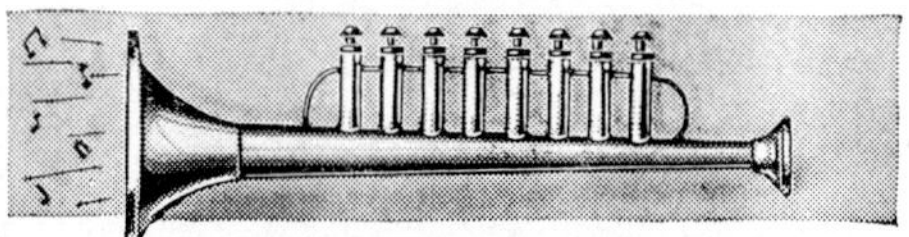

8-Key Gold Color Metal Cornet

Not just a toy—but a 17¾-inch cornet that can be played. Eight spring-valve type notes, like a real cornet and accurately tuned. Nickel plated mouthpiece. Music included. Made in Czechoslovakia. **$1.19**

49 K 2396—Shipping weight, 1 lb. 6 oz.....

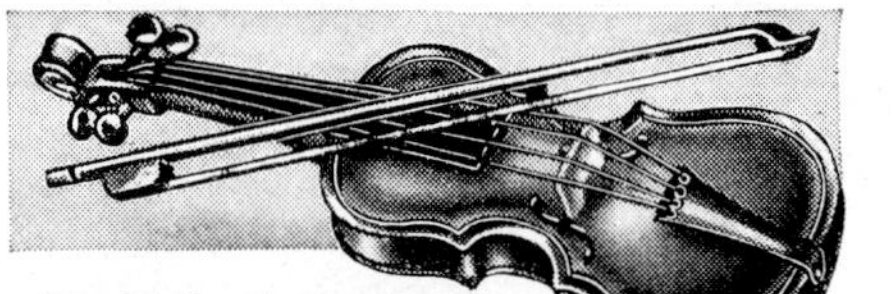

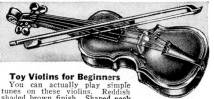

Toy Violins for Beginners

You can actually play simple tunes on these violins. Reddish shaded brown finish. Shaped neck and tail piece. Genuine horse hair bows. Bridge and rosin included. 17½-inch adjustable horsehair bows.

21-Inch Wood Violins—6 Inches Wide
Kiln-dried wood. Made in Germany.
49 K 2332—Shipping weight, 1 lb. 6 oz..$2.29
19¼-Inch Metal Violin 6⅜ inches Wide
Made in Czechoslovakia.
49 K 2335—Shipping weight, 1 lb. 12 oz..$1.00

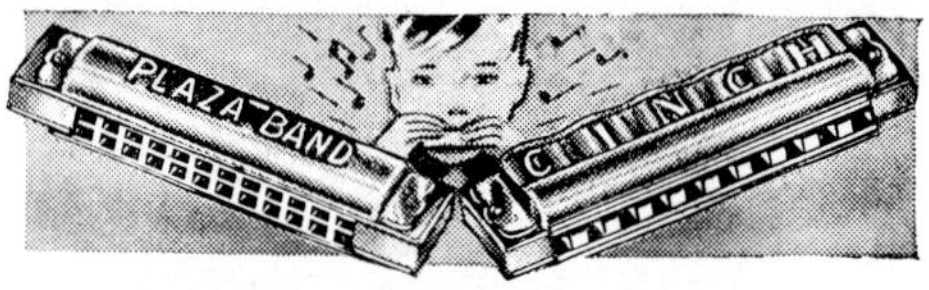

Accurately Tuned Harmonicas

At special low prices. There isn't a youngster anywhere who doesn't want a harmonica. It's fun to play the latest tunes for your friends, at parties or for your own enjoyment. Beautiful nickel plated finish. Assorted styles. Accurately tuned. 2 kinds. Made in Germany.

24 Brassed Reeds
Tremola. 24 single holes. Length, about 4½ in. Shpg. wt., 3 oz. **20c**
49 K 2348 ..

18 Brassed Reeds
10 single holes. Length, about 4 in. Shpg. wt., 3 oz. **12c**
49 K 2345 ..

Little Boy Blue Horn

Two notes. 8¼-inch metal. Carrying cord and wood mouthpiece. Made in Czechoslovakia. Shpg. wt., 6 oz.

49 K 2385....... 29c

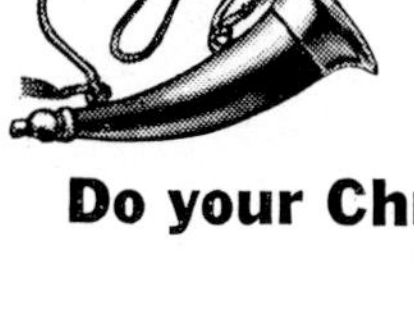

New Improved 45-Piece Stock Farm

Think of it! 45 pieces in all. 44 pieces made of sturdy wood that will last. All parts are specially designed and built to last, not just a large number of cardboard pieces that break easily. What boy or girl wouldn't be happy with the large colorful latest-design barn—16 in. long, 15 in. high to tip of windmill and 9¼ in. across eaves. Take a ruler and visualize its size. Sides and back of barn beautifully printed in colors and a green roof. 40 colored lifelike, cut-out-to-natural-shape animals, a farmer and his family, windmill, farm implements, wagons, etc. made from 3-ply veneer wood (not from cardboard) and printed in 3 colors on both sides; each with wooden stand. 3 wood buildings—a pigpen, chicken coop and a shed for your tractor. They have three walls and roof like real houses and average 5¾x2⅜ in. high. 1 brick red cardboard silo about 9 in. tall. Easily worth $1.50.

79 K 9150—Shipping weight, 6 pounds...................................**98c**

$1.50 Value **98c**

8 Pieces You Need to Play Farmer

Metal, in realistic colors. Includes two tractors; one on real rubber tractor tread, a dump truck—that actually dumps; a thresher-separator; a disc-harrow; two different style plows; and an engine-thresher. Average size, 3 in. long. 1½ in. high; 1⅜ in. wide. Mounted on easy rolling wheels. Realistic—true-to-life. Hours of play. Shpg. wt., 2 lbs. 2 oz.
49 K 5428.......59c

TRU-VUE Machine With One Reel of Fascinating Views Included

Travel with Tru-Vue right in your own home. Magnifies Tru-Vue pictures and shows them in height, breadth and depth in amazing brilliancy. Size, 4¼x1⅞x2¾ in.
49 K 6807—Shipping weight, 11 oz.........**89c**

Non-Inflammable Tru-Vue Films

About 15 views on each film. Shpg. wt., each, 2 oz.

49 K 6814—A Day at the Circus..................	29c
49 K 6816—Around the World...................	29c
49 K 6891—Yellowstone Park..................	29c
49 K 6892—New York City....................	29c

This Watch Ticks!

Boys! What fun to have your own watch! Wind stem, release lever and hands move, making ticking sound. Unbreakable crystal. 1¾ in. across. Assorted designs. Shpg. wt., 2 oz.
49 K 9117...19c

Sears Flying Arrow

Fastest On Any Slide

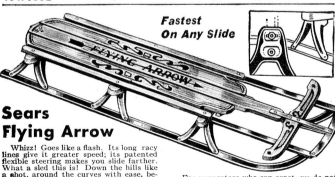

Whizz! Goes like a flash. Its long racy lines give it greater speed; its patented flexible steering makes you slide farther. What a sled this is! Down the hills like a shot, around the curves with ease, because the "FLYING ARROW" steers along the entire length of its runners. A stronger sled, too! The new patented braced knees give much greater strength. Top is of tough hardwood, with spar varnish. Made by a sled maker with 42 years experience. We list only one quality—the best—and sell at the prices of ordinary sleds.

For youngsters who can coast, we do not recommend sleds with steering bar attached way up front, for it limits steering flexibility. That type of sled is about one-fifth cheaper. Sizes given below are measured from bumper to end of runners. The largest sled, 79 KM 8307, has six knees, all others have four patented knees.

Single Cross-bar 30-inch sled for the little tots.
79 K 8302—Shipping weight, 6 pounds...............................**98c**

These Four Sleds Have Double Crossbars

36-Inch Sled	40-Inch Sled	45-Inch Sled	56-Inch Sled
Shpg. wt., 8 lbs.	Shpg. wt., 9 lbs.	Shpg. wt., 10 lbs.	Unmailable. Shpg. wt., 12 lbs. Shipped by Express or Freight.
79 K 8304	79 K 8305	79 K 8306	79 KM 8307
$1.39	**$1.79**	**$2.19**	**$2.79**

730

FAMOUS KEYSTONE MOVIES

SOLD BY MAIL ONLY AT SEARS

New Low Price for Electric Motor Movie

$2.98

Now every boy can own one at this unheard-of low price. Check these features: Non-radio interfering 60-cycle Motor for 110 to 120-volt A.C. current only; shows clear steady pictures of any regular non-inflammable 16 MM film up to 50 ft. length; has tension plate; self-framing device; one reel, made to hold 50 ft. of film; adjustable double projection lens; double claw finger obtains better grip on film; heavy steel body, size over-all, 8x4½x12 in. Use regular house bulb.

Bulb, film or electric cord and plug not included.
79 K 6817—Shpg. wt., 5 lbs. **$2.98**
20 K 671—6-foot Electric Cord and Plug for above movies. Shpg. wt., 7 oz....**17c**

Electric Lighted Hand Crank Movie

At new low price. Similar to 79 K 6817 except without motor but uses regular house current to operate. Bulb, film, electric cord and plug not included.
49 K 6818—Shpg. wt., 2 lbs. 12 oz. **$1.00**

16 MM Non-Inflammable Films — Assorted Subjects for Above Machines

25-Foot Films—Shpg. wt., 2 oz.	Each	50-Foot Films—Shpg. wt., 2 oz.	Each
49 K 6901—Popeye the Sailorman	87c	**49 K 6910**—Popeye the Sailorman	$1.59
49 K 6902—Tom Mix Western	67c	**49 K 6911**—Tom Mix Western	1.29
49 K 6903—Charlie Chaplin Comedy	67c	**49 K 6912**—Charlie Chaplin Comedy	1.29
49 K 6904—Mickey's Hand Organ	87c	**49 K 6913**—Mickey's Blow Out	1.59

$1.98

Sold by Mail Only by Sears

New Mickey Mouse Talkie Jector
Clockwork Motor—Electric Lighted

Imagine hearing voices or music with your movie show! Just wind strong spring motor which operates and keeps record and film synchronized. Clear, flicker-less, cartoon-type moving pictures in colors. Can be shown on any blank wall. Made of metal with Mickey Mouse decoration. 13x7½x12 in. Operates on 110-volt A.C. current. Use regular house bulb. Record, films, bulb or electric cord and plug not included. See below.
79 K 6841—Shipping weight, 4 pounds...............**$1.98**

Sets of two 39 in. Colored Films and one Double-faced 6-in. Record
42c

Music by Irving Berlin. Each film shows story for one side of record. Especially prepared for the little tots. Shipping weight, 1 pound each.

49 K 6960 — Mickey in "Dude Ranch" and "Home Run"......42c	**49 K 6962**—Mickey in "Winning" and "Pal Pluto".........42c	**49 K 6964** — "Sandman" and "Funny Bunnies".........42c
49 K 6961 — Mickey in "Flying Mail" and "Haunted House"...42c	**49 K 6963** — Silly Symphony — "Penguin Land" and "Two Bears" 42c	**49 K 6965**—"Idle Hour" and "Birds in Spring".........42c

Hand Crank Mickey Mouse Movie Jector

Like 79 K 6841, except no talkie attachment and no motor. Use ordinary house bulb. Bulb, cord, plug and film not included. See below.
49 K 6842—Size, 10x9x7½ in. high. Shipping weight, 12 ounces...........**98c**
39-In. Mickey Mouse Films in Color. Shpg. wt., 2 oz. 54-In. Films in Color

49 K 6950—Mickey in "Mickey's Pal Pluto"...10c	**49 K 6952**—"Hansel and Gretel"..............9c
49 K 6951—Mickey in "The Haunted House"...10c	**49 K 6953**—"Treasure Island"..............9c
20 K 671—6-foot Cord and Plug for Talkie or Movie. Shipping weight, 7 ounces........17c	

First Real Motion Picture Film Electric Movie

At this low price every kiddie can have his own movie. Light furnished by 2 batteries. Good lens shows clear steady pictures about 15x18 in. It runs a circular band of non-inflammable film (listed below) giving continuous performance without rewinding. Pocket size. 5x1¾ x 3¼ in. high. Heavy gauge metal, nickel trimmed. Complete with bulb. Batteries and film not included, see below.
49 K 6838—Shipping weight, 1 pound.............**25c**
20 K 1401—1⅜ in. Diam. regular cell Battery. Shpg. wt., 6 oz....**3c**

AS LOW AS **25c**

Non-Inflammable 22-Inch Real Movie Film Loops

Specially prepared new narrow width films. Show a continuous picture as long as desired. Shipping weight, 2 ounces each.

49 K 6970—Popeye in "Says Who".......10c	**49 K 6973**—Popeye in "Stars".........10c	**49 K 6976**—Betty Boop in "Flirt".......10c	**49 K 6979**—Krazy Kat in "Beaned".......10c
49 K 6971—Popeye in "Puff".........10c	**49 K 6974**—Popeye in "The Winner"....10c	**49 K 6977**—Betty Boop in "Dancing".....10c	**49 K 6980**—Krazy Kat in "Wins".......10c
49 K 6972—Popeye in "The Giant".......10c	**49 K 6975**—Popeye in "The Lover".....10c	**49 K 6978**—Betty Boop in "Tripped".....10c	**49 K 6981**—Scrappy in "Pals".........10c

Electric Keystone Radiopticians with 25 Assorted Picture Postcards

They enlarge and project in natural colors, your own travel pictures, photos, comics, etc. Made of sheet steel in crystal finish. Complete with cord and plug. Use your own electric bulbs. Bulbs not included.

Popular Model
3½ in. double convex lens, 2 reflectors, ventilators. Size, 9¾ x 11x12 inches. Shipping weight, 6 lbs.
79 K 6865
$3.98

De Luxe Model
Size, 11x11¾ x12¼ in. Sharper, brighter pictures. Double Plano Convex lens system. Large parabolic reflectors. 2 sliding adjustable picture holders for pictures up to 5½x5¾ in. Shpg. wt., 8 lbs.
79 K 6866......$6.98

Prices in this Sears catalog are for mail orders only

Whole Play Kitchen for Modern Little Housekeeper

An 8⅛-inch all-steel play stove, 2 pans and 2 empty samples. Kitchen walls of heavy cardboard, 36x14 in. Printed in green and white. Built-in cupboard and cabinet, both with doors. Shipping weight, 3 pounds 4 ounces.

49 K 7310—Usual $1.00 Value..........................**69c**

69c

Electric Stove With Switch
$4.50 value! Over 1-ft. high. Real oven heat indicator. Nickel plated cooking top; 4½-ft. cord plugs into 110 to 120-volt current. Pans included. Shpg. wt., 7 lbs. 2 oz.
49 K 7319......$2.98

Little Girl's Electric Stove
Cabinet style, 3 ovens. Cook or bake. Real heat indicator on top oven. Just right for tiny girls. 9⅞ in. wide. 3 pans included. 4½-foot cord plugs into 110 to 120-volt current. Shpg. wt., 5 lbs.
49 K 7308............98c

28½-Inch DOLL HOUSE With Furniture and Automobile

Complete as Shown $1.69 $2.25 Value

Patented Interlocking Joint House—No Metal Clips to Lose
23 Pieces Almost Unbreakable Metal Furniture

We prefer to offer a quality outfit rather than a large number of pieces. Just look at it! A five-room white and green, **strong fiber board Colonial House (not light cardboard)** with breakfast porch and garage and a nice, shiny bright enameled 4-inch metal sedan! The front door of house opens. The back is open so she can arrange the **23 pieces of beautiful colorful furniture.** Mahogany finish radio, settee, table, chair and lamp in the living room. Pink enameled bed, triple mirror vanity, night table, lamp and chair. Orchid enameled bath tub, toilet with removable seat, wash stand, medicine chest and stool. Walnut finish table and four dining room chairs. White kitchen sink, ice box, and range; 23 pieces in all, the largest about 3½ inches. House, 28½x15⅝ inches.

49 K 7149 — House, Breakfast porch, Garage, sedan, 23 pieces of metal furniture. Shipping weight, 4 lbs. 14 oz........**$1.69**
49 K 7130—Furniture only. 23 Pieces. Shpg. wt., 2 lbs. 14 oz...**$1.19**

49 K 7134—House with Breakfast porch, and garage only. (No furniture or sedan.) Shipping weight, 2 lbs. 4 oz....**59c**

LIVING ROOM · BEDROOM · BATHROOM · DINING ROOM · KITCHEN

Popular Cast Iron Stoves
$1.39 10½-Inch

She can "make-believe" cook on them! All brightly nickel plated. Fancy back; each with 4 removable lids; hinged oven door. Pans included.

49 K 7321 — Has all features as shown. 13¾-inch stove. Shipping weight, 11 lbs. 9 oz...**$1.98**
49 K 7320—10½-inch stove. 2 utensils. Shipping wt., 6 lbs. 6 oz.....**1.39**
49 K 7315—6¼-inch stove. 1 pan. Shipping weight, 3 pounds 3 ounces......**.45**

3-Piece Matched Set
A purse her size, a make-believe metal watch with moving hands and elastic wrist strap, and a bead necklace, all in bright colors to match. Shpg. wt., 2 oz.
49 K 9105...21c

New Modernistic Two-Tone Dressers
The smartest we've seen in a decade! And well built, too.

Every girl will want one for her Dolly's clothes. Here it is, pure white enamel with walnut color trim and beveled edge mirror.

79 K 7167—As pictured. 22½x19 in. Shipping wt., 13 lbs.......**$2.98**
79 K 7166—18½x14⅞ in. 3 large drawers. Shipping weight, 7 pounds..........**1.98**
79 K 7165—13½x11½ in. 2 large drawers. Shipping weight, 4 pounds........**.98**

Dolly's Adjustable Ironing Board
To iron Dolly's clothes on! She'll want to iron when Mother does. No rough edges. All smoothly rounded wood. Tapered ironing surface, 34½ inches long, and adjustable to 3 height positions, 21 to 25 inches from floor.
79 K 1775—Shipping weight, 5 lbs. 4 oz......**69c**

Smaller Board for Little Girls
49 K 1777—Same finish but for little girls. Adjustable 12 to 14 inches from floor. 20½ inches long. Shipping weight, 1 lb. 6 oz........**25c**

It's Cleaning Day
7 BIG PIECES FOR ONLY $1.00

And here's a cleaning outfit just her size! (1) Toy Kenmore vacuum cleaner with revolving brush, sateen bag. (2) A Maid of Honor, real colored yarn dust mop with 24-in. wood handle. (3) 12-inch cotton yarn duster, (4) 32-inch broom with enameled wood handle, (5) Green enameled long handle heavy metal dust pan, (6) Dainty color print cotton apron with roomy pocket. (7) pretty maid's cap. Shpg. wt., 4 lbs.
79 K 9187......$1.00

New Improved 7-Piece Laundry Set
98c
Everything for wash day, ironing day. All well-made pieces designed to do their jobs right. 8¾-inch Sunny Suzy Washing Machine with 2 real rubber roll wringers; enameled wash tub; revolving drier; 6 wood clothes pins, 12-inch ironing board and nickel plated iron.
49 K 1712—Shipping weight, 1 pound 9 ounces........**98c**

Cast Iron Sad-iron and Stand
Mrs. Pott's Style. Like Mother's! She can really iron with it! 4¾ in. long. Detachable enameled handle. Shpg. wt., 1 lb. 8 oz.
49 K 1788.....43c

For the Tiny Miss
4-in. size. Not illustrated. Shpg. wt., 12 oz.
49 K 1789.....23c

Girls' Real 4-In. Electric Iron
Red enameled iron and handle. Nickeled heating surface. Asbestos cord and plug. For 110-volt current. Shpg. wt., 1 lb. 13 oz.
49 K 1793......87c

Little Tots' Low Priced Electric Iron
Not Illustrated. Special. Shipping weight, 15 oz.
49 K 1792..........49c

Little Girls' Sewing Machines

With Carrying Case
She can make Dolly's clothes on this 6-inch green enameled sewing machine. Has special thread tension raising foot. It's all ready to sew — with one needle, spool of thread and cloth. Colorful hinge cover 7½ in. cardboard case with 3 drawers. Shpg. wt., 1 lb. 14 oz.
49 K 5802 $1.00

Sew Like Mother
Our best sewing machine. Shaped head like mother's. Makes perfect stitches. Teaches girls to be handy. Size overall, 7½x7⅜x3¾ in. Has drop-foot thread tension and heavy flywheel. Green enameled steel. Nickel plated sewing top. Clamp included. Shpg. wt., 2 lbs. 12 oz.
49 K 5801 $1.39

Doll Trunks
$1.19 14-in.

For Dolly's clothes. Colored metal over wood body. 18⅜ in. long, with leather handles, metal bound edges; lock and key; inside tray.
79 K 8419—Shipping weight, 12 pounds....**$2.49**

14-Inch Trunk
Not shown. With lock, key and tray. Colored artificial leather covering.
79 K 8403—Shpg. wt., 4 lbs. 10 oz...**$1.19**

Sunny Suzy Handy Washing Machine

Your Choice of 2 Sizes 59c
8¾-In. Size

What fun she'll have with it! Turn the crank and it will rotate! Attached wringer has white rollers; adjustable 3 ways.

Large Size, 11¼ in. High.
49 K 1710—Shpg. wt., 3 lbs. 8 oz...**89c**
Medium Size, 8¾ in. High (Not shown)
49 K 1708—Shpg. wt., 3 lbs. 2 oz...**59c**

Do your Christmas shopping from Sears catalogs **737**

OUR BEST
55-Chart Easel Type Solid Oak Blackboard and Desk

$4.98

No Better Blackboard Made

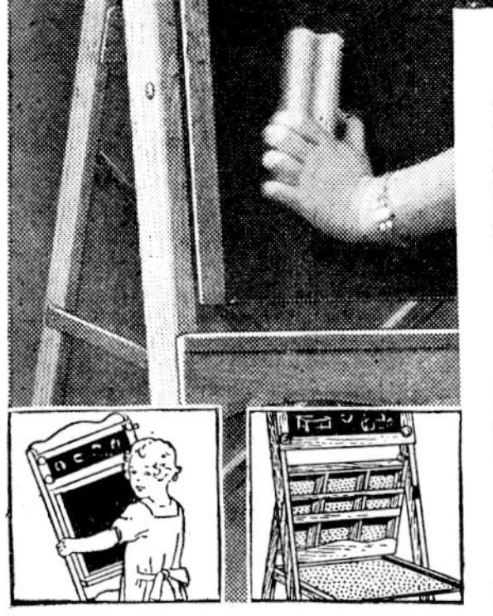

Chalk and Eraser Included

46 inches high; 21⅝ inches wide

We recommend this as the best folding blackboard for young boys and girls. They learn quickly from the 55 up-to-date charts—eight of them in color. The writing surface is heavy slate compound (not just paint). Can be adjusted to form a desk or folded into small space. Strongly braced. Varnished natural finish oak frames. Easy turning rollers. Shipping weight, 18 lbs.
79 K 3811..........................**$4.98**

8-Chart Easel Blackboard and Desk
Regular $2.50 Value

42 inches high; 19½ inches wide

With alphabets, figures, animals, etc. Heavy masonite slate compound surfaced blackboard, with varnished white wood frames, red lacquer trimmed; has chalk rail, easy turning rollers. Chalk and eraser included. Shipping weight, 7 pounds.
79 K 3808.....................**$1.98**

3-Chart Blackboard and Desk
Usually Sells for $1.50

38¾ inches high; 17 inches wide

Varnished white wood. Chalk and eraser included. Exceptional value. Shipping weight, 6 lbs.
79 K 3807.....................**$1.00**

Table and Bench Nailing Set
At Usual Price of Table Alone **$1.00**

Dovetail constructed wood table 19¾x12½x19½ in. Wood bench, 11⅛x7⅛ in., with sturdy steel legs included. One heavy fibrous 11½-in. nailing board. Complete with hammer, assorted non-poisonous colored wood parts, box of nails and instructions. Shipping weight, 6 pounds.
79 K 3685..............**$1.00**

Junior Nailing Set—No Table

Two 11½-in. squares. Complete with hammer and nails. Shipping weight, 3 lbs.
49 K 3686..............**49c**

Extra wood designs and nails.
49 K 3687—Shpg. wt., 8 oz...**21c**

New Early American Logs
Sold by Mail Only by Sears **45c**
42 Pcs.

Make realistic fascinating hewn effect models of log cabins, forts, sawmills, etc. Log sizes, 1½ to 10½ in. long.

145-Piece Big Building Set

Builds many models, including fort illustrated. Box, 18x12¼x1¾ in.
49 K 3647—Shipping wt., 5 pounds................**$1.79**

62-Piece Junior Building Set

Builds cabins, bridges and many other models. Box, 18x12¼x⅞ in.
49 K 3646—Shpg. wt., 2 lbs. 12 oz..**89c**

42-Piece Beginner's Building Set

Log sizes, 1½ to 7½ inches.
49 K 3645—Shpg. wt., 1 lb. 8 oz...**45c**

Make Your Dolly a Quilt
25c

140 colorful 1¾-inch cloth patches. Complete with cotton padding and lining to make quilt size 14x20 in. Shipping wt., 4 oz.
49 K 3869......

New Idea 20-Pc. Embroidery Set With Doll
49c

Think of a 7-in. jointed arm China doll with rayon slip surrounded with 4 pretty print already cut-out dresses, 4 stenciled pieces that make another dress, 2 nighties and romper to fit dolly; 6 skeins of floss, embroidery hoops, scissors, needles and thimble. In 16-in. fancy box.
49 K 3889—Shpg. wt., 2 lbs..........

New Electric Wood Burning Outfit — All the Rage Right Now
89c

Now anyone can make beautiful objects and designs on wood, leather, cork or velvet. Plug in the easy-to-use electric pencil (listed as standard by Underwriters' Laboratories. Heating element embedded in porcelain; cork grip; enameled wood handle. With cord and plug. There are four 3-ply 5x3½ in. plaques in assorted printed designs, and two 5x1½-in. plain plaques.
49 K 3838—Shpg. wt., 1 lb. 8 oz.............**89c**

Assortment of 4 Large Printed Plywood Plaques

One 10x7 in.; two ovals, 10x7 in.; one round, 8-in. diam.
49 K 3836—Shpg. wt., 1 lb. 6 oz.......**4 for 59c**

Assortment of 5 Smaller Printed Plywood Plaques

All 3½x5 inches; attractive designs.
49 K 3835—Shpg. wt., 10 oz..........**5 for 29c**

Fox Educational Boards — Steel Slate Surfaces

13 in. diam. 65 letters, figures, on one side, 45 words and pictures on other side. Shpg. wt., 2 lbs. 11 oz.
49 K 3863..........**$1.19**
$1.50 size..........

13-In. Regular $1.00 Size

No words or pictures. Shpg. wt., 2 lbs. 2 oz.
49 K 3842..........**79c**

9¾-In. Popular 50c Size

48 Letters and figures. Shipping weight, 1 lb. 2 oz.
49 K 3801..........**39c**

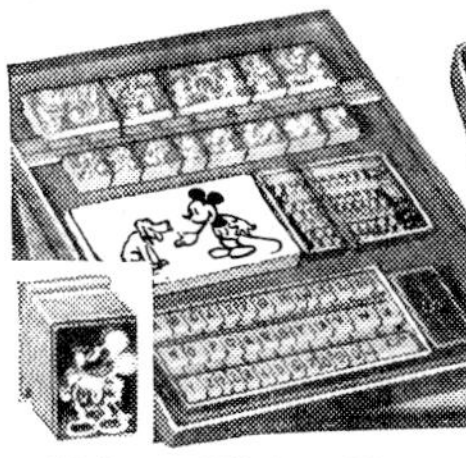

84-Piece Sign Set
49c

Make your own signs. Rubber alphabets of capitals and small letters ½ inch high mounted on wood; numerals; ink pad in metal box, wood ruler, guide. Make show cards with them. Shpg. wt., 13 oz.
49 K 3829.....

63-Piece Mickey Mouse Printing Set
89c

Five 1⅜-in. and eight ¾-in. rubber character stamps. Complete ½-in. alphabet and numerals mounted on wood. Crayons, stamp pad, etc. Shipping weight, 1 lb. 7 oz.
49 K 3866..........**89c**

22-Pc. Mickey Mouse Set
45c

Same 13 figure stamps as above, but no alphabet or numerals. Shpg. wt., 1 lb. 2 oz.
49 K 3865..........

146-Piece Printing Set
25c

Includes 26 A B C's, 10 numerals, $ signs; each ⅜ in. high and mounted on wood. 100 small rubber capital letters, also tweezers, type holder, ink pad in metal box, 4 crayons, paper. Shipping weight, 8 ounces.
49 K 3825......

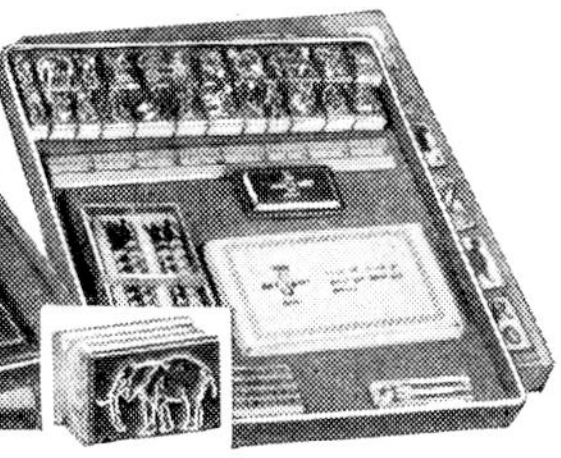

130-Pc. Farm and Jungle Printing Set
59c

Set consists of 21 ⅞-in. barnyard animals, fowls and animals of the jungle. 100 rubber small letters and numerals, ruler, stamp pad, six crayons, a type holder, tweezers and pad of paper. Lithographed box 10¼x9 inches. Shipping weight, 1 pound 3 ounces.
49 K 3867.....

ACTUAL TYPE SIZE

Marx Dial Typewriter
and 100 Sheets of Paper—Only **$1.19**

Less than typewriter price alone last year. Entertaining—educational! Child can actually write real letters on regular size office paper. First popular priced typewriter ever offered for children. Type is securely fastened to dial—cannot drop off. Dial has 40 metal characters including alphabet, numerals, and punctuation marks. Sliding carriage. Heavy lithographed metal, 11½x5¾x6⅛ in.
49 K 3847—Shpg. wt., 3 lbs. 15 oz...**$1.19**

3 Extra Rolls for Typewriter
49 K 3898—Shipping weight, 4 oz........**10c**

Bag of Wood Blocks
59c

About 125 smooth, clean, well shaped wood blocks to build houses, bridges, forts, etc. In a big, red drawstring-top mesh bag. Many shapes, sizes and colors. They'll have lots of fun with these blocks. Can be kept in bag when not in use. Shipping weight, 4 pounds.
49 K 3672 ....**59c**

Big Value Paint Set
25c

For the young artist. Look at all you get! 34 cakes of assorted colored dry paints, two camel's hair brushes in a black enameled metal box, with white enameled inside hinged cover. 9⅝x3½ in. Made in Germany. Shpg. wt., 8 oz.
49 K 3878...**25c**

75c Value Paint Set
49c

A Knockout Value. 48 cakes dry assorted colors, 2 smaller cakes of paints and 2 good camel's hair brushes. Black enameled, white interior metal box with hinged cover. 9¾x 6¾ in. Made in Germany. Shipping weight, 15 ounces.
49 K 3881.....**49c**

De Luxe 48-Pc. Set
89c

Our most practical set. Has 12 tubes moist water colors, 32 cakes dry paints, 2 large cakes and 2 brushes. Black enameled metal box with hinged cover, 9½x5 in. Made in Germany. Shipping weight, 1 lb. 1 oz.
49 K 3882...**89c**

Improved 3-In-1 Set
39c

Look! Stencil, paint and crayon set for the "Kiddies." 22 cardboard stencils and 2 sheets of colored paper 6x4½ in. 12 crayons, 10 water color paints, a pan and brush. Box, 11¼x10¼ inches. Shipping weight, 1 lb. 4 oz.
49 K 3823.... **39c**

Modeling Clay Sets

8 large colored strips, 7 wood design blocks, modeling stick. Shipping weight, 1 lb. 11 oz.
49 K 3751........**39c**

Big Value Modeling Set

8 smaller clay strips, 6 wood design blocks and modeling stick. Shpg.wt., 1 lb. 2 oz.
49 K 3750....**21c**

"Scrappy" Paint Set
49c

Have your own colored movie with the 3 "Scrappy" paper films—mounted on wood rollers, with cardboard stage and 14 colors, paint brush and water pan to paint them. Attractive 10-inch box. Shipping wt., 1 pound 5 ounces.
49 K 3887.....**49c**

Write Sears personal service for suggestions

Electric Lighted Service Station
It Has Streamlined Car, Too

$1.00 Roll the 6-inch streamlined steel coupe up the greasing platform, raise it by pulling the lever and watch the electric lights go on. Beautifully lithographed metal service station with **2 electric lighted "pumps"**, oil service wagon and watering can. 13½x10x5¾ in. high. **Battery included.** Shipping weight 4 pounds. **$1.00**

49 K 5752 .... **$1.00**

Mickey and Minnie Mouse
Take a Ride!

Sold by mail only by Sears. Wind up strong **94c** clockwork motor, release brake and away they go. Their attractively colored shaped composition bodies act like mad while bell rings. 9-in. metal hand car and 6 ft. of circular track.

49 K 5105—Shpg. wt., 2 lbs. 7 oz. **94c**

Fire Truck! Lights! Siren! Ladders!

Off to the fire! Wind the new Marx heavy duty super-power motor and see it go, siren shrieking, electric headlights and searchlight blazing. Pull the brake and mount the two 8-in. ladders on truck for the rescue. It's red enameled heavy steel. 14¼ inches long, with the new streamline fenders and oversize balloon type rubber wheels. **Battery included.** Shipping weight, 4 pounds 5 ounces.

49 K 5796 .... **$1.59**

Garage With 2 Mechanical Autos

Lots of play value! Wind the strong spring motors of the two 6-in. heavy gauge steel streamline automobiles and watch them travel on their easy-rolling wooden wheels. Open garage doors and let cars drive in. Garage is heavy gauge lithographed steel with doors you can lock, and measures 7¼x6⅜x4¾ inches. Shipping weight, 3 pounds 3 ounces.

49 K 5727 .... **59c**

Marx Aluminum Climbing Tractor

Finest tractor ever made. Has new, more powerful clockwork motor. Climbs steep grades and pushes loads bigger than itself. Stop and start lever. Aluminum case over metal housing. 8½ inches long. Shpg. wt., 1 lb. 7 oz. **94c**

49 K 5746 .... **94c**

49 K 5745—Similar to above, but has lithographed metal housing only, not aluminum and less powerful motor. Shipping weight, 1 lb. 7 oz. **59c**

Now! A Heavy Duty Climbing Tank

Here's real fun—wind the new heavy duty super-power clockwork motor—release brake—and watch tank climb up or down hill in real fighting tank fashion. Has oversize 1-inch double traction tread that never misses. A mechanical wonder at a record new low price. It's 9½ in. long by 5¼ in. high. Shiny nickel finish metal. Shpg. wt., 2 lbs. **94c**

49 K 5763 .... **94c**

New Rocket Racer

Latest design, 16 inches long. Tremendous value. Strong spring motor. Bright metal, rubber bumper. Shpg. wt., 1 lb. 6 oz.

49 K 5735 ..... **25c**

Delivery Motorcycle

Every little tot wants one. 9¾ inches long. Bright colored metal, make-believe headlights. Strong spring motor. Shpg. wt., 1 lb. 3 oz.

49 K 5740 .... **25c**

THE LATEST SENSATION
New, Mysterious Tricky Taxi!

39c Daredevil 4½-inch metal taxi with sturdy clockwork motor, whirls and dashes about on the 10-inch colorful metal platform map of city streets, which is included—it goes right to the edges but seldom off—why? Runs on any flat surface.

49 K 5744—Shipping weight, 13 ounces. **39c**

Midget Tractor

Only 5¼ inches long but it actually climbs. Bright metal. Strong spring motor and brake. Shipping weight, 8 ounces.

49 K 5753 ..... **25c**

Moon Mullins Hand Car

6 in. long. Brightly colored. Strong Marx spring motor. They pump the handle up and down and race along. Shpg. wt., 9 oz.

49 K 5772 .... **25c**

New Low Price for Rider Truck

Sit on steel seat, pedal with your feet and steer it like a real truck. Heavy gauge steel, baked-on enamel finish. Holds the weight of a grown-up. Length, overall, 16 inches. Height, to seat from floor, 7½ inches. Shipping weight, 4 pounds 8 ounces.

49 K 5420 .... **59c**

New 13-Piece Municipal Airport

59c Colorful 12x15x12 inch cardboard airport. Easily set up. Famous Tootsie Toy transcontinental tri-motor plane, a TWA cabin plane and a Chrysler automobile of unbreakable metal, averaging 5 inches; 4 passengers and 5 dummy tools. Shipping weight, 2 pounds.

49 K 5411 .... **59c**

24½ In. 4-Car Auto Transport

98c Latest streamline design Double-Decker with electric headlights. Turn lights out, drop unloading platform and let the 3 cars on top roll down easily, just like the big transports. Real dump truck on lower platform.

Transport, 24½ inches long with runway extended. Four streamlined 6-inch cars with shiny sloping radiator fronts. Really 5 toys in one. **Battery included.** Shipping weight, 4 pounds 1 ounce.

49 K 5407 .... **98c**

21-In. Buddy "L" Dump Truck

98c With electric headlights and shiny radiator. Boys! Here's fun! Turn lights on with switch—load your truck, work lever to dump it. Carry sand, toys, anything up to 200 pounds. Biggest value we know of. Heavy gauge steel baked-on enamel and it is Buddy "L" quality. 21 inches long with body raised; 8¾ inches high. Balloon type rubber tires. **Battery included.** Shipping weight, 6 pounds.

79 K 5009 .... **98c**

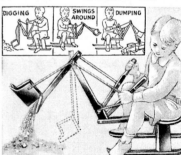

Run a Buddy "L" Digger!

Sit on the strong steel seat. Seat and boom turn on runners to dig and dump wherever you like. It's 28 inches long; with boom extended, 38 inches; largest height, 17 inches. Made of 20-gauge steel, enameled in black and red. Shipping weight, 4 pounds 10 ounces. **98c**

79 K 5002 .... **98c**

Garage and 10 Streamline Cars

A whole fleet of cars with an 11-inch colored strong cardboard garage. Chrysler, several trucks, bus, tanker, roadster, etc. Heavy gauge steel on easy rolling wheels. Average, 6 inches. Shipping wt., 5 lbs. 6 oz. **98c**

49 K 5412 .... **98c**

Big $2.00 Value Last Year—Now Only $1.59
—27-Inch Train—Electric Headlight—Bell—Figure 8 track.

The streamlined engine with clockwork motor, brake and electric headlight and two cars are coupled together like real ones. Watch it speed around the track! They're metal, lithographed in Union Pacific colors. Headlight bulb, battery and Union Pacific Lucky coin included. 160-inches of track.

49 K 5135—Shipping weight, 6 pounds............ **$1.59**

Your Choice
98c Each

Mickey Stokes His Own Freight Train
(A) Brand New—Sold by Mail only by Sears
The faster the train travels, the faster Mickey Mouse stokes the engine and the bell rings. It'll thrill the "kiddies." 7-in. locomotive with powerful clockwork motor and brake release. **Entire train 30 in. long.** Circular track about 80 in. around.

49 K 5104—Shpg. wt., 4 lbs....**98c**

Realistic Watch Sparks Fly
(B) Sparks fly out of smokestack. 29-in. train. Strong Marx clockwork motor. Engine is heavy steel with brake to stop or start. Tender and 3 cars lithographed metal in train colors. Oval track about 74 in. around, banked for speed. **Extra flint included.**

49 K 5133—Shpg. wt., 3 lbs. 13 oz.....**98c**

NEW MICKEY MOUSE CIRCUS TRAIN
With Mechanical Motor
$1.79

Lionel Product

SOLD BY MAIL ONLY BY SEARS

MICKEY STOKES HIS ENGINE   DESIGNS BY WALT DISNEY

Mickey Stokes the New Commodore Vanderbilt Locomotive

30-Inch train, 84 inches of track—a whole circus. Gay 20x9x11 inch high cardboard circus tent, filling station and 5-inch composition Mickey figure. Strong clockwork motor hauls this big circus train with Mickey's kingdom of animals lithographed in beautiful colors on sides of cars. **Headlight flashes, bell rings,** Mickey stokes engine! 7-inch new Commodore Vanderbilt Streamlined engine with brake; tender, circus diner, animal car and band car. Battery included. Shpg. wt., 6 lbs. 6 oz.

49 K 5103—Complete Outfit....................................**$1.79**

SEARS GREATEST ELECTRIC TRAIN VALUES
Complete With Transformer
Nothing Else to Buy

$4.39

$8.79

New Marx Electric
COMMODORE VANDERBILT TRAIN

● 41-inch, 5-car streamlined electric reversible passenger train or 3-car freight train, or combination of both.... 8 beautifully lithographed metal cars in all, one tender and 12-pc. "O"-gauge oval track about 124 in. around... Transformer included.

Have a passenger train—a fast freight or a mixed accommodation! Latest type Commodore Vanderbilt locomotive. Transformer, which is included, changes its speed. Watch the train speed by with headlight piercing the darkness. Red tail light on observation car. For 110-volt 60-cycle A.C. current. Shpg. wt., 8 lbs. 12 oz.

49 K 5158—Complete Outfit.**$4.69**

Same Passenger train as above, but no freight cars. Shpg. wt., 7 lbs. 12 oz.
49 K 5157 ....**$4.29**

$4.29 Without Freight Cars

Marx Streamlined
UNION PACIFIC TRAIN
Save at Sears New Low Price
For This 35-Inch Electric Train

It's the 1935 flying streamline train that goes with a roar over this 124-inch oval track, with headlight streaming ahead. Pull the lever on transformer to change speed or stop it. Wheels mounted to take train at record speed around curves without jumping off track. Four cars in the Union Pacific colors, coupled together. For 110-volt 60-cycle A.C. current. Complete train with 12 pieces "O"-gauge 3-rail track—**Transformer included.** Shipping weight, 8 lbs. 4 oz.

49 K 5156 ....**$4.39**

Distant Control
LIONEL ELECTRIC TRAIN
Sold by Mail Only by Sears
$15.00 Value Last Year

40-inch electric steel train. 9½-inch reversible steel engine; concealed electric headlight; 2 colored pilot lights. Distant controlled so train can be stopped, started or reversed at any point. 6½-inch coal tender. Two 7½-inch pullman cars, and one observation car all have double trucks. 10-piece "O"-gauge oval track about 114 inches around. For 110-volt 60-cycle A.C. current. **Transformer included.** Shipping weight, 11 pounds 13 ounces.

49 K 5155 ....**$8.79**

Electric Train Tracks

"O" Gauge Lionel Track
For train 49 K 5155.   Shpg. wt., 10 oz.
Curved Track   **Straight Track**
49K5235 2 pcs. for...**37c**   **49K5236** 2 pcs. for...**37c**

"O" Gauge Marx Track
For 49 K 5156 and 49 K 5157 and 49 K 5158. Shpg. wt., 11 oz.
Curved   **Straight**
49K5217 4 pcs. for...**39c**   **49K5216** 4 pcs. for...**39c**

Lionel Switches with lamps for "O"-gauge trains. Shpg. wt., 2 lbs. 14 oz.
49 K 5215 **$5.29** Pair

Lionel Crossover for "O"-gauge trains. Shpg. wt., 15 oz.
49 K 5210 **$1.45** Each

MARX Crossover for Trains
49 K 5156, 49 K 5157, and 49 K 5158.
49 K 5238—Shpg. wt., 1 lb......**59c**

Mechanical Train Tracks

Curved Track
For trains 49 K 5103 and 49 K 5104. Shpg. wt., 13 oz.
49K5207 4 pcs. for...**19c**

For trains 49 K 5135 and 49 K 5133. Shpg. wt., 13 oz.
49K5213 4 pcs. for...**19c**

Straight Track
For trains 49 K 5103 and 49 K 5104. Shpg. wt., 13 oz.
49K5206 4 pcs. for...**19c**

For trains 49 K 5135 and 49 K 5133. Shpg. wt., 13 oz.
49K5212 4 pcs. for...**19c**

For All Mechanical Trains
Switches One left and one right. Shpg. wt., 12 oz.
49 K 5203 Pair **39c**

Crossover For making figure eight track. Shpg. wt., 3 oz.
49 K 5205..**19c**

Jefferson Transformer
For "O"-gauge trains. 75 watts, unbroken voltage control 5½ to 22½ volts. 110-volt 60-cycle A.C. Shpg. wt., 3 lbs.
49 K 5277.**$2.79**

Low Priced Transformer
For "O"-gauge trains, 110-volt 60-cycle A.C. Shpg. wt., 3 lbs. 4 oz.
49 K 5288.**$1.19**

WILL HOLD 200 LBS.

$1.29

Ride and Steer This Locomotive
23 inches long. A child can ride on it. Will hold 200 lbs. Heavy 20-gauge steel. 9⅞ in. high. Steering bar on top of boiler. Bright baked-on enamel finish. Steel wheels. Shpg. wt., 9 lbs.
79 K 5024.......**$1.29**

The larger the order the less your postage per pound

743

New! Streamline!
No Increase in Price

Here's the Prize Winner of the New York Toy Show

Oh Boy! Some Bike! Brand new! **Ball bearing front wheel!** Bright red enameled! All-steel! With electric headlight (**1 battery included**)! Gracefully streamlined from the adjustable handlebars to the end of the beautifully shaped all-steel frame; new wide fork, new adjustable spring saddle, new large steel fender, new step plates over rear axle. Rubber pedals, grips. ¾-in. rubber tires. Silvery color spokes.

Measure child from crotch to instep.

Catalog Number	Front Wheel Diam.	Seat to Lower Pedal	Shpg. Wt. Lbs.	Price
79 K 8650	12 in.	18 to 20 in.	21	$4.98
79 K 8651	16 in.	21 to 23 in.	25	5.69
79 K 8652	20 in.	24 to 26 in.	29	6.49

Yes, Sir! Streamline Bikes at Regular Bike Prices

Racy! Light in weight, yet very sturdy! Streamlined from the snub-nose handlebars to the stepplates over the rear axle! **Ball bearing front wheel.** Nicely formed heavy steel red enameled frame, streamlined, comfortable and adjustable spring seat. Fancy steel fender over front wheel. Big handlebars can be raised or lowered. Large rubber grips and pedals. ¾-inch non-skid rubber tires. Strong, sturdy shiny spokes on all wheels.

Measure child from crotch to instep.

Catalog Number	Front Wheel Diam.	Seat to Lower Pedal	Shpg. Wt. Lbs.	Price
79 K 8640	12 inch	17 to 18½ in.	17	$3.69
79 K 8641	16 inch	19 to 21½ in.	23	4.59
79 K 8642	20 inch	22 to 24 in.	29	5.39

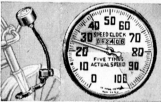

SPEED CLOCK for Velocipedes, Scooters, or Two-Wheelers

Show the speed you can travel on your bike geared up five times actual speed! Shows 50 miles when you go 10. Aluminum case and dial with indicator; convex crystal. Will not fit velocipedes or scooters with large front fender. Complete with flexible shaft and braces for attaching.

79 K 8610—Shpg. wt., 1 lb. **98c**

New MICKEY MOUSE 33½-In. Scooter

With fender and parking stand. Red enameled strong steel frame, 8¼-inch double-disc steel wheels; ⅝-inch rubber tires. Enameled wood handle and corrugated wood footboard. Shipping weight, 11 lbs. **79 K 8801.. $1.49**

Just Out! 1936 Cadillac

1936 Cadillac—All-Steel—Streamlined

He'll dazzle his friends when he races by in this **42½-inch red and cream all-steel Cadillac**, streamlined just like the new cars. It's one of the finest we have ever offered and is worth considerably more than we ask. Silver-color radiator, windshield and bumper; beaver-tail back, heavy fenders and running boards. Real electric headlights with control switch. Big trumpet horn. 9⅜-inch rubber-tired wheels are artillery-type and roller bearing. Adjustable rubber pedals. Drive shafts are set in ball-bearings on rear axle. **No batteries included (two required).** For batteries, see 20 K 1401, Page 592.

79 K 8908—Shipping weight, 48 pounds......................**$9.98**

With Spring Saddle and Ball Bearing Front Wheel

Better value than ever with its new streamlined adjustable seat on flexible spring. Bright red enameled half-oval steel frame with cream color trim . . . curved steel handlebars . . . **ball-bearing front wheel**; ¾-inch rubber tires . . . rubber grips and pedals. Seat may be raised 2¼ in. from measure given.

Measure child from crotch to instep.

Catalog Number	Front Wheel Diam.	Seat to Lower Pedal	Shpg. Wt. Lbs.	Price
79 K 8602	12 in.	16¼ in.	13	$2.79
79 K 8603	16 in.	19 in.	18	3.29

Our Ever-Popular Strong Tubular Steel Bikes

Extra good looking and extra strong! Made like Brother's big bike. Light green and ivory enameled tubular steel frame with **welded joints . . . not usually offered at this price.** Easy riding ball-bearing front wheel, comfortable spring seat; streamline curved steel handlebars with rubber grips, rubber pedals and ¾-inch rubber tires.

Measure child from crotch to instep.

Catalog Number	Front Wheel Diam.	Seat to Lower Pedal	Shpg. Wt. Lbs.	Price
79 K 8684	12 in.	17 to 18½ in.	15	$3.39
79 K 8685	16 in.	19 to 21½ in.	19	3.98
79 K 8686	20 in.	22 to 24 in.	22	4.69

Little Tots Want This Mickey Mouse Wheelbarrow

A Useful Toy—Brightly Colored Almost Two and a Half Feet Long!

It's bound to make any little youngster happy. Green and red enameled steel, with modern streamlined mudguard over the rubber-tired 5-inch wheel. Black enameled steel handles and foot rest. It's strong and well made so that it will stand the rough treatment given it by little hands. They will be delighted with the attractive Mickey Mouse decoration and they'll love this toy for play and use it for work, too. Shipping weight, 5 pounds.

79 K 7626...............98c

DELIGHTS AT SEARS SAVINGS!

28½-INCH DOLL HOUSE

30 Pieces Furniture

$2²⁵ Value $1⁶⁹ Complete

Easy to Set Up...Complete With Wood Furniture

A house fit for a Queen . . . rather than just a lot of pieces . . . and priced within the reach of every little girl, is Sears big idea. Think of it! A 5-room, white and green, **strong fiber board, patented interlocking joint Colonial House** (not light cardboard) with a dining room on one end and a garage on the other. **No metal clips to lose.** Rugs, and drapes, printed on floors and walls; flower boxes printed on outer sides. The front door opens, the back of the house is built open so the little housekeeper can arrange the **30 pieces of colorful wood furniture.** Mahogany finish radio, settee, chair, table, vase and floor lamp in the living room. Pink enameled bed, mirror effect vanity, boudoir lamp, 2 candlesticks and chair in the bedroom. In the bathroom, an ivory enameled tub, toilet, wash-stand, waste basket and electric heater. In the dining room a blue table, 2 chairs, buffet and 3-piece console set; and in the kitchen a green kitchen sink, gas stove, table, 2 chairs and fruit bowl. 30 pieces in all, the largest about 4¼ inches. House, 28½x15x10 inches.

49 D 2125—House, Dining Room, Garage, and 30-Pieces Wood Furniture. Shipping weight, 4 pounds 6 ounces........**$1.69**

49 D 2101—House, Dining Room, and Garage only. (No furniture). Shipping weight, 2 pounds 4 ounces............**59c**

49 D 2120—Wood Furniture Only; 30 Pieces. Shpg. wt., 1 lb. 8 oz.**$1.19**

4-STAR GOLDEN JUBILEE SPECIAL

3-PIECE UNPAINTED FURNITURE SET

Sears tremendous Birthday Party marches on, bringing you value after value; here's one you simply can't overlook! Certainly worthy of the tag we have given it—Four Star Golden Jubilee Special. The biggest buy we have ever offered in a children's furniture outfit. More fun than a picnic to have the kids over for a tea party served on this set, what a thrill they'll get! Strong and durable, massive turned wood legs. Nicely shaped table top of heavy plywood, 26x20 inches, stands 19½-inches from the floor. Fiddle back style chairs, large, shaped seats, 12-inches from the floor. Mom and Dad, you save by buying set unpainted; then paint it the color the kiddies want. Table packed with legs off—easily set up. Dishes not included.

$4.50 Value $2⁴⁹

79 D 8591—Table and 2 Chairs. Shpg. wt., 20 lbs....**$2.49**
79 D 8593—Table Only. Shipping weight, 12 pounds......**1.29**
79 D 8592—2 Chairs Only. Shipping weight, 8 pounds....**1.59**

Again Sears Lead With Toy Dinner Set Values

Even bigger value and prettier than our last year's unprecedented value. Dolly can now have her dinner parties in real style, on real CHINA dishes, at little cost. Two-tone white bodies, ivory borders, rose pink floral sprays, green foliage. Made in Japan.

28-Piece Dinner Set — Service for 6
5¾ in. covered casserole, 4½-in. gravy boat, 6-in. platter; 5¾-in. covered teapot, sugar, creamer. Six, 5-in. plates, 6 cups, 6 saucers; cake plate.
49 D 1669—Shpg. wt., 4 lbs. 8 oz. **98c**

21-Piece Dinner Set — Service for 4 (Not Shown)
4½-in. covered casserole. 3¾ in. gravy boat, 5¾-in. platter; 3⅝-in. covered tea pot, sugar, creamer. Four, 3¾-in. plates; 4 cups, 4 saucers.
49 D 1668—Shpg. wt., 2 lbs. 8 oz... **49c**

"M. Mouse" Metal Tea Sets

Can't hurt these dishes! Mickey and Minnie Mouse in bright lithographed colors! 7⅜-in. tray, 4¼-in. plates.
49 D 1807—21-Piece Set; 6 cups, 6 saucers, 6 plates, a teapot with cover and tray. Shpg. wt., 1 lb. 4 oz. **42c**
49 D 1805—15-Piece Set; 4 cups, 4 saucers, 4 plates, a teapot with cover and tray. Shpg. wt., 1 lb........**25c**

A Dandy, Practical 15-Piece Bake Set

Mm, just imagine the goodies you can make with this outfit—cake, cookies, muffins! Included is an 8-page recipe book which has been prepared and tested by Leone A. Heuer, Sears Cooking Expert. An egg beater, 1-cup flour sifter; 8-in. hardwood bread board and 10¼-in. hardwood rolling pin; cookie sheet, three cookie cutters, measuring cup, muffin tin; tube cake pan, pie pan, bread pan and layer cake pan, all in proportion and the right size. Shpg. wt., 2 lbs. 3 oz.
49 D 1951—15-Piece Set..................... **59c**

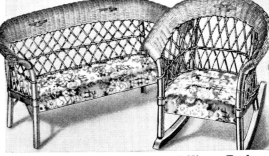

New Fiber Settee

Hand Woven. Child's size; it's strong, practical. Built just like the big ones. Broad back with rolled edge, nicely flared arms, sturdy up-rights. Well padded hardwood seat. It's big; 38-in. long, 18¾-in. high; roomy seat, 12-in. wide, 8¼-in. from floor, covered with durable, colorful cretonne. Two-tone green or two-tone tan, with contrasting woven-in colored designs in back. State color.
79 D 8581—Shipping weight, 16 lbs... **$2⁶⁹**

Hand-Woven Rocker

19½ inch child's fiber rocker **easily worth $2.00!** Made of the same materials as furniture for grown-ups. Well padded hardwood seat, covered with colorful cretonne! Broad back with rolled edge. Nicely flared arms, sturdy uprights. 22 in., shaped, hardwood regular large furniture runners. Two-tone green or two-tone tan with contrasting woven-in color design in back. Roomy seat, 11¼x11¼ in., 8¾ in. from floor. State color.
79 D 8580—Shpg. wt., 9 lbs. **$1²⁹**

Whistling Tea Kettle

Last year Sears were first to introduce this little tea kettle **like mother's.** Here it is again. Whistles merrily when water boils. Pure aluminum. 3⅞ in. wide. 3-in. high. Red lacquer handle. Shpg. wt., 6 oz.
49 D 1871. **20c**

Red Bow-Back Chairs

95c Med. Size

For little boys and girls. Strong and sturdy, yet not too big. Smoothly sanded hardwood, enameled bright red; neat striping. Fancy beaded spindles and panel back.

Choice of Two Sizes

79 D 8564—Medium Size. Seat, 10x10 in. Height, 21¾ in. Shpg. wt., 6 lbs....**95c**
79 D 8556—Small Size. Seat, 9x9 in. Height, 19¾ in. Shpg. wt., 4 lbs........**79c**

Cast Aluminum Cutlery

19 large pieces. Knives, 4¾-in. long, others in proportion. A cotton flannel lined, colorful kiddies design, oilcloth roll; section for each piece. 6 knives, 6 forks, 6 spoons, 1 ladle. Made in Germany. Shipping weight, 6 ounces.
49 D 1960—19-Pc. Set **69c**
49 D 1956—13-Pc. Set. 4 knives, 4 forks, 4 spoons and ladle, display box. Shipping weight, 5 oz.......**39c**

New Toy Aluminum Tea Set—16 Pieces

It's so much fun to have a tea party for Dolly and two of her friends. She'll love this pretty little set—all bright aluminum. New rilled modernistic pattern. So durable, too—will stand lots of hard knocks. **There's service for three;** 3 cups, 3 saucers, 3 spoons. Three 4⁹⁄₁₆-in. plates. Cute, red banded, 4⅝ in. teapot with cover, footed sugar and creamer. An exceptional value considering the quality. Shipping weight, 1 pound 1 ounce.
49 D 1892—16-Piece Set..................... **49c**

SEARS-ROEBUCK · 795

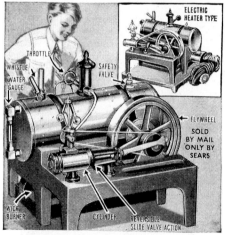

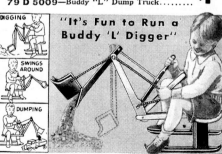

Ace-High Style for Young "Aviators"

Put on the helmet . . . adjust the goggles, and you'll look like a full-fledged pilot! This nifty airman's outfit includes coat and breeches of strong khaki cotton drill. Sam Browne artificial leather belt and puttees, aviator's helmet and goggles. Coat has two big patch pockets and a flyer's emblem. Low priced for the quality!
SIZES: 4, 6, 8, 10, 12, 14 years. State age-size. Shipping weight, 2 lbs. 3 oz.
40 D 4353
6-Piece Aviator's Outfit...... **$1.89**

$1.89

4-STAR JUBILEE FEATURE

$2.59
8 Pieces

You Can Be an "Indian Chief"

Lace front khaki cotton drill coat and pants with colored trim. Large head dress of brightly colored feathers.
SIZES: 4, 6, 8, 10, 12, 14 years. State age-size. Shipping weight, 1 lb. 8 oz.
40 D 4386—3-Pc. Chieftain Suit **$1.49**

Brave's Suit

Similar to above, but lighter weight drill. Less trim. Smaller head dress.
SIZES: 2, 4, 6, 8, 10 yrs. State age-size. Shpg.wt., 1 lb. 1 oz.
40 D 4372—3-Pc. Brave's Suit...... **98c**

$1.49
40 D 4386

40 D 4372

"BUCK" JONES

$4.49
8 Pieces

$3.98
9 Pieces

$1.69
8 Pieces

$1.09
8 Pieces

Ⓐ "Buck Jones" Cowboy Outfit

Our finest cowboy outfit—copied from the real thing! Just like the Western cattlemen wear! Genuine suede leather chaps with bright metal ornaments. Gay plaid cotton flannel shirt. Bright color bandana. Real Western style 10-gallon tan wool felt hat. Lasso, leather belt with leather holster, big 6-shooter toy pistol.
SIZES: 4, 6, 8, 10, 12, 14 years. State age-size. Shipping weight, 4 lbs.
40 D 4376 —8-Piece Cowboy Outfit......... **$4.49**

Ⓑ "Rodeo Rider" 8-Piece Outfit

A "Four-Star" special cowboy suit that's the last word in Western style! Fur front chaps with fancy side trimmings, bright plaid cotton flannel shirt. Bandana. Large toy pistol and holster, cartridge belt, lasso, and black cotton suede cloth hat with white band. Knocks the top off any value near it!
SIZES: 4, 6, 8, 10, 12, 14 yrs. State age-size. Shpg. wt., 3 lbs. 6 oz.
40 D 4365 —8-Pc. Cowboy Outfit......... **$2.59**

Ⓒ "Wild Westerner" Buck Jones Suit

Buck Jones OK's this outfit for the well-dressed cowboy! It has fur front chaps with side trimmings and metal studs. A real cowboy vest to match the chaps. Snappy plaid cotton flannel shirt. Bandana—"six-shooter" toy pistol and holster. Belt with imitation cartridges—lasso—and big tan wool felt "ten-gallon" hat.
SIZES: 4, 6, 8, 10, 12, 14 yrs. State age-size. Shpg. wt., 3 lbs. 15 oz.
40 D 4390 —9-Piece Cowboy Suit............ **$3.98**

Ⓓ Texas Ranger 8-Pc. Outfit

You'll look like your favorite cowboy hero in this suit! Cotton khaki drill cowboy chaps with side trimmings and metal studs. Bright plaid cotton flannel shirt—colorful bandana—cartridge belt. Lasso—extra large "six-shooter" toy pistol and holster. Big cowboy hat with colored band.
SIZES: 4, 6, 8, 10, 12, 14 yrs. State age-size. Shpg. wt., 2 lbs. 12 oz.
40 D 4383—8-Piece Cowboy Outfit.............. **$1.69**

Ⓔ Low Priced 8-Pc. Outfit

A complete cowboy outfit! It means a lot of fun, a lot of long wear, and a lot of saving. Consists of khaki cotton drill chaps with side fringe and elastic waist. Check cotton flannel shirt. Khaki cowboy hat—bright colored bandana—belt—lasso—toy pistol and holster.
SIZES: 4, 6, 8, 10 years. State age-size. Shipping weight, 1 lb. 12 oz.
40 D 4388—8-Piece Cowboy Outfit.............. **$1.09**

MASQUERADE COSTUMES

SHOOTS SPARKS—MAKES RAT-TAT-TAT NOISE

New Low Prices—For Grown-ups and Kiddies

Kiddies' sizes, ages 4 to 14 years. Shipping weight, 1 pound 2 ounces. Adults' sizes, 34 to 44-inch chest. Shipping weights, 1 pound 8 ounces. State children's ages, and adults' chest sizes.

Popeye
Cambric character of "Popeye, the Sailor Man." With buckram mask, corn cob pipe, cap, all the trimmings. Safe, sane noise maker.
Kiddies' Sizes
49 D 4536
$1.19
Adults' Sizes
49 D 4537
$1.79

Mexican
Colorful 4-pc. cambric suit; wire frame sombrero, flared bottom trousers. Vest and sash.
Kiddies' Sizes
49 D 4521
79c
Adults' Sizes
49 D 4531
$1.19

Clown
Colorful 2-pc. cambric. Ruffled at collar, wrist and ankles. Pompons, colored tinsel braid.
Kiddies' Sizes
49 D 4520
79c
Adults' Sizes
49 D 4530
$1.19

Gay "Sixties"
Hoop skirt, long-ago hat, pantalets, half-mask—all the trimmings. Gay print material.
Kiddies' Sizes
49 D 4538
$1.00
Adults' Sizes
49 D 4539
$1.39

M. Mouse
Stiff Cloth mask; cambric waist, pants, or skirt. Yellowcloth gloves. Black rubber tail. Kiddies' sizes only.
Mickey Mouse
49 D 4502
$1.39
Minnie Mouse
49 D 4503
$1.39

G-Man "Tommy" Gun with G-Man's Badge

Hi, fellers! Let's play enforcing the law and be a G Man hero with this keen "Tommy" gun, and get your man. Built mostly of metal, with wood stock and decorated with G-Man pictures in colors. **Wind up long running Marx clockwork motor,** then pull the trigger; **makes rat-tat-tat noise, shoots sparks** and looks just like the "Tommy" guns used by the famous G-Men. It's the most popular gun ever built; 23-inches long, 6 inches high. Has flint inserted, ready to shoot. Shpg. wt., 1 lb. 13 oz.
49 D 5664—G-Man Gun and Badge Complete **94c**

94c

Two Extra Refill Flints
49 D 5787—Shipping weight, 2 oz.   2 Flint Refills for....... **10c**

SAVE on UP-TO-THE-MINUTE SHOOTIN' TOYS

48 Bubblets Included

22 inches Long

8-Inch Bubble Buster
Blow up rubber bubblet by one push of plunger or by pumping slowly. Watch bubblet grow and go bang. Gun is metal. Safe, sane noise maker.
49 D 5659—Shipping weight, 9 ounces........ **19c**
49 D 5662—96 Extra Bubblets. Shpg. wt., 3 oz.....**10c**

Sparkling Pop Gun
Nickel plated! 23-in. long. Wood stock, shiny steel barrel. Automatic action; pull trigger, hear the **sharp pop** and see the sparks fly. 1 flint, ready to shoot. Shpg. wt., 1 lb. 2 oz.
49 D 5674.......... **45c**
49 D 5673—2 Extra Refills. Shpg. wt., 2 oz.....**10c**

Double Barrel Gun
Two triggers break action—just like the real ones. Each barrel fires separately making **sharp pop** noises. Cork enclosed in steel barrels. Varnished wood stock. Shipping weight, 2 pounds.
49 D 5645...♦....**25c**

Water Pistol
New Buck Rogers design. Shoots 15 times with one loading of "Helium" water. Boy! A 7¼-in. streamlined repeater! New action, brilliant colors, futuristic design; sturdy metal. Shpg. wt., 11 oz.
49 D 5646........**23c**

G-Man Automatic
Nickel plated! Key wind gun, 4⅛x3½ in. Pull trigger, hear dull rat-a-tat, see sparks fly! 3 imitation jewels. 2 Keys. Flint inserted. Shpg. wt., 1 lb. 8 oz.
49 D 5675....**45c**
49 D 5676—2 Extra Refills. Shpg. wt., 2 oz..............**10c**

45c

JUBILEE SAVINGS ON REAL TOYS FOR OUTDOOR BOYS

Big 5-Piece Police Outfit
Keep law and order, play enlisting for the police. Cap of dark blue cotton cloth with shiny visor and chief emblem; a loud traffic whistle; polished metal hand cuffs with spring snap. Night stick with wrist strap. Shiny metal badge.
49 D 5609—Shpg. wt., 1 lb. 2 oz....... **59c**

New 4-Piece Cowboy Set
Dress up in real cowboy fashion. Regular Western 10-gallon style hat, fits the average boy's head. 6-ft. lariat; red bandana handkerchief. Baked-on black enameled, 8-in., steel **clicker** gun.
49 D 5699—Shpg. wt., 1 lb. 8 oz.... **59c**

3-Pc. Holster Set
Steel, 6¾ in. **clicker** gun. Cowhide, grain leather, 7-in. holster; leather trimmed. Adjustable belt, shiny buckle.
49 D 5619—Shpg. wt., 7 oz............... **21c**

Texas Ranger Double Holsters
Now with dart shooting guns. Two, 8¼ in. enameled steel guns; 2 darts, with rubber suction cups. Two leather holsters, 9-in. long overall, leather belt, both decorated with metal conchas and leather strips. Printed cowboy scenes, and emblems.
49 D 5647—Shpg. wt., 1 lb. 14 oz..**83c**

7 Pieces for 83c

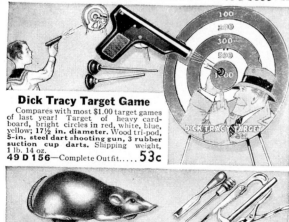

Dick Tracy Target Game
Compares with most $1.00 target games of last year! Target of heavy cardboard, bright circles in red, white, blue, yellow; 17½ in. diameter. Wood tri-pod, 5-in. steel dart shooting gun, 3 rubber suction cup darts. Shipping weight, 1 lb. 14 oz.
49 D 156—Complete Outfit..... **53c**

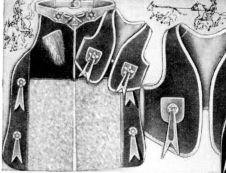

Fools 'Em All—Joke Mouse
Watch him scoot! Real fun, tricky as can be. He might even fool Tabby cat. Mouse colored metal; friction motor. About 3 in. long.
49 D 5719—Shpg. wt., 3 oz... **10c**

Play Tool Set—5 Pieces
Many happy hours for the little carpenter. 5¼-in. hammer; a screwdriver; 4½-in. chisel; 3¾-in. nickel plated pliers; 6¼-in. saw.
49 D 6420—Shpg. wt., 9 oz...**10c**

Low Priced Chaps
Regular $1.00 Value
Tan fleeced cotton leggings, scallop trimmed, bright color, leather-like, cotton suede cloth tops, fur holster pocket; shiny metal conchas. Vest decorated to match. **Even sizes only, 4 to 14 years.** State age. Shpg. wt., 1 lb. 13 oz.
49 D 5693...**79c**

Fur Trimmed Chaps
Regular $2.00 Value
Fluffy, long haired real fur leggings. Cotton, leather-like, suede cloth top. Wide scallops. Bright metal conchas, long cloth strips. Decorated belt. Colorful suede-like cloth vest; big pockets. Fur trimmed holster pocket. Assorted styles. **Even sizes only, 4 to 14 years.** State age. Shpg. wt., 2 lbs.
49 D 5694..**$1.29**

▲ **SEARS-ROEBUCK · 801**

4 STAR JUBILEE SPECIAL

BUZZ BUZZ

PONTOON FENDERS

TUBULAR FRAME

BALL BEARINGS

AIRPLANE HANDLEBARS

NEW BALL BEARING BIKE, ELECTRIC BUZZER, 1/3 SAVING!

$5.95 And Up

A full ball bearing bike like this usually sells for $2.00 more! Wow! Isn't she a beauty! De Luxe in every sense of the word; developed exclusively for Sears, sold only by Sears. Just check these high price features: **(1)** All wheels ball bearing. **(2)** 1-in. black rubber tires; heavy gauge wire spokes. **(3)** Electric buzzer in handlebars, complete with button and two batteries. **(4)** Big, airplane-type, stamped steel handlebars; streamlined rubber grips. **(5)** Semi-tubular, streamlined steel frame; shaped step platform over rear axle. **(6)** Entirely new, pontoon style, steel fenders over each wheel. **(7)** Comfortable, adjustable, genuine Troxel saddle on nickel plated coil springs. **(8)** Streamlined rubber pedals. **(9)** Striking dubonnet (rich wine color) enamel finish, ivory color trim. Three sizes, mailable. **Measure child from crotch to instep.**

Catalog Number	Front Wheel Diameter	Crotch to Instep	Shipping Weight	Price
79 D 8691	12 inches	18 to 19½ inches	26 pounds	$5.95
79 D 8692	16 inches	20 to 22½ inches	32 pounds	6.98
79 D 8693	20 inches	22 to 23½ inches	40 pounds	7.98

Big Savings on Tubular Bikes

$3.39 And Up

BALL BEARING FRONT WHEEL

- **New streamlined rubber pedals and hand grips.**
- **Streamlined handlebars.**
- **Big 3/4-inch rubber tires.**
- **Comfortable, adjustable, steel, spring saddle.**

Priced no higher than ordinary split frame bikes, these popular tubular steel bikes are far stronger and much better looking. Frame, fork and handlebars light green enamel; ivory color wheel rims. Choice of 3 sizes, all mailable. Shipping weights, 15 lbs., 18 lbs., and 22 lbs.

Measure child from crotch to instep.

Cat. No.	Front Wheel Diam.	Crotch to Instep	Price
79 D 8677	12-in.	17 to 18½ in.	$3.39
79 D 8679	16-in.	19 to 21 in.	3.98
79 D 8680	20-in.	21 to 23 in.	4.79

ROLLER BEARING 8-INCH STEEL WHEELS

STREAMLINE STEEL FOOTBOARD

3/4-INCH RUBBER TIRES

$1.49

ENCLOSED MECHANISM

Regular $5.00 Value $3.98

Boycraft Handcar

BALL BEARING DRIVE SHAFT

All Steel Scooter
Easily Worth 50c More

Green enameled steel frame, red wheels. Double bar, steel steering post. Ht., 30 in.
79 D 8817—Mailable.
Shpg. wt., 12 lbs. **$1.49**

New All Steel Hand Car

Streamlined body, 32½-in. long, 13½ in. wide; embossed beavertail back. Rear axle set in ball bearings. Drive forward or backward. Steel, spring saddle, adjustable (back and forth) from 18½ to 21½-in. leg reach. Steel footrests. Tubular steel steering bar, wood handle; dummy headlight. 8½-in. rear wheels, 6¾ in. front wheel; ⅝ in. rubber tires. Baked-on red enamel finish, neatly striped.
79 D 8805—Mailable. Shpg. wt., 20 lbs. **$3.98**

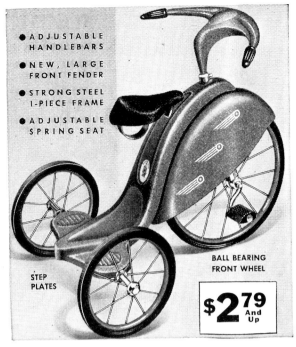

- **ADJUSTABLE HANDLEBARS**
- **NEW, LARGE FRONT FENDER**
- **STRONG STEEL 1-PIECE FRAME**
- **ADJUSTABLE SPRING SEAT**

STEP PLATES

BALL BEARING FRONT WHEEL

$2.79 And Up

Save About $1.50 on These Sturdy Steel Bikes
Streamlined Frame, Fender and Handlebars

Second only to our De Luxe streamliners (at left) are these popular velocipedes! **Each one a sensational value!** Racy, streamlined, yet lightweight! New streamlined steel fender over ball bearing front wheel. Modern, stamped steel handlebars. Improved heavy gauge steel frame, gracefully shaped and turned. **Designed to give longer leg reach. Adjustable, shaped, spring saddle; handlebars can be raised or lowered, too.** Large, rubber grips and pedals; ¾-inch, non-skid, solid rubber tires. Shiny spokes in all wheels. Finished in snappy red crackle enamel; saddle enameled black. Choice of four sizes, all mailable. **Measure child from crotch to instep.**

Catalog Number	Front Wheel Diameter	Crotch to Instep	Shpg. Wt., Lbs.	Price
79 D 8620	10 inches	15 to 16½ in.	12	$2.79
79 D 8621	12 inches	17 to 18½ in.	20	3.69
79 D 8622	16 inches	19 to 21½ in.	25	4.48
79 D 8623	20 inches	22 to 24 in.	29	5.29

Sears Low Price Special

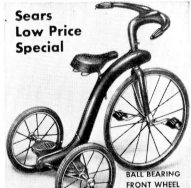

BALL BEARING FRONT WHEEL

25% Savings on Streamlined Bikes

$2.49 And Up

When comparing prices note crotch to instep size, not size of front wheel. Two-piece, S-shaped, stamped steel frame gives longer leg reach. Steel step platform, over rear axle. Adjustable, steel spring saddle. New stamped steel handlebars, rubber grips. Strong wire spokes, ¾-inch black rubber tires; rubber pedals. Striking green and ivory enamel finish; 3 sizes, mailable. Shpg. wts., 11, 13 and 18 lbs. **Measure child from crotch to instep.**

Cat. No.	Front Wheel Diam.	Crotch to Instep, Inches	Price
79 D 8661	10-in.	16 to 17½	$2.49
79 D 8662	12-in.	18 to 19½	2.89
79 D 8663	16-in.	20 to 22	3.49

Fastest on Any Slide

SNOW-BIRD

PATENTED KNEES

Sears New Snow-Bird—Patented Flexible Steering

Whiz! Goes like a flash! Its long racy lines give it greater speed; its patented flexible steering makes you slide farther. What a sled this is! Down the hills like a shot; around the curves with ease, because the Snow-Bird steers along the entire length of the runners. A stronger sled, too! The new patented braced knees give much greater strength. Top of tough hardwood, finished with spar varnish. Made by a sled maker with 43 years experience. We list only one quality—the best—and sell at the prices of ordinary sleds. For youngsters who can coast, we do not recommend sleds with steering bar attached way up front, for it limits steering flexibility. That type of sled is about one-fifth cheaper. Sizes given below are measured from bumper to end of runners. The largest sled, 79 DM 8347, has six knees, all others have four.

Single Crossbar 30-Inch Sled for the Little Tots
79 D 8342—Mailable. Shipping weight, 6 pounds **98c**

These Four Sleds Below Have Double Crossbars—Large Size Unmailable.

36-In. Sled	40-In. Sled	45-In. Sled	56-In. Sled
Shpg. wt., 8 lbs.	Shpg. wt., 9 lbs.	Shpg. wt., 10 lbs.	Shpg. wt., 12 lbs.
79 D 8344	79 D 8345	79 D 8346	79 DM 8347
			By express or freight.
$1.39	$1.79	$2.19	$2.79

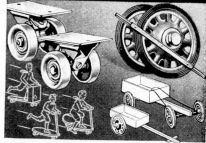

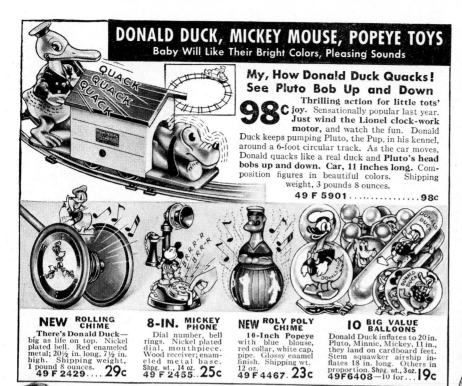

SAVE ON YOUR FAVORITE TOY AT SEARS

"Gee, Sis! what Swell Toys!"

SEARS BIG-VALUE SURPRISE PACKAGES

Have Your Own Surprise Package Party

We search the entire toy market every year to obtain at bargain prices, small quantities of a large variety of toys. We assort them carefully and then make up these superior surprise packages. Here they are, cute toys packed away in big packages. But, what's in those packages is a secret, for if we told, half the fun would be spoiled. Whichever package you get, though, will be full of laughs and surprises. Lots of fun on parties, help to solve your Christmas toy problems, too. Many different toys keep the little folks busy for hours at a time.

4 to 7 Toys for Boys	10 to 12 Toys for Boys	4 to 7 Toys for Girls	10 to 12 Toys for Girls
49F7010—Shpg. wt., about 2 lbs.	49F7012—Shpg. wt., about 3 lbs.	49F7011—Shpg. wt., about 2 lbs.	49F7013—Shpg. wt., about 3 lbs.
A 50c Value **25c**	A $1.00 Value **59c**	A 50c Value **25c**	A $1.00 Value **59c**

SAVE FOR THAT NEW BIKE

3-COIN REGISTERING BANKS
$2.50 Value. Famous Uncle Sam's Bank. Deposit nickels, dimes, or quarters—bell will ring; bank will open at $10. Heavy gauge steel. Size, 6⅛x4½x5¼ in.
49 F 6493
Shpg. wt., 3 lbs. 5 oz..**$1.98**

SAFE BANK
Low Price Special. Deposit the coin, bell rings once for nickels, twice for dimes, 5 times for quarters. Bank opens at $10. Colored metal, 4x4x2½ inches.
49 F 6472
Shpg. wt., 1 lb.......**47c**

Built of sturdy steel, mounted on wheels. Dial combination opens door. Takes bills and coins up to half-dollars. Size, 4¾x3⅛x2¾ inches.
49 F 6478
Shpg. wt., 1 lb.......**25c**

TWO BANKS
A cute Scotty and a funny clown on a round base with clever verse on each. Lock and key. Banks of strong pulp, colored. Each about 5⅝ inches high.
49 F 6436
Shpg. wt., 1 lb. 2 Banks.....**21c**

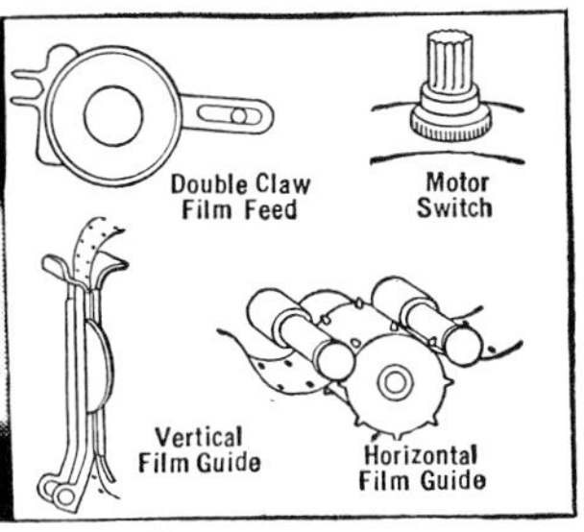

SEARS DE LUXE KEYSTONE MOVIE

Double Claw Film Feed — Motor Switch — Vertical Film Guide — Horizontal Film Guide

16 MM. NON-INFLAMMABLE FILMS
For Use With Any 16MM. Projector
25-FOOT FILM—Shpg. wt., 3 oz.
49 F 6878—Chaplin "My Mistake"		$0.49
49 F 6942—Tom Mix in "The Sheriff"		.49
49 F 6943—Popeye in "Ship Ahoy"		.79
49 F 6988—Mickey in "Narrow Escape"		.79
49 F 6989—Betty Boop in "Bus Trouble"		.79

50-FOOT FILM—Shpg. wt., 4 oz.
49 F 6990—Wolfheart "Saves the Boy"		.98
49 F 6991—Chaplin in "Out of Luck"		.98
49 F 6992—Tom Mix in "Riding West"		.98
49 F 6993—Popeye in "Training Camp"		1.49
49 F 6996—"Mickey and the Gorilla"		1.49

100-FOOT FILM—Shpg. wt., 7 oz.
49 F 6997—Chaplin in "The Boxer"		1.89
49 F 6998—Tom Mix in "CycloneTom"		1.89
49 F 6999—Popeye in "Indian Fighter"		2.98
49 F 7084—"Mickey's Olympic Games"		2.98
49 F 7085—Betty Boop "Kat for Sale"		2.98

Coronation Specials—Just Out
Be first in your community to have one.
49 F 7067—25 Feet—Shpg. wt., 3 oz.		$0.59
49 F 7077—50 Feet—Shpg. wt., 4 oz.		.98

$4.98 Motor Driven GIVES BRIGHTER BETTER PICTURES
Than Former $10.00 Projectors
Again improved in spite of rising costs!
- Every part tested for accuracy.
- Made by Manufacturer of projectors for schools and churches.
- Powerful Condenser lens.
- New, full front, double element, bell-shape lens . . . produces over twice as much light intensity for brighter pictures.
- New, reinforced reel arms built to hold reels for 400-foot film capacity.
- New, direct, film rewind.
- New, convenient on-and-off switch on motor to simplify focusing.
- Fan cooled, non-radio-interfering, 60-cycle, 110-volt A.C. motor with 2 speed pulley . . . no servicing or replacing of worn out brushes with this motor.
- Advance speed and take-up sprockets prevent tearing of film.
- 150 watt rating, concentrated filament, clear glass electric light bulb.
- 4½-foot approved cord and plug.
- 2 empty, 400-ft. capacity metal reels.
- Steel lamp house with heat shield and reflector. Air vents.

Size over-all, 16⅛x13½x5½ in. Tension plate, adjusted lamp base. Film not included, (see at left). Shpg. wt., 10 lbs.
79 F 6837—Motor Driven **$4.98**

Hand Driven Model. (Not shown) One film guide, no condenser lens; two 100-ft. capacity empty reels. Size over-all, 14¼x12¾x5¼ in. Shpg. wt., 7 lbs.
79 F 6831—Hand Driven. **$2.98**

$5 Worth of Play Value!

Above: Painted-on inside back wall.
Below: Stalls set up as real stanchions.

64 PIECE STOCK FARM $1.00

- 44 almost unbreakable, 3-ply wood (not cardboard) people, animals, etc. Color-printed both sides. Cut-to-shape. Wood stands.
- Extra large, green hip-roof, set-up barn, 16¼x14¾ inches high to top of windmill. 9 inches across eaves. Red and black, white trim; stone effect foundation. 2 stalls of 3-ply wood, one side colored; or make stanchions out of them by using stalls as supports for piece which forms stanchions.
- Almost 6 feet of green cardboard fence, 10 interlocking sections.
- 2 tile-type, 10-inch colored cardboard silos.
- 3 all wood outbuildings, chicken coop, pig pen, tool shed, red and green with black printed details. Tool shed, 6x3¼x3¾ inches, others in proportion.
- Two wood dummy ventilators; mailbox, one side colored.

The 2 stalls and stanchions give this matchless barn a realism that has never been equalled before anywhere. Shipping weight, 7 pounds.
79 F 6452—64-Pieces.........**$1.00**

17-PIECE POULTRY SET
Just the thing to add to your toy stock farm. Life-like, composition hens, roosters averaging, 2x1⅞x1 in. Different positions, colors. Green excelsior imitation grass. Shpg. wt., 2 lbs.
49 F 6455...........**23c**

7-PC. RUBBER TRACTOR, ANIMAL SET
Here's the first all rubber tractor with rubber wheels. Length, 4¼ in.; plus, a horse 3¾ in. long; colt 2¼ in. long. Cow, dog, sheep in proportion. 11-in. fence with opening gate. Ideal for little tots, all pieces molded from soft solid rubber. Unbreakable, Sanitary, Life-like, Washable.
49 F 6413—Shipping weight, 1 lb. 8 oz...**49c**

REAL PHONOGRAPH, FIBER HORN
Plays up to 10-in. records. Kiddies will love a phonograph of their own. Clockwork motor. Records not included. Speed control lever. 14-in. overall.
49 F 2433—Shpg. wt., 2 lbs. 10 oz... **$1.00**
6-in. Double Faced Non-Breakable Records
(shown above). Shpg. wt., each, 5 oz..........**10c**
49 F 2362—Old King Cole, Piper's Son
49 F 2357—Mulberry Bush, Simple Simon
49 F 2364—Mary's Lamb, Little Boy Blue

BOYS! GIRLS! Play a Real Uke $1.00
Has real gut strings which can be played correctly and fretted accurately. Play like the big folks do with their guitars and ukuleles you hear over the radio. 17 inches long of frosted red finished wood. Shoulder cord. American made. Shipping weight, 1 pound.
49 F 2446—Ukulele...**$1.00**

PLUTO, THE PUP

ACTION TOY!
Fascinating . . . Fun by the Hour 23c
Pull string, every muscle in his body moves. He'll lie down, stand up, sit down, wag his tail, etc. Beautifully finished wood, trimmings in bright colors. About 7½ in. long. Strung with 50-lb. test fishline. No motor or spring.
49 F 6435—Shpg. wt., 9 oz...**23c**

LOW PRICED HARMONICAS
Accurately tuned. Nickel plated. Assorted styles. Play latest tunes. Made in Germany.
(A) 18 Brassed Reeds 10 holes. About 4 in. long. Shipping weight, 3 oz.
49 F 2345...**12c**
(B) 24 Brassed Reeds Tremola, 24 holes. About 4½ in. long. Shpg. wt., 3 oz.
49 F 2348....**19c**

FOR TODDLERS' GLEE 1 YEAR TO 3

TOYS FOR GOOD GIRLS AND BOYS

INTERLOCKING ABC BLOCKS HALSAM 89c

These Hi-Lo blocks are specially grooved at ends to fit together. 36, 1¾-in. sq. blocks, beautifully embossed; one side with pictures of animals, opposite with pictures or building designs. Other 2 sides painted, grooved.

49 K 3633—36 Blocks. Shpg. wt., 3 lbs. 8 oz...89c
49 K 3632—Same but with 1⁵⁄₁₆-in. square blocks. Shipping weight, 1 pound 12 ounces.............47c

NEW SNOW WHITE ABC BLOCKS 89c

The dwarfs are there, too, all seven of 'em. We wouldn't forget Dopey, Sleepy and the rest. Colorful wood blocks; sides embossed in Snow White, Dwarf, animal and letter designs.

49 K 3614—32-Block Set. 1¾ in. sq. Shpg. wt. 3 lbs. 8 oz......89c
49 K 3613—30-Block Set. 1⁵⁄₁₆ in. sq. Shpg. wt., 1 lb. 12 oz......39c

De Luxe Flirty Eye Bear $1.59

He'll make goo-goo eyes; he'll growl, stand, sit. Golden brown wool pile plush, soft stuffed body. Longer pile and woolier than most bears at higher prices. Head turns; legs and arms move. Black embroidered nose, mouth, claws, feet. Ribbon tie. Made in Germany.

49 K 4342 13¾-In. Bear $1.59 Shpg. wt., 1 lb.
49 K 4343 15¾-In. Bear $2.49 Shpg. wt., 1 lb. 8 oz.

Baby Panda 98c

(A) 12 in. tall. Med. long pile rayon plush. Glass eyes. Head, arms, legs move. Growler voice. Nose, mouth, claws embroidered. Made in America.
49 K 4344 Shpg. wt., 12 oz.....98c

Low Priced Bears 53c

(B) Golden brown medium long rayon pile plush. Moving head, arms and legs, double washer joints. Glass eyes. Noses, mouths, claws embroidered black. Made in Germany.
49 K 4337 Daddy 17¾-in. 98c Shpg. wt. 1 lb. 5 oz.
49 K 4336 Mama 15-in. 79c Shpg. wt., 10 oz.
12⅝-In. Baby Bear
49 K 4335—Shpg. wt. 10 oz..53c

De Luxe Pedal Bike—$2 Value $1.49

Pedal away . . . pedal, pedal! And steer it straight, little fellow! What fun! A swell ride for tots up to 2½ yrs. Pontoon fender over 8-inch front wheel gives a snappy, streamlined appearance. 23 inches long, 16¼ inches wide; leg reach, 14½ inches. Strong step plates over rear axle. Stamped steel handlebars; steel frame and saddle. Rubber grips and pedals and ½-in. tires. Enameled red. Mailable. Shipping weight, 10 pounds.
79 K 8374.............................$1.49
79 K 8376—$1.50 Value! As above, no fender. Shipping weight, 9 pounds..........98c

$2.50 Value Horse Shoofly $1.89

Here's a horsie for Baby to ride . . . he's much fun, good exercise and entirely safe, too, because he's a rocking horse. Baby will love the smooth, gliding motion. Swinging playbox for Baby's toys. Strong, durable, 1-piece 3-ply wood sides; will last through many a hard ride. Steel screws used throughout, no nails to pull out and scratch tender skin. Footrest acts as a guard rail, an extra measure of safety. Bright, colorful finish, pleasing to Baby's eye. 32⅝x15¾ in. high. Mailable.
79 K 7551—Shipping weight, 10 pounds. $1.89

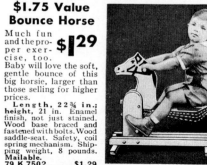

Donald Duck Rolling Chime 29c

There he is, Donald himself, big as life on top. He's having a grand time, too, 'cause he loves to ride. One of the most popular toys ever for little tots. 20½ in. long, 7½ in. high. Nickel plated, tinkling bell will appeal to Baby's ear for music.
49 K 2429—Shpg. wt., 1 lb. 8 oz.............29c

Mickey Phone 25c

8 in. tall. Dial number, bell rings. Nickel plated dial, mouthpiece. Enameled metal base. Shpg. wt., 14 oz.
49 K 2455.....25c

12 Big-Value Balloons 21c

Snow White toss-up inflates to 20 in., Dopey, Grumpy, Pluto, Minnie, Mickey, Donald, to 11 in. 3 pairs cardboard feet. New bubble balloon, 48 in. inflated; serpentine, paddle, stem squawker in proportion.
49 K 6415—Shpg. wt..3 oz. 12 for..21c

$1.75 Value Bounce Horse $1.29

Much fun and the proper exercise, too. Baby will love the soft, gentle bounce of this big horsie, larger than those selling for higher prices.

Length, 22¾ in.; height, 21 in. Enamel finish, not just stained. Wood base braced and fastened with bolts. Wood saddle-seat. Safety, coil spring mechanism. Shipping weight, 8 pounds. Mailable.
79 K 7502......$1.29

SPECIAL TOYS THAT WILL NOT HARM BABY OR FURNITURE

Popular 7-Inch Bouncing Auto 53c

Equipped with huge 1¼-inch sponge rubber tires. Satisfy Baby's desire to throw things—give him this 7-inch bouncing auto. He can toss, pull or push it to his heart's content. Colorful, protected metal body. Shipping weight, 12 oz.
49 K 6120..53c

New Washable Rubber Transport—2 Autos 59c

Baby will love them, they're pliable rubber built to stand all the squeezing and tossing about that little hands can give. Plenty of play-value for older youngsters, too. Colorful tractor-truck; detachable trailer; two, differently colored, 4¾-in. sedans, all roll easily on rubber wheels. Trailer has removable top as loading ramp or so sedans can be carried inside. 11¾ in. long.
49 K 6445—Shipping weight, 2 pounds.................59c

Tot's First Wagon . . . 21x10½-Inch Body 95c

Built like a regular wagon . . . not just a pull toy. Rolled top and bottom; no sharp edges to cut tiny fingers. Heavy steel bolsters, undergearing and tubular tongue, with "D" shape grip, enameled black. Sides and bottom, of red enameled steel body, beaded and embossed for double strength. 4½-in. double disc steel wheels. ½-in. rubber tires.
79 K 7637—Mailable. Shpg. wt., 7 lbs...........95c

OTHER SIDE IS WHITE

WHITEBOARD

AS A DESK

SEARS VALUE LEADER

12-Chart Blackboard Complete With Chair

$1.50 Value

Blackboard for white chalk, whiteboard for colored crayons, desk and chair, all for this low price. 12 charts printed on both sides of 6 cards. Frame sturdy pine, yellow stained, red trimmed. Size overall, 35x16⅜ inches. Chalk rail, 2 colored erasable, wax crayons. 2 pieces chalk, Eraser. Folding chain, 24x10¾ inches wide; seat 9x9½ in. Shipping weight, 5 pounds.

$1.00

79 K 3802—Blackboard and Chair.......$1.00

Popular Telephone Set
Complete With Batteries and Wire

"Hello . . . Isn't this phone great! We can talk from room to room, and Mom and Dad can use it from house to barn or garage." Gives two-way telephone service for 25-ft. distance. Two phones carefully built of steel. Compact size makes them easy to carry. Buzzer coil in each (for signaling other party) operated by switch which opens or cuts off line. **Includes two 25-foot coils of bell wire, also 4 flashlight batteries at Sears low price.** Shipping weight, 3 pounds.
49 K 4749—Complete Outfit................$1.39

$1.39

25 ENVELOPES
35 SHEETS
ERASER
ACTUAL TYPE SIZE

97-Piece Secretary Set with Famous Marx Dial Typewriter

70 sheets of regular size office paper. 25 envelopes. 1 rubber eraser included. Best practical, popular priced typewriter ever offered for children. Type is securely fastened to dial. Dial has 40 metal characters, the alphabet; numerals, punctuation marks. Sliding carriage. Heavy lithographed metal, 11¼x6⅛x5¾ in. New dummy keyboard in red and yellow letters, numbers and characters.

$1.19

49 K 3707—Shipping weight, 3 pounds..........$1.19
3 Extra Ink Rolls for Typewriter
49 K 3898—Shipping weight, 4 ounces..........10c

NOTCHED LOGS

Real Hewn and Embossed Logs
More Pieces Than Usual at This Price

Build Early American towns, chimney gables, blockhouses, forts, cabins, bridges for your toy soldiers; then protect your buildings from redskins; it's keen fun! Realistic rough hewn building logs. Roof boards, clips to hold roof gable ends, and a chimney in each set.

$1.79 163-Pc. Set

49 K 3659
Box, 18x12¼x1¾ in. Shpg. wt., 5 lbs.
163-Pc. **$1.79** Set....

49 K 3658
Box, 18x12¼x⅞ in. Shpg. wt., 2 lbs. 12 oz.
67-Piece Junior Set. **89c**

49 K 3657
Box, 12⅞x10⅛x⅞ in. Shpg. wt., 1 lb. 8 oz.
50-Piece Beginners'.. **42c**

New Electric Pyrograph Set
Water Colors, Brush and 12 Plaques

Listed by Underwriters' Laboratory. Burn beautiful designs. Electric pencil, cork grip, bakelite handle. Approved extension cord, rubber plug. 5 etched, 3-ply wood plaques; 4 are 4½x3½ in., one 7x3½ in. 5, 3½x6-in. wood pulp postcards, 2, 3½x6-in. etched and framed wood pulp plaques. Cord for hangers. 4 paints; brush, palette.
49 K 4714—Instructions. Shpg. wt., 1 lb. 4 oz....89c

89c

7-Piece, 3-Ply Wood Plaque Set
2 pieces, 6½x8½ in., 3, 5x7 in., and 2, 3½x5 in.
49 K 4715—Shipping weight, 8 ounces..........39c

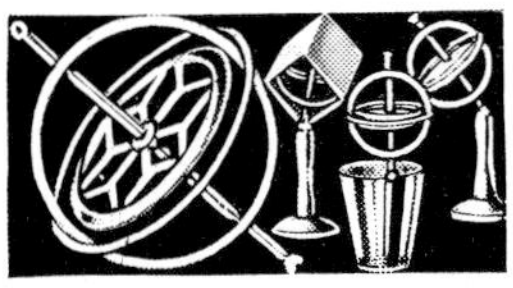

Gyroscope Top

19c

American made. Amusing. Almost defies gravity. It balances at sharp angles; can be made to do unbelievable and startling stunts. Directions, cord and wood stand with each top. Shipping weight, 7 ounces.
49 K 5560.............19c

Big Value Paint Set

34 cakes colored dry paints. Two camel's hair brushes in a black enameled metal box, enameled white inside, hinged cover; Size, 9⅝x3½ in. Made in England and Germany. Shpg. wt., 8 oz.
49 K 3878.............23c

3-in-1 Play Table
Regular $1.50 Value

1. Pound-a-Peg Set.
2. Hammer, Nail Set.
3. Play Table and Bench.
Table alone usual $1.00 value.

$1.00

Youngsters quickly learn to create new designs either by pounding the 40 colored pegs into the holes of separate panel, 11x6 in. or nailing down the 30 colored wood pieces on the sturdy built-in Masonite table top with metal frame and red wooden legs. 18x12x18½ in. high. Red, wood bench, 12x5x9½ in. high. Wood mallet, nails, design sheets. Save on this complete outfit! Shipping weight, 7 lbs.
79 K 3694..............$1.00

225 Colored Wood Blocks

59c

Not just wood pieces, but real blocks, mostly of hardwood cut in multiple. They're smooth, no rough edges to splinter and then scratch little hands; they're clean, they're attractively stained, appealing to the toddler's eye for color harmony. Different sizes and colors . . . build lots of things. All done up in a drawstring cloth and mesh bag to keep them together. Makes a fine gift for youngsters. Shpg. wt., 4 lbs. 6 oz.
49 K 3671—225 Blocks...59c

New Snow White 19-Pc. Stamp Set

47c

Oh boy! Here's real fun . . . make outline pictures with 10 rubber stamps of famous Snow White and her friends, the Seven Dwarfs and Prince Charming. The Queen is there, too, to make things more interesting. Then color the figures with the 6 crayons included. Besides the stamps and crayons, there's an ink pad, 8-in. ruler, pad of paper.
49 K 3862—Shpg. wt., 14 oz..47c

13-Piece Set
49 K 3861—Similar but with 8 stamps, 3 crayons. Shpg. wt., 6 oz. 23c

2 Puppets and Stage

94c

Jointed dressed 7-in. clown and negro mammy, easy to operate by strings attached to control bar; composition head, arms and feet. Heavy cardboard stage 19x5 in. high, scenic background. The "greatest show on earth." Shpg. wt., 1 lb. 8 oz.
49 K 4722..................94c

SEARS ✪ PAGE 909

Up and At 'em

TOYS FOR LITTLE GIRLS AND BOYS

LOAD TRAILER WITH BLOCKS

TRACTOR CLIMBS 40 DEGREE GRADE

SAND SIFTER IS REMOVABLE

Popular 8½-In. Climbing Tractors

A "million" play angles. Extra wide, soft rubber treads for traction power, to protect furniture. Detachable steel road scraper. Climbs up or down steep grades. Clockwork motor, speed governor, brake. Aluminum case over steel. Shipping weight, 1 lb. 7 oz.

94c

49 K 5846—Money-Saving Value..............94c

49 K 5745—Not shown. Colored metal. No road-scraper. Smaller motor. Shipping weight, 1 lb. 7 oz...59c

New 36-Piece Tractor Road Construction Set

Usual $2.50 Value. Federal, state and country roads must be built and improved so let's get our gang together and get busy with this up-to-the-minute road construction outfit consisting of:
1. 8½-inch aluminum cased climbing tractor.
2. Shiny, detachable steel road scraper.
3. Enameled steel, 7¼x4½ in. detachable sand scoop; when attached makes tractor 15½ in. overall.
4. Strong, steel derrick with crank handle.
5. 4¾-inch steel wheel barrow with spade.
6. 9½-in. cement mixer truck; crank to turn mixing drum; latch door that opens.
7. New 8-in. trailer with detachable sand sieve. Crank to shake sieve.
8. About 26 wood blocks colored to look like concrete blocks.
9. 2 steel road signs: "Men Working," "Stop."
10. Outfit packed in colorful cardboard box that can be set up into 11¼ x9½ x7¾ in. size shed.

COMPLETE OUTFIT $1.98

49 K 5879—Shipping weight, 5 lbs....

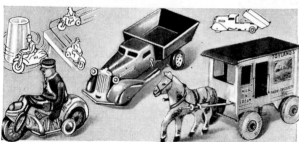

Tricky 'Cycle

Runs on any flat surface right to the edge, but seldom off. Colored metal; 4⅜ in. long; wind-up motor. Fun for everyone. Shpg. wt., 5 oz.
49 K 5743.......**29c**

11-in. Truck

Key wind, spring motor. Pull lever, body actually dumps. Heavy gauge auto fender steel, bright colors. Like a real truck. Shpg. wt., 1 lb. 11 oz.
49 K 5811.........**25c**

Milk Wagon

9½ in. long. Realistic, white finish. Metal. Strong wind-up Marx motor. Real bargain. Shpg. wt., 1 lb.
49 K 5832....**25c**

Mystery Kitty Kat

Soft rubber ears. Little tots can work it with ease. Press down the Kat's tail and away she'll go rolling her wood ball between her paws. Grown-ups, too, will think Kitty Kat amusing. Colored metal; 8½ in. long. Shipping weight, 1 pound.
49 K 5829..................**25c**

25c

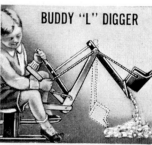

BUDDY "L" DIGGER

Run It Like a Real Steam Shovel

Built by Buddy "L". Auto fender steel, enameled 2 colors. Fun galore to operate your own shovel. Sit on the seat of this big 28-in. digger, load up the scoop and dump it wherever you like. Seat and boom rest easily on runners. 38 in. long, boom extended. Largest height, 17 inches. Play you're excavating for the foundation of a modern skyscraper. Shipping wt., 5 lbs.
79 K 6138......................**98c**

98c

LOAD 'ER UP

SWING 'ER AROUND

DUMP 'ER HERE

Fools 'Em All—3-In. Joke Mouse

Ideal fun for parties. How he can scamper around the floor! Mouse colored metal; friction motor.
49 K 5719—Shipping weight, 3 ounces.............**17c**

Mechanical Tractor

5¼ in. long. Bright metal. Spring motor with brake. Endless rubber treads give power, protect furniture.
49 K 5753—Shpg. wt., 8 oz.**25c**

25c

Big Climbing, Fighting Mechanical Tank

Set for the "Big Push"! Two doughboys in position. Just wind the powerful clockwork motor, release brake, tank climbs up or down hill over obstacles in real fighting fashion. Oversize 1-in. rubber treads. Tank, 9½ x5¼ in. high. Silvery color metal.
49 K 5763—Shipping weight, 2 pounds..............**98c**

98c

Brand New! Repair Shop

Sedan has removable wheels and there are 5 small tools to make wheel changes. Give your customers super service. Send the 5-inch wrecker to tow in the 4-inch sedan. 2 dummy gas pumps; rack with 4 dummy wheels, advertising signs, raised repair platform to do your repair work. Sturdy, steel station realistically colored, size overall, 16¾x10¾x3⅜ inches high. Large machine shop to hold 2 cars. Shipping weight, 3 lbs. 6 oz.
49 K 5755..........**89c**

89c

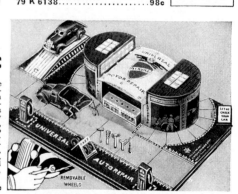

REMOVABLE WHEELS

UNLOADING RAMPS

New 24½-In. Auto Transport

Latest streamline double deck 3-car auto transport. Heavy gauge, steel enamel finish. Coupe, roadster, and dump truck, average 6 in. long with shiny radiators; hauler with trailer has 8 wheels, one spare. 30½ inches long with 2 runways attached to load or unload top Unloading platform on bottom.
49 K 6145—Shipping weight, 4 pounds..............**94c**

94c

Crossover Speedway of the Future, 2 Mechanical Cars

Wind the streamline autos and watch 'em race with breakneck speed over the 2-lane, 144-in., all steel, figure 8 track, one car under the bridge, the other over, or both in the same direction. 3¾-in. cars, powerful motors. Brightly painted. All the thrills of a real race. Shpg. wt., 4 lbs. 10 oz.

$1.89

49 K 5782—Speedway, 2 cars...........$1.89
49 K 5718—Extra 3¾-in. lithographed metal, key wind, high speed racers. Shpg. wt., 10 oz. Each..............................25c

...THE *Newest Thing*

TOP VIEW OF THE DOUBLE-BAR FRAME SHOWING 1-PIECE CONTINUOUS TUBING

THIS TYPE FRAME ON ALL BICYCLES SHOWN ON FIRST THREE PAGES

$39.95 Cash

ONLY $4 DOWN

See Page 1202

BUILT-IN SPEEDOMETER

MODERNISTIC ELECTRIC HEADLIGHT

TEAR-DROP HORN AND BATTERY CASE

STEEL CARRIER WITH RED REFLECTOR

REAR FENDER TIP WITH DEEP BEADING

PATENT APPLIED FOR

4-STAR FEATURE

New Continuous Tube Frame Revolutionizes Bike Design

WORLD'S GREATEST BICYCLE SCOOP—presented by Sears! *The only bikes anywhere with suspension bridge construction* combined with mechanical improvements that are part of the bike and not just gadgets put on to make it look complete.

Five great engineers and three great artists were assigned the task of designing a completely new line of bicycles—built on an entirely new principle. From fender to fender these bikes are radically different, and embody the strength and ruggedness of suspension bridge construction with the sleek, streamlined styling of modern automobiles.

In place of the conventional frame—made of short pieces of steel connected by 22 joints—Sears new double-bar frame is made of continuous steel trusses from front to rear and welded at only 4 points. This is the strongest construction ever devised and eliminates the necessity for the upright tube between saddle and sprocket housing. When subjected to "Torture Tests" on a special machine, Sears new double-bar frame withstood a much greater amount of punishment than it will ever get under actual riding conditions during the entire life of the bicycle.

See Sears new, complete line on the following pages. You'll find new style, new colors—from lowest price to most elaborate model.

PAGE 916 ★ SEARS

NEW ELGIN DELUXE TWIN 60

- Sears exclusive double-bar frame of continuous steel tubing. (Patent Applied For). New, ultra-modern ornamental tank.
- Powerful electric beam-light built into the streamlined head. X-pert speedometer registers miles per hour and total mileage traveled.
- Highly polished, chrome plated luggage carrier and streamlined battery case with raised bead. Contains electric horn. Use No. 6 lantern battery (battery not included, see Page 953).
- Chrome plated full length Gothic chain guard.
- Extra fine quality 3-coat enamel finish.

The peak of perfection on every count! Note the sweep of the bright, sparkling, polished fenders with raised center bead—the comfortable top grain leather saddle on flexible auto-like leaf springs—other features, such as full weighted streamlined pedals which always remain in horizontal position—streamlined handlebar grips. Drop forged handlebar stem, practically unbreakable. Kick-up stand. Fine ALL-STATE balloon tires, 26x2⅛ in. with inner tubes. Chrome plated rims, sprockets, air cooled brake (Pat. No. 101999). Equipped with Sears Exclusive Alemite Pressure Lubricating system. Full size frame with saddle adjustable from 29 to 34 in. from seat to pedal.

For Boys and Men

Black with White trim or Red 517 with White trim. State color. Number after color refers to COLORGRAPH following Index pages in back of book.
6 KM 5085—Shpg. wt., 83 lbs...................**$39.95**

See Opposite Page For Shipping Points

Bikes as New as a *Streamliner* ...Save Up to ⅓!

Full Ball Bearing $3.98 12-in.
WORTH $2.00 MORE

- 1¼-in. tubular steel frame welded to U-shaped tubular steel back bone and head. Strongest, safest, best-looking construction.
- Full 1-in. rubber tires. Adjustable, shaped steel saddle on double coil springs.
- New, modern, 1-piece, beautifully embossed steel step plate over rear axle.
- Graceful front fender; regular bike fork.

The easiest pedaling bike we know of! Fast ball bearings in all three wheels. Rubber cushioned steering. Streamlined, adjustable handlebar; rubber grips. Rubber pedals. Big hubs. Red enamel finish, ivory color trim.

All mailable. Be sure to measure child from crotch to instep.

Cat. No.	Front Wheel	Crotch to Instep Adj.	Shpg. Wt.	Price
79 D 8644	12 in.	16 to 18 in.	19 lbs.	$3.98
79 D 8645	16 in.	18 to 20 in.	22 lbs.	4.98
79 D 8646	20 in.	20 to 22 in.	24 lbs.	5.98

Single Tube Frame $2.19 10-in.
BUILT LIKE $5 BIKES

- High Speed Steel Bearings! Frame is 1¼-in. steel tubing (not cheap ⅞ or 1-in. size) welded to tubular steel head and rear axle. Exceptionally speedy, safe and strong!
- 1-piece steel rear step plate.
- Adjustable, shaped steel saddle.
- Rubber cushion between regular bike fork and head for easy turns.

The biggest bike bargain in years! Adjustable steel handlebar, rubber grips. Rubber pedals; ⅝-inch rubber tires. Red enamel finish, ivory color trim; cadmium plated, rust resisting metal parts.

All mailable. Be sure to measure child from crotch to instep.

Cat. No.	Front Wheel	Crotch to Instep Adj.	Shpg. Wt.	Price
79 D 8634	10 in.	14 to 15 in.	17 lbs.	$2.19
79 D 8635	13 in.	16 to 17 in.	19 lbs.	2.69
79 D 8636	16 in.	18 to 19 in.	21 lbs.	3.29

BRAND NEW
OUR FINEST BIKE!

CAN'T HURT THESE TIRES—THEY'RE PUNCTURE-PROOF..SEMI-PNEUMATIC

When Buying Velocipedes Order Next Larger Size. Gives Longer Service, Won't Be Quickly Outgrown.

Ball Bearing Front Wheel $6.48 12-in.
NEW FEATURES—SAVE ⅓

- Big 1½-in. puncture-proof semi-pneumatic molded rubber tires. Non-skid, straight tread.
- Strong, safe, handsome. Frame is 1¼-in. steel tubing, welded to tubular steel head. Gracefully curves to tubular steel backbone and is welded again. The best velocipede construction known!
- Embossed, 1-piece steel rear step plate.
- Adjustable, shaped, molded rubber saddle is mounted on nickel plated coil springs.
- Chrome plated tubular steel handlebars; adjustable up or down, and for angle; large rubber grips.
- Double bar rubber pedals.

Get on and really GO! This fine bike takes you safely, easily, swiftly. Drive wheel is ball bearing for more effortless miles. Big 1½-in. tires absorb bumps. Finished in dubonnet (maroon) enamel, ivory color trim. All mailable. Be sure to measure child from crotch to instep.

Cat. No.	Front Wheel	Crotch to Instep Adj.	Shpg. Wt.	Price
79 D 8654	12 in.	17½ to 19½ in.	21 lbs.	$6.48
79 D 8655	16 in.	19½ to 21½ in.	25 lbs.	7.48
79 D 8656	20 in.	21½ to 23½ in.	29 lbs.	8.48

Time for Toys Says St. Nick. See the Extra Big Selection in Sears new Christmas Catalog. Ready About November 15.

PAGE 894 ✳ ▣ SEARS

1200-Mile Wheels $1.10

Tested Congo bearings in two 9½-in. double disc red enameled steel wheels; ¾-in. rubber tires. Flared journals, fancy hub caps. 17-in. steel axle with brace; washers, pins. Shipping weight, 7 lbs.
79D7622—Complete $1.10
79D7621—Has 8-in. wheels. Shpg. wt., 5 lbs........89c

Big Speedy Hand Car $2.29

Push and pull; away you speed! To stop, hold the handle tight. Undergearing is flexible steel to take the bumps in stride. Shaped wood 11x7-inch spring seat movable back and forth (See A); leg reach adjustable from 19½ to 22½ in. Size overall, 32x15½ in. rear and 6-in. front double disc steel wheels, all enameled red; ½-in. rubber tires. Shipping weight, 14 pounds.
79 D 8802—Mailable...........$2.29

Deluxe With Seat—Save! $2.98

Get 'er goin' fast, then sit down and coast! Blue enameled steel frame scooter, 30½ in. high, 39 in. long. Black enameled, folding (See A) wood seat, 20 in. high. Double disc steel, artillery spoke, 10-in. wheels are yellow enameled and roller bearing. Tubular steel handle; rubber grips, 1-in. tires. Streamlined wood footboard. Parking stand and brake. Mailable.
79 D 8813—Shpg. wt., 18 lbs.....$2.98

Bargain Scooter $1.00

One of the best scooter values ever! Strong steel, 33 in. long and 30 in. high; easy rolling double disc steel wheels are 7 in. in diameter; ¾-in. rubber tires. Roomy steel platform, 12½x4 in. Red and green enameled. Shipping weight, 9 pounds. Mailable.
79 D 8811 ....$1.00

Big Savings, Too!

HOOD FOLDS

STROLLER TYPE DROP FRONT

FOLDS

All Steel Buggy $1.19
Holds up to 18-inch dolls! Large, streamlined and practical. Push handle 20¾ in. and top of hood 20½ in. from floor. Embossed, 17⅞x8-in. body and adjustable hood with triangular windows, enameled light green; 5-in. wheels, ¼-in. rubber tires.
79 D 8112—Shpg. wt., 7 lbs..$1.19

New Folding Buggy $1.87
Body, 22x11x7½ inch has extension footend, will hold 24-inch dollies! Four-bow folding hood, sun visor, Blue enameled, rolled steel frame, front drops to make stroller; folds flat. Body and hood blue-white mixture cloth, bound in yellow. Handle 27½ in. high; 5¼-in. ivory color steel spoke wheels; ½-in. rubber tires.
79 D 8202—Shipping weight, 9 pounds..$1.87

IN HOME

AS ROCKER

Write for Sears New Play Yard Equipment Catalog—670D

Portable All Steel 2-in-1 Rock-A-Swing $3.49
Swing high, swing low indoors or out. Unsnap the chains and presto you have a modern, streamlined rocker. Brand new fun for youngsters 2 to 7. Lightweight but rugged frame is red enameled tubular steel with black striping. All parts are socketed together, no nuts and bolts to loosen or sheer off. Reinforced 1-piece steel top. Rubber feet prevent creeping indoors — can be removed so frame digs in and grips ground outdoors. Cadmium plated steel swing chains.
Rocker has black, tubular steel extra long runners and arm rests. Red enameled, shaped steel backrest and seat. Adjustable safety strap.
Height overall, 48 inches; ground or floor space needed, 28x34 inch Rocker shipped set up; frame taken apart, easily assembled. Shipping wt., 10 lbs. Not mailable.
79 DM 7560.......$3.49

7-Inch Bouncing Auto 53c
With soft huge 1¼-inch sponge rubber tires. Satisfy Baby's desire to throw things —He can toss, pull or push this toy to his heart's content, without harm to himself or furniture. It always lands right side up, too (See A above). Colorful, protected metal body. Hear the soft click-click. Shpg. wt., 12 oz.
49 D 6120.................53c

Sturdy Double-Sewed Seams $1.15 UP
United States flags with 48 stars sewed on each side. Heavy canvas headings, brass grommets. Pole not included.

Cat. No.	Each	Size, Ft.	Shpg. Wt.	
49 D 6270	$2.65	3x5	1 lb.	All Wool Fast Color
49 D 6271	3.75	4x6	1 lb. 8 oz.	
49 D 6272	6.35	5x8	2 lbs. 2 oz.	
49 D 6280	1.15	3x5	1 lb.	2-Ply Fast Color Cotton
49 D 6281	1.55	4x6	1 lb. 8 oz.	
49 D 6282	2.45	5x8	2 lbs. 2 oz.	

13-Piece Electric Wood Burning Set 89c
Listed by Underwriters' Laboratory and easily worth $1.50! Burn beautiful designs in the two 2-pc. bookends and 4-pc. tie rack. When finished as shown, they'll be unusually handsome and really useful at home. Set also includes an electric pencil with cork grip bakelite handle, approved extension cord and rubber plug. Four water colors; brush, pallette. Two, etched, 3-ply wood placques, 6x4¼ in. Four, wood pulp, 6x3½-in. postcards—etch your own designs. Full instructions. Shipping weight, 1 pound 4 ounces.
49 D 4769.................89c

7, 3-Ply Wood Placques
Range in size from 9½x7¾ in. to 5x3½ in. Shipping weight, 8 ounces.
49 D 4757.................39c

Washable Rubber Transport 49c
Little tots will love this combination of transport and 2 autos. They're pliable rubber built to stand lots of squeezing and tossing about. Plenty of play-value for older youngsters, too. Colorful tractor-truck; detachable trailer; two, differently colored, 4¾-in. sedans, all roll easily on rubber wheels. Trailer has removable top as loading ramp or so sedans can be carried inside. 11¾ in. long. Shipping weight, 2 pounds.
49 D 6445.................49c

Rolling Chimes 29c
With new balloon type wheels. And there's Donald Duck, himself, big as life on top... My, how he is enjoying the ride! Built of strong red enameled metal; 20½ in. long, 7½ in. high. Nickel plated, tinkling bell will appeal to Baby's ear for music. Shipping weight, 1 pound 8 ounces.
49 D 2429.................29c

12 Big Value Balloons 21c
Large, and colorful! Little tots will love 'em! Four with stem squawkers. Toss tumbling dummy in the air; he lands on cardboard feet; inflates to 20 in. high. Dopey inflates to 13 in. high. Range in size from 7-in. diam. to 30 in. long when inflated. Other assorted round and long, airship and fancy serpentine shapes. Shipping weight, 3 ounces.
49 D 6409.................21c

He'll Be Here Soon—Santa. And His Pack'll Be Brimming With Toys. See Them in Sears New Christmas Catalog.. Mailed About November 15.

SEARS ● PAGE 897